New Zealand

Wines

2018

Michael Cooper's Buyer's Guide

upstart press

A catalogue record for this book is available from the National Library of New Zealand

ISBN 978-1-988516-06-6

An Upstart Press Book
Published in 2017 by Upstart Press Ltd
Level 4, 15 Huron Street, Takapuna
Auckland, New Zealand

Designed by www.cvdgraphics.nz
Printed by Opus Group Pty Ltd

Front cover photograph: Dawn breaks over the vines in the Omarunui Valley, Hawke's Bay. — Getty Images

Reviews of the latest editions

'The softcover book that first made its presence felt in 1992 has become somewhat of a bible for wine lovers here at home and, more recently via his website, overseas.' – Tessa Nicholson, *New Zealand Winegrower*

'With totally independent, unbiased ratings and tasting notes on over 3000 New Zealand wines, the book is my "bible" . . .' – *Beattie's Book Blog*

'Michael is deeply entrenched in the landscape of New Zealand wine . . . We consider his extensive knowledge and long experience vital as a benchmark tool when reflecting on our wines.' – Dry River

'A remarkable book . . . I don't believe there is a better one, certainly in Australasia and possibly even in the world, of tasting notes for the latest vintages . . . Arguably the best buyer's guide on the planet.' – Leighton Smith, *Newstalk ZB*

'A "must-have" for all lovers of New Zealand wine.' – Bob Campbell, *The Real Review*

'When Michael Cooper says a wine is great — and great value — you sit up and listen.' – Josie Steenhart, *Stuff*

Michael Cooper is New Zealand's most acclaimed wine writer, with 42 books and several major literary awards to his credit, including the Montana Medal for the supreme work of non-fiction at the 2003 Montana New Zealand Book Awards for his magnum opus, *Wine Atlas of New Zealand*. In the 2004 New Year Honours, Michael was appointed an Officer of the New Zealand Order of Merit for services to wine writing.

Author of the country's biggest-selling wine book, the annual *New Zealand Wines: Michael Cooper's Buyer's Guide*, now in its 26th edition, he was awarded the Sir George Fistonich Medal in recognition of services to New Zealand wine in 2009. The award is made each year at the country's largest wine competition, the New Zealand International Wine Show, to a 'living legend' of New Zealand wine. The weekly wine columnist for the *New Zealand Listener*, he was also until recently New Zealand editor of Australia's *Winestate* magazine and chairman of its New Zealand tasting panel.

In 1977 he obtained a Master of Arts degree from the University of Auckland with a thesis entitled 'The Wine Lobby: Pressure Group Politics and the New Zealand Wine Industry'. He was marketing manager for Babich Wines from 1980 to 1990, and since 1991 has been a full-time wine writer.

Michael's other major works include *100 Must-Try New Zealand Wines* (2011); the much-extended second edition of *Wine Atlas of New Zealand* (2008); *Classic Wines of New Zealand* (second edition 2005); *The Wines and Vineyards of New Zealand* (published in five editions from 1984 to 1996); and *Pocket Guide to Wines of New Zealand* (second edition 2000). He is the New Zealand consultant for Hugh Johnson's annual, best-selling *Pocket Wine Book* and the acclaimed *World Atlas of Wine*.

Michael's comprehensive, frequently updated website, *MichaelCooper.co.nz*, was launched in 2011.

Contents

The Winemaking Regions of New Zealand

Area in producing vines 2018 (percentage of national producing vineyard area)

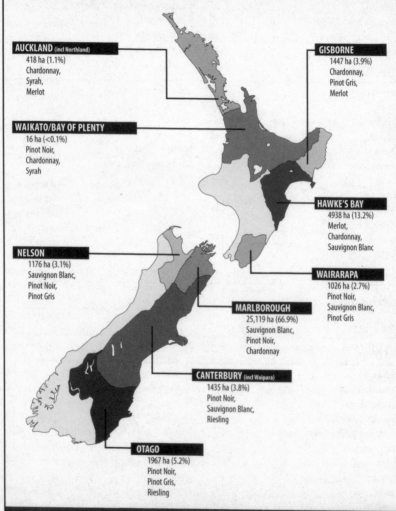

AUCKLAND (incl Northland)
418 ha (1.1%)
Chardonnay,
Syrah,
Merlot

GISBORNE
1447 ha (3.9%)
Chardonnay,
Pinot Gris,
Merlot

WAIKATO/BAY OF PLENTY
16 ha (<0.1%)
Pinot Noir,
Chardonnay,
Syrah

HAWKE'S BAY
4938 ha (13.2%)
Merlot,
Chardonnay,
Sauvignon Blanc

NELSON
1176 ha (3.1%)
Sauvignon Blanc,
Pinot Noir,
Pinot Gris

WAIRARAPA
1026 ha (2.7%)
Pinot Noir,
Sauvignon Blanc,
Pinot Gris

MARLBOROUGH
25,119 ha (66.9%)
Sauvignon Blanc,
Pinot Noir,
Chardonnay

CANTERBURY (incl Waipara)
1435 ha (3.8%)
Pinot Noir,
Sauvignon Blanc,
Riesling

OTAGO
1967 ha (5.2%)
Pinot Noir,
Pinot Gris,
Riesling

These figures (rounded to the closest percentages) are from New Zealand Winegrowers'
Vineyard Register Report 2015–2018. During the period 2015 to 2018, the total area of producing
vines was predicted to expand from 35,463 to 37,542 hectares – a rise of 6 per cent.

Preface

New Zealand is one of the world's youngest, most innovative wine-producing countries, but many wineries have recently passed milestone anniversaries. Babich is a standout example, in 2016 celebrating a century of family-owned production, but a host of other producers have now been in action for decades. Felton Road's first wines flowed 20 years ago; Lawson's Dry Hills' 25 years ago; Ata Rangi's 33 years ago; Hunter's 35 years ago; Seifried's more than 40 years ago.

Amid the familiar buzz of new labels and new vintages, it's easy to overlook fundamental changes in the wine industry. 'Our vineyards have been under organics and biodynamics for 15 years now,' a Central Otago winemaker told me recently. 'Lots of other producers are farming this way now. Fifteen to 25-year-old vines are increasingly the norm. Many of the viticulturists and winemakers have been in the one spot for up to 20 years. . . . The whole industry is significantly more mature, even compared to five years ago. We haven't started on wine style and quality!'

But further north, many top Marlborough producers believe their global reputation is being eroded by bulk wine exports, which account for almost 40 per cent of the region's output. Under a new proposed scheme, tentatively called Pure Marlborough, member companies will use a brand that guarantees their wines are made entirely from Marlborough grapes, grown with specific – as yet undefined – maximum grape yields, and bottled in New Zealand.

After the remnants of two cyclones dumped torrential rain in April – the main harvest month – most wineries agreed the 2017 vintage had been 'challenging'. Pegasus Bay summed up the problem as 'quite simply, rain, and too much of it'.

Almost 80 per cent of the country's grapes were harvested in Marlborough. Some fruit rotted on the vines, while other, contract-grown grapes were turned away by the wineries, but top-end producers, who ripened and picked their grapes earlier, reported Chardonnay and Pinot Noir of 'outstanding' quality. In the deep south, protected by the mountains from the series of late summer and autumn rainstorms, Central Otago's winegrowers also enthused about picking 'superb' Riesling, Chardonnay and Pinot Noir.

In another positive move, the long-postponed New Zealand Geographical Indications (Wine and Spirits) Registration Act finally came into force in July. '"Geographical Indications" – the names and places where our wines come from – are at the very heart of the New Zealand wine story,' says Philip Gregan, CEO of New Zealand Winegrowers.

To date, some of the Geographical Indications (GIs) apply solely to regions (such as Marlborough), while others cover regions and their sub-regions (such as Auckland, Matakana, Kumeu and Waiheke Island). Registration implies nothing about permitted grape varieties or production methods, but guarantees that the names are reserved exclusively for wines from the stated area.

To qualify for a GI, 'there also has to be some quality or reputation or characteristic of the wine that is associated with that place,' says Jeffrey Clarke, GM of Advocacy at New Zealand Winegrowers. 'It is about telling the story . . .'

Until this year, New Zealand was the only significant wine-producing country without a GI system.

— *Michael Cooper*

Vintage Charts 2008–2017

WHITES	Auckland	Gisborne	Hawke's Bay	Wairarapa	Nelson	Marlborough	Canterbury	Otago
2017	3	4	4	3	3	2–5	3–4	5
2016	3	4	4	5	3	4–5	5–6	5
2015	5	5	5	5	4	6	6	4
2014	6	6	5–6	5–6	5–6	5	3–5	5
2013	7	7	7	6	5	6–7	6–7	5–6
2012	3–4	2	3–4	3–4	4	4–5	4–5	4–6
2011	3	3	4	4	4	4	4	3
2010	7	6–7	7	6	7	7	6	6
2009	4	6–7	4	5	6	5	6	3–5
2008	5–6	3–4	3–5	5–7	4	2–5	3–6	5–6

REDS	Auckland	Gisborne	Hawke's Bay	Wairarapa	Nelson	Marlborough	Canterbury	Otago
2017	2	3	3	3	3	3–5	3–4	5
2016	3	4	4	5	3	5	5–6	5
2015	4	4	4	5	4	5	6	4
2014	5–6	5–6	5–6	5–6	5–6	5	3–5	5
2013	6–7	7	6–7	6	6	6–7	6–7	5–6
2012	3–5	2	3	3–4	4	4–5	4–5	4–6
2011	2	2	3–4	4	3	4	4	3
2010	7	6	6	5	6	6–7	5	5–6
2009	5	6–7	6	5	6	6	6	3–5
2008	5–7	3–4	3–5	5–7	4	2–5	3–6	5–6

7 = Outstanding   6 = Excellent   5 = Above average   4 = Average   3 = Below average   2 = Poor   1 = Bad

2017 Vintage Report

'"Challenging" is the word you'll hear from everyone,' a wine company executive told me shortly after the 2017 vintage. 'What was the problem?' asked Pegasus Bay in its Spring 2017 newsletter. 'Quite simply, rain, and too much of it.'

In Marlborough, where nearly 80 per cent of the country's grapes were harvested, some fruit rotted on the vines, when the remnants of two cyclones dumped torrential rain in early April. However, top-end producers, who picked their grapes earlier, reported Chardonnay and Pinot Noir of 'outstanding' quality.

At 396,000 tonnes, 2017 was our third-largest vintage, trailing only the record 2014 and 2016 harvests. Hawke's Bay, the second-largest wine region, produced 9 per cent of the crop, followed by Gisborne with 4 per cent. Central Otago produced about 2 per cent of the country's wine, as did Nelson and Canterbury.

Around the country, a generally warm spring was followed by a cool, dry start to the summer. February, however, was markedly wetter than usual in Marlborough, Gisborne and – especially – Hawke's Bay. In early autumn, north-westerly winds dumped record high rainfall in the upper North Island, while south-easterly airflows over the South Island brought cool, wet conditions to east coast regions. April – the core harvest month – experienced 'more north-easterly wind flow than normal,' reported NIWA, 'bringing with it moist tropical air masses and record-high rainfall for parts of the North Island. . . . This pattern also led to a very wet month for the northern and eastern South Island.'

Most of the regions' winegrowers had to battle exceptionally wet weather before the harvest, which slowed ripening and encouraged the spread of botrytis rot. Quality-focused growers, who crop their vines lightly, ripened their grapes relatively early, but for those aiming for a bumper crop, there was no 'get out of jail' card. Some grape-growers had their unripe fruit rejected by the wineries; others picked nothing at all.

In Auckland, red-wine varieties 'really bore the brunt of the challenging weather,' says the Northern Winegrowers Association, and were 'somewhat diluted'. The *Gisborne Herald* reported crop losses due to the adverse autumn weather, but after very selective picking, producers were still bullish about wine quality.

In Hawke's Bay, a favourably warm, dry summer was followed by a miserable autumn. A top producer reported 'pretty good' Chardonnay and Merlot, but Syrah was 'a struggle'. Grape-grower Xan Harding predicted some top wines would emerge, 'but not as many as in 2013 to 2016'.

In Marlborough, 'it was a rough ride,' reported *Winepress*, the local industry magazine, 'that resulted in lower brix [natural grape sugar levels], disease pressure, and reduced harvest expectations for many.' Spy Valley reported 'quite solid' Sauvignon Blanc and 'lovely' Pinot Gris. Nautilus expects its Sauvignon Blancs to be 'slightly more restrained than some years, but delightful to drink and unmistakably Marlborough'.

The most upbeat reports flowed from Central Otago, where after a very cool, windy summer, but favourable autumn, most winegrowers reported harvesting small crops of disease-free, ripely flavoured Pinot Noir.

Auckland

The two northernmost regions, Auckland (934 tonnes) and Northland (121 tonnes), together accounted for less than 0.3 per cent of the national grape harvest.

'Overall, temperatures were cooler than normal,' according to the Northern Winegrowers Association, 'with more wind and cloud cover than average.' A wet, cool spring triggered 'a moderate flowering, resulting in fairly loose clusters and lower [grape] yields'.

Summer was described by Kumeu River as 'quite ordinary', with maximum temperatures of 26°C, compared to the usual peaks of 30°C. However, on 1 February, a fire ban was in place in Northland. 'January and February were beautiful, building up the colours and phenolics,' enthused Frenchmans Hill Estate, on Waiheke Island. 'Approaching the harvest, things looked good.'

In early autumn, however, a slow-moving subtropical low brought 'several extreme rainfall events', reported Northern Winegrowers. Warkworth recorded its third-highest ever March rainfall. On 28 March, Heron's Flight, at Matakana, declared: 'We've had more rain these past couple of weeks than we've had in 30 years at this time.'

There was no let-up in mid-autumn, when Warkworth recorded its wettest April on record. Pinot Gris and Chardonnay showed 'the effect of dilution,' says Northern Winegrowers, 'with lower than usual sugar levels and low acidity as well.' Red-wine varieties 'really bore the brunt of the challenging weather . . .'.

On Waiheke Island, though, Frenchmans Hill reported its vineyards on steep, well-drained sites performed well. 'We got the white grapes off before the big rains.' Red-wine varieties were harvested with lower brixes (natural sugar levels), but no splitting. 'The colours and aromas are rich; there are no issues with concentration. Syrah looks really good.'

Gisborne

At 16,338 tonnes, Gisborne growers picked 4.3 per cent of the national grape crop. After a very positive start to the season, expectations were high by the end of summer, but a damp autumn triggered a rushed harvest.

Bud-burst started in mid-September with 'fantastic spring weather,' reported James Millton. 'Conditions were warm and dry.' However, an extended period of flowering 'resulted in variable fruit set,' according to Villa Maria, with lots of 'hen and chicken' – large and small berries – on the same bunch.

Following an exceptionally dry January, by 1 February a total fire ban was in place. In mid-February, Villa Maria stated that 'December and January have both been very dry and the season has continued to be very warm.' At the end of summer, though, NIWA reported the region's total monthly February rainfall had been well above average.

Autumn began with a warm, wet March. By 15 March, Gisborne Winegrowers noted that due to heavy rain, 'we have not been able to wait for perfect ripeness'. April – the region's fourth-wettest on record – brought well over double the average rainfall.

On 7 April, the *Gisborne Herald* reported that for some growers, 'the weather got the better of the crops before they could be harvested'. Winemaker Steve Voysey described his early season grapes for sparkling wines and Pinot Gris as 'outstanding . . . but dampness in the ground meant we struggled to get the full brix'.

'It won't go down in history as the best vintage of the decade,' admitted Matawhero, 'but we feel we have a strong line-up of wines.' At Millton, the wet weather at harvest led to 'a very selective pick, which delivered significantly lower yields, while maintaining great flavours and balance'.

Hawke's Bay

'We will still see some great wines from the vintage, but not as many as 2013 to 2016,' admits Xan Harding, one of Hawke's Bay's most prominent grape-growers. At 33,679 tonnes, the region's crop was 8.8 per cent of the national harvest and significantly smaller than 2016 (42,958 tonnes).

After a cool spring, north-westerly winds gave the region 'very mild daytime temperatures' in early summer, according to *Hawke's Bay Wine*, 'while the rest of New Zealand struggled with below-average temperatures'. In late January, Harding told the *New Zealand Herald* that 'so far the growing season has been as close to perfect as we could wish for'.

After a very dry January, a total fire ban was in place at the start of February. 'It could have been a stunner,' says Chris Scott, senior winemaker at Church Road, about the 2017 crop, after 'lots of days over 30°C in January and early February'. But after three days of heavy rain in the second half of the month, February's rainfall was more than double the long-term average.

Autumn 'was a miserable end to the season,' according to *Hawke's Bay Wine*. March was warm but very wet, NIWA reported. In April, Hastings recorded its third-highest ever rainfall for the month – more than double the long-term average.

Babich reported 'lower brix levels than usual', but also 'no green notes in the Cabernets'. The winemaker for one of the biggest companies views 2017 as 'challenging', but better than 2011 and 2012. 'Harvest was very wet, but we had a fantastic summer. Chardonnay looks good. Reds were a mixed bag, with pretty good Merlot from the Gimblett Gravels, but Syrah was a struggle.'

For both Chardonnay and Merlot, he expected good wines in the middle tiers, but doubted the company's most prestigious labels would appear from 2017.

Wairarapa

At 3822 tonnes, Wairarapa winegrowers harvested just 1 per cent of the national grape crop. 'Unfortunately, the season has not been ideal,' admitted Palliser Estate, 'and in summary has been very challenging.'

A dry spring was followed by a 'quite poor' summer, says Big Sky, at Martinborough. By the end of March, one well-established producer said everyone was 'a bit nervous down here, waiting for the sporadic drizzle to stop'.

In autumn, Martinborough and Gladstone, in the northern Wairarapa, had their wettest Aprils on record. As early as 2 April, Dry River reported 'managing one of our more challenging vintages in recent history'.

On 11 April, Brodie Estate, in Martinborough, reported summer drizzle has 'created perfect conditions for powdery mildew. . . . The rain is causing problems with an increase in botrytis and the weather preventing picking. As soon as we get some dry days, all the fruit will need to be picked.'

Further north, Gladstone Vineyard predicted 'subtle, lower in alcohol' wines from the 2017 vintage.

Nelson

'To say the grape harvest of 2017 threw out some challenges would be an understatement,' says Waimea Estate, one of Nelson's largest wine producers. At 8540 tonnes, the region's winegrowers processed just over 2 per cent of the national grape crop.

'Spring was basically free of cold nights and frosts, allowing the vines a great start,' noted *New Zealand Winegrower*. But Villa Maria described early summer as 'very unsettled', followed by 'significant' rain in January. At the end of summer, Mahana Estates reported that 'low temperatures and strong winds have been the prevailing weather conditions. . . . Normal bunch numbers have been produced, but the berry numbers are low on those bunches.'

In autumn, a damp March was followed by a notably wet April, with at least twice the usual rainfall. On 4 April, Seifried Estate told *Stuff* 'the grapes are fairly fragile, after all the rain they've had. . .'. Brightwater Vineyard was reported to have rushed to bring in its grapes – apart from the later-ripening varieties, Riesling and Merlot – although the fruit was 'nice and clean' and 'fully ripe'.

Marlborough

At 302,396 tonnes, the region's growers picked their third-biggest harvest, about 8 per cent smaller than the record 2014 crop. 'Vintage 2017 was one of the most challenging Marlborough's wine industry has experienced,' acknowledged *Winepress*, 'with the major November earthquake [which caused two deaths], inclement summer and extraordinary January winds, followed by a series of major rain events during a drawn-out and humid harvest. It was a rough ride that resulted in lower brix, disease pressure and reduced harvest expectations for many.'

Spring started with a cloudy, dry September, followed by a warm October and warm, wet November. 'There was regular rainfall at the beginning of the growing season,' reported Villa Maria, 'and elevated soil moisture levels meant canopies generally grew well.'

Summer, however, was 'a bummer,' according to Framingham. *New Zealand Winegrower* reported 'mixed conditions in December, just as Sauvignon Blanc began to flower. The earlier part of the month was cool and wet, with temperatures and sunshine not emerging until the end. That has resulted in variability in crop levels.'

In the middle of summer, January was warm, sunny, dry and windy. 'Most of January felt very windy,' according to Villa Maria, 'with no let-up from the dry north-westerly winds.' Wine Marlborough reported 'the winds sent vines into survival mode, instead of ripening fruit'. According to *New Zealand Winegrower*, the winds meant 'spray coverage was less effective, allowing powdery mildew to become a major issue in the humid growing season, and leaving the fruit more susceptible to botrytis infection'.

A total fire ban was in place by 1 February, but although slightly warmer and sunnier than usual, February also proved significantly wetter, with rainfall 44 per cent above the average.

In autumn, heavy rain in mid-March 'lit the fire,' according to Wine Marlborough, causing berries to split and allowing botrytis to spread. The warm, but cloudy and damp, March weather also slowed the grapes' ripening.

April, the key harvest month, was also warm, overcast and wet. 'April was a month of two distinct halves,' reported Marlborough Research Centre. 'The first half of April recorded very high rainfall and little sunshine,' but the second half of the month proved dry and sunny.

Overall, however, April rainfall in Marlborough was 248 per cent of the long-term average. According to one grower, in early April, a lot of grapes 'stalled at about 14 brix' on the vines and were rejected by the wineries. Some growers were reported to be unable to harvest their crops.

Many grapes were harvested at lower ripeness levels than normal. Plant & Food Research, at the Marlborough Research Centre, monitors eight vineyards. 'In most cases, the blocks would never have been able to achieve 21.5 brix [the usual target for natural grape sugars], due to the disease pressure that forced most blocks to be harvested before optimum maturity.'

However, Wine Marlborough declared quality-focused growers picked 'clean, lower-brix Sauvignon Blanc fruit with pure aromatics and flavours'. Pinot Noir and Chardonnay, harvested before the rain and humidity, were 'fantastic'.

Nautilus also praised its Chardonnay and Pinot Noir as among 'the best Nautilus has ever made'. The company expects its Sauvignon Blancs to be 'slightly more restrained than some years, but delightful to drink and unmistakably Marlborough'.

Spy Valley reported its Sauvignon Blanc looked 'quite solid, considering the conditions. We will see lower alcohol . . . due to earlier picking.' However, its Pinot Gris showed 'lovely flavours and richness'.

Canterbury

At 8247 tonnes, Canterbury, including Waipara, produced just 2.1 per cent of the country's wine in 2017.

After a frost-free spring, according to *New Zealand Winegrower*, Villa Maria reported that 'leading into Christmas, the vineyards in Waipara were looking great'. In late summer, NIWA recorded a record dry February in Waipara and Akaroa.

At the start of autumn, Greystone reported 'very dry conditions', small berries on the vines and very little disease pressure. But April proved far wetter than expected, with NIWA stations at Waipara West and Akaroa, on Banks Peninsula, both recording their second-highest ever rainfall for April.

On 27 April, Greystone enthused the harvest had been 'really good. No humidity after the rain, so no disease pressure.' On 8 May, Bishop's Head reported 'some outstanding sticky sweet wines'.

Reflecting on the vintage, Pegasus Bay observed that 'prolonged humidity tends to attract fungal growth on ripe fruit. . . . We had to do a lot of extra work in the vineyard, removing any substandard fruit, and stringently triaging [sorting] what was brought to the winery to make certain only the best was used to make wine. . . . We achieved good ripeness and concentration in our wines . . . although the quantity is well down.'

Otago

2017 was the lightest grape crop in Central Otago since 2012 – even smaller than the 2008 vintage – but quality expectations are high. The region's 'southerly, mountainous location afforded us great protection against the unsettled late summer and early autumn weather,' says Felton Road. 'Consequently, we were fortunately never challenged by rain or grey skies leading up to or during harvest.'

'We had the worst-ever start to the season,' reported Chard Farm. Villa Maria says spring was 'very cool with late flowering and a couple of frost events'.

In December, 'windy weather during flowering took its toll on yields,' according to Felton Road. In early to mid-summer, December and January were both cooler than average, says Quartz Reef. Wooing Tree summed up summer as 'fairly dismal, with strong winds and cold temperatures'.

But at the end of a dry March, one winery told me: 'Surprise, surprise, I think we are going to have a good vintage after all down here.' On 5 April, Rippon Vineyard reported 'beautiful weather in March and the fruit is tasting sensational'.

It was a very cool growing season. At Alexandra, Grasshopper Rock reported its coolest December to March period for at least 15 years. Misha's Vineyard experienced its coolest-ever season – even colder than 2009.

Most producers reported a later harvest than usual. 'While yields for the Pinot Noir were low due to the light bunch weights, the flavour ripeness was exceptional, so this year we harvested at lower sugar levels,' says Amisfield. 'All indications are for a beautiful year for Pinot Noir.'

'Quality across our three varieties is superb with lovely balance, depth and focus to all the wines,' enthused Felton Road. 'There's little doubt that 2017 will make rather profound wines.' Grasshopper Rock also predicted 'really interesting and complex wine'.

Best Buys of the Year

Best White Wine Buy of the Year

Mud House Waipara Valley Riesling 2016
★★★★, $14.99

Offering terrific value, this is a distinctly medium style of Riesling, with loads of drink-young charm. Attractively scented, it has strong, vibrant, citrusy flavours, hints of passionfruit and ginger, and mouth-watering acidity. Rieslings of excellent, four-star quality typically sell in the $20 to $25 category, so at under $15, this is a steal.

Past vintages of Mud House Waipara Valley Riesling, a wine with a long, impressive track record in competitions, were priced at $20. So when I tasted the 2016 vintage ($14.99), I jotted down: 'Unusually rich for a sub-$15 wine – check the price.' When the lower price was confirmed, I added: 'Great value.'

Others agree. Judges at the 2017 Royal New Zealand Easter Show Wine Awards gave the wine a silver medal, while *Cuisine* awarded it a four-star rating and Best Buy status.

The quality of the Mud House Riesling reflects the superb growing season in Waipara. As the region's most famous producer, Pegasus Bay, put it: 'If the rest of New Zealand had half the vintage we had, 2016 will surely go down as one of the crackers of the last 20 years.' A warm spring was followed by a hot summer and long, dry autumn.

For Mud House winemaker Cleighten Cornelius, the Indian summer created the opportunity for 'a sweet change of tack'. As the berries grew riper and riper, boosting their natural grape sugar levels, one option was to harvest swiftly, to make a drier style of Riesling. Instead, the decision was made to leave the fruit on the vines, in pursuit of a richer, sweeter wine, with greater personality.

The grapes were estate-grown in the Deans and The Mound vineyards at Waipara, planted in gravelly loams overlying alluvial sub-soils. At the winery, the fruit was pressed gently, and part of the blend was given six to 12 hours' skin contact, 'to enhance varietal character and add structure and depth'. The juice was then cool-fermented with selected yeasts in stainless steel tanks.

Harbouring 28 grams per litre of residual sugar, this is clearly a 'medium' style, rather than the medium-dry style of Riesling most common in New Zealand. 'The shift towards a sweeter style is something we have been toying with for a while,' says Cornelius. He believes the higher level of sweetness 'raises the volume of the mouthfeel, but the wine is not overtly sweet and retains its dry finish'.

It's currently hard to resist, but Mud House suggests the wine can also be cellared for up to five years, to develop toasty, bottle-aged complexities. At Mud House Restaurant & Café, they like to serve it with 'feasts like juicy barbecue chicken and fresh, crunchy vegetables with an aromatic Thai dressing'.

Best Red Wine Buy of the Year

Vidal Reserve Gimblett Gravels Hawke's Bay Merlot/Cabernet Sauvignon 2015
★★★★☆, $19.99

Pinot Noir is our most popular and fashionable red-wine variety, but the best buys are Merlot-based. This wine is frequently a steal – the 2010, 2013 and 2014 vintages all ranked among this country's finest red-wine bargains.

Now comes the irresistible 2015. Already delicious, but still unfolding, it's a blend of Merlot (75 per cent), Cabernet Sauvignon (18 per cent) and Malbec (7 per cent). Deeply coloured, mouthfilling, vibrantly fruity and supple, it offers excellent density of ripe, plummy, spicy flavours, with a long, finely poised finish. A refined, savoury, age-worthy red, likely to be at its best from 2019 onwards, it's as classy as many producers' $40 reds.

If you shop around, you won't even have to pay $19.99 – several online retailers are offering it at $16.99 to $17.99. 'We were quite taken with this wine at our Vidal tasting with winemaker Hugh Crichton,' reports Christchurch-based Vino Fino, 'but we were absolutely blown away by the fact you can get a wine of this quality at this kind of price. Wow!' Wine critics have been equally enthusiastic, including Raymond Chan (18.5/20 and *****), Cameron Douglas (91/100) and Sam Kim (93/100).

From a cooler growing season than 2014, but warmer than 2013, the 2015 Hawke's Bay reds are generally very good, especially the blends of the two classic Bordeaux varieties, Merlot and Cabernet Sauvignon. After a damp early autumn but favourably dry summer, Hawke's Bay Winegrowers singled out Merlot as the red-wine 'standout'.

Grown on free-draining, low-vigour sites in the Gimblett Gravels, the grapes for the Vidal Reserve red were harvested in early to mid-April. The wine was matured for 16 months in French oak barrels (24 per cent new), before bottling on 1 November 2016. After deciding not to produce the estate's most prestigious, $70 reds, branded Vidal Legacy, in 2015, the wines tentatively earmarked for that label were all declassified into the Vidal Reserve Merlot/Cabernet Sauvignon.

A dense but smooth red, Vidal Reserve Gimblett Gravels Hawke's Bay Merlot/Cabernet Sauvignon 2015 is already delicious, but should mature gracefully over the next five years. Enjoy it with hard cheeses, lamb and beef.

Other shortlisted wines

Whites

Gunn Estate Reserve Hawke's Bay Chardonnay 2016 ★★★★ $17
Villa Maria Cellar Selection Hawke's Bay Chardonnay 2016 ★★★★ $18
Villa Maria Cellar Selection Marlborough Dry Riesling 2016 ★★★★☆ $18

Reds

Delegat Awatere Valley Pinot Noir 2016 ★★★★ $25
Te Kairanga Runholder Martinborough Pinot Noir 2015 ★★★★☆ $29

MichaelCooper.co.nz

Since the 20th anniversary edition of the *Buyer's Guide* was published six years ago, the contents of the book have been available globally via the Internet, on the website www.michaelcooper.co.nz

Those who have since signed up to the website, from New Zealand and around the world, include wine lovers and professionals – producers, distributors, retailers and sommeliers. Membership of the website provides access to about 3000 recent reviews of New Zealand wine, together with all the reviews from the five previous editions, topped up by reviews added in most months (including those based on the finest quality and best-value wines tasted).

Wineries sending samples for review in the book and on the website do not pay entry fees, although there is a charge for a guaranteed quick review on the website. To preserve the independence that is essential when evaluating wines with a critical eye, the book and the website are also free of advertising.

Members' benefits also include access to uniquely detailed, region-by-region vintage reports; vintage charts; and regional maps from the prize-winning *Wine Atlas of New Zealand*.

The website also offers free content – a 'best buy' and 'treat yourself' (renewed monthly); best buys of the year; information on cellaring; a list of classic wines of New Zealand; event notification (updated regularly); information on grape varieties and the key wine regions; and links to my weekly wine columns in the *New Zealand Listener*, with a brief outline of their topics.

The website is intended to supplement the book, for those who can't conveniently buy the print version or prefer to get their information online.

Classic Wines of New Zealand

A crop of two new Classics and 14 Potential Classics are the features of this year's closely revised list of New Zealand wine classics.

What is a New Zealand wine classic? It is a wine that in quality terms consistently ranks in the very forefront of its class. To qualify for selection, each label must have achieved an outstanding level of quality for at least three vintages; there are no flashes in the pan here.

By identifying New Zealand wine classics, my aim is to transcend the inconsistencies of individual vintages and wine competition results, and highlight consistency of excellence. When introducing the elite category of Super Classics, I restricted entry to wines which have achieved brilliance in at least five vintages (compared to three for Classic status). The Super Classics are all highly prestigious wines, with a proven ability to mature well (even the Sauvignon Blancs, compared to other examples of the variety).

The Potential Classics are the pool from which future Classics will emerge. These are wines of outstanding quality which look likely, if their current standards are maintained or improved, to qualify after another vintage or two for elevation to Classic status. All the additions and elevations on this year's list are identified by an asterisk.

Note: A few wines featured on the classics list are not reviewed every year. If a wine is not currently on sale, this generally reflects a lack of favourable weather in recent vintages.

Super Classics

Branded and Other White Wines
Cloudy Bay Te Koko, Dog Point Vineyard Section 94

Chardonnay
Ata Rangi Craighall; Church Road Grand Reserve Hawke's Bay; Clearview Reserve; Clos de Ste Anne Naboth's Vineyard; Dry River; Fromm Clayvin Vineyard Marlborough; Kumeu River Estate; Kumeu River Hunting Hill; Kumeu River Mate's Vineyard; Neudorf Moutere; Sacred Hill Riflemans; Te Mata Elston; Villa Maria Reserve Barrique Fermented Gisborne; Villa Maria Single Vineyard Keltern

Gewürztraminer
Johanneshof Marlborough; Lawson's Dry Hills Marlborough

Pinot Gris
Dry River

Riesling
Dry River Craighall Vineyard; Felton Road Bannockburn; Pegasus Bay

Sauvignon Blanc
Cloudy Bay; Palliser Estate Martinborough; Saint Clair Wairau Reserve Marlborough; Seresin Marlborough

Sweet Whites
Dry River Late Harvest Craighall
Riesling; Forrest Estate Botrytised
Riesling; Villa Maria Reserve Noble
Riesling

Bottle-fermented Sparklings
Deutz Marlborough Cuvée Blanc de
Blancs; Nautilus Cuvée Marlborough

Branded and Other Red Wines
Church Road Tom; Craggy Range
Le Sol; Esk Valley The Terraces;
Stonyridge Larose; Te Mata Coleraine

Merlot
Esk Valley Winemakers Reserve
Merlot-predominant blend; Villa
Maria Reserve Hawke's Bay

Pinot Noir
Ata Rangi; Dry River; Felton Road
Block 3; Felton Road Block 5; Fromm
Clayvin Vineyard Marlborough;
Neudorf Moutere; Pegasus Bay Prima
Donna; Pegasus Bay Waipara Valley;
Villa Maria Reserve Marlborough

Syrah
Passage Rock Reserve; Te Mata
Estate Bullnose; Trinity Hill Homage
Gimblett Gravels Hawke's Bay

Classics

Chardonnay
Babich Irongate; Church Road Tom;
Cloudy Bay; Dog Point Vineyard; Esk
Valley Winemakers Reserve; Felton
Road Block 2; Greenhough Hope
Vineyard; Martinborough Vineyard;
Pegasus Bay; Seresin Reserve; Te
Whau Vineyard Waiheke Island; Villa
Maria Reserve Marlborough

Chenin Blanc
Millton Te Arai Vineyard

Gewürztraminer
Dry River Lovat Vineyard;
Framingham Marlborough; Pegasus
Bay; Vinoptima Ormond Reserve

Pinot Gris
Greystone Waipara; Neudorf Moutere;
Villa Maria Single Vineyard Seddon

Riesling
Carrick Bannockburn; **Carrick
Josephine; Neudorf Moutere; Rippon

Sauvignon Blanc
Brancott Estate Letter Series 'B'
Brancott Marlborough; Clos Henri
Marlborough; Greywacke Marlborough
Wild; Lawson's Dry Hills Marlborough;
Staete Landt Annabel Marlborough;
Te Mata Cape Crest; Villa Maria
Reserve Clifford Bay; Villa Maria
Reserve Wairau Valley

Viognier
Clos de Ste Anne Les Arbres;
Te Mata Estate Zara

**New Classic

Sweet Whites
Framingham F-Series Riesling
Trockenbeerenauslese; Framingham
Noble Riesling; Pegasus Bay Encore
Noble Riesling

Bottle-fermented Sparklings
Deutz Marlborough Cuvée Brut NV;
Deutz Marlborough Prestige Cuvée;
Quartz Reef MéthodeTraditionnelle
[Vintage]

Branded and Other Red Wines
Alpha Domus AD The Aviator;
Babich The Patriarch; Craggy Range
Aroha; Craggy Range Sophia; Destiny
Bay Magna Praemia; Destiny Bay
Mystae; Newton Forrest Estate
Cornerstone; Puriri Hills Reserve;
Sacred Hill Brokenstone; Sacred Hill
Helmsman; Te Whau The Point

Cabernet Sauvignon-predominant Reds
Babich Irongate Cabernet/Merlot/
Franc; Brookfields Reserve Vintage
['Gold Label'] Cabernet/Merlot; Te
Mata Awatea Cabernets/Merlot; Villa
Maria Reserve Cabernet Sauvignon/
Merlot

Pinot Noir
Akarua Bannockburn Central Otago;
Bannock Brae Central Otago; Carrick
Bannockburn Central Otago; Dog
Point Vineyard Marlborough; Felton
Road Bannockburn Central Otago;
Felton Road Cornish Point Central
Otago; Fromm Fromm Vineyard;
Gibbston Valley Le Maitre; Gibbston
Valley Reserve; Grasshopper Rock
Earnscleugh Vineyard; Greenhough
Hope Vineyard; Mt Difficulty Single
Vineyard Target Gully; Palliser Estate
Martinborough; Pisa Range Estate
Black Poplar Block; Quartz Reef
Bendigo Estate Vineyard; Quartz
Reef Central Otago Single Vineyard;
Rippon Tinker's Field Mature Vine;
Valli Bannockburn Vineyard Central
Otago; Villa Maria Single Vineyard
Seddon Marlborough; Villa Maria
Single Vineyard Southern Clays
Marlborough

Syrah
**Church Road Grand Reserve
Hawke's Bay; Esk Valley Winemakers
Reserve Gimblett Gravels; Mills Reef
Elspeth; Sacred Hill Deerstalkers
Hawke's Bay; Stonecroft Gimblett
Gravels Reserve; La Collina;
Stonyridge Pilgrim Syrah/Mourvedre/
Viognier/Grenache; Villa Maria
Reserve Hawke's Bay

Potential Classics

Branded and Other White Wines
Seresin Chiaroscuro

Arneis
Clevedon Hills

Chardonnay
Auntsfield Single Vineyard
Southern Valleys Marlborough;
*Carrick Cairnmuir Terraces EBM;
Greystone Erin's Reserve; Greywacke
Marlborough; John Forrest Collection
Wairau Valley Marlborough; Kumeu
River Coddington; Mahi Twin Valleys
Marlborough; Mission Jewelstone;
Nautilus Marlborough; Spy Valley
Envoy Marlborough; Trinity Hill
Hawke's Bay [Black Label]; Vidal
Legacy Hawke's Bay; Villa Maria
Reserve Hawke's Bay; Villa Maria
Single Vineyard Taylors Pass

Chenin Blanc
Clos de Ste Anne La Bas

Gewürztraminer
Greystone Waipara Valley; Lawson's
Dry Hills The Pioneer; Seifried
Winemaker's Collection Nelson; Spy
Valley Envoy Marlborough; Stonecroft
Old Vine; Villa Maria Single Vineyard
Ihumatao

Pinot Gris
Blackenbrook Vineyard Nelson;
Church Road McDonald Series;
Greywacke Marlborough; Misha's
Vineyard Dress Circle; Seresin
Marlborough; *Spy Valley Envoy
Marlborough

Riesling
Felton Road Dry; Framingham
Classic; Framingham F-Series Old
Vine; Greystone Waipara Valley;
Greywacke Marlborough; Misha's
Vineyard Limelight; Misha's Vineyard
Lyric; Muddy Water James Hardwick
Waipara; Saint Clair Pioneer Block 9
Big John

Sauvignon Blanc
Auntsfield Single Vineyard Southern
Valleys; Church Road Grand
Reserve Barrel Fermented Hawke's
Bay; Churton Marlborough; Clos
Marguerite Marlborough; Dog Point
Vineyard Marlborough; Giesen
Marlborough The August; Greywacke
Marlborough; Hans Herzog
Marlborough Barrell Fermented
Sur Lie; Jackson Estate Grey Ghost
Marlborough; Jackson Estate Stich
Marlborough; Pegasus Bay Sauvignon/
Sémillon; Seresin Marama; *Spy
Valley Envoy Johnson Vineyard;
Villa Maria Single Vineyard Graham
Marlborough;Villa Maria Single
Vineyard Taylors Pass Marlborough

Sweet White Wines
Alpha Domus AD Noble Selection;
Felton Road Block 1 Riesling;
Framingham F-Series Gewürztraminer
VT; Framingham F-Series Riesling
Auslese; Framingham Select Riesling;
Pegasus Bay Aria Late Picked Riesling;
Trinity Hill Gimblett Gravels Hawke's
Bay Noble Viognier; Vinoptima
Noble Ormond Gewürztraminer

*New Potential Classic

Rosé Wines

Terra Sancta Bannockburn Central Otago Pinot Noir Rosé

Branded and Other Red Wines

Alluviale; Clearview Old Olive Block; Clearview The Basket Press; Destiny Bay Destinae; *Frenchman's Hill Estate Blood Creek 8; Gillman; Hay Paddock, The; Messenger; Obsidian, The; Puriri Hills Pope; Trinity Hill The Gimblett

Cabernet Sauvignon-predominant Reds

Church Road McDonald Series Cabernet Sauvignon; Mills Reef Elspeth Cabernet Sauvignon; Mills Reef Elspeth Cabernet/Merlot; Vidal Legacy Gimblett Gravels Cabernet Sauvignon/Merlot

Malbec

Stonyridge Luna Negra Waiheke Island Hillside

Merlot

Church Road McDonald Series Hawke's Bay; Hans Herzog Spirit of Marlborough Merlot/Cabernet

Montepulciano

Hans Herzog Marlborough; Obsidian Waiheke Island

Pinot Noir

Amisfield Central Otago; Burn Cottage Central Otago; *Carrick Excelsior Central Otago; Craggy Range Te Muna Road Vineyard Martinborough; Doctors Flat Central Otago; Felton Road Calvert Central Otago; Gibbston Valley China Terrace Bendigo; Gibbston Valley School House Central Otago; *Greystone Thomas Brothers; Hans Herzog Marlborough; Julicher Martinborough; *Lowburn Ferry Home Block; Lowburn Ferry The Ferryman Reserve; Mondillo Central Otago; Mount Edward Muirkirk; Mt Difficulty Single Vineyard Pipeclay Terrace; Muddy Water Slowhand; Nautilus Four Barriques Marlborough; Peregrine Central Otago; *Rippon 'Rippon' Mature Vine; Rockburn Central Otago; Tatty Bogler Central Otago; *Terra Sancta Jackson's Block; *Two Paddocks Proprietor's Reserve The Last Chance Earnscleugh Vineyard; Valli Gibbston Vineyard Otago; Villa Maria Single Vineyard Taylors Pass Marlborough; Voss Reserve Martinborough; Wooing Tree Central Otago

Syrah

*Awaroa Melba Peach Waiheke Island; *Brookfields Hillside; Church Road McDonald Series; Clos de Ste Anne The Crucible; Craggy Range Gimblett Gravels Vineyard; *Elephant Hill Reserve Hawke's Bay; Kennedy Point; Man O' War Dreadnought; Mission Huchet; *Mission Jewelstone; Mudbrick Reserve; Passage Rock; Trinity Hill Gimblett Gravels Hawke's Bay; Vidal Legacy Gimblett Gravels; Villa Maria Cellar Selection Hawke's Bay

The following wines are not at the very forefront in quality terms, yet have been produced for many vintages, are extremely widely available and typically deliver good to excellent quality and value. They are all benchmark wines of their type – a sort of Everyman's classic.

Chardonnay
Church Road Hawke's Bay; Stoneleigh Marlborough

Gewürztraminer
Seifried Nelson

Pinot Gris
Waimea Nelson

Riesling
Hunter's Marlborough; Lawson's Dry Hills Marlborough; Seifried Nelson; Waimea Classic Nelson

Sauvignon Blanc
Brancott Estate Marlborough; Oyster Bay Marlborough; Saint Clair Marlborough; Stoneleigh Marlborough; Tohu Marlborough; Villa Maria Private Bin Marlborough

Sparkling
Lindauer Brut; Lindauer Special Reserve; Soljans Fusion Sparkling Muscat

Merlot
Church Road Hawke's Bay Merlot/Cabernet/Malbec; Te Mata Estate Vineyards Merlot/Cabernets

Pinot Noir
Akarua Rua Central Otago; Pencarrow Martinborough; Villa Maria Private Bin Marlborough

Cellar Sense

Most wine in New Zealand is young and consumed on the day it is bought. Some small producers, such as Puriri Hills and Hans Herzog, regularly offer bottle-aged vintages for sale, but around the country, barely 1 per cent of the wine we buy is cellared for even a year.

So, it's great news that more and more wineries are releasing or rereleasing mature, bottle-aged wines, up to a decade old. Dog Point Vineyard in 2017 rereleased its 2007 Section 94 (a barrel-fermented Sauvignon Blanc, currently in magnificent shape), 2007 Chardonnay and 2007 Pinot Noir. Villa Maria recently launched three Cabernet Sauvignon and Merlot-based reds from 2009 and 2010, labelled 'Library Release'; and Pegasus Bay rereleased its 2007 Riesling and Pinot Noir under an 'Aged Release' label. Age has not wearied these beauties, proving the country's finest wines can mature well for a decade or longer.

Sauvignon Blanc, which accounts for about two-thirds of New Zealand wine, is not usually seen as a variety that needs time to develop. Only a decade ago, Marlborough winemakers often stated that the region's Sauvignon Blanc 'should be picked, pressed and pissed by Christmas'.

Today, most Sauvignon Blancs develop soundly for a couple of years, but the popularity of New Zealand Pinot Noir has done far more to persuade consumers around the world that this country's wine can mature gracefully – as it must, if New Zealand is to be accepted as a serious wine producer.

'To gain true international recognition, an industry has to be capable of making wines that improve with age – that's the ultimate quality factor,' stresses John Buck, co-founder of Te Mata Estate, acclaimed for its long-lived Hawke's Bay Cabernet/Merlots. 'People need to be able to put wine into their cellars with confidence and know that when they pull them out they will be a damn sight better than when they put them in.'

But do all winemakers share that view? Geoff Kelly, a Wellington-based critic, believes too much emphasis is placed on young wines in New Zealand, partly because many wine judges are winemakers. 'Generalising, winemakers . . . speak most highly of fresh and fruity smells and flavours in wine. How else can they sell their young wines? Consequently, it is quite rare to find New Zealand winemakers who really enjoy old wines or attend tastings of them.'

If you are keen to build up a cellar of distinguished Chardonnays, Rieslings, Pinot Noirs or Cabernet/Merlots, how do you decide what to buy? Confidence comes from 'vertical' tastings, where several vintages of a wine are tasted side by side. Vertical tastings, staged more and more frequently in New Zealand, let you assess the overall quality of a wine, the evolution of its style, the impact of vintage variation and its maturation potential.

To sum up, I suggest drinking most New Zealand Sauvignon Blancs at nine months to two years old. Screwcaps preserve the wines' freshness markedly better than corks did. Most fine-quality Chardonnays are at their best at two to five years old; top Rieslings at three to seven years old.

Middle-tier Pinot Noirs, Merlots and Syrahs typically drink well for five years; outstanding examples can flourish for much longer. New Zealand's top Cabernet/ Merlot blends from Hawke's Bay and Waiheke Island are still the safest bet for long-term cellaring over decades.

Cellaring Guidelines

Grape variety	Best age to open
White	
Sauvignon Blanc	
(non-wooded)	6–24 months
(wooded)	1–3 years
Arneis	1–3 years
Albariño	1–4 years
Gewürztraminer	1–4 years
Grüner Veltliner	1–4 years
Viognier	1–4 years
Pinot Gris	1–4 years
Sémillon	1–4 years
Chenin Blanc	2–5 years
Chardonnay	2–5 years
Riesling	2–7+ years
Red	
Pinotage	1–3 years
Malbec	1–5 years
Cabernet Franc	2–5 years
Montepulciano	2–5 years
Merlot	2–5+ years
Pinot Noir	2–5+ years
Syrah	2–5+ years
Tempranillo	2–5+ years
Cabernet Sauvignon	3–7+ years
Cabernet/Merlot	3–7+ years
Other	
Sweet whites	2–5 years
Bottle-fermented sparklings	
(vintage-dated)	3–5+ years

How to Use this Book

It is essential to read this brief section to understand how the book works. Feel free to skip any of the other preliminary pages, but not these.

The majority of wines have been listed in the book according to their principal grape variety, as shown on the front label. Lawson's Dry Hills Marlborough Sauvignon Blanc, for instance, can be located simply by turning to the Sauvignon Blanc section. Wines with front labels that do not refer clearly to a grape variety or blend of grapes, such as Cloudy Bay Te Koko, can be found in the Branded and Other Wines sections for white and red wines.

Most entries are firstly identified by their producer's name. Wines not usually called by their producer's name, such as Kim Crawford Marlborough Sauvignon Blanc (from Constellation New Zealand), or Triplebank Awatere Valley Marlborough Pinot Noir (from Pernod Ricard NZ), are listed under their most common name.

The star ratings for quality reflect my own opinions, formed where possible by tasting a wine over several vintages, and often a particular vintage several times. *The star ratings are therefore a guide to each wine's overall standard in recent vintages*, rather than simply the quality of the latest release. However, to enhance the usefulness of the book, in the body of the text I have also given a *quality rating for the latest vintage of each wine*; sometimes for more than one vintage. (Since April 2010 wineries have been able to buy stickers to attach to their bottles, based on these ratings.)

I hope the star ratings give interesting food for thought and succeed in introducing you to a galaxy of little-known but worthwhile wines. It pays to remember, however, that wine-tasting is a business fraught with subjectivity. You should always treat the views expressed in these pages for what they are – one person's opinion. The quality ratings are:

★★★★★	Outstanding quality (gold medal standard)
★★★★☆	Excellent quality, verging on outstanding
★★★★	Excellent quality (silver medal standard)
★★★☆	Very good quality
★★★	Good quality (bronze medal standard)
★★☆	Average quality
★★	Plain
★	Poor
No star	To be avoided

These quality ratings are based on comparative assessments of New Zealand wines against one another. A five-star Merlot/Cabernet Sauvignon, for instance, is an outstanding-quality red judged by the standards of other Merlot/Cabernet Sauvignon blends made in New Zealand. It is not judged by the standards of overseas reds of a similar style (for instance Bordeaux), because the book is focused solely on New Zealand wines and their relative merits. (Some familiar New Zealand wine brands in recent years have included varying proportions of overseas wine. To be featured in this book, they must still include at least some New Zealand wine in the blend.)

Where brackets enclose the star rating on the right-hand side of the page, for example (★★★), this indicates the assessment is only tentative, because I have tasted very few vintages of the wine. A dash is used in the relatively few cases where a wine's quality has oscillated over and above normal vintage variations (for example ★–★★★).

Super Classic wines, Classic wines and Potential Classic wines (see page 20) are highlighted in the text by the following symbols:

                                🍇

Super Classic   Classic   Potential Classic

Each wine has also been given a dryness-sweetness, price and value-for-money rating. The precise levels of sweetness indicated by the four ratings are:

DRY	Less than 5 grams/litre of residual sugar
MED/DRY	5–14 grams/litre of residual sugar
MED	15–49 grams/litre of residual sugar
SW	50 and over grams/litre of residual sugar

Less than 5 grams of residual sugar per litre is virtually imperceptible to most palates – the wine tastes fully dry. With between 5 and 14 grams, a wine has a hint of sweetness, although a high level of acidity (as in Rieslings or even Marlborough Sauvignon Blancs, which often have 4 to 6 grams per litre of residual sugar) reduces the perception of sweetness. Where a wine harbours over 15 grams, the sweetness is clearly in evidence.

At above 50 grams per litre, most wines are unabashedly sweet, although high levels of acidity can still disguise the degree of sweetness. Most wines that harbour more than 50 grams per litre of sugar are packaged in half bottles, made to be served with dessert, and can be located in the Sweet White Wines section. However, a growing number of low-alcohol, sweet but not super-sweet, mouth-wateringly crisp Rieslings, not designed as dessert wines and usually packaged in 750-ml bottles, can also be found in the Riesling section.

Prices shown are based on the average price in a supermarket or wine shop (as indicated by the producer), except where most of the wine is sold directly to consumers from the winery, either over the vineyard counter or via mail order or the Internet.

The art of wine buying involves more than discovering top-quality wines. The real challenge – and the greatest satisfaction – lies in identifying wines at varying quality levels that deliver outstanding value for money. The symbols I have used are self-explanatory:

–V	=	Below average value
AV	=	Average value
V+	=	Above average value

The ratings discussed thus far are all my own. Many of the wine producers themselves, however, have also contributed individual vintage ratings of their own top wines over the past decade and the 'When to drink' recommendations. (The symbol **WR** indicates Winemaker's Rating, and the symbol **NM** alongside a vintage means the wine was not made that year.) Only the producers have such detailed knowledge of the relative quality of all their recent vintages (although in some cases, when the information was not forthcoming, I have rated a vintage myself). The key point you must note is that *each producer has rated each vintage of each wine against his or her highest quality aspirations for that particular label, not against any absolute standard.* Thus, a 7 out of 7 score merely indicates that the producer considers that particular vintage to be an outstanding example of that particular wine; not that it is the best-quality wine he or she makes.

The 'When to drink' (Drink) recommendations (which I find myself referring to constantly) are largely self-explanatory. The P symbol for PEAKED means that a particular vintage is already at, or has passed, its peak; no further benefits are expected from aging.

Here is an example of how the ratings work:

Ata Rangi Pinot Noir   ★★★★★

One of the greatest of all New Zealand wines, this Martinborough red is powerfully built and concentrated, yet seductively fragrant and supple. 'Intense, opulent fruit with power beneath' is founder Clive Paton's goal. 'Complexity comes with time.' The grapes are drawn from numerous sites, including the estate vineyard, planted in 1980, and the vines, up to 37 years old, have a very low average yield of 4.5 tonnes of grapes per hectare. The wine is fermented with indigenous yeasts and maturation is for 11 months in French oak barriques (35 per cent new in 2015). From a dry, low-yielding season, the classy 2015 vintage (★★★★★) is deeply coloured, mouthfilling and savoury, with highly concentrated, ripe cherry, plum and spice flavours, hints of dried herbs and nuts, excellent complexity and a finely poised, lasting finish. Still youthful, it shows obvious potential; best drinking 2020+.

Vintage	15	14	13	12	11	10	09	08
WR	7	7	7	7	7	7	7	7
Drink	17-27	17-26	17-25	17-24	17-23	17-22	17-21	17-20

DRY $75 AV

The winemaker's own ratings indicate that the 2015 vintage is of excellent quality for the label, and is recommended for drinking between 2017 and 2027.

Describes 'Classic' status, ranging from 🍇🍇🍇 for Super Classic, 🍇🍇 for Classic to 🍇 for Potential Classic. This is a wine that in quality terms ranks in the forefront of its class.

Dryness-sweetness rating, price and value for money. This wine is dry in style (below 5 grams/litre of residual sugar). At $75 it is average value for money.

Quality rating, ranging from ★★★★★ for outstanding to no star (–), to be avoided. This is generally a wine of outstanding quality.

White Wines

Albariño

Coopers Creek's 2011 bottling was the first true example of Albariño from New Zealand or Australia. Called Albariño in Spain and Alvarinho in Portugal, this fashionable variety produces light, crisp wines described by Riversun Nurseries at Gisborne as possessing 'distinctive aromatic, peachy characteristics, similar to Viognier'. With its loose clusters, thick skins and good resistance to rain, Albariño could thrive in this country's wetter regions. New Zealand's 30 hectares of bearing Albariño vines in 2018 are mostly in Gisborne (12 hectares), Hawke's Bay (7 hectares) and Marlborough (4 hectares), but there are also pockets in Nelson and Auckland.

Aronui Single Vineyard Nelson Albariño ★★★★

The impressive 2015 vintage (★★★★☆) was estate-grown and hand-picked at Upper Moutere. Aromatic and full-bodied, it is a strongly varietal wine, with good vigour and intensity of peach, grapefruit and spice flavours, dryish (7 grams/litre of residual sugar), crisp, finely balanced and long.

MED/DRY $25 AV

Astrolabe Vineyards Sleepers Vineyard Marlborough Albariño ★★★★

Grown at Kekerengu, the youthful 2016 vintage (★★★★) was hand-harvested and fermented in an even split of tanks and old French oak barrels. Made in a fully dry style, it is a fresh, tasty, medium-bodied wine with vibrant citrusy flavours, a slightly salty streak, and very good vigour and intensity. The refreshing 2015 vintage (★★★★☆), also grown at Kekerengu, was mostly tank-fermented, but a small portion of the blend was fermented and matured in old French barrels. Light lemon/green, it is attractively scented, with strong, vibrant, citrusy, slightly salty flavours, a touch of complexity, and a dry, harmonious, lingering finish.

DRY $25 AV

Babich Family Estates Headwaters Organic Marlborough Albariño ★★★★

The lively 2016 vintage (★★★★) was estate-grown in the Headwaters Vineyard, on the north side of the Wairau Valley, hand-harvested from organically certified vines, tank-fermented and bottled young. Full-bodied and vibrantly fruity, it is drinking well in its youth, with strong, fresh, citrusy, slightly spicy flavours, crisp, dryish (5.2 grams/litre of residual sugar) and lingering.

MED/DRY $27 –V

Coopers Creek Select Vineyards Bell-Ringer Gisborne Albariño ★★★★

The refreshing 2016 vintage (★★★★) was hand-harvested in the Bell Vineyard and tank-fermented. Crisp and lively, it's a finely balanced, dry wine (4 grams/litre of residual sugar), with strong, ripe, citrusy, slightly spicy flavours and an appealingly floral bouquet.

Vintage	16	15	14	13	12	11
WR	6	7	7	7	4	4
Drink	17-18	P	P	P	P	P

DRY $23 AV

Doubtless Albariño   (★★★)

Grown at Doubtless Bay, in Northland, the steely 2015 vintage (★★★) was fermented in old oak casks. Light lemon/green, it is medium to full-bodied, with good depth of lively, citrusy flavours, mouth-watering acidity and a dry finish. A good food wine.

Vintage	15
WR	5
Drink	17-20

DRY $22 –V

Forrest Marlborough Albariño   (★★★★☆)

Delicious young but age-worthy too, the 2016 vintage (★★★★☆) is an attractively scented, full-bodied, vibrantly fruity wine with strong personality. It has an array of lively ripe-fruit flavours, showing good intensity, a slightly salty streak and a crisp, dry, persistent finish.

DRY $25 V+

Hihi Gisborne Albariño   ★★★☆

The 2015 vintage (★★★☆) was estate-grown at Ormond. Made in an easy-drinking style, it is mouthfilling, with ripe, peachy flavours, showing good vigour, a distinct splash of sweetness (14 grams/litre of residual sugar), and a crisp, smooth finish.

MED/DRY $20 AV

Left Field Gisborne Albariño   ★★★★☆

The 2016 vintage (★★★★) is from grapes hand-picked and mostly handled in stainless steel (tanks and barrels); 5 per cent of the blend was fermented in seasoned French oak puncheons. Lemon-scented, it is a fresh, vibrant, strongly varietal wine, full-bodied and tangy, with excellent depth of citrusy, slightly spicy and salty flavours, appetisingly dry (3.9 grams/litre of residual sugar) and crisp. (From Te Awa.)

Vintage	16
WR	6
Drink	17-21

DRY $25 V+

Mahurangi River Winery Matakana Albariño   ★★★★

Grown at Matakana, north of Auckland, the 2015 vintage (★★★★) was fermented in a mix of tanks (80 per cent) and barrels (20 per cent). It is mouthfilling, with generous, citrusy, slightly spicy flavours, complexity from the delicate oak seasoning, appetising acidity and a fresh, finely poised finish.

Vintage	15	14
WR	6	7
Drink	17-18	P

DRY $29 –V

Maison Noire Hawke's Bay Albariño   (★★★★)

The characterful 2016 vintage (★★★★) was hand-picked near Maraekakaho, tank-fermented and then lees-aged for three months in old barrels. Pale yellow, it is medium to full-bodied, with strong, ripe, peachy, citrusy, slightly spicy flavours, crisp but not high acidity and a fully dry, balanced finish. Showing considerable complexity, it's already drinking well.

Vintage	16
WR	6
Drink	17-19

 DRY $22 V+

Matua Single Vineyard Hawke's Bay Albariño   ★★★★★

Consistently impressive. Full of personality, the 2015 vintage (★★★★★) is richly scented and mouthfilling, with a strong surge of vibrant, peachy, spicy, slightly limey flavours, mouth-watering acidity and a dry (3 grams/litre of residual sugar), lingering finish.

 DRY $35 AV

Nautilus Marlborough Albariño   ★★★★

Delicious from the start, the aromatic 2016 vintage (★★★★☆) is a single-vineyard wine, handled without oak. Bright, light lemon/green, it is mouthfilling, sweet-fruited and dry (4 grams/litre of residual sugar), with strong, peachy, slightly spicy flavours, a slightly salty streak and good complexity.

 DRY $29 –V

Neudorf Moutere Albariño   ★★★★★

Full of youthful impact, the classy 2016 vintage (★★★★★) was estate-grown and hand-picked in Rosie's Block, at Upper Moutere, and tank-fermented with indigenous yeasts. Handled entirely without oak, it is vibrant, concentrated and tangy, with deep, citrusy, slightly limey and spicy flavours, a salty streak, and an appetisingly crisp, dryish (6 grams/litre of residual sugar), lasting finish.

Vintage	16	15
WR	6	7
Drink	17-18	P

 MED/DRY $33 AV

Ransom Matakana Albariño   ★★★★

The 2015 vintage (★★★☆) is mouthfilling, crisp and dry, with vibrant, citrusy, slightly spicy flavours that linger well. A very refreshing, appetising summer wine.

DRY $26 –V

Redmetal Vineyards Block Five Hawke's Bay Albariño   (★★★★)

The debut 2016 vintage (★★★★) was grown in the Bridge Pa Triangle and handled without oak. Bright, light lemon/green, it is enjoyable young, with ripe, peachy, spicy flavours, showing good vigour and concentration, and a dry (3 grams/litre of residual sugar), well-rounded finish.

Vintage	16
WR	5
Drink	17-22

 DRY $23 AV

Rod McDonald One Off Gisborne Albariño   ★★★☆

The 2015 vintage (★★★☆) was hand-picked and tank-fermented with indigenous yeasts. Light lemon/green, it is vibrantly fruity, with good varietal character, a slightly salty streak and citrusy, appley flavours that linger well.

DRY $28 –V

Sileni Estate Selection Advocate Hawke's Bay Albariño   ★★★★

The light lemon/green 2016 vintage (★★★★) was estate-grown in the Bridge Pa Triangle, tank-fermented and lees-aged. A full-bodied, dry wine (2.2 grams/litre of residual sugar), it has good intensity of fresh, ripe tropical-fruit flavours, lively but not high acidity, and lots of drink-young appeal.

Vintage	16	15
WR	6	6
Drink	17-22	17-21

DRY $25 AV

Spade Oak Vineyard Heart of Gold Gisborne Albariño   ★★★☆

The 2015 vintage (★★★☆) was hand-picked and made in a dryish style (5 grams/litre of residual sugar). Medium-bodied, it is fresh and vibrantly fruity, with ripe, peachy flavours, a slightly salty note, balanced acidity and very good depth.

MED/DRY $23 –V

Stanley Estates Single Vineyard Awatere Valley Marlborough Albariño   ★★★★

Drinking well now, the 2016 vintage (★★★★) was handled in tanks (60 per cent) and seasoned French oak casks (40 per cent). Bright, light lemon/green, it is lively and tangy, with citrusy, limey, slightly nutty flavours, showing a distinct touch of complexity, and a finely balanced, dry (2.7 grams/litre of residual sugar), minerally finish.

Vintage	16
WR	5
Drink	17-22

DRY $23 AV

Villa Maria Cellar Selection Gisborne Albariño   ★★★★☆

The 2016 vintage (★★★★☆) is full of personality and great value. Mostly hand-picked and handled without oak, it is scented and fleshy, with strong tropical-fruit flavours to the fore, a salty, minerally thread, appetising acidity and a fully dry (1.9 grams/litre of residual sugar) finish.

Vintage	17
WR	7
Drink	17-20

DRY $19 V+

Villa Maria Single Vineyard Braided Gravels Hawke's Bay Albariño   (★★★★★)

The classy 2016 vintage (★★★★★) was mostly tank-fermented, but 25 per cent of the blend was fermented with indigenous yeasts in seasoned French oak puncheons. A powerful, fresh, full-bodied wine, it is dry (2.2 grams/litre of residual sugar), with very vibrant flavours, showing excellent intensity, complexity and length.

Vintage	16
WR	7
Drink	17-20

 DRY $32 AV

Waimea Nelson Albariño   ★★★☆

The 2016 vintage (★★★☆) is a mouth-wateringly crisp, medium-bodied wine with lively, citrusy, slightly spicy and salty flavours, showing good depth. A tangy, dry style (4.3 grams/litre of residual sugar), it's already drinking well.

 DRY $23 –V

Wairau River Marlborough Albariño   ★★★★

This single-vineyard wine is estate-grown on the north side of the Wairau Valley. The 2016 vintage (★★★★) is aromatic, crisp and dryish (7 grams/litre of residual sugar), with strong grapefruit and green-apple flavours, lively, refreshing and lingering.

Vintage	16	15
WR	6	6
Drink	17-18	P

MED/DRY $20 V+

Arneis

Still fairly rare here, with 33 hectares of bearing vines in 2018, Arneis is one of the most distinctive emerging varieties. Pronounced 'Are-nay-iss', it is a traditional grape of Piedmont, in north-west Italy, where it yields soft, early-maturing wines with slightly herbaceous aromas and almond flavours. The word 'Arneis' means 'little rascal', which reflects its tricky character in the vineyard; a vigorous variety, it needs careful tending. First planted in New Zealand in 1998 at the Clevedon Hills vineyard in South Auckland, its potential is now being explored by numerous producers. Coopers Creek released the country's first varietal Arneis from the 2006 vintage. Most of the bearing vines in 2018 are in Gisborne (16 hectares), Hawke's Bay (13 hectares) and Marlborough (4 hectares).

Clevedon Hills Arneis ★★★★★

Estate-grown in South Auckland, in favourable seasons like 2013 (★★★★★) and 2010 (★★★★★) this is an outstanding wine. The 2014 vintage (★★★★☆) is weighty (14 per cent alcohol) and dry. Sweet-fruited, it has ripe lychee, pear and slight spice flavours that build to a strong, finely textured finish.

DRY $27 V+

Coopers Creek SV Gisborne Arneis The Little Rascal ★★★★

Top years are richly scented, with substantial alcohol and strong, slightly spicy and herbal flavours. Hand-picked in the Bell Vineyard and tank-fermented, the 2014 (★★★★☆) is fragrant and full-bodied, with concentrated, ripe tropical-fruit flavours, finely balanced, dry and lengthy. The 2015 vintage (★★★★) is delicately scented, with good weight, generous, citrusy, slightly peachy and spicy flavours, fresh acidity and a lingering, dryish (5.6 grams/litre of residual sugar) finish.

Vintage	15	14	13	12	11	10
WR	6	7	7	NM	5	7
Drink	17-19	17-18	17-18	NM	P	P

DRY $23 AV

Hans Herzog Marlborough Arneis ★★★★

Organically certified, the 2014 vintage (★★★★) was matured on its yeast lees for 10 months in French oak puncheons. It's a mouthfilling, 'serious' wine, with strong, ripe citrus-fruit and pineapple flavours, balanced acidity, a gentle oak influence and a bone-dry finish.

Vintage	14	13
WR	7	7
Drink	17-19	17-18

DRY $39 –V

Villa Maria Cellar Selection Hawke's Bay Arneis ★★★★

The 2015 vintage (★★★★☆) is a powerful wine, lemon-scented, with substantial body (14.5 per cent alcohol) and a strong surge of peachy, citrusy, slightly spicy flavours, showing a touch of complexity (5 per cent barrel-fermented). Vibrantly fruity, with fresh acidity and a dry finish (2.7 grams/litre of residual sugar), it's a distinctive wine, with good aging potential.

Vintage	15	14	13
WR	7	6	7
Drink	17-19	17-18	P

DRY $18 V+

Branded and Other White Wines

Cloudy Bay Te Koko, Dog Point Vineyard Section 94 – in this section you'll find all the white wines that don't feature varietal names. Lower-priced branded white wines can give winemakers an outlet for grapes like Chenin Blanc, Sémillon and Riesling that otherwise can be hard to sell. They can also be an outlet for coarser, less delicate juice ('pressings'). Some of the branded whites are quaffers, but others are highly distinguished.

Aurum Central Otago Amber Wine (★★★★★)

Looking for something completely different, made by ancient techniques? The 2014 vintage (★★★★★) is an amber-hued Pinot Gris, estate-grown, made with indigenous yeast fermentation and prolonged skin maceration, barrique-aged for over a year, and bottled unfined and unfiltered. Mouthfilling, it shows good complexity, with strong apricot and spice flavours, a touch of tannin, and a dry, structured finish. Certified organic.

DRY $45 AV

Bellbird Spring Home Block White ★★★★

The 2015 vintage (★★★☆) is a field blend of four aromatic grape varieties – Pinot Gris, Riesling, Muscat and Gewürztraminer – hand-picked at Waipara and fermented and lees-aged for five months in old oak barrels. Pale yellow, it is medium-bodied, with peachy, slightly spicy flavours, gentle sweetness, fresh acidity, a touch of complexity, and a smooth finish.

MED $32 –V

Bellbird Spring Sous Voile (★★★★★)

The non-vintage wine (★★★★★) released in 2015 is unique for New Zealand, but echoes wines from Jura, France, and amontillado sherry. Made in a deliberately 'oxidative' style from Waipara Pinot Gris, it was fermented dry and matured for four years in old oak barriques under a layer of yeast ('sous voile' means 'under veil'). Light gold, it is an unfortified wine (although harbouring 15.5 per cent alcohol), with substantial body and strong, dry, peachy, yeasty, nutty flavours. Well worth discovering.

DRY $40 (500 ML) AV

Cloudy Bay Te Koko ★★★★★

Te Koko o Kupe ('The Oyster Dredge of Kupe') is the original name for Cloudy Bay; it is also the name of the Marlborough winery's intriguing oak-aged Sauvignon Blanc. The 2014 vintage (★★★★☆), grown in the Wairau Valley, was fermented in French oak barrels (only 8 per cent new, to ensure a subtle oak influence), and matured in wood on its yeast lees for 15 months. Light yellow/green, it is fresh, mouthfilling and vibrant, with concentrated tropical-fruit flavours, a herbaceous undercurrent, lively acidity, well-integrated oak and a dry (3.5 grams/litre of residual sugar) finish. Te Koko lies well outside the mainstream regional style of Sauvignon Blanc, but it is well worth discovering.

Vintage	14	13	12	11	10
WR	7	7	6	7	7
Drink	17-20	17-20	17-18	17-18	P

DRY $53 AV

Craggy Range Te Muna Four

The 2014 vintage (★★★★) is a Martinborough 'field blend' (hand-harvested together) of a quartet of Alsatian varieties – Riesling, Pinot Gris, Gewürztraminer and Pinot Blanc. Fermented with indigenous yeasts and matured for six months in seasoned French oak barriques, it's a medium-bodied, tightly structured wine, scented and vibrantly fruity, with concentrated, citrusy, peachy, spicy flavours, a real sense of drive through the palate, and a long, dry (2.4 grams/litre of residual sugar) finish. (The 2015 vintage is a blend of the same four varieties, made in a dry style with barrel-ferment complexity.)

Dog Point Vineyard Section 94 ★★★★★

This ranks among the country's greatest oak-aged Sauvignon Blancs. Looking for 'texture, rather than rich aromatics', Dog Point fermented and lees-aged the 2015 vintage (★★★★★) for 18 months in seasoned French oak casks. Hand-harvested in the Dog Point Vineyard (for which 'Section 94' was the original survey title), at the confluence of the Brancott and Omaka valleys, and fermented with indigenous yeasts, it is light yellow/green, fragrant and mouthfilling. A fleshy, complex, tightly structured wine, it has deep, ripe, non-herbaceous fruit flavours, gently seasoned with oak, that build to a finely balanced, very long finish. Already highly enjoyable, it should be long-lived. (The 2007 vintage has been rereleased at a decade old in mid-2017, at $52 per bottle in six-packs. Still remarkably fresh and vigorous, it is ripely scented and mouthfilling, with penetrating grapefruit and lime flavours, showing excellent complexity, and notable vigour and depth.)

Vintage	15	14	13	12	11	10	09	08
WR	7	7	7	5	7	7	5	6
Drink	17-24	17-23	17-22	17-19	17-21	17-19	P	P

Expatrius Waiheke Island Advenus ★★★★☆

This sturdy blend of Sauvignon Blanc (principally) and Viognier is fermented in tanks and new oak barrels. The 2014 vintage (★★★★☆), 25 per cent barrel-fermented, is ripely fragrant, weighty and rounded, in a sweet-fruited style with concentrated, peachy, spicy flavours, fresh and lively, a subtle seasoning of oak, and an off-dry finish. Showing excellent personality and harmony, it's ready to roll.

Hans Herzog Marlborough Mistral ★★★★★

The delicious 2013 vintage (★★★★★) is a blend of traditional Rhône Valley grape varieties – Viognier (mostly), Marsanne and Roussanne. Fermented with indigenous yeasts and matured for 18 months in French oak puncheons, it is powerful, fleshy and dry, with highly concentrated, ripe stone-fruit flavours to the fore, finely integrated oak, and a very harmonious, slightly buttery, lasting finish. Certified organic.

Vintage	13	12
WR	7	7
Drink	17-23	17-22

Hunky Dory The Tangle   ★★★

From Huia, this is an estate-grown Marlborough blend of Pinot Gris (55 per cent), Gewürztraminer (35 per cent) and Riesling (10 per cent). Made in a dry style, it is typically a good, 'all-purpose' wine, freshly scented and mouthfilling, with lively acidity and satisfying depth of peach, pear, lychee and spice flavours. Certified organic.

Vintage	14
WR	6
Drink	17-18

DRY $18 AV

Kaimira Estate Nelson Hui Katoa   (★★★★)

Certified organic, the 2015 vintage (★★★★) is a blend (Hui Katoa means 'All Together') of Pinot Blanc, Viognier, Riesling and Gewürztraminer, estate-grown and barrel-fermented. The bouquet is floral; the palate is mouthfilling, with generous flavours of peaches, lychees, pears and spices, fresh and dryish (5 grams/litre of residual sugar).

MED/DRY $25 AV

Kaipara Estate Nine Lakes   ★★★☆

Estate-grown on the South Head peninsula of the Kaipara Harbour, this is a barrel-aged, Chardonnay-based wine, with smaller portions of such varieties as Pinot Gris, Arneis and Viognier. The 2014 vintage (★★★☆) is a light gold, mouthfilling, slightly toasty wine with a touch of sweetness (5 grams/litre of residual sugar) and strong, peachy, slightly honeyed flavours. Ready.

MED/DRY $36 –V

Man O' War Gravestone   ★★★★

Still on sale, the 2013 vintage (★★★★☆) is an age-worthy blend of Sauvignon Blanc (70 per cent) and Sémillon (30 per cent), grown at the eastern end of Waiheke Island and partly barrel-fermented. Mouthfilling, with ripely herbaceous flavours, a hint of toasty oak, and excellent concentration, drive and complexity, it's now in full stride.

DRY $33 –V

Peter Yealands Marlborough PGR   (★★★)

The 2015 vintage (★★★) is an 'aromatic blend' of Pinot Gris, Gewürztraminer and Riesling. Lemon-scented, it is medium-bodied, with vibrant, citrusy, slightly peachy and spicy flavours, a sliver of sweetness (7 grams/litre of residual sugar), balanced acidity, and an easy-drinking appeal. The 2016 vintage is a medium-bodied, off-dry (5.3 grams/litre of residual sugar) blend of Pinot Gris (47 per cent), Riesling (35 per cent) and Gewürztraminer (18 per cent).

Vintage	15
WR	7
Drink	17-18

MED/DRY $16 V+

Pushmi (★★★★)

Launched in mid-2017, this non-vintage wine (★★★★) from Gladstone Vineyard is a rare marriage of Sauvignon Blanc and Viognier, produced for the Arts Foundation. Grown in the northern Wairarapa and fermented in an even split of tanks and old barrels, it is fresh, youthful and mouthfilling. Vibrantly fruity, with peachy, slightly limey flavours, subtle oak adding a touch of complexity and a fully dry, crisp finish, it's currently more restrained than the label description of a 'generous, full-flavoured beast'. Best drinking 2018+.

DRY $31 –V

Quest Farm Alpino Central Otago Vin Gris ★★★☆

Made entirely from Pinot Noir, the 2014 vintage (★★★☆) is a pale pink, fully dry wine with vibrant strawberry, peach and spice flavours, mouthfilling, crisp and lively. Maturing gracefully, it's ready to roll.

DRY $21 AV

Ransom Matakana Compleat Pig (★★★★)

The very distinctive 2015 vintage (★★★★) is an 'orange' wine, made from Pinot Gris grapes left on their skins for a week, then drained to seasoned oak barrels for the rest of the fermentation (with indigenous yeasts) and several months of lees-aging. Pale orange, it is mouthfilling, with strong, peachy, spicy flavours, dry, lively and lingering.

DRY $27 –V

Richmond Plains Nelson Blanc de Noir ★★★☆

Certified organic, the fruity 2016 vintage (★★★☆) is a faintly pink wine, made from hand-picked Pinot Noir. Freshly aromatic, it's a very easy-drinking style, with good depth of vibrant, peachy, slightly spicy flavours and a smooth (9.5 grams/litre of residual sugar) finish. A summertime charmer.

MED/DRY $23 AV

Schubert Tribianco (★★★★)

The 2016 vintage (★★★★) is a distinctive Martinborough blend of Chardonnay, Müller-Thurgau and Pinot Gris. Hand-picked and fermented in French oak barriques and puncheons (15 per cent new), it's a floral, full-bodied wine with fresh, dry, peachy, slightly spicy flavours, showing excellent depth. Certified organic.

DRY $33 –V

Seresin Chiaroscuro ★★★★★

This organic Marlborough wine is a blend of equal portions of Chardonnay (for 'structure'), Pinot Gris (for 'texture'), and Riesling (for 'fruity acidity'). Estate-grown – mostly in the Raupo Creek Vineyard, in the Omaka Valley – the 2012 vintage (★★★★☆) was hand-picked and fermented with indigenous yeasts in old oak puncheons. Mouthfilling and vibrantly fruity, with strong, peachy, citrusy, slightly spicy and buttery flavours, woven with fresh acidity, it has good complexity and a long, tight finish. A wine of strong personality, it's still available and ready to roll.

Vintage	12	11	10
WR	6	7	7
Drink	17-18	17-18	P

DRY $65 AV

Sileni Estate Selection Hawke's Bay Alba ★★★★

The 2016 vintage (★★★★) is an unusual blend of Pinot Gris, Sauvignon Blanc, Albariño, Muscat and Chardonnay, barrel-aged for five months. Weighty, fleshy and dry (2.9 grams/litre of residual sugar), it's a bright, light lemon/green, aromatic wine, with peach, pear and spice flavours, showing excellent complexity and depth.

Vintage	16	15
WR	6	7
Drink	17-25	17-25

 DRY $33 –V

Terra Sancta Mysterious Diggings Mysterious White ★★★☆

Still on sale, the 2014 vintage (★★★☆) is a blend of Muscat, Gewürztraminer, Pinot Gris and Riesling, estate-grown and co-harvested at Bannockburn, in Central Otago, and partly (10 per cent) fermented in old oak puncheons. It is mouthfilling, vibrantly fruity and dry (4.7 grams/litre of residual sugar), with citrus-fruit, pear, lychee and spice flavours, showing a touch of complexity.

 DRY $25 –V

Tincan Wilful White New Zealand Natural Wine (★★★☆)

From a company based at Upper Moutere, in Nelson, the debut 2016 vintage (★★★☆) is a blend of Pinot Gris (50 per cent), Chardonnay, Sauvignon Blanc and Riesling. Made without sulphur-dioxide additions, fining and filtering, and bottled with a cork closure, it has slightly hazy, orange/brown colour. Medium to full-bodied, it has stone-fruit and spice flavours, with hints of oranges and apricots, good depth and a dry finish. Ready.

 DRY $28 –V

Wooing Tree Blondie ★★★☆

This 'blanc de noir' – a white (or rather faintly pink) Central Otago wine – is estate-grown at Cromwell. It is made from hand-picked Pinot Noir grapes; the juice is held briefly in contact with the skins and then fermented in tanks. Already enjoyable, the 2017 vintage (★★★☆) is pale, with the merest hint of pink. Still very youthful, it is freshly scented, with lots of lively, strawberryish, slightly spicy flavour, and a gently sweet (6.2 grams/litre of residual sugar), smooth finish.

MED/DRY $28 –V

Yealands Estate Single Vineyard Awatere Valley Marlborough PGR ★★★★

The 2015 vintage (★★★★) is a blend of Pinot Gris, Gewürztraminer and Riesling, estate-grown at Seaview, in the lower Awatere Valley. Scented and mouthfilling, it is a vibrantly fruity, off-dry wine (5.5 grams/litre of residual sugar), with generous, citrusy, peachy flavours, spicy notes, and excellent delicacy and length. The 2016 vintage is a blend of Pinot Gris (45 per cent), Riesling (40 per cent) and Gewürztraminer (15 per cent), made in a dry style (3 grams/litre of residual sugar).

Vintage	16	15	14
WR	7	7	7
Drink	17-19	17-18	17-18

 MED/DRY $23 AV

Breidecker

A nondescript crossing of Müller-Thurgau and the white hybrid Seibel 7053, Breidecker is rarely seen in New Zealand. There were 32 hectares of bearing vines recorded in 2003, but only 0.6 hectares in 2017 (in Otago and Marlborough). Its early-ripening ability is an advantage in cooler regions, but Breidecker typically yields light, fresh quaffing wines, best drunk young.

Hunter's Marlborough Breidecker ★★★

A drink-young charmer, 'for those who are new to wine'. Grown in the Wairau Valley, this wine is typically floral, light and lively, with a splash of sweetness, fresh acidity and ripe, citrusy, slightly peachy and spicy flavours.

MED/DRY $18 AV

Chardonnay

Do you drink Chardonnay? Sauvignon Blanc is our biggest-selling white-wine variety by far, and Pinot Gris is riding high, but neither of these popular grapes produces New Zealand's greatest dry whites. Chardonnay wears that crown. It's less fashionable than 20 or 30 years ago, but Chardonnay is our most prestigious white-wine variety. No other dry whites can command such lofty prices; many New Zealand Chardonnays are on the shelves at $50 or more. And although it has lost ground to Sauvignon Blanc and Pinot Gris, Chardonnay is still a big seller. Winegrowers are currently reporting a surge in sales, suggesting that Chardonnay is coming back into fashion. However, New Zealand Chardonnay has yet to make the huge international impact of our Sauvignon Blanc. Our top Chardonnays are classy, but so are those from a host of other countries in the Old and New Worlds. In 2017, Chardonnay accounted for 2.4 per cent by volume of New Zealand's wine exports (far behind Sauvignon Blanc, with over 86 per cent). There's an enormous range to choose from. Most wineries – especially in the North Island and upper South Island – make at least one Chardonnay; many produce several and the big wineries produce dozens. The hallmark of New Zealand Chardonnays is their delicious varietal intensity – the leading labels show notably concentrated aromas and flavours, threaded with fresh, appetising acidity.The price of New Zealand Chardonnay ranges from under $10 to over $100. The quality differences are equally wide, although not always in relation to their prices. Lower-priced wines are typically fermented in stainless steel tanks and bottled young with little or no oak influence; these wines rely on fresh, lemony, uncluttered fruit flavours for their appeal. Chardonnays labelled as 'unoaked' were briefly popular a few years ago, as winemakers with an eye on overseas markets worked hard to showcase New Zealand's fresh, vibrant fruit characters. But without oak flavours to add richness and complexity, Chardonnay handled entirely in stainless steel tanks can be plain – even boring. The key to the style is to use well-ripened, intensely flavoured grapes.

Mid-price wines may be fermented in tanks and matured in oak casks, which adds to their complexity and richness, or fermented and/or matured in a mix of tanks and barrels (or handled entirely in tanks, with oak chips or staves suspended in the wine). The top labels are fully fermented and matured in oak barrels (normally French barriques, with varying proportions of new casks); there may also be extended aging on (and regular stirring of) yeast lees and varying proportions of a secondary, softening malolactic fermentation (sometimes referred to in the tasting notes as 'malo'). The best of these display the arresting subtlety and depth of flavour for which Chardonnay is so highly prized.

Chardonnay plantings have been far outstripped in recent years by Sauvignon Blanc, as wine producers respond to overseas demand, and in 2018 will constitute 8.8 per cent of the bearing vineyard. The variety is spread throughout the wine regions, particularly Marlborough (where 34 per cent of the vines are concentrated), Hawke's Bay (32 per cent) and Gisborne (22 per cent). Gisborne is renowned for its softly mouthfilling, ripe, peachy Chardonnays, which offer very seductive drinking in their youth; Hawke's Bay yields sturdy wines with rich grapefruit-like flavours, power and longevity; and Marlborough's Chardonnays are slightly leaner in a cool-climate, appetisingly crisp style.

Chardonnay has often been dubbed 'the red-wine drinker's white wine'. Chardonnays are usually (although not always, especially cheap models) fully dry, as are all reds with any aspirations to quality. Chardonnay's typically mouthfilling body and multi-faceted flavours are another obvious red-wine parallel.

Broaching a top New Zealand Chardonnay at less than two years old can be unrewarding – the finest of the 2014s will offer excellent drinking during 2018. If you must drink Chardonnay when it is only a year old, it makes sense to buy one of the cheaper, less complex wines specifically designed to be enjoyable in their youth.

Aitken's Folly Riverbank Road The Reserved Barrel
Wanaka Central Otago Chardonnay   (★★★★)

Well worth cellaring, the 2014 vintage (★★★★) was estate-grown, barrel-fermented and oak-aged for 18 months (compared to 10 months for the 'standard' wine). Pale straw, it is mouthfilling, with strong, citrusy, slightly peachy flavours, firm acid spine, and a long, steely, slightly toasty finish. Best drinking 2018+.

DRY $35 –V

Aitken's Folly Riverbank Road Wanaka Central Otago Chardonnay   (★★★★)

The 2014 vintage (★★★★) is the only wine in the country based solely on Chardonnay clone 548. Estate-grown, it was fermented in French oak barriques (30 per cent new), given a full, softening malolactic fermentation, and barrel-aged for 10 months. Lemon-scented, it is a distinctly cool-climate, tightly structured style, with very good vigour and intensity of citrusy, slightly buttery flavours, showing good complexity.

DRY $28 AV

Akarua Central Otago Chardonnay   ★★★★

The estate-grown 2014 vintage (★★★★) was hand-harvested at Bannockburn and fermented and matured in French oak barrels (10 per cent new). Mouthfilling, it is creamy and biscuity, with grapefruit-like flavours to the fore, fresh acidity, a hint of spice, and good complexity and length. Subtle and finely poised, it should be at its best 2018+.

Vintage	14	13	12
WR	6	6	6
Drink	17-21	17-20	17-19

DRY $29 AV

Ake Ake Northland Chardonnay   (★★★☆)

The 2014 vintage (★★★☆) was fermented and matured for eight months, with weekly lees-stirring, in French and American oak casks (new and seasoned). It has a nutty bouquet, leading into a mouthfilling, dry wine with strong, ripe, peachy, toasty flavours, balanced acidity, and a slightly buttery finish.

DRY $25 –V

Alchemy Hawke's Bay Chardonnay   ★★★★☆

Offering excellent value, the 2015 vintage (★★★★☆) is a single-vineyard wine, hand-picked at Puketapu, in the Dartmoor Valley, and fermented and matured for a year in French oak barrels (30 per cent new). Bright, light lemon/green, with a fragrant bouquet, it is a full-bodied, sweet-fruited wine, with fresh, strong, peachy flavours, seasoned with toasty oak, and excellent complexity. Delicious now, it should also reward cellaring for a year or two.

DRY $29 V+

Alexander Martinborough Chardonnay   ★★★★☆

Delicious now, the 2015 vintage (★★★★☆) was matured for 11 months in French oak hogsheads (one year old). Lemon-scented, it is fragrant and full-bodied, with generous citrus and stone-fruit flavours, gently seasoned with toasty oak, good complexity and a long finish. It's still developing; drink now or cellar. The 2016 vintage (★★★★) was hand-picked and fermented in French oak barriques (one year old). Light lemon/green, it is fresh and youthful, with mouthfilling body, strong, ripe grapefruit-like flavours, well-integrated oak and obvious potential; open mid-2018+.

Vintage	16	15
WR	5	6
Drink	18-22	18-22

DRY $29 V+

Allan Scott Eli Marlborough Chardonnay   (★★★★☆)

The debut 2016 vintage (★★★★☆) is rare – just one barrel was produced. Fermented with indigenous yeasts and given 'lots' of lees-stirring, it's a weighty, harmonious wine, concentrated and finely textured, with deep, citrusy, peachy flavours, biscuity and well-rounded.

 DRY $100 –V

Allan Scott Generations Marlborough Chardonnay   ★★★★

The debut 2015 vintage (★★★★) is an upfront style, estate-grown in the Wallops Vineyard and matured for 16 months in French oak puncheons (80 per cent new). Light lemon/green, it has a creamy bouquet, leading into a mouthfilling, sweet-fruited, slightly buttery, smoothly textured wine, with ripe, peachy, toasty flavours, showing very good depth and complexity. The 2016 vintage (★★★★) was fermented in puncheons and hogsheads (mostly seasoned). Already enjoyable, it's a weighty wine, with generous stone-fruit flavours, slightly biscuity and well-rounded.

 DRY $30 –V

Alpha Domus AD Hawke's Bay Chardonnay   ★★★★☆

The classy 2015 vintage (★★★★★) is a single-vineyard wine, estate-grown in the Bridge Pa Triangle. Fermented and matured for a year in French oak casks (60 per cent new), it is mouthfilling and tightly structured, with youthful grapefruit and stone-fruit flavours, showing excellent intensity, delicacy and complexity, fresh acidity and a finely poised, lasting finish. Best drinking 2019+.

 DRY $38 –V

Alpha Domus First Solo Hawke's Bay Chardonnay   ★★★★

The generous 2014 vintage (★★★★) was estate-grown in the Bridge Pa Triangle and French oak-fermented (25 per cent new). Fleshy and sweet-fruited, it is slightly toasty and creamy, with strong, ripe, citrusy, peachy flavours and a well-rounded finish.

Vintage	14	13	12	11
WR	7	7	6	5
Drink	17-18	P	P	P

DRY $26 AV

Alpha Domus The Pilot Hawke's Bay Chardonnay ★★★

Drinking well now, the 2015 vintage (★★★☆) was estate-grown in the Bridge Pa Triangle and partly barrel-fermented. Light lemon/green, it's a 'fruit-driven' style, finely balanced, with a subtle oak seasoning and very good depth of fresh citrusy, peachy, slightly buttery flavours.

DRY $19 AV

Alpha Domus The Skybolt Hawke's Bay Chardonnay (★★★☆)

The 2016 vintage (★★★☆) is a single-vineyard wine, estate-grown in the Bridge Pa Triangle and fermented in French oak barriques. Fresh and full-bodied, it is vibrant and sweet-fruited, with slightly biscuity, buttery notes adding complexity, finely balanced acidity and plenty of drink-young appeal.

DRY $28 –V

Anchorage Family Estate Nelson Chardonnay ★★☆

The 2014 vintage (★★☆) is a medium-bodied wine, made in a vibrant, 'fruit-driven' style with crisp, lemony, slightly buttery flavours.

DRY $19 –V

Anchorage Family Estate Reserve Nelson Chardonnay ★★★☆

Made in an upfront style, the good-value 2014 vintage (★★★☆) is a single-vineyard wine, barrel-fermented. Pale straw, it is mouthfilling, with strong, peachy, slightly toasty flavours and a creamy-smooth finish. Drink now.

DRY $18 V+

Archangel Central Otago Chardonnay ★★★☆

The 2014 vintage (★★★☆) has a creamy, biscuity bouquet. The palate shows good depth of peachy, citrusy, slightly spicy flavours, with nutty notes and considerable complexity.

Vintage	14	13
WR	7	6
Drink	17-20	17-18

DRY $26 –V

Aronui Single Vineyard Nelson Chardonnay ★★★★

The creamy-textured 2014 vintage (★★★★) was hand-picked and French oak-fermented. Mouthfilling, it shows good complexity, with ripe, peachy, slightly toasty flavours, balanced acidity and excellent depth and harmony. (From Kono, also owner of the Tohu brand.)

DRY $25 AV

Ash Ridge Estate Hawke's Bay Chardonnay ★★★★

Priced sharply, the 2016 vintage (★★★★) was estate-grown in the Bridge Pa Triangle, fully barrel-fermented (10 per cent new), and 90 per cent of the blend went through a secondary, softening malolactic fermentation. Enjoyable from the start, it has strong, vibrant peach and grapefruit flavours, well-integrated oak and a finely textured, slightly buttery finish.

DRY $20 V+

Ash Ridge Premium Hawke's Bay Chardonnay   (★★★★)

Still very youthful, the 2016 vintage (★★★★) was grown in the Bridge Pa Triangle and fermented in French oak casks (30 per cent new). It has a fragrant, complex bouquet, leading into a medium to full-bodied wine with vibrant, ripe, citrusy, peachy flavours, oak and lees-aging notes adding complexity, and fresh, finely balanced acidity. Best drinking mid-2018+.

DRY $30 –V

Ash Ridge Reserve Hawke's Bay Chardonnay   ★★★★☆

Estate-grown in the Bridge Pa Triangle, the 2016 vintage (★★★★☆) was fermented and matured in French oak casks (45 per cent new). Designed for cellaring, it is an elegant, youthful wine, medium to full-bodied, with concentrated, citrusy, peachy flavours, showing excellent vibrancy and complexity, and a tightly structured, long finish. Open 2019+.

DRY $40 –V

Ashwell Martinborough Chardonnay   ★★★★

Barrique-fermented, the 2016 vintage (★★★★) is a youthful, full-bodied wine with strong, ripe stone-fruit flavours, well-integrated oak adding complexity, fresh acidity and a dry, lasting finish. Best drinking 2019+.

Vintage	15
WR	5
Drink	17-20

DRY $28 AV

Askerne Hawke's Bay Chardonnay   ★★★

Fleshy and high-flavoured, the 2014 vintage (★★★★) was estate-grown, hand-picked and matured for nine months in seasoned French and Hungarian oak barrels. Mouthfilling and sweet-fruited, it has generous stone-fruit flavours, oak complexity and a well-rounded finish. The 2015 vintage (★★☆), fully barrel-fermented, is a solid, slightly honeyed wine.

DRY $22 –V

Askerne Reserve Hawke's Bay Chardonnay   ★★★★☆

The 2014 vintage (★★★★) is a classic regional style. Hand-picked and barrel-fermented (45 per cent new oak), it is fleshy and sweet-fruited, with generous, peachy flavours, finely integrated oak adding complexity, and a well-rounded finish. Retasted in mid-2016, it's maturing well.

DRY $30 AV

Astrolabe Province Marlborough Chardonnay   ★★★★

The 2015 vintage (★★★★) was hand-picked at two sites (Astrolabe Farm Vineyard, in the lower Wairau Valley, and Wrekin Vineyard, in the Southern Valleys), and fermented and matured for 10 months in French oak barriques and puncheons. Bright, light lemon/green, it is mouthfilling and vibrant, with strong grapefruit and peach flavours, slightly buttery and toasty notes, and good complexity. Drink now or cellar.

DRY $26 AV

Ata Rangi Craighall Martinborough Chardonnay   ★★★★★

This memorable wine has notable richness, complexity and downright drinkability. From a company-owned block of low-yielding Mendoza-clone vines in the Craighall Vineyard, planted in 1983, it is hand-picked, whole-bunch pressed and fermented with indigenous yeasts in French oak barriques (typically 25 per cent new). Bright, light lemon/green, the 2016 vintage (★★★★★) is an elegant, very youthful and tightly structured wine. Weighty and generous, it has ripe grapefruit and peach flavours, gently seasoned with toasty oak, excellent depth, delicacy and complexity, fine acidity and a very long finish. Still a baby, it should flourish with cellaring; open 2019 onwards.

Vintage	15	14	13	12	11	10
WR	7	7	7	6	7	7
Drink	17-23	17-22	17-21	17-19	17-19	17-18

DRY $38 AV

Ata Rangi Petrie Wairarapa Chardonnay   ★★★★☆

This single-vineyard wine is grown at East Taratahi, south of Masterton, in the Wairarapa. Based on mature vines (over 20 years old), it is hand-picked and fermented and lees-aged in French oak casks. Lemon-hued, the 2015 vintage (★★★★☆) is mouthfilling, with strong, vibrant, grapefruit and peach flavours, biscuity and buttery notes adding complexity, fresh acidity and a finely poised finish. Best drinking 2018+.

DRY $28 V+

Ataahua Waipara Chardonnay   ★★★★

The 2015 vintage (★★★★☆) is fragrant, with a slightly buttery bouquet. A high-flavoured, sweet-fruited wine, it was barrel-fermented and given a full, softening malolactic fermentation. Mouthfilling, with generous, peachy, slightly spicy and mealy flavours, a hint of butterscotch and good complexity, it is well worth cellaring, but already delicious.

DRY $30 –V

Auntsfield Cob Cottage Southern Valleys Marlborough Chardonnay   ★★★★★

This single 'block' – rather than just single 'vineyard' – wine is estate-grown on the south side of the Wairau Valley. The 2014 vintage (★★★★★) is powerful, weighty and sweet-fruited. Matured for 10 months in French oak casks (35 per cent new), it is light lemon/green, with highly concentrated, ripe stone-fruit flavours, youthful, complex and lasting. Best drinking 2018+.

Vintage	14
WR	6
Drink	17-24

DRY $49 AV

Auntsfield Single Vineyard Southern Valleys Marlborough Chardonnay   ★★★★★

This consistently rewarding wine is estate-grown on the south side of the Wairau Valley, hand-picked and fermented and matured in French oak barrels (18 per cent new in 2014). The 2014 vintage (★★★★☆) is light lemon/green, with a slightly creamy bouquet. Mouthfilling, it is tightly structured, with strong, peachy, slightly appley and smoky flavours, woven with fresh acidity, well-integrated oak adding complexity, and a lingering finish.

Vintage	14	13	12	11	10
WR	7	7	6	7	6
Drink	17-20	17-20	17-19	17-18	P

DRY $33 AV

Aurum Central Otago Chardonnay   ★★★★

Drinking well from the start, the 2014 vintage (★★★★) is a creamy-textured wine, fermented with indigenous yeasts and barrel-aged for 16 months (20 per cent new). It has strong, citrusy, appley, slightly peachy flavours, showing good complexity, balanced acidity, and a rounded, lingering finish.

DRY $45 –V

Awatere River by Louis Vavasour Marlborough Chardonnay   ★★★★

The 2015 vintage (★★★★) is a single-vineyard wine, hand-picked and fermented and matured in French oak barriques (15 per cent new). Pale straw, it is mouthfilling, with vibrant grapefruit and peach flavours, balanced acidity, well-integrated nutty oak adding complexity, and a slightly creamy finish. Best drinking 2018+.

Vintage	15
WR	6
Drink	17-21

DRY $32 –V

Babich Family Estates Headwaters Organic Marlborough Chardonnay   ★★★★

The 2015 vintage (★★★★☆), certified organic, was partly barrel-fermented, with some use of new oak, and 60 per cent of the blend went through a softening malolactic fermentation. It has an invitingly fragrant, slightly creamy and nutty bouquet. A youthful, fleshy wine, it has generous, ripe, peachy, citrusy and slightly spicy flavours, showing good complexity, a minerally streak, and excellent vigour, depth and harmony. Best drinking 2018+.

DRY $27 AV

Babich Hawke's Bay Chardonnay   ★★★☆

The 2016 vintage (★★★☆) is an unoaked style. Full-bodied and dry, it has fresh, ripe stone-fruit flavours to the fore, a slightly buttery note (from 15 to 20 per cent malolactic fermentation), and lots of drink-young appeal.

DRY $22 AV

Babich Irongate Chardonnay   ★★★★★

Babich's flagship Chardonnay. A stylish wine, Irongate was traditionally markedly leaner and tighter than other top Hawke's Bay Chardonnays, while performing well in the cellar, but the latest releases have more drink-young appeal. It is based on hand-picked fruit from the shingly Irongate Vineyard in Gimblett Road, fully barrel-fermented (about 20 per cent new), and lees-matured for up to 10 months. Malolactic fermentation was very rare up to the 2002, but has since exerted a growing influence. The 2015 vintage (★★★★☆) was mostly fermented with indigenous yeasts (80 per cent). Light yellow/green, it is an elegant, fragrant, mouthfilling wine with very youthful, citrusy, peachy flavours, finely integrated oak, good complexity and a lasting finish. Best drinking 2019+.

Vintage	15	14	13	12	11
WR	7	6	7	4	6
Drink	17-26	17-25	17-25	17-18	17-20

DRY $37 AV

Beach House Selection Hawke's Bay Chardonnay (★★★★)

Enjoyable young, the 2016 vintage (★★★★) was hand-harvested at four sites – Bay View, Te Awanga, Twyford and in the Gimblett Gravels – barrel-fermented (15 per cent new) and given a full, softening malolactic fermentation. Bright, light lemon/green, with a fragrant, slightly buttery bouquet, it is weighty, with rich, peachy flavours, showing good complexity, and a creamy-smooth finish. Drink now or cellar.

Beach House The Levels Stoney Beach Gravels Hawke's Bay Chardonnay (★★★★★)

The multi-faceted 2016 vintage (★★★★★) was estate-grown in The Levels Vineyards, at Te Awanga, hand-picked, and fermented and matured for 10 months in French oak casks of varying sizes (33 per cent new). Bright, light lemon/green, it has a fragrant bouquet, showing indigenous yeast notes. A classic regional style, it is mouthfilling and lively, with concentrated, ripe stonefruit-like flavours, enriched with oak, excellent complexity and obvious potential; open 2019 onwards. Fine value.

Beach House The Track Gimblett Gravels Hawke's Bay Chardonnay (★★★★☆)

The elegant, very youthful 2016 vintage (★★★★☆) was estate-grown and hand-picked in Mere Road, fermented with indigenous yeasts in French oak barrels (28 per cent new), and mostly (75 per cent) given a softening malolactic fermentation. Light lemon/green, it has vibrant, grapefruit-like flavours, showing excellent delicacy and depth, a subtle seasoning of oak, and impressive complexity and harmony. It's crying out for cellaring; open 2019+.

Bell Bird Bay Reserve Hawke's Bay Chardonnay (★★★)

The easy-drinking 2014 vintage (★★★) was grown in the Bridge Pa Triangle and matured on its yeast lees for 10 months, with some use of French oak. Light lemon/green, it is mouthfilling and sweet-fruited, with fresh, ripe, peachy flavours to the fore, buttery notes and a smooth finish. (From Alpha Domus.)

Bent Duck Bay of Islands Chardonnay ★★★☆

The 2014 vintage (★★★☆) of this Northland wine was barrel-fermented and oak-aged for nine months. Made in an upfront style, it is weighty and fleshy, with generous, ripe stone-fruit flavours, a toasty oak influence and a slightly creamy finish. (From Byrne Wines.)

DRY $25 –V

Bespoke Mills Reef Hawke's Bay Chardonnay (★★★★☆)

The debut 2016 vintage (★★★★☆) was designed to 'pay tribute to the famous old-school style', with 'lashings of toasty oak'. Already drinking well, it was grown at Maraekakaho, in the Bridge Pa Triangle, barrel-fermented, matured for over a year in a 3:1 mix of French and American oak casks, and given a full, softening malolactic fermentation. Pale straw, it has an oaky, creamy bouquet. A softly mouthfilling wine, it is fat and generous, with concentrated, peachy, toasty flavours and a rich, well-rounded finish. Best drinking mid-2018+.

Bilancia Hawke's Bay Chardonnay ★★★★★

The youthful 2015 vintage (★★★★☆) was estate-grown, hand-picked and fermented with indigenous yeasts in French oak puncheons (30 per cent new). Light lemon/green, with a fragrant, smoky ('struck match') bouquet, it is full-bodied, with excellent depth of vigorous, grapefruit-like flavours, integrated oak, and a dry, lingering finish. Best drinking 2019+.

Vintage	15	14	13
WR	6	6	7
Drink	17-22	17-20	17-18

 DRY $34 AV

Bishop's Head Waipara Valley Chardonnay (★★★★)

The 2014 vintage (★★★★) is an elegant, tightly structured wine. Hand-picked, fermented with indigenous yeasts in French oak barrels (30 per cent new) and lees-aged for 11 months, it is medium to full-bodied, with vibrant, citrusy, slightly buttery flavours, good acid spine, and mealy, biscuity notes adding complexity.

 DRY $30 –V

Black Barn Barrel Fermented Chardonnay ★★★★☆

Estate-grown in the Havelock North hills, hand-picked and barrel-fermented, this is typically a classy wine, in a classic regional style. The 2014 vintage (★★★★) is mouthfilling and still youthful, with vibrant, peachy, biscuity flavours, barrel-ferment complexity, and very good depth and potential.

 DRY $35 –V

Black Barn Unoaked Chardonnay (★★★☆)

Bottled by July, the 2017 vintage (★★★☆) was estate-grown and hand-picked at Havelock North, in Hawke's Bay. Still very youthful, it is full-bodied and dry, with plenty of ripe, peachy flavours, showing good freshness and vigour.

 DRY $25 –V

Black Cottage Reserve Marlborough Chardonnay (★★★☆)

Offfering good value, the 2014 vintage (★★★☆) is a single-vineyard wine, hand-picked and fermented and matured for 11 months in French oak barrels. Full-bodied, it has very good depth of peachy, citrusy, slightly mealy and buttery flavours, showing considerable complexity, and a rounded finish.

 DRY $18 V+

Black Estate Home Chardonnay ★★★★☆

The 2016 vintage (★★★★) is from the Home Vineyard at Omihi, Waipara, where the oldest vines were planted in 1994. Hand-picked and fermented with indigenous yeasts in French oak barrels (20 per cent new), it was given a full, softening malolactic fermentation and bottled unfiltered. Light lemon/green, it is mouthfilling, with very youthful, grapefruit-like flavours, hints of peaches and nectarines, mealy notes adding complexity, a subtle seasoning of oak and fresh acidity. An elegant, restrained, distinctly cool-climate style, it needs time; open 2019+.

DRY $45 –V

Black Estate Netherwood Waipara Valley Chardonnay ★★★★☆

The 2015 vintage (★★★★★) was grown on a south-facing block in the Netherwood Vineyard at Omihi, planted in 1986 and now owned by Black Estate. A rare wine (49 cases only), it was hand-picked, fermented with indigenous yeasts in old French oak casks, given a full, softening malolactic fermentation, and bottled unfined and unfiltered. A highly distinctive, thought-provoking wine, it is minerally, citrusy and gently oaked, in a restrained, subtle style with good intensity and a long, crisp finish. Still very youthful, it is tightly structured and should be long-lived.

DRY $65 –V

Black Ridge Central Otago Chardonnay (★★★☆)

Still on the market and maturing soundly, the 2013 vintage (★★★☆) was grown at Alexandra and lees-stirred in seasoned oak barrels. Light lemon/green, it is moderately complex, with fresh, citrusy, peachy, gently toasty flavours and a crisp, slightly buttery finish. Drink now.

Vintage	13
WR	6
Drink	17-22

DRY $26 –V

Blackenbrook Family Reserve Nelson Chardonnay ★★★★

The powerful 2014 vintage (★★★★) was matured for a year in American oak casks (43 per cent new). Pale straw, it has substantial body (15 per cent alcohol), with generous, peachy, citrusy flavours, strongly seasoned with oak, considerable complexity and a creamy-smooth finish. If you like a bold style of Chardonnay, try this.

Vintage	14
WR	6
Drink	17-25

DRY $38 –V

Blackenbrook Nelson Chardonnay ★★★★

The sturdy 2016 vintage (★★★★) was estate-grown, hand-harvested, partly barrel-fermented, and matured for a year in American (62 per cent) and French (38 per cent) oak casks (6 per cent new). Pale lemon/green, it is mouthfilling, with generous, vibrant, peachy, slightly toasty flavours, showing considerable complexity, and a well-rounded finish. Enjoyable young.

Vintage	16
WR	7
Drink	17-21

DRY $25 AV

Boneline, The, Barebone Waipara Chardonnay (★★★★☆)

If you are looking for an unoaked, Chablis-style Chardonnay, this North Canterbury beauty is hard to beat. The 2016 vintage (★★★★☆) is not at all brash, but still full of personality. Pale, with mouthfilling body, it is lemon-scented, very fresh and vibrant, with pure, delicate, citrusy, peachy flavours, lively acidity, a minerally streak, and excellent vigour and length. Fine value.

DRY $23 V+

Boneline, The, Sharkstone Waipara Chardonnay ★★★★★

The distinguished 2016 vintage (★★★★★) was estate-grown, hand-picked from 20-year-old vines and fermented with indigenous yeasts in French oak barrels (22 per cent new). An elegant, distinctly cool-climate style, it is full-bodied, with youthful, very fresh, pure and delicate flavours, citrusy, peachy, vaguely buttery and persistent. A finely poised, very harmonious wine, it should flourish with cellaring; open 2019+.

DRY $35 AV

Boric French Oak Barrel Fermented Chardonnay (★★★★)

Produced by Boric Food Market, the 2016 vintage (★★★★) is a rare wine. Grown in the Kerr Vineyard at Kumeu, in West Auckland, it was hand-picked and fermented and matured for nine months in a single new French oak barrel. Light lemon/green, it is weighty, with deep, ripe stone-fruit flavours, strongly seasoned with oak, and a well-rounded finish. Best drinking 2019+.

DRY $30 –V

Boundary Vineyards Tuki Tuki Road Hawke's Bay Chardonnay ★★★☆

Pernod Ricard NZ's wine is grown near the coast, at Te Awanga, fermented in Hungarian oak barriques, and much of the blend is given a softening malolactic fermentation. The 2015 vintage (★★★★) is a great buy. Bright, light yellow, it is mouthfilling and vibrantly fruity, with good concentration of peach and grapefruit flavours, a hint of butterscotch and a tight finish.

DRY $20 AV

Brancott Estate Letter Series 'O' Marlborough Chardonnay ★★★★★

Named after the company's Omaka Vineyard, this typically refined wine is hand-picked at sites on the south side of the Wairau Valley, fermented with indigenous yeasts in French oak barriques (about 40 per cent new), and given a full, softening malolactic fermentation. The 2015 vintage (★★★★☆) has a fragrant, complex, nutty bouquet. Highly expressive in its youth, it is full-bodied, with very generous, ripe, peachy, slightly buttery and toasty flavours, showing excellent concentration and complexity. Drink now or cellar.

DRY $33 V+

Brancott Estate Marlborough Chardonnay (★★★☆)

Priced sharply, the 2015 vintage (★★★☆) is drinking well from the start. Full-bodied, it has peachy, slightly spicy and creamy flavours, showing good depth, a touch of complexity and a well-rounded finish.

DRY $17 V+

Brancott Estate Terroir Series Southern Valleys Marlborough Chardonnay (★★★★)

The debut 2014 vintage (★★★★) was grown in the Southern Valleys sub-region and fermented and matured for seven months in large new French oak cuves. Full-bodied, dry and sweet-fruited, it has strong, citrusy, peachy flavours, slightly buttery and smooth, a subtle seasoning of oak, and excellent depth and harmony. Delicious young.

DRY $20 V+

Brightside Nelson Chardonnay ★★★

From Kaimira, the 2015 vintage (★★★) was fermented in a 50:50 split of tanks and barrels. It is mouthfilling, with peachy, slightly buttery flavours, fresh acidity and a smooth finish. Certified organic.

DRY $18 AV

Brightside Organic Chardonnay (★★★)

Bargain-priced, the 2015 vintage (★★★) was fermented in seasoned oak barrels. It has youthful colour, with fresh, ripe-fruit flavours to the fore, slightly buttery and toasty notes, balanced acidity, and current-drinking appeal.

DRY $16 V+

Brightwater Vineyards Lord Rutherford Barrique Chardonnay ★★★★☆

The 2014 vintage (★★★★☆) is a single-vineyard, estate-grown, Nelson wine, hand-picked and fermented in French oak barriques (25 per cent new). Barrel-matured for a year and given a full, softening malolactic fermentation, it is a powerful, full-bodied, concentrated wine, with generous, ripe stone-fruit flavours and biscuity, buttery notes adding richness and complexity. A bold style of Chardonnay, it's likely to be at its best 2018+.

Vintage	14	13	12	11	10
WR	7	6	7	NM	7
Drink	17-20	17-19	17-18	NM	P

DRY $40 –V

Brightwater Vineyards Nelson Chardonnay ★★★★

The 2014 vintage (★★★★) was estate-grown, hand-picked, and fermented and matured for 11 months in French oak barriques (20 per cent new). It is mouthfilling and vibrantly fruity, with peach and grapefruit flavours, showing good concentration, a gentle seasoning of toasty oak, and a slightly buttery finish.

Vintage	14
WR	6
Drink	P

DRY $25 AV

Brodie Estate Martinborough Chardonnay ★★★★

The 2015 vintage (★★★☆) was fermented and lees-aged in oak barrels (20 per cent new). Softly mouthfilling, it has good depth of fresh, ripe, peachy, slightly toasty flavours, showing considerable complexity, and a creamy-smooth finish.

DRY $30 –V

Bronte Nelson Chardonnay ★★★☆

From Rimu Grove, the 2016 vintage (★★★☆) was grown at Moutere and French oak-aged. Light lemon/green, with a fragrant, citrusy, peachy bouquet, it is full-bodied and vibrant, with ripe-fruit flavours to the fore, fresh acidity and good depth. Enjoyable young.

Vintage	16	15
WR	6	7
Drink	17-27	17-26

DRY $24 AV

Brookfields Bergman Chardonnay   ★★★☆

Named after the Ingrid Bergman roses in the estate garden, this wine is grown alongside the winery at Meeanee, in Hawke's Bay, hand-picked, and fermented and matured on its yeast lees in seasoned French and American oak casks. The 2016 vintage (★★★☆) is full-bodied, with generous, ripe citrus and stone-fruit flavours, showing a touch of complexity, and a smooth finish. Enjoyable young.

Vintage	16	15
WR	7	7
Drink	17-21	18-20

 DRY $20 AV

Brookfields Marshall Bank Chardonnay   ★★★★☆

Brookfields' top Chardonnay is named after proprietor Peter Robertson's grandfather's property in Otago. Grown in a vineyard adjacent to the winery at Meeanee and fermented and matured (with weekly stirring of its yeast lees) in French oak barriques (50 per cent new in 2015), it is a powerful, classy, concentrated Hawke's Bay wine. The 2015 vintage (★★★★☆), oak-matured for 10 months, is still youthful. Fragrant, with rich, citrusy, peachy, biscuity, nutty flavours, ripe and rounded, it is savoury and complex, with obvious potential; best drinking 2018+.

Vintage	15
WR	7
Drink	18-21

 DRY $30 AV

Bushmere Estate Classic Gisborne Chardonnay   (★★★★)

Delicious young, the 2015 vintage (★★★★) was French oak-fermented. A fresh, medium to full-bodied wine, it is vibrantly fruity, with generous, ripe, peachy flavours, finely integrated oak, gentle acidity, and good texture and harmony.

 DRY $25 AV

Byrne Northland Puketotara Chardonnay   ★★★★☆

This powerful wine is grown in the Fat Pig Vineyard. Bright, light lemon/green, the 2016 vintage (★★★★☆) was fermented in French oak barriques (33 per cent new). Fragrant and mouthfilling, it is fresh and creamy-textured, in a concentrated, strongly oak-influenced style, complex and lingering. Best drinking mid-2018+.

DRY $30 AV

C.J. Pask Chardonnays – see Pask

Cable Bay Awatere Valley Marlborough Chardonnay   (★★★☆)

The 2014 vintage (★★★☆) is a fruit-driven style, mostly handled in tanks; 12 per cent was fermented and matured in new French oak barrels. Fresh, lively and weighty, it has citrusy, slightly appley flavours and a finely textured, slightly creamy finish.

Vintage	14
WR	5
Drink	17-25

 DRY $25 –V

Cable Bay Waiheke Chardonnay ★★★★

Blended from three estate vineyards at the western end of the island, the 2015 vintage (★★★★) was fermented and matured for a year in French oak puncheons and barriques (20 per cent new). A still-youthful, creamy-textured wine, it is medium-bodied, with citrusy, appley, mealy, slightly biscuity flavours, showing very good depth, vigour and complexity. Best drinking 2018+.

Vintage	16	15
WR	5	6
Drink	17-27	17-24

 DRY $45 –V

Carrick Bannockburn Central Otago Chardonnay ★★★★☆

Certified organic, this consistently impressive wine is estate-grown, fermented with indigenous yeasts, matured for almost a year in French oak barriques (10 per cent new), and bottled unfined and unfiltered. The 2015 vintage (★★★★☆) is an elegant, tightly structured wine with a fragrant bouquet, showing good complexity. Mouthfilling, it is fresh and vibrant, with strong, youthful grapefruit and peach flavours, finely integrated oak and good acid spine. The 2016 vintage (★★★★☆) is similar – tightly structured, with ripe, citrusy flavours, showing good intensity, gentle mealy, toasty notes adding complexity, fresh acidity and obvious potential; best drinking 2019+.

Vintage	16	15	14	13	12	11
WR	6	5	6	7	7	6
Drink	18-23	17-21	17-21	17-20	17-18	P

 DRY $38 –V

Carrick Cairnmuir Terraces EBM Chardonnay ★★★★★

From a region producing increasingly fine, often underrated Chardonnays, this is one of the best. EBM means 'extended barrel maturation'. The impressive 2014 vintage (★★★★★), estate-grown at Bannockburn, was fermented and matured for 18 months in French oak barrels (12 per cent new). Light lemon/green, it is a mouthfilling, highly complex wine, with rich grapefruit and peach flavours, overlaid with mealy, nutty characters, and excellent harmony and personality. Certified organic, the 2015 vintage (★★★★☆) is still very youthful. Full-bodied, it is finely poised, with fresh acidity woven through its peachy, citrusy, slightly biscuity and toasty flavours, which show good complexity. Best drinking 2019+.

Vintage	15	14	13	12	11	10	09	08
WR	5	6	7	7	6	6	7	5
Drink	17-22	17-21	17-20	17-19	P	P	P	P

 DRY $47 AV

Cathedral Cove Hawke's Bay Chardonnay (★★★)

Looking for a cheap, satisfying Chardonnay? The 2014 vintage (★★★) is mouthfilling, with youthful colour, decent depth of tight, citrusy, peachy flavours, slightly toasty notes emerging, and a dry finish. Worth discovering.

 DRY $10 V+

Chard Farm Closeburn Central Otago Chardonnay   ★★★☆

Delicious young, the 2016 vintage (★★★★) was fermented and lees-aged in tanks, with no oak handling. Bright, light lemon/green, it is fresh, mouthfilling and creamy-textured, in a 'fruit-driven' style, with ripe, peachy flavours, showing good concentration, and a smooth, dry finish.

Vintage	16		DRY $28 –V
WR	6		
Drink	18-22		

Chard Farm Judge & Jury Central Otago Chardonnay   (★★★★☆)

The 2016 vintage (★★★★☆) was designed to showcase its delicious, vibrant fruit characters – 70 per cent of the blend was handled in tanks, but 30 per cent was matured in old and new oak barrels. Pale lemon/green, with a creamy, slightly citrusy and biscuity bouquet, it is mouthfilling and buoyantly fruity, with fresh, rich, grapefruit-like flavours to the fore, very generous, smooth and harmonious. It's already highly enjoyable.

Vintage	16		DRY $39 –V
WR	6		
Drink	18-23		

Church Road Grand Reserve Hawke's Bay Chardonnay   ★★★★★

This very classy wine sits above the McDonald Series (but below Tom) in the Church Road hierarchy. Hand-picked at two sites (Tuki Tuki and Haumoana, both cooled by sea breezes), and fermented with indigenous yeasts in French oak barrels (partly new), the pale straw 2015 vintage (★★★★★) is a classic regional style, built to last. A powerful, multi-faceted wine, it is highly fragrant, with a hint of 'struck match'. Mouthfilling and generous, with good acidity, it has impressively concentrated, well-ripened stone-fruit and toasty oak flavours, revealing outstanding complexity, harmony and length. Already delicious, it's also well worth cellaring to 2019+.

DRY $40 AV

🍇🍇🍇

Church Road Hawke's Bay Chardonnay   ★★★★

This mouthfilling, rich wine is made by Pernod Ricard NZ at Church Road winery in Hawke's Bay. Described by winemaker Chris Scott as 'unashamedly just a little bit old school', it is typically fleshy and smooth, with ripe stone-fruit flavours, showing good complexity and depth. The 2016 vintage (★★★★) was fermented in Hungarian and French oak barrels (30 per cent new), given a full, softening malolactic fermentation, and oak-matured for six months. Light lemon/green, it is sweet-fruited and soft, with generous, peachy, slightly toasty and buttery flavours, showing good complexity and harmony. As usual, a top buy.

Vintage	16	15	14	13	12	11	10	DRY $18 V+
WR	5	7	7	7	5	5	7	
Drink	17-19	17-19	17-18	P	P	P	P	

Church Road McDonald Series Hawke's Bay Chardonnay ★★★★★

Fragrant, with a complex, slightly smoky bouquet, the classy 2016 vintage (★★★★☆) was grown principally (67 per cent) in the company's Tuki Tuki Vineyard and 97 per cent of the blend was fermented and lees-aged for seven months in French and Hungarian oak barriques (15 per cent new); 3 per cent was handled in large oak cuves. Bright, light lemon/green, it is mouthfilling and youthful, with generous, ripe grapefruit/peach flavours, toasty and yeasty notes adding complexity, and good potential; open 2018+.

Vintage	16	15	14	13	12	11
WR	5	7	7	7	6	5
Drink	17-20	17-20	17-19	17-18	P	P

DRY $27 V+

Church Road Tom Chardonnay ★★★★★

The 2014 vintage (★★★★★), released in mid-2017, is Chardonnay on the grand scale. Grown mostly (92 per cent) in the company's Tuki Tuki Vineyard, planted on a west-facing clay slope cooled by afternoon sea breezes, it was hand-picked, fermented with indigenous yeasts and matured for 11 months on its full yeast lees, with periodic stirring, in French oak barriques (28 per cent new). After another four months in old oak casks, it was then lees-aged in tanks for a further year, prior to bottling. Light yellow/green, it has a very rich, ripe, complex bouquet, leading into a powerful, mouthfilling wine with good acidity, deep, peachy, complex flavours, well-integrated oak, and a vaguely toasty, long finish. Best drinking 2019+.

Vintage	14	13	12	11	10	09
WR	7	7	NM	NM	7	6
Drink	17-21	17-20	NM	NM	P	P

DRY $150 –V

🍇🍇

Clearview Beachhead Hawke's Bay Chardonnay ★★★★☆

This Hawke's Bay winery has a reputation for powerful Chardonnays, and top vintages of this label are no exception. Estate-grown and hand-picked on the coast at Te Awanga, the 2016 vintage (★★★★) was fermented and matured for eight months in French oak barrels (10 per cent new). Light lemon/green, with a slightly buttery, oaky bouquet, it is full-bodied, in an upfront style, with generous, peachy, slightly creamy and toasty flavours. Still very youthful, it has considerable complexity; open mid-2018+.

Vintage	16	15	14	13	12	11	10	09
WR	5	7	7	7	5	5	7	6
Drink	17-21	17-21	17-20	17-19	P	P	P	P

DRY $27 V+

Clearview Coastal Hawke's Bay Chardonnay ★★★★

Offering great value, the 2016 vintage (★★★★) was grown at Te Awanga, tank-fermented and briefly barrel-aged. Light lemon/green, it's an excellent 'fruit-driven' style, fresh, vibrant and smooth, with strong, peachy, slightly appley flavours, a minerally streak, and a real sense of youthful drive and vigour.

DRY $19 V+

Clearview Endeavour Hawke's Bay Chardonnay   ★★★★☆

One of New Zealand's highest-priced Chardonnays, this wine is estate-grown at Te Awanga, hand-picked from vines planted in 1989, fermented with indigenous yeasts and matured for an unusually long period in barrels. It typically makes a very bold statement. The 2013 vintage (★★★★☆) was matured for 30 months in all-new French oak barriques. Light lemon/green, it is a powerful wine, weighty and concentrated, with rich, grapefruit-like flavours, mealy and complex, and a very strong seasoning of toasty oak. Still unfolding, it shows excellent cellaring potential and should be at its best 2018+.

Vintage	13
WR	7
Drink	17-20

DRY $165 –V

Clearview Reserve Hawke's Bay Chardonnay   ★★★★★

For his premium Chardonnay label, winemaker Tim Turvey aims for a 'big, grunty, upfront' style – and hits the target with ease. It's typically a hedonist's delight – an arrestingly bold, intense, savoury, mealy, complex wine with layers of flavour. The 2016 vintage (★★★★★) was hand-picked from vines up to 29 years old at Te Awanga, fermented and matured for 14 months in French oak barriques (49 per cent new), and given a full, softening malolactic fermentation. Bright, light lemon/green, it is fragrant, mouthfilling and sweet-fruited, with deep, grapefruit-like flavours, showing excellent delicacy and vibrancy, and a long, citrusy, creamy, very harmonious finish. A finely poised, vigorous young wine, it should break into full stride 2019 onwards.

Vintage	16	15	14	13	12	11	10	09	08
WR	6	7	7	7	6	6	7	7	7
Drink	17-26	17-25	17-25	17-23	17-21	17-20	17-20	17-19	17-18

DRY $45 AV

Clearview Three Rows Hawke's Bay Chardonnay   (★★★★☆)

The stylish, debut 2015 vintage (★★★★☆) was selected from three rows in the estate vineyard at Te Awanga, and fermented and lees-aged for 10 months in French oak puncheons (one and two years old). An elegant, youthful wine, it has generous, vibrant grapefruit and peach flavours, with biscuity, mealy notes adding complexity, and excellent drive and depth through the palate. Well worth cellaring, it should be in full stride 2018+.

DRY $32 AV

Clearview White Caps Hawke's Bay Chardonnay   (★★★☆)

The 2014 vintage (★★★☆) was designed as a return 'to the excesses of the 1980s', with 'loads of oak'. Estate-grown and hand-picked at Te Awanga, and 'fermented with new French oak', it is full-bodied and vibrantly fruity. It lacks the complexity of its Beachhead stablemate from the same vintage, but offers strong, citrusy, peachy flavours.

DRY $30 –V

Clifford Bay Marlborough Chardonnay   (★★★)

The bright light lemon/green 2014 vintage (★★★) is mouthfilling, with good depth of grapefruit and peach flavours, fresh acidity, and toasty, buttery notes adding a touch of complexity.

DRY $16 V+

Clos de Ste Anne Chardonnay Naboth's Vineyard   ★★★★★

Millton's exceptional Chardonnay is based on ungrafted, unirrigated vines, over 25 years old, in the steep, north-east-facing Naboth's Vineyard in the Poverty Bay foothills. Grown biodynamically and hand-harvested, it is fermented with indigenous yeasts in mostly second-fill French oak barriques, and has usually not been put through malolactic fermentation, 'to leave a pure, crisp mineral flavour'. A powerful wine, it is also notably stylish and complete. The 2015 vintage (★★★★☆) is a good but not great vintage. Bright, light yellow/green, it has a restrained bouquet, leading into a weighty, rich palate with deep grapefruit and peach flavours, showing excellent complexity, fresh acidity, and a well-structured, faintly buttery, long finish. Still youthful, it should be at its best 2019+.

Vintage	15	14	13	12	11	10	09	08	07
WR	6	7	7	NM	NM	7	7	6	7
Drink	17-29	17-29	17-28	NM	NM	17-25	17-21	P	P

DRY $75 AV

Cloudy Bay New Zealand Chardonnay   ★★★★★

A powerful Marlborough wine with impressively concentrated, savoury, lemony, mealy flavours and a proven ability to mature well over the long haul. The grapes are sourced from numerous company-owned and growers' vineyards at Brancott, Fairhall, Benmorven and in the Central Wairau Valley. The wine is fermented with indigenous yeasts in French oak barriques (18 per cent new in 2015), lees-aged in barrels for a year to 15 months, and most goes through a softening malolactic fermentation. Light lemon/green, the 2015 vintage (★★★★☆) is a very elegant, youthful wine, full-bodied and tightly structured, with vibrant, citrusy flavours, showing excellent vigour and depth, a subtle seasoning of oak, good complexity and obvious potential; drink now or cellar.

Vintage	15	14	13	12	11
WR	7	7	7	7	7
Drink	17-20	17-20	17-19	17-20	17-19

DRY $34 V+

Cognoscenti Gisborne Chardonnay   (★★★★☆)

Offering top value, the 2016 vintage (★★★★☆) is from Waimata Vineyards, a commercial arm of EIT-Tairawhiti. Hand-picked at two sites, it was fermented (mostly with indigenous yeasts) in European oak barriques (25 per cent new), and 30 per cent of the blend went through a secondary, softening malolactic fermentation. Pale lemon/green, it is a powerful, youthful wine, full-bodied, with rich, peachy, mealy flavours, hints of pears and spices, integrated oak, good complexity and a slightly creamy finish. Best drinking mid-2018+.

DRY $20 V+

Collaboration Aurulent Hawke's Bay Chardonnay   ★★★★☆

Hand-harvested at 'select vineyard sites', the stylish 2016 vintage (★★★★☆) was fermented and lees-aged for a year in French oak casks (25 per cent new). Pale lemon/green, it has a fragrant, fresh bouquet, showing very good complexity. Mouthfilling, it is youthful, with concentrated, grapefruit-like flavours, well-integrated, biscuity oak adding complexity, balanced acidity and excellent cellaring potential; best drinking 2019+.

Vintage	16	15	14	13	12	11
WR	6	7	7	7	6	5
Drink	17-23	17-23	17-22	17-21	17-19	17-18

Collaboration Impression Hawke's Bay Chardonnay   (★★★★)

A fresh, lively, fruit-driven style, the 2016 vintage (★★★★) was matured for six months in seasoned French oak barrels and given a full, softening malolactic fermentation. Light lemon/green, it has strong, peachy, citrusy fruit flavours to the fore, a minerally streak, and subtle, yeasty, nutty notes adding considerable complexity. Drink now onwards.

Coniglio Hawke's Bay Chardonnay   ★★★★☆

Still unfolding, the 2014 vintage (★★★★☆) was estate-grown in the inland, elevated Riverview Vineyard, hand-picked, and fermented with indigenous yeasts in French oak barrels (50 per cent new). Bright, light lemon/green, it is full-bodied, with rich citrus and stone-fruit flavours, biscuity and buttery notes, finely balanced acidity, and excellent complexity. Best drinking mid-2018+.

Coopers Creek Gisborne Chardonnay   ★★★☆

The 2015 vintage (★★★☆) was fermented in barrels (70 per cent) and tanks. Mouthfilling and vibrantly fruity, it has good depth of peach and grapefruit flavours, slightly toasty and smooth (4 grams/litre of residual sugar). Enjoyable young.

DRY $18 V+

Coopers Creek Select Vineyards Big + Buttery Gisborne Chardonnay   (★★★★)

Revisiting the bold, upfront Chardonnay style that was highly popular in the 1980s, the 2016 vintage (★★★★) was fermented and matured for 11 months in American oak barrels (33 per cent new), and given a full, softening malolactic fermentation. Fresh, full-bodied and fleshy, it has generous, peachy, citrusy flavours, toasty and nutty, and a smooth finish. Best drinking 2019+.

DRY $25 AV

Coopers Creek SV Limeworks Hawke's Bay Chardonnay   ★★★★

Estate-grown at Havelock North, this is crafted in a 'full-on' style. The vibrantly fruity 2015 vintage (★★★★) was fully barrel-fermented in American oak casks (50 per cent new). Fresh, tightly structured and moderately complex, it has a nutty oak influence and very good depth, vigour and harmony.

Coopers Creek SV Plainsman Hawke's Bay Chardonnay   (★★★☆)

The 2015 vintage (★★★☆) is finely balanced for current drinking. Full-bodied, it was fermented in seasoned oak barrels and most (90 per cent) of the blend went through a softening malolactic fermentation. Fresh and weighty, it's a peachy, moderately complex style with a hint of butterscotch and satisfying depth.

DRY $22 AV

Coopers Creek Swamp Reserve Chardonnay   ★★★★☆

Based on the winery's best Hawke's Bay grapes, this seductive Chardonnay has a finely judged balance of rich, citrusy, peachy fruit flavours and toasty oak. Hand-picked in the company's Middle Road Vineyard at Havelock North, it is fermented and matured in French oak barriques (40 per cent new in 2016), and given a full, softening malolactic fermentation. The youthful 2016 vintage (★★★★☆) is typically weighty and generous. Light lemon/green, it is fragrant and full-bodied, with ripe stone-fruit flavours, seasoned with biscuity, toasty oak, excellent complexity and a long finish. Already enjoyable, it should break into full stride during 2019.

Vintage	16
WR	7
Drink	17-22

DRY $39 –V

Craft Farm Home Vineyard Hawke's Bay Chardonnay   (★★★★☆)

Delicious young, the 2015 vintage (★★★★☆) was estate-grown at Havelock North, fermented with indigenous yeasts in French oak casks (30 per cent new), barrel-matured for nine months, and given a full, softening malolactic fermentation. Light lemon/green, it is fragrant, weighty and concentrated, with ripe, rounded, peachy, biscuity flavours, showing excellent richness and harmony.

DRY $35 –V

Craggy Range Block 19 Gimblett Gravels Chardonnay   (★★★★★)

The very refined debut 2014 vintage (★★★★★) was hand-picked from seven-year-old vines and fermented with indigenous yeasts in French oak barriques (40 per cent new). Barrel-aged for 11 months, it's a full-bodied, finely textured wine, powerful yet subtle, with ripe stone-fruit flavours, a hint of toasty oak, and lovely mouthfeel, delicacy and depth. Best drinking 2018 onwards.

DRY $60 –V

Craggy Range Gimblett Gravels Vineyard Hawke's Bay Chardonnay   ★★★★☆

This stylish wine is typically mouthfilling and savoury, with complexity from fermentation and maturation in French oak barriques (28 per cent new in 2015). The 2015 vintage (★★★★★) was hand-harvested, fermented with indigenous yeasts and barrel-aged for 10 months. The bouquet is fragrant and complex; the palate is mouthfilling, with subtle grapefruit and nut flavours, showing excellent vibrancy, delicacy, harmony and persistence. A very elegant, rather than high-impact, wine, it's already delicious, but well worth cellaring.

DRY $32 AV

Crazy by Nature Gisborne Shotberry Chardonnay ★★★☆

From Millton, this is an unoaked style. The 2015 vintage (★★★☆) is a light lemon/green, medium-bodied wine with vibrant, peachy, citrusy flavours, fresh acidity and good depth. Certified organic.

Vintage	15	14
WR	6	5
Drink	17-19	17-18

DRY $22 AV

Crossroads Milestone Series Hawke's Bay Chardonnay ★★★★

A consistently good buy, this is a classic regional style, weighty, ripe and rounded. The 2014 vintage (★★★★) was mostly grown inland, at Mangatahi, and predominantly (66 per cent) fermented in French oak barriques. Mouthfilling, it's a very harmonious wine, with strong, ripe stone-fruit flavours, finely integrated nutty oak, and good complexity.

Vintage	14	13
WR	6	6
Drink	17-24	17-20

DRY $20 V+

Crossroads Winemakers Collection Hawke's Bay Chardonnay ★★★★☆

The 2014 vintage (★★★★★) was grown in the Kereru Vineyard, inland at Mangatahi, hand-picked and fermented and lees-aged for 10 months in French oak barriques (25 per cent new). A refined wine, it is fragrant and mouthfilling, youthful and tightly structured, with strong, vibrant, citrusy, peachy flavours, finely integrated oak, and very impressive delicacy, complexity and harmony. Well worth cellaring.

Vintage	14	13	12
WR	7	7	6
Drink	17-25	17-24	17-20

DRY $40 –V

Cypress Hawke's Bay Chardonnay ★★★☆

The 2014 vintage (★★★☆) was estate-grown and gently oak-influenced (20 per cent of the blend was barrel-fermented). Full-bodied and buoyantly fruity, it has fresh, ripe, peachy flavours, showing a touch of complexity, and plenty of drink-young appeal.

Vintage	14	13	12
WR	7	7	6
Drink	P	P	P

DRY $21 AV

Cypress Terraces Hawke's Bay Chardonnay ★★★★☆

From a sloping, 2-hectare site at Roys Hill, the highly attractive 2016 vintage (★★★★☆) was hand-harvested and fermented with indigenous yeasts in French oak casks (25 per cent new). A classic Hawke's Bay style, it is full-bodied and sweet-fruited, with generous, ripe stone-fruit flavours, a subtle seasoning of toasty oak, slightly buttery notes, and excellent complexity and harmony. Best drinking mid-2018+.

Vintage	16	
WR	7	DRY $32 AV
Drink	17-21	

Darling, The, Marlborough Chardonnay (★★★★★)

Certified organic, the 2013 vintage (★★★★★) is a very elegant, tightly structured, single-vineyard wine, grown in the Southern Valleys and handled in seasoned oak casks. The bouquet is fragrant and complex; the palate is weighty, with penetrating grapefruit and nut flavours, good acid spine and a finely poised, lasting finish. Best drinking 2018+.

DRY $33 V+

Dashwood Marlborough Chardonnay ★★★☆

The 2015 vintage (★★★☆) is a bright, light lemon/green wine, with a slightly creamy bouquet. Drinking well in its youth, it is mouthfilling, with peachy, slightly spicy flavours, generous depth and a smooth finish. (From Foley Family Wines.)

DRY $17 V+

De La Terre Hawke's Bay Chardonnay (★★★★)

Handled without oak, the 2014 vintage (★★★★) was hand-picked on limestone terraces at Havelock North. It is freshly scented, with ripe, citrusy, peachy flavours in an elegant, slightly minerally style with obvious cellaring potential.

DRY $24 V+

De La Terre Hawke's Bay Chardonnay Barrique Ferment (★★★★★)

Showing obvious potential, the classy 2015 vintage (★★★★★) was estate-grown at Havelock North and fermented in French oak barriques (15 per cent new). Light lemon/green, it has a fragrant, complex bouquet, leading into an elegant, tightly structured wine with excellent intensity of grapefruit-like flavours, mealy, biscuity notes adding complexity, good acid spine and a lengthy finish. Best drinking 2018+.

Vintage	15	
WR	6	DRY $30 V+
Drink	17-18	

De La Terre Reserve Hawke's Bay Chardonnay ★★★★★

The classy, finely structured 2014 vintage (★★★★★) was hand-picked at 23 brix at Havelock North and fermented, partly with indigenous yeasts, in French oak barriques (50 per cent new). Full-bodied, with a minerally streak, it has intense, citrusy, peachy, spicy flavours, fresh acidity, well-integrated oak, and excellent complexity, vigour and length. Best drinking 2018+.

The 2015 vintage (★★★★☆) was also fermented in French oak barriques (50 per cent new). A powerful, tight-knit wine, it is youthful, with rich grapefruit and stone-fruit flavours, slightly buttery and complex, a minerally thread, and excellent cellaring potential; open 2019+.

Vintage	15	14	13
WR	6	7	6
Drink	17-22	17-23	17-22

DRY $40 AV

Delegat Crownthorpe Terraces Chardonnay   ★★★★

From one vintage to the next, this is a great buy. The 2016 vintage (★★★★☆) was grown at the company's cool, elevated, inland site at Crownthorpe, in Hawke's Bay, and fermented and matured for a year in French oak barrels (new and one year old). Very fresh and lively, with a slightly nutty, buttery bouquet, it is rich and mouthfilling, with strong, vibrant peach and grapefruit flavours, and a harmonious, well-rounded finish. Bargain-priced.

DRY $20 V+

Dog Point Vineyard Marlborough Chardonnay   ★★★★★

This classy, single-vineyard wine is grown on the south side of the Wairau Valley, hand-picked, fermented and matured for 18 to 20 months in French oak barriques (15 to 25 per cent new), and given a full, softening malolactic fermentation. Bright, light lemon/green, the 2015 vintage (★★★★★) is mouthfilling, concentrated and very youthful, with intense grapefruit-like flavours, showing good complexity, fresh acid spine and a tight, persistent finish. A wine with a powerful presence, it should be at its best 2020+. (The 2007 vintage has been released again at a decade old in mid-2017, at $52 per bottle in six-packs. Delicious now, it is a full-bodied wine, with bright, light yellow colour, a strong surge of peachy, vaguely toasty flavours, lively acidity and a lasting finish.)

Vintage	15	14	13	12	11	10	09	08
WR	7	7	7	5	7	6	5	7
Drink	17-27	17-26	17-21	P	17-19	P	P	P

DRY $36 AV

Domain Road Defiance Vineyard Central Otago Chardonnay   (★★★★)

Well worth cellaring, the 2015 vintage (★★★★) is a single-vineyard wine, grown at Bannockburn and fermented and matured for 10 months in French oak casks. Light lemon/green, it is still very fresh and youthful, with mouthfilling body, balanced acidity and vibrant, citrusy, slightly peachy and biscuity flavours. Showing considerable complexity, it should be at its best mid-2018+.

DRY $28 AV

Domaine Rewa Central Otago Chardonnay ★★★★☆

The distinguished 2014 vintage (★★★★★) was estate-grown in the Epicurious Vineyard, in the Cromwell Basin, and fermented and matured for nine months in French oak barriques (25 per cent new). Pale lemon/green, it is fragrant and youthful, with deep, vibrant, grapefruit-like flavours, finely integrated oak, balanced acidity and a long finish. Still full of vigour, it's a drink-now or cellaring proposition.

Vintage	14	13	12
WR	7	7	7
Drink	17-20	17-19	17-18

 DRY $38 –V

Dry River Martinborough Chardonnay ★★★★★

Elegance, restraint and subtle power are the key qualities of this classic wine. It's not a bold, upfront style, but tight, savoury and seamless, with rich grapefruit and nut flavours that build in the bottle for several years. Based on low-cropping, Mendoza-clone vines in the Craighall and Dry River Estate vineyards, it is hand-harvested, whole-bunch pressed and fermented in French oak barrels (with a low percentage of new casks). The proportion of the blend that has gone through a softening malolactic fermentation has never exceeded 15 per cent. The 2015 vintage (★★★★★) is a typically elegant, fragrant, complex wine. Mouthfilling, with a slightly biscuity, mealy bouquet, it is still very youthful, with deep grapefruit and peach flavours, gently seasoned with oak, balanced acidity and a tightly structured finish. A very age-worthy wine, it should be at its best 2018+. The 2016 vintage (★★★★★) is a very 'complete' wine. Bright, light lemon/green, it is mouthfilling, with rich, ripe stone-fruit flavours, nutty, complex and finely textured, and impressive depth and harmony. Already a delicious mouthful, it should be at its best 2019+.

Vintage	16	15	14	13	12	11	10	09	08	07
WR	7	7	7	7	5	7	7	7	7	7
Drink	18-25	17-25	17-24	17-23	17-22	17-20	17-20	17-20	P	17-18

 DRY $65 AV

Durvillea by Astrolabe Marlborough Chardonnay (★★★)

The refreshing 2016 vintage (★★★) is a 'fruit-driven' style, hand-harvested in the Wairau Valley, 60 per cent barrel-fermented and 100 per cent barrel-aged. Bright, light lemon/green, it is a fresh, medium-bodied wine, with lively, citrusy, peachy flavours, a hint of biscuity oak and a dry, smooth finish.

 DRY $17 AV

Easthope Skeetfield Hawke's Bay Chardonnay ★★★★

Grown at Ohiti and fermented in French oak barrels (25 per cent new), the 2013 vintage (★★★★) is an elegant, tightly structured wine with a long finish, well worth cellaring. The 2014 vintage (★★★★) is more open and expressive in its youth, showing good complexity and richness.

Vintage	15
WR	6
Drink	17-19

DRY $40 –V

Elephant Hill Hawke's Bay Chardonnay   ★★★★☆

The elegant, age-worthy 2015 vintage (★★★★☆) was estate-grown and hand-picked at Te Awanga, fermented with indigenous yeasts in French oak barriques (25 per cent new), and lees-aged in barrels for 11 months. Light lemon/green, with a fragrant, slightly nutty bouquet, it is weighty, with vibrant grapefruit and peach flavours, showing excellent vigour and complexity, and a lasting finish. Best drinking 2018+.

Vintage	15	14	13
WR	6	7	6
Drink	17-22	P	P

DRY $29 V+

Elephant Hill Reserve Hawke's Bay Chardonnay   ★★★★★

Estate-grown at Te Awanga, the very youthful and tightly structured 2015 vintage (★★★★★) was hand-harvested, fermented with indigenous yeasts and matured for a year in French oak barrels (30 per cent new). Highly fragrant, with citrusy, mealy aromas, it is mouthfilling, sweet-fruited and finely poised, with fresh, intense, slightly peachy and toasty flavours, good acid spine and obvious potential. A classy, complex wine, it's well worth cellaring to 2019+.

Vintage	15
WR	6
Drink	17-25

DRY $49 AV

Eradus Second Pick Special Reserve Marlborough Chardonnay   (★★★★)

Already drinking well, the 2016 vintage (★★★★) was estate-grown in the Awatere Valley and oak-aged. Light lemon/green, it is sturdy (14.5 per cent alcohol), vibrant and sweet-fruited, with rich peachy flavours, integrated oak and lots of drink-young appeal.

DRY $25 AV

Esk Valley Hawke's Bay Chardonnay   ★★★★

Top vintages can offer irresistible value. The 2015 vintage (★★★★) was fully fermented and matured in French oak barriques (15 per cent new), and half the blend went through a softening malolactic fermentation. A classic regional style, it is a generous, sweet-fruited wine, mouthfilling, with youthful grapefruit and peach flavours, a subtle seasoning of oak, fresh acidity and a slightly mealy, finely textured finish. It's one of the best-value Chardonnays on the market.

Vintage	16	15	14	13	12	11	10
WR	7	7	6	6	5	5	6
Drink	17-20	17-19	17-18	P	P	P	P

DRY $20 V+

Esk Valley Winemakers Reserve Hawke's Bay Chardonnay   ★★★★★

Often one of the region's most distinguished Chardonnays. Fragrant, with a smoky, 'struck match' bouquet, the classy, youthful 2016 vintage (★★★★★) was grown and hand-picked at two sites in northern Hawke's Bay (including the Esk Valley home block), and fermented and matured for 11 months in French oak barriques (30 per cent new). Weighty, vibrant and tightly structured, it has deep grapefruit-like flavours, biscuity, mealy notes adding complexity, fresh acidity and obvious potential; best drinking 2019+.

Vintage	16	15	14	13	12
WR	7	7	7	7	6
Drink	17-23	17-23	17-20	17-20	17-18

DRY $32 V+

Fairhall Downs Single Vineyard Marlborough Chardonnay   (★★★☆)

The 2016 vintage (★★★☆) is a Brancott Valley wine, hand-picked and fermented and lees-aged for 10 months in French oak barrels (30 per cent new). Full-bodied and youthful, it is citrusy and distinctly yeasty, with integrated oak, slightly buttery notes, balanced acidity and some complexity.

DRY $30 –V

Falconhead Hawke's Bay Chardonnay   ★★★

Drinking well now, the 2014 vintage (★★★) was partly barrel-fermented. Light lemon/green, it is fresh and full-bodied, with ripe, peachy flavours, showing a touch of complexity and good depth. Priced right.

DRY $16 V+

Felton Road Bannockburn Central Otago Chardonnay   ★★★★★

Forging ahead in quality, this classy, distinctive wine is grown at Bannockburn and matured in French oak barriques, with limited use of new oak. Pale lemon/green, the elegant 2016 vintage (★★★★☆) was estate-grown in The Elms and Cornish Point vineyards, and barrel-aged for a year (15 per cent new). Full-bodied, it is still very youthful, with vibrant, grapefruit-like flavours, slightly biscuity notes adding complexity, and a long, harmonious finish. A subtle wine with obvious potential, it's well worth cellaring to mid-2018 onwards.

Vintage	16	15	14	13	12	11	10	09	08
WR	7	7	7	7	7	6	7	7	6
Drink	17-30	17-29	17-28	17-24	17-26	17-22	17-22	17-20	17-18

DRY $47 AV

Felton Road Block 2 Central Otago Chardonnay   ★★★★★

This outstanding wine is grown in a 'special part of The Elms Vineyard in front of the winery', which has the oldest vines. Handled with no new oak influence, it is bottled unfined and unfiltered. The 2015 vintage (★★★★★) is bright, light lemon/green, mouthfilling, fresh and youthful, with concentrated, grapefruit-evoking flavours, mealy notes adding complexity, a subtle seasoning of oak, and a very long finish. Best drinking 2018+.

Vintage	15	14	13	12
WR	7	7	7	7
Drink	17-31	17-30	17-27	17-26

DRY $56 AV

Felton Road Block 6 Central Otago Chardonnay   (★★★★★)

Estate-grown in The Elms Vineyard at Bannockburn, the debut 2015 vintage (★★★★★) was handled principally in seasoned oak casks (6 per cent new), and bottled unfined and unfiltered. Highly fragrant, it is full-bodied, with concentrated, citrusy, slightly peachy flavours, mealy, toasty notes adding complexity, and a lasting finish. Still youthful, it is slightly richer and rounder than its Block 2 stablemate, offering an intriguing style comparison.

Vintage	15
WR	7
Drink	17-31

 DRY $56 AV

Forrest Marlborough Chardonnay   ★★★★

Still fresh and lively, the 2014 vintage (★★★★) was fermented and matured in a 50:50 split of tanks and barrels. Bright, light lemon/green, it has a fragrant, citrusy, slightly toasty bouquet, leading into a full-bodied wine with good intensity of grapefruit-like flavours, gently seasoned with oak, good acid spine, and an emerging, bottle-aged complexity. Drink now to 2018.

 DRY $25 AV

Framingham F-Series Marlborough Chardonnay   ★★★★★

The classy, youthful 2016 vintage (★★★★★) has a fragrant, slightly smoky bouquet. Bright, light lemon/green, it is full-bodied, with concentrated, ripe stone-fruit flavours, showing excellent complexity, and a long, savoury finish. Best drinking mid-2018+.

 DRY $35 AV

Framingham Marlborough Chardonnay   ★★★★

The elegant 2016 vintage (★★★★) was fermented and matured in a 50:50 split of tanks and barrels. Fresh and vibrantly fruity, it's still youthful, with citrusy, peachy flavours, showing very good depth, and savoury, biscuity notes adding complexity. Best drinking mid-2018 onwards.

DRY $25 AV

French Peak Banks Peninsula Chardonnay   (★★★☆)

From mature, 27-year-old vines in Canterbury, the 2015 vintage (★★★☆) was barrel-fermented. Light straw, with a creamy bouquet, it is a medium to full-bodied style, with peachy, slightly buttery flavours, showing very good depth, and firm acid spine. Enjoyable young, it should mature well.

 DRY $35 –V

Frenchmans Hill Estate Waiheke Island Ted's Chardonnay   (★★★★)

Light gold, with a toasty bouquet, the 2014 vintage (★★★★) was grown at Te Rere Cove Vineyard and fermented and matured for a year in all-new French oak barriques. A powerful, full-bodied wine, it is sweet-fruited, with rich, ripe stone-fruit flavours, strongly seasoned with toasty oak. Best drinking 2017 onwards.

DRY $58 –V

Fromm Clayvin Vineyard Marlborough Chardonnay ★★★★★

Fromm's finest Chardonnay is grown on the southern flanks of the Wairau Valley, where the clay soils, says winemaker Hätsch Kalberer, give 'a less fruity, more minerally and tighter character'. Fermented with indigenous yeasts in French oak barriques, with little or no use of new wood, it is barrel-aged for well over a year. It is a rare wine – only three barrels were produced in 2013 – and top vintages mature well for a decade. The 2013 vintage (★★★★★) is pale lemon/green, with a highly fragrant, complex bouquet. It is very refined and harmonious, with concentrated, ripe grapefruit-like flavours, a subtle seasoning of oak, a slightly creamy texture, and lovely delicacy, poise and persistence. Best drinking 2018+. (There is no 2014 vintage, but the label returns from 2015.)

Vintage	13	12	11	10	09	08
WR	7	NM	7	6	7	NM
Drink	17-23	NM	17-21	17-18	17-19	NM

DRY $68 AV

Fuder, The, Single Vineyard Selection Clayvin Marlborough Chardonnay ★★★★★

From Giesen, this wine is grown in the famous Clayvin Vineyard, in the Brancott Valley, and fermented and matured in 1000-litre German oak casks (fuders), which 'develop greater complexity and refinement, but the oak doesn't dominate'. The tight, youthful, age-worthy 2014 vintage (★★★★★) is bright, light lemon/green, with a fragrant, complex, slightly smoky bouquet. Mouthfilling, it is elegant, with concentrated grapefruit and peach flavours, integrated oak, fine acidity, and a powerful, lasting finish.

Vintage	14	13
WR	7	7
Drink	17-23	17-22

DRY $60 AV

Gibbston Valley 95 China Terrace Central Otago Chardonnay (★★★★★)

The 2016 vintage (★★★★☆) is a single-vineyard Bendigo wine, estate-grown at 320 metres above sea level, and hand-picked solely from highly regarded clone 95 vines. Fermented with indigenous yeasts in French oak barriques and puncheons (22 per cent new), and barrel-aged for a year, it is a light lemon/green, mouthfilling wine with deep, ripe, youthful, peachy flavours, finely integrated oak and impressive complexity. Approachable now but full of potential, it's well worth cellaring to 2019+.

DRY $55 –V

Gibbston Valley China Terrace Bendigo Single Vineyard Chardonnay ★★★★☆

Here's more evidence that Central Otago has great Chardonnay potential. The 2015 vintage (★★★★☆) was estate-grown, at 320 metres above sea level, and fermented and matured for 11 months in French oak barriques and puncheons (25 per cent new). Light lemon/green, it is very fresh and poised, with an aromatic, slightly smoky bouquet. A distinctly cool-climate style, it is tightly structured, with strong, youthful, grapefruit-like flavours, a subtle seasoning of biscuity oak, and obvious cellaring potential. Best drinking 2018+.

DRY $39 –V

Giesen Hawke's Bay Chardonnay   (★★☆)

The 2014 vintage (★★☆) is a fresh, medium-bodied wine, vibrant and fruity, with citrusy flavours and a smooth (4 grams/litre of residual sugar) finish.

Vintage	14
WR	4
Drink	P

Giesen The Brothers Marlborough Chardonnay   ★★★★☆

The 2014 vintage (★★★★☆) is a fragrant, generous wine. Grown in the Wairau Valley and the Southern Valleys, it was fermented with indigenous yeasts in French and German oak fuders (big, 1000-litre barrels). The bouquet is complex, with ripe-fruit aromas and hints of toasty oak; the flavours are rich, peachy and slightly buttery, with excellent depth and harmony.

Glazebrook Regional Reserve Hawke's Bay Chardonnay   ★★★☆

Ngatarawa's second-tier Chardonnay is named after the Glazebrook family, once partners in the Hawke's Bay venture. The youthful 2016 vintage (★★★☆) is mouthfilling and vibrantly fruity, with ripe, citrusy, peachy flavours to the fore, a gentle toasty oak influence, moderate complexity and a fresh, finely balanced finish. Drink now or cellar.

Goldie Estate Reserve Waiheke Island Chardonnay   ★★★★☆

Grown on Waiheke Island by Goldie Wines, owned by the University of Auckland, the 2014 vintage (★★★★☆) was hand-picked and fermented and matured for a year in French oak barriques (30 per cent new). A powerful, full-bodied wine, it is fragrant and sweet-fruited, with generous, peachy, slightly buttery flavours, showing good complexity, and a well-rounded finish.

Goldwater Wairau Valley Marlborough Chardonnay   ★★★★

This is a consistently attractive, generous, sweet-fruited wine. The 2014 vintage (★★★★) is mouthfilling, with strong, fresh stone-fruit flavours, gently seasoned with toasty oak. It's a well-rounded, harmonious wine, delicious young. (From Foley Family Wines.)

Greenhough Hope Vineyard Chardonnay   ★★★★★

This impressive wine is estate-grown at Hope, in Nelson, hand-picked, barrel-fermented with indigenous yeasts and matured in French oak barriques (in 2015, 66 per cent of the barrels were one year old and only 7 per cent were new). Certified organic, the powerful 2015 vintage (★★★★★) is a light lemon/green, sturdy wine with generous, ripe stone-fruit flavours, deep and savoury, a slightly toasty oak influence, and excellent complexity. Still developing, it should be in peak form mid-2018+.

Vintage	15	14	13	12	11	10	09	08
WR	5	7	6	6	6	NM	6	6
Drink	17-20	17-20	17-19	17-18	17-18	NM	P	P

Greenhough Nelson Chardonnay ★★★★

This consistently enjoyable wine is designed to express a 'fresh, taut' style, with background oak providing 'some subtle, savoury complexities'. Certified organic, the 2016 vintage (★★★★☆) was grown at Hope, in the Morison and Greenhough vineyards, barrel-fermented (13 per cent new) and French oak-aged for nine months. Light yellow/green, it has a complex bouquet, fresh and inviting. A stylish, mouthfilling wine, it has good concentration of ripe, citrusy, peachy flavours, finely integrated oak and a slightly creamy texture. Already delicious, it's a drink-now or cellaring proposition.

Vintage	16	15	14	13	12	11	10
WR	5	6	6	6	6	6	6
Drink	17-20	17-20	17-19	17-18	17-18	P	P

 DRY $26 AV

Greyrock Hawke's Bay Chardonnay (★★★)

From Sileni, the 2015 vintage (★★★) is a 'lightly oaked' style. Lemon-scented, it is mouthfilling and vibrantly fruity, with fresh acidity, a slightly creamy texure and good depth of citrusy, peachy flavours. Enjoyable young.

 DRY $17 AV

Greystone Erin's Waipara Valley Chardonnay ★★★★★

Greystone views Chardonnay as 'the finest white wine variety'. The outstanding 2015 vintage (★★★★★) is exceptionally rare – just 44 cases were produced. Grown on steep, north-facing limestone slopes, it was hand-harvested, fermented with indigenous yeasts, given a full, softening malolactic fermentation, and matured for 15 months in French oak casks (50 per cent new). Bright, light lemon/green, it is a highly fragrant, weighty wine (14.5 per cent alcohol), tightly structured and youthful, with intense grapefruit and peach flavours that have effortlessly lapped up the new oak. Showing lovely mouthfeel, complexity and length, it's a memorable mouthful. Best drinking 2019+.

Vintage	15
WR	6
Drink	17-28

 DRY $95 –V

Greystone Waipara Valley Chardonnay ★★★★☆

The classy 2015 vintage (★★★★★) was hand-picked, fermented with indigenous yeasts in French oak barrels (20 per cent new), and given a full, softening malolactic fermentation. Light yellow/green, it is full-bodied, with concentrated, peachy, slightly buttery flavours, finely integrated oak, good acid spine, excellent complexity and a long finish.

Vintage	16	15	14	13	12
WR	6	7	7	7	7
Drink	17-25	17-26	17-20	17-19	17-18

DRY $42 –V

Greywacke Marlborough Chardonnay ★★★★★

Light lemon/green, the 2015 vintage (★★★★☆) was fermented with indigenous yeasts in French oak barriques (20 per cent new), and wood-aged for 18 months. An elegant, youthful wine, it is mouthfilling, with rich, vibrant, grapefruit-like flavours, well-integrated oak, slightly buttery notes, fresh acidity, and obvious potential; open 2019+.

Vintage	15	14	13	12	11	10	09
WR	6	6	6	5	6	6	5
Drink	18-25	17-24	17-23	17-20	17-21	17-20	17-19

 DRY $41 AV

Grove Mill Wairau Valley Marlborough Chardonnay ★★★☆

Enjoyable young, the 2015 vintage (★★★☆) is a pale yellow, full-bodied wine, mostly barrel-fermented, with peachy, citrusy, well-rounded flavours, slightly toasty and generous. It's drinking well now.

Vintage	14	13
WR	7	7
Drink	17-19	17-18

 DRY $22 AV

Gunn Estate Reserve Hawke's Bay Chardonnay ★★★☆

Offering great value, the 2016 vintage (★★★★) was fermented in French oak barrels and lees-aged for eight months. Light lemon/green, it is fragrant and finely balanced, with mouthfilling body, ripe peach and grapefruit flavours, a buttery note, and good complexity and harmony. Drink now or cellar.

Vintage	16	15
WR	6	7
Drink	17-20	17-18

 DRY $17 V+

Haha Hawke's Bay Chardonnay (★★★☆)

Drinking well in its youth, the 2016 vintage (★★★☆) was partly oak-aged. Light yellow/green, it is full-bodied and dry, with fresh, ripe stone-fruit flavours to the fore, toasty and buttery notes adding a touch of complexity, and good depth. Fine value.

 DRY $16 V+

Haha Marlborough Chardonnay ★★★☆

The 2016 vintage (★★★☆) is still unfolding. Partly oak-aged, it is full-bodied, fresh and youthful, with good depth of vibrant, citrusy, peachy flavours, showing a touch of complexity, and a smooth, dry finish. Bargain-priced.

Vintage	16	15	14	13
WR	7	7	7	7
Drink	17-20	17-19	17-18	P

DRY $16 V+

Hans Herzog Marlborough Chardonnay   ★★★★☆

At its best, this is a notably powerful wine with layers of peach, butterscotch, grapefruit and nut flavours. The pale straw 2013 vintage (★★★★☆) was hand-picked, fermented with indigenous yeasts in French oak puncheons, barrel-aged for 18 months and given a full, softening malolactic fermentation. A mouthfilling wine, it has rich, ripe grapefruit and peach flavours, seasoned with biscuity oak, and a tight, slightly creamy finish. Certified organic.

Vintage	13	12	11
WR	7	7	7
Drink	17-23	17-22	17-19

 DRY $44 –V

Harakeke Farm Nelson Chardonnay   ★★★★☆

This impressive, single-vineyard, Upper Moutere wine is hand-picked, fermented with indigenous yeasts in French oak puncheons and given a full, softening malolactic fermentation. The powerful 2014 vintage (★★★★★) is sturdy (14.5 per cent alcohol), sweet-fruited and rich, with concentrated, peachy, mealy, gently toasty and buttery flavours, balanced acidity and a highly fragrant, complex bouquet. Already delicious, it's a 'full-on' style, likely to be at its best 2018+.

Vintage	14	13	12
WR	7	7	6
Drink	17-18	P	P

 DRY $30 AV

Hihi The Full Monty Gisborne Chardonnay   (★★★)

Made in the 'old school' (big and buttery) Gisborne style, the 2016 vintage (★★★) was grown at Patutahi and fermented in polyethylene, rather than oak, barrels, with American and French oak 'additions'. Light lemon/green, it is mouthfilling, with peachy, creamy flavours, showing a touch of complexity, and a rounded finish. Drink young.

 DRY $17 AV

Hitchen Road Chardonnay   ★★★☆

The 2014 vintage (★★★★) is a bargain. Estate-grown and hand-picked at 23.5 brix at Pokeno, in North Waikato, it was barrel-aged, with lees-stirring, for seven months. Mouthfilling, sweet-fruited and generous, it has strong, citrusy, peachy, slightly buttery flavours, integrated oak, considerable complexity and a well-rounded finish. Delicious young.

 DRY $18 V+

Huia Marlborough Chardonnay   ★★★★☆

Certified organic, the 2014 vintage (★★★★☆) is a single-vineyard wine, mouthfilling, sweet-fruited and fleshy. It has deep, peachy, slightly biscuity flavours, showing excellent concentration and complexity. The 2015 vintage (★★★★☆), also certified organic, is full-bodied and savoury, with generous, citrusy, peachy flavours, nutty, biscuity notes adding complexity, and a dry, rich finish. Drink now or cellar.

DRY $34 AV

Hunter's Marlborough Chardonnay   ★★★★

This good-value wine has traditionally placed its accent on vibrant fruit flavours, overlaid with very subtle wood-aging characters. The 2016 vintage (★★★★), estate-grown at Rapaura and Omaka, was fermented – with indigenous yeasts – and lees-aged for 10 months in French oak casks (20 per cent new). Already drinking well, it is mouthfilling, with generous, ripe peach and grapefruit flavours, lightly seasoned with toasty oak, gentle acidity, a slightly creamy texture, and good complexity and harmony.

Vintage	16	15	14	13	12	11	10
WR	7	7	7	6	6	5	6
Drink	18-21	17-20	17-19	17-18	P	P	P

DRY $22 V+

Hunter's Succession Marlborough Chardonnay   (★★★★☆)

The debut 2013 vintage (★★★★☆) is a tightly structured, very elegant wine, likely to be long-lived. Matured in all-new French oak casks, it has youthful colour, with strong grapefruit-like flavours that have lapped up the new oak influence. Smoky and complex, with a long finish, it should be at its best 2018+.

DRY $39 –V

Hunter's Unoaked Marlborough Chardonnay   ★★★☆

A delicious example of the unoaked style, the 2016 vintage (★★★★) is a single-vineyard wine, handled solely in tanks, rather than barrels, with a small amount of lees-stirring. Opening out really well in mid-2017, it is mouthfilling, very fresh and lively, with strong, vibrant, grapefruit and peach flavours, moderate acidity, and a long, fully dry finish.

DRY $19 V+

Invivo Gisborne Chardonnay   (★★★)

'There's nothing subtle in this bottle', says the back label on the easy-drinking, 'big, bold' 2016 vintage (★★★). Bright, light lemon/green, it is fresh, sweet-fruited and mouthfilling, with ripe, citrusy, peachy flavours, slightly creamy and toasty notes adding complexity, and a rounded finish.

DRY $20 –V

Isabel Marlborough Chardonnay   (★★★★☆)

This label has a chequered past, but is now owned by Australian supermarket giant, Woolworths. The 2016 vintage (★★★★☆) was estate-grown and matured in French oak casks (40 per cent new). Light lemon/green, it has a fresh bouquet, showing good complexity. Mouthfilling, it is vibrant and sweet-fruited, with ripe stone-fruit flavours, showing excellent delicacy and depth, well-integrated oak, and a tightly structured, smooth finish. Already enjoyable, it should unfold well; open 2019+.

DRY $30 AV

Jackson Estate Shelter Belt Single Vineyard Marlborough Chardonnay   ★★★★

The 2014 vintage (★★★☆) was estate-grown and hand-picked in the Homestead Vineyard, in the heart of the Wairau Valley, and mostly barrel-fermented; 25 per cent of the blend was handled in tanks. Mouthfilling and smooth, it's drinking well now, with gentle acidity and generous, peachy, slightly buttery and toasty flavours.

Vintage	14	13
WR	6	6
Drink	17-18	P

 DRY $25 AV

Johner Martinborough Chardonnay   ★★★☆

The 2015 vintage (★★★☆) was fermented and matured in French oak casks (25 per cent new). Woven with fresh acidity, it has good depth of citrusy, slightly mealy and creamy flavours, showing considerable complexity. Best drinking 2018+.

Vintage	15
WR	5
Drink	17-19

 DRY $26 –V

Johner Wairarapa Chardonnay   ★★★☆

Handled in seasoned oak, the 2016 vintage (★★★☆) is a fruit-driven style, lively and mouthfilling, with very good depth of grapefruit and spice flavours, leesy notes adding a touch of complexity, and lots of drink-young appeal.

Vintage	16
WR	6
Drink	17-21

 DRY $26 –V

Jules Taylor Gisborne Chardonnay   ★★★☆

The attractive 2014 vintage (★★★★) was partly barrel-fermented and made with some use of indigenous yeasts and malolactic fermentation. Mouthfilling and slightly creamy, it is a refined wine with strong grapefruit-like flavours, a hint of spice, fresh, balanced acidity, a subtle oak influence, and good weight, vibrancy, texture and harmony.

Vintage	14
WR	5
Drink	17-18

 DRY $22 AV

Jules Taylor Marlborough Chardonnay   ★★★★

Offering good value, the 2016 vintage (★★★★) was grown at three sites in the Southern Valleys. Just over half of the blend was handled in tanks, but 45 per cent was barrel-fermented (with one-third of the barrels being new). Finely balanced for early enjoyment, it has a slightly creamy bouquet, leading into a mouthfilling, 'fruit-driven' wine with vibrant, citrusy, slightly spicy flavours, mealy notes adding complexity, and excellent harmony and depth.

Vintage	16	15
WR	6	6
Drink	17-21	17-20

DRY $24 V+

Jules Taylor OTQ Limited Release Single Vineyard Marlborough Chardonnay   (★★★★★)

The complex, youthful 2016 vintage (★★★★★) was grown in the Meadowbank Vineyard, on the south side of the Wairau Valley, and matured for 10 months in French oak barrels (33 per cent new). Pale lemon/green, it is richly fragrant, mouthfilling and sweet-fruited, with deep stone-fruit flavours, finely integrated oak, mealy notes adding complexity, balanced acidity and a long, very harmonious finish. Already delicious, it should break into full stride mid-2018+.

Vintage	16
WR	7
Drink	17-22

 DRY $35 AV

Junction Corner Post Central Hawke's Bay Chardonnay   (★★★☆)

Grown in Central Hawke's Bay, the 2015 vintage (★★★☆) was barrel-fermented (30 per cent new) and given a full, softening malolactic fermentation. Fresh and lively, it has crisp, grapefruit-like flavours to the fore, a minerally streak and very good depth.

DRY $27 –V

Kaimira Estate Brightwater Chardonnay   ★★★☆

Certified organic, the 2016 vintage (★★★★) was estate-grown at Brightwater, in Nelson, fermented in French oak barrels (30 per cent new), and oak-aged for nearly a year. Bright, light lemon/green, it is mouthfilling and fleshy, with generous, ripe, peachy, slightly biscuity flavours, a slightly creamy texture, and good harmony. It's already drinking well.

Vintage	16	15
WR	6	6
Drink	17-22	17-20

 DRY $25 –V

Kakapo Barrel Fermented Marlborough Chardonnay   (★★★★)

The 2015 vintage (★★★★) from wine distributor Sanz Global is a mouthfilling, vibrantly fruity wine. Showing good delicacy, it has ripe, peachy, citrusy flavours, strongly seasoned with nutty oak, and obvious potential; drink now or cellar.

Vintage	15
WR	4
Drink	17-21

DRY $24 AV

Karikari Estate Calypso Chardonnay   ★★★☆

Grown in Northland, the 2014 vintage (★★★★) is fragrant and softly mouthfilling, with finely integrated oak and generous, ripe, peachy, slightly spicy flavours. It's an excellent example of the powerful northern style.

DRY $29 –V

Karikari Estate Chardonnay ★★★★☆

Estate-grown in Northland, the 2014 vintage (★★★★☆) is mouthfilling, rich and well-rounded, with ripe, peachy, slightly toasty flavours, poised and lively, and excellent depth and complexity. It's already highly enjoyable, but also worth cellaring.

DRY $45 –V

Kidnapper Cliffs Hawke's Bay Chardonnay ★★★★★

From Te Awa (owned by Villa Maria), the classy 2014 vintage (★★★★★) was estate-grown, mostly in the Bridge Pa Triangle, hand-picked, fermented with indigenous yeasts in French oak hogsheads (40 per cent new), and barrel-aged for 10 months. Bright light lemon/green, it has a fragrant, complex bouquet, with a distinct whiff of 'struck match'. Still fresh and youthful in 2017, it is mouthfilling, with concentrated peach and grapefruit flavours, a subtle seasoning of oak, and very impressive vibrancy, poise and length. An elegant, tightly structured wine, it's still unfolding; best drinking 2019+.

Vintage	14	13
WR	7	6
Drink	17-21	17-20

DRY $55 AV

Kim Crawford Hawke's Bay Small Parcels Chardonnay (★★★★☆)

Already delicious, the age-worthy 2016 vintage (★★★★☆) was fermented with indigenous yeasts and matured in French oak barriques (36 per cent new). Bright, light lemon/green, it is fragrant and mouthfilling, with rich, ripe stone-fruit flavours, very good complexity and a long, harmonious finish. Best drinking 2019+. Fine value.

Vintage	16
WR	6
Drink	17-22

DRY $25 V+

Kim Crawford New Zealand Chardonnay (★★★)

The very easy-drinking 2016 vintage (★★★) was grown in Marlborough and Hawke's Bay. It's a weighty, fleshy style with ripe, peachy flavours to the fore, a distinct hint of butterscotch, and an ultra-smooth (4.4 grams/litre of residual sugar) finish. Priced right.

Vintage	16
WR	5
Drink	17-20

DRY $17 AV

Kina Beach Vineyard Reserve Nelson Chardonnay (★★★★☆)

The stylish 2014 vintage (★★★★☆) was estate-grown on the coast, fermented with indigenous yeasts in French oak casks, and wood-aged for seven months. Light lemon/green, it is fragrant, with strong, vibrant peach and grapefruit flavours, gently seasoned with oak, excellent complexity and a finely structured, lengthy finish. Best drinking 2019+.

Vintage	14
WR	6
Drink	17-22

DRY $36 –V

Kumeu River Coddington Chardonnay   ★★★★★

Launched from the 2006 vintage, this powerful, rich wine is grown in the Coddington Vineyard, between Huapai and Waimauku. The grapes, cultivated on a clay hillside, achieve an advanced level of ripeness (described by Kumeu River as 'flamboyant, unctuous, peachy'). Mouthfilling, complex and slightly nutty, it's typically a lusher, softer wine than its Hunting Hill stablemate (below). The 2016 vintage (★★★★★) was hand-picked, fermented with indigenous yeasts in French oak barriques and wood-matured for 11 months. Bright, light lemon/green, it is still very youthful, with a complex bouquet and fresh, tightly structured palate. Full-bodied, it's a classy wine with deep, vibrant, grapefruit-like flavours, showing excellent complexity, fresh acidity and a long, finely poised finish. Best drinking 2019+.

Vintage	16	15	14	13	12	11	10	09
WR	6	7	7	7	5	5	7	7
Drink	17-22	17-22	17-21	17-20	17-18	P	17-19	P

Kumeu River Estate Chardonnay   ★★★★★

This wine ranks fourth in the company's hierarchy of five Chardonnays, after three single-vineyard labels, but is still outstanding. Grown at Kumeu, in West Auckland, it is powerful, with rich, beautifully interwoven flavours and a seductively creamy texture, but also has good acid spine. The key to its quality lies in the vineyards, says winemaker Michael Brajkovich: 'We manage to get the grapes very ripe.' Grown in several blocks around Kumeu, hand-picked, fermented with indigenous yeasts and lees-aged (with weekly or twice-weekly lees-stirring) in Burgundy oak barriques (typically 25 per cent new), the wine normally undergoes a full, softening malolactic fermentation. The 2016 vintage (★★★★★) is a top buy. Pale lemon/green, it is fragrant, mouthfilling and youthful, with finely balanced acidity and ripe, citrusy, peachy, slightly biscuity and toasty flavours, showing excellent depth, complexity and harmony. Already enjoyable, it should be at its best 2019+.

Vintage	16	15	14	13	12	11	10	09
WR	6	6	7	7	5	5	7	7
Drink	17-21	17-20	17-20	17-19	P	P	17-19	P

Kumeu River Hunting Hill Chardonnay   ★★★★★

This outstanding, single-vineyard wine – my favourite in the Kumeu River range – is grown on slopes above Mate's Vineyard, directly over the road from the winery at Kumeu (originally planted in 1982, the site was replanted in 2000). A notably elegant wine, in its youth it is generally less lush than its Coddington stablemate (above), but with good acidity and citrusy, complex flavours that build well across the palate. The 2016 vintage (★★★★★) was hand-picked, fermented with indigenous yeasts in French oak barriques and wood-aged for 11 months. Attractively scented and mouthfilling, it has a real sense of youthful vigour. Intense and vibrantly fruity, with searching, peachy, lemony, slightly biscuity and toasty flavours, it shows excellent ripeness and complexity, with a very long, tight finish. Best drinking 2019+.

Vintage	16	15	14	13	12	11	10	09
WR	6	7	7	7	5	5	7	6
Drink	17-23	17-22	17-21	17-20	17-18	P	17-19	P

DRY $50 AV

DRY $32 V+

DRY $60 AV

Kumeu River Mate's Vineyard Kumeu Chardonnay   ★★★★★

This extremely classy single-vineyard wine is Kumeu River's flagship. It is made entirely from the best of the fruit harvested from Mate's Vineyard, planted in 1990 on the site of the original Kumeu River vineyard purchased by Mate Brajkovich in 1944. Strikingly similar to Kumeu River Estate Chardonnay, but slightly more opulent and concentrated, it offers the same rich and harmonious flavours of grapefruit, peach and butterscotch, typically with a stronger seasoning of new French oak (about 30 per cent). For winemaker Michael Brajkovich, the hallmark of Mate's Vineyard is 'a pear-like character on the nose, with richness and length on the palate after two to three years'. The 2016 vintage (★★★★★) was hand-picked, barrel-fermented and oak-aged for 11 months. Bright, light lemon/green, it is still a baby, with mouthfilling body and vibrant, very youthful, citrusy, peachy flavours, slightly toasty, complex, lively and long. A tightly structured wine with obvious potential, it's best opened 2020+.

Vintage	16	15	14	13	12	11	10	09	08
WR	6	7	7	7	5	5	7	7	6
Drink	17-23	17-22	17-21	17-20	17-18	P	17-19	P	P

 DRY $70 AV

Kumeu Village Hand Harvested Chardonnay   ★★★☆

Kumeu River's lower-tier, drink-young wine is hand-picked from heavier-bearing Chardonnay clones than the Mendoza commonly used for the top wines, and is typically fermented with indigenous yeasts in a mix of tanks (principally) and seasoned French oak casks. The 2016 vintage (★★★★), grown in Kumeu and Hawke's Bay, was 25 per cent fermented in old French oak barriques; the rest was handled in tanks. Instantly appealing, it is fresh and mouthfilling, with generous, peachy, slightly biscuity flavours, finely balanced acidity, considerable complexity and good length. Offering excellent value, it should be at its best mid-2018+.

DRY $18 V+

Lake Chalice Marlborough Chardonnay   ★★★☆

The 2016 vintage (★★★☆) is the latest release of a wine previously labelled 'The Haast'. Grown in the Wairau Valley, it was fermented and lees-aged for six months in tanks and oak casks. Light lemon/green, it is mouthfilling and vibrantly fruity, with fresh, grapefruit-like flavours, subtle oak and lees-aging notes adding complexity, and a finely balanced, dry finish. Best drinking 2018+.

 DRY $20 AV

Lake Chalice The Haast Marlborough Chardonnay   (★★★☆)

The 2015 vintage (★★★☆) was made in an easy-drinking, 'upfront' style, mouthfilling and creamy-textured, with generous, ripe, peachy, slightly toasty flavours and a very smooth finish. (The 2016 – see above – is not labelled as 'The Haast'.)

 DRY $20 AV

Lake Chalice The Nest Marlborough Chardonnay   (★★★☆)

Attractive young, the 2016 vintage (★★★☆) is a vibrant, 'fruit-driven' style. Offering very easy drinking, it is freshly scented, with mouthfilling body, plenty of ripe, peachy, slightly toasty flavours, and a creamy-smooth finish. Fine value.

 DRY $18 V+

Lake Chalice The Raptor Marlborough Chardonnay ★★★★☆

Unexpectedly classy for its price, the refined 2016 vintage (★★★★☆) was hand-picked in the Reed Vineyard, in the Wairau Valley, barrel-fermented with indigenous yeasts and matured for 10 months in French oak barriques (partly new). Light lemon/green, it is fragrant, mouthfilling, fresh and creamy-textured, with vibrant peach and grapefruit flavours, leesy, biscuity notes adding excellent complexity, and a finely poised, persistent finish.

 DRY $23 V+

Landing, The, Bay of Islands Chardonnay ★★★★☆

From a coastal site in the northern Bay of Islands, the 2015 vintage (★★★★☆) was fermented and matured in French oak casks (30 per cent new). An elegant, mouthfilling wine, it shows good complexity, with deep, ripe, citrusy, slightly buttery and smoky flavours, threaded with fresh acidity, and a lingering finish. Drink now to 2019.

Vintage	16	15	14	13
WR	4	5	5	6
Drink	17-20	17-20	17-19	P

DRY $40 –V

Last Shepherd, The, Gisborne Chardonnay (★★★★)

Enjoyable from the start, but worth cellaring, the 2016 vintage (★★★★) is a full-bodied, sweet-fruited wine with strong, vibrant, citrusy, peachy flavours to the fore, a subtle seasoning of oak adding complexity, and a finely textured finish.

 DRY $25 AV

Lawson's Dry Hills Marlborough Chardonnay ★★★☆

The 2016 vintage (★★★★) is an excellent example of the almost unoaked Chardonnay style. Fermented with indigenous yeasts and lees-stirred in tanks, with some malolactic fermentation, it is mouthfilling and vibrantly fruity, with good weight, strong, ripe, citrusy, peachy flavours and a fully dry, slightly creamy finish. Best drinking mid-2018+.

Vintage	16	15	14
WR	6	6	6
Drink	18-21	17-20	P

 DRY $20 AV

Lawson's Dry Hills Reserve Marlborough Chardonnay ★★★★☆

Estate-grown and hand-harvested in the Chaytors Road Vineyard, in the Wairau Valley, the 2015 vintage (★★★★☆) was fermented with indigenous yeasts in French oak barriques (25 per cent new). Bright, light lemon/green, it has a fragrant, slightly toasty bouquet. Fresh, full-bodied and dry, it is concentrated and complex, with good acid spine and strong, vibrant, citrusy, peachy flavours, gently seasoned with oak. A finely balanced wine, it's a drink-now or cellaring proposition. Good value.

Vintage	15	14	13
WR	7	6	6
Drink	17-22	17-20	17-18

 DRY $28 V+

Le Pont Chardonnay ★★★★☆

The 2015 vintage (★★★★☆) will appeal to fans of bold, 'upfront' Chardonnays. Hand-picked in the Ormond and Patutahi districts of Gisborne, it was fermented and matured for 14 months in French and Hungarian oak barrels (25 per cent new), with some use of indigenous yeasts and malolactic fermentation. Light lemon/green, it is a generous, full-bodied wine, with rich, ripe, stone-fruit flavours, biscuity, mealy, nutty notes adding complexity, balanced acidity and a slightly creamy texture. Still youthful, it should break into full stride 2018+. (From Poverty Bay Wine.)

DRY $34 AV

Left Field Hawke's Bay Chardonnay ★★★☆

From Te Awa, the 2016 vintage (★★★★) was fermented and matured in a mix of tanks (40 per cent) and French oak puncheons and hogsheads (60 per cent). It has a slightly smoky bouquet, mouthfilling body and generous, grapefruit-like flavours, showing excellent freshness, complexity and depth. Fine value.

Vintage	16	15
WR	5	5
Drink	17-19	17-19

DRY $18 V+

Leveret Estate Hawke's Bay Chardonnay ★★★

Maturing well, the 2014 vintage (★★★★) is a fresh, elegant wine, offering good value. Mouthfilling and smooth, with a hint of gunflint, it is citrusy and peachy, slightly buttery and toasty, with lively acidity and good complexity and length.

DRY $22 –V

Leveret Estate Reserve Hawke's Bay Chardonnay ★★★★

The elegant 2014 vintage (★★★★☆) was estate-grown at cool inland sites and barrel-fermented. Mouthfilling, it is finely poised, with concentrated, grapefruit-like flavours, slightly smoky and toasty notes adding complexity, and a long, tightly structured finish. Best drinking 2018+.

DRY $30 –V

Linden Estate Esk Valley Hawke's Bay Chardonnay ★★★☆

The 2015 vintage (★★★☆) was estate-grown in the Esk Valley, hand-picked and barrel-aged for 15 months. Fresh and full-bodied, it is weighty, ripe, peachy and toasty, with slightly buttery notes and an 'upfront' appeal. Best drinking 2018+.

Vintage	15
WR	4
Drink	17-18

DRY $25 –V

Linden Estate Reserve Hawke's Bay Chardonnay   (★★★★)

Still unfolding, the 2015 vintage (★★★★) was hand-harvested in the Esk Valley and fermented with indigenous yeasts in French oak barrels. Light lemon/green, it is mouthfilling and fresh, with concentrated, youthful grapefruit-like flavours, a gentle toasty streak and barrel-ferment complexity. Open mid-2018 onwards.

DRY $35 –V

Vintage	15
WR	6
Drink	17-18

Longview Estate Unoaked Chardonnay   (★★★)

From a hillside vineyard in Northland, the 2014 vintage (★★★) is mouthfilling and rounded, with ripe peach, apple and pear flavours. It's not a complex style, but shows good freshness, vigour and depth.

DRY $26 –V

Luna Eclipse Martinborough Chardonnay   (★★★☆)

The 2015 vintage (★★★☆) is a distinctive, medium-bodied wine with a slightly creamy bouquet. Citrusy and appley, with fresh acidity and considerable complexity, it is lively and youthful, with cellaring potential. (From Murdoch James.)

DRY $35 –V

Ma Maison Martinborough Chardonnay   (★★★★☆)

Worth cellaring, but already drinking well, the 2015 vintage (★★★★☆) was grown in the estate vineyard and at a neighbouring site, barrel-fermented and matured for 11 months on its full yeast lees. Bright, light yellow, it is rich, peachy and complex, with strong stone-fruit and toasty oak flavours, balanced acidity and a long finish.

DRY $45 –V

Mad Dog Vineyard Bay of Islands Chardonnay   (★★★★)

The 2014 vintage (★★★★), French oak-matured for 10 months, is a weighty, generous Northland style. Fleshy and creamy, it has fresh, strong grapefruit and peach flavours and a well-rounded finish. Enjoyable in its youth.

DRY $24 V+

Mahi Marlborough Chardonnay   ★★★★☆

The 2015 vintage (★★★★☆) was hand-picked at three sites, all towards the western end of the Wairau Valley, fermented with indigenous yeasts in French oak barrels and wood-aged for 11 months. A very elegant wine, it is mouthfilling and sweet-fruited, with ripe, peachy flavours, showing excellent delicacy and depth, mealy, biscuity notes adding complexity, and a long finish. Drink now or cellar.

DRY $29 AV

Vintage	16	15	14	13	12	11	10	09
WR	6	6	6	6	6	6	6	6
Drink	17-22	17-21	17-21	17-18	P	P	P	P

Mahi Twin Valleys Vineyard Marlborough Chardonnay ★★★★★

Grown and hand-picked in the Twin Valleys Vineyard, at the junction of the Wairau and Waihopai valleys, the classy 2015 vintage (★★★★★) was fermented with indigenous yeasts and matured for 15 months in French oak barriques. Bright, light lemon/green, it is mouthfilling and tightly structured, with concentrated, youthful grapefruit and stone-fruit flavours, integrated oak, fresh acidity and excellent complexity and cellaring potential. Best drinking mid-2018+.

Vintage	15	14	13	DRY $39 AV
WR	6	6	6	
Drink	17-23	17-22	17-22	

Mahurangi River Winery Field of Grace Chardonnay ★★★★☆

Estate-grown at Matakana, this consistently impressive wine is grown in the Field of Grace Block, hand-harvested and matured in French oak barriques (8 per cent new in 2014). The 2014 vintage (★★★★☆) is a wine of subtle power. Sweet-fruited, it has deep, vibrant grapefruit and peach flavours, very subtle oak, good mouthfeel and complexity, and a slightly mealy, rounded finish.

Vintage	14	13	DRY $36 –V
WR	6	6	
Drink	17-20	17-19	

Mahurangi River Winery Field of Grace Reserve Chardonnay ★★★★★

The 2014 vintage (★★★★★) was hand-picked at Matakana and fermented and matured in French oak barrels (64 per cent new). Fragrant, with a complex bouquet, it is a powerful, rich wine, with generous, ripe stone-fruit flavours, biscuity notes adding complexity, and a long, well-rounded finish. Distinctly classy.

Vintage	14	13	DRY $58 AV
WR	6	6	
Drink	17-21	17-20	

Main Divide Chardonnay ★★★☆

The Main Divide range, from Pegasus Bay, is based on South Island grapes. The 2015 vintage (★★★☆), grown in North Canterbury, was fermented with indigenous yeasts and lees-matured for a year in old French oak casks, 'restricting any pick-up of oak flavours and allowing the fruit to express itself'. Bright, light lemon/green, it is full-bodied, with good depth of peachy, slightly spicy and honeyed flavours, fresh acidity and a touch of complexity. Drink now to 2018. The 2016 vintage (★★★★) is a blend of North Canterbury and Marlborough grapes. Fermented with indigenous yeasts and matured for a year in old French oak barrels, it is light yellow/green, mouthfilling and generous, with ripe, peachy flavours, balanced acidity, considerable complexity and a slightly creamy finish. Already drinking well, it should be at its best during 2018.

Vintage	16	15	14	13	DRY $21 AV
WR	7	6	6	6	
Drink	18-25	17-18	P	P	

Maison Noire Hawke's Bay Chardonnay

The 2016 vintage (★★★★) was grown at three sites and fermented in one to two-year-old barrels. Mouthfilling, fresh and lively, it is savoury, with ripe grapefruit and peach flavours, gentle mealy notes adding complexity, and excellent harmony and personality. An elegant wine, it's already drinking well, but also worth cellaring.

Vintage	16
WR	6
Drink	17-21

DRY $25 AV

Man O' War Valhalla Waiheke Island Chardonnay   ★★★★

This tautly structured wine is estate-grown at the remote, eastern end of Waiheke Island. Hand-harvested and fermented with indigenous yeasts in French oak casks, the powerful, light yellow 2016 vintage (★★★★☆) is full-bodied, with very generous, ripe, peachy, slightly nutty flavours, complex, dry and long. Best drinking 2019+.

DRY $42 –V

Map Maker Marlborough Chardonnay Pure   ★★★★

From Staete Landt, the 2014 vintage (★★★★) was grown and hand-harvested at Rapaura, in the Wairau Valley. A weighty, creamy-textured wine, it was barrel-fermented, but not barrel-aged, and bottled young. An excellent drink-young style, it is fleshy and forward, with some complexity and strong, citrusy, peachy, slightly nutty flavours. Fine value.

Vintage	14
WR	6
Drink	P

DRY $20 V+

Margrain Martinborough Chardonnay   ★★★★

Maturing very gracefully, the 2014 vintage (★★★★☆) was fermented and matured for 10 months in French oak barriques (10 per cent new). Light lemon/green, it is mouthfilling, with strong, vibrant, grapefruit-like flavours to the fore, a subtle seasoning of oak, good vigour and a slightly minerally, lingering finish. Best drinking 2018+.

Vintage	14
WR	6
Drink	17-26

DRY $28 AV

Marsden Bay of Islands Black Rocks Chardonnay   ★★★★☆

Grown at Kerikeri, this Northland wine is impressive in favourably dry seasons – sturdy, with concentrated, ripe sweet-fruit flavours, well seasoned with toasty oak, in a typically lush, upfront, creamy-smooth style. The classy 2016 vintage (★★★★★) was fermented and matured for 10 months in French oak barriques (35 per cent new). Bright, light lemon/green, it has a fragrant, mealy bouquet. Full-bodied, it is concentrated and complex, with generous, ripe stone-fruit flavours, slightly buttery and toasty notes, gentle acidity and a smooth, very harmonious finish. Already delicious, it should break into full stride from mid-2018 onwards.

Vintage	16	15	14	13	12	11	10
WR	6	6	6	6	4	5	6
Drink	17-23	17-22	17-19	17-18	P	P	P

DRY $40 –V

Martinborough Vineyard Chardonnay ★★★★★

Mouthfilling, peachy and mealy, this is a powerful, harmonious wine, rich and complex. Made from grapes grown on the gravelly Martinborough Terrace, including the original Mendoza-clone vines planted in 1980, it is hand-picked, fermented with indigenous yeasts and lees-aged for a year in French oak barriques (20 per cent new in 2012). The 2013 vintage (★★★★☆) has a fragrant, stylish, complex bouquet. A finely poised wine with concentrated flavours of grapefruit, peach and biscuity oak, it is savoury and complex, with obvious potential; open 2017 onwards.

Vintage	13	12	11	10	09	08
WR	7	6	6	7	7	7
Drink	17-19	P	P	P	P	P

DRY $39 AV

Martinborough Vineyard Home Block Chardonnay (★★★★★)

Already delicious, the 2014 vintage (★★★★★) is a fragrant, generous, age-worthy wine. Light lemon/green, it is finely poised, with rich, ripe stone-fruit flavours, showing good complexity, slightly smoky notes, finely integrated oak and a long finish. Best drinking 2018+.

DRY $40 AV

Matahiwi Estate Hawke's Bay Chardonnay ★★☆

The light lemon/green 2015 vintage (★★★) from this Wairarapa-based producer was grown at two sites in Hawke's Bay. Enjoyable young, it is fresh and vibrantly fruity, with good depth of ripe, peachy, slightly buttery and toasty flavours.

DRY $22 –V

Matahiwi Estate Holly Hawke's Bay Chardonnay ★★★★

The 2014 vintage (★★★★), barrel-fermented (35 per cent new), is fragrant, rich and rounded, with generous, slightly buttery flavours. The 2015 vintage (★★★★) is tightly structured, with mouthfilling body and ripe, peachy, slightly toasty flavours, woven with fresh acidity. Best drinking 2018+.

DRY $25 AV

Matakana Estate Matakana Chardonnay ★★★★☆

The 2014 vintage (★★★★☆) is a classy wine, fermented with indigenous yeasts in French oak casks (25 per cent new). It is full-bodied, with strong grapefruit and peach flavours, mingled with biscuity oak, fresh acidity, good complexity, and a long, savoury finish.

DRY $30 AV

Matawhero Church House Barrel Fermented Gisborne Chardonnay ★★★★

The 2015 vintage (★★★★☆) is a generous, 'upfront' style, already offering a lot of pleasure, but worth cellaring. Fermented in American oak casks (30 per cent new), and given a full, softening malolactic fermentation, it is full-bodied and sweet-fruited, with a hint of butterscotch and ripe, peachy, slightly creamy and toasty flavours, showing excellent vigour and richness. The 2016 vintage (★★★☆) is a medium-bodied wine, with delicate, citrusy, peachy fruit flavours, indigenous yeasts adding a touch of complexity, and a smooth, lengthy finish.

DRY $26 AV

Matawhero Single Vineyard Gisborne Chardonnay

Handled without oak, the 2016 vintage (★★★☆) was given a full, softening malolactic fermentation. Fleshy and creamy-textured, it offers very satisfying depth of fresh, ripe stone-fruit flavours, in an attractive, drink-young style.

DRY $23 AV

Vintage	14	13
WR	7	7
Drink	P	P

Matua Single Vineyard Marlborough Chardonnay

The 2014 vintage (★★★★★) was grown in the centre of the Wairau Valley and barrel-fermented, with some use of indigenous yeasts and new oak. The bouquet is fragrant, smoky and complex; the palate is mouthfilling and very savoury, with generous, peachy, citrusy flavours, integrated oak, and a very persistent finish. Best drinking 2018+.

DRY $58 AV

Maude Mt Maude Vineyard Wanaka Chardonnay

The 2014 vintage (★★★★☆), hand-picked from estate-grown, 20-year-old vines, was fermented and matured in seasoned French oak puncheons. Fragrant and full-bodied, it is a rich, elegant style with concentrated, citrusy, peachy flavours, slightly buttery notes, excellent complexity and a long finish. Best 2018+.

DRY $28 V+

Milcrest Nelson Reserve Chardonnay

The 2014 vintage (★★★☆) is a single-vineyard wine, fermented and matured for 11 months in French and American oak barriques. It is full-bodied, with very good depth of peachy, citrusy, slightly yeasty and toasty flavours, showing considerable complexity. Enjoyable young.

DRY $42 –V

Mill Road Hawke's Bay Chardonnay (★★☆)

Looking for a fruity Chardonnay, priced sharply? The 2015 vintage (★★☆) is mouthfilling, with citrusy, peachy flavours in a 'fruit-driven' style, simple but lively.

DRY $10 V+

Mills Reef Elspeth Gimblett Gravels Hawke's Bay Chardonnay

Mills Reef's flagship Chardonnay is consistently rewarding and a classic regional style. The 2014 vintage (★★★★☆) was hand-picked and fermented, partly with indigenous yeasts, in French oak casks (23 per cent new). It is mouthfilling, with concentrated, peachy, toasty flavours, showing good complexity. A generous, tightly structured wine, it has obvious cellaring potential and should be at its best 2018+. The 2015 (★★★★★) is a top vintage. Bright, light lemon/green, it is fragrant, with rich, vibrant grapefruit and stone-fruit flavours, a slightly buttery note, and a long, very harmonious finish. Already delicious, it's a very elegant and age-worthy wine.

DRY $40 –V

Vintage	15	14	13	12	11	10	09
WR	7	7	7	NM	7	7	6
Drink	17-21	17-20	17-18	NM	P	P	P

Mills Reef Estate Hawke's Bay Chardonnay   ★★★

The 2015 vintage (★★★) was grown at Meeanee, Maraekakaho and Crownthorpe. A fruit-driven style, it was mostly handled in tanks; 14 per cent of the blend was barrel-fermented. Medium to full-bodied, it has lively, citrusy, appley, slightly spicy flavours, showing a touch of complexity, and a fresh, smooth finish. Enjoyable young.

Vintage	15	14
WR	7	6
Drink	17-18	P

 DRY $18 AV

Mills Reef Reserve Hawke's Bay Chardonnay   ★★★★

Mills Reef's middle-tier Chardonnay. The attractive 2016 vintage (★★★★) was fermented and matured for 10 months in barrels (two-thirds French, one-third American, 27 per cent new). Grown at Maraekakaho, Meeanee and in the Gimblett Gravels, it is an 'upfront' style, mouthfilling and fresh, with vibrant, peachy, citrusy flavours, showing good richness, mealy and toasty notes adding complexity, and a slightly buttery finish. Drink now onwards.

Vintage	16	15	14	13	12	11	10
WR	6	7	7	7	6	7	7
Drink	17-20	17-19	17-18	P	P	P	P

 DRY $25 AV

Millton Clos de Ste Anne Chardonnay – see Clos de Ste Anne Chardonnay

Millton Opou Vineyard Gisborne Chardonnay   ★★★★

Certified organic, the impressive 2015 vintage (★★★★☆) was fermented with indigenous yeasts in French oak barrels (15 per cent new), and oak-aged for 15 months. Pale straw, it has a fragrant, complex bouquet. Mouthfilling, it is rich, sweet-fruited, peachy and biscuity, with a slightly oily texture and excellent depth and harmony.

Vintage	15	14
WR	6	6
Drink	17-25	17-24

 DRY $29 AV

Mission Barrique Reserve Hawke's Bay Chardonnay   ★★★★☆

For Mission's classy, upper-tier Chardonnay, the style goal is a wine that 'emphasises fruit characters rather than oak, but offers some of the benefits of fermentation and maturation in wood'. The classy 2016 vintage (★★★★☆) was fermented and matured in French oak barriques. Pale lemon/green, it is mouthfilling, with concentrated, ripe, peachy flavours, seasoned with nutty notes, smoky notes adding complexity, and a long, tightly structured finish. Best drinking 2019+.

Vintage	15	14	13	12	11	10
WR	5	7	7	5	5	5
Drink	17-20	17-21	17-20	17-18	17-18	P

DRY $29 V+

Mission Hawke's Bay Chardonnay ★★★

The 2015 vintage (★★★★) is a skilfully crafted wine with a slightly buttery bouquet. Full-bodied, it has peachy, slightly toasty flavours, showing excellent depth and harmony. Great value.

DRY $18 AV

Mission Huchet Hawke's Bay Chardonnay (★★★★★)

Full of potential, the debut 2013 vintage (★★★★★) is a notably refined wine. Hand-harvested and fermented with indigenous yeasts in French oak casks (33 per cent new), it was given a full, softening malolactic fermentation. The bouquet is fragrant and complex; the palate is mouthfilling, rich and layered, with highly concentrated peach and grapefruit flavours, integrated oak, fine acidity, and a very persistent finish. Best drinking 2018+.

DRY $80 –V

Mission Jewelstone Hawke's Bay Chardonnay ★★★★★

Classy stuff. Hand-picked from mature vines, the 2015 vintage (★★★★★) was barrel-fermented (French, 26 per cent new) and lees-aged for 10 months. A powerful, rich wine with a real sense of drive and potential, it is weighty, with a hint of butterscotch, ripe, grapefruit-like flavours, finely integrated oak, a slightly creamy texture and a lengthy finish. The 2016 vintage (★★★★★) is a single-vineyard wine, hand-harvested from 'old vines' and barrel-fermented. Bright, light lemon/green, it is a restrained, youthful, classic cellaring style, with grapefruit and peach flavours, showing excellent delicacy and depth, oak complexity and a finely poised, lasting finish. Best drinking 2020+.

Vintage	15	14	13	12	11	10	09
WR	7	7	6	5	NM	7	6
Drink	17-22	17-21	17-20	P	NM	17-20	17-18

DRY $40 AV

Mission Vineyard Selection Hawke's Bay Chardonnay ★★★☆

The pale yellow 2016 vintage (★★★☆) is a 'lightly oaked' style. Delicious young, it is mouthfilling, with ripe, citrusy flavours, showing very good vibrancy and depth.

DRY $20 AV

Misty Cove Signature Marlborough Chardonnay ★★★☆

The 2014 vintage (★★★) was estate-grown at Rapaura, in the Wairau Valley. Mouthfilling and sweet-fruited, it has good depth of fresh, peachy, slightly toasty and buttery flavours, a hint of honey, and drink-young appeal.

DRY $30 –V

Monarch Estate Vineyard Matakana Chardonnay (★★★★)

The elegant 2014 vintage (★★★★) was estate-grown, hand-picked and barrel-fermented (33 per cent new oak). It's a full-bodied wine, with vibrant, citrusy, peachy flavours, integrated oak, savoury notes adding complexity and a tight finish. Well worth cellaring.

DRY $25 AV

Montana Reserve Gisborne Chardonnay   (★★★☆)

The debut 2016 vintage (★★★☆) is a generous, upfront style, enjoyable young. Bright, light yellow, it is full-bodied and smooth, with a slightly toasty bouquet, good depth of fresh, ripe, peachy flavours, a hint of butterscotch, gentle acidity and moderate complexity.

DRY $17 V+

Mount Riley 17 Valley Marlborough Chardonnay   ★★★★☆

The 2014 vintage (★★★★★) is very refined. Estate-grown at three sites, and fermented and matured in French oak barriques (30 per cent new), it is an immaculate wine, mouthfilling and rich, with concentrated, peachy, citrusy flavours, finely balanced oak, and a long, finely textured finish. Best drinking 2018+.

Vintage	14	13	12	11	10	09
WR	7	7	7	7	7	7
Drink	17-21	17-20	17-19	17-18	P	P

DRY $31 AV

Mount Riley Marlborough Chardonnay   ★★★

The 2014 vintage (★★★) was mostly (70 per cent) fermented in French oak barriques; 30 per cent of the blend was tank-fermented. Grown in the Wairau Valley, it is a fruit-driven style, with mouthfilling body, vibrant, citrusy flavours to the fore, a very gentle seasoning of oak, fresh acidity, and good depth.

DRY $17 AV

Moutere Hills Nelson Chardonnay   ★★★★

The single-vineyard 2016 vintage (★★★★☆) was estate-grown, hand-picked and fermented and matured for 11 months in French oak barrels. Pale straw, it is weighty, with deep, ripe peach and grapefruit flavours, balanced acidity, a slightly creamy texture, and excellent complexity. It's already quite open and expressive, but also well worth cellaring.

DRY $34 –V

Moutere Hills Sarau Reserve Chardonnay   ★★★★☆

The powerful, fragrant 2015 vintage (★★★★★) is an estate-grown, single-vineyard Nelson wine, hand-picked and fermented and matured for 11 months in French oak barriques. Light yellow/green, it is full-bodied and fresh, with vibrant, citrusy, peachy flavours, showing excellent concentration and complexity, balanced acidity, and a lasting finish. Best drinking 2019+.

DRY $55 –V

Mt Beautiful North Canterbury Chardonnay   ★★★★

Estate-grown at Cheviot, north of Waipara, the 2015 vintage (★★★★) was handled in an even split of tanks and seasoned French oak casks. Pale lemon/green, it has a creamy bouquet, leading into a mouthfilling, softly textured wine with vibrant, ripe stone-fruit flavours to the fore, hints of biscuity oak adding complexity, balanced acidity and a slightly buttery finish. Drink now or cellar.

Vintage	15	14
WR	6	5
Drink	17-21	17-20

DRY $30 –V

Mt Difficulty Grower's Series Lowburn Valley Chardonnay ★★★★

Still unfolding, the youthful 2015 vintage (★★★★☆) was hand-picked at two sites at Lowburn, in Central Otago, and fermented with indigenous yeasts in French oak barrels (17 per cent new). Light lemon/green, it is lemon-scented, with mouthfilling body, strong, vibrant, citrusy flavours, well-integrated oak, good complexity and excellent length. Best drinking mid-2018+.

Vintage	15	14
WR	6	6
Drink	17-25	17-25

 DRY $39 –V

Mud House Sub Region Series Omaka Marlborough Chardonnay (★★★☆)

The debut 2015 vintage (★★★☆) was handled in tanks (70 per cent) and barrels (30 per cent). A mouthfilling, creamy-textured wine, it has ripe stone-fruit flavours to the fore, with gentle toasty notes, a touch of complexity, and a smooth finish. Enjoyable young.

DRY $20 AV

Muddy Water Waipara Chardonnay ★★★★☆

Certified organic, the elegant, youthful 2015 vintage (★★★★☆) was hand-picked from 22-year-old vines and fermented with indigenous yeasts in French oak puncheons (15 per cent new). Light lemon/green, it is weighty, with rich stone-fruit and spice flavours, a subtle seasoning of oak, fresh acidity, and strong personality. Best drinking 2018+.

Vintage	15	14	13	12	11	10
WR	7	6	6	6	6	6
Drink	17-26	17-22	17-21	17-20	17-18	17-18

DRY $38 AV

Nanny Goat Vineyard Central Otago Chardonnay ★★★☆

The 2014 vintage (★★★☆) is a mouthfilling, creamy wine with fresh acidity and very good depth of citrusy, slightly mealy and biscuity flavours. It should reward cellaring.

 DRY $36 –V

Nautilus Marlborough Chardonnay ★★★★★

Hand-harvested, barrel-fermented and lees-stirred (in 25 per cent new oak), the 2015 (★★★★★) is a top vintage. Light lemon/green, it is fragrant, rich and harmonious, with fresh, ripe, peachy flavours, integrated oak and excellent complexity. A classy young wine, with lovely balance and freshness, it is very age-worthy; best drinking 2018+.

Vintage	15	14	13	12	11	10
WR	7	6	7	7	6	7
Drink	17-20	17-19	17-18	P	P	P

DRY $35 AV

Neudorf Moutere Chardonnay $\qquad$ ★★★★★

Superbly rich but not overblown, with arrestingly intense flavours enlivened with fine acidity, this multi-faceted Nelson wine enjoys a reputation second to none among New Zealand Chardonnays. Grown in clay soils threaded with gravel at Upper Moutere, it is hand-harvested from mature vines, fermented with indigenous yeasts, and lees-aged, with regular stirring, for a year in French oak barriques (12 per cent new in 2016). Bright, light yellow/green, the 2016 vintage (★★★★★) is richly fragrant, with ripe, peachy, slightly toasty flavours, showing lovely vibrancy, complexity and depth. Threaded with fresh, appetising acidity, it is still youthful, but already a memorable mouthful. Best drinking 2019+. Certified organic.

Vintage	16	15	14	13	12	11	10	09	08	DRY $74 AV
WR	6	7	6	6	7	6	7	7	6	
Drink	19-23	18-22	17-21	17-20	17-20	17-18	17-18	P	P	

Neudorf Rosie's Block Nelson Chardonnay $\qquad$ ★★★★☆

Already enjoyable, the stylish 2016 vintage (★★★★☆) was hand-harvested in Rosie's Block and the Home Block, both in Upper Moutere. Fermented with indigenous yeasts and lees-aged for 10 months in French oak casks (15 per cent new), it was given a full, softening malolactic fermentation. Light lemon/green, it is mouthfilling, with concentrated, vibrant fruit flavours, woven with appetising acidity, very good complexity, and a long, dry, slightly biscuity finish. Drink now or cellar.

Vintage	16	15	DRY $33 AV
WR	6	7	
Drink	17-21	17-21	

Neudorf Twenty Five Rows Moutere Chardonnay $\qquad$ ★★★★☆

'The inspiration is unabashedly Chablis' for this organically certified wine, which is very lightly exposed to oak. The 2016 vintage (★★★★☆), estate-grown and hand-harvested at Upper Moutere, was fermented with indigenous yeasts in tanks and then matured on its yeast lees, with some handling in old oak puncheons. Bright, light lemon/green, it is mouthfilling, fresh and youthful, with ripe, citrusy, peachy flavours to the fore, excellent vibrancy and intensity, mealy notes adding complexity, and a tightly structured finish. A very elegant wine, it should be at its best mid-2018+.

Vintage	16	15	14	13	DRY $33 AV
WR	6	7	6	6	
Drink	18-21	17-20	17-19	17-18	

Nga Waka Home Block Martinborough Chardonnay $\qquad$ ★★★★☆

This single-vineyard wine is from vines planted in 1988. At its best, it is an authoritative wine, weighty and concentrated, with strong personality. The 2016 vintage (★★★★☆) was fermented and matured for 10 months in French oak casks (30 per cent new), and given a full, softening malolactic fermentation. Bright, pale yellow, it is full-bodied, vibrant, sweet-fruited and slightly creamy, with concentrated fruit flavours, slightly oily and buttery notes, balanced acidity and plenty of personality. Best drinking mid-2018+.

Vintage	16	15	14	13	12	11	10	09
WR	6	6	7	7	6	7	NM	7
Drink	17-22	17-21	17-20	P	P	P	NM	P

DRY $40 –V

Nga Waka Martinborough Chardonnay ★★★★

This is a consistently rewarding wine. The 2016 vintage (★★★★) was fermented and matured for 10 months in French oak casks (20 per cent new). Already enjoyable, it is ripely fragrant and full-bodied, with generous stone-fruit flavours, a well-integrated, biscuity oak influence, good complexity and a harmonious, well-rounded finish. Best drinking mid-2018+.

Vintage	16	15	14	13	12	11	10
WR	6	6	7	7	6	7	7
Drink	17-20	17-19	17-18	P	P	P	P

DRY $30 –V

Ngatarawa Proprietors' Reserve Hawke's Bay Chardonnay ★★★★☆

The second, 2014 vintage (★★★★☆) was grown at two sites in the Bridge Pa Triangle, fermented and lees-aged in French oak barriques (33 per cent new), and given a full, softening malolactic fermentation. A fragrant, youthful wine, it is weighty, with strong, vibrant, peachy, slightly biscuity and mealy flavours, complex and savoury, and a dry, very harmonious finish. Best drinking 2018+.

DRY $35 –V

Ngatarawa Stables Reserve Hawke's Bay Chardonnay ★★★

Bottled early, the 2015 vintage (★★★) is full-bodied, with vibrant stone-fruit flavours, a touch of complexity, and plenty of drink-young appeal. (For the 2016 vintage, see Stables Reserve Hawke's Bay Chardonnay.)

Vintage	15	14
WR	7	5
Drink	17-20	17-19

DRY $20 –V

Nikau Point Reserve Hawke's Bay Chardonnay (★★☆)

Ready to roll, the 2014 vintage (★★☆) is a mouthfilling, sweet-fruited wine with uncomplicated, peachy fruit flavours, still fresh and lively.

DRY $14 AV

Nikau Point Select Hawke's Bay Chardonnay (★★★)

Enjoyable now, the bargain-priced 2013 vintage (★★★) was made with 'light use of oak'. Still youthful in colour, it is fresh, vibrantly fruity and smooth, with grapefruit-like flavours, showing good depth.

DRY $10 V+

Obsidian Reserve Waiheke Island Chardonnay ★★★★☆

This reserve bottling, from 'small hillside vineyards', is based on 'the best fruit parcels and barrels'. The 2015 vintage (★★★★☆) is fragrant and mouthfilling, with layers of rich, ripe, peachy flavours, seasoned with toasty oak, excellent complexity, and a finely textured, harmonious finish. Delicious from the start, it should be at its best 2018+. The 2016 vintage (★★★★) is an elegant, savoury, youthful wine with generous, ripe grapefruit and peach flavours, integrated toasty oak (French, 40 per cent new), and good complexity. Well worth cellaring, it should be at its best mid-2018+.

Vintage	15	14	13	12
WR	6	6	7	6
Drink	17-21	17-20	17-19	17-18

 DRY $48 –V

Obsidian Waiheke Island Chardonnay ★★★★

The 2014 vintage, matured in French oak barriques for 10 months, is mouthfilling, with fresh, generous peach and grapefruit flavours, gently seasoned with biscuity oak. A subtle, finely poised, youthful wine, it should be at its best 2018+.

 DRY $29 AV

Odyssey Gisborne Chardonnay ★★★

The 2014 vintage (★★★☆), grown in the Kawatiri Vineyard, was handled in tanks (60 per cent) and barrels (40 per cent). Full-bodied and fleshy, it has fresh, ripe, peachy, slightly nutty and buttery flavours, in a moderately complex style with a rounded finish – and lots of drink-young appeal.

 DRY $20 –V

Odyssey Reserve Iliad Gisborne Chardonnay ★★★★☆

Top vintages represent Gisborne Chardonnay at its finest. Hand-picked from mature vines in the Kawatiri Vineyard at Hexton and fermented and lees-aged in French oak barriques (27 per cent new), the 2014 vintage (★★★★☆) is a mouthfilling wine with strong, ripe stone-fruit flavours, biscuity and nutty notes adding complexity, and good power and potential. Best drinking 2018+.

Vintage	14	13
WR	6	6
Drink	17-18	17-18

DRY $34 AV

Ohinemuri Estate Patutahi Reserve Chardonnay ★★★★

The elegant, barrel-fermented 2014 vintage (★★★★) is one of the best yet. Mouthfilling, it has generous, ripe stone-fruit flavours, showing good complexity, a subtle oak influence, slightly buttery notes and excellent freshness and harmony. Retasted in mid-2017, it's maturing gracefully; drink now or cellar.

Vintage	14
WR	6
Drink	17-21

 DRY $25 AV

Old Coach Road Nelson Chardonnay ★★★

Drinking well now, the 2016 vintage (★★★) is mouthfilling, peachy and slightly buttery, with plenty of flavour and a smooth finish.

Vintage	16
WR	6
Drink	17-22

DRY $15 V+

Old Coach Road Unoaked Nelson Chardonnay ★★☆

Balanced for early drinking, the 2017 vintage (★★☆) from Seifried is a fresh, fruity, uncomplicated wine, with peachy, slightly buttery flavours and a fully dry finish.

Vintage	17
WR	6
Drink	17-19

DRY $13 V+

Omaka Springs Falveys Single Vineyard Marlborough Chardonnay ★★★☆

Offering good value, the 2016 vintage (★★★★) was estate-grown in the Omaka Valley and French oak-matured. Light lemon/green, it is fragrant, finely poised and youthful, with very satisfying depth of peachy, slightly creamy flavours, enriched with biscuity oak. Showing very good complexity and harmony, it's a drink-young or cellaring proposition.

DRY $23 AV

Osawa Prestige Collection Hawke's Bay Chardonnay ★★★☆

Estate-grown at Mangatahi, the 2014 vintage (★★★☆) has pale, lemon/green colour. Full-bodied, it is sweet-fruited, with generous, peachy, slightly toasty flavours, threaded with fresh acidity, and slightly earthy notes adding complexity. It tastes ready.

DRY $50 –V

Osawa Winemaker's Collection Hawke's Bay Chardonnay ★★★★☆

Tasted in mid-2017, the elegant, youthful 2013 vintage (★★★★☆) was hand-picked and French oak-aged. Light lemon/green, it is still developing, with fresh, strong grapefruit-like flavours, finely balanced oak, good complexity and a tight-knit, long finish.

DRY $85 –V

Oyster Bay Marlborough Chardonnay ★★★☆

This huge-selling, moderately priced wine is designed to showcase Marlborough's incisive fruit flavours. About half the blend is handled solely in tanks; the other half is fermented, lees-stirred and matured in French oak barrels. It typically offers strong, ripe grapefruit-like flavours, threaded with appetising acidity. The 2016 vintage (★★★★) was grown in the Wairau and Awatere valleys. Instantly appealing, it is mouthfilling, with vibrant, citrusy, slightly buttery flavours, showing good richness, balanced acidity, considerable complexity, and a well-rounded finish. Drink now onwards.

DRY $20 AV

Pa Road Marlborough Chardonnay

Bargain-priced, the 2016 vintage (★★★★) was hand-picked in the Southern Valleys, partly barrel-fermented, and lees-aged for six months. Bright, light lemon/green, it has lots of youthful impact, in a fruit-driven style with vibrant, peachy, citrusy flavours, appetising acidity and a dry, slightly buttery finish. Delicious young. (From Te Pa.)

DRY $17 V+

Paddy Borthwick New Zealand Chardonnay   ★★★★

Estate-grown in the northern Wairarapa, the 2016 vintage (★★★★) is a single-vineyard wine, fermented and matured in French oak casks (20 per cent new). Bright, light lemon/green, it is a fragrant, medium to full-bodied wine with fresh, youthful, citrusy flavours, a subtle seasoning of oak, and very good vigour, depth and potential.

DRY $26 AV

Palliser Estate Martinborough Chardonnay   ★★★★★

The key attributes of this wine are finesse and harmony, rather than power. A celebration of rich, ripe fruit flavours, it is gently seasoned with oak (French, typically 25 per cent new), producing a delicious wine with subtle winemaking input and concentrated varietal flavours. The 2015 vintage (★★★★☆) is a very elegant, youthful wine. Fragrant, full-bodied and finely poised, it has generous, citrusy, slightly spicy flavours and a well-integrated, toasty, nutty oak influence.

Vintage	15	14	13
WR	7	7	7
Drink	17-22	17-21	17-18

DRY $39 AV

Paroa Bay Bay of Islands Chardonnay   ★★★☆

The 2014 vintage (★★★☆) was estate-grown at Russell and barrel-fermented. Weighty, it has very good depth of ripe, peachy, citrusy flavours and a subtle seasoning of nutty, toasty oak.

DRY $35 –V

Pask Declaration Gimblett Gravels Chardonnay   ★★★★☆

The winery's top Chardonnay is estate-grown in the Gimblett Gravels, Hawke's Bay. The 2015 vintage (★★★★★) was fermented and matured for 11 months in French oak puncheons (78 per cent new). Bright, light lemon/green, it is weighty and youthful, with concentrated, ripe stone-fruit flavours, mealy and biscuity notes adding complexity, and excellent delicacy, texture and length. Best drinking 2018+.

Vintage	15	14	13	12	11	10
WR	7	7	7	5	6	NM
Drink	17-24	17-21	17-20	17-19	17-18	NM

DRY $40 –V

Pask Gimblett Gravels Chardonnay

This second-tier Hawke's Bay Chardonnay is designed to highlight its vibrant fruit characters, with a subtle wood influence from partial barrel fermentation. The 2015 vintage (★★★☆) is elegant and fruity, with ripe, peachy flavours, gently seasoned with oak, and fresh acidity keeping things lively.

Vintage	15	14	13	12	11	10
WR	6	7	7	5	5	7
Drink	17-21	17-19	17-18	P	P	P

DRY $22 AV

Pask Small Batch Gimblett Road Wild Ferment Chardonnay

Estate-grown in Hawke's Bay, the attractive 2016 vintage (★★★★☆) was fermented with indigenous ('wild') yeasts and matured for a year in seasoned French oak casks. Light lemon/green, it is fresh, elegant and youthful, with lively, citrusy, peachy flavours, gently seasoned with oak, good complexity and harmony, and a fragrant bouquet. Drink now to 2019.

Vintage	16
WR	5
Drink	17-22

DRY $25 AV

Peacock Sky Waiheke Island Chardonnay ★★★

The 2016 vintage (★★★) was hand-picked and fermented with indigenous yeasts. Made in a 'lightly oaked' style, it is mouthfilling and vibrantly fruity, with fresh, peachy, citrusy, slightly appley flavours, offering pleasant, easy drinking.

DRY $39 –V

Pegasus Bay Chardonnay ★★★★★

Strapping yet delicate, richly flavoured yet subtle, this sophisticated North Canterbury wine is one of the country's best Chardonnays grown south of Marlborough. Muscular and taut, it typically offers a seamless array of fresh, crisp, citrusy, biscuity, complex flavours and great concentration and length. Estate-grown at Waipara, it is based on ungrafted, Mendoza-clone vines (about 30 years old) and given lengthy oak aging (the 2016 vintage was fermented and lees-aged for a year in French oak puncheons, 30 per cent new). The 2015 vintage (★★★★★) is light lemon/green, with a fragrant, youthful bouquet. Weighty, sweet-fruited and smooth, it has very generous, peachy, mealy, slightly buttery and spicy flavours, and a long, dry, savoury, seamless finish. Drink now or cellar. The 2016 vintage (★★★★★) has a complex, fragrant bouquet, leading into a youthful, very harmonious wine with concentrated grapefruit and peach flavours, fresh acidity, a gentle seasoning of toasty oak, excellent complexity, and a well-structured, long finish. Already delicious, it should be at its best 2019+.

DRY $42 AV

Vintage	16	15	14	13	12	11	10	09	08
WR	6	6	5	7	6	6	6	7	6
Drink	17-28	17-27	17-23	17-23	17-24	17-23	17-20	17-18	P

Pegasus Bay Virtuoso Chardonnay ★★★★★

Blended from several of the 'best barrels', this wine is hand-picked from the company's mature, Mendoza-clone vines at Waipara. Fermented with indigenous yeasts, it is lees-aged for a year in French oak puncheons (40 per cent new in 2015), matured in tanks on light lees for several more months before bottling, and then bottle-aged for a year prior to its release. The 2015 vintage (★★★★★) is a rich, stylish, youthful wine, likely to be long-lived. Light yellow/green, it is full-bodied, with deep, ripe stone-fruit flavours, showing excellent delicacy and complexity, good acid spine, a slightly minerally streak, and a lasting finish. Open 2019+.

Vintage	15
WR	6
Drink	17-28

DRY $55 AV

Petane Station Esk Valley Hawke's Bay Chardonnay (★★★★☆)

The refined 2016 vintage (★★★★☆) was harvested from young, first-crop vines at Eskdale, in the Esk Valley, and fermented and matured in French oak barrels (one and two years-old). It has a fragrant, peachy, slightly mealy bouquet. A medium to full-bodied wine, it is instantly appealing, with fresh, ripe stone-fruit flavours, showing excellent delicacy and depth, gentle toasty notes adding complexity, moderate acidity, and a very harmonious, creamy-textured finish. A quietly satisfying wine, already delicious, it's a drink-now or cellaring proposition.

DRY $30 AV

Peter Yealands Reserve Hawke's Bay Chardonnay (★★★)

Made in a 'fruit-driven' style, the gently oak-influenced 2014 vintage (★★★) is an attractive, harmonious wine with ripe melon and peach flavours, mealy, biscuity notes adding a touch of complexity, and good harmony.

Vintage	14
WR	7
Drink	17-18

DRY $21 –V

Poderi Crisci Waiheke Island Chardonnay (★★★★)

The 2016 vintage (★★★★) was barrel-matured for 10 months. Light lemon/green, it is a medium to full-bodied, very youthful wine with a yeasty, complex, slightly funky bouquet. The palate shows good concentration, with grapefruit and peach flavours, lots of barrel-stir complexity, and obvious potential. Best drinking 2019+.

DRY $49 –V

Prospect, The, Gisborne Chardonnay (★★★★)

From Spade Oak, the light lemon/green 2015 vintage (★★★★) was grown in the Ormond and Patutahi districts, and fermented and matured for 11 months in French oak casks (21 per cent new). Made with 'lashings of toasty vanillin oak' (according to the back label), in fact it's a harmonious wine, mouthfilling, with concentrated, ripe, peachy flavours, biscuity notes adding complexity, a hint of development, and lots of current-drinking appeal.

DRY $28 AV

Pyramid Valley Growers Collection Marlborough Chardonnay (★★★★☆)

The stylish 2014 vintage (★★★★☆) was grown in Kerner Estate Vineyard, in the Waihopai Valley, and matured in seasoned French oak puncheons. Mouthfilling, it has deep, citrusy flavours, a restrained oak influence, and a very harmonious, smooth, slightly buttery finish. Drink now or cellar.

DRY $48 –V

Quarter Acre Hawke's Bay Chardonnay ★★★★☆

The 2014 vintage (★★★★☆), grown in the coastal Doc's Block Vineyard at Haumoana, was hand-picked from 20-year-old vines and fermented with indigenous yeasts in French oak barriques (60 per cent new). Mouthfilling, it has fresh, ripe, peachy flavours, showing excellent depth and complexity, and a slightly buttery, well-rounded finish.

DRY $35 –V

Ra Nui Marlborough Wairau Valley Chardonnay ★★★☆

Drinking well in 2017, the 2013 vintage (★★★☆) was hand-picked and fermented in seasoned French oak barriques. Full-bodied, it has very good depth of citrusy, peachy flavours, well-integrated oak and a slightly creamy, harmonious finish.

DRY $30 –V

Rapaura Springs Marlborough Chardonnay ★★★☆

The 2016 vintage (★★★☆) is an easy-drinking wine, partly barrel-aged. Light lemon/green, it is mouthfilling, with very good depth of fresh, vibrant, citrusy, peachy flavours, and a dry (2.1 grams/litre of residual sugar) finish.

Vintage	16	15
WR	6	7
Drink	17-22	17-21

DRY $17 V+

Rapaura Springs Reserve Marlborough Chardonnay ★★★★

Offering fine value, the 2016 vintage (★★★★) was partly barrel-fermented. Pale lemon/green, it is full-bodied and fleshy, with strong, vibrant melon and peach flavours, a gentle seasoning of oak, balanced acidity and a fully dry finish.

Vintage	16	15
WR	6	7
Drink	17-23	17-24

DRY $19 V+

Renato Nelson Chardonnay ★★★★

Estate-grown on the Kina Peninsula, hand-picked and fermented and matured for 10 months in French oak barriques (15 per cent new), the 2015 vintage (★★★★) of this single-vineyard wine is fresh and youthful. Mouthfilling, with a fragrant, slightly buttery bouquet, it has strong, ripe, peachy flavours, woven with fresh acidity, finely integrated oak, and very good depth.

Vintage	15	14	13	12	11	10	09
WR	6	6	NM	7	NM	6	7
Drink	17-21	17-20	NM	17-18	NM	P	P

DRY $25 AV

Richmond Plains Nelson Chardonnay ★★★☆

Certified organic, the 2015 vintage (★★★★) was handled in a 2:1 mix of oak barrels (15 per cent new) and tanks. Light lemon/green, it is lemon-scented, with mouthfilling body, vibrant, citrusy, slightly buttery flavours, a subtle seasoning of oak, and good persistence. An elegant, youthful wine, it should be at its best 2018+.

DRY $25 –V

Rimu Grove Nelson Chardonnay ★★★★☆

This wine is typically full of personality. Estate-grown near the coast in the Moutere hills and fermented and lees-matured for 11 months in French oak casks, the pale straw 2016 vintage (★★★★☆) is weighty and smooth, with concentrated, well-ripened stone-fruit flavours, seasoned with toasty oak, excellent complexity and lots of drink-young appeal.

Vintage	16	15	14	13	12	11	10	09
WR	7	7	7	7	7	NM	7	6
Drink	18-30	17-30	17-25	17-28	17-27	NM	17-25	17-18

DRY $39 –V

Rock Ferry 3rd Rock Marlborough Chardonnay ★★★★★

Certified organic, the 2014 vintage (★★★★★) was estate-grown in The Corners Vineyard, at Rapaura. Hand-picked, it was fermented with indigenous yeasts in a French oak cuve, and matured in French oak barriques (25 per cent new). Bright, light lemon/green, it is rich, ripe and rounded, with a fragrant bouquet, good weight and very generous, peachy, citrusy, mealy flavours, gently seasoned with oak. A very harmonious, creamy-textured wine, it's delicious now. Fine value.

DRY $30 V+

Rongopai Hawke's Bay Chardonnay (★★☆)

The 2015 vintage (★★☆) is an uncomplicated wine, vibrantly fruity, with lemony, appley flavours, fresh and direct. (From Babich.)

DRY $20 –V

Rossendale Marlborough Chardonnay ★★★

Priced sharply, the 2015 vintage (★★★) is a barrel-fermented, medium-bodied wine, with fresh, crisp, lively, citrusy flavours to the fore, slightly peachy and toasty notes, a touch of complexity and satisfying depth.

DRY $16 V+

Sacred Hill Halo Hawke's Bay Chardonnay ★★★★

The fleshy, generous 2016 vintage (★★★★) was grown in the elevated Riflemans Vineyard and barrel-fermented. Bright, light lemon/green, it is full-bodied, with fresh, strong, peachy, slightly buttery and toasty flavours, and a well-rounded finish. Already approachable, it should be at its best 2018+.

DRY $28 AV

Sacred Hill Hawke's Bay Chardonnay ★★★☆

The 2016 vintage (★★★☆) is a 'fruit-driven' style, mouthfilling and moderately complex, with vibrant, citrusy flavours to the fore, a subtle seasoning of oak, and good delicacy and harmony. Drink now onwards. Fine value.

Vintage	16	15
WR	6	6
Drink	17-19	17-18

DRY $17 V+

Sacred Hill Reserve Hawke's Bay Chardonnay ★★★★

The attractive 2016 vintage (★★★★☆) was estate-grown and barrel-fermented. Already delicious, it is fragrant, sweet-fruited and mouthfilling, with fresh, generous peach, grapefruit and toasty oak flavours, showing very good complexity. A stylish, finely balanced wine, still unfolding, it's well worth cellaring.

Vintage	16	15
WR	7	5
Drink	17-20	P

DRY $25 AV

Sacred Hill Riflemans Chardonnay ★★★★★

Sacred Hill's flagship Chardonnay is one of New Zealand's greatest – powerful yet elegant, with striking intensity and outstanding cellaring potential. Grown in the cool, inland, elevated (100 metres above sea level) Riflemans Terraces Vineyard in the Dartmoor Valley of Hawke's Bay, it is hand-picked from mature, own-rooted, Mendoza-clone vines and fermented with indigenous yeasts in French oak barriques (new and one year old), with some malolactic fermentation. The 2016 vintage (★★★★★) is bright, light lemon/green. An elegant, mouthfilling wine, it has concentrated, vibrant grapefruit and peach flavours, seasoned with nutty oak, and lovely freshness, delicacy, poise and complexity. Already delicious, it's a tight-knit wine with obvious potential; best drinking 2019+.

Vintage	16	15	14	13	12	11	10	09
WR	7	6	7	7	NM	NM	7	7
Drink	17-23	17-22	17-20	17-19	NM	NM	P	P

DRY $70 AV

Sacred Hill Virgin Chardonnay ★★★★

This Chablis-style wine is hand-picked in the company's acclaimed Riflemans Terraces Vineyard, in the upper Dartmoor Valley, tank-fermented and lees-aged. Harvested relatively early to preserve its lively acidity, it is handled without oak or malolactic fermentation, and promoted as a 'pure, natural Chardonnay'. The 2015 vintage (★★★★) has a strong presence, with mouthfilling body and crisp, tightly structured, citrusy, peachy flavours that linger well. Drink now or cellar.

Vintage	15	14
WR	6	6
Drink	18-28	17-19

 DRY $30 –V

Sacred Hill Wine Thief Hawke's Bay Chardonnay ★★★★☆

Designed as a 'richer and toastier' style than the flagship Riflemans Chardonnay (above), this wine is grown in the same vineyard, hand-picked and fermented with indigenous yeasts in new and one-year-old French oak barriques. The 2016 vintage (★★★★☆) is a high-flavoured wine, already very expressive. Bright, light yellow/green, it is mouthfilling, with fresh, peachy, toasty, faintly buttery flavours, showing excellent complexity, and finely balanced acidity. Best drinking mid-2018+.

Vintage	16	15
WR	6	6
Drink	17-20	17-19

 DRY $35 –V

Saint Clair James Sinclair Marlborough Chardonnay ★★★★

The 2016 vintage (★★★★) was grown in the Awatere Valley, fermented and matured in seasoned French and American oak barriques, and given a full, softening malolactic fermentation. A drink-now or cellaring proposition, it is fresh and mouthfilling, with balanced acidity, plenty of peachy, slightly toasty flavours, creamy notes, good harmony and lots of drink-young appeal.

DRY $24 V+

Saint Clair Marlborough Chardonnay ★★★☆

Finely balanced for early drinking, the 2016 vintage (★★★☆) is a fresh, mouthfilling, moderately complex wine with a slightly creamy texture and generous, citrusy, slightly peachy and toasty flavours. Grown in the Wairau Valley, it was fermented in a mix of tanks and French and American oak barrels.

DRY $22 AV

Saint Clair Omaka Reserve Marlborough Chardonnay ★★★★☆

This is typically a fat, creamy wine, weighty and rich, made in a bold, upfront style. Grown in the Southern Valleys – mostly in the company's vineyard in the Omaka Valley – it is fermented and lees-aged for 10 months in American oak casks (50 per cent new in 2016), and given a full, softening malolactic fermentation. Bright, light lemon/green, the youthful 2016 vintage (★★★★☆) is mouthfilling, sweet-fruited and savoury, with good complexity and a creamy-textured, very harmonious finish. Best drinking mid-2018+.

Vintage	16	15	14	13	12	11	10
WR	7	7	7	7	7	7	7
Drink	17-20	17-19	17-18	P	P	P	P

 DRY $38 –V

Saint Clair Pioneer Block 10 Twin Hills Marlborough Chardonnay ★★★★☆

This powerful wine is grown principally in the company's vineyard in the Omaka Valley, a warm site with clay-based soils. The refined 2016 vintage (★★★★☆) was fermented and lees-aged in French oak barriques. It is pale, mouthfilling and creamy, with vibrant, ripe grapefruit and peach flavours, a gentle seasoning of toasty oak, mealy, leesy notes adding complexity, fresh acidity and a finely textured finish. Well worth cellaring.

DRY $33 AV

Saint Clair Pioneer Block 11 Cell Block Marlborough Chardonnay ★★★★☆

The 2015 vintage (★★★★☆) was grown at Dillons Point, in the lower Wairau Valley, fermented and lees-aged for 10 months in French oak barriques (100 per cent new), and given a full, softening malolactic fermentation. Bright, light lemon/green, with a fragrant, complex bouquet, it is mouthfilling, with deep, peachy, slightly buttery and toasty flavours, balanced acidity and a lasting finish. Drinking well now, it should be at its best mid-2018+.

DRY $33 AV

Saint Clair Pioneer Block 4 Sawcut Marlborough Chardonnay ★★★★

Grown in the Sawcut Vineyard, in the Ure Valley, half-way between Blenheim and Kaikoura, this is a consistently good wine. The 2015 vintage (★★★★) was hand-picked, fermented and lees-aged for 10 months in French oak barriques (25 per cent new), and given a full, softening malolactic fermentation. Bright, light lemon/green, it has a fresh, complex bouquet, leading into a mouthfilling wine with vibrant, peachy, toasty flavours, lively acidity and a slightly creamy finish. Drink now or cellar.

DRY $33 –V

Saint Clair Unoaked Marlborough Chardonnay ★★★

This refreshing wine is cool-fermented and lees-aged in tanks, using malolactic fermentation to add complexity and soften the acidity. Enjoyable young, the 2015 vintage (★★★) is a medium to full-bodied wine, with fresh, citrusy flavours, hints of apples and spices, a slightly creamy texture and a smooth (4.2 grams/litre of residual sugar) finish.

DRY $22 –V

Saint Clair Vicar's Choice Marlborough Chardonnay ★★★

The 2014 vintage (★★★☆), fermented in a 50:50 split of tanks and seasoned oak barrels, was matured on its yeast lees for several months and given a full, softening malolactic fermentation. Fresh and moderately complex, it's a highly attractive, drink-young style, with generous, vibrant, peachy flavours to the fore, a hint of sweet oak, and a creamy-smooth finish.

DRY $19 AV

Sanctuary Marlborough Chardonnay ★★★

The 2015 vintage (★★★) of this flavoursome, 'lightly oaked' wine is pale straw, with slightly buttery aromas and flavours. Vibrantly fruity, with spicy, toasty notes, it's enjoyable young.

DRY $18 AV

Satyr Kereru Hawke's Bay Chardonnay   (★★★★)

The 2014 vintage (★★★★) is a mouthfilling wine, with ripe peach/grapefruit flavours, a slightly buttery, creamy texture, and good complexity. It's maturing well. (From Sileni.)

DRY $34 –V

Sea Level Home Block Nelson Chardonnay   ★★★★

The 2014 vintage (★★★★), estate-grown at Mariri, was matured for 10 months in seasoned French oak puncheons. Skilfully crafted, it is fragrant and finely poised, in a medium to full-bodied style with concentrated, vibrant, peachy flavours, showing good delicacy and length, balanced acidity and obvious cellaring potential.

Vintage	14
WR	6
Drink	17-20

DRY $25 AV

Seifried Nelson Chardonnay   ★★★☆

Priced sharply, the 2016 vintage (★★★☆) was matured for a year in French oak barriques (new, one and two years old). Pale yellow, it's a peachy, slightly toasty and honeyed, full-flavoured wine, already drinking well, likely to be at its best during 2018.

Vintage	16	15	14	13
WR	6	6	6	6
Drink	17-26	17-25	17-24	17-21

DRY $18 V+

Seifried Winemaker's Collection Nelson Barrique Fermented Chardonnay   ★★★★

This is typically a bold style, concentrated and creamy, with loads of flavour. The 2015 vintage (★★★★) was fermented and matured for a year in French oak barriques. Full-bodied, it is a generous wine with concentrated, ripe, peachy, slightly spicy flavours, showing good complexity, and a well-rounded finish. Drink now or cellar.

Vintage	15
WR	7
Drink	17-25

DRY $26 AV

Selaks Founders Limited Edition Hawke's Bay Chardonnay   ★★★★☆

Delicious young, the powerful 2016 vintage (★★★★☆) was barrel-fermented. Light lemon/green, it is a weighty, slightly buttery wine, with strong peach and grapefruit flavours, showing good complexity and harmony, and a fragrant bouquet. Priced right.

Vintage	16
WR	6
Drink	18-21

DRY $25 V+

Selaks Reserve Hawke's Bay Chardonnay ★★★

Enjoyable young, the 2016 vintage (★★★) is full-bodied and fruity, with citrusy, slightly buttery and toasty flavours, fresh, ripe and smooth.

Vintage	16
WR	5
Drink	17-18

 DRY $16 V+

Selaks The Taste Collection Hawke's Bay Buttery Chardonnay (★★★★)

If you like soft, buttery Chardonnays, try this. The debut 2016 vintage (★★★★) was principally (70 per cent) fermented and matured in French oak barriques (30 per cent new); 30 per cent of the blend was handled in tanks. Light lemon/green, with a toasty bouquet, it is mouthfilling, with ripe, peachy flavours, coupled with strong buttery and toasty notes – as you would expect – but also freshness and vivacity. Skilfully crafted for instant appeal, it offers good value.

 DRY $22 V+

Seresin Chardonnay Reserve ★★★★★

Finesse is the keynote quality of this organically certified Marlborough wine. Estate-grown in the Raupo Creek Vineyard, in the Omaka Valley, the classy 2013 vintage (★★★★★) was hand-picked, fermented with indigenous yeasts and lees-aged for 11 months in French oak barrels (20 per cent new), then blended and matured for a further four months in seasoned oak puncheons. It shows excellent depth, complexity and potential. Sweet-fruited, with concentrated, citrusy, slightly toasty flavours, a minerally streak, and impressive vigour and length, it should be at its best during 2018.

Vintage	13	12	11	10	09	08
WR	7	7	6	7	7	6
Drink	17-22	17-22	17-20	17-20	P	P

 DRY $40 AV

Seresin Marlborough Chardonnay ★★★★☆

This stylish, BioGro-certified wine is designed to 'focus on the textural element of the palate rather than emphasising primary fruit characters'. It is typically a full-bodied and complex wine with good mouthfeel, ripe melon/citrus characters shining through, subtle toasty oak and fresh acidity. The 2014 vintage (★★★★☆) was estate-grown in the Raupo Creek Vineyard, in the Omaka Valley, hand-picked, fermented with indigenous yeasts and lees-aged for 11 months in French oak barriques (8 per cent new), and given a full, softening malolactic fermentation. It's a mouthfilling, fleshy wine with generous, ripe grapefruit and peach flavours, finely integrated oak, good complexity and a well-rounded finish. Drink now or cellar.

DRY $30 AV

Sherwood Estate Stoney Range Waipara Valley Chardonnay (★★★☆)

Offering fine value, the 2015 vintage (★★★☆) was partly handled in tanks, but 75 per cent of the blend was barrel-fermented with indigenous yeasts. A full-bodied, fleshy wine, it has ripe peach/nectarine flavours and a slightly creamy finish.

 DRY $17 V+

Sileni Cellar Selection Hawke's Bay Chardonnay   ★★★

Enjoyable young, the 2016 vintage (★★★) was 'lightly' oaked and half the blend went through a softening malolactic fermentation. Freshly scented, it is a medium-bodied, vibrantly fruity wine, with citrusy flavours and a smooth, dry finish.

DRY $20 –V

Sileni Exceptional Vintage Hawke's Bay Chardonnay   ★★★★☆

Sileni's flagship Chardonnay is produced only in top vintages, such as 2010 and 2013. The 2013 vintage (★★★★★), fermented and matured in French oak casks (60 per cent new), is powerful, with a hint of butterscotch on the nose. Weighty, with rich stone-fruit flavours, buttery, toasty and nutty notes adding complexity, and lots of drink-young appeal, it's a drink-now or cellaring proposition.

Vintage	15	14	13	12	11	10
WR	NM	NM	6	NM	NM	7
Drink	NM	NM	17-22	NM	NM	17-19

DRY $65 –V

Sileni The Lodge Hawke's Bay Chardonnay   ★★★★☆

The elegant 2016 vintage (★★★★☆) was fermented and matured in French oak barriques (30 per cent new), and given a full, softening malolactic fermentation. Bright, light yellow/green, it is mouthfilling and sweet-fruited, with vibrant, grapefruit-like flavours, slightly buttery notes, well-integrated oak, and excellent harmony and richness. Drink now or cellar.

Vintage	16	15	14	13	12	11	10
WR	6	6	6	6	5	5	6
Drink	17-22	17-21	17-21	17-19	17-19	P	P

DRY $33 AV

Soho Carter Waiheke Island Chardonnay   ★★★★☆

The 2016 vintage (★★★★) is an estate-grown, single-vineyard wine, hand-picked at Onetangi and fermented and matured in French oak barriques (28 per cent new). Bright, light lemon/green, it has a fresh, slightly biscuity bouquet. A mouthfilling, sweet-fruited wine, it is still very youthful, with vibrant, peachy, citrusy flavours, finely integrated oak, good complexity and a slightly creamy finish. Best drinking mid-2018+.

DRY $37 –V

Spade Oak Vigneron Gisborne Chardonnay   (★★★★☆)

Still unfolding, the 2015 vintage (★★★★☆) was grown in the Ashwood Vineyard, fermented with indigenous yeasts in oak barrels (25 per cent new), and given a full, softening malolactic fermentation. Light lemon/green, it is full-bodied, with generous, ripe, peachy, slightly toasty flavours, showing good complexity, and a finely balanced, creamy-smooth finish. Best drinking 2018+.

DRY $32 AV

Spade Oak Vineyard Voysey Series Gisborne Chardonnay ★★★☆

The 2014 vintage (★★★☆) offers good value. Mouthfilling, it is a fleshy, sweet-fruited, moderately complex style with strong, ripe, peachy fruit flavours to the fore, gentle acidity and a well-rounded finish. Ready.

Spinyback Nelson Chardonnay ★★★

From Waimea Estates, the 2014 vintage (★★★) was tank-fermented and then 'aged with a selection of French oak'. Light lemon/green, it is mouthfilling and vibrantly fruity, with ripe, peachy, slightly spicy flavours, offering smooth, easy drinking.

Spy Valley Envoy Johnson Vineyard Marlborough Chardonnay ★★★★★

This distinguished wine is estate-grown in the Waihopai Valley, hand-picked, fermented with indigenous yeasts and lees-aged in French oak barriques (mostly seasoned) for up to 20 months. Elegant and youthful, the 2014 vintage (★★★★☆) is fragrant and tightly structured, with fresh, concentrated, peachy, slightly toasty and creamy flavours, a minerally streak, good acid spine and obvious cellaring potential. Best drinking 2018+.

Vintage	14	13	12	11	10	09	08
WR	6	6	6	NM	6	6	6
Drink	17-20	17-21	17-18	NM	P	P	P

Spy Valley Marlborough Chardonnay ★★★★

A consistently attractive, top-value wine. The 2015 vintage (★★★★) was hand-picked, barrel-fermented and oak-aged for nearly a year. Light lemon/green, it is fragrant and mouthfilling, with very youthful, vibrant, citrusy flavours to the fore, a subtle seasoning of oak, good acid spine and a bone-dry, slightly buttery, lingering finish.

Vintage	15	14	13	12
WR	6	7	7	7
Drink	18-25	17-20	17-19	17-18

Stables Reserve Hawke's Bay Chardonnay (★★★)

Enjoyable young, the 2016 vintage (★★★) is a full-bodied, sweet-fruited wine with ripe, peachy, slightly buttery flavours, showing good depth, and a very smooth finish. (From Ngatarawa.)

Staete Landt Josephine Marlborough Chardonnay ★★★★☆

This single-vineyard wine is estate-grown at Rapaura. The fragrant, weighty 2015 vintage (★★★★☆) was hand-harvested, barrel-fermented (in French oak puncheons, 10 per cent new) and wood-aged for 15 months. Light lemon/green, it is still very youthful, with generous, ripe, citrusy, peachy flavours, balanced acidity, biscuity notes adding complexity and a lingering finish. Best drinking 2019+.

Stanley Estates Reserve Single Vineyard
Awatere Valley Marlborough Chardonnay   ★★★★

Already drinking well, the 2016 vintage (★★★★) was fermented with indigenous yeasts in French oak barrels (25 per cent new), and wood-aged for 10 months. Light lemon/green, it is mouthfilling and vibrant, with strong, citrusy, slightly peachy flavours, well-integrated oak, a minerally streak and a finely balanced, slightly creamy finish.

Vintage	16
WR	6
Drink	17-24

 DRY $28 AV

Starborough Single Vineyard Awatere Valley Chardonnay   (★★★★☆)

Delicious young, the lush 2015 vintage (★★★★☆) was estate-grown at Dashwood, hand-picked, fermented with indigenous yeasts in French oak casks (25 per cent new), and given a full, softening malolactic fermentation. Bright, light yellow/green, it is sturdy, rich and rounded, with generous, peachy, slightly buttery flavours, showing good complexity, and lots of drink-young appeal.

 DRY $30 AV

Stone Bridge Gisborne Chardonnay   ★★★★

The 2015 vintage (★★★★) was hand-picked and fermented and matured for over a year in French oak barrels (25 per cent new). Bright, light yellow, it is mouthfilling and fleshy, with generous, ripe, peachy, toasty flavours and a smooth, slightly buttery finish. A very typical regional style, it's drinking well now and likely to be at its best during 2018.

 DRY $25 AV

Stonecroft Gimblett Gravels Hawke's Bay Chardonnay   ★★★★

Certified organic, the 2016 vintage (★★★★) was estate-grown and matured for six months in seasoned French oak barrels. Still unfolding, it is full-bodied, with ripe, peachy flavours to the fore, toasty and buttery notes adding complexity, balanced acidity and excellent depth. Best drinking mid-2018+.

Vintage	16	15	14	13
WR	5	6	6	6
Drink	17-22	17-22	17-21	17-20

 DRY $27 AV

Stonecroft Old Vine Gimblett Gravels Hawke's Bay Chardonnay   ★★★★★

The impressive 2016 vintage (★★★★★) is a rare wine – only two barrels were made. From vines planted in Mere Road in 1992, it was hand-picked, fermented and matured for a year in French oak casks (50 per cent new), and given a full, softening malolactic fermentation. Light lemon/green, it is mouthfilling and highly concentrated, with layers of stone-fruit, grapefruit and biscuity oak flavours, revealing excellent complexity, and a very long, savoury finish. A classy young wine, it should be at its peak 2020+.

Vintage	16	15
WR	6	6
Drink	18-25	18-24

DRY $47 AV

Stoneleigh Latitude Marlborough Chardonnay   ★★★☆

The 2014 vintage (★★★★) is a mouthfilling wine, grown at Rapaura. Softly textured, with strong, ripe grapefruit-like flavours and nutty, savoury elements adding complexity, it's enjoyable from the start. Also attractive young, the 2015 vintage (★★★) has good depth of ripe, peachy flavours, with a well-rounded finish.

DRY $22 AV

Stoneleigh Marlborough Chardonnay   ★★★☆

From Pernod Ricard NZ, this wine is always enjoyable and good value on special. It is typically about two-thirds wood-fermented, in French and Hungarian barrels, small and large; the rest is handled in tanks. The 2015 vintage (★★★) is bright, light yellow. Fleshy, with satisfying depth of citrusy, slightly buttery flavours, it is a moderately complex wine, fresh and lively, with drink-young appeal.

DRY $17 V+

Vintage	15	14	13	12	11	10
WR	7	6	6	6	6	7
Drink	17-18	P	P	P	P	P

Stoneleigh Rapaura Series Marlborough Chardonnay   ★★★★

This single-vineyard wine is fermented and matured in new and one-year-old French oak casks. The 2015 vintage (★★★☆) is mouthfilling, with good depth of citrusy, slightly peachy and biscuity flavours, showing a touch of complexity.

DRY $28 AV

Vintage	15	14	13	12	11
WR	7	6	6	6	6
Drink	P	P	P	P	P

Stoneleigh Wild Valley Marlborough Chardonnay   (★★★☆)

The debut 2015 vintage (★★★☆) was grown at Rapaura, in the Wairau Valley, and fermented with indigenous ('wild') yeasts in a 50:50 split of tanks and French oak barrels. Mouthfilling and smooth, it has ripe, peachy, slightly toasty flavours and gentle acidity, in a moderately concentrated, creamy-textured style, enjoyable young. Priced right.

DRY $19 V+

Stonyridge Fallen Angel Hawke's Bay Chardonnay   (★★★★)

The 2014 vintage (★★★★) was barrel-fermented and lees-aged for 10 months. Pale straw, it is mouthfilling and creamy-textured, with generous, ripe, slightly spicy and toasty flavours, finely balanced for enjoyable, early drinking.

DRY $45 –V

Sugar Loaf Marlborough Chardonnay   (★★★★)

Priced sharply, the 2014 vintage (★★★★) is a single-vineyard wine, hand-picked in the lower Wairau Valley and barrel-fermented. Full-bodied, ripe and rounded, it is vibrant and sweet-fruited, with strong, peachy, citrusy flavours, a hint of butterscotch, and good complexity and harmony.

DRY $22 V+

Summerhouse Marlborough Chardonnay ★★★★

The fine-value 2016 vintage (★★★★) was fully barrel-fermented and oak-aged for nine months. Bright, light lemon/green, it is mouthfilling, with strong, vibrant, peachy, slightly buttery flavours, dry and harmonious. Delicious young.

Vintage	16	15	14
WR	7	7	7
Drink	17-25	17-23	17-22

DRY $19 V+

Supper Club Marlborough Chardonnay (★★★☆)

Offering good value, the 2014 vintage (★★★☆) is a blend of upper Awatere Valley (principally) and lower Wairau Valley fruit, mostly handled in tanks, but 30 per cent barrel-fermented. Mouthfilling, it has citrusy, peachy flavours to the fore, with savoury, slightly buttery notes adding complexity, and very good depth and harmony.

DRY $19 V+

Tantalus Cachette Reserve Waiheke Island Chardonnay (★★★★)

Estate-grown at Onetangi, the 2015 vintage (★★★★) was fermented and matured for 10 months in French oak casks. Light lemon/green, with a fragrant, creamy bouquet, it is mouthfilling, with fresh, ripe stone-fruit flavours, well-integrated oak and balanced acidity. Enjoyable young, it should be at its best 2018+.

Vintage	15
WR	5
Drink	17-19

DRY $45 –V

Te Awa Single Estate Hawke's Bay Chardonnay ★★★★☆

The 2016 vintage (★★★★☆) is an estate-grown wine, hand-harvested and fermented with indigenous yeasts in French oak hogsheads. A very elegant, youthful wine, it is full-bodied, with concentrated, grapefruit-like flavours, smoky, biscuity notes adding complexity, and excellent depth and harmony. Best drinking 2019+.

Vintage	16	15	14
WR	7	7	6
Drink	17-25	17-25	17-24

DRY $30 AV

Te Awanga Estate Hawke's Bay Chardonnay ★★★★

Already delicious, the 2015 vintage (★★★★☆), from 12 to 19-year-old vines, was partly barrel-fermented with indigenous yeasts, given a full, softening malolactic fermentation, and lees-aged for 10 months. Bright, light lemon/green, it is mouthfilling and finely poised, with strong, vibrant grapefruit/peach flavours, a subtle seasoning of toasty oak, slightly buttery notes, and excellent harmony and drink-young appeal. Drink now or cellar.

DRY $25 AV

Te Kairanga John Martin Martinborough Chardonnay ★★★★

The 2014 vintage (★★★★☆), made from the 'best vineyard parcels', was fermented and matured in French oak puncheons (15 per cent new), and given a full, softening malolactic fermentation. It is an elegant, sweet-fruited wine with rich, youthful peach, grapefruit and subtle oak flavours, and a long, finely balanced finish. The 2015 vintage (★★★★) has a toasty bouquet, leading into a generous, ripely flavoured wine with a creamy-smooth finish and plenty of drink-young appeal.

Vintage	15	14	13
WR	7	7	7
Drink	17-23	17-22	17-22

 DRY $35 –V

Te Kairanga Martinborough Chardonnay ★★★★

The 2014 vintage (★★★★) was fermented in French oak puncheons (15 per cent new) and given a full, softening malolactic fermentation. It is mouthfilling and slightly creamy, with generous, ripe, peachy, slightly biscuity flavours and a well-rounded, harmonious finish.

Vintage	14	13
WR	7	6
Drink	17-20	17-20

 DRY $24 V+

Te Mania Nelson Chardonnay ★★★

The 2015 vintage (★★★☆) was handled in tanks (85 per cent) and barrels (15 per cent). Light lemon/green, it is mouthfilling and vibrantly fruity, with fresh, citrusy aromas and flavours to the fore, slightly creamy, buttery notes, lively acidity and very good depth.

 DRY $22 –V

Te Mania Reserve Nelson Chardonnay (★★★★)

The lively 2015 vintage (★★★★) was fermented and matured for 10 months in French oak barrels (25 per cent new). Fleshy, with strong, fresh grapefruit, peach and toasty oak flavours, balanced acidity and good complexity, it's well worth cellaring to 2018+.

 DRY $30 –V

Te Mata Elston Chardonnay ★★★★★

One of New Zealand's most illustrious Chardonnays, Elston is a stylish, intense, slowly evolving Hawke's Bay wine. At around four years old, it is notably complete, showing concentration and finesse. The grapes are grown and hand-picked principally at two sites in the Te Mata hills at Havelock North, and the wine is fully fermented in French oak barriques (35 per cent new), with full malolactic fermentation. The pale straw 2015 vintage (★★★★★) is mouthfilling and still very youthful. Weighty and sweet-fruited, it has peachy, slightly spicy flavours, integrated oak, balanced acidity, and a tightly structured, poised and persistent finish. Best drinking 2019+.

Vintage	15	14	13	12	11	10	09
WR	6	7	7	7	7	7	7
Drink	17-23	17-19	17-18	P	P	P	P

 DRY $35 AV

Te Mata Estate Vineyards Hawke's Bay Chardonnay ★★★★

This consistently attractive wine is sourced from the company's vineyards at Woodthorpe Terraces, in the Dartmoor Valley, the Bridge Pa Triangle and at Havelock North. Fermented and lees-aged in a mix of tanks and French oak barrels, it is typically a harmonious wine with fresh, ripe grapefruit characters to the fore, a gentle seasoning of biscuity oak, very good depth and a touch of complexity. The 2016 vintage (★★★★) is finely balanced for early drinking. A fragrant, mouthfilling, fleshy wine, it is sweet-fruited, with vibrant grapefruit and peach flavours to the fore, mealy, biscuity notes adding complexity, fresh acidity and a slightly buttery finish.

Vintage	16	15
WR	6	6
Drink	17-20	17-19

 DRY $22 V+

Te Pa Marlborough Chardonnay (★★★★☆)

Priced right, the 2016 vintage (★★★★☆) is a single-vineyard wine, hand-harvested in the Southern Valleys and fermented and matured for 11 months in French oak casks (30 per cent new). Light lemon/green, it has a fresh, attractive, slightly smoky bouquet. Mouthfilling, it is lively, with rich, peachy, slightly buttery and toasty flavours, appetising acidity, and excellent complexity, texture and depth. Already enjoyable, it should be at its best mid-2018+.

 DRY $25 V+

Te Rere Waiheke Island Chardonnay (★★★★☆)

Delicious young, the 2014 vintage (★★★★☆) was grown at the western end of the island. It is mouthfilling, rich, sweet-fruited and creamy-textured, with impressively concentrated, ripe stone-fruit flavours and a nutty, fragrant bouquet.

DRY $45 –V

Te Whau Vineyard Waiheke Island Chardonnay ★★★★★

For its sheer vintage-to-vintage consistency, this has been Te Whau's finest wine. Full of personality, it has beautifully ripe fruit characters showing excellent concentration, nutty oak and a long, finely poised finish. The 2015 vintage (★★★★★) was hand-harvested and fermented and lees-aged for nine months in French oak barriques. Light lemon/green, it is fragrant and weighty, with youthful, rich, peachy, slightly toasty flavours, excellent complexity, and a well-rounded finish. Best drinking 2018+.

Vintage	15	14	13	12	11	10	09
WR	7	7	7	6	5	7	6
Drink	17-21	17-20	17-20	P	P	P	P

DRY $95 –V

Terra Sancta Riverblock Bannockburn Central Otago Chardonnay ★★★★

Drinking well now, the 2015 vintage (★★★★☆) was fermented with indigenous yeasts and matured in French oak puncheons and barriques (10 per cent new). Bright, light lemon/green, it is fragrant, with strong, fresh, citrusy, gently oaked flavours, showing excellent vigour, complexity and length.

Vintage	15	14
WR	7	7
Drink	18-21	17-22

Theory & Practice Hawke's Bay Chardonnay ★★★★

Offering great value, the 2015 vintage (★★★★☆) was grown near the coast, hand-harvested, fermented and matured for 10 months in French oak barrels (28 per cent new), and given a full, softening malolactic fermentation. Light lemon/green, it has a complex bouquet, leading into a mouthfilling, savoury palate with generous, ripe, peachy, slightly mealy and nutty flavours, showing good complexity, balanced acidity, and a well-rounded, persistent finish. It's already delicious.

Thomas Waiheke Island Chardonnay (★★★★☆)

From Batch winery, the 2014 vintage (★★★★☆) was hand-picked at Onetangi and fermented and matured for 11 months in seasoned French oak barriques. The bouquet is fragrant and complex; the palate is mouthfilling and sweet-fruited, with strong, peachy, citrusy flavours, a gentle oak influence, excellent delicacy and harmony, and a lingering finish.

Thornbury Gisborne Chardonnay ★★★☆

Mouthfilling, with a slightly nutty bouquet, the 2016 vintage (★★★★) has ripe stone-fruit flavours, considerable complexity and a dry, creamy-smooth finish. A warmer-climate style, with good texture and mouthfeel, it's bargain-priced. (From Villa Maria.)

Three Paddles Martinborough Chardonnay ★★★

From Nga Waka, the 2016 vintage (★★★) is a 'fruit-driven' style. Mouthfilling, it has fresh, youthful, peachy flavours, slightly toasty and creamy notes, and lively acidity. Enjoyable young.

Vintage	16
WR	7
Drink	17-20

DRY $18 AV

Ti Point Hawke's Bay Chardonnay ★★★☆

The 2015 vintage (★★★☆) has strong, drink-young appeal. Pale yellow, it is mouthfilling and slightly creamy, in a moderately complex style with generous, citrusy, peachy flavours, slightly buttery notes, and a dry finish. (From Sacred Hill.)

Tiki Hawke's Bay Chardonnay   ★★★

The 2015 vintage (★★★) was given a full, softening malolactic fermentation. Light lemon/green, it is vibrantly fruity, with fresh, citrusy, slightly appley and buttery notes, and good depth. Enjoyable young.

DRY $20 –V

Tiki Koro Hawke's Bay Chardonnay   ★★★★

The 2015 vintage (★★★★) was hand-picked and fermented and lees-aged for 11 months in French oak barriques (70 per cent new). Light lemon/green, it is mouthfilling, sweet-fruited and creamy, with rich stone-fruit flavours, slightly buttery notes and a well-rounded finish. Delicious young.

DRY $33 –V

Tiki Single Vineyard Hawke's Bay Chardonnay   (★★★★)

The elegant, vibrantly fruity 2014 vintage (★★★★) was fermented in French oak barriques (40 per cent new). Fresh and finely balanced, it has strong grapefruit-like flavours, a subtle seasoning of oak, and very good vigour and depth.

DRY $23 AV

Tohu Gisborne Chardonnay   ★★★☆

Enjoyable young, the 2015 vintage (★★★☆) was partly barrel-fermented and given a full, softening malolactic fermentation. Pale straw, with a slightly buttery and toasty bouquet, it is mouthfilling and creamy, with ripe, peachy flavours, gentle acidity and very good depth.

DRY $22 AV

Tohu Hemi Reserve Marlborough Chardonnay   ★★★★☆

The youthful 2015 vintage (★★★★☆) is a rare wine (60 cases), hand-picked from estate-grown vines in the Awatere Valley and handled in French oak barriques. Pale lemon/green, it is fragrant, mouthfilling and sweet-fruited, with strong, ripe stone-fruit flavours, a slightly creamy texture, and good delicacy and complexity. Best drinking 2018+.

DRY $35 –V

Tohu Single Vineyard Marlborough Chardonnay   ★★★

The 2014 vintage (★★★) was grown at Rapaura, in the Wairau Valley, handled entirely without oak, and given a full, softening malolactic fermentation. Mouthfilling, it is sweet-fruited, with fresh, ripe, peachy flavours and gentle acidity, in a very easy-drinking style.

DRY $22 –V

Toi Toi Gisborne Chardonnay   ★★☆

The easy-drinking 2016 vintage (★★☆) is a pale lemon/green, medium-bodied wine with peachy, slightly spicy flavours, fresh and smooth.

DRY $18 –V

Toi Toi Reserve New Zealand Chardonnay ★★★★

The 2016 vintage (★★★★) was grown in Marlborough, hand-harvested, and fermented and lees-aged for nine months in French oak barriques (partly new). Light lemon/green, it is a fleshy, softly mouthfilling wine with generous, peachy, slightly toasty flavours, and lots of drink-young appeal.

Vintage	16	15
WR	7	7
Drink	17-21	17-20

DRY $26 AV

Tony Bish Skeetfield Hawke's Bay Chardonnay ★★★★★

The impressive 2016 vintage (★★★★★) is based on mature, Mendoza-clone vines at Ohiti. Hand-harvested, it was fermented in French oak barriques (60 per cent new), lees-aged for a year, and given a full, softening malolactic fermentation. A very 'complete' wine, it is delicious in its youth, with a fragrant, complex bouquet. Weighty and rounded, it has highly concentrated stone-fruit flavours, a real sense of depth through the palate, and a faintly buttery, finely textured, very harmonious finish. Drink now or cellar.

DRY $60 AV

Trinity Hill Gimblett Gravels Chardonnay ★★★★★

The winery's flagship 'black label' Chardonnay from Hawke's Bay is typically intense and finely structured. Grown in the Gimblett Gravels and fermented and matured for a year in French oak puncheons (30 per cent new), the 2016 vintage (★★★★☆) is bright, light lemon/green, with a toasty bouquet. Still youthful, it is very fresh, elegant and lively, with strong, vibrant grapefruit and stone-fruit flavours, mealy, biscuity notes adding complexity, and obvious potential; open mid-2018+.

Vintage	16	15	14	13	12	11	10
WR	7	6	7	7	6	6	6
Drink	17-24	17-23	17-21	17-20	17-18	P	P

DRY $35 AV

Trinity Hill Hawke's Bay Chardonnay ★★★☆

From 'cooler' sites, the 2014 vintage (★★★☆) is a 'low oak-influenced' style. An elegant, mouthfilling wine, vibrantly fruity, it has subtle mealy, biscuity notes adding complexity and a finely poised, harmonious finish.

Vintage	14	13	12	11	10
WR	7	7	5	6	6
Drink	17-18	P	P	P	P

DRY $20 AV

TW CV Gisborne Chardonnay/Viognier (★★★★)

The 2014 vintage (★★★★) is a bright, light lemon/green, mouthfilling wine with generous, ripe stone-fruit flavours and a slightly buttery finish. Lush, with good richness and roundness, and some bottle-aged complexity, it's drinking well now.

DRY $20 V+

TW Estate Gisborne Chardonnay ★★★☆

Priced sharply, the 2015 vintage (★★★☆) is a mouthfilling, fruit-driven wine with very good depth of peachy, slightly buttery flavours, a distinct hint of butterscotch, and a well-rounded finish. It's drinking well now.

DRY $17 V+

TW Reserve Gisborne Chardonnay (★★★★)

Ready for drinking, the 2014 vintage (★★★★) was harvested from estate-grown vines on the Golden Slope, up to 30 years old, and fermented and matured for 10 months in a mix of French, American and Hungarian oak barriques (20 per cent new). Pale yellow, it is full-bodied, with generous, ripe stone-fruit flavours, biscuity and buttery notes adding complexity, and a mature bouquet.

DRY $27 AV

Two Rivers Clos Des Pierres Marlborough Chardonnay ★★★★

From a stony Wairau Valley site ('Clos des Pierres' means 'Place of Stones'), this wine is hand-picked, fermented with indigenous yeasts in French oak barrels (25 per cent new in 2015), and given a full, softening malolactic fermentation. The 2015 vintage (★★★★) is pale yellow, with a fresh, buttery bouquet. Mouthfilling, it has strong, peachy, citrusy flavours, fresh acidity, buttery and toasty notes, and good complexity. Drink now or cellar.

Vintage	15
WR	6
Drink	17-21

DRY $36 –V

Vavasour Anna's Vineyard Awatere Valley Marlborough Chardonnay ★★★★★

From a site within the original, terraced vineyard in the lower Awatere Valley, the 2015 vintage (★★★★★) was barrel-fermented with indigenous yeasts and wood-aged for 11 months. Pale yellow, it is mouthfilling, with rich, citrusy, peachy, slightly mealy and buttery flavours, showing excellent delicacy, vigour and harmony, and a fragrant, complex bouquet.

DRY $41 AV

Vavasour Awatere Valley Marlborough Chardonnay ★★★★☆

This powerful, rich, creamy-textured wine is grown in the Awatere Valley, given a full, softening malolactic fermentation and lees-aged in French oak barrels. The 2015 vintage (★★★★☆) is pale yellow/green, with a creamy, slightly oaky bouquet. Full-bodied, it has deep, peachy, mealy, toasty flavours, in an open, expressive style, fleshy, smooth and already drinking well.

DRY $31 AV

Vidal Anthony Joseph Vidal 1888 Hawke's Bay Chardonnay (★★★★★)

'The absolute pinnacle of Vidal Estate', the 2014 vintage (★★★★★) is an extremely rare wine – only 61 cases were made, released in mid to late 2017. Hand-picked from vines then 18 years old, in the Lyons Vineyard, in the Gimblett Gravels, it was fermented with indigenous yeasts in French oak barriques (50 per cent new), and matured on its yeast lees in oak for 11 months. Bright, light lemon/green, it has a rich, smoky, complex bouquet. Still developing, it is weighty, fleshy and multi-layered, with concentrated, vibrant, peachy, mealy, biscuity flavours, showing notable power and complexity, and a tightly structured, dry, very persistent finish. Best drinking 2019+.

 DRY $120 –V

Vidal Hawke's Bay Chardonnay ★★★☆

The 2016 vintage (★★★☆) is a top buy. Fermented and matured in tanks (principally) and seasoned French oak barriques, it has a slightly smoky bouquet, leading into a mouthfilling wine with fresh, dry, grapefruit-like flavours, showing very good depth.

Vintage	16	15	14	13
WR	6	6	7	7
Drink	17-20	17-18	P	P

 DRY $16 V+

Vidal Legacy Hawke's Bay Chardonnay ★★★★★

The 2016 vintage (★★★★★) of Vidal's flagship Chardonnay was grown at three sites, hand-harvested, fermented with indigenous yeasts and matured for 10 months in French oak barriques (43 per cent new). Bright, light lemon/green, it has a complex, slightly smoky bouquet. Mouthfilling and tightly structured, it is notably youthful and complex, with intense, grapefruit-like flavours, subtle oak influence, and a crisp, dry, very long finish. Best drinking 2020+.

Vintage	16	15	14	13	12	11	10
WR	7	7	7	7	7	6	7
Drink	18-24	17-25	17-23	17-20	17-19	P	P

 DRY $60 –V

Vidal Reserve Hawke's Bay Chardonnay ★★★★

This middle-tier label consistently offers great value. The 2016 vintage (★★★★) was fermented and matured for nine months in French oak barriques (19 per cent new), with some use of indigenous yeasts and malolactic fermentation. Light lemon/green, it is vibrant and sweet-fruited, with strong, grapefruit-like flavours to the fore, slightly peachy notes, a subtle seasoning of biscuity oak, fresh acidity, and a real sense of youthful vigour. Best drinking mid-2018+.

Vintage	16	15	14	13	12
WR	7	7	7	7	6
Drink	17-21	17-20	17-18	17-18	P

 DRY $20 V+

Villa Maria Cellar Selection Gisborne Chardonnay (★★★★)

The bargain-priced 2016 vintage (★★★★) was fermented and matured for nine months in French and Hungarian oak barriques (35 per cent new). Already drinking well, it's a full-bodied, fresh, harmonious wine with well-ripened stone-fruit flavours, gentle biscuity, toasty notes adding complexity, finely poised acidity and a dry, slightly buttery finish.

Vintage	16
WR	7
Drink	17-21

DRY $18 V+

Villa Maria Cellar Selection Hawke's Bay Chardonnay   ★★★★

A top buy. The 2016 vintage (★★★★) was 40 per cent hand-picked and fully barrel-fermented (mostly French, 24 per cent new). Already delicious, it is mouthfilling, with generous, ripe stone-fruit flavours, showing good complexity, and a dry, very harmonious finish.

Vintage	16	15	14
WR	7	7	7
Drink	17-21	17-20	17-19

DRY $18 V+

Villa Maria Cellar Selection Marlborough Chardonnay   ★★★★

A stylish, great-value wine. The 2016 vintage (★★★★☆), grown in the Wairau and Awatere valleys, was partly hand-picked, fully fermented in oak barriques (15 per cent new), and barrel-matured for eight months. Fragrant, it shows good complexity, with strong, vibrant, citrusy, peachy flavours and a fully dry, slightly buttery finish.

Vintage	16	15	14	13	12	11	10
WR	6	6	6	6	6	6	6
Drink	17-20	17-20	17-20	17-18	P	P	P

DRY $18 V+

Villa Maria Library Release Hawke's Bay Chardonnay   (★★★★★)

The debut 2010 vintage (★★★★★) was released as a mature but still lively wine in 2015. Grown in the company's Ngakirikiri and Keltern vineyards, it was fermented, mostly with indigenous yeasts, and matured for 10 months in French oak barriques (38 per cent new). It's rare – only 190 cases were produced. It shows good maturity and complexity, with toasty, bottle-aged notes emerging, but also vibrant, citrusy, peachy fruit flavours. Still very lively, complex and long, it's a drink-now or cellaring proposition.

Vintage	10
WR	7
Drink	17-20

DRY $50 AV

Villa Maria Private Bin East Coast Chardonnay   ★★★

The 2016 vintage (★★★), a regional blend, is mouthfilling, with fresh, ripe, peachy, slightly biscuity and spicy flavours. Vibrantly fruity, with good depth, it offers fine value at $12 on special.

DRY $17 AV

Villa Maria Reserve Barrique Fermented Gisborne Chardonnay   ★★★★★

This acclaimed wine is usually sourced principally from the company's Katoa and McDiarmid Hill vineyards. The 2016 vintage (★★★★★) was mostly (94 per cent) grown and hand-picked at McDiarmid Hill, in the Patutahi district, fermented – mostly with indigenous yeasts – in French oak barriques (half new), oak-aged for 10 months, and given a full, softening malolactic fermentation. It's a powerful, weighty, lush wine, very generous, peachy, toasty and buttery, but also complex and finely structured. Already delicious, it should break into full stride 2019+.

Vintage	16	15	14	13	12	11	10	09
WR	7	7	7	7	7	7	7	6
Drink	17-24	17-23	17-22	17-21	17-19	17-18	17-18	P

DRY $40 AV

Villa Maria Reserve Hawke's Bay Chardonnay ★★★★★

The 2016 vintage (★★★★★) was grown at three sites, fermented – mostly with indigenous yeasts – in French oak barriques (40 per cent new), and oak-matured for 10 months. Weighty and very finely balanced, it has fresh, concentrated, citrusy, peachy flavours, gently seasoned with nutty oak, smoky notes adding complexity, and a rich, rounded finish. Best drinking 2019+.

Vintage	16	15	14	13	12	11	10	09	08
WR	7	7	7	7	6	6	7	7	7
Drink	17-24	17-23	17-22	17-21	17-19	17-18	17-18	P	P

DRY $35 AV

Villa Maria Reserve Marlborough Chardonnay ★★★★★

With its rich, slightly mealy, citrusy flavours, this is a distinguished wine, concentrated and finely structured. A marriage of intense, ripe Marlborough fruit with French oak, it is one of the region's greatest Chardonnays. It is typically grown and hand-picked in the warmest sites supplying Chardonnay grapes to Villa Maria, in the Awatere and Wairau valleys. The highly refined 2015 vintage (★★★★★) was fermented and matured for nine months in French oak barriques and puncheons (30 per cent new), and given a full, softening malolactic fermentation. The bouquet is fragrant and complex; the palate is highly concentrated, with rich, peachy, citrusy flavours, integrated oak, and a long finish. The 2016 vintage (★★★★★) is tightly structured and complex, with intense, youthful, grapefruit-like flavours, well-integrated oak and a long, dry finish. Best drinking 2019+.

Vintage	16	15	14	13	12	11	10	09
WR	7	7	7	7	7	7	7	7
Drink	18-23	17-22	17-22	17-20	17-20	17-18	P	P

DRY $35 AV

Villa Maria Single Vineyard Ihumatao Chardonnay ★★★★★

This impressive wine is estate-grown at Mangere, in South Auckland. The 2016 vintage (★★★★★) was hand-picked, fermented with indigenous yeasts in French oak barriques (31 per cent new), oak-aged for 11 months, and mostly (90 per cent) given a secondary, softening malolactic fermentation. Likely to be long-lived, it is mouthfilling and vibrant, with concentrated, ripe citrus and stone-fruit flavours, gently seasoned with nutty, biscuity oak, smoky and buttery notes adding richness, and a dry, persistent finish. Best drinking 2019+.

Vintage	16	15	14	13	12	11	10	09
WR	7	NM	7	7	6	6	7	6
Drink	17-22	NM	17-22	17-21	17-19	17-18	17-18	P

DRY $40 AV

Villa Maria Single Vineyard Keltern Hawke's Bay Chardonnay ★★★★★

Grown at the Keltern Vineyard, a warm, inland site east of Maraekakaho, this consistently impressive wine is hand-picked, fermented with indigenous yeasts and lees-aged in French oak barriques (30 per cent new in 2016). The 2016 vintage (★★★★★), barrel-aged for 10 months, is striking. The bouquet is rich and complex; the palate is highly concentrated, with vibrant grapefruit and stone-fruit flavours, slightly smoky, tight-knit, dry and sustained. A potentially great wine, it's well worth cellaring to 2020+.

Vintage	16	15	14	13	12	11	10	09
WR	7	7	7	7	6	7	7	6
Drink	17-24	17-23	17-22	17-21	17-19	17-18	17-18	P

DRY $50 AV

Villa Maria Single Vineyard Taylors Pass Chardonnay ★★★★★

Grown in the company's Taylors Pass Vineyard in Marlborough's Awatere Valley, this wine is hand-picked and barrel-fermented. The very refined 2015 vintage (★★★★☆) was fermented and lees-aged for nine months in French oak puncheons and barriques (25 per cent new), and given a full, softening malolactic fermentation. An elegant, tightly structured wine, it is citrusy and slightly smoky, with a subtle seasoning of oak and excellent vigour and potential. Open 2018+. Already lovely, the 2016 vintage (★★★★★) is highly refined, with a fragrant, citrusy bouquet, deep, vibrant grapefruit and peach flavours, nutty, smoky notes adding complexity, and a long, dry finish. Best drinking 2019+.

Vintage	15	14	13	12	11	10
WR	7	7	7	7	7	7
Drink	17-22	17-22	17-20	17-20	17-18	P

DRY $35 AV

VNO Hawke's Bay Chardonnay ★★★

The 2015 vintage (★★★☆) is an upfront style from Constellation NZ, offering good value. Enjoyable young, it is a partly barrel-fermented style, fleshy and smooth, with ripe, peachy flavours, slightly buttery and toasty, and good depth.

DRY $17 AV

Waiheke Road Gisborne Reserve Chardonnay (★★★★)

From Awaroa, based on Waiheke Island, the 2015 vintage (★★★★) was grown in Gisborne and barrel-aged for nine months. Bright, light lemon/green, it is weighty, generous and youthful, with strong grapefruit and peach flavours, integrated oak, slightly buttery notes and lots of drink-young appeal.

Vintage	15
WR	6
Drink	18-20

DRY $38 –V

Waiheke Road Waiheke Island Reserve Chardonnay (★★★★☆)

The refined, youthful 2014 vintage (★★★★☆) has a fragrant, slightly creamy and biscuity bouquet. Full-bodied, with strong, ripe grapefruit and peach flavours, it has mealy and toasty notes adding complexity, and a finely balanced, long finish. Best drinking 2018+. (From Awaroa Vineyard.)

DRY $38 –V

Waimea Nelson Chardonnay ★★★★

Enjoyable young, the 2014 vintage (★★★★) was fermented in French oak barriques and puncheons (partly new). Mouthfilling, it is creamy-textured, with fresh acidity, strong, ripe, peachy flavours, gently seasoned with biscuity oak, and good harmony.

Vintage	14	13	12	11	10
WR	6	6	6	6	7
Drink	17-18	P	P	P	P

DRY $23 V+

Waipara Springs Reserve Premo Chardonnay   (★★★☆)

The youthful 2016 vintage (★★★☆) was fermented in tanks and barrels, then fully barrel-matured. Medium-bodied, it is vibrantly fruity, with appetising acidity and toasty, buttery notes adding complexity. Best drinking mid-2018+.

DRY $22 AV

Wairau River Marlborough Chardonnay   ★★★☆

The 2015 vintage (★★★☆) was handled in tanks and French oak casks. Fresh and lively, it has citrusy, slightly peachy flavours, showing a touch of complexity, and very good vigour and depth.

Vintage	15	14	13	12	11
WR	6	6	6	5	6
Drink	17-19	17-19	P	P	P

DRY $20 AV

Wairau River Reserve Marlborough Chardonnay   ★★★★

Grown and hand-picked at two sites adjacent to the Wairau River, on the north side of the valley, the 2015 vintage (★★★★) was fermented and matured for a year in French oak barriques (25 per cent new), and given a full, softening malolactic fermentation. Lemon-scented, it is mouthfilling and sweet-fruited, with a subtle seasoning of oak, good complexity, and a slightly buttery finish. Well worth cellaring.

Vintage	15	14
WR	6	6
Drink	17-22	17-19

DRY $30 –V

Walnut Block Nutcracker Marlborough Chardonnay   ★★★★☆

Certified organic, the 2015 vintage (★★★★☆) is a characterful wine, hand-picked from 21-year-old vines, fermented with indigenous yeasts and fermented in French oak puncheons (20 per cent new). Full-bodied and youthful, it is finely textured, with strong, ripe, peachy, biscuity flavours, complex and savoury, and a lasting, very harmonious finish. Best drinking 2018+.

Vintage	15
WR	6
Drink	17-22

DRY $32 AV

West Brook Barrique Fermented Chardonnay   ★★★★

The bright lemon/green 2015 vintage (★★★★), grown in Marlborough, was fermented and matured in French oak barriques (20 per cent new). Delicious now, it is mouthfilling, sweet-fruited and vibrant, with finely integrated oak adding complexity, balanced acidity, slightly creamy notes, and very good freshness, vigour and depth.

Vintage	15
WR	5
Drink	17-20

DRY $25 AV

West Brook Waimauku Chardonnay   (★★★★☆)

Still youthful, the 2015 vintage (★★★★☆) was estate-grown in West Auckland and fermented and matured in French oak barriques (20 per cent new). Pale lemon/green, it is a subtle, very age-worthy wine with rich, ripe stone-fruit characters, showing excellent delicacy, fresh acidity, hints of toasty oak and gunflint, and complex flavours that build well across the palate to a long finish. Open mid-2018+.

Vintage	15
WR	6
Drink	17-24

 DRY $35 –V

Whitehaven Marlborough Chardonnay   ★★★★

The 2016 vintage (★★★★) is fresh and mouthfilling, with slightly creamy notes on the nose and palate. Still youthful, it has vibrant grapefruit-like flavours to the fore and well-integrated, biscuity oak adding complexity. Best drinking mid-2018+.

 DRY $25 AV

Wither Hills Single Vineyard Benmorven Marlborough Chardonnay   (★★★★☆)

The fine-value 2015 vintage (★★★★☆) was hand-picked and fermented in oak hogsheads and barriques (40 per cent new). The bouquet is savoury; the palate is mouthfilling, with concentrated, vibrant, citrusy, peachy flavours, showing excellent harmony, and a well-rounded finish.

 DRY $25 V+

Wooing Tree Central Otago Chardonnay   ★★★★

The 2016 vintage (★★★★) was estate-grown at Cromwell, hand-picked and fermented and matured for eight months in French oak casks (30 per cent new.) Light lemon/green, it shows good weight and harmony, with mouthfilling body, strong, ripe grapefruit/apple flavours and a subtle seasoning of oak adding complexity. Drink now or cellar.

 DRY $38 –V

Wrights Reserve Gisborne Chardonnay   ★★★★

Certified organic, the 2015 vintage (★★★★☆) was fermented and lees-stirred in new French oak barrels and given a full, softening malolactic fermentation. A powerful, robust wine (15 per cent alcohol), it is very age-worthy, with concentrated, youthful peach and grapefruit flavours, showing good richness and complexity, and a long finish. Best drinking mid-2018+.

 DRY $38 –V

Zephyr Marlborough Chardonnay   (★★★★)

The 2014 vintage (★★★★) is a subtle wine, estate-grown in the lower Wairau Valley, hand-picked and fermented with indigenous yeasts in large oak barrels. Light lemon/green, it is full-bodied and fleshy, with generous, ripe, citrusy flavours, a gentle seasoning of nutty oak, and a finely textured, lengthy finish. Drink now or cellar.

DRY $32 –V

Chenin Blanc

Today's Chenin Blancs are markedly riper, rounder and more enjoyable to drink than the sharply acidic, austere wines of the 1980s, when Chenin Blanc was far more extensively planted in New Zealand. Yet this classic grape variety is still struggling for an identity. In recent years, several labels have been discontinued – not for lack of quality or value, but lack of buyer interest.

A good New Zealand Chenin Blanc is fresh and buoyantly fruity, with melon and pineapple-evoking flavours and a crisp finish. In the cooler parts of the country, the variety's naturally high acidity (an asset in the warmer viticultural regions of South Africa, the United States and Australia) can be a distinct handicap. But when the grapes achieve full ripeness here, this classic grape of Vouvray, in the Loire Valley, yields sturdy wines that are satisfying in their youth yet can mature for many years, gradually unfolding a delicious, honeyed richness.

Only three wineries have consistently made impressive Chenin Blancs over the past decade: Millton, Margrain and Esk Valley. Many growers, put off by the variety's late-ripening nature and the susceptibility of its tight bunches to botrytis rot, have uprooted their vines. Plantings have plummeted from 372 hectares in 1983 to 24 hectares of bearing vines in 2018.

Chenin Blanc is the country's thirteenth most widely planted white-wine variety (behind Albariño and Arneis), with plantings concentrated in Hawke's Bay, Marlborough and Gisborne. In the future, winemakers who plant Chenin Blanc in warm, sunny vineyard sites with devigorating soils, where the variety's vigorous growth can be controlled and yields reduced, can be expected to produce the ripest, most concentrated wines. New Zealand winemakers have yet to get to grips with Chenin Blanc.

Amisfield Central Otago Chenin Blanc ★★★★

Estate-grown at Pisa, in the Cromwell Basin, the 2016 vintage (★★★☆) was hand-harvested and partly barrel-fermented. A youthful, tightly structured wine with obvious potential, it is full-bodied, lemony, appley and slightly spicy, with a sliver of sweetness (5.7 grams/litre of residual sugar) and mouth-watering acidity. Best drinking 2019+.

MED/DRY $30 –V

Astrolabe Vineyards Wrekin Vineyard Chenin Blanc ★★★★☆

Offering great value, the pale lemon/green 2015 vintage (★★★★★) was hand-picked in the Southern Valleys and partly fermented with indigenous yeasts in old oak barrels. A fully dry style (2.1 grams/litre of residual sugar), it has strong personality, with a real sense of youthful drive and vigour. An ideal all-purpose wine, it has deep, vibrant fruit flavours, suggestive of grapefruit and lime, a minerally streak, moderate acidity and excellent structure, delicacy, complexity and length. A thought-provoking wine, it should be long-lived.

DRY $25 V+

Bishop's Head Waipara Valley Chenin Blanc (★★★★)

The 2015 vintage (★★★★) was hand-picked, fermented with indigenous yeasts and lees-aged for 11 months in oak barrels (20 per cent new). Vibrant, with peachy, slightly mealy and toasty flavours, it shows good complexity, with a slightly buttery, dry, lingering finish.

DRY $30 –V

Clos de Ste Anne La Bas Chenin Blanc   ★★★★★

Certified biodynamic, the 2014 vintage (★★★★★) is from a section of the vineyard 'down there' (La Bas). Grown in Millton's Clos de Ste Anne hillside vineyard at Manutuke, in Gisborne, and fermented with indigenous yeasts, it was matured for nine months in large, 600-litre oak barrels ('demi-muids'). A mouthfilling, fleshy wine, it is unusually ripe and well-rounded for Chenin Blanc, with concentrated peach and pineapple flavours, showing excellent complexity, gentle acidity, and a long, dry (2.1 grams/litre of residual sugar) finish. Drink now or cellar.

Forrest Marlborough Chenin Blanc   ★★★☆

This is a rare beast – a Chenin Blanc from the South Island. Estate-grown in the Wairau Valley, the 2015 vintage (★★★★) is still unfolding and likely to be long-lived. Light lemon/green, it is an attractively scented, medium-bodied wine, vibrant and youthful, with good varietal character, a sliver of sweetness and appetising acidity. Best drinking mid-2018+.

Margrain Martinborough Chenin Blanc   ★★★★

When Margrain bought the neighbouring Chifney property, they acquired Chenin Blanc vines now around 30 years old. The 2016 vintage (★★★★) is crisp and gently sweet (22 grams/litre of residual sugar), with very good depth of peach, lemon and pear flavours, lively acidity, good balance and obvious potential. Best drinking 2018+.

Vintage	16	15
WR	7	6
Drink	17-26	17-25

Margrain Old Vine Martinborough Chenin Blanc   (★★★★★)

The striking 2016 vintage (★★★★★) is based solely on the estate's original, 35-year-old vines, planted by Stan Chifney. Handled entirely in tanks, it's a pale lemon/green, highly scented wine, medium-bodied, with gentle sweetness (16 grams/litre of residual sugar), appetising acidity, and rich, vibrant, lemony, appley flavours, showing lovely purity, delicacy and intensity. Already delicious, it should flourish in the bottle for many years.

Vintage	16
WR	7
Drink	17-29

MED $65 AV

Matawhero Church House Single Vineyard Gisborne Chenin Blanc ★★★★

The 2016 vintage (★★★★) was harvested from young vines at Patutahi. Light lemon/green, it is very fresh and lively, with strong, citrusy, appley flavours. Already delicious, it's a dryish style (5.2 grams/litre of residual sugar), with moderate acidity for Chenin Blanc and excellent delicacy, poise and depth. Drink now or cellar.

MED/DRY $28 –V

Vintage	16	15	14	13
WR	6	7	7	6
Drink	17-19	17-18	P	P

Millton Chenin Blanc Te Arai Vineyard ★★★★★

Certified organic, this Gisborne wine is New Zealand's best-known Chenin Blanc. It's a richly varietal wine with concentrated, fresh, vibrant fruit flavours to the fore in some vintages, nectareous scents and flavours in others. The grapes are hand-picked at up to four stages of ripening, culminating in some years ('It's in the lap of the gods,' says James Millton) in a final harvest of botrytis-affected fruit. Fermentation is in tanks and large, 600-litre French oak casks, used in the Loire for Chenin Blanc. The 2016 vintage (★★★★☆) is bright, light yellow/green. A medium-bodied wine, with plenty of personality, it has vibrant, peachy, faintly honeyed fruit flavours, showing good concentration and complexity, a sliver of sweetness (7 grams/litre of residual sugar), moderate acidity, and good aging potential. Best drinking 2019+.

MED/DRY $30 AV

Vintage	16	15	14	13	12	11	10	09	08
WR	6	6	7	7	NM	6	7	6	6
Drink	17-26	17-25	17-26	17-25	NM	P	17-22	17-21	P

Moutere Hills Nelson Chenin Blanc (★★★★☆)

Full of personality, the 2016 vintage (★★★★☆) is a single-vineyard wine, hand-picked from 23-year-old vines and matured for 11 months in old French oak casks. Pale straw, it is mouthfilling, with concentrated, vibrant, peachy fruit flavours, good complexity, fresh acidity and a faintly buttery, dry, very harmonious finish. Drink now or cellar.

DRY $34 –V

Mt Difficulty Single Vineyard Long Gully Bannockburn Chenin Blanc ★★★★☆

The lovely 2016 vintage (★★★★★) is rich, vibrant and finely poised. Bright, light lemon/green, it is full-bodied (14 per cent alcohol), with fresh, intense fruit flavours, hints of spices and honey, abundant sweetness (51 grams/litre of residual sugar), mouth-watering acidity and a lasting finish. Full of youthful drive, it's already delicious; drink now or cellar.

MED $30 –V

Fiano

A traditional low-yielding variety of Campania, in south-west Italy, Fiano is also grown in Sicily, Argentina and Australia. It is not listed separately in New Zealand Winegrowers' *Vineyard Register Report 2015–2018*, but its age-worthy wines have been praised by UK writer Oz Clarke as 'exciting' and 'distinctive'.

Bushhawk Vineyard Bella's Block Hawke's Bay Fiano ★★★★☆

The 2014 vintage (★★★★☆) is impressive. Grown in the Bridge Pa Triangle, hand-picked, and fermented and lees-aged for six months in small stainless steel 'barrels', it is full-bodied, with finely balanced acidity and a powerful surge of fresh, ripe fruit flavours, reminiscent of peaches and pineapples. Sturdy and dry, it's a drink-now or cellaring proposition.

DRY $25 V+

Coopers Creek Single Barrel Single Vineyard Gisborne Fiano (★★★☆)

The rare 2016 vintage (★★★☆) was barrel-fermented and briefly oak-aged. Pale straw, it is mouthfilling and dry (4 grams/litre of residual sugar), with lively, slightly citrusy and spicy, vaguely toasty flavours, fresh acidity, and very good depth. Drink now or cellar.

DRY $25 –V

Flora

A California crossing of Gewürztraminer and Sémillon, in cool-climate regions Flora produces aromatic, spicy wine. Some of New Zealand's 'Pinot Gris' vines were more than a decade ago positively identified as Flora, but the country's total area of bearing Flora vines in 2018 will be just 3 hectares, almost all in Auckland and Northland.

Shipwreck Bay Northland Flora   ★★★

The 2015 vintage (★★★) is a fresh, medium-bodied wine, estate-grown in Northland, with lively acidity woven through strong, citrusy, peachy flavours, balanced for easy drinking. (From Okahu Estate.)

MED/DRY $20 –V

Gewürztraminer

Only a trickle of Gewürztraminer is exported (0.01 per cent of our total wine shipments), and the majority of New Zealand bottlings lack the power and richness of the great Alsace model. Yet this classic grape is starting to get the respect it deserves from grape-growers and winemakers here.

For most of the 1990s, Gewürztraminer's popularity was on the wane. Between 1983 and 1996, New Zealand's plantings of Gewürztraminer dropped by almost two-thirds. A key problem is that Gewürztraminer is a temperamental performer in the vineyard, being particularly vulnerable to adverse weather at flowering, which can decimate grape yields. Now there is proof of a strong renewal of interest: the area of bearing vines has surged from 85 hectares in 1998 to 258 hectares in 2018. Most of the plantings are in Marlborough (34 per cent of the national total), Hawke's Bay (19 per cent) and Gisborne (18 per cent), but there are also significant pockets in Nelson, Canterbury and Otago. Gewürztraminer is a high-impact wine, brimming with scents and flavours. 'Spicy' is the most common adjective used to pinpoint its distinctive, heady aromas and flavours; tasters also find nuances of gingerbread, freshly ground black pepper, cinnamon, cloves, mint, lychees and mangoes. Once you've tasted one or two Gewürztraminers, you won't have any trouble recognising it in a blind tasting – it's one of the most forthright, distinctive white-wine varieties of all.

Allan Scott Generations Marlborough Gewürztraminer (★★★★☆)

The debut 2016 vintage (★★★★☆) is a single-vineyard wine, promoted as 'the perfect combination of sassy and sweet'. Pale, it is delicately perfumed, with pear, lychee and spice aromas. Fresh and full-bodied, it is very harmonious, with deep, ripe, vibrant fruit flavours, a slightly oily texture, gentle sweetness (15 grams/litre of residual sugar), and a softly seductive finish. Drink now or cellar.

MED $25 V+

Anchorage Family Estate Nelson Gewürztraminer ★★★☆

Offering good value, the 2014 vintage (★★★★) is mouthfilling and fleshy, with ripe-fruit flavours and a slightly oily texture. Made in a medium style, it is harmonious, well-rounded and ripely perfumed.

MED/DRY $19 V+

Aronui Nelson Gewürztraminer ★★★☆

The 2015 vintage (★★★☆) is a single-vineyard wine, hand-picked in the Moutere hills. Mouthfilling (14 per cent alcohol), it is a dryish style (5 grams/litre of residual sugar), with fresh, delicate peach, lychee and spice flavours, showing good varietal character, and a perfumed bouquet.

MED/DRY $22 AV

Askerne Hawke's Bay Gewürztraminer ★★★★

Partly barrel-fermented, this is a consistently good, easy-drinking wine, priced right. The 2015 vintage (★★★★) is gently perfumed, mouthfilling and well-rounded, with a gentle splash of sweetness (11 grams/litre of residual sugar), plenty of ripe, citrusy, spicy flavour, and excellent harmony.

MED/DRY $22 V+

Ataahua Waipara Gewürztraminer ★★★★☆

Exotically perfumed and mouthfilling, the 2014 vintage (★★★★☆) is a partly barrel-fermented wine (20 per cent) with soft, rich flavours. Peachy, spicy and slightly gingery, it is concentrated, with good complexity, gentle sweetness and a seductively smooth finish. Showing strong personality, the 2015 vintage (★★★★★) is an enticingly perfumed, complex, intensely varietal wine, full-bodied, with an oily texture and concentrated, peachy, gingery, spicy flavours, dryish, rounded and rich.

Vintage	15	14	13	12	11	10
WR	6	6	6	7	7	6
Drink	17-20	17-19	17-20	17-19	17-18	P

MED/DRY $27 AV

Babich Family Estates Gimblett Gravels Gewürztraminer ★★★☆

Grown in Hawke's Bay, the 2014 vintage (★★★★) is very open and expressive from the start. Mouthfilling, it has ripe, peachy, slightly spicy flavours in a strongly varietal style, showing good body and fragrance.

Vintage	14	13	12	11
WR	7	7	5	7
Drink	17-18	P	P	P

DRY $25 –V

Black Ridge Central Otago Old Vine Gewürztraminer (★★★★)

Estate-grown at Alexandra, the 2013 vintage (★★★★), still on sale in 2017, is drinking well. Light lemon/green, it is fragrant, with mouthfilling body and strong varietal characteristics. Peachy and spicy, with a hint of ginger, it's a medium-dry style (8 grams/litre of residual sugar), with toasty, bottle-aged notes adding complexity and excellent depth.

MED/DRY $26 –V

Blackenbrook Vineyard Nelson Gewürztraminer ★★★★

A consistently attractive wine. The refined 2017 vintage (★★★★) was mostly handled in tanks, but 12 per cent of the blend was matured in old barrels. Pale and ripely perfumed, it is a medium-dry style (8 grams/litre of residual sugar), with mouthfilling body and a vibrant array of pear, peach, lychee and spice flavours, showing excellent delicacy and depth. Best drinking mid-2018+.

Vintage	17	16
WR	7	5
Drink	17-21	17-20

MED/DRY $25 AV

Bladen Marlborough Gewürztraminer ★★★★☆

Hand-harvested in the Tilly Vineyard, the 2015 vintage (★★★★☆) was very expressive in its youth. Exotically perfumed, it is mouthfilling (14.5 per cent alcohol), with concentrated, peachy, spicy flavours, a hint of apricots, gentle sweetness (12 grams/litre of residual sugar), and lots of drink-young appeal.

MED/DRY $25 V+

Brancott Estate Letter Series 'P' Marlborough Gewürztraminer ★★★★☆

The 2015 vintage (★★★★) is a highly perfumed, strongly varietal wine, with fresh, pure, well-spiced flavours. Mouthfilling, it has a lush, oily texture and a gently sweet finish.

 MED/DRY $33 –V

Charcoal Gully Sally's Pinch Central Otago Gewürztraminer ★★★☆

The 2014 vintage (★★★☆) was hand-picked at Pisa, in the Cromwell Basin. Offering good drinkability, it's a fresh, medium-dry style (8 grams/litre of residual sugar), with a slightly oily texture, good depth of lively, finely balanced lemon, apple and spice flavours, and a floral, spicy bouquet. Ready; no rush.

Vintage	14
WR	5
Drink	17-22

 MED/DRY $21 AV

Cicada Marlborough Gewürztraminer ★★★★

The refined 2014 vintage (★★★★☆) is a perfumed, mouthfilling, vibrantly fruity wine with deep, peachy, spicy flavours. A strongly varietal wine, it has good vigour and harmony, with a gentle splash of sweetness (9 grams/litre of residual sugar) and a slightly oily richness. (From Riverby Estate.)

 MED/DRY $25 AV

Clearview Te Awanga Gewürztraminer ★★★★

Exotically perfumed, the 2015 vintage (★★★★) is a refined wine with fresh pear and spice flavours, showing good balance of sweetness and acidity. A strongly varietal wine, with excellent delicacy and depth, it should mature well.

 MED/DRY $19 V+

Craft Farm Home Vineyard Hawke's Bay Gewürztraminer (★★★★☆)

The 2014 vintage (★★★★☆) is enticingly perfumed. Full-bodied (14.5 per cent alcohol), it's a medium style (17 grams/litre of residual sugar) with impressive weight, concentrated lychee and spice flavours, gentle acidity and a slightly oily richness.

 MED $32 –V

Crossroads Milestone Series Hawke's Bay Gewürztraminer ★★★★

The 2014 vintage (★★★★), grown at Fernhill, is perfumed, with mouthfilling body, delicate lychee and spice flavours and a dryish (5 grams/litre of residual sugar) finish. An intensely varietal wine, it should blossom in the bottle.

Vintage	14
WR	6
Drink	17-24

MED/DRY $20 V+

Dry River Lovat Vineyard Gewürztraminer ★★★★★

From mature, 24-year-old vines in Martinborough, the powerful and delicious 2016 vintage (★★★★★) was hand-harvested in four stages, concluding with some heavily botrytised fruit. It was mostly handled in tanks; about 10 per cent of the blend was barrel-fermented. Pale straw, with a perfumed, spicy bouquet, it is mouthfilling and fleshy, with rich, peachy, spicy flavours, gentle acidity and a slightly sweet (20 grams/litre of residual sugar), lingering finish. Very 'open' in its youth, it's an intensely varietal, very harmonious wine; drink now or cellar.

Vintage	16	15	14	13
WR	6	6	6	6
Drink	17-28	17-27	17-26	17-25

MED $47 AV

Dunstan Road Central Otago Gewürztraminer (★★★☆)

From a single row of vines, in a 2-hectare vineyard between Clyde and Alexandra, the easy-drinking 2014 vintage (★★★☆) was briefly wood-aged (for a month) and made in a medium style. Fresh, lively and harmonious, it is mouthfilling, with good depth of ripe lychee and spice flavours, showing a touch of complexity, a gentle splash of sweetness, and a rounded finish.

MED $20 AV

Ellero Central Otago Gewürztraminer ★★★☆

The 2014 vintage (★★★☆) was grown in two neighbouring vineyards at Pisa, in the Cromwell Basin, and fermented in a tank and an old oak puncheon. Full-bodied and fresh, it has pear, lychee and spice flavours, gentle acidity and a dry (4 grams/litre of residual sugar), lingering, spicy finish.

DRY $27 –V

Falconhead Hawke's Bay Gewürztraminer (★★★)

Ready to roll, the easy-drinking 2014 vintage (★★★) is a perfumed, medium style, with mouthfilling body, peachy, slightly spicy and gingery flavours, and a smooth, slightly sweet finish. Priced right.

MED $16 V+

Forrest Marlborough Gewürztraminer ★★★☆

The 2016 vintage (★★★☆) is full-bodied, with strong, ripe, peachy, slightly gingery flavours, a sliver of sweetness, and plenty of drink-young appeal.

MED/DRY $25 –V

Gibson Bridge Reserve Marlborough Gewürztraminer ★★★★

Still unfolding, the attractive 2014 vintage (★★★★) of this single-vineyard, hand-harvested wine is freshly scented and mouthfilling, with strong, youthful lychee and pear flavours, lively acidity and a slightly sweet, gently spicy finish. Best drinking 2018+.

MED/DRY $28 –V

Giesen The Brothers Marlborough Gewürztraminer   (★★★★☆)

From sites at Rapaura and in the lower Wairau Valley, the 2014 vintage (★★★★☆) is exotically perfumed and fleshy. It has concentrated, gently sweet lychee, pear and spice flavours, showing a touch of complexity, and a slightly oily richness.

MED/DRY $33 –V

Greystone Waipara Valley Gewürztraminer   ★★★★★

An emerging star. The 2015 vintage (★★★★☆) was estate-grown, hand-picked and briefly matured on its yeast lees. Bright, light lemon/green, it is beautifully perfumed and very full-bodied (14.5 per cent alcohol). Still youthful, it is a powerful wine, with deep, delicate lychee, pear and spice flavours, an oily texture and obvious potential; open 2018+.

Vintage	15	14	13	12	11
WR	6	6	7	7	7
Drink	17-25	17-18	P	P	P

MED/DRY $33 AV

Huia Marlborough Gewürztraminer   ★★★★☆

The delicious 2014 vintage (★★★★★) is a striking wine. Estate-grown in the lower Wairau Valley and certified organic, it was partly fermented and fully matured for 10 months in old French oak puncheons. Fragrant and softly mouthfilling, it has rich, ripe, peachy, spicy, faintly gingery flavours, showing excellent complexity, and loads of personality. A dry style (4 grams/litre of residual sugar), it is finely textured, with good potential and notable harmony.

DRY $28 V+

Hunter's Marlborough Gewürztraminer   ★★★★☆

The 2016 vintage (★★★★), estate-grown at Rapaura, on the north side of the Wairau Valley, is a perfumed and spicy, full-bodied wine, strongly varietal, with fresh, youthful lychee, pear and spice flavours, showing excellent depth. A fleshy, dry style (4 grams/litre of residual sugar) with gentle acidity, it's enjoyable from the start. The 2017 vintage (★★★★) is still very youthful. Pale lemon/green, it is perfumed and mouthfilling, with pear, ginger and spice flavours, showing excellent delicacy and purity, fresh acidity and a dryish finish. Open mid-2018+.

MED/DRY $25 V+

Johanneshof Cellars Marlborough Gewürztraminer   ★★★★★

This beauty is one of the country's greatest Gewürztraminers. Exotically perfumed, the rich 2015 vintage (★★★★★) was hand-harvested and handled without oak. Light lemon/green, it is mouthfilling and smooth, with a gentle splash of sweetness (20 grams/litre of residual sugar) and a lovely surge of fresh, ripe, peachy, spicy flavours, finely textured and harmonious. The 2016 vintage (★★★★★) has a fragrant, invitingly scented bouquet. Full-bodied, it is a fleshy, rich, medium-dry style (11 grams/litre of residual sugar), with deep, peachy, gently spicy flavours, good complexity, a slightly oily texture and a soft, lasting finish. Full of personality, it's a drink-now or cellaring proposition.

Vintage	16	15	14	13	12	11	10	09	08
WR	7	6	7	7	7	6	7	6	6
Drink	17-25	17-24	17-24	17-23	17-21	17-20	17-20	P	P

MED $31 AV

Kaimira Estate Brightwater Gewürztraminer ★★★☆

The 2015 vintage (★★★☆), certified organic, is a perfumed, strongly varietal wine with lively acidity and very good depth of peachy, spicy flavour, fresh and slightly sweet (7 grams/litre of residual sugar). Drink now or cellar.

MED/DRY $22 AV

Konrad Marlborough Gewürztraminer ★★★

Estate-grown and hand-picked in the Waihopai Valley, the 2014 vintage (★★★☆) is mouthfilling, with a spicy bouquet, strong, citrusy, spicy flavours and a dryish finish. Showing good varietal character, it's certified organic.

MED/DRY $19 AV

Kumeu River Estate Gewürztraminer ★★★★

The 2014 vintage (★★★☆) was hand-picked from mature vines at Kumeu, in West Auckland, and fermented with indigenous yeasts in tanks. Full-bodied, it is gently sweet, with fresh lychee and spice flavours, balanced acidity and good length.

MED/DRY $25 AV

Lawson's Dry Hills Marlborough Gewürztraminer ★★★★★

One of the country's most impressive Gewürztraminers. Grown in the Home Block and nearby Woodward Vineyard, at the foot of the Wither Hills, it is typically harvested at about 24 brix and mostly fermented in stainless steel tanks; a key part of the blend (about 15 per cent) is given 'the full treatment', with a high-solids, indigenous yeast ferment in seasoned French oak barriques, malolactic fermentation and lees-stirring. The 2016 vintage (★★★★★) is benchmark stuff. Bright, light lemon/green, it is weighty and well-rounded, with generous, youthful peach, pear, lychee and spice flavours and a rich, slightly sweet (7.5 grams/litre of residual sugar), very harmonious finish. It's already delicious.

Vintage	16	15	14	13	12	11	10	09
WR	7	7	6	7	7	7	7	7
Drink	17-24	17-24	17-22	17-20	17-18	P	17-18	P

MED/DRY $25 V+

Lawson's Dry Hills The Pioneer Marlborough Gewürztraminer ★★★★★

The delicious 2015 vintage (★★★★★) is a weighty (14.5 per cent alcohol), fleshy, Alsace-style wine, estate-grown in the Home Block and barrel-fermented with indigenous yeasts. Bright, light lemon/green, it is fresh and complex, with concentrated, ripe, peachy, spicy flavours, a gentle splash of sweetness (18.6 grams/litre of residual sugar), and lovely depth and harmony. Drink now or cellar.

Vintage	15	14	13
WR	7	6	7
Drink	17-24	17-24	17-20

MED $30 AV

Leveret Estate Hawke's Bay Gewürztraminer (★★★☆)

Drinking well now, the light lemon/green 2016 vintage (★★★☆) is mouthfilling, with very good depth of fresh peach and pear flavours, hints of spices and ginger, and a slightly sweet finish.

Vintage	16	MED/DRY $23 –V
WR	7	
Drink	18-22	

Linden Estate Esk Valley Hawke's Bay Gewürztraminer (★★★)

The 2014 vintage (★★★) is aromatic and fleshy, with strong pear, lychee and spice flavours and a dry (4 grams/litre of residual sugar) finish. It shows a slight lack of delicacy, but plenty of body and flavour.

DRY $20 –V

Loveblock Marlborough Gewürztraminer ★★★★

Certified organic, the 2014 vintage (★★★★) was harvested at a hilltop site in the lower Awatere Valley and made in a medium-dry style (14 grams/litre of residual sugar). Light lemon/green, it is fleshy and soft, with gentle acidity and strong, ripe peach, lychee and spice flavours. A harmonious wine with good varietal character, it's ready to roll.

MED/DRY $25 AV

Mahi Twin Valleys Marlborough Gewürztraminer ★★★★

The 2015 vintage (★★★★) is a single-vineyard wine, grown at the junction of the Wairau and Waihopai valleys, hand-picked and fermented with indigenous yeasts in tanks (mostly) and seasoned French oak barriques. It has a perfumed, strongly varietal bouquet, leading into a mouthfilling, fleshy, dry palate (3 grams/litre of residual sugar), with rich, youthful lychee and spice flavours, showing considerable complexity, and a softly textured finish.

Vintage	15	DRY $24 AV
WR	7	
Drink	17-20	

Main Divide Marlborough Gewürztraminer (★★★★)

The 2015 vintage (★★★★) has a perfumed, distinctly spicy bouquet, leading into a mouthfilling wine (14 per cent alcohol), with strong, peachy, spicy, slightly gingery flavours and a dryish (12 grams/litre of residual sugar) finish. (From Pegasus Bay.)

Vintage	15	MED/DRY $21 V+
WR	6	
Drink	17-22	

Main Divide North Canterbury Gewürztraminer ★★★★

From a 'great' year for Gewürztraminer, the 2016 vintage (★★★★) is a weighty, fleshy, very harmonious wine. Matured for six months in old French oak puncheons, it has plenty of fresh, peachy, distinctly spicy flavour, a touch of complexity, and a slightly sweet (12 grams/litre of residual sugar), well-rounded finish. Drink now or cellar. (From Pegasus Bay.)

Vintage	16
WR	7
Drink	17-22

MED/DRY $21 V+

Margrain Martinborough Gewürztraminer (★★★★)

Pale straw, the 2016 vintage (★★★★) is a distinctly medium style (31 grams/litre of residual sugar). Full-bodied, with a strong surge of peachy, spicy flavours, and hints of ginger and honey, it's already drinking well.

Vintage	16
WR	7
Drink	17-23

MED $38 –V

Marsden Bay of Islands Gewürztraminer (★★★★)

Who says you can't make good Gewürztraminer in the north? Grown at Mangawhai, the 2015 vintage (★★★★) is a pale straw, faintly pink wine with a spicy, gingery bouquet. Mouthfilling, it is gently sweet (21 grams/litre of residual sugar), with strong, peachy, spicy, vaguely honeyed flavours, ripe and fresh, and a long, well-spiced finish.

Vintage	15
WR	6
Drink	17-18

MED $29 –V

Matawhero Single Vineyard Gisborne Gewürztraminer ★★★★

Grown in the Matawhero Vineyard, the 2016 vintage (★★★☆) is gently perfumed, with a hint of sweetness (7 grams/litre of residual sugar) and vibrant, citrusy, spicy flavours, showing very good balance, delicacy and depth.

MED/DRY $23 AV

Millton Riverpoint Vineyard Gewürztraminer ★★★★☆

The 2015 vintage (★★★★★) of this Gisborne wine makes a big statement. Certified organic, it was fermented on its skins for several days, emerging with gold/amber colour and a well-spiced bouquet. Full of personality, it is sturdy (14.5 per cent alcohol), peachy, spicy and slightly honeyed, with hints of ginger and passionfruit, an oily richness and an off-dry (9.5 grams/litre of residual sugar) finish.

Vintage	15	14
WR	6	6
Drink	17-19	17-18

MED/DRY $26 AV

Misha's Vineyard The Gallery Central Otago Gewürztraminer ★★★★☆

The 2014 vintage (★★★★☆), estate-grown and hand-harvested at Bendigo, was fermented in seasoned French oak casks, partly (25 per cent) with indigenous yeasts. Weighty (14.5 per cent alcohol), it has strong, ripe lychee and spice flavours, showing excellent delicacy and depth, good complexity, gentle acidity, and a slightly sweet (13 grams/litre of residual sugar), well-rounded finish. Drink now or cellar.

Vintage	14	13	12	11	10	09	08
WR	6	6	7	6	6	6	7
Drink	17-23	17-23	17-21	17-20	17-20	17-18	17-18

 MED/DRY $32 –V

Mission Hawke's Bay Gewürztraminer ★★★★

Bargain-priced, the 2015 vintage (★★★★) is a full-bodied, medium style (15 grams/litre of residual sugar), with an attractively perfumed bouquet, lively acidity and strong, fresh, well-spiced, slightly gingery flavours. Drink now to 2018.

 MED $18 V+

Mount Riley Marlborough Gewürztraminer ★★★☆

The 2014 vintage (★★★☆), grown in the Omaka Valley, was mostly handled in tanks; 10 per cent of the blend was barrel-fermented. Mouthfilling, it is weighty and smooth, with a sliver of sweetness (8 grams/litre of residual sugar) and very good depth of fresh, citrusy, peachy, spicy flavour.

 MED/DRY $17 V+

Mt Difficulty Growers Series Station Block Pisa Range
Central Otago Gewürztraminer ★★★★

Delicious young, the 2015 vintage (★★★★) is a single-vineyard wine, grown in the Cromwell Basin. Pale lemon/green, it is attractively perfumed, fresh and mouthfilling, with concentrated pear, lychee and spice flavours, gently sweet (20 grams/litre of residual sugar), well-rounded and harmonious. Best drinking 2018+.

 MED $26 –V

Ohinemuri Estate Matawhero Gewürztraminer ★★★☆

The 2015 vintage (★★★★) was grown in Gisborne and mostly handled in tanks, but 10 per cent of the blend was fermented and matured for four months in oak barrels. It is already drinking well, but worth cellaring. Light lemon/green, it is mouthfilling, slightly sweet (15 grams/litre of residual sugar) and smooth, with fresh, peachy, gently spicy flavours. Finely balanced, it's a strongly varietal wine, youthful and enticingly perfumed.

Vintage	15
WR	5
Drink	17-19

MED $24 –V

Old Coach Road Nelson Gewürztraminer ★★★☆

Bargain-priced, the 2016 vintage (★★★☆) is fresh, citrusy and gently spicy, with a sliver of sweetness (11 grams/litre of residual sugar), balanced acidity, and good varietal definition and depth. Fine value from Seifried Estate.

MED/DRY $13 V+

Ostler Waitaki Valley North Otago Gewürztraminer (★★★★)

Attractively perfumed, the debut 2015 vintage (★★★★) is still youthful. Mouthfilling, it is a slightly sweet style (7 grams/litre of residual sugar), with balanced acidity and ripe, peachy, well-spiced flavours, showing very good drive, delicacy and depth. Well worth cellaring.

MED/DRY $27 –V

Pegasus Bay Gewürztraminer ★★★★★

Grown at Waipara and fermented with indigenous yeasts in large old barrels, the outstanding 2016 vintage (★★★★★) was made from 'very ripe' grapes, with 'some noble botrytis'. Powerful (14.5 per cent alcohol), it has a beautifully perfumed, spicy bouquet, leading into a weighty wine with rich, well-spiced flavours, gentle sweetness (14 grams/litre of residual sugar) and acidity, and unusual complexity and harmony. Highly expressive in its youth, it's already delicious.

Vintage	16	15	14	13	12	11	10
WR	5	NM	7	7	7	6	6
Drink	17-22	NM	17-22	17-21	17-20	P	P

MED/DRY $30 AV

Rimu Grove Nelson Gewürztraminer ★★★★

The 2016 vintage (★★★★☆) is already delicious. Light lemon/green, it is perfumed, weighty and finely textured, in a slightly sweet style (12 grams/litre of residual sugar) with gentle acidity, generous peach, spice and slight ginger flavours, showing excellent depth and harmony, and lots of drink-young appeal.

Vintage	16	15	14
WR	6	7	7
Drink	17-27	17-26	17-25

MED/DRY $26 –V

Ruru Central Otago Gewürztraminer ★★★☆

The 2017 vintage (★★★☆), grown at Alexandra, is a pale, youthful, delicately scented wine. Mouthfilling, it has good varietal character, with moderately rich pear, lychee and spice flavours, gentle sweetness (7.2 grams/litre of residual sugar), and a distinctly spicy finish. Best drinking 2019+.

MED/DRY $26 –V

Saint Clair Marlborough Gewürztraminer ★★★☆

Attractively perfumed, the 2014 vintage (★★★★) is grown at two sites in the Wairau Valley. It's a richly varietal wine with very good depth of fresh, ripe lychee, pear and spice flavours, a slightly oily texture, gentle acidity and a slightly sweet (9 grams/litre of residual sugar), soft finish. Delicious young.

MED/DRY $22 AV

Saint Clair Pioneer Block 12 Lone Gum Marlborough Gewürztraminer   ★★★★☆

Grown at a warm site in the lower Omaka Valley, the 2015 vintage (★★★★☆) is an attractively perfumed, softly seductive wine. It is fleshy and smooth, with concentrated, peachy, spicy flavours, a slightly oily texture, and a gently sweet (16 grams/litre of residual sugar), rich finish.

 MED $27 AV

Saint Clair Vicar's Choice Marlborough Gewürztraminer   ★★★

Enjoyable young, the 2014 vintage (★★★) is full-bodied, fresh and smooth, with good depth of vibrant lychee, peach and spice flavours, and a dryish (7 grams/litre of residual sugar), well-rounded finish.

MED/DRY $19 AV

Seifried Nelson Gewürztraminer   ★★★★

Typically a floral, well-spiced wine, offering excellent quality and value. The 2016 vintage (★★★★) is fresh and finely poised, with a sliver of sweetness (7 grams/litre of residual sugar) amid its youthful, vibrant peach, pear and spice flavours. Tightly structured, with good potential, it should be at its best 2018+. The 2017 vintage (★★★★) is already delicious. Mouthfilling, it is perfumed, with strong, fresh pear, lychee and spice flavours, gentle sweetness (12 grams/litre of residual sugar), and a smooth, very harmonious finish.

Vintage	17	16	15	14	13	12
WR	6	6	6	6	6	6
Drink	17-21	17-20	17-20	P	P	P

MED/DRY $18 V+

Seifried Winemaker's Collection Nelson Gewürztraminer   ★★★★★

This is typically a powerful wine with loads of personality. The 2016 vintage (★★★★☆) is richly perfumed and full-bodied, with concentrated, fresh, strongly spicy, slightly gingery flavours and a bone-dry finish. It's already very expressive; drink now or cellar.

Vintage	16	15	14	13
WR	7	6	6	6
Drink	17-21	17-21	17-19	17-18

DRY $26 V+

Sileni Estate Selection 1,000 Vines Hawke's Bay Gewürztraminer   (★★★★)

The debut 2015 vintage (★★★★) has a musky perfume, good weight and strong, fresh lychee, pear and spice flavours. Fleshy and dryish (7 grams/litre of residual sugar), with a touch of complexity, it's well worth cellaring.

Vintage	15
WR	6
Drink	17-23

MED/DRY $28 –V

Sileni G2 Hawke's Bay Gewürztraminer (★★★★)

The 'G2' refers to Graeme Avery (the owner) and Grant Edmonds (chief winemaker), the two key figures at Sileni. Grown in the Bridge Pa Triangle, the 2014 vintage (★★★★) is a mouthfilling, fleshy, soft wine with off-dry (6 grams/litre of residual sugar) flavours of peaches, apricots, lychees and spices, a slightly oily texture, and loads of drink-young charm.

Vintage	14
WR	6
Drink	17-22

 MED/DRY $35 –V

Spy Valley Envoy Johnson Vineyard Marlborough Gewürztraminer ★★★★★

Estate-grown in the lower Waihopai Valley, hand-harvested from mature vines and fermented in small oak vessels, the light yellow/green 2016 vintage (★★★★★) has a powerful presence. Late-harvested, it is medium-bodied, with fresh, lush, highly concentrated stone-fruit, peach and ginger flavours, abundant sweetness (105 grams/litre of residual sugar), and a very harmonious, softly seductive finish. (Past vintages have been made in a medium style.)

Vintage	16	15	14	13	12
WR	7	7	6	7	5
Drink	17-22	17-20	17-19	17-20	17-18

 SW $32 AV

Spy Valley Single Vineyard Marlborough Gewürztraminer ★★★★

Estate-grown in the Waihopai Valley and fermented in tanks and old oak vessels, this wine is consistently impressive. The 2016 vintage (★★★★) is mouthfilling and gently sweet (12.5 grams/litre of residual sugar), with peachy, slightly spicy and gingery flavours, showing a touch of complexity, moderate acidity, and excellent depth and harmony. Drink now or cellar.

Vintage	16	15	14	13	12	11	10
WR	6	6	7	6	6	7	6
Drink	18-22	17-19	17-18	P	P	P	P

MED/DRY $23 AV

Stonecroft Gimblett Gravels Hawke's Bay Gewürztraminer ★★★★☆

Certified organic, the 2015 vintage (★★★★☆) was estate-grown and a small part of the blend was fermented in old oak casks. Sturdy (14.5 per cent alcohol) and gently sweet (10 grams/litre of residual sugar), it has concentrated, ripe, citrusy, spicy flavours, with hints of ginger and honey, and a well-rounded finish. Already delicious, it should mature gracefully.

Vintage	17
WR	6
Drink	18-24

 MED/DRY $27 AV

Stonecroft Old Vine Gewürztraminer ★★★★★

The Gewürztraminers from this tiny Hawke's Bay winery are among the finest in the country. This 'Old Vine' wine is made entirely from grapes hand-picked from the original Mere Road plantings in 1983. Certified organic, the 2015 vintage (★★★★★) is a pale gold, mouthfilling (14.5 per cent alcohol), very rich wine, with lush, ripe, peachy, spicy flavours, gentle acidity, and a smooth, gently sweet (20 grams/litre of residual sugar), lasting finish. Drink now or cellar.

Vintage	15	14		MED $47 AV
WR	6	6		
Drink	17-24	17-23		

Te Awanga Estate Hawke's Bay Gewürztraminer (★★★★)

The 2014 vintage (★★★★) was hand-harvested at an inland site, tank-fermented and matured on its yeast lees. It has a perfumed, spicy bouquet, leading into a mouthfilling, off-dry wine with strong, citrusy, peachy, spicy flavours, fresh, harmonious and long.

MED/DRY $25 AV

Te Mania Nelson Gewürztraminer ★★★☆

The 2014 vintage (★★★) is a charming wine with lemony, gently spicy flavours in a fresh, off-dry style, well balanced for early appeal.

MED/DRY $23 –V

Two Gates Hawke's Bay Gewürztraminer (★★★☆)

Grown at Maraekakaho, the 2014 vintage (★★★☆) is a single-vineyard wine, hand-picked and fermented with indigenous yeasts in tanks and French oak puncheons. The bouquet is spicy, with some 'funky' notes; the palate is medium-bodied, with good depth of peachy, spicy, slightly gingery, dryish flavours.

MED/DRY $28 –V

Villa Maria Private Bin East Coast Gewürztraminer ★★★★

This regional blend, grown at sites stretching from Auckland to Waipara, typically offers very good value. The 2016 vintage (★★★★) is a great buy. The bouquet is fragrant and well-spiced; the palate is mouthfilling, with a sliver of sweetness (7.8 grams/litre of residual sugar) and rich peach, spice and ginger flavours. The 2017 vintage (★★★★) is mouthfilling, soft and slightly sweet, with fresh and lively, very generous, peachy, spicy flavours. Delicious young.

Vintage	17	16	15	14	13	12	MED/DRY $16 V+
WR	6	7	6	7	7	6	
Drink	17-20	17-19	P	P	P	P	

Villa Maria Private Bin Hawke's Bay Organic Gewürztraminer ★★★★

A consistently good buy. The 2016 vintage (★★★★) is full-bodied, with good concentration of citrusy, peachy, spicy flavours and a dryish, well-rounded finish. Certified organic.

Vintage	16	15	14	MED/DRY $17 V+
WR	7	6	7	
Drink	17-19	P	P	

Villa Maria Single Vineyard Ihumatao Gewürztraminer ★★★★★

Estate-grown in South Auckland, this wine is partly fermented with indigenous yeasts in seasoned French oak barriques; the rest is handled in tanks. The 2014 vintage (★★★★☆), 10 per cent barrel-fermented, is perfumed and weighty, with concentrated, ripe pear and lychee flavours, showing excellent delicacy and richness. An off-dry style (7 grams/litre of residual sugar), it has an oily texture and good cellaring potential.

Vintage	14	13
WR	7	7
Drink	17-20	P

MED/DRY $28 V+

Vinoptima Ormond Reserve Gewürztraminer ★★★★★

This wine, launched from 2003, is from Nick Nobilo's vineyard at Ormond, in Gisborne, devoted exclusively to the variety, and is fermented in tanks and large 1200-litre German oak ovals. The 2010 vintage (★★★★★), dubbed 'Delicatum', is fleshy, with strong, peachy, citrusy, gently spicy flavours, showing good vigour and bottle-aged complexity. Released in October 2015, it's probably at its peak now to 2018.

Vintage	10	09	08
WR	7	NM	6
Drink	17-20	NM	17-18

MED $75 –V

Waimea Nelson Gewürztraminer ★★★★

The 2015 vintage (★★★★) is attractively perfumed and mouthfilling, with ripe, peachy, spicy, slightly gingery flavours, showing excellent delicacy and vibrancy. Made in an off-dry style (11 grams/litre of residual sugar), it is a finely textured wine with a distinctly spicy finish.

MED/DRY $23 AV

Wairau River Marlborough Gewürztraminer ★★★☆

The 2016 vintage (★★★☆) is a youthful wine with mouthfilling body and very good depth of fresh, ripe, peachy, spicy flavours. Made in an off-dry style (8 grams/litre of residual sugar), it should be at its best 2018+.

Vintage	16	15	14	13
WR	6	5	5	6
Drink	17-19	17-18	P	P

MED/DRY $20 AV

West Brook Marlborough Gewurztraminer ★★★★

Drinking well now, the 2014 vintage (★★★★) was mostly handled in tanks; 9 per cent was fermented in old oak barrels. Bright, light lemon/green, it is still fresh and vibrant, with mouthfilling body, ripe peach, lychee and spice flavours, a sliver of sweetness (8 grams/litre of residual sugar), bottle-aged complexity and a smooth, harmonious finish.

Vintage	14
WR	5
Drink	17-22

MED/DRY $23 AV

Whitehaven Marlborough Gewürztraminer   ★★★★☆

Offering fine value, the delicious 2016 vintage (★★★★☆) was hand-picked, fermented in tanks and made in a medium-dry style (14.6 grams/litre of residual sugar). Exotically perfumed, it is mouthfilling and soft, with strong, youthful lychee, pear and spice flavours, showing excellent delicacy and richness, and a well-rounded finish. Drink now or cellar.

MED/DRY $22 V+

Zephyr Marlborough Gewürztraminer   ★★★★☆

Richly perfumed, the youthful 2015 vintage (★★★★☆) was estate-grown in the lower Wairau Valley and mostly tank-fermented; 5 per cent was handled in old oak. Light lemon/green, it is sturdy (14.5 per cent alcohol) and smooth, with ripe pear, lychee and spice flavours, showing excellent delicacy and depth. A powerful, harmonious wine with a touch of complexity, it shows strong personality.

MED/DRY $24 V+

Grüner Veltliner

Grüner Veltliner, Austria's favourite white-wine variety, is currently stirring up interest in New Zealand, especially in the south. 'Grü-Vee' is a fairly late ripener in Austria, where it yields medium-bodied wines, fruity, crisp and dry, with a spicy, slightly musky aroma. Most are drunk young, but the finest wines, with an Alsace-like substance and perfume, are more age-worthy. Coopers Creek produced New Zealand's first Grüner Veltliner from the 2008 vintage. Of the country's 46 hectares of bearing Grüner Veltliner vines in 2018, most are now clustered in Marlborough (33 hectares), with Nelson (6 hectares) a distant second.

Aronui Single Vineyard Nelson Grüner Veltliner (★★★)

The debut 2014 vintage (★★★) was estate-grown at Upper Moutere, hand-harvested and tank-fermented. Mouthfilling, it's a fully dry style with vibrant, citrusy, slightly appley and spicy flavours, moderate acidity and good vigour.

DRY $25 –V

Ata Mara Central Otago Grüner Veltliner (★★★)

The 2014 vintage (★★★) is a basically dry style (4.2 grams/litre of residual sugar), from vines planted in 2008. Medium-bodied, it has good freshness and vigour, with crisp, slightly appley flavours that linger well.

DRY $20 –V

Babich Family Estates Headwaters Organic Block
Marlborough Grüner Veltliner ★★★☆

Certified organic, the 2016 vintage (★★★☆) was estate-grown in the Headwaters Vineyard, in the Wairau Valley, and fermented in tanks and old oak puncheons. Invitingly aromatic, it's a lively, medium-bodied wine, with vibrant, citrusy flavours, hints of herbs and spices, and a dry (1.8 grams/litre of residual sugar) finish.

Vintage	16	15	14	13
WR	7	7	7	7
Drink	17-19	17-18	P	P

DRY $27 –V

Bannock Brae Marlene's Central Otago Grüner Veltliner ★★★★☆

Finely balanced for early drinking, the delicious 2016 vintage (★★★★★) was hand-harvested at Bannockburn and fermented in seasoned French oak barriques. Light lemon/green, it is mouthfilling, sweet-fruited and dry (2.4 grams/litre of residual sugar), with excellent intensity of peachy, citrusy, spicy flavours, slightly toasty notes adding complexity, fresh acidity and a persistent finish. Offering fine value, it should be at its best 2018 onwards.

Vintage	16	15	14
WR	7	7	6
Drink	17-22	17-21	17-20

DRY $24 V+

Forrest Marlborough Grüner Veltliner   (★★★☆)

Still youthful, the light yellow/green 2015 vintage (★★★☆) is a medium-bodied wine, scented and vibrantly fruity, with good depth of lively, peachy, spicy flavours and a dry, tangy finish. Drink now to 2019.

DRY $22 AV

Hans Herzog Marlborough Grüner Veltliner   ★★★★

Estate-grown on the north side of the Wairau Valley, the age-worthy 2013 vintage (★★★★) was fermented and matured for 18 months in French oak puncheons. A dry style (3 grams/litre of residual sugar), it is medium to full-bodied, with vibrant grapefruit, peach and spice flavours, gently seasoned with oak, fresh acidity and good cellaring potential. Certified organic.

Vintage	13	12
WR	7	7
Drink	17-20	P

DRY $44 –V

Jules Taylor Marlborough Grüner Veltliner   ★★★★☆

The stylish 2016 vintage (★★★★☆) was mostly grown in the Griffith Vineyard and cool-fermented in tanks, but 32 per cent of the blend, grown in the Anderson Vineyard, was fermented with indigenous yeasts in seasoned French oak casks and went through a secondary, softening malolactic fermentation. Light lemon/green, it is fragrant, mouthfilling and vibrantly fruity, with good intensity of peachy, citrusy, spicy flavours, a touch of complexity, balanced acidity and a dry (1.2 grams/litre of residual sugar), slightly minerally finish. A very harmonious wine with layers of flavour, it's well worth cellaring.

Vintage	16	15	14
WR	6	6	5
Drink	17-20	17-19	17-18

DRY $24 V+

Lime Rock Grüner Veltliner   (★★★★★)

Full of personality, the light lemon/green 2016 vintage (★★★★★) was estate-grown in Central Hawke's Bay, hand-picked and made in a dry style (3 grams/litre of residual sugar). Enticingly fragrant, it is an intensely varietal wine, full-bodied, with fresh, concentrated flavours, peachy and slightly spicy, and is already very expressive. A top example of New Zealand Grüner Veltliner.

Vintage	16
WR	7
Drink	18-21

DRY $28 V+

Lime Rock Single Barrique Ferment Grüner Veltliner   (★★★★☆)

Estate-grown in Central Hawke's Bay, the 2017 vintage (★★★★☆) is a rare wine, fermented in a seasoned oak barrel. Light lemon/green, it's a youthful, gently oaked, full-bodied wine, with good concentration of vibrant, peachy, slightly spicy flavours, and a well-rounded, dry (4.6 grams/litre of residual sugar), harmonious finish. Best drinking mid-2018+.

Vintage	17
WR	7
Drink	18-25

DRY $36 –V

Margrain Martinborough Grüner Veltliner   ★★★

Promoted as a sort of 'potbellied Riesling', the 2016 vintage (★★★☆) was partly barrel-fermented. Light lemon/green, it is a medium to full-bodied, slightly sweet style (20 grams/litre of residual sugar), with lively, peachy, appley flavours, crisp acidity, and good depth. Best drinking 2018+.

Vintage	16
WR	6
Drink	17-22

MED $30 –V

Nautilus Marlborough Grüner Veltliner   ★★★★☆

Showing good personality, the 2015 vintage (★★★★☆) was handled without oak and made in a bone-dry style. Weighty and tangy, with strong, citrusy, slightly spicy flavours, it is very fresh and lively, with a crisp, finely balanced, lasting finish. The 2016 vintage (★★★★☆) is fragrant, fresh and full-bodied, with generous, vibrant, citrusy, peachy flavours, dry, finely balanced and lingering. Drink now or cellar.

Vintage	16	15	14
WR	7	7	6
Drink	17-20	17-19	17-18

DRY $29 AV

Riverby Estate Marlborough Grüner Veltliner   ★★★☆

A single-vineyard wine, grown and hand-picked in the heart of the Wairau Valley, the 2014 vintage (★★★☆) was handled in stainless steel tanks and made in a dry style (3.9 grams/litre of residual sugar). Medium to full-bodied, it has finely balanced acidity and very good depth of fresh, citrusy, slightly spicy flavours.

Vintage	14	13
WR	6	6
Drink	17-19	17-18

DRY $24 –V

Saint Clair Marlborough Grüner Veltliner   ★★★★

The 2015 vintage (★★★★) is a full-bodied, dry wine (2.5 grams/litre of residual sugar), grown in the Omaka and Wairau valleys, and made with some use of old oak and malolactic fermentation. Vibrantly fruity, it shows very good vigour and depth of citrusy, spicy flavours, with hints of peaches and ginger, gentle acidity and a well-rounded finish. Delicious young.

DRY $21 V+

Saint Clair Pioneer Block 5 Bull Block Marlborough Grüner Veltliner   ★★★★

Still youthful, the 2015 vintage (★★★★) is a mouthfilling, tightly structured wine, grown in the Omaka Valley. Pale lemon/green, it has fresh, generous, peachy, slightly spicy flavours, good drive through the palate and a dry (2.7 grams/litre of residual sugar), lengthy finish. Best drinking 2018+.

DRY $27 –V

Seifried Nelson Grüner Veltliner ★★★☆

The 2016 vintage (★★★☆) is medium to full-bodied, with fresh, citrusy, slightly spicy and peachy flavours, showing very good vibrancy and depth. Made in a fully dry style, it's still youthful; open 2018 onwards.

Vintage	16	15	14	13	12
WR	6	6	6	6	6
Drink	17-18	17-18	P	P	P

DRY $25 –V

Soul by Waipara Hills Waipara Valley Grüner Veltliner (★★★★★)

A very auspicious debut, the classy 2016 vintage (★★★★★) is from first-crop vines in The Mound Vineyard. Hand-picked and lees-aged for eight months, it's an attractively scented, full-bodied wine (14 per cent alcohol), with vibrant, peachy, slightly biscuity flavours, fresh acidity and a dryish (6 grams/litre of residual sugar), lingering finish. Showing considerable complexity, it's an immaculate, very harmonious wine, likely to reward cellaring to mid-2018+.

MED/DRY $28 V+

Waimea Nelson Grüner Veltliner ★★★★

The easy-drinking 2016 vintage (★★★★) was grown at three sites on the Waimea Plains. Mouthfilling, smooth and dry (3 grams/litre of residual sugar), it has fresh, peachy, slightly citrusy and spicy flavours, showing excellent depth and harmony.

DRY $23 AV

Wairau River Marlborough Grüner Veltliner (★★★☆)

A single-vineyard, estate-grown wine, the 2014 vintage (★★★☆) is mouthfilling and dry (2 grams/litre of residual sugar), with citrusy, slightly peachy and spicy flavours, showing good freshness and vigour.

DRY $25 –V

Whitehaven Marlborough Grüner Veltliner (★★★★)

The fragrant 2015 vintage (★★★★) is enjoyable from the start. Full-bodied, with gentle acidity, it has strong, vibrant, peachy, spicy flavours, with a slightly creamy texture and a dry (4.7 grams/litre of residual sugar), well-rounded finish.

DRY $23 AV

Yealands Estate Single Vineyard Awatere Valley Marlborough Grüner Veltliner ★★★★☆

Consistently good. The 2015 vintage (★★★★☆) is mouthfilling, fleshy and dry (3 grams/litre of residual sugar), with rich, ripe stone-fruit and spice flavours, strong, vibrant, finely balanced and lingering. It's already very open and expressive.

Vintage	15	14
WR	7	7
Drink	17-19	17-18

DRY $23 V+

Marsanne

Cultivated extensively in the northern Rhône Valley of France, where it is often blended with Roussanne, Marsanne yields powerful, sturdy wines with rich pear, spice and nut flavours. Although grown in Victoria since the 1860s, it is extremely rare in New Zealand, with 0.3 hectares of bearing vines in 2018, clustered in Gisborne and Auckland.

Coopers Creek SV Gisborne Allison Marsanne ★★★★

The 2015 vintage (★★★☆) is mouthfilling, fleshy and dry, with delicate aromas and fresh, ripe, slightly peachy and spicy flavours, showing good depth.

DRY $24 AV

Vintage	14
WR	7
Drink	P

Trinity Hill Gimblett Gravels Marsanne/Viognier ★★★★☆

Already drinking well, the 2016 vintage (★★★★☆) is a weighty, softly seductive blend of Marsanne (51 per cent) and Viognier (49 per cent), hand-picked and fermented and matured for 14 months in seasoned French oak puncheons. Bright, light lemon/green, it has an inviting, floral, ripely scented bouquet. Mouthfilling, it has fresh, peachy, slightly buttery flavours, showing good richness, very gentle acidity and a smooth (5 grams/litre of residual sugar), persistent finish.

MED/DRY $35 –V

Vintage	16	15	14
WR	6	6	6
Drink	17-21	17-20	17-20

Muscat

Muscat vines grow all over the Mediterranean, but Muscat is rarely seen in New Zealand as a varietal wine, because it ripens late in the season, without the lushness and intensity achieved in warmer regions. Of the country's 37 hectares of bearing Muscat vines in 2018, 30 hectares are clustered in Gisborne. Most of the grapes are used to add an inviting, musky perfume to low-priced sparklings, modelled on the Asti Spumantes of northern Italy.

Blackenbrook Nelson Muscat ★★★★

The 2014 vintage (★★★★) is a rare example of South Island Muscat (the 2010 was the first). Estate-grown, hand-picked at 22.6 brix and lees-aged in tanks, it is scented and vibrant, with good body, poise and richness. Made in an off-dry style (5 grams/litre of residual sugar), it is full-bodied, with lychee, pear and orange flavours, showing excellent purity, delicacy and varietal precision.

Vintage	14
WR	6
Drink	P

MED/DRY $24 AV

Millton Te Arai Vineyard Gisborne Muskats at Dawn ★★★★

Certified organic, the 2015 vintage (★★★★) is 'just off-dry', according to the label, but it tastes a lot sweeter than that. Highly perfumed, it is vibrantly fruity, with rich peach, pear and lychee flavours, balanced acidity, and lots of drink-young charm. Imagine an Asti Spumante, without the bubbles.

Vintage	15
WR	6
Drink	P

SW $22 V+

Pegasus Bay Muscat ★★★★★

This rare, estate-grown Waipara Valley wine is made in a sturdy, Alsace style and matured for six months in old oak puncheons. The 2016 vintage (★★★★☆) is gently perfumed and mouthfilling (14 per cent alcohol), with peach, orange and spice flavours, a splash of sweetness (18 grams/litre of residual sugar) and fresh acidity. It's still very youthful; open mid-2018+. The 2015 vintage (★★★★★) is invitingly scented and full-bodied, with generous peach, orange and spice flavours, showing good complexity, slight sweetness (15 grams/litre of residual sugar) and strong personality. Delicious now, it's maturing very gracefully and well worth discovering.

MED $30 AV

Pinot Blanc

If you love Chardonnay, try Pinot Blanc. A white mutation of Pinot Noir, Pinot Blanc is highly regarded in Italy and California for its generous extract and moderate acidity, although in Alsace and Germany the more aromatic Pinot Gris finds greater favour.

With its fullness of weight and subtle aromatics, Pinot Blanc can easily be mistaken for Chardonnay in a blind tasting. The variety is still rare in New Zealand, but in 2018 there will be 12 hectares of bearing vines, mostly in Marlborough and Central Otago.

Gibbston Valley Red Shed Bendigo Single Vineyard
Central Otago Pinot Blanc ★★★★☆

The 2016 vintage (★★★★) was estate-grown and hand-picked at Bendigo, fermented with indigenous yeasts in old French barriques, and lees-aged in oak for 10 months; 90 per cent of the blend also had a softening malolactic fermentation. Pale lemon/green, it is fleshy and creamy, with very youthful, citrusy, slightly appley flavours, showing good complexity, fresh acidity and obvious potential; best drinking 2019+.

DRY $39 –V

Greenhough Hope Vineyard Nelson Pinot Blanc ★★★★☆

Based principally on Pinot Blanc vines planted at Hope in 1976, the impressive 2015 vintage (★★★★★) is a blend of Pinot Blanc (94 per cent) and Pinot Gris (6 per cent), estate-grown, hand-harvested, and fermented and matured for 16 months in seasoned French oak barriques and puncheons. Bright, light lemon/green, it is weighty, fleshy, youthful and finely poised, with concentrated, vibrant, citrusy, peachy flavours, showing excellent complexity, and a fully dry, slightly creamy finish. Best drinking mid-2018+. Certified organic.

Vintage	15
WR	6
Drink	17-20

DRY $36 –V

Kaimira Estate Brightwater Nelson Pinot Blanc ★★★★

Certified organic, the 2016 vintage (★★★★) was estate-grown and partly wood-aged. Pale lemon/green, it is weighty and fleshy, with strong, youthful, peachy flavours, showing considerable complexity, a slightly creamy texture and a very harmonious, fully dry finish. It's an age-worthy wine; drink now or cellar.

DRY $25 AV

Nevis Bluff Merrill's Block Central Otago Pinot Blanc ★★★★

The fresh, full-bodied 2015 vintage (★★★★) was grown at Pisa and fermented and matured in tanks, with no use of oak. Pale lemon/green, it is weighty, with youthful, delicate, citrusy, appley flavours, hints of pears and spices, and a dry, well-rounded finish. Still unfolding, it's a finely textured wine, likely to be at its best mid-2018+.

DRY $35 –V

Pyramid Valley Growers Collection Kerner Estate
Vineyard Marlborough Pinot Blanc   ★★★★☆

Grown in the Waihopai Valley, the 2014 vintage (★★★★) was hand-picked and fermented with indigenous yeasts in seasoned French oak puncheons. It is mouthfilling and fleshy, with strong, ripe, peachy flavours, showing considerable complexity, balanced acidity and a dry, slightly creamy finish.

DRY $32 –V

Rock Ferry Orchard Vineyard Marlborough Pinot Blanc   ★★★★

Certified organic, the 2014 vintage (★★★★☆) is a single-vineyard wine, grown at Rapaura, in the Wairau Valley, hand-picked, and fermented in tanks (88 per cent) and seasoned oak puncheons (12 per cent). Full-bodied and dryish (5 grams/litre of residual sugar), it has good weight and personality, with concentrated, vibrant, peachy, slightly spicy flavours, showing a distinct touch of complexity, moderate acidity and a well-rounded finish. Drink now or cellar.

MED/DRY $30 –V

Pinot Gris

New Zealanders' love affair with Pinot Gris shows no signs of abating, and the wines are also starting to win an international reputation. The variety is spreading like wildfire – from 130 hectares of bearing vines in 2000 to 2579 hectares in 2018 – and accounts for nearly 6.9 per cent of the total producing vineyard area. New Zealand's third most extensively planted white-wine variety, with plantings more than triple those of Riesling, Pinot Gris is trailing only Sauvignon Blanc and Chardonnay.

A mutation of Pinot Noir, Pinot Gris has skin colours ranging from blue-grey to reddish-pink, sturdy extract and a fairly subtle, spicy aroma. It is not a difficult variety to cultivate, adapting well to most soils, and ripens with fairly low acidity to high sugar levels. In Alsace, the best Pinot Gris are matured in large casks, but the wood is old, so as not to interfere with the grape's subtle flavour.

What does Pinot Gris taste like? Imagine a wine that couples the satisfying weight and roundness of Chardonnay with some of the aromatic spiciness of Gewürztraminer. A popular and versatile wine, Pinot Gris is well worth getting to know.

In terms of style and quality, however, New Zealand Pinot Gris vary widely. Many of the wines lack the enticing perfume, mouthfilling body, flavour richness and softness of the benchmark wines from Alsace. These lesser wines, typically made from heavily cropped vines, are much leaner and crisper – more in the tradition of cheap Italian Pinot Grigio.

Popular in Germany, Alsace and Italy, Pinot Gris is now playing an important role here too. Well over half of the country's plantings are concentrated in Marlborough (41 per cent) and Hawke's Bay (17 per cent), but there are also significant pockets of Pinot Gris in Gisborne, Otago, Canterbury, Nelson, Wairarapa and Auckland.

8 Ranges Tussock Ridge Central Otago Pinot Gris ★★★☆

From Tussock Ridge Vineyard, between Alexandra and Clyde, the 2015 vintage (★★★☆) was estate-grown and hand-picked. A floral, vibrantly fruity wine, it has very good depth of fresh pear, lychee and peach flavours, with finely balanced acidity and a dryish finish.

`MED/DRY $25 –V`

12,000 Miles Wairarapa Pinot Gris ★★★☆

From Gladstone Vineyard, the 2015 vintage (★★★☆) was grown in the northern Wairarapa, briefly lees-aged and handled without oak. Fresh and full-bodied, it's enjoyable young, with ripe, peachy, slightly spicy flavours, balanced acidity and a basically dry (4.7 grams/litre of residual sugar) finish.

`DRY $20 AV`

Akarua Rua Central Otago Pinot Gris ★★★☆

Estate-grown at Bannockburn and Gibbston, the 2016 vintage (★★★☆) was hand-picked and tank-fermented. Freshly scented and mouthfilling, it is vibrantly fruity, with good depth of citrusy, peachy flavours, hints of lychees and pears, a sliver of sweetness (10 grams/litre of residual sugar) and appetising acidity.

`MED/DRY $23 –V`

Ake Ake Vineyard Northland Pinot Gris ★★★☆

Hand-picked at Kerikeri, the 2015 vintage (★★★) was handled without oak and made in a medium-dry style (7 grams/litre of residual sugar). It's a fresh, medium to full-bodied wine, with finely balanced acidity and lively, peachy, slightly spicy flavours. Good, easy drinking.

`MED/DRY $25 –V`

Alexandra Wine Company alex.gold Pinot Gris ★★★

Grown in Central Otago, the 2014 vintage (★★☆) is a lively, citrusy, appley wine with a sliver of sweetness (11 grams/litre of residual sugar) and fresh, crisp acidity.

MED/DRY $17 AV

Allan Scott Marlborough Pinot Gris ★★★

Very pale pink, the easy-drinking 2016 vintage (★★★) was grown in the Wairau (mostly) and Awatere valleys, and made with a 'short period of skin contact, to extract colour and flavour'. Full-bodied, it is a smooth, off-dry style (6 grams/litre of residual sugar), with plenty of fresh, peachy, slightly spicy flavour. Enjoyable young, it's already very open and expressive.

MED/DRY $18 AV

Amisfield Central Otago Pinot Gris ★★★★

The 2016 vintage (★★★★), estate-grown and hand-picked at Pisa, in the Cromwell Basin, was mostly fermented and lees-aged in tanks; 30 per cent of the blend was fermented with indigenous yeasts in large, seasoned French oak barrels. Mouthfilling and smooth, it's a youthful wine with ripe, peachy, citrusy flavours, showing a touch of complexity, fresh acidity, a sliver of sweetness (8.2 grams/litre of residual sugar), and good richness and harmony. Best drinking 2018+.

MED/DRY $30 –V

Anchorage Family Estate Nelson Pinot Gris ★★★

The 2015 vintage (★★★) is mouthfilling and well-rounded, with a sliver of sweetness (5.8 grams/litre of residual sugar) amid its ripe, peachy, slightly spicy flavours, and hints of pears and ginger. Fresh and finely balanced, it's enjoyable young.

MED/DRY $17 AV

Ant Moore Signature Series Marlborough Pinot Gris (★★★)

The 2015 vintage (★★★) is a peachy, spicy, gingery wine, slightly Gewürztraminer-like, with fresh acidity, a sliver of sweetness, and drink-young charm.

MED/DRY $23 –V

Ara Single Estate Marlborough Pinot Gris ★★★☆

Estate-grown in the lower Waihopai Valley, the 2015 vintage (★★★★) has excellent depth of fresh pear and spice flavours, hints of peaches and honey, a gentle splash of sweetness (8 grams/litre of residual sugar) and lively acidity.

Vintage	15
WR	6
Drink	P

MED/DRY $22 AV

Archangel Central Otago Pinot Gris ★★★★

The highly attractive, fleshy 2014 vintage (★★★★) is scented and full-bodied, with strong lychee, pear and apple flavours, showing excellent freshness, delicacy and purity, and a dryish (5 grams/litre of residual sugar), well-rounded finish.

MED/DRY $25 AV

Aronui Single Vineyard Nelson Pinot Gris   ★★★☆

From Kono – also owner of the Tohu brand – the 2016 vintage (★★★☆) was estate-grown and hand-picked at Upper Moutere, and briefly lees-aged. Made in an off-dry style (5.5 grams/litre of residual sugar), it is full-bodied and vibrantly fruity, with youthful citrus-fruit and lychee flavours, hints of apples, pears and spices, and good depth.

 MED/DRY $22 AV

Ash Ridge Hawke's Bay Estate Pinot Gris   (★★★☆)

The debut 2016 vintage (★★★☆) is a medium-bodied wine, partly barrel-fermented. Attractively scented, it is vibrantly fruity, with good depth of ripe peach, pear and spice flavours, a touch of complexity, and a finely balanced, dryish (5 grams/litre of residual sugar) finish.

 MED/DRY $20 AV

Askerne Hawke's Bay Pinot Gris   ★★★☆

The 2015 vintage (★★★★) is soft and generous, in a finely textured style with mouthfilling body, concentrated, peachy flavours, gentle sweetness, and a floral, slightly honeyed and toasty bouquet.

 MED/DRY $22 AV

Astrolabe Province Marlborough Pinot Gris   ★★★★

Freshly scented, mouthfilling and drier than most New Zealand Pinot Gris, the 2016 vintage (★★★★) was grown at sites in the Wairau Valley, Awatere Valley and further south, at Kekerengu. Pale and fragrant, it shows good varietal character, with vibrant, delicate flavours of pears and lychees, a gentle spiciness, and a dry (3 grams/litre of residual sugar), persistent finish. Best drinking mid-2018+.

 DRY $23 AV

Astrolabe Valleys Kekerengu Coast Pinot Gris   ★★★★

The youthful, very lively 2016 vintage (★★★★) was grown in the Sleepers Vineyard, hand-picked and tank-fermented. Light lemon/green, it is mouthfilling, with good intensity of pear and lychee flavours, a minerally streak, and a fully dry, crisp finish. Still unfolding, it should be at its best mid-2018+.

DRY $25 AV

Ata Mara Central Otago Pinot Gris   (★★★★)

From estate-grown, 12-year-old vines in the Cromwell Basin, the 2014 vintage (★★★★) was made in an 'Alsace' style. Fragrant pear and spice aromas lead into a full-bodied wine (13.4 per cent alcohol) with strong, vibrant fruit flavours, a sliver of sweetness (6.5 grams/litre of residual sugar), gentle acidity and loads of drink-young charm.

MED/DRY $19 V+

Ata Rangi Lismore Pinot Gris   ★★★★☆

Grown in the Lismore Vineyard in Martinborough, 400 metres from the Ata Rangi winery, the 2015 vintage (★★★★☆) has a fragrant, ripe, peachy bouquet. Full-bodied, it has concentrated stone-fruit flavours, a hint of spice, a slightly oily texture and an off-dry, rich finish.

Vintage	14	13	12	11	10
WR	7	7	6	6	7
Drink	17-18	P	P	P	P

MED/DRY $28 AV

Aurum Central Otago Pinot Gris   ★★★☆

Certified organic, the 2014 vintage (★★★☆) was estate-grown and hand-picked at Lowburn, tank-fermented and lees-stirred. A mouthfilling wine, it has citrusy flavours, hints of apples, pears and spices, and a dryish (7 grams/litre of residual sugar), tightly structured finish.

Vintage	14	13	12	11	10
WR	5	6	6	6	7
Drink	17-20	17-18	P	P	P

MED/DRY $26 –V

Awatere River by Louis Vavasour Marlborough Pinot Gris   ★★★★

The 2016 vintage (★★★★) is fragrant and mouthfilling. Pale, it has fresh, youthful, pear-like flavours, with hints of peaches and spices, a slightly oily texture, and excellent depth and harmony. Made in an off-dry style (5.7 grams/litre of residual sugar), it's already drinking well.

Vintage	16	15
WR	6	7
Drink	18-21	17-20

MED/DRY $24 AV

Babich Black Label Marlborough Pinot Gris   ★★★★

Sold principally in restaurants, the 2015 vintage (★★★★) was grown in the Waihopai and Wairau valleys and mostly handled in tanks; 15 per cent of the blend spent four months in old oak. A mouthfilling, fleshy wine, it has rich, ripe peach, pear and spice flavours, a hint of almonds, and a balanced, dry (3 grams/litre of residual sugar) finish.

DRY $25 AV

Babich Marlborough Pinot Gris   ★★★★

The 2015 vintage (★★★★) was partly barrel-fermented and made in a fully dry style (1 gram/litre of residual sugar). Fleshy, with peachy, spicy, slightly gingery flavours, showing very good depth, it's a drink-now or cellaring proposition.

DRY $22 V+

Bald Hills Central Otago Pinot Gris   ★★★★

Maturing gracefully, the 2015 vintage (★★★★) was grown at Bannockburn and made in an off-dry style. Floral and fleshy, it is mouthfilling, fresh and vibrant, with strong peach, lychee, pear and spice flavours, showing good delicacy and purity, and a dryish finish (7.6 grams/litre of residual sugar). The 2016 vintage (★★★★) is scented, mouthfilling and slightly sweet (6 grams/litre of residual sugar), with vibrant pear, peach, lychee and spice flavours, balanced acidity, a slightly oily texture and good concentration. Drink now or cellar.

Vintage	16	15
WR	6	5
Drink	17-21	17-21

MED/DRY $32 –V

Beach House Ohiti Road Hawke's Bay Pinot Gris   ★★★☆

The 2016 vintage (★★★☆) is a pale lemon/green, fresh, medium-bodied wine, with very good depth of ripe, peachy, slightly spicy flavours, showing a touch of complexity, a sliver of sweetness (6 grams/litre of residual sugar), and a well-rounded finish.

MED/DRY $20 AV

Bellbird Spring Waipara Valley Block 8 Pinot Gris   ★★★★

The 2015 vintage (★★★★) is a medium style, barrel-aged for five months. Straw-hued, it has generous, peachy, slightly spicy and gingery flavours, showing good complexity, and a gently sweet, well-rounded finish. Ready.

MED $32 –V

Bellbird Spring Waipara Valley Dry Pinot Gris   ★★★★☆

Showing strong personality, the 2016 vintage (★★★★☆) is already drinking well. Fermented in old oak barrels, it is mouthfilling and fleshy, with concentrated, peachy, slightly spicy and buttery flavours, a slightly oily texture and a rich, dry finish.

DRY $32 –V

Bilancia Hawke's Bay Pinot Gris   ★★★★

Delicious now, but still maturing, the 2016 vintage (★★★★☆) is a mouthfilling, dry style (4 grams/litre of residual sugar), with generous, ripe stone-fruit flavours, a slightly creamy texture, and excellent ripeness and richness.

Vintage	16
WR	6
Drink	17-21

DRY $27 –V

Bird Gisborne Pinot Gris   (★★★☆)

The 2015 vintage (★★★☆) is a medium-bodied wine with ripe, peachy, slightly spicy flavours. Made in an off-dry style, with balanced acidity, it is fresh and lively, with good depth.

MED/DRY $20 AV

Black Barn Hawke's Bay Pinot Gris   ★★★★

Estate-grown and hand-picked at Havelock North, the 2017 vintage (★★★★) is a powerful, full-bodied and fleshy wine, aromatic, with pear and lychee flavours, dryish, fresh and strong.

MED/DRY $26 –V

Black Cottage Marlborough Pinot Gris ★★★

From Two Rivers, the 2016 vintage (★★★☆) is a gently floral, dry style, with pear, lychee and spice flavours, lively acidity, and very good freshness, delicacy and depth.

DRY $18 AV

Blackenbrook Nelson Pinot Gris ★★★★★

An emerging classic. Estate-grown and hand-picked, the 2017 vintage (★★★★) was handled in a mix of tanks (91 per cent) and old oak barrels (9 per cent). Pale, it is aromatic and softly mouthfilling, with richly varietal lychee, pear and spice flavours, showing excellent vibrancy, delicacy and depth. Made in a medium-dry style (12 grams/litre of residual sugar), it should break into full stride mid-2018+.

Vintage	17	16	15	14	13	12	11	10
WR	6	5	6	7	5	7	6	7
Drink	17-21	17-19	17-19	17-19	P	P	P	P

MED/DRY $25 V+

Bladen Marlborough Pinot Gris ★★★☆

Estate-grown and hand-picked, the 2015 vintage (★★★★) is mouthfilling, with excellent varietal character and strong, vibrant peach, pear and spice flavours. Made in an off-dry style (5.6 grams/litre of residual sugar), with fresh, balanced acidity, it's a very harmonious wine.

MED/DRY $25 –V

Boundary Vineyards Paper Lane Waipara Pinot Gris ★★★★

The 2014 vintage (★★★★) from Pernod Ricard NZ is attractively scented, with mouthfilling body and vibrant, citrusy, slightly sweet flavours, showing excellent depth and harmony.

MED/DRY $21 V+

Brancott Estate Flight Marlborough Pinot Gris ★★☆

This low-alcohol wine is harvested early and made in a slightly sweet style, with high acidity. The 2016 vintage (★★☆) is light-bodied (9 per cent alcohol), with fresh, simple, lemony, appley flavours.

MED $17 –V

Brancott Estate Hawke's Bay Pinot Gris ★★★

The 2016 vintage (★★★☆) is full-bodied and fresh, with generous pear, lychee and spice aromas and flavours. Made in a smooth, off-dry style, it's finely balanced and enjoyable young. Good value.

MED/DRY $17 AV

Brancott Estate Letter Series 'F' Marlborough Pinot Gris ★★★★☆

The 2016 vintage (★★★★☆) is delicious young. Made in a medium-dry style (12 grams/litre of residual sugar), it was estate-grown in the Brancott Vineyard, mostly hand-harvested, and fermented in a large, 10,000-litre oak cuve (85 per cent) and French oak puncheons (15 per cent). Mouthfilling and soft, it is vibrantly fruity, with an array of ripe peach, pear, lychee and spice flavours, showing excellent freshness, delicacy and depth.

MED/DRY $33 –V

Brancott Estate Living Land Series Marlborough Pinot Gris ★★★☆

Certified organic, the 2014 vintage (★★★☆) is a full-bodied, off-dry wine with good depth of fresh, citrusy, slightly peachy and spicy flavours, and a smooth, harmonious finish.

MED/DRY $20 AV

Brancott Estate Terroir Series Awatere Valley Marlborough Pinot Gris ★★★★

Attractively scented, the 2016 vintage (★★★★) is fleshy and soft, with strong stone-fruit flavours, showing a touch of complexity, gentle acidity, a slightly oily texture and a long, harmonious finish. Fine value.

MED/DRY $20 V+

Brick Bay Matakana Pinot Gris ★★★★

At its best, this estate-grown wine is weighty, rich and rounded. Hand-harvested and lees-aged, it is made in an off-dry style. The 2014 vintage (★★★☆) is medium-bodied, fresh and tightly structured, with pear, lychee and spice flavours, a hint of apricot, and crisp acidity.

MED/DRY $32 –V

Brightside New Zealand Organic Pinot Gris (★★★☆)

Certified organic, the 2016 vintage (★★★☆) was produced by Kaimira Estate, based in Nelson. Made in an off-dry style (10 grams/litre of residual sugar), it is a medium to full-bodied wine, with good varietal character and depth of vibrant pear, lychee and spice flavours.

MED/DRY $18 V+

Brightwater Vineyards Lord Rutherford Nelson Pinot Gris (★★★★☆)

The instantly attractive 2014 vintage (★★★★☆) is finely textured, with a long finish. Hand-picked and made in a medium style (28 grams/litre of residual sugar), it is fresh and lively, with concentrated, ripe peach, pear and spice flavours.

MED $30 –V

Brightwater Vineyards Nelson Pinot Gris ★★★★

The 2016 vintage (★★★★) is a fleshy, Alsace-style Pinot Gris, grown and hand-picked at Hope. Full-bodied, it is very harmonious, with peach, pear and lychee flavours, spicy notes, moderate acidity, a gentle splash of sweetness (15 grams/litre of residual sugar) and a well-rounded, lingering finish. Fine value.

Vintage	16	15	14	13	12	11	10
WR	6	7	6	6	6	6	5
Drink	17-19	17-18	17-18	P	P	P	P

 MED $20 V+

Bronte Nelson Pinot Gris ★★★☆

Rimu Grove's second-tier label. Hand-picked in the Moutere hills and mostly handled in tanks (6 per cent French oak-aged), the 2015 vintage (★★★★) is an off-dry style (11 grams/litre of residual sugar), attractively scented and mouthfilling, with vibrant, peachy, slightly spicy flavours, showing good concentration. Delicious young.

 MED/DRY $22 AV

Brookfields Robertson Hawke's Bay Pinot Gris ★★★★

Bright, light lemon/green, the 2016 vintage (★★★★) is a mouthfilling, off-dry wine (6 grams/litre of residual sugar). Full-bodied, it's an Alsace-style wine, with strong, ripe peach, lychee and spice flavours, gentle sweetness and a rich, rounded finish. The pale 2017 vintage (★★★☆) is full-bodied and slightly sweet (7 grams/litre of residual sugar), with balanced acidity and very good depth of peachy, citrusy, slightly spicy flavours.

Vintage	17	16
WR	7	7
Drink	18-20	18-20

 MED/DRY $20 V+

Cable Bay Awatere Valley Marlborough Pinot Gris ★★★★

The pale gold 2015 vintage (★★★★) is a characterful, estate-grown wine, 'pushed' for fruit ripeness, given 'lots of skin contact', and lees-aged for seven months. Full-bodied and dry, it has strong, peachy, spicy, gingery, vaguely honeyed flavours, a touch of tannins, and loads of interest and personality. Ready.

Vintage	15
WR	5
Drink	P

 DRY $23 AV

Carrick Bannockburn Central Otago Pinot Gris ★★★★☆

Certified organic, the classy 2016 vintage (★★★★★) was estate-grown and partly handled in tanks; 60 per cent of the blend was fermented with indigenous yeasts and lees-aged for six months in old French oak barrels. Fleshy and rich, it is sturdy, with strong, ripe, peachy, slightly spicy flavours, showing good complexity, and a dry (4 grams/litre of residual sugar), well-rounded, persistent finish. A distinctive, finely balanced wine with loads of personality, it's the best vintage yet.

DRY $27 AV

Catalina Sounds Marlborough Pinot Gris ★★★★

The distinctive 2015 vintage (★★★★) was estate-grown in the Waihopai Valley, hand-picked and fermented in tanks (80 per cent) and seasoned French oak puncheons (20 per cent). Made in a dry style, it is full-bodied, with concentrated, ripe peach, pear and spice flavours, oak and lees-aging notes adding a touch of complexity, and a finely balanced finish. The 2016 vintage (★★★★) is attractively scented, with mouthfilling body, strong, ripe peach and pear flavours, slightly mealy notes, and a fresh, finely textured finish.

DRY $25 AV

Cathedral Cove Hawke's Bay Pinot Gris (★★★)

Priced sharply, the 2016 vintage (★★★) is drinking well now. Light lemon/green, it is full-bodied and smooth, with a sliver of sweetness, fresh acidity and ripe, peachy, slightly spicy flavours.

MED/DRY $10 V+

Ceres Composition Central Otago Pinot Gris ★★★★

The 2014 vintage (★★★★) is a mouthfilling, fleshy Bannockburn wine with strong, ripe peach, lychee and pear flavours, gentle acidity and a slightly spicy, off-dry (9 grams/litre of residual sugar), smooth finish.

MED/DRY $28 –V

Ceres Swansong Vineyard Central Otago Pinot Gris ★★★★

From two sites at Bannockburn, the powerful, age-worthy 2015 vintage (★★★★) is sturdy (14.5 per cent alcohol), with strong, peachy, citrusy, spicy flavours and an off-dry, creamy-textured finish.

MED/DRY $28 –V

Chard Farm Sur Lie Central Otago Pinot Gris ★★★★

The 2015 vintage (★★★★☆) of this consistently enjoyable wine was hand-picked at Parkburn, in the Cromwell Basin, and fermented and lees-aged in tanks. It is attractively scented and mouthfilling, with vibrant, pure lychee, pear and spice flavours, showing excellent delicacy and richness, gentle acidity, a slightly oily texture and a dry (2 grams/litre of residual sugar), well-rounded finish. Delicious young.

DRY $27 –V

Cherry Orchard, The, Bannockburn Single Vineyard Central Otago Pinot Gris (★★★☆)

From a 1-hectare site and partly barrel-fermented, the weighty, dry 2014 vintage (★★★☆) is drinking well in 2017. Light lemon/green, it is mouthfilling, with fresh acidity woven through its citrusy, slightly minerally flavours. Good food wine.

DRY $22 AV

Church Road Hawke's Bay Pinot Gris   ★★★★

Estate-grown in Pernod Ricard NZ's relatively cool, elevated, inland site at Matapiro, this is a consistently impressive and enjoyable, weighty, Alsace-style wine, bargain-priced. Delicious from the start, the pale straw 2016 vintage (★★★★) is ripely scented and sturdy (14.5 per cent alcohol), with strong pear, lychee and spice flavours, gentle sweetness and a softly seductive finish. Fine value.

MED $20 V+

Church Road McDonald Series Hawke's Bay Pinot Gris   ★★★★★

If you like Alsace-style Pinot Gris, try the 2016 vintage (★★★★★). Full of personality, it is a fleshy, sturdy wine (14.5 per cent alcohol), grown at a cool, elevated, inland site and fermented with indigenous yeasts in old French oak cuves. Straw-hued, it is deliciously concentrated, oily-textured and well-rounded, with deep, ripe stone-fruit flavours, a vague hint of honey, gentle sweetness, soft acidity, and excellent richness, complexity and harmony.

MED $27 AV

Circuit North Canterbury Pinot Gris   (★★★★)

Full of personality, the debut 2015 vintage (★★★★) was hand-picked in the Falcon Crest Vineyard at Waipara, and mostly fermented with indigenous yeasts in old French oak puncheons; 10 per cent of the blend was co-fermented on its skins with Riesling from the same vineyard and held on its skins for seven months, before pressing. Pale straw, with a fragrant, spicy bouquet, it is rich and peachy, with excellent flavour depth, good complexity and a slightly sweet (9 grams/litre of residual sugar), faintly honeyed finish. (From Black Estate.)

MED/DRY $23 AV

Clark Estate Single Vineyard Upper Awatere Marlborough Pinot Gris   ★★★☆

The 2014 vintage (★★★) is an easy-drinking style, with fresh, ripe, peachy, slightly spicy and gingery flavours and an off-dry, smooth finish. Ready.

MED/DRY $23 –V

Clearview Haumoana Hawke's Bay Pinot Gris   ★★★

The 2015 vintage (★★★☆) is a fresh, lively, medium to full-bodied wine, hand-picked and fermented in seasoned oak barrels. Made in an off-dry style (11 grams/litre of residual sugar), it has appetising acidity and very good depth of finely balanced, ripe, peachy, slightly spicy flavours. Drink now or cellar.

MED/DRY $19 AV

Clifford Bay East Coast Pinot Gris   ★★★☆

The 2015 vintage (★★★) is a light lemon/green, fresh, medium-bodied wine, vibrantly fruity, with good depth of pear, lychee and spice flavours, slightly sweet and crisp.

MED/DRY $20 AV

Coopers Creek New Zealand Pinot Gris ★★★

The 2016 vintage (★★★) is a blend of Auckland (75 per cent) and Gisborne (25 per cent) grapes. Bright, light lemon/green, it is a full-bodied, easy-drinking wine with ripe, peachy, slightly spicy flavours, a creamy texture and lots of current-drinking appeal.

MED/DRY $18 AV

Coopers Creek SV The Pointer Marlborough Pinot Gris ★★★☆

The 2015 vintage (★★★) is a floral, medium-bodied style, enjoyable now, with lively acidity, a gentle splash of sweetness (6.7 grams/litre of residual sugar), and good freshness and flavour depth.

Vintage	14
WR	7
Drink	P

 MED/DRY $23 –V

Couper's Shed Hawke's Bay Pinot Gris ★★★★

Grown at Pernod Ricard NZ's elevated, inland Matapiro site, the 2015 vintage (★★★★) is a pale yellow, weighty (14.5 per cent alcohol), Alsace-style Pinot Gris. It has generous, peachy, slightly spicy aromas and flavours and a slightly sweet, smooth finish. Good value.

 MED/DRY $20 V+

Crab Farm Winery Hawke's Bay Pinot Gris ★★★

The 2014 vintage (★★★) is a sturdy, fleshy wine with ripe, peachy, slightly yeasty flavours and a fully dry finish. It's ready to roll.

DRY $17 AV

Crafters Union Hawke's Bay Pinot Gris (★★★☆)

A drink-now or cellaring proposition, the pale straw 2016 vintage (★★★☆) is mouthfilling and gently sweet, with very good depth of vibrant peach and pear flavours, balanced acidity, and a slightly spicy finish. (From Constellation NZ.)

Vintage	16
WR	6
Drink	17-18

 MED/DRY $22 AV

Craggy Range Te Muna Road Vineyard Martinborough Pinot Gris ★★★★

Hand-harvested at over 23 brix, the 2015 vintage (★★★★) is a full-bodied, dry style (4 grams/litre of residual sugar). Attractively scented and fleshy, with fresh, vibrant pear, lychee and spice flavours, and finely balanced acidity, it should be at its best 2018+.

 DRY $27 –V

Crossings, The, Awatere Valley Marlborough Pinot Gris ★★★☆

The 2015 vintage (★★★) is mouthfilling, with fresh, lively, peachy, spicy flavours and a finely balanced, dryish (5 grams/litre of residual sugar) finish. Enjoyable young.

Vintage	15
WR	6
Drink	P

MED/DRY $20 AV

Crossroads Milestone Series Hawke's Bay Pinot Gris ★★★☆

Fermented in tanks (92 per cent) and barrels (8 per cent), the 2014 vintage (★★★☆) is a scented, medium to full-bodied wine with peach, apricot and spice flavours, showing good depth, a touch of complexity and a finely balanced, dry (4 grams/litre of residual sugar) finish.

Vintage	15	14	13	12
WR	6	6	7	5
Drink	17-19	17-19	17-18	P

DRY $20 AV

Cypress Hawke's Bay Pinot Gris (★★★★)

The 2014 vintage (★★★★) is a dry style (3 grams/litre of residual sugar), mostly handled in tanks, but 20 per cent of the blend was barrel-fermented, with lots of lees-stirring. Grown at Bridge Pa, it is lively, with strong, ripe stone-fruit and spice flavours, a touch of complexity, and a finely textured, well-rounded finish.

DRY $26 AV

Dashwood Marlborough Pinot Gris ★★★★

The 2015 vintage (★★★★) is a tightly structured, youthful wine with good weight, fresh, strong pear, apple and spice flavours, and a finely textured, lengthy finish. Excellent value.

MED/DRY $19 V+

De Vine Dry Nelson Pinot Gris (★★★☆)

The 2015 vintage (★★★☆) offers fine value. Medium to full-bodied, it's a dryish wine with balanced acidity and fresh peach, pear and spice flavours, showing very good vigour and depth.

MED/DRY $16 V+

Devil's Staircase Central Otago Pinot Gris ★★★☆

From Rockburn, the lively 2016 vintage (★★★☆) is drinking well now. Pale lemon/green, it is mouthfilling, with good depth of vibrant pear, peach and spice flavours, a gentle splash of sweetness (14 grams/litre of residual sugar), fresh acidity, and lots of drink-young charm.

MED/DRY $25 –V

Dry River Martinborough Pinot Gris ★★★★★

From the first vintage in 1986, for many years Dry River towered over other New Zealand Pinot Gris, by virtue of its exceptional body, flavour richness and longevity. A sturdy Martinborough wine, it has peachy, spicy characters that can develop great subtlety and richness with maturity (at around five years old for top vintages, which also hold well for a decade). It is grown in the estate and nearby Craighall vineyards, where the majority of the vines are over 25 years old. To avoid any loss of varietal flavour, it is not oak-aged. Already delicious but very age-worthy, the 2016 vintage (★★★★★) is a ripely scented, mouthfilling wine with highly concentrated, peachy, slightly spicy flavours, a gentle splash of sweetness (20 grams/litre of residual sugar), moderate acidity, a slightly oily texture and a harmonious, well-rounded, lasting finish. Drink now or cellar.

Vintage	16	15	14	13	12	11	10	09	08
WR	7	7	7	6	7	7	7	7	7
Drink	17-28	17-27	17-26	17-25	17-22	17-21	17-20	17-19	17-18

MED $55 AV

Dunstan Road Central Otago Pinot Gris (★★★☆)

From a single row of vines in a small vineyard, between Clyde and Alexandra, the 2014 vintage (★★★☆) was briefly oak-aged. It is light-bodied (10.5 per cent alcohol), with strong, peachy, spicy flavours, showing a touch of complexity, plentiful sweetness (46 grams/litre of residual sugar) and a smooth finish.

MED $20 AV

Durvillea D by Astrolabe Marlborough Pinot Gris ★★★

The 2016 vintage (★★★☆) was grown at sites from the Waihopai Valley to Kekerengu. Pale lemon/green, it is fresh, full-bodied and dry (3 grams/litre of residual sugar), with ripe, delicate pear, peach and spice flavours, and a well-rounded finish. Enjoyable young, it offers good value.

DRY $15 V+

Easthope Blackhawk Hawke's Bay Dry Pinot Gris (★★★★)

Grown in the Te Awanga and Bridge Pa Triangle sub-regions, the 2015 vintage (★★★★) is an attractively scented, dry style (3 grams/litre of residual sugar). It has mouthfilling body, balanced acidity, and strong, vibrant lychee, pear and spice flavours.

DRY $25 AV

Elder, The, Martinborough Pinot Gris ★★★★☆

The 2015 vintage (★★★★) is a distinctive, youthful, single-vineyard wine, tank-fermented with indigenous yeasts and lees-aged for six months in old barriques. Mouthfilling, it has vibrant, pure lychee, pear and spice flavours, showing excellent delicacy and depth, a very subtle oak influence, and a dry, lingering finish.

Vintage	15	14	13	12	11
WR	6	7	6	7	6
Drink	17-20	17-20	17-19	17-18	P

DRY $45 –V

Elephant Hill Hawke's Bay Pinot Gris ★★★★

Finely scented, the 2016 vintage (★★★★☆) was estate-grown at Te Awanga, hand-harvested, and fermented in tanks and seasoned oak barriques. Delicious from the start, it is mouthfilling, sweet-fruited and vibrantly fruity, with strong, pure, delicate pear and lychee flavours, a very subtle seasoning of oak, a sliver of sweetness (6 grams/litre of residual sugar), balanced acidity, and plenty of personality. Drink now or cellar.

MED/DRY $26 –V

Eradus Awatere Valley Single Vineyard Marlborough Pinot Gris   ★★★☆

The attractive 2016 vintage (★★★★) is a mouthfilling, very fresh and vibrant wine, with lychee, pear and spice flavours that linger well. Made in a basically dry style, it is finely balanced and worth cellaring to mid-2018+.

DRY $19 V+

Esk Valley Hawke's Bay Pinot Gris   ★★★★

Winemaker Gordon Russell says this wine 'stylistically hints more at the fuller end of Pinot Grigio than the original Alsace model'. Fermented in tanks (70 per cent) and old oak barriques, the 2016 vintage (★★★☆) has a spicy bouquet, leading into a softly mouthfilling wine with fresh stone-fruit flavours, gently seasoned with oak, moderate acidity and a dry (3.7 grams/litre of residual sugar) finish. The 2017 vintage (★★★★) was estate-grown at Maraekakaho and mostly tank-fermented; 15 per cent was fermented in old French oak casks. Mouthfilling, it is vibrantly fruity, with fresh, pure pear and spice flavours, a gentle splash of sweetness (7.6 grams/litre of residual sugar) and good concentration.

Vintage	17
WR	6
Drink	17-20

DRY $20 V+

Fairhall Downs Single Vineyard Marlborough Pinot Gris   (★★★★☆)

Already delicious, the 2016 vintage (★★★★☆) was grown in the Brancott Valley and partly barrel-fermented. Highly fragrant, it's a dryish style (5 grams/litre of residual sugar), with concentrated, ripe peach, pear and lychee flavours, a touch of complexity, balanced acidity and strong personality. Fine value.

MED/DRY $24 V+

Fairmont Estate Pinot Gris   (★★★★)

Grown in the northern Wairarapa, the 2014 vintage (★★★★) is a full-bodied, fleshy wine, with generous, ripe, peachy flavours, showing a touch of complexity. Priced sharply.

DRY $18 V+

Falconhead Hawke's Bay Pinot Gris   (★★☆)

The 2014 vintage (★★☆) is faintly pink. Medium-bodied, it's an easy-drinking style with solid depth of peachy, slightly spicy flavours and a fresh, slightly sweet (7 grams/litre of residual sugar), smooth finish.

Vintage	14
WR	6
Drink	P

MED/DRY $16 AV

Fern Ridge Hawke's Bay Pinot Gris   (★★★)

The pale 2015 vintage (★★★) is a fresh, dryish wine with mouthfilling body and vibrant, citrusy, slightly appley and spicy flavours. It's a very easy-drinking wine, priced sharply.

MED/DRY $16 V+

Forrest Marlborough Pinot Gris ★★★☆

Enjoyable young, the 2017 vintage (★★★☆) is pale, with a freshly scented bouquet. Mouthfilling and smooth, it has vibrant pear and peach flavours, a hint of spice, good depth and a slightly sweet finish. Showing good varietal character, it's skilfully balanced for easy drinking.

 MED/DRY $22 AV

Framingham Marlborough Pinot Gris ★★★★☆

The weighty, generous 2016 vintage (★★★★☆) was hand-picked and fermented (mostly with indigenous yeasts) in tanks and old oak barrels. A distinctly 'Alsace style' Pinot Gris, it is full-bodied and vibrantly fruity, with ripe stone-fruit flavours, showing excellent depth and harmony, a slightly oily texture and an off-dry, smooth finish.

 MED/DRY $25 V+

French Peak Banks Peninsula Pinot Grigio (★★★☆)

Hand-harvested at French Farm, on the shores of Akaroa Harbour, the 2015 vintage (★★★☆) is medium-bodied and smooth. Fresh and finely balanced, it has good depth of lemony, slightly appley flavours, with hints of pears and lychees, lively acidity and a dryish (5 grams/litre of residual sugar) finish. Ready.

 MED/DRY $28 –V

Fromm La Strada Marlborough Pinot Gris ★★★★☆

Certified organic, the youthful 2016 vintage (★★★★) was partly barrel-fermented. Pale straw, it is mouthfilling, well-rounded and dryish, with ripe, peachy, slightly spicy flavours, showing excellent depth, gentle acidity, a touch of complexity, and good aging potential.

Vintage	16	15	14	13
WR	6	7	6	6
Drink	17-19	17-18	P	P

 MED/DRY $28 AV

Georges Road Selection Waipara Pinot Gris ★★★★☆

Full of personality, the 2015 vintage (★★★★★) is a powerful, rich wine, estate-grown, hand-picked and fermented with indigenous yeasts in seasoned oak barrels. Fragrant, fleshy and creamy-textured, it is full-bodied (14.5 per cent alcohol), with concentrated, ripe stone-fruit flavours, hints of ginger and spice, and good complexity. Made in a dryish style, it's very open and expressive.

 MED/DRY $24 V+

Gibbston Valley Central Otago Pinot Gris ★★★★

At its best, this wine is full of personality. The 2014 vintage (★★★★) is mouthfilling, with vibrant peach, citrus-fruit and spice flavours, showing good concentration, a sliver of sweetness (5.9 grams/litre of residual sugar), fresh acidity, and a tight, slightly creamy finish. (This label was recently replaced by the GV Collection Pinot Gris – see that wine.)

Vintage	14	13
WR	7	7
Drink	17-20	17-20

MED/DRY $28 –V

Gibbston Valley Gold River Central Otago Pinot Gris ★★★★

Delicious young, the 2015 vintage (★★★★) is mouthfilling, fresh and finely balanced. From hand-picked grapes, it has strong, lively, peachy, slightly spicy flavours, a gentle splash of sweetness (8 grams/litre of residual sugar) and appetising acidity.

MED/DRY $23 AV

Gibbston Valley GV Collection Central Otago Pinot Gris ★★★★

Hand-picked at Bendigo and Lowburn, the very age-worthy 2017 vintage (★★★★) was handled entirely in tanks and made in a dry style (4 grams/litre of residual sugar). Pale and freshly scented, it is mouthfilling and vibrant, with very youthful pear and lychee flavours, showing exellent delicacy and harmony. Best drinking 2019+.

DRY $28 –V

Gibbston Valley La Dulcinée Bendigo Single Vineyard Pinot Gris ★★★★☆

Estate-grown and hand-picked at over 350 metres above sea level, in the La Dulcinée Vineyard at Bendigo, in Central Otago, the 2016 vintage (★★★★☆) was fermented and lees-aged for a year in stainless steel barriques (85 per cent) and French acacia puncheons (15 per cent). Bright, light lemon/green, it is still very youthful, with mouthfilling body, concentrated, vibrant peach and pear flavours, showing good complexity, fresh acidity and a dryish (5 grams/litre of residual sugar), finely poised finish. Best drinking 2019+. Certified organic.

MED/DRY $39 –V

Gibson Bridge Estate Blend Marlborough Pinot Gris (★★★★)

The distinctive 2015 vintage (★★★★) was estate-grown, hand-harvested and mostly tank-fermented. Blended with barrique-fermented Gewürztraminer (12 per cent), it was all barrel-matured and finally bottled in April 2017. Gold/amber, it is weighty and slightly honeyed, with concentrated peach, apricot and spice flavours, oak complexity, a dry finish and plenty of personality. Ready.

DRY $38 –V

Gibson Bridge Reserve Marlborough Pinot Gris ★★★★☆

Invitingly scented, the 2016 vintage (★★★★☆) is an estate-grown, single-vineyard wine, hand-harvested in the Wairau Valley and fermented and lees-aged in tanks. Full-bodied and vibrantly fruity, it has fresh, pure varietal flavours of pears and lychees, showing excellent delicacy and depth, that build across the palate to a slightly spicy, dryish, long finish. Still very youthful, it should be at its best mid-2018+.

DRY $34 –V

Giesen New Zealand Pinot Gris ★★★

From vineyards in Marlborough, Hawke's Bay and Waipara, the 2016 vintage (★★★) is fresh, medium-bodied and smooth, with lively peach, pear and spice flavours, a gentle splash of sweetness (8 grams/litre of residual sugar) and balanced acidity.

Vintage	16
WR	5
Drink	P

MED/DRY $17 AV

Gladstone Vineyard Pinot Gris ★★★★

The distinctive 2016 vintage (★★★★) was grown in the northern Wairarapa and fermented and lees-aged in an even split of tanks and old French oak barrels. Pale straw, it is a fresh, medium to full-bodied wine, still unfolding, with concentrated, peachy flavours, showing a touch of complexity, gentle sweetness (23.9 grams/litre of residual sugar), balanced acidity and good potential; open mid-2018+.

MED $25 AV

Gold Star XIV Pinot Gris (★★★)

The 2014 vintage (★★★) from Pukeora Estate, in Central Hawke's Bay, was predominantly (73 per cent) barrel-fermented with indigenous yeasts; the rest was handled in tanks. It's a weighty, fully dry wine, with a touch of complexity and good depth of peachy, spicy, slightly buttery flavours. Ready.

DRY $23 –V

Goldwater Wairau Valley Pinot Gris ★★★☆

Drinking well young, the 2015 vintage (★★★☆) is ripely scented and fleshy, with generous, vaguely honeyed stone-fruit and spice flavours.

MED/DRY $22 AV

Greyrock Hawke's Bay Pinot Gris ★★★

From Sileni, the 2015 vintage (★★★) is an easy-drinking, medium-bodied style, with good depth of fresh peach, pear and spice flavours and an off-dry finish. Priced right.

MED/DRY $14 V+

Greystone Sand Dollar Waipara Pinot Gris ★★★★☆

The stylish 2016 vintage (★★★★☆) is a slightly off-dry style (6 grams/litre of residual sugar), estate-grown in the Omihi Vineyard and mostly handled in tanks; 10 per cent of the blend was fermented with indigenous yeasts in old French oak barrels. Light lemon/green, it is mouthfilling and richly varietal, with generous, ripe stone-fruit and spice flavours, a slightly oily texture and a lasting finish.

DRY $28 AV

Vintage	16	15
WR	6	7
Drink	17-24	17-22

Greystone Waipara Valley Pinot Gris ★★★★★

At its best, this is one of the finest Pinot Gris in the country. Estate-grown, it is mostly handled in tanks; a small portion of the blend (5 per cent in 2016) is fermented with indigenous yeasts in old oak barriques. The delicious 2016 vintage (★★★★★) is a richly scented, mouthfilling (13.5 per cent alcohol), distinctly Alsace-style wine, off-dry in style (10 grams/litre of residual sugar), with rich, ripe stone-fruit and spice flavours, showing good complexity, a slightly oily texture, and lovely harmony and depth. Drink now or cellar.

Vintage	16	15	14	13	12	11	10
WR	6	7	7	7	7	6	6
Drink	17-22	17-19	P	P	P	P	P

MED/DRY $25 V+

Greywacke Marlborough Pinot Gris   ★★★★★

Grown in the Brancott Valley (principally) and at Rapaura, the 2015 vintage (★★★★★) was mostly (80 per cent) fermented with indigenous yeasts in old oak barrels and wood-matured for seven months; 20 per cent of the blend was handled with cultured yeasts in tanks. A lovely young wine, showing greater complexity than most Pinot Gris, it is fleshy and vibrantly fruity, with mouthfilling body and deep, ripe peach/pear flavours, slightly sweet (10 grams/litre of residual sugar) and well-rounded. A rich, subtle, finely poised wine, it should be at its best 2018+.

Vintage	15	14	13	12	11	10
WR	6	6	6	6	5	5
Drink	17-21	17-20	17-20	17-19	P	17-18

 MED/DRY $29 V+

Grove Mill Marlborough Pinot Gris   ★★★☆

Floral, full-bodied and fleshy, the 2016 vintage (★★★★) was grown in the Wairau Valley and partly (15 per cent) barrel-fermented. It has stone-fruit flavours, showing very good ripeness and depth, and a slightly sweet, finely balanced finish.

MED/DRY $20 AV

Gunn Estate Reserve Marlborough Pinot Gris   ★★★☆

Priced sharply, the 2017 vintage (★★★☆) is a fleshy style, grown in the Southern Valleys. Mouthfilling, with a distinct splash of sweetness (13.5 grams/litre of residual sugar), it is freshly scented, with very good depth of vibrant pear and lychee flavours, and a slightly spicy finish.

Vintage	17	16
WR	5	6
Drink	17-20	17-18

 MED/DRY $17 V+

Haha Hawke's Bay Pinot Gris   ★★★☆

The 2016 vintage (★★★★) offers fine value. Grown in 'the high country of Hawke's Bay', it was fermented and lees-stirred in tanks. Freshly aromatic, it is a medium-bodied, clearly varietal wine with vibrant peach, pear and spice flavours, strong, off-dry (8 grams/litre of residual sugar) and finely balanced for early enjoyment.

MED/DRY $16 V+

Hans Herzog Marlborough Pinot Gris   ★★★★☆

Prepare for something different! Estate-grown on the north side of the Wairau Valley, the 2016 vintage (★★★★★) is a thought-provoking wine. Apricot-coloured, from long skin contact with the juice, it is mouthfilling, sweet-fruited and dry, with fresh, concentrated peach, apricot and spice flavours, hints of watermelon and strawberry, a gentle touch of tannin, an oily richness and loads of personality. Best drinking 2018+. Certified organic.

DRY $39 –V

Harwood Hall Marlborough Pinot Gris ★★★

The 2014 vintage (★★★☆) was blended from Awatere Valley (90 per cent) and Rarangi (10 per cent) fruit, and mostly handled in tanks; 10 per cent was barrel-fermented. It's a fleshy, full-bodied style with very good depth of lemon, apple and pear flavours, balanced acidity, and a dryish, slightly nutty finish. Enjoyable young.

 MED/DRY $19 AV

Hawkshead Central Otago Pinot Gris ★★★★

Estate-grown and hand-picked at Gibbston, the 2014 vintage (★★★★) is fully dry (2 grams/litre of residual sugar). Mouthfilling and smooth, it has strong, ripe peach/pear flavours, gentle acidity, a slightly creamy texture and a floral bouquet.

Vintage	14	13	12
WR	7	7	5
Drink	P	P	P

 DRY $26 –V

Hills & Rivers Hawke's Bay Pinot Gris (★★★☆)

The 2015 vintage (★★★☆) is a top buy. Pale pink, with a fragrant bouquet of pears and spices, it has very good body, ripeness and flavour depth, in an off-dry (6 grams/litre of residual sugar) style, delicious young. (From Ash Ridge.)

 MED/DRY $14 V+

Huia Marlborough Pinot Gris ★★★★

Certified organic, the powerful 2016 vintage (★★★★☆) is mouthfilling and fleshy, with rich pear, peach and spice flavours, slightly sweet (6 grams/litre of residual sugar) and well-rounded. A distinctly Alsace-style wine, it's already delicious.

MED/DRY $28 –V

Hunter's Marlborough Pinot Gris ★★★★

A consistently good buy. The 2016 vintage (★★★★) was mostly handled in tanks, but a small part of the blend was fermented with indigenous yeasts in seasoned French oak casks. Aromatic and fleshy, it is sturdy (14.5 per cent alcohol), with strong, peachy, spicy flavours, a vague hint of honey, a harmonious, dry finish (3 grams/litre of residual sugar) and plenty of personality. Drink now or cellar. The 2017 vintage (★★★☆) was grown at Rapaura and Omaka and partly barrel-fermented.

 DRY $21 V+

Hyperion Phoebe Matakana Pinot Gris (★★★★)

The 2014 vintage (★★★★) is a sturdy, dry style, with fresh, strong, citrusy, slightly spicy flavours, a slightly oily texture and a lingering finish.

DRY $27 –V

Invivo Marlborough Pinot Gris   ★★★☆

The 2016 vintage (★★★☆) is full-bodied and fresh, with clear-cut varietal character. A dryish wine (5.8 grams/litre of residual sugar), it has pear, lychee and spice flavours, showing good depth, and a smooth finish. The 2017 vintage (★★★) is mouthfilling, with a slightly earthy bouquet, pear, peach and spice flavours, a sliver of sweetness (5.5 grams/litre of residual sugar), fresh acidity and youthful vigour.

MED/DRY $19 V+

Johanneshof Marlborough Pinot Gris   ★★★★

Drinking well young, the 2016 vintage (★★★★) is a faintly pink, full-bodied wine, hand-picked and handled entirely in tanks. Vibrantly fruity, with pear, lychee and spice flavours, showing good delicacy, it has hints of peach and apricot, a sliver of sweetness (10 grams/litre of residual sugar), and excellent freshness and depth.

MED/DRY $28 –V

Johner Estate Wairarapa Pinot Gris   ★★★★

The 2016 vintage (★★★★) was fully fermented in seasoned oak barrels and made in a dry style (4 grams/litre of residual sugar). It is vibrantly fruity, with strong pear, lychee and spice flavours, showing very good delicacy and harmony, and a touch of complexity. Well worth cellaring, it should be at its best 2018+.

Vintage	16	15	14	13	12
WR	6	6	6	6	6
Drink	17-21	17-20	P	P	P

DRY $24 AV

Jules Taylor Marlborough Pinot Gris   ★★★★

Grown in the Awatere and Wairau valleys, the 2016 vintage (★★★★) was made with some use of hand-picking, indigenous yeasts and old barrel fermentation. Produced in a dry style (2.4 grams/litre of residual sugar), it is mouthfilling and vibrantly fruity, with finely poised, peachy, slightly spicy flavours, a creamy texture, and very good freshness, delicacy and depth. Best drinking 2018+.

Vintage	16
WR	6
Drink	17-19

DRY $24 AV

Junction Pastime Central Hawke's Bay Pinot Gris   (★★★☆)

Ripely scented, the 2015 vintage (★★★☆) has mouthfilling body and very good depth of fresh, slightly sweet, peachy, spicy flavours.

MED/DRY $22 AV

Kaimira Estate Brightwater Pinot Gris   ★★★☆

Certified organic, the 2015 vintage (★★★★) is fleshy and dry (4.8 grams/litre of residual sugar), with ripe peach, pear and spice flavours, finely balanced and generous.

DRY $22 AV

Kainui Road Bay of Islands Pinot Gris ★★★

The 2015 vintage (★★★) was estate-grown and hand-picked at Kerikeri. Faintly pink, it's an easy-drinking wine with fresh, peachy, spicy flavours and an off-dry finish.

MED/DRY $25 –V

Kakapo Central Otago Pinot Gris (★★★★)

The 2015 vintage (★★★★) from distributor Sanz Global is full-bodied and vibrantly fruity. Mouthfilling, it has fresh, strong pear, lychee and spice flavours and a dryish, very harmonious finish.

MED/DRY $24 AV

Kapiro Vineyard Kerikeri Pinot Gris ★★★☆

Hand-harvested at Kerikeri, in Northland, the 2015 vintage (★★★☆) is a mouthfilling wine with fresh, ripe peach, lychee and spice flavours, a gentle splash of sweetness (13 grams/litre of residual sugar), balanced acidity and very good depth.

Vintage	14	13	12	11	10
WR	7	7	6	5	7
Drink	P	P	P	P	P

MED/DRY $25 –V

Kate Radburnd Sun Kissed Hawke's Bay Pinot Gris ★★☆

From Pask, the 2014 vintage (★★☆) was grown in the Gimblett Gravels. It's a light-bodied, off-dry wine with decent depth of pear and spice flavours.

MED/DRY $18 –V

Kim Crawford Marlborough Pinot Gris ★★★☆

Enjoyable young, the 2017 vintage (★★★☆) is mouthfilling and vibrantly fruity, with very good depth of ripe peach, pear and lychee flavours, a hint of spice, and a dry (3.3 grams/litre of residual sugar), very harmonious finish. Good value.

Vintage	16
WR	4
Drink	17-20

DRY $17 V+

Kina Cliffs Nelson Pinot Gris ★★★★

Grown in a coastal vineyard, the 2015 vintage (★★★☆) was hand-picked and mostly handled in tanks; 10 per cent was barrel-fermented. A medium to full-bodied wine, it has vibrant pear, nectarine and spice flavours, fresh acidity and a finely balanced, dryish finish.

MED/DRY $22 V+

Kumeu River Pinot Gris ★★★★

This consistently attractive wine is grown at Kumeu, in West Auckland, aged on its yeast lees, but not oak-matured. Made in a medium-dry style, it is typically floral and weighty, with a slightly oily texture, finely balanced acidity and peach, pear and spice aromas and flavours, vibrant and rich. Light lemon/green, the 2016 vintage (★★★★) is freshly scented and mouthfilling, with strong, vibrant, youthful pear, citrus-fruit and spice flavours, lively acidity and a touch of complexity. Best drinking mid-2018+.

Vintage	16	15	14	13	12	11	10
WR	6	7	7	7	5	5	7
Drink	17-20	17-19	17-18	P	P	P	P

MED/DRY $25 AV

Kumeu Village Pinot Gris ★★★☆

From Kumeu River, the 2014 vintage (★★★☆) was hand-picked, fermented in tanks with indigenous yeasts and matured on its yeast lees. An ideal, all-purpose wine, it is full-bodied, with vibrant peach, pear and slight spice flavours, showing very good depth, balanced acidity, and a dryish finish. Bargain-priced.

MED/DRY $15 V+

Lake Chalice Marlborough Pinot Gris ★★★☆

The 2016 vintage (★★★☆) is a fresh, lively wine, grown in the Wairau and Waihopai valleys, and made with some use of barrel fermentation and lees-aging. Clearly varietal, it shows very good vigour and depth of pear, lychee and spice flavours, with a dryish (4.8 grams/litre of residual sugar), finely balanced finish.

DRY $20 AV

Lake Chalice The Raptor Marlborough Pinot Gris (★★★☆)

Estate-grown in the Eyrie Vineyard, in the Southern Valleys, the 2016 vintage (★★★☆) is a fresh, full-bodied wine, with slightly creamy notes and vibrant, peachy, spicy, dryish flavours (6 grams/litre of residual sugar) that linger well.

MED/DRY $25 –V

Lake Hayes Central Otago Pinot Gris ★★★☆

From Amisfield, the 2016 vintage (★★★☆) is freshly scented and mouthfilling, with very good depth of peach, lychee and spice flavours, and a slightly sweet (10 grams/litre of residual sugar), smooth finish. Enjoyable from the start.

MED/DRY $20 AV

Lawson's Dry Hills Marlborough Pinot Gris ★★★★

Mostly estate-grown in the Waihopai Valley, the 2016 vintage (★★★★) was principally handled in tanks, but 10 per cent of the blend was fermented with indigenous yeasts in seasoned French oak barrels. Pale straw, it is freshly scented and mouthfilling, with strong, vibrant pear, lychee and spice flavours, hints of ginger and peach, a touch of complexity, and a dryish (6.8 grams/litre of residual sugar) finish. Best drinking mid-2018+.

Vintage	16	15	14	13	12	11	10
WR	7	7	7	7	7	6	7
Drink	17-20	17-20	P	P	P	P	P

MED/DRY $25 AV

Lawson's Dry Hills The Pioneer Marlborough Pinot Gris ★★★★☆

Late-picked, the 2015 vintage (★★★★☆) was fermented with indigenous yeasts in old French oak casks. Light lemon/green, it is scented and slightly honeyed, with mouthfilling body and an array of peach, pear, spice, lychee and honey flavours. An off-dry style (14 grams/litre of residual sugar), with good complexity, it should be at its best mid-2018+.

Vintage	15
WR	7
Drink	17-20

MED/DRY $30 –V

Left Field Hawke's Bay Pinot Gris ★★★☆

The easy-drinking 2016 vintage (★★★☆) was fermented in tanks and stainless steel barrels. Medium-bodied, it has vibrant pear and spice flavours, fractional sweetness (5.5 grams/litre of residual sugar) and lots of drink-young appeal. The 2017 vintage (★★★☆) is a very finely balanced, medium-bodied wine with fresh, lively pear/spice flavours, a sliver of sweetness (5 grams/litre of residual sugar), and plenty of drink-young charm. (From Te Awa.)

Vintage	17	16
WR	5	5
Drink	17-19	17-19

MED/DRY $18 V+

Lime Rock Central Hawke's Bay Pinot Gris ★★★★

Estate-grown near Waipawa, the pale lemon/green 2015 vintage (★★★★) was fermented in tanks and old oak barriques. Attractively scented, with pear-like aromas, it is mouthfilling, with strongly varietal pear, lychee and spice flavours, showing very good delicacy and freshness, and a dryish finish. Maturing very gracefully, the 2014 vintage (★★★★) is still lively, with fresh, delicate pear, lychee and spice flavours, appetising acidity, and very good depth and harmony.

MED/DRY $24 AV

Linden Estate Hawke's Bay Pinot Gris ★★★☆

The 2015 vintage (★★★☆) was grown at Te Awanga. Pale straw, it's a medium-dry style (13 grams/litre of residual sugar), with good body and depth of peachy, spicy, slightly gingery flavours. Enjoyable young.

MED/DRY $20 AV

Luminary, The, Wairarapa Pinot Gris (★★★☆)

From Palliser Estate, the 2016 vintage (★★★☆) is a medium to full-bodied wine, enjoyable young. Fresh and smooth, it has good depth of finely balanced, peachy, slightly spicy flavours, slightly sweet and smooth. Fine value.

MED/DRY $17 V+

Lynfer Estate Wairarapa Pinot Gris ★★★★

Grown at Gladstone, the 2014 vintage (★★★★) is mouthfilling, with good intensity of ripe, peachy, slightly spicy flavours, hints of lychees and pears, a touch of complexity, and a dry (3 grams/litre of residual sugar), slightly honeyed finish.

DRY $21 V+

Mahana Blood Moon Pinot Gris   (★★★★)

Certified organic, the 2014 vintage (★★★★) was hand-picked in Nelson from estate-grown vines and the nearby Tibbs Vineyard. Orange-hued, it was fermented with indigenous yeasts on its skins for four weeks, then matured in old oak barriques for a year, followed by another year of lees-aging in tanks, before bottling. Full-bodied, it has strong, spicy, peachy flavours, showing good complexity, and a firm, dry finish.

Mahi Marlborough Pinot Gris   ★★★★

The 2016 vintage (★★★★) is a single-vineyard wine, hand-picked near Ward, in the Awatere Valley, and mostly handled in tanks; 10 per cent of the blend was barrel-fermented. Mouthfilling and fleshy, with a touch of complexity, it is vibrantly fruity, with moderate acidity and generous, ripe peach, pear and spice flavours, dry (2 grams/litre of residual sugar) and smooth.

Vintage	17	16	15	14
WR	6	6	NM	6
Drink	17-21	17-20	NM	17-20

DRY $22 V+

Mahi Ward Farm Marlborough Pinot Gris   (★★★★☆)

The 2015 vintage (★★★★☆) is a single-vineyard wine, grown near Ward, in the Awatere Valley. Hand-picked, it was fermented with indigenous yeasts in French oak barriques and matured on its yeast lees in oak for over a year. Light lemon/green, it is a mouthfilling, dry style (3 grams/litre of residual sugar), in a 'serious', slightly Chardonnay-like style. Showing plenty of personality, it is finely textured, with strong stone-fruit and spice flavours, a hint of toasty oak, and good complexity.

Vintage	15
WR	7
Drink	17-21

DRY $35 –V

Main Divide Pokiri Reserve North Canterbury Late Picked Pinot Gris   ★★★★☆

Currently on sale, the 2014 vintage (★★★★) is gold/amber, with a strong botrytis influence. Full-bodied, with a fragrant bouquet of honey and spice, it is sweetish (76 grams/litre of residual sugar), with concentrated, apricot-like flavours, showing bottle-aged complexity. Full of personality, it's drinking well now.

Vintage	14
WR	5
Drink	17-22

SW $25 V+

Main Divide Waipara Valley Pinot Gris   ★★★★

From Pegasus Bay, this is consistently a great buy. The 2015 vintage (★★★★) is drinking well now. Bright, light yellow/green, it has a gently honeyed bouquet, leading into a full-bodied wine with concentrated, peachy, spicy flavours, slightly sweet (9 grams/litre of residual sugar) and crisp. Revealing a clear botrytis influence, it's already very open and expressive.

Vintage	15	14	13	12	11	10
WR	7	7	5	7	6	6
Drink	17-22	17-20	17-19	17-18	17-18	P

Man O' War Exiled Pinot Gris ★★★★

The 2016 vintage (★★★☆) was grown on Waiheke and Ponui islands, and 20 per cent of the blend was handled in seasoned French oak casks. Pale straw, it is medium-bodied and gently sweet (28 grams/litre of residual sugar), with vibrant peach, pear and ginger flavours, fresh acidity, and very good drive and depth.

Vintage	16	15
WR	7	6
Drink	17-22	17-19

MED $34 –V

Man O' War Paradise Pinot Gris (★★★★)

The 2016 vintage (★★★★) was grown on Ponui Island, off the eastern end of Waiheke Island, and made in a medium style (15 grams/litre of residual sugar). Pale lemon/green, it is fresh and light-bodied (10.5 per cent alcohol), with strong pear and lychee flavours, hints of peaches and spices, and obvious potential. Best drinking 2018+.

Vintage	16
WR	6
Drink	17-21

MED $29 –V

Maori Point Central Otago Pinot Gris ★★★☆

A single-vineyard wine, grown in the Cromwell Basin, the 2015 vintage (★★★☆) was fermented in old oak casks. An easy-drinking style, it is medium-bodied, with good depth of fresh, citrusy, peachy flavours, hints of ginger and spice, a sliver of sweetness (7.8 grams/litre of residual sugar), and an appetisingly crisp finish.

MED/DRY $24 –V

Map Maker Marlborough Pinot Gris ★★★★

From Staete Landt, the easy-drinking 2015 vintage (★★★☆) was estate-grown at Rapaura, in the Wairau Valley, and part of the blend was fermented in old French oak puncheons. Faintly pink, with a fresh, spicy bouquet, it is mouthfilling and smooth, with good depth of ripe, peachy, spicy flavours, showing a touch of complexity, and a dry finish.

DRY $21 V+

Margrain Martinborough Pinot Gris ★★★☆

The 2015 vintage (★★★☆) is a bone-dry style, mostly lees-aged for 10 months in tanks; a small percentage of the blend was fermented in old barrels. Bright, light lemon/green, it is mouthfilling, with ripe, peachy, gently spicy flavours, slightly toasty, bottle-aged notes emerging, and very good depth.

Vintage	15	14	13
WR	7	6	5
Drink	17-27	17-26	17-20

DRY $26 –V

Marsden Bay of Islands Pinot Gris ★★★★

In favourable seasons, this Kerikeri, Northland winery produces an impressive Pinot Gris. The 2015 vintage (★★★★) is mouthfilling, fresh and generous, with a gently spicy bouquet. Showing good varietal character, it has vibrant, peachy, citrusy, spicy flavours, a sliver of sweetness (8 grams/litre of residual sugar), balanced acidity, and good concentration.

Vintage	15	14	13
WR	6	5	6
Drink	17-18	P	P

 MED/DRY $25 AV

Martinborough Vineyard Te Tera Martinborough Pinot Gris ★★★☆

Partly barrel-fermented, the 2016 vintage (★★★☆) is attractively scented, with good weight, ripe peach, pear and spice flavours, a sliver of sweetness, and very good vibrancy and depth.

 MED/DRY $22 AV

Matahiwi Estate Wairarapa Pinot Gris ★★★

The 2015 vintage (★★★) is an off-dry style, full-bodied, with a slightly minerally streak and good depth of peachy, spicy flavours.

MED/DRY $22 –V

Matakana Estate Marlborough Pinot Gris (★★★☆)

A fresh, medium-bodied style, the 2015 vintage (★★★☆) has pale straw colour. Vibrantly fruity, it has good depth of distinctly peachy, slightly spicy and buttery flavours, fresh acidity and a dry finish.

 DRY $22 AV

Matawhero Gisborne Pinot Gris ★★★☆

The 2016 vintage (★★★☆) is full-bodied, with generous, pear-like flavours, a gentle splash of sweetness (11.8 grams/litre of residual sugar) and a slightly creamy finish. Enjoyable from the start, the 2017 vintage (★★★☆) is scented and mouthfilling, with fresh, ripe, peachy flavours and a slightly sweet (13 grams/litre of residual sugar) finish.

 MED/DRY $23 –V

Maude Central Otago Pinot Gris ★★★★

Grown at several sites – including Mount Maude Vineyard at Wanaka – the youthful 2016 vintage (★★★★) was fermented in tanks (60 per cent) and old oak barriques (40 per cent). A fleshy, dryish wine (5.2 grams/litre of residual sugar), it has good intensity of vibrant pear, peach and spice flavours, fresh acidity, a touch of complexity and obvious potential. Best drinking 2018+.

 MED/DRY $25 AV

Maui Marlborough Pinot Gris (★★★☆)

The fine-value 2016 vintage (★★★☆) was estate-grown in the upper Wairau Valley. Mouthfilling and fleshy, with very good depth of fresh peachy, spicy, slightly gingery flavours, it's drinking well in its youth. (From Tiki.)

MED/DRY $19 V+

Milcrest Estate Nelson Pinot Gris ★★★

The 2014 vintage (★★★☆) was grown at Hope and mostly handled in tanks; 4 per cent of the blend was French oak-aged. It is mouthfilling, with very good depth of ripe, peachy, slightly appley and spicy flavours, a gentle splash of sweetness (14 grams/litre of residual sugar) and balanced acidity.

MED/DRY $24 –V

Mill Road Hawke's Bay Pinot Gris (★★)

Priced right, the 2014 vintage (★★) is a pale, medium-bodied wine with pleasant, citrusy, appley flavours and an off-dry finish. Ready.

MED/DRY $10 AV

Mills Reef Estate Hawke's Bay Pinot Gris ★★★

The 2015 vintage (★★★☆) is a medium to full-bodied, finely balanced wine, fresh and vibrantly fruity, with citrusy, peachy, slightly spicy flavours, showing very good depth. It's ready to roll.

DRY $18 AV

Mills Reef Reserve Hawke's Bay Pinot Gris ★★★★

The 2016 vintage (★★★★), a single-vineyard wine grown at Maraekakaho, was tank-fermented and briefly lees-aged. Ripely scented, it is mouthfilling, with strong, peachy, spicy flavours, very gentle acidity and a fully dry (1 gram/litre of residual sugar), seductively smooth finish. Enjoyable from the start.

DRY $25 AV

Misha's Vineyard Dress Circle Central Otago Pinot Gris ★★★★★

The 2016 vintage (★★★★☆) was estate-grown and hand-harvested at 23.5 to 24.4 brix at Bendigo. It was mostly handled in tanks, but 40 per cent of the blend was fermented with indigenous yeasts in old French oak barrels. Made in an off-dry style (7 grams/litre of residual sugar), it is ripely scented, fleshy and strongly varietal, with mouthfilling body and fresh, youthful peach, pear, lychee and spice flavours, showing excellent delicacy, depth, complexity and harmony. Best drinking mid-2018+.

Vintage	16	15	14	13	12	11	10
WR	6	7	6	6	7	6	6
Drink	17-23	17-23	17-22	17-21	17-20	17-19	17-18

MED/DRY $28 V+

Mission Hawke's Bay Pinot Gris ★★★

The Mission has long been a standard-bearer for Pinot Gris. The 2015 vintage (★★★☆) is full-bodied, with very good depth of ripe, peachy, spicy flavours, fresh acidity and a smooth, dryish (5 grams/litre of residual sugar) finish.

MED/DRY $18 AV

Mission Marlborough Pinot Gris (★★★)

The light lemon/green 2016 vintage (★★★) is a full-bodied wine, with good depth of fresh lemon and pear flavours, hints of ginger and spices, and an off-dry finish.

MED/DRY $18 AV

Mission Pinot Gris Lighter in Alcohol ★★☆

The light lemon/green 2016 vintage (★★☆) is not labelled by region, but is mostly from grapes estate-grown and hand-harvested early in the vintage at Taradale, in Hawke's Bay. Stop-fermented with low alcohol (10 per cent), it is an off-dry style (8 grams/litre of residual sugar), light-bodied, with fresh, crisp, lemony flavours.

MED/DRY $16 AV

Mission Vineyard Selection Marlborough Pinot Gris ★★★☆

Estate-grown in the Awatere Valley, the 2016 vintage (★★★☆) has citrusy, slightly sweet flavours, balanced by appetising acidity, and very good vibrancy and depth.

MED/DRY $20 AV

Momo Marlborough Pinot Gris ★★★★

From Seresin, the organically certified 2014 vintage (★★★★☆) is a wonderful buy. Estate-grown, it was hand-harvested and fermented with indigenous yeasts in a mix of tanks and old French oak barriques. A distinctly 'Alsace-style' Pinot Gris, it is full-bodied, with a sliver of sweetness and strong, ripe stone-fruit and spice flavours. A very harmonious wine, it has a slightly oily texture, complexity and excellent richness.

MED/DRY $23 AV

Montana Festival Block Waipara Pinot Gris ★★★☆

The 2014 vintage (★★★☆) is mouthfilling, with generous, ripe, citrusy, peachy flavours, slightly sweet and smooth. Enjoyable from the start.

MED/DRY $20 AV

Montana Reserve Hawke's Bay Pinot Gris (★★★☆)

Offering good value, the 2016 vintage (★★★☆) is ripely scented, weighty (14.5 per cent alcohol) and smooth. Fleshy and slightly sweet, it is clearly varietal, with satisfying depth of fresh, ripe stone-fruit and pear flavours, a slightly creamy texture and good harmony. Enjoyable young.

MED/DRY $17 V+

Montana Winemakers' Series Hawke's Bay Pinot Gris ★★★

The 2016 vintage (★★★) is mouthfilling, vibrantly fruity and smooth, with fresh pear, lychee and spice flavours, skilfully balanced for early drinking.

MED/DRY $15 V+

Morepork Vineyard Northland Pinot Gris ★★★★

Estate-grown and hand-harvested at a very small, single-variety vineyard in Kerikeri, the 2017 vintage (★★★★) is delicious from the start. Attractively scented, it is full-bodied and gently sweet (5 grams/litre of residual sugar), with balanced acidity and vibrant pear and lychee flavours, showing very good varietal character and depth. Best drinking mid-2018+.

Vintage	17
WR	7
Drink	17-18

MED/DRY $24 AV

Mount Brown Estates Waipara Valley Pinot Gris ★★★☆

Priced sharply, the 2016 vintage (★★★☆) is a strongly varietal wine. Full-bodied, with plenty of fresh, gently sweet (8 grams/litre of residual sugar), peachy, slightly spicy and gingery flavour, it's drinking well in its youth.

Vintage	16	15
WR	6	6
Drink	17-21	17-20

MED/DRY $16 V+

Mount Brown Grand Reserve Waipara Pinot Gris ★★★★☆

The 2016 vintage (★★★★☆) is an Alsace-style Pinot Gris, already delicious. Full-bodied, rich, ripe and rounded, it has concentrated stone-fruit and spice flavours, a sliver of sweetness, vague hints of honey, and excellent depth and harmony.

Vintage	15
WR	7
Drink	17-22

MED/DRY $23 V+

Mount Riley Marlborough Pinot Gris ★★★★

Offering excellent value, the 2016 vintage (★★★★) was grown in the Wairau and Awatere valleys and mostly handled in tanks; 10 per cent of the blend was barrel-fermented. It's a fresh, weighty, finely poised wine, with very good depth of vibrant, strongly varietal pear, lychee and spice flavours, and a dryish (9 grams/litre of residual sugar) finish.

Vintage	16	15	14
WR	6	7	6
Drink	17-19	17-18	P

MED/DRY $18 V+

Mount Vernon Marlborough Pinot Gris ★★★

The 2015 vintage (★★★) is a fresh, medium to full-bodied wine with good depth of ripe, peachy, slightly spicy and gingery flavours, and a dryish (5 grams/litre of residual sugar) finish. (From Lawson's Dry Hills.)

MED/DRY $19 AV

Moutere Hills Nelson Pinot Gris   ★★★★

Estate-grown and hand-picked at Upper Moutere, the 2016 vintage (★★★☆) is a dry style
(4 grams/litre of residual sugar). Medium-bodied, it has fresh peach, pear and spice flavours,
a touch of barrel-ferment complexity (5 per cent of the blend), and good vigour and depth.

DRY $23 AV

Mt Beautiful North Canterbury Pinot Gris   ★★★★

The 2015 vintage (★★★★) was estate-grown at Cheviot and handled in tanks (90 per cent)
and old oak casks (10 per cent). Light lemon/green, it is sturdy (14.5 per cent alcohol), fleshy
and rounded, with generous, ripe, peachy, slightly spicy flavours and a fully dry, creamy-smooth
finish.

Vintage	15	14
WR	5	6
Drink	17-19	17-18

DRY $27 –V

Mt Difficulty Bannockburn Pinot Gris   ★★★★

Grown and hand-picked at Bannockburn, in Central Otago, and lees-aged in tanks, the 2016
vintage (★★★★☆) is a vibrant, full-bodied wine (14.5 per cent alcohol), attractively scented,
with concentrated, ripe, peachy flavours, a vague hint of sweetness (5 grams/litre of residual
sugar), finely balanced acidity, and loads of drink-young appeal. Already delicious, it should
break into full stride 2018+.

MED/DRY $27 –V

Mud House Marlborough Pinot Gris   ★★★★

The 2015 vintage (★★★★) is mouthfilling and vibrantly fruity, with a fragrant bouquet, good
intensity of ripe, peachy, spicy flavours, and an off-dry, smooth finish. Delicious young.

MED/DRY $18 V+

Mud House Single Vineyard Home Block Waipara Valley Pinot Gris   ★★★★

The 2014 vintage (★★★★) was partly barrel-fermented and made in a dry style (4 grams/
litre of residual sugar). Mouthfilling, it is vibrantly fruity, with strong yet delicate flavours of
lychees, pears and spices, hints of peaches and nectarines, a touch of complexity, and excellent
freshness and length.

DRY $24 AV

Mud House Sub Regional Series Grovetown Marlborough Pinot Gris   (★★★★)

Attractively scented, the debut 2016 vintage (★★★★) is a full-bodied wine, with strong,
youthful pear, lychee and spice flavours, showing clear-cut varietal character, and hints of
peaches and ginger. An off-dry style with gentle acidity, it should be at its best 2018+.

MED/DRY $20 V+

Nautilus Marlborough Pinot Gris   ★★★★☆

The delicious 2016 vintage (★★★★☆) is a full-bodied, dry style (4 grams/litre of residual
sugar), grown mostly in the Awatere Valley, hand-picked, and mostly tank-fermented (8 per
cent of the blend was fermented in old oak casks). Light lemon/green, with a fresh, attractive

bouquet, it is mouthfilling, vibrantly fruity and smooth, with strongly varietal, pear, peach, lychee and spice flavours, showing a distinct touch of complexity, and a rich, very harmonious finish.

Vintage	16	15	14	13	12	11	10
WR	7	7	7	7	7	6	7
Drink	17-20	17-19	P	P	P	P	P

DRY $29 AV

Neudorf Maggie's Block Nelson Pinot Gris ★★★★

The 2015 vintage (★★★★) was grown in the Balquidder Vineyard, at Brightwater, on the Waimea Plains, hand-picked, and fermented in tanks (79 per cent) and old oak puncheons (21 per cent). Made in an off-dry style (7 grams/litre of residual sugar), it is freshly scented and mouthfilling, with citrusy, peachy, slightly spicy flavours, showing a touch of complexity, and very good vigour, harmony and depth.

Vintage	15	14	13	12	11	10
WR	6	6	6	6	6	6
Drink	17-20	17-19	17-18	17-18	P	P

MED/DRY $25 AV

Neudorf Moutere Pinot Gris ★★★★★

The youthful 2016 vintage (★★★★☆) was hand-picked from mature vines in the Home Vineyard and fermented with indigenous yeasts in tanks (83 per cent) and old French oak puncheons (17 per cent). An off-dry style (5.5 grams/litre of residual sugar), it is a pale lemon/green, full-bodied wine, vibrantly fruity, with pear, citrus-fruit and peach flavours, showing excellent delicacy, vigour and depth. A finely poised wine, it should break into full stride mid-2018+.

Vintage	16	15	14	13	12
WR	6	7	6	7	6
Drink	17-21	17-20	17-19	17-18	17-18

MED/DRY $29 V+

Nevis Bluff Central Otago Pinot Gris ★★★★

Delicious now, the 2014 vintage (★★★★) was estate-grown at Pisa, in the Cromwell Basin, and handled entirely in tanks. Light lemon/green, it is fleshy and well-rounded, with strong, vibrant pear, lychee, peach and spice flavours, and a fully dry, smooth finish.

DRY $33 –V

Nevis Bluff Oak Aged Central Otago Pinot Gris ★★★★☆

The distinctive 2014 vintage (★★★★☆) was hand-harvested at Pisa, in the Cromwell Basin, and fermented and matured for nine months in seasoned oak casks. Bright, light lemon/green, it is weighty and generous, with concentrated, ripe, peachy flavours, a subtle seasoning of oak, good complexity and a smooth, fully dry finish. It's still unfolding; best drinking mid-2018+.

DRY $35 –V

Nevis Bluff Vendanges Tardives Central Otago Pinot Gris   (★★★★☆)

The 2014 vintage (★★★★☆) is a floral, gently sweet wine (55 grams/litre of residual sugar) picked at Pisa, in the Cromwell Basin, six weeks after the main harvest. Bright, light lemon/green, it is weighty, with vibrant, peachy, spicy flavours, hints of pears and ginger, a slightly oily texture, and excellent richness and roundness.

MED $35 (500ML) –V

Ngatarawa Stables Reserve Hawke's Bay Pinot Gris   (★★★☆)

The 2015 vintage (★★★☆) is weighty and finely textured, with good depth of vibrant peach, pear and spice flavours, and a fully dry finish. Enjoyable from the start.

Vintage	15
WR	7
Drink	P

DRY $20 AV

Nikau Point Reserve Marlborough Pinot Gris   (★★☆)

Priced right, the 2014 vintage (★★☆) is a fresh, medium-bodied wine, with peachy, slightly gingery and spicy flavours, and a slightly sweet finish. It's enjoyable now.

MED/DRY $14 AV

Nikau Point Select Hawke's Bay Pinot Gris   (★★☆)

Still fresh, the easy-drinking 2014 vintage (★★☆) is medium-bodied, with lively pear and lychee flavours, a splash of sweetness, and a very smooth finish. Fine value.

MED $12 V+

Obsidian Waiheke Island Pinot Gris   ★★★☆

The 2015 vintage (★★★☆) is a single-vineyard wine, attractively scented. Full-bodied and fleshy, it is a dryish style, with ripe, citrusy, peachy flavours, showing good depth, and a well-rounded finish.

MED/DRY $27 –V

Odyssey Marlborough Pinot Gris   ★★★☆

Estate-grown in the Brancott Valley, the characterful 2014 vintage (★★★★) was hand-picked and fermented in old French oak casks. It's a sturdy, fleshy wine with peachy, slightly spicy and toasty flavours, showing more complexity than most Pinot Gris, and a well-rounded, dry (3.5 grams/litre of residual sugar) finish. Certified organic.

DRY $25 –V

Ohinemuri Estate Central Valley Poverty Bay Pinot Gris   ★★★☆

The 2015 vintage (★★★☆) was fermented with indigenous yeasts in seasoned oak barrels. Made in a medium-dry style (11 grams/litre of residual sugar), it is a fresh, medium to full-bodied wine, with very good depth of peachy, slightly spicy and gingery flavours, and a smooth finish. Drink now to 2018.

Vintage	15
WR	6
Drink	17-22

 MED/DRY $27 –V

Old Coach Road Nelson Pinot Gris ★★☆

From Seifried, the vibrantly fruity 2017 vintage (★★☆) is a pale, fresh, medium-bodied wine with citrusy, peachy flavours, crisp acidity and a dry (3 grams/litre of residual sugar) finish. Priced right.

DRY $15 V+

Vintage	17
WR	5
Drink	17-18

Omaha Bay Vineyard Matakana Pinot Gris ★★★★

The 2014 vintage (★★★★) is impressive – fleshy, ripe and rounded, with good concentration of stone-fruit and spice flavours, a slightly creamy texture and a dry finish.

DRY $30 –V

Vintage	14	13
WR	6	6
Drink	17-19	P

Omaka Springs Marlborough Pinot Gris ★★★☆

Offering easy drinking, the 2016 vintage (★★★☆) was estate-grown in the Omaka Valley and handled entirely in tanks. A fresh, medium-bodied, clearly varietal wine, it is vibrantly fruity and smooth, with good depth of peach, pear, lychee and spice flavours, and a slightly sweet (12 grams/litre of residual sugar), finely balanced finish.

MED/DRY $20 AV

Opawa Marlborough Pinot Gris ★★★☆

This wine is made in a 'lighter, crisper' style than its Nautilus Estate stablemate. Hand-picked in the Wairau Valley and tank-fermented, the 2016 vintage (★★★☆) is mouthfilling and dry (3 grams/litre of residual sugar), with vibrant, peachy, slightly spicy flavours, showing very good depth. Enjoyable from the start.

DRY $22 AV

Ostler Audrey's Waitaki Valley Pinot Gris ★★★★☆

Retasted in mid-2017, the 2015 vintage (★★★★★) is maturing very gracefully. It was mostly handled in tanks, but 25 per cent of the blend was fermented with indigenous yeasts in demi muids – large, old barrels, holding 600 litres. Light lemon/green, it is highly scented and richly varietal, with pear, lychee and spice flavours, showing excellent vibrancy, delicacy, poise and depth, and a long, off-dry (8 grams/litre of residual sugar) finish. Still unfolding, with good complexity, it should be at its best mid-2018+.

MED/DRY $34 –V

Ostler Lakeside Vines Waitaki Valley Pinot Gris ★★★★☆

The impressive 2016 vintage (★★★★☆) was grown at Lake Waitaki and partly (20 per cent) fermented with indigenous yeasts in old oak barriques. Pale lemon/green, it is gently sweet (14 grams/litre of residual sugar), mouthfilling and vibrantly fruity, with strong pear and lychee flavours, showing excellent varietal definition, hints of peaches, ginger and spices, and a well-rounded finish. It's already delicious.

MED/DRY $29 AV

Overstone Hawke's Bay Pinot Gris ★★☆

The 2015 vintage (★★☆) is a dryish wine, medium-bodied, with fresh acidity and ripe, peachy, spicy flavours, balanced for easy drinking. Good value from Sileni.

MED/DRY $13 V+

Oyster Bay Hawke's Bay Pinot Gris ★★★☆

Grown mostly at Crownthorpe, a relatively cool, elevated, inland district, this is a good, all-purpose wine, modelled on dry Italian Pinot Grigio rather than the richer, sweeter Pinot Gris of Alsace. Handled without oak, the 2016 vintage (★★★☆) is fleshy, with fresh, ripe, peachy, slightly creamy flavours, very good depth and a smooth, dry (3 grams/litre of residual sugar) finish.

DRY $20 AV

Pa Road Marlborough Pinot Gris ★★★☆

From Te Pa, the 2017 vintage (★★★☆) is good value. A blend of Pinot Gris (95 per cent) and Gewürztraminer (5 per cent), grown principally in the Awatere Valley, it was mostly handled in tanks; 7 per cent was barrel-fermented. Light lemon/green, it is mouthfilling, with fresh, ripe peach, pear and spice flavours, slightly earthy notes, balanced acidity, gentle sweetness (7 grams/litre of residual sugar), and good depth.

 MED/DRY $17 V+

Paddy Borthwick New Zealand Pinot Gris ★★★★

Estate-grown at Gladstone, in the northern Wairarapa, the 2016 vintage (★★★☆) is mouthfilling, with stone-fruit and spice flavours to the fore, slightly toasty notes (from 25 per cent barrel fermentation), and a dry (3.5 grams/litre of residual sugar), slightly buttery finish. It's already drinking well; open now to 2018.

DRY $22 V+

Palliser Estate Martinborough Pinot Gris ★★★★

The easy-drinking 2016 vintage (★★★★) was fermented and lees-aged for three months in tanks. Fresh and full-bodied, it is a slightly sweet style (6.8 grams/litre of residual sugar), with vibrant, ripe, peachy, spicy flavours, showing very good depth, and a smooth, slightly creamy finish. Still youthful, it should be at its best mid-2018+. High-priced.

 MED/DRY $30 –V

Pass, The, Gisborne Pinot Gris (★★☆)

From Vavasour, the easy-drinking 2016 vintage (★★☆) is fresh-scented and mouthfilling, with gentle acidity and pleasant peach, pear and spice flavours, ripe and smooth.

 MED/DRY $17 –V

People's, The, Hawke's Bay Pinot Gris ★★★

Offering very easy drinking, the 2014 vintage (★★★) includes a splash (3 per cent) of Gewürztraminer. It is smooth and mouthfilling, with plenty of citrusy, peachy, slightly spicy flavour, dryish and well-rounded. (From Constellation New Zealand.)

 MED/DRY $16 V+

Peregrine Central Otago Pinot Gris   ★★★★

Grown and hand-picked at Bendigo and Pisa, the 2016 vintage (★★★★) was mostly handled in tanks; 10 per cent of the blend was barrel-fermented. Ripely scented, it is mouthfilling, vibrant and smooth, with strong pear, peach and spice flavours, a sliver of sweetness (5 grams/litre of residual sugar), a slightly creamy texture, and lots of drink-young appeal.

 MED/DRY $29 –V

Peter Yealands Lighter in Alcohol Marlborough Pinot Gris   (★★)

The 2015 vintage (★★) is fresh, light (9.5 per cent alcohol), lemony and slightly appley, with a slightly sweet (6 grams/litre of residual sugar), crisp finish. Pleasant, but plain.

Vintage	15
WR	7
Drink	P

 MED/DRY $16 –V

Peter Yealands Marlborough Pinot Gris   ★★★

The 2016 vintage (★★★) is mouthfilling, fresh and smooth, with good depth of peachy, slightly spicy flavours and a crisp, dry (4 grams/litre of residual sugar) finish. Lively, easy drinking. Priced sharply.

 DRY $15 V+

Peter Yealands Reserve Awatere Valley Marlborough Pinot Gris   ★★★☆

The 2016 vintage (★★★★) is mouthfilling, with strong stone-fruit, pear and spice flavours and a finely balanced, dry (4 grams/litre of residual sugar) finish. Enjoyable young, it offers fine value.

Vintage	16	15	14
WR	6	7	6
Drink	17-18	P	P

 DRY $18 AV

Pied Stilt Nelson Pinot Gris   ★★★

A single-vineyard Motueka wine, the 2014 vintage (★★★) is sturdy and creamy-textured, with peach, pear, lychee and spice flavours, and a dry (3 grams/litre of residual sugar) finish. Ready.

DRY $20 –V

Prophet's Rock Central Otago Pinot Gris   ★★★★☆

Estate-grown and hand-picked at two Bendigo sites, in the Cromwell Basin, the classy, attractively scented 2016 vintage (★★★★★) is full of personality. Fermented with indigenous yeasts and made with some use of old oak, it is light lemon/green, mouthfilling, fresh and youthful. Fleshy, it is an off-dry style (11 grams/litre of residual sugar), with concentrated, ripe, peachy flavours, hints of apples and lychees, a slightly creamy texture, and a real sense of youthful drive. A subtle, complex wine with gentle acidity, it should be at its best mid-2018+.

Vintage	16	15
WR	7	6
Drink	17-28	17-22

MED/DRY $40 –V

Quartz Reef Bendigo Single Vineyard Pinot Gris ★★★★☆

Certified biodynamic, the refined 2016 vintage (★★★★☆) was estate-grown at Bendigo, in Central Otago, hand-picked and fermented and lees-aged in tanks. Pale, mouthfilling and vibrantly fruity, it has pear and citrus-fruit flavours, showing excellent depth and roundness, and a long, dry (3 grams/litre of residual sugar), finely textured finish. Already delicious, it's well worth cellaring.

Vintage	16	15	14	13	12	11	10
WR	7	7	7	6	7	7	7
Drink	17-21	17-19	17-18	P	P	P	P

DRY $29 AV

Quest Farm Silver Lining Central Otago Pinot Gris (★★★☆)

The 2014 vintage (★★★☆) is a fully dry style (2 grams/litre of residual sugar), with a small portion (about 5 per cent) of Gewürztraminer and Viognier in the blend. Full-bodied, it is vibrantly fruity, with stone-fruit and pear flavours, fresh, appetising acidity, and very good depth and immediacy.

DRY $25 –V

Ra Nui Wairau Valley Marlborough Pinot Gris ★★★☆

Enjoyable young, the distinctive 2016 vintage (★★★★) includes splashes of Gewürztraminer (3 per cent) and Viognier (2 per cent), and was partly barrel-fermented. Light lemon/green, it is fragrant, mouthfilling and well-rounded, with fractional sweetness (4 grams/litre of residual sugar) and plenty of soft, peachy, spicy, slightly toasty flavour, showing good complexity.

DRY $25 –V

Rapaura Springs Marlborough Pinot Gris ★★★☆

The easy-drinking 2017 vintage (★★★☆) is fragrant, full-bodied and vibrantly fruity, with gentle sweetness (6.5 grams/litre of residual sugar) and very good depth of citrusy, peachy flavours. Instantly appealing.

Vintage	17	16	15	14
WR	4	7	7	7
Drink	17-19	17-19	17-18	17-18

MED/DRY $17 V+

Rapaura Springs Reserve Marlborough Pinot Gris ★★★★

The dryish 2016 vintage (★★★★) was mostly handled in tanks; 5 per cent of the blend was barrel-fermented. Full-bodied, it has generous stone-fruit and spice flavours, with a hint of ginger, slight sweetness (5 grams/litre of residual sugar), a touch of complexity, and lots of drink-young appeal. The 2017 vintage (★★★★) is pale and fresh, with strong pear, lychee and spice flavours, showing a touch of complexity, and a dryish (7.2 grams/litre of residual sugar) finish. Best drinking 2018+.

Vintage	17	16
WR	6	7
Drink	17-20	17-20

 MED/DRY $19 V+

Renato Nelson Pinot Gris   ★★★☆

Estate-grown on the coast, at Kina, and hand-picked, the 2016 vintage (★★★☆) is still youthful, with vibrant pear, citrus-fruit and spice flavours, lees-aging notes adding a touch of complexity, and a finely balanced, slightly sweet (7 grams/litre of residual sugar), lingering finish. Best drinking 2018+.

Vintage	16	15	14	13	12	11	10
WR	6	7	7	NM	6	6	7
Drink	17-20	17-21	17-20	NM	17-19	P	P

MED/DRY $20 AV

Ribbonwood Marlborough Pinot Gris   ★★★☆

From Framingham, the 2014 vintage (★★★☆) was partly (15 per cent) barrel-matured. Full-bodied (14 per cent alcohol), it is a dryish style (6 grams/litre of residual sugar), with citrusy, slightly peachy and spicy flavours, showing good depth, and a scented bouquet. An attractive, all-purpose wine.

MED/DRY $20 AV

Richmond Plains Nelson Pinot Gris   ★★★☆

The highly attractive 2016 vintage (★★★★) is an off-dry (7 grams/litre of residual sugar) style. Fragrant, with pear-like aromas, it is full-bodied and fresh, with an array of stone-fruit, lychee, pear and spice flavours, showing very good delicacy and depth, and a slightly sweet (7 grams/litre of residual sugar), harmonious finish. Drink now or cellar.

MED/DRY $22 AV

Rimu Grove Bronte Pinot Gris – see Bronte Pinot Gris

Riverby Estate Marlborough Pinot Gris   ★★★☆

A single-vineyard wine, grown in the heart of the Wairau Valley, the 2014 vintage (★★★) is full-bodied, with fresh, moderately concentrated pear, lychee and spice flavours and an off-dry (8 grams/litre of residual sugar), smooth finish.

MED/DRY $22 AV

Roaring Meg Central Otago Pinot Gris   ★★★☆

From Mt Difficulty, the light lemon/green 2016 vintage (★★★★) was hand-harvested in the Cromwell Basin and made in a medium-dry style (10 grams/litre of residual sugar). Delicious young, it is vibrantly fruity, with mouthfilling body, ripe, peachy, slightly spicy flavours, refreshing acidity and excellent freshness, harmony and depth. Drink now to 2019.

MED/DRY $23 –V

Rock Ferry 3rd Rock Marlborough Pinot Gris   ★★★★☆

(This label recently replaced the former Rock Ferry Marlborough Pinot Gris.) Still youthful, the 2014 vintage (★★★★☆) was hand-picked in The Corners and Orchard vineyards at Rapaura, in the Wairau Valley, and mostly handled in tanks; 15 per cent of the blend was fermented in seasoned oak puncheons. Light lemon/green, it is mouthfilling (14 per cent alcohol), fleshy and rounded, with vibrant, ripe stone-fruit flavours, a subtle seasoning of oak adding complexity, and a dryish (6.5 grams/litre of residual sugar), finely textured finish. A distinctly 'Alsace' style of Pinot Gris, it offers delicious drinking from 2017 onwards. Certified organic.

Rock Ferry Trig Hill Vineyard Central Otago Pinot Gris   ★★★★★

Certified organic, the lovely 2014 vintage (★★★★★) was estate-grown in the Trig Hill Vineyard at Bendigo, hand-picked and mostly tank-fermented; 20 per cent was fermented in seasoned French oak puncheons. The entire blend was then matured for six months in a seasoned French oak cuve, prior to bottling. Light lemon/green, it is weighty (14 per cent alcohol) and complex, with rich, vibrant stone-fruit flavours to the fore, fresh acidity, excellent depth and harmony, and a long, dryish (6.4 grams/litre of residual sugar), very finely poised finish.

Rockburn Central Otago Pinot Gris   ★★★☆

Grown at Parkburn, in the Cromwell Basin, and at Gibbston, the 2016 vintage (★★★★) is a pale, attractively scented wine, mouthfilling and vibrant, with strong, citrusy, peachy flavours, fresh acidity and a dry (4 grams/litre of residual sugar) finish. Finely balanced, with good intensity, it's delicious in its youth, but also worth cellaring.

Rod McDonald One Off Hawke's Bay Pinot Gris Rhymes With Orange   (★★★☆)

The debut 2015 vintage (★★★☆) is described by the producer as 'a typical orange wine, with sweet upfront fruit and drying finish'. Hand-picked at Maraekakaho and held on its skins for nine months, it is medium to full-bodied, with an onion-skin hue and a spicy, peachy bouquet. The flavours are strong, with stone-fruit and spice notes, a hint of apricots, more personality than most Pinot Gris, and a firm, dry finish. Worth trying.

Rossendale Marlborough Pinot Gris   ★★☆

Priced sharply, the estate-grown 2016 vintage (★★☆) is a sound but not memorable wine, with fresh lemon, apple and spice flavours, and a dryish finish.

Ruru Central Otago Pinot Gris   (★★★)

Grown and hand-picked at Alexandra, the 2016 vintage (★★★) is a medium-bodied wine, with fresh, lively pear and lychee flavours, a sliver of sweetness, and good vigour and immediacy.

MED/DRY $19 AV

Ruru Reserve Central Otago Pinot Gris

The youthful 2017 vintage (★★★★) was estate-grown, hand-picked in the Immigrant's Vineyard at Alexandra, and mostly handled in tanks; 10 per cent of the blend was oak-aged. Invitingly scented, it is full-bodied and sweet-fruited, with fresh, strong peach, lychee and nectarine flavours, a gentle splash of sweetness (8.8 grams/litre of residual sugar) and lively acidity. Best drinking mid-2018+.

MED/DRY $24 AV

Sacred Hill Marlborough Pinot Gris

★★★☆

The 2017 vintage (★★★☆) was grown in the Southern Valleys. Mouthfilling and smooth, it is vibrantly fruity, with pear, lychee, peach and spice flavours, a gentle splash of sweetness (12.7 grams/litre of residual sugar), and very good depth and harmony. Enjoyable from the start.

MED/DRY $17 V+

Saint Clair Godfrey's Creek Reserve Marlborough Pinot Gris

★★★☆

Made in a full-bodied, dryish style (5.2 grams/litre of residual sugar), the 2016 vintage (★★★☆) is a single-vineyard, Brancott Valley wine, tank-fermented and lees-aged. It is mouthfilling and fleshy, with fresh pear, lychee and spice flavours, showing very good delicacy and depth.

MED/DRY $31 –V

Saint Clair James Sinclair Marlborough Pinot Gris

(★★★)

The debut 2015 vintage (★★★) is a blend of Pinot Gris (87.5 per cent) with small amounts of Gewürztraminer, Riesling, Grüner Veltliner and Muscat. Grown in the Southern Valleys and Awatere Valley, it is fresh and full-bodied, in a dryish (4.5 grams/litre of residual sugar), 'grigio' style, with plenty of crisp, slightly spicy flavour.

DRY $22 –V

Saint Clair Pioneer Block 5 Bull Block Marlborough Pinot Gris

★★★★

Grown in the lower Omaka Valley, the 2014 vintage (★★★★) was made in a 'tardive' (late-harvest) style. An elegant wine with citrusy, appley aromas and flavours, it has good vigour and delicacy, with hints of peaches, spices and ginger, gentle acidity and a finely balanced, slightly sweet (10 grams/litre of residual sugar) finish. Very age-worthy.

MED/DRY $27 –V

Saint Clair Vicars Choice Bright Light Marlborough Pinot Gris

(★★☆)

The 2014 vintage (★★☆) is a pleasant, light wine (9.5 per cent alcohol), with fresh pear, lychee and spice flavours and a slightly sweet (8.6 grams/litre of residual sugar) finish. It's a clearly varietal wine, offering smooth, easy, no-fuss drinking.

MED/DRY $19 –V

Saint Clair Vicar's Choice Marlborough Pinot Gris

★★★

The 2015 vintage (★★★) includes splashes of Grüner Veltliner (7 per cent) and Viognier (6 per cent) in the blend. Made in a 'grigio' style, it is medium-bodied, fresh and crisp, with pear, citrus and spice flavours and a dry finish.

DRY $19 AV

Sanctuary Gisborne Pinot Gris

The 2016 vintage (★★☆) is a medium-bodied wine with decent depth of fresh, ripe citrus-fruit, pear and spice flavours, balanced for easy drinking.

MED/DRY $18 –V

Satyr Hawke's Bay Pinot Gris   ★★☆

From Sileni, the easy-drinking 2015 vintage (★★☆) is a medium-bodied, crisp and lively wine with dryish, citrusy, appley flavours. Priced sharply.

MED/DRY $14 AV

Sea Level Home Block Nelson Pinot Gris   ★★★★

The 2014 vintage (★★★★) was estate-grown at Mariri. Freshly scented, it is mouthfilling, with strong, vibrant pear, lychee and spice flavours, showing excellent varietal character, and a finely balanced, off-dry (6 grams/litre of residual sugar) finish.

Vintage	14
WR	7
Drink	P

MED/DRY $18 V+

Seifried Nelson Pinot Gris   ★★★

Enjoyable young, the 2017 vintage (★★★) is a medium-bodied wine with fresh, peachy, slightly spicy flavours, showing decent depth, and a dry (3 grams/litre of residual sugar), smooth finish.

Vintage	17	16	15	14	13
WR	6	6	6	5	6
Drink	17-18	17-18	P	P	P

DRY $18 AV

Selaks Founders Limited Edition Hawke's Bay Pinot Gris   (★★★★)

The refined 2014 vintage (★★★★), grown mostly at Moteo, is a mouthfilling, dry style (3 grams/litre of residual sugar). It is ripely flavoured, peachy and spicy, with balanced acidity and very good drive, delicacy and depth through the palate.

DRY $26 –V

Selaks Reserve Hawke's Bay Pinot Gris   ★★★

The 2017 vintage (★★★) is a good buy – mouthfilling, with good depth of vibrant, ripe, peachy, slightly spicy flavours, well-balanced, slightly sweet and smooth.

Vintage	17
WR	5
Drink	18-19

MED/DRY $16 V+

Seresin Marlborough Pinot Gris   ★★★★★

Certified organic, this is one of the region's most distinctive Pinot Gris. The 2016 vintage (★★★★) was estate-grown and hand-picked at two sites – Raupo Creek Vineyard, in the Omaka Valley (70 per cent), and Noa Vineyard, in the western Wairau Valley (30 per cent).

Fermented and lees-aged in a mix of tanks (60 per cent) and old oak barriques (40 per cent), it's a pale straw, complex, dryish wine (6.8 grams/litre of residual sugar), with vibrant pear, citrus-fruit and spice flavours, showing good complexity, fresh acidity and a lively, lingering finish.

MED/DRY $25 V+

Sherwood Estate Stoney Range Waipara Valley Pinot Gris   (★★★☆)

Already drinking well, the 2017 vintage (★★★☆) was partly barrel-fermented and made in a dry style (3.5 grams/litre of residual sugar). Bright, light lemon/green, it is mouthfilling and vibrant, with good depth of peachy, spicy, slightly gingery flavours.

DRY $17 V+

Sherwood Waipara Valley Pinot Gris   ★★★☆

This is the 'signature' wine of Sherwood Estate. Bright, light lemon/green, the 2017 vintage (★★★☆) is a dry style (1.5 grams/litre of residual sugar), partly barrel-fermented. Fresh, mouthfilling and youthful, with ripe, peachy, slightly spicy flavours, showing very good depth, it's already drinking well.

DRY $19 V+

Sileni Cellar Selection Hawke's Bay Pinot Gris   ★★★

Already enjoyable, the 2017 vintage (★★★) is a fresh, medium-bodied wine, with gentle sweetness and good depth of peachy, slightly spicy flavours.

MED/DRY $20 –V

Sileni Estate Selection Priestess Hawke's Bay Pinot Gris   ★★★★

The 2015 vintage (★★★★) is a distinctive, dry wine (4.5 grams/litre of residual sugar), hand-picked and fermented in an even split of tanks and old oak barrels. Light lemon/green, it is mouthfilling, with vibrant, peachy flavours, showing good richness, balanced acidity, and the subtle oak influence giving a distinct touch of complexity.

DRY $25 AV

Sileni Wisp Cellar Selection Lo Cal Pinot Gris   (★★☆)

The 2014 vintage (★★☆) is a light style (9.5 per cent alcohol), with pleasant, lemony, appley flavours, hints of pears and peaches, and a smooth, slightly sweet (7 grams/litre of residual sugar) finish. Forward, easy drinking.

MED/DRY $17 –V

Silver Fern Marlborough Pinot Gris   (★★★☆)

The 2014 vintage (★★★☆) is full-bodied and creamy-textured, in a very easy-drinking style with stone-fruit, pear and spice flavours, showing very good freshness and depth. (From Yealands.)

MED/DRY $21 AV

Soho Jagger Marlborough Pinot Gris ★★★★

The 2015 vintage (★★★★) was mostly handled in tanks; 5 per cent of the blend was fermented in seasoned French oak barrels. A scented, mouthfilling wine, it has very good depth of pear, lychee, peach and spice flavours, showing a touch of complexity, and a smooth, dryish finish.

Vintage	15
WR	5
Drink	17-18

 MED/DRY $26 –V

Soho White Collection Marlborough Pinot Gris ★★★☆

The 2015 vintage (★★★☆) is fragrant and full-bodied, with fresh acidity woven through its peachy, slightly spicy flavours, which show good depth. An off-dry style, it's skilfully balanced for enjoyable, early drinking.

Vintage	15
WR	4
Drink	P

 MED/DRY $20 AV

Soljans Kumeu Pinot Gris ★★★

Estate-grown and hand-picked in West Auckland and tank-fermented, the 2014 vintage (★★★) is a freshly scented, medium-bodied wine with ripe, peachy, slightly spicy and gingery flavours, a touch of sweetness (12 grams/litre of residual sugar), and an easy-drinking charm.

Vintage	14
WR	7
Drink	P

 MED/DRY $19 AV

Spade Oak Vineyard Voysey Gisborne Pinot Gris ★★★

The 2014 vintage (★★☆) is an easy-drinking style, peachy and slightly spicy, with considerable sweetness (16 grams/litre of residual sugar), gentle acidity and a smooth finish.

 MED $19 AV

Spinyback Nelson Pinot Gris ★★★☆

From Waimea Estate, the sharply priced 2016 vintage (★★★☆) is an attractively scented, mouthfilling wine with peachy, slightly spicy and gingery flavours, a sliver of sweetness (7 grams/litre of residual sugar), and lots of drink-young appeal.

MED/DRY $15 V+

Springs, The, Waipara Pinot Gris ★★★

Priced sharply, the 2016 vintage (★★★) is an aromatic, medium-bodied wine, with satisfying depth of vibrant pear and spice flavours and a slightly sweet (10 grams/litre of residual sugar), smooth finish.

MED/DRY $15 V+

Spy Valley Envoy Johnson Vineyard Waihopai Valley Marlborough Pinot Gris   ★★★★★

Estate-grown in the lower Waihopai Valley, the 2016 vintage (★★★★★) was late-harvested from vines planted in 1999. Made from ultra-ripe grapes, with some shrivel and noble rot, and wood-fermented, it is a lovely mouthful. Light lemon/green, it is richly scented, with mouthfilling body and highly concentrated, peachy, slightly spicy, gingery and honeyed flavours. Fresh, gently sweet (65 grams/litre of residual sugar) and soft, it's a very harmonious wine, highly seductive in its youth. Drink now or cellar.

Vintage	16
WR	6
Drink	17-22

SW $32 AV

Spy Valley Marlborough Pinot Gris   ★★★★★

Bargain-priced, the instantly appealing 2016 vintage (★★★★★) was mostly hand-harvested and made with some use of indigenous yeasts and wood fermentation. Freshly perfumed, full-bodied and vibrantly fruity, it has ripe stone-fruit flavours to the fore, showing excellent delicacy and richness, a slightly oily texture, and a slightly sweet (14.9 grams/litre of residual sugar), soft, lasting finish. Drink now or cellar.

Vintage	16	15	14	13	12	11	10
WR	6	7	7	6	6	6	6
Drink	18-22	17-20	17-19	P	P	P	P

MED/DRY $24 V+

Staete Landt State of Bliss Marlborough Pinot Gris   ★★★★☆

Fleshy and smooth, the 2016 vintage (★★★★☆) is a 'serious' style of Pinot Gris, hand-picked and fermented (partly with indigenous yeasts) in old French barrels. Light lemon/green, it is mouthfilling, with concentrated, dry, peachy, gently spicy flavours, a slightly creamy texture and good complexity.

DRY $25 V+

Stanley Estates Single Vineyard Awatere Valley Marlborough Pinot Gris   ★★★★

Well worth cellaring, the lively 2016 vintage (★★★★) is a tightly structured, dry style (2.9 grams/litre of residual sugar), handled in tanks (80 per cent) and seasoned French oak barrels (20 per cent). Pale and full-bodied, it is vibrantly fruity, with strong pear and spice flavours, showing good delicacy and complexity, and a fresh, crisp, lengthy finish.

Vintage	16
WR	7
Drink	17-22

DRY $23 AV

Starborough Family Estate Marlborough Pinot Gris   ★★★☆

The 2016 vintage (★★★☆) is a 2:1 blend of Wairau Valley and Awatere Valley grapes, mostly handled in tanks; 10 per cent of the blend was barrel-aged. Pale, it shows good varietal character, with good depth of fresh, delicate pear and lychee flavours, fractional sweetness (5.5 grams/litre of residual sugar) and balanced acidity.

MED/DRY $20 AV

Stoneleigh Latitude Marlborough Pinot Gris   ★★★★

Estate-grown on the northern side of the Wairau Valley, the 2016 vintage (★★★★) was fermented in a mix of tanks (84 per cent) and old oak cuves (16 per cent). Mouthfilling and generous, it has strong, fresh, peachy, slightly spicy flavours, a sliver of sweetness (7.7 grams/litre of residual sugar) and a very harmonious finish.

MED/DRY $24 AV

Stoneleigh Marlborough Lighter Pinot Gris   (★★)

The 2016 vintage (★★) is a light style (9.8 per cent alcohol). Freshly scented, with lemony, appley flavours and a sliver of sweetness (7.6 grams/litre of residual sugar), it's a pleasant lunchtime sipper, but lacks real body, ripeness and richness.

MED/DRY $17 –V

Stoneleigh Marlborough Pinot Gris   ★★★☆

Offering excellent value, the 2016 vintage (★★★★) is a full-bodied, weighty wine with good intensity of fresh, ripe pear, peach and spice flavours, gentle acidity, and a slightly sweet (12 grams/litre of residual sugar), well-rounded finish.

MED/DRY $17 V+

Stoneleigh Rapaura Series Marlborough Pinot Gris   ★★★★

Delicious young, the 2016 vintage (★★★★) of this single-vineyard wine was mostly fermented and lees-aged in tanks; 8 per cent of the blend was barrel-fermented. Pale straw, it is full-bodied (14.5 per cent alcohol), with gentle sweetness (14 grams/litre of residual sugar), and peachy, spicy, slightly gingery flavours, vaguely honeyed, fresh and strong.

MED/DRY $28 –V

Stoney Range Reserve Waipara Pinot Gris   (★★★☆)

Enjoyable young, the flavour-packed 2017 vintage (★★★☆) was partly barrel-fermented and made in a dry style (3.5 grams/litre of residual sugar). Light lemon/green, with a fresh, spicy bouquet, it is full-bodied, with strong, spicy, gingery, faintly honeyed flavours. Very forward in its appeal, it will probably be at its best during 2018. (From Sherwood Estate.)

DRY $22 AV

Summerhouse Marlborough Pinot Gris   ★★★☆

The attractive 2017 vintage (★★★☆) was fermented in tanks and old oak barriques. Full-bodied, it is a slightly sweet style (6.4 grams/litre of residual sugar), with fresh, delicate pear and spice flavours, balanced acidity, and very good harmony and depth.

Vintage	17
WR	7
Drink	17-22

MED/DRY $19 V+

Takatu Matakana Pinot Gris ★★★★

Grown on a north-facing hillside, this is a sophisticated wine. The 2014 vintage (★★★★) was handled in a mix of seasoned oak puncheons and barriques (60 per cent of the blend) and stainless steel tanks. Mouthfilling, it is richly scented, with strong, vibrant, citrusy, peachy flavours, balanced acidity and a tight, dry finish (1.5 grams/litre of residual sugar).

DRY $35 –V

Tantalus Estate Waiheke Island Pinot Gris (★★★★)

Grown at Onetangi, the 2015 vintage (★★★★) was French oak-aged for six months. Fleshy and well-rounded, it has strong, ripe pear and lychee flavours, showing good varietal character, a touch of complexity and a dry (3 grams/litre of residual sugar) finish.

Vintage	15
WR	5
Drink	17-18

DRY $35 –V

Tarras Vineyards Central Otago Pinot Gris (★★★★)

Grown at Alexandra, the 2014 vintage (★★★★) is a gently perfumed wine, displaying good varietal character. It has dryish pear and quince flavours, showing excellent balance and length.

MED/DRY $29 –V

Tatty Bogler Waitaki Pinot Gris ★★★★

Still unfolding, the 2016 vintage (★★★★) is a bright, light lemon/green, finely scented wine from the Waitaki Valley, North Otago. Lively and youthful, it is full-bodied, with vibrant, peachy, spicy, slightly sweet flavours, showing excellent vigour and depth. Best drinking 2018+. (From Forrest Estate.)

MED/DRY $25 AV

Te Amo Central Otago Pinot Gris (★★★★☆)

The highly attractive 2016 vintage (★★★★☆) is invitingly scented, with pear and lychee aromas. Fresh and full-bodied, it is dryish, with strong peach, pear and spice flavours, finely textured, very harmonious and long. Drink now or cellar.

MED/DRY $28 AV

Te Awanga Estate Hawke's Bay Pinot Gris ★★★

The 2014 vintage (★★★) was hand-picked at an inland site, tank-fermented and lees-aged. It's a mouthfilling wine with vibrant pear, lychee and spice flavours and a dry (under 3 grams/litre of residual sugar) finish.

DRY $25 –V

Te Kairanga Martinborough Pinot Gris ★★★★

Partly barrel-fermented, the 2016 vintage (★★★★☆) is fragrant and full-bodied, with concentrated, ripe stone-fruit and spice flavours, a touch of complexity, a creamy texture and a fresh, dry (3 grams/litre of residual sugar), lasting finish.

DRY $25 AV

Te Mania Nelson Pinot Gris

★★★★

The 2015 vintage (★★★★) was grown at two sites, on the plains and in the hills. It is full-bodied and vibrantly fruity, with strong pear, lychee and spice flavours, fractional sweetness (6.5 grams/litre of residual sugar), and very good varietal character and harmony.

 MED/DRY $22 V+

Te Pa Marlborough Pinot Gris

(★★★☆)

The pale straw 2016 vintage (★★★☆) is a single-vineyard wine, grown in the Awatere Valley. Tank-fermented and lees-aged, it is mouthfilling, with very good depth of vibrant, slightly gingery and spicy flavours, and a dryish (5 grams/litre of residual sugar) finish. Ready.

 MED/DRY $20 AV

Terra Sancta Lola's Block Bannockburn Central Otago Pinot Gris

★★★★

The 2016 vintage (★★★★) was estate-grown, hand-harvested, and fermented and matured in old oak barrels. Mouthfilling, it is a weighty, very harmonious wine, with a touch of complexity, slight sweetness (5.4 grams/litre of residual sugar), and peachy, slightly spicy flavours, strong and well-rounded.

Vintage	16
WR	6
Drink	18-21

 MED/DRY $28 –V

Terra Sancta Mysterious Diggings Bannockburn Central Otago Pinot Gris

★★★★

Estate-grown and hand-picked, the 2017 vintage (★★★★) is delicious young. Mouthfilling, it is vibrantly fruity, with generous pear, lychee and spice flavours, woven with fresh acidity, and a dry (4.7 grams/litre of residual sugar), finely balanced finish.

Vintage	17
WR	7
Drink	18-22

DRY $24 AV

Terrace Edge Waipara Pinot Gris

★★★★☆

Already delicious, the 2016 vintage (★★★★☆) is a sturdy, fleshy, Alsace-style wine, hand-picked and fermented with indigenous yeasts in a mix of seasoned French oak barrels (60 per cent) and tanks. Full-bodied and soft, it has rich stone-fruit and spice flavours, a splash of sweetness (14 grams/litre of residual sugar) and a slightly oily texture. Drink now or cellar.

Vintage	16	15	14	13	12	11
WR	7	7	6	7	7	6
Drink	17-23	17-22	17-19	17-18	P	P

 MED/DRY $25 V+

Theory & Practice Hawke's Bay Pinot Gris   (★★★★)

Offering great value, the 2016 vintage (★★★★) was grown in two coastal vineyards and fermented in tanks (60 per cent) and large German oak fuders (40 per cent). Light lemon/green, it is invitingly scented, mouthfilling and rounded, with generous, peachy, faintly buttery flavours, slight sweetness (8.5 grams/litre of residual sugar) and a finely balanced finish. Drink now.

MED/DRY $19 V+

Thornbury Waipara Pinot Gris   ★★★☆

Offering great value, the 2017 vintage (★★★☆) was grown in the Waiata Vineyard, in North Canterbury, and fermented and lees-aged in tanks. Very fresh and lively, it is medium-bodied, with strong, vibrant pear and lychee flavours and a gently sweet (13.6 grams/litre of residual sugar), smooth finish. (From Villa Maria.)

Vintage	17	16	15	14	13
WR	4	7	7	5	7
Drink	17-19	17-18	17-18	P	P

MED/DRY $14 V+

Tiki Estate Marlborough Pinot Gris   ★★★☆

Estate-grown in the upper Wairau Valley, the 2016 vintage (★★★★) is attractively scented, with mouthfilling body and strong, ripe peach, pear, lychee and spice flavours, showing good varietal character. Made in a dryish style, it's a drink-now or cellaring proposition.

MED/DRY $20 AV

Tinpot Hut Marlborough Pinot Gris   ★★★

The 2014 vintage (★★★) was grown in the Home Block and neighbouring McKee Vineyard, in the Awatere Valley. Mouthfilling, it has decent depth of vibrant, ripe citrus-fruit and pear flavours, with hints of apples and spices, and a dry (3.9 grams/litre of residual sugar) finish.

DRY $22 –V

Tohu Awatere Valley Marlborough Pinot Gris   ★★★☆

The youthful 2016 vintage (★★★☆) is full-bodied, with vibrant peachy, spicy flavours, showing very good depth, and an off-dry (5 grams/litre of residual sugar) finish.

MED/DRY $22 AV

Toi Toi Brookdale Reserve Marlborough Pinot Gris   ★★★☆

The 2016 vintage (★★★★) is a mouthfilling, generous, dryish wine (6 grams/litre of residual sugar), weighty and finely textured, with very good depth of ripe, peachy, citrusy, slightly spicy and gingery flavours, showing a touch of complexity, and a well-rounded finish.

Vintage	16
WR	7
Drink	17-20

MED/DRY $22 AV

Toi Toi Marlborough Pinot Gris ★★☆

Showing good varietal character, the 2016 vintage (★★★) is a mouthfilling, off-dry wine with ripe pear, lychee and spice flavours, fresh and well-balanced for early appeal.

MED/DRY $17 –V

Torea Marlborough Pinot Gris ★★★☆

From an Auckland-based company, the 2014 vintage (★★★☆) is a fleshy, very easy-drinking wine with good depth of ripe, peachy flavours and a slightly sweet, creamy-smooth finish.

MED/DRY $17 V+

Torrent Bay Nelson Pinot Gris ★★☆

The 2014 vintage (★★☆) is medium-bodied, with decent depth of vibrant lemon, apple and spice flavours, slightly sweet and crisp. Fresh, easy drinking.

MED/DRY $17 –V

Trinity Hill Hawke's Bay Pinot Gris ★★★☆

The 2014 vintage (★★★☆) is a medium-bodied style, with dry, peachy, spicy flavours, showing very good depth, and toasty, bottle-aged notes emerging. Ready.

DRY $22 AV

Triplebank Awatere Valley Marlborough Pinot Gris ★★★☆

Pernod Ricard NZ's wine is typically aromatic and flavourful. The 2016 vintage (★★★★) is scented and mouthfilling, with vibrant pear, lychee and spice flavours, gentle acidity and a well-rounded finish. Delicious young.

MED/DRY $20 AV

Tupari Awatere Valley Marlborough Pinot Gris ★★★★

A single-vineyard wine, the 2015 vintage (★★★★) is maturing gracefully. Fresh and lively, it is full-bodied, with good concentration of ripe, peachy flavours, a slightly oily texture and a dry (4 grams/litre of residual sugar) finish. Drink now to 2018.

Vintage	15	14	13
WR	6	6	6
Drink	17-18	P	P

DRY $27 –V

Turanga Creek Le Pur Pinot Gris (★★★★☆)

Well worth discovering, the 2015 vintage (★★★★☆) was estate-grown and hand-picked at Whitford, in South Auckland. Made in a fully dry style, it is sturdy (14.5 per cent alcohol) and sweet-fruited, with concentrated, ripe stone-fruit and spice flavours, lively and long. Certified organic.

DRY $27 AV

Two Rivers of Marlborough Brookby Hill Pinot Gris   (★★★★)

From 16-year-old vines in the Omaka Valley, the 2016 vintage (★★★☆) was hand-picked and partly (10 per cent) barrel-fermented. Fresh, with citrus-fruit and pear-like flavours, it is lively and youthful, with a touch of complexity and a dry (4 grams/litre of residual sugar) impression.

DRY $24 AV

Vintage	16
WR	6
Drink	17-20

Two Rivers of Marlborough Wairau Selection Pinot Gris   ★★★☆

The 2015 vintage (★★★) is medium to full-bodied, with vibrant pear and apple flavours, and a fresh, dryish (5 grams/litre of residual sugar), finely balanced finish.

MED/DRY $25 –V

Vintage	15	14	13
WR	6	6	7
Drink	P	P	P

Two Sisters Central Otago Pinot Gris   ★★★★

The impressive 2015 vintage (★★★★☆) is a single-vineyard wine, hand-harvested at Lowburn, in the Cromwell Basin, and fermented in seasoned oak casks. Fragrant and weighty (14.5 per cent alcohol), it is intensely varietal, with ripe, peachy, citrusy, spicy flavours, showing excellent delicacy and depth. Made in a fully dry style, with a slightly creamy texture, it's a drink-now or cellaring proposition.

DRY $29 –V

Urlar Gladstone Pinot Gris   ★★★★

Weighty and rich, this northern Wairarapa wine is hand-picked and fermented and matured in seasoned French oak casks, with extended lees-aging and lees-stirring. The 2015 vintage (★★★★) is full-bodied, with ripe stone-fruit flavours, showing very good complexity and depth, and a dry finish. Certified organic.

DRY $28 –V

Valli Gibbston Vineyard Central Otago Pinot Gris   ★★★★

The 2016 vintage (★★★★☆) was estate-grown at Gibbston and handled entirely in tanks. A scented wine, it is a dry style (4 grams/litre of residual sugar), full-bodied and vibrantly fruity, with fresh, rich pear, lychee and spice flavours, showing excellent purity, depth and harmony. Still youthful, it's well worth cellaring; open 2018+.

DRY $30 –V

Vintage	16
WR	7
Drink	17-24

Vavasour Awatere Valley Marlborough Pinot Gris   ★★★★☆

A consistently impressive wine, bargain-priced. Floral, very fresh and lively, the partly barrel-fermented 2016 vintage (★★★★★) was estate-grown in the lower Awatere Valley. Vibrant, with pure, ripe lychee, pear and spice flavours, it has a leesy, nutty complexity and a finely textured, dryish (5.3 grams/litre of residual sugar) finish.

MED/DRY $23 V+

Vidal Hawke's Bay Pinot Gris   (★★★☆)

The 2017 vintage (★★★☆) was grown at Te Awanga and in the Bridge Pa Triangle, blended with small amounts of Gewürztraminer and Viognier, and made in a dryish style (7.9 grams/litre of residual sugar). Enjoyable from the start, it has fresh, strong pear, lychee and spice aromas and flavours, threaded with lively acidity.

Vintage	17
WR	6
Drink	17-19

MED/DRY $16 V+

Villa Maria Cellar Selection Marlborough Pinot Gris   ★★★★

The great-value 2016 vintage (★★★★☆) was 5 per cent oak-aged. Grown in the Wairau and Awatere valleys, it's an off-dry style (7.8 grams/litre of residual sugar), with mouthfilling body and rich stone-fruit and spice flavours, finely textured and well-rounded. A very harmonious wine, it's a drink-now or cellaring proposition.

Vintage	17	16	15	14	13
WR	6	6	6	6	6
Drink	17-19	17-19	17-18	17-18	P

MED/DRY $18 V+

Villa Maria Private Bin East Coast Pinot Gris   ★★★☆

The 2017 vintage (★★★☆) is already drinking well. Grown in Marlborough, Gisborne and Waipara, it is an aromatic, medium-bodied wine with very good depth of strongly varietal pear, lychee and spice flavours, vibrant, slightly sweet (6.5 grams/litre of residual sugar) and smooth. Fine value.

Vintage	17	16	15	14	13
WR	7	6	7	7	7
Drink	17-20	17-18	17-18	P	P

MED/DRY $16 V+

Villa Maria Single Vineyard Seddon Marlborough Pinot Gris   ★★★★★

One of the country's top Pinot Gris, this Awatere Valley wine is typically sturdy, beautifully scented and intense. Hand-picked and fermented in tanks (75 per cent) and seasoned French oak barriques (25 per cent), the 2016 vintage (★★★★★) is a fleshy, dryish style (7 grams/litre of residual sugar), floral and luscious, soft and ripe, with vibrant, rich stone-fruit flavours, gentle acidity and a long, finely textured finish.

Vintage	16	15	14	13
WR	7	7	7	7
Drink	17-20	17-20	17-18	17-19

MED/DRY $32 AV

Vista Nelson Pinot Gris ★★★☆

Priced right, the 2015 vintage (★★★☆) is a single-vineyard wine, grown at Kina. Mouthfilling and dry (4 grams/litre of residual sugar), it has very good depth of peach, pear and spice flavours, woven with appetising acidity.

DRY $18 V+

VNO Hawke's Bay Pinot Gris ★★★

Mouthfilling, with a slightly oily texture, the 2015 vintage (★★★☆) includes a splash of Gewürztraminer (5 per cent). Well balanced for easy drinking, it has good depth of pear, lychee and spice flavours, with a dryish, very smooth finish. Good value.

MED/DRY $17 AV

VNO Skinny Hawke's Bay Pinot Gris (★★)

The pale, easy-drinking 2015 vintage (★★) is a light style (9 per cent alcohol). It has gentle pear and spice flavours, fresh acidity, a sliver of sweetness and a smooth finish.

MED/DRY $17 –V

Waimea Nelson Pinot Gris ★★★★

In top seasons, this is one of the country's best-value Pinot Gris. The 2016 vintage (★★★☆), estate-grown on the Waimea Plains, is mouthfilling, with very good depth of ripe, peachy, slightly spicy flavours, a gentle splash of sweetness (10.7 grams/litre of residual sugar), moderate acidity, and lots of drink-young charm.

MED/DRY $17 V+

Waipara Hills Waipara Valley Pinot Gris ★★★★

Bargain-priced, the 2016 vintage (★★★★☆) is full-bodied and vibrantly fruity, with strong, ripe stone-fruit and spice flavours and a slightly sweet (5.6 grams/litre of residual sugar), finely balanced finish. Drink now or cellar.

MED/DRY $17 V+

Wairau River Marlborough Pinot Gris ★★★★

Estate-grown, the 2016 vintage (★★★★) was handled mostly in tanks, but a small part of the blend was barrel-fermented. Mouthfilling, it is slightly creamy-textured, with a sliver of sweetness (7 grams/litre of residual sugar) and vibrant citrusy, slightly peachy and spicy flavours, showing very good vigour and depth.

MED/DRY $20 V+

Vintage	16	15	14	13
WR	6	7	7	5
Drink	17-19	17-20	17-19	17-18

West Brook Waimauku Pinot Gris   (★★★☆)

Worth cellaring, the 2016 vintage (★★★☆) was grown in West Auckland and mostly handled in tanks; 9 per cent was fermented in seasoned oak casks. Freshly aromatic, it is medium-bodied, with youthful citrus-fruit, apple and pear flavours, showing a touch of complexity, a sliver of sweetness (5.7 grams/litre of residual sugar), lively acidity and very good depth. Best drinking mid-2018+.

Vintage	16
WR	5
Drink	17-22

MED/DRY $23 –V

Whitehaven Featherweight Marlborough Pinot Gris/Sauvignon Blanc   (★★★)

Fresh, lively and smooth, the 2016 vintage (★★★) is a low-alcohol style (9.5 per cent), with gentle sweetness (9 grams/litre of residual sugar) and crisp acidity. It has lemon, pear and spice flavours, in a refreshing style, enjoyable young.

MED/DRY $20 –V

Whitehaven Marlborough Pinot Gris   ★★★★

The 2014 vintage (★★★★) is a fragrant, full-bodied, vibrantly fruity wine, partly hand-harvested, with strong, peachy, slightly spicy and gingery flavours, and a dryish (6 grams/litre of residual sugar), finely balanced finish. Delicious young.

MED/DRY $23 AV

Wild Rock Marlborough Pinot Gris   (★★★☆)

From Craggy Range, the 2016 vintage (★★★☆) has a scented, slightly spicy bouquet. Mouthfilling, it has fresh, citrusy, peachy flavours, showing very good depth, and a finely balanced, dry (4 grams/litre of residual sugar) finish.

DRY $19 V+

Wooing Tree Central Otago Pinot Gris   ★★★

Grown at Alexandra, the 2016 vintage (★★★) was hand-harvested, fermented in a mix of tanks (30 per cent) and old French oak barrels (70 per cent), and made in an off-dry (10.7 grams/litre of residual sugar) style. Pale, it is fresh, peachy and vibrantly fruity, in an uncomplicated, easy-drinking style with a smooth, slightly creamy finish.

MED/DRY $32 –V

Yealands Estate Land Made Marlborough Pinot Gris   ★★★☆

The 2015 vintage (★★★☆) is mouthfilling and dry (4 grams/litre of residual sugar), with fresh acidity and vibrant pear/spice flavours that linger well.

Vintage	15	14
WR	6	7
Drink	P	P

DRY $20 AV

Yealands Estate Single Vineyard Marlborough Pinot Gris   ★★★★

Estate-grown in the Seaview Vineyard, in the Awatere Valley, and partly (10 per cent) barrel-fermented, the 2016 vintage (★★★★) is aromatic, full-bodied and vibrantly fruity, with very good depth of ripe peach, pear and almond flavours, gentle acidity, and a finely textured, dry (3.9 grams/litre of residual sugar), lingering finish. The 2017 vintage (★★★★) is freshly scented, mouthfilling, vibrantly fruity and smooth, with gentle acidity and clearly varietal pear, lychee and spice flavours, showing very good depth, delicacy and harmony.

DRY $23 AV

Vintage	16	15	14
WR	6	6	6
Drink	17-18	P	P

Riesling

Riesling isn't yet one of New Zealand's great successes in overseas markets and most New Zealand wine lovers also ignore Riesling. The favourite white-wine variety of many winemakers, Riesling barely registers on the wine sales charts in supermarkets, generating about 1 per cent of the dollar turnover.

Around the world, Riesling has traditionally been regarded as Chardonnay's great rival in the white-wine quality stakes, well ahead of Sauvignon Blanc. So why are wine lovers here slow to appreciate Riesling's stature?

Riesling is usually made in a slightly sweet style, to balance the grape's natural high acidity, but this obvious touch of sweetness runs counter to the fashion for dry wines. And fine Riesling demands time (at the very least, a couple of years) to unfold its full potential; drunk in its infancy, as it so often is, it lacks the toasty, minerally, honeyed richness that is the real glory of Riesling.

After being overhauled by Pinot Gris in 2007, Riesling ranks as New Zealand's fourth most extensively planted white-wine variety. Between 2007 and 2018, its total area of bearing vines has contracted slightly, from 868 to 765 hectares.

The great grape of Germany, Riesling is a classic cool-climate variety, particularly well suited to the cooler growing temperatures and lower humidity of the South Island. Its two strongholds are Marlborough (where 40 per cent of the vines are clustered) and Canterbury (38 per cent), but the grape is also extensively planted in Otago, Nelson and Wairarapa.

Riesling styles vary markedly around the world. Most Marlborough wines are medium to full-bodied (12 to 13.5 per cent alcohol), with just a touch of sweetness. However, a new breed of Riesling has emerged in the past decade – lighter (only 7.5 to 10 per cent alcohol) and markedly sweeter. These refreshingly light, sweet Rieslings offer a more vivid contrast in style to New Zealand's other major white wines, and are much closer in style to the classic German model.

Abbey Cellars Hawke's Bay Medium Dry Riesling ★★★☆

Estate-grown and hand-picked in the Bridge Pa Triangle, the 2014 vintage (★★★★) is a tightly structured, medium-bodied (11 per cent alcohol) wine, with citrusy flavours, showing excellent vibrancy and depth.

MED/DRY $22 AV

Akarua Central Otago Riesling ★★★☆

The 2015 vintage (★★★) was hand-picked at Bannockburn at 19.8 brix. Still youthful, it is an off-dry style (9 grams/litre of residual sugar) with fresh, restrained, citrusy, appley flavours.

MED/DRY $28 –V

Allan Scott Family Winemakers Marlborough Riesling ★★★★

The 2015 vintage (★★★☆) is a mouthfilling (13 per cent alcohol), medium-dry wine with a slightly minerally bouquet. Showing some early development, it is fleshy, ripe and citrusy, with slightly toasty notes and a rounded finish. Priced right.

MED/DRY $18 V+

Allan Scott Generations Marlborough Dry Riesling   (★★★★)

The debut 2015 vintage (★★★★) is a generous wine, estate-grown in the Moorlands Vineyard, in the heart of the Wairau Valley. Mouthfilling, with a dry feel (5 grams/litre of residual sugar), it has strong, ripe, citrusy, slightly peachy flavours, balanced acidity, and lots of drink-young appeal, but should also reward cellaring.

 MED/DRY $26 –V

Allan Scott Generations Marlborough Riesling   (★★★★)

Launched from the 2015 vintage (★★★★), this estate-grown wine is from the Moorlands Vineyard, in the heart of the Wairau Valley, with some botrytis-affected grapes in the blend. It has a gently honeyed bouquet, moderate acidity, gentle sweetness (34 grams/litre of residual sugar), and strong, peachy, slightly spicy flavours. An age-worthy wine, it's also delicious young.

 MED $26 –V

Amisfield Dry Central Otago Riesling   ★★★★☆

Estate-grown at Pisa, in the Cromwell Basin, the 2015 vintage (★★★★☆) was hand-harvested and fermented with cultured and indigenous yeasts. Pale lemon/green, it has a fragrant, slightly toasty bouquet. Still tight and youthful, it's an age-worthy wine, with fresh, strong, citrusy, dryish flavours (9 grams/litre of residual sugar), tangy acidity, and a slightly minerally, lingering finish. Showing excellent vigour and intensity, it should be at its best 2019+.

 MED/DRY $25 V+

Amisfield Lowburn Terrace Central Otago Riesling   ★★★★☆

Estate-grown in the Cromwell Basin, the 2015 vintage (★★★★☆) was hand-picked and made in a low-alcohol (9 per cent), gently sweet style (57 grams/litre of residual sugar). Bright, light lemon/green, it's a Mosel-like wine, with strong, vibrant lemon/lime flavours, very fresh and punchy, appetising acidity, and excellent poise. Still youthful, it should be at its best 2019+.

 SW $25 V+

Anchorage Family Estate Classic Nelson Riesling   ★★★☆

Light and lively, with low alcohol (9 per cent), the 2015 vintage (★★★☆) has strong, crisp lemon/lime flavours, a sliver of sweetness (7.1 grams/litre of residual sugar) and tangy acidity. Finely balanced for early drinking, it's priced sharply.

 MED/DRY $17 V+

Anchorage St Urbanus Nelson Riesling   (★★★)

The 2014 vintage (★★★) is a partly barrel-fermented, dry wine (2.5 grams/litre of residual sugar). Medium-bodied, it is citrusy, with moderate acidity (for Riesling) and good freshness, depth and drinkability.

DRY $19 AV

Aronui Single Vineyard Nelson Riesling (★★★★)

The finely balanced 2014 vintage (★★★★) was grown on the Waimea Plains and made in a medium-dry style (11 grams/litre of residual sugar). It has moderate acidity for Riesling and strong, lively, citrusy, slightly spicy and gingery flavours, showing good vigour, depth and harmony.

MED/DRY $25 AV

Astrolabe Astrolabe Farm Marlborough Dry Riesling (★★★★)

The 2016 vintage (★★★★) was grown at Grovetown, in the lower Wairau Valley, and tank-fermented to dryness (4.1 grams/litre of residual sugar). Pale lemon/green, it is a lemon-scented, medium to full-bodied wine with fresh, crisp, citrusy flavour, a slightly minerally streak, and very good vigour and depth. Drink now or cellar.

DRY $23 AV

Astrolabe Province Marlborough Dry Riesling ★★★★

The 2015 vintage (★★★★) was hand-picked at Grovetown, in the lower Wairau Valley, and tank-fermented to dryness (4 grams/litre of residual sugar). It is very finely poised, with good intensity of fresh, lemony, slightly appley and spicy flavours, lively but not high acidity, a minerally streak, and obvious cellaring potential.

DRY $23 AV

Astrolabe Valleys Wairau Valley Marlborough Riesling ★★★★

The 2014 vintage (★★★★) was grown at Grovetown, in the lower Wairau Valley, and tank-fermented. Made in a medium-dry style (6.8 grams/litre of residual sugar), it has strong, ripe grapefruit/lime flavours, fresh, balanced acidity, slightly toasty, bottle-aged characters emerging and good harmony.

MED/DRY $20 V+

Ata Mara Central Otago Riesling (★★★★)

The 2014 vintage (★★★★) is a tightly structured and vigorous wine, with good intensity of fresh, lemony, limey flavours, slightly sweet (17 grams/litre of residual sugar), crisp and strong.

MED $27 –V

Ataahua Waipara Riesling ★★★★

Maturing well, the 2015 vintage (★★★★) is a distinctly medium style, with strong, ripe citrus, passionfruit and lime flavours, a vague hint of honey, balanced acidity and good harmony. Drink now or cellar.

MED $27 –V

Aurum Central Otago Riesling ★★★★☆

Freshly scented, lively and tangy, the 2014 vintage (★★★★★) is a medium-bodied wine with intense lemon/lime flavours, a minerally streak and a finely poised, dryish, very long finish. Full of personality and potential, it's certified organic.

Vintage	14
WR	6
Drink	18-24

 MED/DRY $26 AV

Babich Family Estates Cowslip Valley Marlborough Riesling ★★★★

Estate-grown in the Waihopai Valley, the 2015 vintage (★★★☆) is a medium-bodied, dryish style, with a scented, lemony bouquet. Peachy and citrusy, with hints of spices and ginger, and an appetisingly crisp finish, it should be at its best from 2018 onwards. Showing strong personality, the 2016 vintage (★★★★) was harvested with some 'noble rot' influence. Full-bodied, with good concentration of lemony, slightly sweet and honeyed flavours, it's already drinking well.

 MED/DRY $25 AV

Bald Hills Central Otago Riesling ★★★★☆

The 2015 vintage (★★★★☆) was grown at Bannockburn. An elegant, tightly structured wine, it has excellent depth of vibrant, delicate lemon/lime flavours, in a medium style (23 grams/litre of residual sugar) with finely balanced acidity. Delicious young, it should mature gracefully. The classy 2016 vintage (★★★★★), also grown at Bannockburn, has a scented, minerally bouquet. Light lemon/green, it is already drinking well, with concentrated, ripe, citrusy, peachy flavours, gentle sweetness (17 grams/litre of residual sugar), good acid spine, and a very long finish.

Vintage	16
WR	6
Drink	17-23

MED $30 –V

Bannock Brae Central Otago Dry Riesling ★★★★

Grown at Bendigo, the highly distinctive 2016 vintage (★★★★☆) reflects 'traditional German winemaking techniques', including fermentation and lees-aging in old oak barrels. Still youthful, but already approachable, it is a fresh, medium-bodied wine (12 per cent alcohol), showing unusual complexity, with strong, citrusy, peachy, slightly spicy flavours and a crisp, dryish (7.4 grams/litre of residual sugar), finely balanced finish.

MED/DRY $25 AV

Beach House Stoney Beach Gravels Hawke's Bay Riesling ★★★★

The 2016 vintage (★★★★☆) is a vivacious wine, hand-picked in The Levels Vineyard, at Te Awanga. Bright, light lemon/green, it is lemon-scented and light-bodied, with good intensity of citrusy, appley, slightly peachy flavours, gently sweet (30 grams/litre of residual sugar) and mouth-wateringly crisp. The 2017 vintage (★★★★) is also a light-bodied, medium style (25 grams/litre of residual sugar), with fresh, penetrating lemony, appley flavours, racy acidity, and good harmony and vigour. Best drinking 2019+.

 MED $20 V+

Betty by Soho Marlborough Riesling   (★★★★☆)

The delicious, debut 2015 vintage (★★★★☆) is promoted as a 'lower alcohol' style (9.4 per cent). A hand-picked, single-vineyard wine, it is pale lemon/green, with a scented bouquet. Intense, vibrantly fruity and steely, with a high level of acidity balanced by ample sweetness (44 grams/litre of residual sugar), it has concentrated, appley flavours, a minerally streak, slightly toasty notes developing, and a real sense of vigour and drive. Drink now onwards.

MED $22 V+

Black Estate Damsteep Waipara Valley Riesling   (★★★★☆)

From vines planted in 1999, the 2015 vintage (★★★★☆) was hand-picked at 19.8 to 23.6 brix and fermented with indigenous yeasts in tanks (95 per cent) and old 500-litre barrels (5 per cent). It is mouthfilling and fleshy, in a dryish style (6 grams/litre of residual sugar), with concentrated, peachy flavours, slightly spicy, gingery and honeyed, finely balanced acidity, and excellent vigour and harmony. Drink now or cellar.

MED/DRY $28 AV

Black Estate Waipara Valley Riesling   ★★★★

For the 2014 vintage (★★★★), Black Estate 'sourced a parcel of local, hand-harvested fruit'. A slightly honeyed wine, it has rich, citrusy, peachy, spicy flavours, good complexity, and a dryish finish.

MED/DRY $24 AV

Black Peak Wanaka Central Otago Riesling   ★★★★

The 2015 vintage (★★★★) is an instantly appealing, vivacious wine, light (8.9 per cent alcohol) and gently sweet (48 grams/litre of residual sugar), with a freshly scented bouquet, strong, vibrant lemon/lime flavours, good acid spine and a lengthy finish. Drink now or cellar.

MED $26 –V

Black Ridge Central Otago Old Vine Riesling   ★★★★☆

Showing good personality, the 2016 vintage (★★★★) was estate-grown at Alexandra and made in a dry style (4 grams/litre of residual sugar). Light lemon/green, it is lemon-scented and full-bodied, with very satisfying depth of youthful, lemony, appley flavours, a minerally streak, and obvious cellaring potential; open 2019+.

Vintage	16
WR	5
Drink	17-22

DRY $26 AV

Black Stilt Waitaki Valley Riesling   ★★★☆

Priced sharply, the 2014 vintage (★★★☆) is a medium-bodied North Otago wine with good depth of lemony, slightly peachy and appley flavours and a finely balanced, off-dry, smooth finish.

MED/DRY $18 V+

Brancott Estate Flight Waipara Riesling ★★★

Offering very easy drinking, the 2015 vintage (★★☆) is a light wine (9 per cent alcohol), gently sweet, with decent depth of tangy, citrusy, limey flavours.

MED $17 AV

Brancott Estate Waipara Riesling ★★★☆

Priced right, the 2016 vintage (★★★☆) is a vibrantly fruity, crisp, medium-bodied wine with a sliver of sweetness and good depth of citrusy, slightly spicy flavours, fresh and finely balanced.

MED/DRY $17 V+

Brightside Organic Riesling ★★★☆

From Kaimira Estate, in Nelson, the 2016 vintage (★★★☆) is an off-dry style (10 grams/litre of residual sugar). Light lemon/green, it is medium-bodied, with vibrant, lemony, appley flavours, well balanced for easy drinking, and good depth. Certified organic, it's priced sharply.

MED/DRY $16 V+

Brightwater Vineyards Nelson Riesling ★★★★☆

Estate-grown and hand-picked on the Waimea Plains, the classy 2015 vintage (★★★★★) is richly scented, with incisive lemon, lime and passionfruit flavours, and an off-dry (14 grams/litre of residual sugar), mouth-wateringly crisp finish. Very fresh and concentrated, with a minerally streak, it's a beautifully poised wine, already highly expressive, but well worth cellaring. A top buy.

Vintage	15	14
WR	6	5
Drink	17-19	17-18

MED/DRY $20 V+

Burn Cottage Central Otago Riesling/Grüner Veltliner ★★★★☆

The 2015 vintage (★★★★☆) is an estate-grown blend of Riesling (54 per cent) and Grüner Veltliner (46 per cent), fermented and matured for 11 months in stainless steel barrels and old oak barriques. Light lemon/green, it is full-bodied, with a fresh, citrusy bouquet. Full of youthful drive, it has strong, lemony, slightly spicy and peachy flavours, showing good complexity, a minerally thread, and a long, crisp, dryish (6.3 grams/litre of residual sugar) finish. Best drinking 2019+.

MED/DRY $55 –V

Camshorn Classic Riesling ★★★★

The 2015 vintage (★★★★) from Pernod Ricard NZ is a good buy. Attractively scented and light-bodied (10.5 per cent alcohol), with generous, ripe, peachy flavours, moderate acidity and a smooth finish, it's drinking well now.

MED $20 V+

Carrick Bannockburn Central Otago Riesling ★★★★★

Certified organic, the classy 2016 vintage (★★★★★) is pale lemon/green, youthful and vibrant, with excellent intensity of grapefruit and lime flavours, a gentle splash of sweetness, good acid spine and a long, very harmonious finish. Approachable now, it should flourish with cellaring; open 2019+.

Vintage	16	15	14	13	12	11	10
WR	7	6	7	7	7	6	7
Drink	17-22	17-20	17-20	17-18	17-18	P	P

Carrick Central Otago Dry Riesling ★★★★☆

Certified organic, the 2016 vintage (★★★★☆) has a scented, minerally bouquet. Tightly structured, with strong, fresh, citrusy flavours, firm acid spine and a steely, dryish (less than 10 grams/litre of residual sugar) finish, it is slightly austere in its infancy, with obvious potential; open 2019+.

MED/DRY $27 AV

Carrick Josephine Central Otago Riesling ★★★★★

Instantly appealing, the finely poised 2016 vintage (★★★★★) was estate-grown in Lot 8 Vineyard at Bannockburn, hand-picked and made in a low-alcohol (9 per cent), sweetish style. A lovely young wine, it is light and vivacious, with fresh, rich peach, lemon and lime flavours, abundant sweetness balanced by racy acidity, and a lively, long finish. Drink now or cellar. Certified organic.

Vintage	16	15	14	13	12	11	10
WR	7	7	7	7	7	6	7
Drink	17-21	17-20	17-19	17-18	17-18	P	P

Ceres Black Rabbit Bannockburn Central Otago Riesling ★★★★★

Already delicious, the classy, flavour-packed 2017 vintage (★★★★★) was grown in the Black Rabbit Vineyard at Bannockburn, fermented with indigenous yeasts and made in a medium-sweet (45 grams/litre of residual sugar) style. Pale lemon/green, it is richly scented, very lively, intense and racy, with penetrating, lemony, appley, slightly peachy flavours, vibrant, finely poised and long. Drink now or cellar.

MED $28 V+

Ceres Composition Central Otago Riesling (★★★★)

The 2014 vintage (★★★★) is a fragrant Bannockburn wine with strong, citrusy, limey aromas and flavours, showing good freshness and vigour, tangy acidity, and a finely balanced, slightly sweet, appetisingly crisp finish.

MED/DRY $23 AV

Chard Farm Central Otago Riesling ★★★★

The delicious 2016 vintage (★★★★★) was hand-harvested in the Cromwell Basin. Light lemon/green, it has a scented, citrusy bouquet. A fresh, medium-bodied wine, it is instantly appealing, with vibrant lemon/lime flavours, showing excellent delicacy and depth, a gentle splash of sweetness (15 grams/litre of residual sugar), lively acidity and a finely poised, long finish.

Vintage	16
WR	6
Drink	17-22

 MED $25 AV

Cherry Orchard, The, Bannockburn Single Vineyard Central Otago Riesling (★★★★)

Drinking well now, the 2013 vintage (★★★★) is still on the market. A strongly varietal, medium style, it has very good depth of citrusy, slightly toasty flavours, bottle-aged complexity and a lingering finish.

 MED $22 V+

Clark Estate Upper Awatere Block 8 Marlborough Riesling ★★★★

The 2015 vintage (★★★★) of this single-vineyard Riesling is fresh-scented, light (8 per cent alcohol) and lively, with good acid spine and strong, citrusy, appley, slightly peachy flavours. Delicious young, it's also worth cellaring.

 MED $28 –V

Coney The Ritz Martinborough Riesling ★★★☆

The 2014 vintage (★★★☆) is a 'spritzig' (faintly sparkling) wine, light (9 per cent alcohol) and crisp, with a splash of sweetness (31 grams/litre of residual sugar) amid its tangy, lemony, limey flavours, which show good freshness, balance and depth.

 MED $20 AV

Coopers Creek Marlborough Riesling ★★★☆

The 2015 vintage (★★★☆) is medium-bodied and tangy, in an off-dry style with fresh, lemony, slightly limey flavours, showing very good depth and vigour.

 MED/DRY $18 V+

Craggy Range Te Muna Road Vineyard Martinborough Riesling ★★★☆

The 2014 vintage (★★★☆) was hand-picked at 19.8 brix and fermented with some use of indigenous yeasts. Aromatic, it is fresh, light (11.5 per cent alcohol) and lively, with very good vigour and depth of lemony, limey flavours, dryish (7 grams/litre of residual sugar) and racy.

 MED/DRY $27 –V

Dashwood Marlborough Riesling ★★★☆

The 2015 vintage (★★★★) is a floral, medium-bodied, reasonably dry but not austere wine, vibrantly fruity. It has finely balanced acidity, with citrusy, limey flavours, showing very good delicacy and depth.

MED/DRY $19 V+

Doctors', The, Marlborough Riesling ★★★★

From Forrest, this is a low-alcohol style. Delicious now, the 2016 vintage (★★★★) is bright, light lemon/green, with strong, lemony scents, fresh and inviting. Light (9 per cent alcohol) and gently sweet, it is citrusy and appley, with finely balanced acidity, and excellent vigour, harmony and depth.

Vintage	16
WR	7
Drink	17-26

 MED $22 V+

Domaine Rewa Central Otago Riesling ★★★★

Drinking well now, but still maturing, the 2014 vintage (★★★★☆) is a single-vineyard, Cromwell Basin wine, with a scented, slightly toasty bouquet. A medium style (25 grams/litre of residual sugar), it is vibrantly fruity, with penetrating, citrusy, limey flavours, gentle sweetness, balanced acidity and a lingering finish.

 MED $25 AV

Drowsy Fish by Crown Range Cellar Waipara Riesling (★★★★)

The 2015 vintage (★★★★) was hand-harvested and produced in a distinctly medium style (23 grams/litre of residual sugar). It is fleshy, with peachy, slightly spicy flavours, showing a touch of complexity, finely balanced acidity, and a long, harmonious finish.

 MED $50 –V

Dry River Craighall Vineyard Martinborough Riesling ★★★★★

One of the finest Rieslings in the country, this is typically a wine of exceptional purity, delicacy and depth, with a proven ability to flourish in the cellar for many years. The grapes are sourced from a small block of mature vines, mostly over 20 years old, in the Craighall Vineyard, with yields limited to an average of 6 tonnes per hectare, and the wine is stop-fermented just short of dryness. The impressive 2016 vintage (★★★★★) is pale lemon/green, with a fragrant, minerally bouquet. An intensely varietal wine, it is medium-bodied, with incisive lemon/lime flavours, fresh, appetising acidity, a sliver of sweetness (6 grams/litre of residual sugar) and a finely poised, lasting finish. Already very expressive, it should break into full stride from 2019 onwards.

MED/DRY $47 AV

Dry River Craighall Vineyard Selection Martinborough Riesling ★★★★★

This wine is made to 'produce a Riesling with low alcohol, high residual sugar and high acidity, in order to create a tension between these components'. The 2016 vintage (★★★★★) has obvious potential, but is already a delicious mouthful. Bright, light lemon/green, it is medium-bodied (9.5 per cent alcohol), with intense, citrusy, peachy flavours, ripe and fresh, hints of honey and spices, gentle sweetness (55 grams/litre of residual sugar) and appetising acidity. The 2017 vintage (★★★★★), harvested at 19 to 28 brix, with some botrytis infection, is even sweeter (95 grams/litre of residual sugar). Bright, light lemon/green, it is richly scented, with concentrated, vibrant lemon, apple and peach flavours, lovely sugar/acid harmony, and a lasting finish. For such a young wine, it's already offering great pleasure.

 SW $69 –V

Esk Valley Marlborough Riesling   ★★★★

The 2015 vintage (★★★★) is from mature vines, grown in the Wairau Valley. Made in an appetisingly crisp, dryish style (6.5 grams/litre of residual sugar), it is lemon-scented, with good intensity of finely balanced, citrusy, slightly limey flavours.

MED/DRY $20 V+

Felton Road Bannockburn Central Otago Riesling   ★★★★★

Estate-grown in The Elms Vineyard, this gently sweet style has deep flavours woven with fresh acidity. It offers more drink-young appeal than its Dry Riesling stablemate, but invites long-term cellaring. Hand-picked and tank-fermented with indigenous yeasts, it is bottled with a high level of residual sugar (63 grams/litre in 2016). The 2016 vintage (★★★★★) is bright, light lemon/green. A Mosel-like wine, it is light (9.5 per cent alcohol), with vibrant lemon/lime flavours, a hint of sherbet, and lovely depth, balance and freshness. Delicious from the start, it's a drink-now or cellaring proposition.

Vintage	16
WR	7
Drink	17-36

SW $35 AV
🍇🍇🍇

Felton Road Block 1 Riesling – see Sweet White Wines

Felton Road Dry Riesling   ★★★★★

Based on low-yielding vines in schisty soils at Bannockburn, in Central Otago, this wine is hand-picked in The Elms Vineyard and fermented with indigenous yeasts. The 2016 vintage (★★★★★) is pale/lemon green, with an inviting fragrance. Mouthfilling (13.5 per cent alcohol) and vibrant, it is finely balanced, with intense, citrusy, slightly spicy flavours, fresh acidity, a whisker of sweetness (5.3 grams/litre of residual sugar), and a lasting finish. Best drinking 2018+.

Vintage	16
WR	7
Drink	17-31

DRY $35 V+

Framingham Classic Marlborough Riesling   ★★★★★

Top vintages of this Marlborough wine are strikingly aromatic, richly flavoured and zesty. The 2014 vintage (★★★★☆) is a full-bodied wine, with concentrated, lemony, limey, slightly spicy flavours, a gentle splash of sweetness (17 grams/litre of residual sugar) and fresh, tangy acidity. It's highly enjoyable in its youth, but also has obvious potential. The 2015 vintage (★★★★★) is certified organic. Medium-bodied, it has rich, citrusy flavours and lively acidity, with toasty, bottle-aged complexities emerging. A very 'complete' wine, it's a drink-now or cellaring proposition.

MED $25 V+

Framingham F-Series Old Vine Marlborough Riesling   ★★★★★

From estate vines planted at Renwick over 30 years ago, the 2014 vintage (★★★★★) of this organically certified wine is promoted as an 'Old World style, with more texture and complexity'. Full-bodied, it has fresh, ripe, peachy flavours, gentle acidity for Riesling, and a distinct touch of complexity (19 per cent of the blend was matured for 10 months in old oak barrels). Weighty, finely textured and lingering, it's a distinctive, dryish (8.5 grams/litre of residual sugar), 'food-worthy' Riesling, for drinking now or cellaring. The 2016 vintage (★★★★★) is dryish (under 8 grams/litre of residual sugar), fragrant and mouthfilling, with intense, vibrant, citrusy flavours and a very long finish.

MED/DRY $40 AV

Framingham F-Series Riesling Kabinett   ★★★★☆

The 2015 is only the second vintage of this label, after the slightly sweeter 2011. The 2015 vintage (★★★★☆) is a medium-sweet style (48 grams/litre of residual sugar), handled in tanks (60 per cent) and old oak casks (40 per cent). Light-bodied (9 per cent alcohol), it has fresh, incisive, lemony, appley, slightly peachy and spicy flavours, gentle sweetness (48 grams/litre of residual sugar), good acid spine, a minerally streak, and a long finish. Still youthful, it should mature gracefully.

MED $35 –V

Framingham Marlborough Dry Riesling   (★★★★☆)

Currently on sale, the decade-old, but still very energetic, 2007 vintage (★★★★☆) is light lemon/green, with a gently toasty bouquet. Medium to full-bodied, it has good intensity of lemony, slightly appley and minerally flavours, bottle-aged complexity, and a crisp, basically dry, long finish. Ready; no rush.

MED/DRY $30 –V

Gibbston Valley Central Otago Riesling   ★★★★

Estate-grown in the Red Shed Vineyard, at Bendigo, the 2014 vintage (★★★☆) is mouthfilling, with very good depth of citrusy, slightly peachy and spicy flavours, a touch of sweetness (8.7 grams/litre of residual sugar), lively acidity and obvious potential. (This label has been replaced by the GV Collection Central Otago Riesling – see below.)

Vintage	14	13
WR	7	7
Drink	17-25	17-20

MED/DRY $28 –V

Gibbston Valley GV Collection Central Otago Riesling   ★★★★

Still very youthful, the 2017 vintage (★★★★) is an estate-grown, single-vineyard wine, hand-picked at Bendigo. Bright, light lemon/green, it is mouthfilling (13.5 per cent alcohol) and slightly minerally, with citrusy, appley flavours, lively acidity, a touch of sweetness (7.9 grams/litre of residual sugar), and very good balance, delicacy and depth. Best drinking 2019+.

MED/DRY $28 –V

Gibbston Valley Le Fou Riesling ★★★★★

Estate-grown in the Red Shed Vineyard, at Bendigo, in Central Otago, the 2015 (★★★★★) is the first vintage not based on old vines at Gibbston. Hand-picked, it is pale lemon/green, with lovely freshness, delicacy and poise. It has concentrated, citrusy, slightly limey and spicy flavours that build across the palate to a very harmonious, lasting finish. A very classy, medium wine (28 grams/litre of residual sugar), it's already delicious; drink now or cellar.

Vintage	15	14	13	12	11	10	09	08	07
WR	7	7	7	7	NM	7	6	7	7
Drink	17-26	17-25	17-25	17-25	NM	17-23	17-20	17-20	17-18

MED $39 AV

Giesen Marlborough Riesling ★★★★

The 2015 vintage (★★★★) is a low-alcohol (10 per cent), medium-sweet style (44 grams/litre of residual sugar). Grown in Marlborough and Waipara, it is fresh and vibrantly fruity, with crisp, citrusy flavours, showing good intensity. A poised, vivacious wine, it's a drink-now or cellaring proposition.

MED $17 V+

Gladstone Vineyard Wairarapa Riesling (★★★★☆)

Certified organic, the stylish 2016 vintage (★★★★☆) was hand-picked from 25-year-old, estate-grown vines and matured for six months on its full yeast lees. Light-bodied, it's a medium-dry style (11 grams/litre of residual sugar), with youthful lemon/lime flavours, showing excellent freshness, delicacy, poise and length. Best drinking 2019+.

MED/DRY $25 V+

Glasnevin Limited Release Waipara Valley Riesling ★★★★☆

Showing good personality, the 2015 vintage (★★★★☆) is a distinctly medium style (26 grams/litre of residual sugar). Bright, light lemon/green, it is medium-bodied, fresh and elegant, with rich, citrusy, appley flavours, a hint of passionfruit, balanced acidity, and excellent delicacy, depth and harmony. Best drinking 2018+.

MED $24 V+

Grava Martinborough Riesling (★★★★)

The 2015 vintage (★★★★) was estate-grown south of Martinborough, at a site formerly called Hudson Vineyard. It's an instantly appealing, off-dry style (12 grams/litre of residual sugar), medium-bodied, with vibrant, citrusy, peachy flavours, a hint of passionfruit, and excellent freshness and harmony. Drink now or cellar.

MED/DRY $30 –V

Greenhough Apple Valley Nelson Riesling ★★★★

Grown and hand-picked at Upper Moutere, the 2016 vintage (★★★★) is light-bodied (9.8 per cent alcohol) and gently sweet (28 grams/litre of residual sugar). Light lemon/green, it is aromatic and lively, with fresh, strong, citrusy, appley flavours, tangy acidity and obvious potential; best drinking 2019+.

Vintage	16	15	14	13	12	11	10	09	MED $22 V+
WR	7	6	7	7	7	7	6	6	
Drink	17-21	17-20	17-20	17-19	17-18	P	P	P	

Greenhough Hope Vineyard Nelson Riesling ★★★★☆

This wine is hand-picked from vines that average over 20 years old. Certified organic, the 2014 vintage (★★★★) was mostly handled in tanks, but 30 per cent was fermented in old oak barrels, to 'enhance palate texture and richness'. Pale lemon/green, it has a highly scented, slightly toasty bouquet. Medium-bodied, it is a distinctive, tangy wine, with a minerally streak and strong, lively, slightly sweet (11.5 grams/litre of residual sugar) flavours.

Vintage	14	13	12	11	10	09	MED/DRY $24 V+
WR	7	6	6	6	7	7	
Drink	17-21	17-20	17-19	P	P	P	

Greystone Sea Star Waipara Valley Riesling ★★★★☆

A top example of dry Riesling, the 2016 vintage (★★★★★) was estate-grown, hand-picked, fermented and lees-stirred in tanks, and bottled unfined. Fleshy and full-bodied (13 per cent alcohol), with moderate acidity for Riesling, it has penetrating, youthful, peachy, lemony, slightly limey flavours, that build to a very finely balanced, dry (4.7 grams/litre of residual sugar), lasting finish. Already drinking well, it should also reward cellaring.

Vintage	16	DRY $28 AV
WR	6	
Drink	17-25	

Greystone Waipara Valley Riesling ★★★★★

Greystone sees this wine as 'the truest expression of the variety for us'. Estate-grown and hand-harvested at over 23 brix, with a small percentage of 'noble rot', the 2015 vintage (★★★★★) is a medium style (23 grams/litre of residual sugar). A lovely young wine, it is full-bodied, with strong, ripe, citrusy, peachy flavours, hints of lime, spice and honey, and excellent concentration and harmony. Instantly appealing.

Vintage	15	14	13	12	11	10	09	08	07	MED $27 V+
WR	6	5	7	6	7	7	6	6	5	
Drink	17-30	17-20	17-22	17-20	17-21	17-20	P	P	P	

Greywacke Marlborough Riesling ★★★★★

The 2015 vintage (★★★★☆) was hand-picked from mature vines at Fairhall. Half of the juice was fermented with indigenous yeasts in old French oak barrels, and all of the wine was oak-aged for five months. Made in a medium style (20 grams/litre of residual sugar), it is instantly attractive, with ripe-fruit flavours of peaches, passionfruit and limes, gentle sweetness, a touch of complexity, and excellent harmony and concentration. Best drinking 2018+.

Vintage	15	14	13	12	11	10	09
WR	5	5	6	5	6	5	6
Drink	17-21	17-21	17-20	17-18	17-19	17-20	P

 MED $29 V+

Grove Mill Wairau Valley Marlborough Riesling ★★★☆

The 2015 vintage (★★★☆) is fragrant and fleshy, with strong, ripe, citrusy, limey flavours, showing good freshness, acidity and length.

MED $21 AV

Hans Herzog Marlborough Riesling ★★★★☆

Certified organic, the characterful 2013 vintage (★★★★★) was estate-grown in the Wairau Valley and matured for a year in French oak puncheons. Bright, light lemon/green, it is mouthfilling and vibrantly fruity, with good intensity of grapefruit and lime flavours, a very subtle seasoning of oak adding richness, inconspicuous sweetness (6 grams/litre of residual sugar) and excellent harmony. Best drinking 2018+.

Vintage	13
WR	7
Drink	17-23

 MED/DRY $44 –V

Hawkshead Central Otago Riesling ★★★★

Grown at Lowburn, hand-picked and tank-fermented, the 2014 vintage (★★★★) is a slightly sweet style (10 grams/litre of residual sugar). Full-bodied, it has generous, citrusy, limey flavours, a minerally streak, good acid spine, and a lingering finish. Finely balanced for easy drinking, it's a drink-now or cellaring proposition.

Vintage	14	13	12
WR	6	6	6
Drink	17-19	17-18	P

 MED/DRY $23 AV

Highfield Marlborough Riesling ★★★★

The 2015 vintage (★★★★) is drinking well now. Made in a gently sweet style (24 grams/litre of residual sugar), it is a medium-bodied wine, vaguely honeyed, with ripe, peachy, slightly limey and toasty flavours, showing good concentration.

Vintage	15
WR	6
Drink	17-19

 MED $21 V+

Huia Marlborough Riesling ★★★★

Certified organic, the 2015 vintage (★★★★) is a distinctive, weighty, fleshy wine with strong, citrusy flavours, dryish (5.3 grams/litre of residual sugar), well-rounded and lingering. It's drinking well now.

MED/DRY $28 –V

Hunter's Marlborough Riesling ★★★★

This wine is consistently good and bargain-priced. The fresh, youthful 2016 vintage (★★★★) is an off-dry style (7 grams/litre of residual sugar), with good intensity of lively, citrusy, slightly peachy and spicy flavours, tightly structured and tangy. The 2017 vintage (★★★★) was grown in the Rapaura and Brancott districts. Light lemon/green, it is scented and vibrantly fruity, in a medium-bodied style with strong, lemony, appley flavours, dryish and tangy. Best drinking 2019+.

MED/DRY $20 V+

Invivo Central Otago Riesling ★★★★

The 2014 vintage (★★★★) is a tangy, medium style (25 grams/litre of residual sugar), with punchy, ripe, peachy, slightly limey and spicy flavours, strong, fresh and finely balanced for early enjoyment. It is drinking well now, with toasty, bottle-aged aromas and flavours emerging.

Vintage	14
WR	6
Drink	17-24

MED $22 V+

Jackson Estate Homestead Marlborough Dry Riesling ★★★★

Worth cellaring, the 2015 vintage (★★★★) is a bone-dry but not austere style, estate-grown in the Wairau Valley. Full-bodied, with strong, ripe, citrusy, slightly spicy flavours, woven with fresh acidity, it has very good vigour, balance and depth.

DRY $24 AV

Johanneshof Marlborough Riesling Medium-Dry ★★★★

Youthful, vibrantly fruity and tightly structured, the 2016 vintage (★★★★☆) is a mouthfilling, medium style (19.5 grams/litre of residual sugar). Bright, light lemon/green, it has strong, crisp, citrusy flavours, a vague hint of honey, and excellent poise and persistence. Best drinking 2019+.

MED $25 AV

Johner Estate Wairarapa Riesling ★★★★

The 2016 vintage (★★★★) is a tangy, vivacious wine, medium-dry (11 grams/litre of residual sugar), with lively, citrusy, appley flavours, showing good intensity and harmony. Best drinking 2018+.

Vintage	16	15
WR	6	7
Drink	17-22	17-25

MED/DRY $24 AV

Julicher Martinborough Riesling   ★★★★

The 2014 vintage (★★★★) was estate-grown at Te Muna. Light-bodied (10.5 per cent alcohol), it is a vivacious wine with moderate acidity – for Riesling – and very good depth of ripe, peachy, gently sweet (11 grams/litre of residual sugar), slightly spicy flavours. Delicious young.

MED/DRY $20 V+

Junction Runaway Riesling   (★★★☆)

Grown in Central Hawke's Bay, the attractively scented 2015 vintage (★★★☆) is an off-dry style, with lively acidity threaded through its vibrant, grapefruit-like flavours, which show good freshness and depth.

MED/DRY $22 AV

Kaimira Estate Brightwater Riesling   ★★★☆

This estate-grown, Nelson wine typically matures well. Bright, light lemon/green, the 2015 vintage (★★★☆) is fresh and vibrant, with lemon/lime flavours, slightly peachy notes, good depth and a finely balanced, dry (4.9 grams/litre of residual sugar) finish. Certified organic.

Vintage	15	14	13
WR	5	5	5
Drink	17-23	17-20	17-19

DRY $22 AV

Kaimira Estate Iti Selection Brightwater Riesling   ★★★☆

Made in a low-alcohol style ('Iti' is Maori for 'Small'), the 2016 vintage (★★★☆) is light-bodied (10.5 per cent), with lively, lemony, appley, slightly sweet flavours (15.4 grams/litre of residual sugar), showing good depth, and an appetisingly crisp finish. it's certified organic.

Vintage	16
WR	5
Drink	17-23

MED $22 AV

Kalex Central Otago Riesling   ★★★★

Instantly appealing, the 2014 vintage (★★★★) is a light (9.5 per cent alcohol), gently sweet style, grown at Bendigo, in the Cromwell Basin. Tangy, ripe, peachy and slightly spicy, it has good concentration and harmony.

MED $26 –V

Konrad Dry Marlborough Riesling   ★★★☆

Estate-grown in the Waihopai Valley, the 2015 vintage (★★★★) has a scented, slightly toasty bouquet. Showing good personality, it is bright, light yellow/green, with moderate alcohol (10.5 per cent) and strong, lemony, appley, minerally flavours, crisp, dryish and finely balanced for current drinking.

MED/DRY $23 –V

Lake Chalice The Falcon Marlborough Riesling ★★★★

The 2014 vintage (★★★★) is a single-vineyard, Awatere Valley wine, harvested early and stop-fermented to produce a low-alcohol (9.5 per cent) style. It is light-bodied, very vibrant and racy, with a splash of sweetness (30 grams/litre of residual sugar), strong lemon/apple flavours, a hint of sherbet, and a finely poised, tangy finish.

MED $21 V+

Lawson's Dry Hills Marlborough Riesling ★★★★

The 2016 vintage (★★★★) is a single-vineyard wine, grown in the Waihopai Valley. Light lemon/green, it is medium-bodied, with fresh, youthful, citrusy, slightly appley flavours, showing very good depth, and a finely balanced, off-dry (9 grams/litre of residual sugar) finish. Best drinking mid-2018+.

Vintage	16	15	14
WR	6	7	6
Drink	17-24	17-22	17-20

MED/DRY $20 V+

Linden Estate Martinborough Riesling (★★★★)

The 2014 vintage (★★★★) is a ripely scented wine, crisp and lively. Light-bodied (10.2 per cent alcohol), it has good intensity of lemon/lime flavours, with a sliver of sweetness (8 grams/litre of residual sugar), fresh, appetising acidity and toasty, bottle-aged complexities starting to emerge.

MED/DRY $20 V+

Loveblock Bone Dry Marlborough Riesling ★★★★

The 2014 vintage (★★★★) was estate-grown in the lower Awatere Valley. Showing some toasty, bottle-aged development, it is a bright lemon/green wine, full-bodied, with tangy acidity, a minerally streak and a strong surge of ripe, peachy, slightly spicy, fully dry (1.4 grams/litre of residual sugar) flavours. Certified organic.

Vintage	14	13	12	11
WR	6	NM	NM	6
Drink	17-22	NM	NM	P

DRY $25 AV

Mahana Riesling (★★★★)

Grown in Nelson, the 2016 vintage (★★★★) has a slightly 'funky' bouquet, leading into a light-bodied wine (8.5 per cent alcohol) with strong, lively, citrusy flavours, gentle sweetness (40 grams/litre of residual sugar), a minerally streak and good acid spine. Drink now or cellar.

MED $29 –V

Main Divide Waipara Valley Riesling ★★★★

Offering fine value, the 2014 vintage (★★★★) has good personality. Bright, light yellow/green, it is medium-bodied and tangy, with strong citrus and passionfruit flavours to the fore, hints of oranges, toast and honey, gentle sweetness (20 grams/litre of residual sugar) and lively acidity. (From Pegasus Bay.)

Vintage	14	13
WR	6	7
Drink	17-27	17-22

 MED $21 V+

Marble Point Hanmer Springs Riesling Dry ★★★★

Estate-grown in North Canterbury and matured for two months in old barrels, the 2014 vintage (★★★★) has a fragrant, citrusy, slightly honeyed bouquet. It shows very good freshness, vigour and depth, with strong, lemony flavours, hints of peaches, limes and spices, mouth-watering acidity, good sugar/acid balance (13 grams/litre of residual sugar) and lots of personality.

Vintage	14
WR	6
Drink	17-25

 MED/DRY $22 V+

Margrain Martinborough Riesling (★★★★)

The 2017 vintage (★★★★) is a vibrant, medium-bodied wine, with good intensity of citrusy, appley flavours. Made in a medium-dry style (12 grams/litre of residual sugar), it has good acid spine and plenty of drink-young appeal, but should also mature well.

Vintage	17
WR	6
Drink	17-27

MED/DRY $26 –V

Margrain Proprietor's Selection Martinborough Riesling (★★★★)

Well worth cellaring, the 2016 vintage (★★★★) is an off-dry style (9 grams/litre of residual sugar). Medium to full-bodied, it is fresh, crisp and youthful, with good intensity of lemon, apple and lime flavours, slightly sweet and tangy. Best drinking 2018+.

Vintage	16
WR	7
Drink	17-26

MED/DRY $24 AV

Martinborough Vineyard Manu Riesling ★★★★

The 2016 vintage (★★★★☆) is quietly classy. A medium-dry style (14 grams/litre of residual sugar), it is fresh and finely poised, with ripe, citrusy, peachy flavours, showing excellent delicacy, richness and harmony. Best drinking mid-2018+.

 MED/DRY $28 –V

Maude Mt Maude Vineyard East Block Wanaka Riesling   ★★★★☆

From vines planted in 1994 on a steep, north-facing slope at Wanaka, in Central Otago, the 2016 vintage (★★★★★) is highly aromatic, light and vivacious, with strong lemon/apple flavours, gentle sweetness (34 grams/litre of residual sugar), racy acidity and obvious potential; open 2019+.

MED $32 –V

Maude Mt Maude Vineyard Wanaka Dry Riesling   ★★★★☆

Hand-picked from vines planted in 1994, the richly scented 2016 vintage (★★★★★) is very refined, intense and minerally, with deep lemon, apple and spice flavours, a sliver of sweetness (9 grams/litre of residual sugar) and mouth-watering acidity. Best drinking 2019+.

MED/DRY $32 –V

Millton Opou Vineyard Riesling   ★★★★☆

Typically scented, with rich, lemony, often honeyed flavours, this is the country's northernmost fine-quality Riesling. Harvested from Gisborne vines of varying ages – the oldest planted in 1981 – it is gently sweet, in a less racy style than South Island wines. The grapes, grown in the Opou Vineyard at Manutuke, are hand-picked over a month at three stages of ripening, usually culminating in a final pick of botrytis-affected fruit. The very youthful 2015 vintage (★★★★☆) is a low-alcohol (8.5 per cent), gently sweet wine (36 grams/litre of residual sugar). Bright, light lemon/green, it is light and tangy, with intense, vibrant lemon/lime flavours, appetising acidity, and excellent poise and vigour. Best drinking 2019+. Certified organic.

Vintage	15	14	13	12
WR	6	6	7	6
Drink	17-25	17-25	17-22	17-20

MED $28 AV

Misha's Vineyard Limelight Riesling   ★★★★★

This single-vineyard wine is hand-harvested at Bendigo, in Central Otago. The 2014 vintage (★★★★★) is a highly scented, vibrantly fruity wine, made in a medium style (33 grams/litre of residual sugar), with complexity gained by fermenting 25 per cent of the blend with indigenous yeasts in old French oak barrels. Fleshy, with concentrated, citrusy, limey flavours, appetising acidity and a rich, finely poised finish, it's already delicious, but likely to be at its best 2018+.

Vintage	14	13	12	11	10	09	08
WR	6	7	7	6	6	7	6
Drink	17-21	17-20	17-18	17-19	17-18	17-18	P

MED $28 V+

Misha's Vineyard Lyric Riesling   ★★★★★

This is the sort of 'dry' Riesling New Zealand needs a lot more of. Estate-grown at Bendigo, in Central Otago, the 2013 vintage (★★★★★) is fractionally off-dry (5.5 grams/litre of residual sugar). It was mostly handled in tanks, but 41 per cent of the blend was fermented with indigenous yeasts in old French oak barrels. Lemon-scented, it is elegant and tightly structured, with rich, citrusy, appley, slightly spicy flavours. Weighty, with good complexity and harmony and a long, dry finish, it's enjoyable now but also very age-worthy. (There is no 2014, but the label returns from the 2015 vintage.)

Vintage	14	13	12	11	10	09
WR	NM	7	7	6	6	7
Drink	NM	17-22	17-21	17-20	17-19	17-18

Mission Hawke's Bay Riesling   ★★★☆

Finely balanced for easy drinking, the 2016 vintage (★★★☆) is a single-vineyard wine, grown at Ohiti. Pale lemon/green, it is medium-bodied, with strong, lemony, slightly appley flavours, a sliver of sweetness, and lots of drink-young appeal.

MED/DRY $18 V+

Misty Cove Marlborough Riesling   (★★★★)

The fleshy, full-bodied 2015 vintage (★★★★), branded 'Signature' on the back label, was hand-picked at Rapaura and lees-aged for 16 weeks. It has generous, ripe grapefruit/lime flavours, with a hint of honey, gentle sweetness and balanced acidity. Drink now or cellar.

MED/DRY $24 AV

Mondillo Central Otago Riesling   ★★★★

Estate-grown at Bendigo, the 2015 vintage (★★★★) is an almost fully dry style (2.6 grams/litre of residual sugar). Light lemon/green, it is mouthfilling, with strong, youthful lemon/lime flavours, crisp acidity, a minerally streak and good vigour and length. Best drinking 2018+.

Vintage	15	14	13	12	11	10
WR	7	7	7	NM	7	NM
Drink	17-21	17-24	17-22	NM	17-20	NM

Montana Waipara Riesling   ★★★

The 2014 vintage (★★★) offers great value, with moderate alcohol (11 per cent) and plenty of fresh, lively, lemony flavour.

MED $12 V+

Mount Brown Estates Grand Reserve Waipara Valley Riesling   (★★★★)

Forward in its appeal, the 2016 vintage (★★★★) is a late-picked, medium style (18 grams/litre of residual sugar), with a scented, slightly honeyed bouquet. Citrusy, with moderate acidity, it is full-flavoured, with a vague hint of botrytis and very good balance and depth.

MED $23 AV

Mount Brown Estates Waipara Valley Riesling   ★★★

Priced right, the 2016 vintage (★★★) is an easy-drinking, gently sweet wine (8 grams/litre of residual sugar), medium-bodied, with citrusy, appley flavours, hints of pears and spices, and good harmony. Drink now or cellar.

Vintage	16
WR	7
Drink	17-22

MED/DRY $16 V+

Mount Edward Central Otago Riesling   ★★★★☆

The 2014 vintage (★★★★☆) is a single-vineyard wine, grown at Lowburn. It is a tight, medium-bodied style with good intensity of vibrant lemon/lime flavours, a minerally streak, and a gently sweet, racy finish.

MED/DRY $25 V+

Mount Riley Marlborough Riesling   ★★★☆

The 2015 vintage (★★★☆), grown in the Wairau Valley, is medium-bodied, with strong, lemony, slightly limey flavours and an off-dry (7.9 grams/litre of residual sugar), crisp finish.

Vintage	15	14
WR	6	6
Drink	17-18	P

MED/DRY $17 V+

Moutere Hills Single Vineyard Nelson Riesling   ★★★☆

The 2014 vintage (★★★☆) was grown and hand-picked on the Waimea Plains. A finely balanced, lively, light-bodied wine (under 10 per cent alcohol), it has good depth of fresh, peachy, spicy flavours, a hint of apricot, and gentle sweetness (21 grams/litre of residual sugar) balanced by appetising acidity.

MED $29 –V

Mt Beautiful North Canterbury Riesling   ★★★★

Estate-grown at Cheviot, the racy 2016 vintage (★★★★) is a pale lemon/green, highly scented wine, light to medium-bodied, with strong, lively lemon/apple flavours, a minerally streak, and a gently sweet (13 grams/litre of residual sugar), crisp finish. Drink now or cellar.

Vintage	16	15
WR	7	7
Drink	17-25	17-25

MED/DRY $31 –V

Mt Difficulty Bannockburn Central Otago Dry Riesling   ★★★★

Estate-grown at Bannockburn, the 2016 vintage (★★★★☆) is one of the best yet. Bright, light lemon/green, it is full-bodied and fleshy, with strong grapefruit, lime and peach flavours, dry but not austere, and a long, harmonious finish. Already drinking well, it should be at its best 2019+.

DRY $26 –V

Mt Difficulty Growers Series Packspur Vineyard Lowburn Valley Riesling   ★★★★

Already delicious, the 2016 vintage (★★★★☆) is mouthfilling (13.5 per cent alcohol), with rich, ripe, peachy, slightly gingery and honeyed flavours, plentiful sweetness (53 grams/litre of residual sugar) and a well-rounded finish.

SW $26 –V

Mt Difficulty Target Bannockburn Medium Riesling   ★★★★☆

From Central Otago, the 2016 vintage (★★★★☆) is an instantly appealing, medium-sweet style (43 grams/litre of residual sugar). Bright, light lemon/green, it is medium-bodied and vibrant, with rich, ripe, peachy, limey flavours, hints of passionfruit, marmalade and honey, and a lovely balance of sweetness and appetising acidity.

MED $26 AV

Mud House Single Vineyard The Mound Waipara Valley Riesling   ★★★★

The 2014 vintage (★★★☆) is a poised, vibrantly fruity wine with lemon/lime flavours, showing very good depth, and a slightly sweet, mouth-wateringly crisp finish.

Vintage	14	13
WR	5	7
Drink	17-18	17-18

MED/DRY $24 AV

Mud House Waipara Valley Riesling   ★★★★

Offering terrific value, the estate-grown 2016 vintage (★★★★) is a distinctly medium style (28 grams/litre of residual sugar), with loads of drink-young charm. Bright, light lemon/green, it is attractively scented, with strong, vibrant, citrusy flavours, hints of passionfruit and ginger, mouth-watering acidity and a persistent finish. Drink now or cellar.

MED $15 V+

Muddy Water James Hardwick Waipara Riesling   ★★★★★

Certified organic, the 2015 vintage (★★★★☆) is a medium-dry style, hand-harvested (with a touch of botrytis) and fermented with indigenous yeasts. The bouquet is scented; the palate is rich, citrusy and peachy, with a hint of passionfruit, a minerally streak, and excellent complexity and depth. Best drinking 2018+.

Vintage	15
WR	7
Drink	17-30

MED/DRY $28 V+

Neudorf Moutere Riesling ★★★★★

A copybook cool-climate style with excellent intensity, estate-grown at Upper Moutere. The 2014 vintage (★★★★★) was hand-picked in Rosie's Block at 19.7 brix, fermented with indigenous yeasts, and stop-fermented in a medium-sweet style, with just 9.5 per cent alcohol and 48 grams per litre of residual sugar. Very expressive in its youth, with a slightly minerally streak and deep, peachy, slightly spicy flavours, it's a drink-now or cellaring proposition.

 MED $30 AV

Neudorf Moutere Riesling Dry ★★★★☆

The 2016 vintage (★★★★☆) was estate-grown at Upper Moutere, in Nelson, hand-harvested and fermented in tanks (81 per cent) and old oak puncheons (19 per cent). Pale lemon/green, it is a youthful, medium-bodied wine, with searching, delicate, lemony and appley flavours, biscuity and minerally notes, and a dryish (7.5 grams/litre of residual sugar), long finish. A very age-worthy wine, it should be at its best 2019+.

Vintage	16	15	MED/DRY $27 AV
WR	6	7	
Drink	18-26	17-25	

Nga Waka Martinborough Dry Riesling ★★★★☆

Drinking well now, but still developing, the 2015 vintage (★★★★☆) is a light lemon/green, attractively scented wine, with strong, citrusy flavours, dryish (5 grams/litre of residual sugar) and harmonious, and some toasty, bottle-aged notes. An intensely varietal wine, it shows good personality.

Vintage	15	MED/DRY $25 V+
WR	6	
Drink	18-28	

Ohinemuri Estate Waikato Riesling ★★★☆

Karangahake Gorge-based winemaker Horst Hillerich usually draws his Riesling grapes from Gisborne, but the 2014 vintage (★★★☆) was hand-picked near Cambridge, in the Waikato, and fermented in tanks (mostly) and old oak barrels (7 per cent). Retasted in mid-2017, it is still youthful, with tight, lemony flavours, slight sweetness (12 grams/litre of residual sugar), crisp acidity and good length. Best drinking 2018+.

Vintage	14	MED/DRY $20 AV
WR	6	
Drink	17-21	

Old Coach Road Lighter in Alcohol Nelson Riesling (★★★)

From Seifried, the 2015 vintage (★★★) is crisp and slightly sweet (17 grams/litre of residual sugar), with a low level of alcohol (9.5 per cent), vibrant, lemony, appley, limey flavours, firm acid spine, and lots of drink-young charm.

 MED $13 V+

Vintage	16
WR	7
Drink	17-22

Old Coach Road Nelson Riesling ★★★

From Seifried, this is an enjoyable, drink-young style, priced sharply. The 2015 vintage (★★★☆) is a medium-dry style (8.5 grams/litre of residual sugar). Mouthfilling, it is crisp and lively, with plenty of fresh, citrusy, slightly spicy flavour.

 MED/DRY $13 V+

Vintage	15
WR	6
Drink	17-22

Omeo Blackman's Gully Central Otago Riesling ★★★★

Grown at Alexandra, the 2015 vintage (★★★★) is a lively, still youthful wine. Bright, light lemon/green, it is very fresh and tangy, with strong lemon/lime flavours, gentle sweetness (13 grams/litre of residual sugar) and appetising acidity. The 2016 vintage (★★★★) is similar. Mouthfilling, it is vibrantly fruity, with incisive, citrusy, slightly sweet flavours (12 grams/litre of residual sugar), mouth-watering acidity, and very good vigour and harmony. Best drinking 2019+.

MED/DRY $23 AV

Vintage	16	15	14
WR	6	7	5
Drink	17-24	17-23	17-22

Ostler Lakeside Riesling Spatlese (★★★★★)

Grown in the Waitaki Valley, North Otago, the 2015 vintage (★★★★★) is a lovely young wine. Light lemon/green, it is full of youthful impact. Light-bodied, it is vivacious, with penetrating, citrusy, peachy flavours, gently sweet (29 grams/litre of residual sugar) and mouth-wateringly crisp, and a very long finish. Already delicious, it's well worth cellaring.

MED $29 V+

Paddy Borthwick New Zealand Riesling ★★★☆

Slightly austere in its youth, the 2016 vintage (★★★) was estate-grown at Gladstone, in the Wairarapa. Bright, light lemon/green, it is tightly structured and minerally, with lemon and green-apple flavours, firm acidity and just a sliver of sweetness (4.5 grams/litre of residual sugar). It needs time; open 2019+.

 DRY $22 AV

Palliser Estate Martinborough Riesling   ★★★★

Already very approachable, the 2016 vintage (★★★★) is a finely poised, youthful wine. Medium-bodied, with an attractive array of ripe, peachy, citrusy, limey, spicy flavours, it is a vibrantly fruity, off-dry style (8 grams/litre of residual sugar), showing very good depth. Best drinking 2019+.

MED/DRY $24 AV

Pegasus Bay Aria Late Picked Riesling – see Sweet White Wines

Pegasus Bay Bel Canto Riesling Dry   ★★★★★

Bel Canto means 'Beautiful Singing'. Late-harvested at Waipara, in North Canterbury, from mature vines and made with 'a good portion' of noble rot, the 2015 vintage (★★★★★) is full of personality. Bright, light yellow/green, with a slightly honeyed bouquet, it is full-bodied (13.4 per cent alcohol) and fleshy, with highly concentrated, ripe flavours, a hint of marmalade, gentle sweetness (7.5 grams/litre of residual sugar) and loads of current-drinking appeal.

Vintage	15
WR	6
Drink	17-21

MED/DRY $35 AV

Pegasus Bay Riesling   ★★★★★

Classy stuff. Estate-grown at Waipara, in North Canterbury, in top vintages it is richly fragrant and thrillingly intense, with flavours of citrus fruits and honey, complex and luscious. Based on mature vines and stop-fermented in a distinctly medium style, it breaks into full stride at about three years old and can mature well for a decade. The 2015 vintage (★★★★★) is from a growing season in which 'open bunches [of grapes] meant less botrytis'. Still very youthful, it is medium-bodied, with gentle sweetness (26 grams/litre of residual sugar) and deep, pure, citrusy, peachy flavours, crisp and minerally. It should flourish with cellaring; open 2019+.

Vintage	15	14	13	12	11	10
WR	6	7	6	7	6	7
Drink	17-32	17-28	17-27	17-27	17-25	17-22

MED $30 AV

🍇🍇🍇

Pegasus Bay Riesling Aged Release   (★★★★★)

The debut 2007 vintage (★★★★★) of this 'Aged Release' label in 2017 is a re-release of the decade-old Waipara Valley classic – the first of a planned annual release of 10-year-old wines. Still full of vigour, with a bright, light lemon/green hue and a scented, faintly honeyed bouquet, it is gently sweet and crisp, with lovely poise and energy. Light and vivacious, with deep grapefruit and slight honey flavours, very vibrant and racy, it promises to be very long-lived.

MED $40 AV

Peregrine Central Otago Riesling   (★★★★)

Well worth cellaring, the 2016 vintage (★★★★) is a pale, basically dry wine (5 grams/litre of residual sugar), with a scented, lemony, minerally bouquet. Slightly austere in its youth, it has strong, citrusy, appley flavours, crisp and long; open 2019+.

MED/DRY $27 –V

Peter Yealands Marlborough Riesling   ★★★

The 2015 vintage (★★★☆) is a lively, medium-bodied wine with lemony, limey flavours, gentle sweetness (7 grams/litre of residual sugar), fresh acidity, and very good varietal character, depth and harmony. Priced right.

Vintage	15	14
WR	7	5
Drink	17-18	17-18

MED/DRY $16 V+

Pisa Range Estate Pisa Central Otago Riesling   ★★★★

The 2014 vintage (★★★☆) was grown at Pisa, tank-fermented and lees-aged in tanks. It is a dry style (4 grams/litre of residual sugar), with strong, lemony, slightly peachy and spicy flavours.

Vintage	14
WR	7
Drink	17-18

DRY $28 –V

Prophet's Rock Central Otago Dry Riesling   ★★★★★

Estate-grown and hand-picked at Bendigo, in the Cromwell Basin, the outstanding 2015 vintage (★★★★★) was fermented with indigenous yeasts and lees-aged, partly in old oak barrels. Light lemon/green, it is mouthfilling, with concentrated, vigorous, citrusy flavours, a hint of marmalade, and a dryish (9 grams/litre of residual sugar), very sustained finish. Already a lovely mouthful, it's a drink-now or cellaring proposition.

Vintage	15	14
WR	7	6
Drink	17-28	17-26

MED/DRY $40 AV

Ribbonwood Marlborough Riesling   ★★★☆

From Framingham, the 2014 vintage (★★★) is a freshly scented wine. It has good depth of lemon, lime and apple flavours, in a medium-dry style (12 grams/litre of residual sugar), with tangy acidity and drink-young appeal.

MED/DRY $20 AV

Rimu Grove Nelson Riesling   ★★★★

Balanced for easy drinking, the bright, light lemon/green 2016 vintage (★★★☆) is light to medium-bodied (10 per cent alcohol), with youthful lemon/apple flavours, showing very good delicacy and depth, a slightly minerally streak, and an off-dry (10 grams/litre of residual sugar) finish. Best drinking 2018+.

Vintage	16	15	14	13	12	11
WR	6	7	6	7	7	6
Drink	17-27	17-26	17-25	17-21	17-20	17-19

MED/DRY $26 –V

Rippon Mature Vine Riesling ★★★★★

This single-vineyard, Lake Wanaka, Central Otago wine is a distinctly cool-climate style, steely, long-lived and penetratingly flavoured. Based on mature vines, it is fermented with indigenous yeasts and given extended lees-aging. The 2015 vintage (★★★★★) is bright, light lemon/green, with a slightly yeasty fragrance. Full-bodied, it is weighty, deep and unusually complex, with fresh, concentrated, citrusy, slightly spicy flavours that build across the palate to a dryish, resounding finish. Already delicious, it should be long-lived; best drinking 2020+.

Riverby Estate Eliza Marlborough Riesling ★★★★☆

Instantly appealing, the 2014 vintage (★★★★) is an estate-grown, Wairau Valley wine, hand-picked from vines planted in 1990. A distinctly medium style (40 grams/litre of residual sugar), it has a slightly honeyed bouquet, leading into a medium to full-bodied wine with strong, ripe, peachy, slightly gingery and honeyed flavours, and a smooth finish.

Vintage	14	13
WR	6	7
Drink	17-20	17-20

Riverby Estate Sali's Block Marlborough Riesling ★★★☆

The 2014 vintage (★★★) is a mouthfilling, medium-dry style (14 grams/litre of residual sugar), with lemony aromas and flavours, slightly spicy notes, fresh acidity and good depth.

Vintage	14	13
WR	6	7
Drink	17-20	17-20

Roaring Meg Central Otago Riesling ★★★★

Enjoyable young, the light lemon/green 2016 vintage (★★★★) is a full-bodied, medium style (25 grams/litre of residual sugar) with lively, lemony, slightly appley and peachy flavours, a hint of honey, and excellent depth and harmony. (From Mt Difficulty.)

Rock Ferry 3rd Rock Marlborough Riesling ★★★★

The attractively scented 2014 vintage (★★★★) was hand-picked in The Corners Vineyard, at Rapaura, in the Wairau Valley, fermented in tanks and given extended lees contact. Fleshy, it has ripe stone-fruit and spice flavours, showing good concentration, and a finely textured, off-dry (7.5 grams/litre of residual sugar) finish. Drinking well now, it's certified organic.

MED/DRY $27 –V

Rockburn Central Otago Tigermoth Riesling   ★★★★☆

Estate-grown at Parkburn, in the Cromwell Basin, and made in a low-alcohol (8.5 per cent) style, the 2016 vintage (★★★★☆) was 'inspired by the spatlese wines of Germany'. Pale lemon/green, it is light and lively, with excellent vibrancy, delicacy and depth, and a gently sweet (59 grams/litre of residual sugar), mouth-wateringly crisp finish. It's already delicious.

SW $39 –V

Vintage	16	15	14	13	12	11
WR	6	6	6	6	6	7
Drink	17-30	17-30	17-30	17-30	17-25	17-25

Sailfish Cove Northland Riesling   (★★☆)

A rare example of Riesling from the north, the 2014 vintage (★★☆) is less scented than Rieslings grown in cooler regions to the south, but very sound, with decent depth of crisp, dry, citrusy flavours.

DRY $19 –V

Saint Clair Marlborough Riesling   ★★★★

Typically an attractive, finely balanced wine. The 2015 vintage (★★★★) – which has minor amounts of Grüner Veltliner, Chardonnay, Pinot Gris and Sauvignon Blanc, totalling 9 per cent of the blend – is very open and expressive in its youth. Lively, tangy and slightly sweet (8.5 grams/litre of residual sugar), it is medium-bodied, with penetrating, lemony, spicy, slightly gingery flavours, woven with steely acidity.

MED/DRY $22 V+

Saint Clair Pioneer Block 9 Big John Marlborough Riesling   ★★★★★

Grown at Woodbourne, in the Wairau Valley, the 2016 vintage (★★★★) was stop-fermented with low alcohol (9 per cent) and abundant sweetness (40 grams/litre of residual sugar). Crisp and lively, it has appetising, citrusy, appley flavours, showing very good freshness and intensity.

SW $27 AV

Saint Clair Vicar's Choice Marlborough Riesling Bright Light   (★★★)

The debut 2014 vintage (★★★) is a low-alcohol style (9 per cent), from grapes harvested early in the Awatere Valley. Fresh and light, with lemony, appley flavours, it is a tangy, medium style (26 grams/litre of residual sugar) with an easy-drinking balance.

MED $19 AV

Sanctuary Marlborough Riesling   (★★★☆)

The 2014 vintage (★★★☆) is a crisp, lively, medium-bodied wine with very good depth of fresh lemon/lime flavours, slightly sweet and tangy.

MED/DRY $18 V+

Seifried Nelson Riesling ★★★★

From a pioneer of Riesling in New Zealand, the 2017 vintage (★★★☆) is typically good value. It is crisp and medium-bodied, with vibrant, citrusy, appley flavours, a gentle splash of sweetness (13 grams/litre of residual sugar), and very good depth.

Vintage	17	16	15	14	13	12	11	10	09
WR	4	5	6	6	6	6	6	6	6
Drink	18-21	17-21	17-25	17-21	17-20	17-19	P	P	P

MED/DRY $18 V+

Soho Maren Marlborough Riesling ★★★★

The 2015 vintage (★★★☆) is a lively, medium-bodied wine with strong, slightly sweet, lemony, appley flavours. Finely poised, it's a youthful wine with good depth, vigour and harmony.

Vintage	15
WR	6
Drink	17-28

MED/DRY $26 –V

Spinyback Nelson Riesling ★★★

The 2016 vintage (★★★) from Waimea Estates is a lemon-scented, medium-bodied wine, fresh and crisp, with peachy, slightly spicy flavours and a gently sweet finish. Balanced for easy, early drinking, it's priced sharply.

MED/DRY $15 V+

Spy Valley Envoy Johnson Vineyard Waihopai Valley Marlborough Dry Riesling ★★★★★

Estate-grown and hand-picked at 23.9 brix from the oldest vines, the 2016 vintage (★★★★☆) is a bright, light lemon/green, dry wine (3.7 grams/litre of residual sugar), barrel-fermented with indigenous yeasts. A notably powerful, weighty style of Riesling (14 per cent alcohol), with good acid spine and strong, ripe, grapefruit-evoking flavours, it's a highly distinctive wine (promoted as 'more reminiscent of Old World wines'), crying out for cellaring; open 2020+.

Vintage	16
WR	6
Drink	18-26

DRY $32 AV

Spy Valley Envoy Single Vineyard Marlborough Riesling ★★★★☆

Estate-grown in the lower Waihopai Valley, the 2011 vintage (★★★★★), released in mid-2017, was hand-picked, with no botrytis influence, and barrel-fermented. Pale lemon/green, it has an inviting, scented, minerally bouquet. Light and lovely, it is low in alcohol (8.6 per cent), with searching, citrusy, appley flavours, sweet (72 grams/litre of residual sugar) and tangy, poised and persistent. Acquiring excellent bottle-aged complexity, with a strong sense of depth, delicacy and drive, it should be long-lived; drink now or cellar.

Vintage	11
WR	7
Drink	17-21

SW $32 –V

Spy Valley Marlborough Riesling ★★★★

The 2015 vintage (★★★★) is a mouthfilling, dry style (4.7 grams/litre of residual sugar), fermented in tanks and old oak vessels. Bright, light lemon/green, with good body and depth of ripe, citrusy, slightly peachy and spicy flavours, moderate acidity and a touch of complexity, it's a distinctive, age-worthy Riesling, unusually fleshy and dry for New Zealand.

Vintage	15	14	13	12
WR	7	6	6	6
Drink	17-23	17-20	P	P

DRY $23 V+

Stoneleigh Marlborough Riesling ★★★★

Priced sharply, the 2016 vintage (★★★☆) is medium-bodied and vibrantly fruity, with a gentle splash of sweetness and good depth of fresh, citrusy, limey flavours.

MED/DRY $17 V+

Stoney Range Waipara Riesling ★★★☆

The 2015 vintage (★★★) from Sherwood Estate is a lively, finely poised wine with strong, lemony, slightly sweet flavours and a slightly funky bouquet.

MED $17 V+

Stonyridge Fallen Angel Marlborough Riesling (★★★★)

The 2014 vintage (★★★★) is a generous, tangy wine with strong lemon/lime flavours, a minerally streak, slightly toasty, bottle-aged notes adding complexity and an off-dry (11 grams/litre of residual sugar), crisp finish.

MED/DRY $30 –V

Tatty Bogler Central Otago Riesling ★★★★

The 2014 vintage (★★★☆) is enjoyable now. Light lemon/green, it is medium-bodied, with gentle, lemony, appley flavours, slight sweetness and a touch of bottle-aged complexity. (From Forrest Estate.)

MED/DRY $25 AV

Te Kairanga Martinborough Riesling ★★★★

The 2015 vintage (★★★) has a moderately fresh bouquet, leading into a mouthfilling, dryish style with citrusy, limey flavours, firm acid spine and a minerally streak.

MED/DRY $23 AV

Te Mania Nelson Riesling ★★★☆

The 2015 vintage (★★★★) is delicious young. Medium-bodied, it has appetising acidity, generous, ripe, lemony, slightly peachy and spicy flavours, and a slightly sweet, finely balanced finish.

MED/DRY $22 AV

Terra Sancta Miro's Block Bannockburn Central Otago Dry Riesling   ★★★★☆

The highly satisfying 2015 vintage (★★★★☆) was estate-grown and harvested from 'seven rows of old vines'. A dry style (4.8 grams/litre of residual sugar), it has strong, lively, citrusy, limey flavours, slightly toasty notes adding complexity, and excellent depth and harmony. Drink now or cellar.

Vintage	15	MED/DRY $28 AV
WR	6	
Drink	18-22	

Terrace Edge Classic Waipara Valley Riesling   ★★★☆

Certified organic, the 2016 vintage (★★★☆) is an off-dry style (12.5 grams/litre of residual sugar). Bright, light lemon/green, it is full-bodied, with ripe peach and passionfruit-like flavours, a hint of honey, slightly earthy notes, and lots of drink-young appeal.

Vintage	16	MED/DRY $19 V+
WR	7	
Drink	17-23	

Terrace Edge Liquid Geography Waipara Valley Riesling   ★★★★☆

As a medium style of Riesling (35 grams/litre of residual sugar) for drinking young, the 2016 vintage (★★★★☆) is hard to beat, especially at the price. Hand-picked, with some botrytis influence, it is attractively scented, with a vague hint of honey, moderate acidity, and excellent delicacy and depth of citrusy, peachy flavours. Certified organic.

Vintage	16	15	MED $20 V+
WR	7	7	
Drink	17-24	17-24	

Thornbury Waipara Riesling   ★★★☆

The 2016 vintage (★★★☆) is a medium style (18 grams/litre of residual sugar), fresh and lively, with good depth of citrusy, slightly spicy flavours, woven with appetising acidity. Finely balanced for early drinking, it offers good value. (From Villa Maria.)

Vintage	16	MED $16 V+
WR	6	
Drink	17-21	

Three Paddles Martinborough Riesling   ★★★☆

The 2016 vintage (★★★☆) from Nga Waka is already enjoyable. Bright, light lemon/green, it is medium-bodied, with good depth of fresh, ripe, citrusy, peachy, slightly limey flavours, gentle sweetness (10 grams/litre of residual sugar) and an easy-drinking balance.

Vintage	16	MED/DRY $18 V+
WR	6	
Drink	17-21	

Tohu Single Vineyard Marlborough Riesling ★★★☆

Estate-grown in the upper Awatere Valley, the 2015 vintage (★★★☆) is a dryish style (8.5 grams/litre of residual sugar). Tangy and lively, with a slightly toasty bouquet, it has citrusy, slightly limey flavours, a minerally streak, and good depth.

MED/DRY $22 AV

Vintage	15	14	13	12	11
WR	7	6	7	6	7
Drink	17-19	17-18	17-18	P	P

Toi Toi Reserve Marlborough Riesling ★★★★

The 2014 vintage (★★★★) is a ripely scented, medium-bodied wine, grown at Omaka. It has strong, citrusy flavours, a gentle splash of sweetness (14 grams/litre of residual sugar), lively acidity, and very good freshness, balance and length. It's drinking well now.

MED/DRY $22 V+

Tupari Awatere Valley Riesling (★★★★)

Delicious young, the 2016 vintage (★★★★) is a medium style (25 grams/litre of residual sugar), with excellent depth of fresh, citrusy, limey flavour, woven with appetising acidity. Drink now or cellar.

MED $23 AV

Two Paddocks Picnic Central Otago Riesling ★★★★

Estate-grown in the Red Banks Vineyard, at Earnscleugh, near Alexandra, the 2015 vintage (★★★★) is an off-dry style. Lemon-scented, it is a medium-bodied, citrusy, appley wine, fresh, finely balanced and full-flavoured.

MED/DRY $22 V+

Two Rivers of Marlborough Juliet Riesling ★★★★

The 2016 vintage (★★★★) was harvested from 16-year-old vines in the Wairau Valley. Tangy and lively, it has ripe, peachy, slightly sweet flavours (12.5 grams/litre of residual sugar), with a hint of passionfruit, and very good vigour and depth. Approachable from the start, it should be at its best 2018+.

MED/DRY $25 AV

Vintage	16
WR	6
Drink	17-21

Two Sisters Central Otago Riesling ★★★★★

Estate-grown on a steeply sloping site at Lowburn, in the Cromwell Basin, the finely balanced 2010 vintage (★★★★★) was released in 2016. Finely scented and mouthfilling, it is lively, with moderate acidity and peachy, slightly toasty flavours, showing excellent ripeness, delicacy, depth and harmony. A medium style (18 grams/litre of residual sugar), it's a drink-now or cellaring proposition.

MED $29 V+

Valli Waitaki North Otago Riesling   ★★★★☆

Already delicious, the light lemon/green 2016 vintage (★★★★☆) is attractively scented, with fresh, rich, citrusy, peachy flavours, showing excellent delicacy and vibrancy, gentle sweetness (18 grams/litre of residual sugar), good acid spine and a finely poised finish. Drink now or cellar.

MED $30 –V

Vavasour Awatere Valley Marlborough Riesling   (★★★☆)

The 2015 vintage (★★★☆) is scented, with fresh, citrusy, slightly appley flavours, showing very good depth, racy acidity and a hint of bottle-aged toastiness.

MED/DRY $21 AV

Vidal Marlborough Riesling   ★★★☆

Offering great value, the 2015 vintage (★★★★) is drinking well now, but also worth cellaring. Grown in the Awatere Valley (42 per cent), Waihopai Valley (42 per cent) and the central Wairau Valley (16 per cent), it is very fresh and lively, with good weight, crisp, medium-dry flavours (8.7 grams/litre of residual sugar), citrusy and limey, and a persistent finish.

Vintage	15
WR	6
Drink	17-23

MED/DRY $16 V+

Villa Maria Cellar Selection Marlborough Dry Riesling   ★★★★

A great buy, the skilfully crafted 2016 vintage (★★★★☆) was grown in the Wairau Valley. Fragrant, with a touch of bottle-aged toastiness emerging, it is medium to full-bodied, with strong, ripe, citrusy flavours, dryish (9 grams/litre of residual sugar), rich and very finely balanced for current drinking.

Vintage	16	15	14	13	12	11	10	09
WR	6	7	7	6	6	6	6	7
Drink	17-22	17-22	17-20	17-18	P	P	P	P

MED/DRY $19 V+

Villa Maria Private Bin Marlborough Dry Riesling   ★★★☆

Grown in the Awatere and Wairau valleys, the 2017 vintage (★★★☆) is a slightly sweet style (15 grams/litre of residual sugar), medium-bodied, with very good depth of fresh lemon/lime flavours and appetising acidity to keep things lively. Enjoyable young, it offers fine value.

Vintage	17	16	15	14	13	12	11	10
WR	6	5	6	6	6	6	6	6
Drink	17-20	17-20	17-20	17-18	P	P	P	P

MED $16 V+

Waimea Classic Nelson Riesling   ★★★★

This luscious wine is balanced for easy drinking, consistently impressive – and good value. Estate-grown on the Waimea Plains, the 2015 vintage (★★★★) has good intensity of peachy, slightly gingery and honeyed flavours, and a slightly sweet (12.5 grams/litre of residual sugar), mouth-wateringly crisp finish.

MED/DRY $17 V+

Waipara Hills Waipara Valley Riesling ★★★★

The 2015 vintage (★★★★) is freshly scented, vibrant and tangy, with citrusy, limey, slightly peachy and spicy flavours, a gentle splash of sweetness, and excellent vigour, balance and depth.

MED/DRY $22 V+

Waipara Springs Waipara Riesling ★★★☆

The 2016 vintage (★★★) is light-bodied, with fresh, lively, citrusy flavours, gentle sweetness (20 grams/litre of residual sugar), and drink-young appeal.

MED $18 V+

Wairau River Marlborough Riesling ★★★☆

A single-vineyard wine from 23-year-old vines in the Wairau Valley, the 2015 vintage (★★★☆) is an off-dry style (7 grams/litre of residual sugar). Full-bodied, it has fresh, ripe lemon/lime flavours, crisp and strong.

Vintage	15	14	13
WR	7	6	5
Drink	17-22	17-21	17-20

MED/DRY $20 AV

Wairau River Summer Marlborough Riesling ★★★★

The 2016 vintage (★★★★) was made 'to be supped with frivolous frivolity'. Fresh and light-bodied (9.5 per cent alcohol), it is medium-sweet (41 grams/litre of residual sugar), with good intensity of peachy, citrusy flavours, fresh and tangy. Delicious from the start.

Vintage	16	15	14	13
WR	6	7	6	5
Drink	17-19	17-18	P	P

MED $20 V+

West Brook Marlborough Riesling ★★★★☆

This label is well worth discovering. Offering great value, the 2015 vintage (★★★★★) is richly scented. Pale lemon/green, it is medium-bodied, with vibrant, ripe grapefruit/lime flavours, penetrating and lively, and a long, off-dry (16 grams/litre of residual sugar), appetisingly crisp finish. Fresh and finely poised, intense and racy, it should reward long-term cellaring. The 2014 vintage (★★★★☆) is drinking well now. Light lemon/green, it is medium-bodied, with strong, ripe grapefruit/lime flavours, a splash of sweetness (11 grams/litre of residual sugar), toasty, bottle-aged notes emerging, and a long, lively finish.

Vintage	15	14
WR	5	5
Drink	17-25	17-24

MED/DRY $20 V+

Whitehaven Marlborough Riesling ★★★★

The 2016 vintage (★★★★) is invitingly scented, with strong, citrusy, slightly appley flavours. Made in a medium-dry style (11 grams/litre of residual sugar), it is a finely balanced, youthful wine, already drinking well, but likely to be at its best 2019+.

MED/DRY $22 V+

Yealands Estate Land Made Marlborough Riesling   ★★★☆

The 2015 vintage (★★★☆) is a fragrant wine, slightly sweet (7 grams/litre of residual sugar) and crisp, with strong lemon/lime flavours, a minerally streak and a tangy finish.

Vintage	15	14
WR	7	5
Drink	17-18	17-18

Yealands Estate Single Vineyard Awatere Valley Marlborough Riesling   ★★★☆

Estate-grown in the Seaview Vineyard, the youthful 2016 vintage (★★★★) is a dryish style (6 grams/litre of residual sugar). Medium to full-bodied, it is tightly structured, with vibrant, citrusy, peachy flavours, showing good richness, and a finely balanced finish. Best drinking 2018+.

Zephyr Marlborough Riesling   ★★★★

Estate-grown at Dillons Point, in the lower Wairau Valley, the 2014 vintage (★★★★) is a medium-dry style, finely poised, with fresh acidity, strong, citrusy, slightly spicy flavours and good harmony.

MED/DRY $25 AV

Roussanne

Roussanne is a traditional ingredient in the white wines of France's northern Rhône Valley, where typically it is blended with the more widely grown Marsanne. Known for its fine acidity and 'haunting aroma', likened by some tasters to herbal tea, it is also found in the south of France, Italy and Australia, but this late-ripening variety is extremely scarce in New Zealand, with only 0.2 hectares bearing in 2018, north of Auckland.

Mahurangi River Winery Roussanne/Viognier ★★★★☆

The elegant 2014 vintage (★★★★) was estate-grown and hand-picked near Matakana. A blend of Roussanne (54 per cent) and Viognier (46 per cent), it is youthful, with fresh, strong pear and citrus-fruit flavours, good acid spine and a tight finish. A powerful, dry wine, showing good delicacy and complexity, it's well worth cellaring.

Vintage	14	13
WR	5	6
Drink	17-20	17-20

DRY $39 –V

Ransom Roussanne Matakana (★★★★)

Delicious young, the vibrantly fruity 2014 vintage (★★★★) was made from bought-in grapes and handled entirely in tanks. Full-bodied, it is sweet-fruited, with ripe stone-fruit flavours, fresh and strong, and a dry finish.

DRY $26 –V

Sauvignon Blanc

Sauvignon Blanc is New Zealand's major calling card in the wine markets of the world, often – but not always, due to the rising challenge from Chile – winning trophies at big competitions in the UK. For countless wine lovers overseas, New Zealand 'is' Sauvignon Blanc, almost invariably from Marlborough. The rise to international stardom of New Zealand Sauvignon Blanc was remarkably swift. Government Viticulturist Romeo Bragato imported the first Sauvignon Blanc vines from Italy in 1906, but it was not until 1974 that Matua Valley marketed New Zealand's first varietal Sauvignon Blanc, grown in West Auckland. Montana first planted Sauvignon Blanc vines in Marlborough in 1975; its first bottling of Marlborough Sauvignon Blanc flowed in 1979. In 2017, 86.1 per cent by volume of all New Zealand's wine exports were based on Sauvignon Blanc.

Sauvignon Blanc is by far New Zealand's most extensively planted variety, in 2018 comprising 58 per cent of the bearing national vineyard. Almost 90 per cent of the vines are concentrated in Marlborough, with further significant plantings in Hawke's Bay, Nelson, Canterbury and Waipara. Between 2005 and 2018, the area of bearing Sauvignon Blanc vines will surge from 7277 hectares to 21,901 hectares.

The flavour of New Zealand Sauvignon Blanc varies according to fruit ripeness. At the herbaceous, under-ripe end of the spectrum, vegetal and fresh-cut grass aromas hold sway; riper wines show capsicum, gooseberry and melon-like characters; very ripe fruit displays tropical-fruit flavours.

Intensely herbaceous Sauvignon Blancs are not hard to make in the viticulturally cool climate of the South Island and the lower North Island (Wairarapa). 'The challenge faced by New Zealand winemakers is to keep those herbaceous characters in check,' says Kevin Judd, of Greywacke Vineyards, formerly chief winemaker at Cloudy Bay. 'It would be foolish to suggest that these herbaceous notes detract from the wines; in fact I am sure that this fresh edge and intense varietal aroma are the reason for its international popularity. The better of these wines have these herbaceous characters in context and in balance with the more tropical-fruit characters associated with riper fruit.'

There are two key styles of Sauvignon Blanc produced in New Zealand. Wines handled entirely in stainless steel tanks – by far the most common – place their accent squarely on their fresh, direct fruit flavours. Alternatively, many top labels are handled principally in tanks, but 5 to 15 per cent of the blend is barrel-fermented, adding a touch of complexity without subduing the wine's fresh, punchy fruit aromas and flavours.

Another major style difference is regionally based: the crisp, incisively flavoured wines of Marlborough contrast with the softer, less pungently herbaceous Hawke's Bay style. These are wines to drink young (traditionally within 18 months of the vintage) while they are irresistibly fresh, aromatic and tangy, although the oak-matured, more complex wines can mature well for several years.

The swing since the 2001 vintage from corks to screwcaps has also boosted the longevity of the wines. Rather than running out of steam, many are still highly enjoyable at two years old.

12,000 Miles Gladstone Sauvignon Blanc ★★★☆

From Gladstone Vineyard, in the northern Wairarapa, the 2016 vintage (★★★☆) was grown at four sites, tank-fermented and lees-aged. Mouthfilling and sweet-fruited, it has ripe tropical-fruit flavours, very gentle acidity and a well-rounded, bone-dry finish.

DRY $20 AV

Allan Scott Marlborough Sauvignon Blanc ★★★☆

Grown in the central Wairau Valley, the 2017 vintage (★★★) was tank-fermented. It's an aromatic, medium-bodied wine, briskly herbaceous, with fresh, lively, green capsicum-like flavours, and fractional sweetness (4 grams/litre of residual sugar) balanced by tangy acidity.

DRY $17 V+

Alluviale Hawke's Bay Sauvignon Blanc/Sémillon (★★★★☆)

The mouthfilling, fleshy 2015 vintage (★★★★☆) was grown at the Craft Farm and Askerne vineyards at Havelock North. A blend of Sauvignon Blanc (81 per cent), Sémillon (14 per cent) and Muscat (5 per cent), partly barrel-fermented, it has strong, ripe tropical-fruit flavours, a very subtle seasoning of oak, good complexity, and a crisp, dry, lingering finish.

DRY $24 V+

Alluviale Marlborough Sauvignon Blanc (★★★★)

Ripely scented, the 2016 vintage (★★★★) was grown at sites in the lower Wairau Valley and Waihopai Valley, and lees-aged for three months. Weighty and sweet-fruited, it has generous melon, passionfruit and lime flavours, lively acidity, and a dry (2.8 grams/litre of residual sugar) finish. Good value.

DRY $20 V+

Alpine Valley Marlborough Sauvignon Blanc (★★★)

Vibrantly fruity, the 2016 vintage (★★★) is a full-bodied wine with lively melon, capsicum and green-apple flavours, woven with appetising acidity, and a fresh, crisp, easy-drinking appeal. (From Tiki.)

DRY $17 AV

Amisfield Central Otago Sauvignon Blanc ★★★★

The 2016 vintage (★★★★), estate-grown at Pisa, was mostly handled in tanks, but a small portion of the blend was fermented with indigenous yeasts in old French oak barriques. Aromatic and tangy, it is bone-dry, with good intensity of tropical-fruit and herbaceous flavours, a touch of complexity, and very good balance, vigour and depth.

DRY $25 AV

Amisfield Fumé Central Otago Sauvignon Blanc (★★★★)

The 2014 vintage (★★★★) was estate-grown at Pisa, hand-harvested at 24 to 25 brix, barrel-fermented with indigenous yeasts, and oak-aged for well over a year. Light lemon/green, it's a 'serious', full-bodied style, with fresh, concentrated, ripely herbaceous flavours and a smooth (5 grams/litre of residual sugar), finely balanced finish.

MED/DRY $35 –V

Aotea by Seifried Nelson Sauvignon Blanc ★★★★

From Seifried Estate, the bright, light lemon/green 2017 vintage (★★★★) has a punchy bouquet, leading into a mouthfilling, appetisingly crisp wine with penetrating passionfruit/lime flavours. Vibrantly fruity, with firm acidity, it is a basically dry style (4 grams/litre of residual sugar), likely to be at its best mid-2018+.

Vintage	17
WR	6
Drink	17-18

 DRY $26 –V

Ara Single Estate Marlborough Sauvignon Blanc ★★★★

Ara in a glass, the 2015 vintage (★★★★) from this Waihopai Valley producer is bright, light lemon/green, with a freshly aromatic bouquet. Crisp and lively, it has strong passionfruit/lime flavours, a touch of bottle-aged complexity, and a dry (3.5 grams/litre of residual sugar), lingering finish.

Vintage	15
WR	6
Drink	P

 DRY $22 V+

Ash Ridge Hawke's Bay Estate Sauvignon Blanc ★★★☆

The 2016 vintage (★★★) was fermented in old barrels (70 per cent) and tanks (30 per cent). It's a fresh, medium-bodied wine with ripely herbaceous flavours, showing a touch of complexity, and a dry (3 grams/litre of residual sugar), crisp finish.

 DRY $20 AV

Ashwell Martinborough Sauvignon Blanc ★★★☆

Estate-grown on the Martinborough Terraces, the 2017 vintage (★★★) is a pale lemon/green, freshly scented wine, medium-bodied, with plenty of citrusy, appley flavour, dry and tangy.

 DRY $20 AV

Astrolabe Province Marlborough Sauvignon Blanc ★★★★

The 2016 vintage (★★★★) is a regional blend, grown in the Awatere Valley (56 per cent), Southern Valleys (17 per cent), Wairau Valley (14 per cent) and Kekerengu (13 per cent). Made in a fully dry style, it is freshly aromatic, mouthfilling and slightly minerally, with melon/lime flavours, pure, crisp and strong. Good drinking now to 2018.

DRY $23 AV

Astrolabe Valleys Awatere Valley Sauvignon Blanc ★★★★☆

Grown at two sites in the Awatere Valley, the classy 2016 vintage (★★★★★) is a very typical sub-regional style, currently in full stride. Light lemon/green, it is full-bodied and bone-dry, with pure, penetrating melon and green-capsicum flavours, racy, harmonious and long.

 DRY $25 V+

Astrolabe Valleys Kekerengu Coast Marlborough Sauvignon Blanc   ★★★★☆

Grown at Kekerengu, south of the Awatere Valley, the 2015 vintage (★★★★☆) is currently in full stride. It was mostly handled in tanks, but one-sixth of the blend was fermented and matured in French oak barrels. Bright, light lemon/green, it is still very fresh and lively, with strong, vibrant melon and green-capsicum flavours, a slightly 'salty' streak, and a crisp, dry, lasting finish.

DRY $25 V+

Astrolabe Vineyards Taihoa Vineyard Marlborough Sauvignon Blanc   ★★★★★

Grown at Kekerengu, south of the Awatere Valley, the 2015 vintage (★★★★★) was hand-picked at 24.4 brix and fermented and matured in old French oak barrels. Bright, light lemon/green, it's a powerful wine with strong personality, still unfolding. Weighty and fully dry, it has deep, ripely herbaceous flavours, crisp, complex and long. A vigorous, finely structured wine, it's well worth cellaring.

DRY $32 AV

Auntsfield Single Vineyard Southern Valleys
Marlborough Sauvignon Blanc   ★★★★★

Estate-grown on the south side of the Wairau Valley, on the site where the region's first wines were made in the 1870s, the 2016 vintage (★★★★☆) was mostly fermented in tanks; a small percentage was handled in old oak casks. Bright, light lemon/green, it is freshly scented, mouthfilling and dry, with excellent intensity of tropical-fruit flavours, tight and youthful. Best drinking 2018+.

DRY $23 V+

Awatere River by Louis Vavasour Marlborough Sauvignon Blanc   ★★★☆

The 2016 vintage (★★★★) is a 'full-on', punchy style. Mouthfilling, it is lively, sweet-fruited and herbaceous, with strong melon and green-capsicum flavours, dry (3.8 grams/litre of residual sugar) and appetisingly crisp.

Vintage	16
WR	6
Drink	17-19

DRY $23 –V

Babich Black Label Marlborough Sauvignon Blanc   ★★★★☆

The 'Black Label' wines are mostly seen in restaurants. The outstanding 2016 vintage (★★★★★), partly barrel-fermented, is a mouthfilling, vibrantly fruity, finely textured wine with concentrated, ripe passionfruit and lime flavours to the fore, subtle oak/lees-aging notes adding complexity, and a rich, dry (2.9 grams/litre of residual sugar), well-rounded finish.

DRY $25 AV

Babich Family Estates Headwaters Organic Block
Marlborough Sauvignon Blanc ★★★★

This subtle, fully dry wine is grown in the Wairau Valley. The 2016 vintage (★★★★) is mouthfilling, with good vigour and depth of ripe tropical-fruit flavours, slightly spicy and minerally notes, and a long, tight finish. Certified organic.

Babich Marlborough Sauvignon Blanc ★★★★

Babich favours 'a fuller, riper, softer' Sauvignon Blanc. 'It's not a jump out of the glass style, but the wines develop well.' The latest releases reflect a rising input of grapes from the company's Cowslip Valley Vineyard in the Waihopai Valley, which gives less herbaceous fruit characters than its other Marlborough vineyards. The 2016 vintage (★★★★) is typical. The bouquet is fresh, with ripe tropical-fruit aromas; the palate is mouthfilling and dry (3.5 grams/litre of residual sugar), with strong, vibrant, passionfruit-evoking flavours, in a non-herbaceous, but still lively and appetisingly crisp, style.

Babich Winemakers Reserve Barrel Fermented
Marlborough Sauvignon Blanc ★★★★☆

A stylish example of gently oak-influenced Sauvignon Blanc. Estate-grown in the Cowslip Valley Vineyard, in the Waihopai Valley, the impressive 2016 vintage (★★★★★) was partly handled in tanks, but most of the blend was fermented and lees-aged for six months in seasoned French oak barriques. Instantly appealing, it is still youthful, with mouthfilling body and concentrated, ripe tropical-fruit flavours, showing excellent freshness and complexity. Finely textured, with moderate acidity and a dry (1.6 grams/litre of residual sugar), harmonious finish, it should be at its peak during 2018.

Baby Doll Marlborough Sauvignon Blanc ★★★★

The 2016 vintage (★★★★) is mouthfilling, with strong, ripe tropical-fruit flavours, enlivened by appetising acidity. Fine value. (From Yealands.)

Beach House Otihi Road Hawke's Bay Sauvignon Blanc (★★★)

The distinctive 2016 vintage (★★★) is a single-vineyard wine, made in an off-dry style (8 grams/litre of residual sugar). Light lemon/green, it is a fresh, lively, medium-bodied wine with good depth of citrusy, appley flavours, balanced for smooth, easy drinking.

Beach House Reserve Wild Ferment Hawke's Bay Sauvignon Blanc ★★★★

From two sites at Te Awanga, the distinctive 2016 vintage (★★★☆) was fermented with indigenous yeasts in seasoned oak barrels, and wood-matured for six months. Aromatic and tangy, it's an off-dry style (10 grams/litre of residual sugar), fresh, vibrant and medium-bodied, with punchy, herbaceous flavours, a touch of complexity, and steely acidity.

MED/DRY $25 AV

Bel Echo by Clos Henri Marlborough Sauvignon Blanc ★★★★☆

This well-priced wine is grown in the more clay-based soils at Clos Henri (the top wine, sold as 'Clos Henri', is from the stoniest blocks). Drinking well now and still on sale, the 2015 vintage (★★★★☆) was hand-picked, tank-fermented and matured on its yeast lees for six months. Mouthfilling and sweet-fruited, it has generous tropical-fruit flavours, showing a touch of bottle-aged complexity, and a long, bone-dry finish. Certified organic.

Vintage	15	14
WR	6	7
Drink	17-21	17-20

DRY $26 AV

Bellbird Spring Block Eight Waipara Sauvignon Blanc ★★★★☆

This distinctive wine is hand-picked and fermented with indigenous yeasts in old oak barriques. The 2016 vintage (★★★★☆), barrel-matured for five months, is a bright, light yellow/green, mouthfilling wine with fresh, strong, ripely herbaceous flavours. A generous wine, with well-integrated oak adding richness and complexity, slightly buttery notes and excellent harmony, it's a drink-now or cellaring proposition.

DRY $32 –V

Bishop's Head Waipara Valley Fumé Blanc ★★★

The 2015 vintage (★★★☆) was hand-picked and fermented with indigenous yeasts in acacia barrels, which give 'a nice, lifted sweetness on the palate'. Full-bodied, with fresh acidity and generous, ripely herbal, slightly nutty flavours, it's a distinctly cool-climate expression of Sauvignon Blanc, showing considerable complexity.

DRY $30 –V

Black Cottage Marlborough Sauvignon Blanc ★★★☆

From Two Rivers, the 2017 vintage (★★★☆) is a blend of fruit from the Wairau and Awatere valleys. A good-value wine, with lots of drink-young appeal, it is medium-bodied, with finely balanced melon/lime flavours, a hint of passionfruit, good depth and a dry (3.6 grams/litre of residual sugar) finish.

Vintage	17	16
WR	5	5
Drink	17-18	P

DRY $18 V+

Blackenbrook Nelson Sauvignon Blanc ★★★★

Estate-grown at Tasman, hand-picked and handled in tanks (mostly) and old oak barrels (4 per cent), the 2017 vintage (★★★☆) is a pale, aromatic wine, lively and herbaceous. Medium-bodied, it has melon, green-capsicum and slight passionfruit flavours, appetisingly crisp, dry (4 grams/litre of residual sugar) and strong.

Vintage	17	16	15	14	13
WR	6	6	5	7	6
Drink	17-18	P	P	P	P

DRY $21 V+

Blind River Awatere Valley Marlborough Sauvignon Blanc   ★★★★

This single-vineyard wine is partly (10 per cent) barrel-fermented. Light lemon/green, the 2016 vintage (★★★★) is aromatic, mouthfilling and freshly herbaceous, with lively tropical-fruit and green-capsicum flavours, showing good intensity, and a crisp, dry (3.5 grams/litre of residual sugar) finish. Already drinking well, the 2017 vintage (★★★★) has a punchy, aromatic bouquet, leading into a mouthfilling, lively, smooth wine with melon, lime and capsicum flavours, a slightly 'salty' streak, and a distinct touch of complexity.

Vintage	16	DRY $25 AV
WR	7	
Drink	17-21	

Blind River Tekau Awatere Valley Marlborough Sauvignon Blanc   ★★★★★

Drinking well now, the 2016 vintage (★★★★☆) is a single-vineyard wine, fermented with indigenous yeasts in French oak barrels (6 per cent new). Light lemon/green, it is full-bodied, with rich tropical-fruit and herbaceous flavours, slightly toasty notes adding complexity, and excellent depth and harmony.

Vintage	16	DRY $30 AV
WR	7	
Drink	17-23	

Boatshed Bay Marlborough Sauvignon Blanc   ★★★☆

The 2016 vintage (★★★☆) is mouthfilling and vibrantly fruity, with good weight and depth of fresh passionfruit, melon and green-capsicum flavours, crisp and lively. (From Foley Family Wines.)

DRY $20 AV

Brancott Estate Chosen Rows Marlborough Sauvignon Blanc   ★★★★★

From the company that planted the region's first Sauvignon Blanc vines in 1975, Chosen Rows is promoted as 'the ultimate expression of Marlborough Sauvignon Blanc'. The goal is to create 'an age-worthy wine with great palate weight and texture . . . a sophisticated, thought-provoking wine'. The second, 2013, vintage (★★★★★) was grown in the historic Brancott Vineyard, hand-picked from 15 to 17-year-old vines, fermented with indigenous yeasts in large French oak cuves, and lees-aged for eight months. Bottled in June 2014 and released in December 2015, it is a powerful (14.5 per cent alcohol) wine, weighty and fleshy, with firm acid spine, very ripe melon/lime flavours, showing excellent concentration and complexity, and a dry, lasting finish. Drink now or cellar.

Vintage	13	12	11	10	DRY $80 –V
WR	7	NM	NM	7	
Drink	17-20	NM	NM	P	

Brancott Estate Flight Marlborough Sauvignon Blanc   ★★☆

This is a low-alcohol style (below 10 per cent) with a gentle splash of sweetness. The 2016 vintage (★★☆) is aromatic and light-bodied, with fresh, delicate, citrusy, appley, green-edged flavours, threaded with firm acidity.

MED/DRY $17 –V

Brancott Estate Letter Series 'B' Brancott Marlborough Sauvignon Blanc ★★★★★

This wine is promoted by Pernod Ricard NZ as 'our finest expression of Marlborough's most famous variety' – and lives up to its billing. 'Palate weight, concentration and longevity' are the goals. It has traditionally been grown in the company's sweeping Brancott Vineyard, on the south, slightly cooler side of the Wairau Valley, and a significant portion is fermented and lees-aged in French oak puncheons and large French oak cuves, to add 'some toast and spice as well as palate richness'. The 2016 vintage (★★★★★) is a powerful, weighty wine, richly scented, with excellent concentration of ripe tropical-fruit flavours, intense and lingering. The 2017 vintage (★★★★) is mouthfilling and vibrantly fruity, with strong, ripe passionfruit/lime flavours, woven with fresh acidity. It's a 'forward' vintage, likely to be at its best mid-2018+.

Brancott Estate Living Land Series Marlborough Sauvignon Blanc ★★★☆

Certified organic, the 2016 vintage (★★★★) is from vineyards on the south side of the Wairau Valley. Intensely aromatic, it is mouthfilling and vibrantly fruity, with rich, incisive, ripely herbaceous flavours. Fine value.

Brancott Estate Marlborough Sauvignon Blanc ★★★☆

This famous wine is promoted as 'the original Marlborough Sauvignon Blanc', since it is descended directly from the pioneering label, Montana Marlborough Sauvignon Blanc, launched in 1979. The 2017 vintage (★★★☆) has a punchy, aromatic bouquet. Medium-bodied, it has strong, freshly herbaceous flavours of melons and green capsicums, lively and well balanced for early drinking. Fine value.

Brancott Estate Terroir Series Awatere Valley
Marlborough Sauvignon Blanc ★★★★☆

Looking for a classic expression of Sauvignon Blanc from the Awatere Valley? Don't miss the great-value 2016 vintage (★★★★★). A fresh, strong, intensely varietal wine with penetrating melon and green-capsicum flavours, woven with appetising acidity, it is powerful and rich, with a lasting finish – the Awatere in a glass.

Brightside Organic Sauvignon Blanc ★★★☆

The 2016 vintage (★★★☆) from Kaimira Estate, in Nelson, offers great value. Light lemon/green, it is fresh, tangy and mouthfilling, with ripely herbaceous flavours of passionfruit and lime, a slightly minerally streak, and a dry (4 grams/litre of residual sugar), appetisingly crisp finish. Drink now to 2018. Certified organic.

DRY $16 V+

Brightwater Vineyards Lord Rutherford Barrique Nelson Sauvignon Blanc   ★★★★☆

Still unfolding, the 2016 vintage (★★★★☆) was estate-grown at Hope, hand-picked, fermented with indigenous yeasts in seasoned French oak casks, and lees-aged in barrels for six months. Light lemon/green, with a slightly toasty bouquet, it is full-bodied and savoury, with fresh, ripe tropical-fruit flavours, showing good complexity, balanced acidity, and a dry, youthful finish. Best drinking 2018+.

DRY $30 –V

Brightwater Vineyards Lord Rutherford Nelson Sauvignon Blanc   ★★★★☆

Grown at Hope, on the Waimea Plains, the 2016 vintage (★★★★☆) is a single-vineyard wine, low-cropped, tank-fermented and briefly lees-aged. Light lemon/green, it is ripely scented, mouthfilling and vibrantly fruity, with fresh, crisp, passionfruit/lime flavours, showing good intensity and vigour, and a dry (2 grams/litre of residual sugar), lengthy finish.

Vintage	16	15	14	13	12
WR	6	6	6	6	7
Drink	17-21	17-20	17-19	17-18	P

DRY $25 V+

Brightwater Vineyards Nelson Sauvignon Blanc   ★★★★

Grown at Hope, on the Waimea Plains, this is a consistently attractive, ripely flavoured wine, fresh and punchy. The 2016 vintage (★★★★), harvested from vines up to 23 years old, is dry (2 grams/litre of residual sugar) and ripely scented, with generous passionfruit and lime flavours, vibrant and appetisingly crisp. Enjoyable from the start.

Vintage	16	15	14
WR	6	7	6
Drink	17-18	P	P

DRY $20 V+

Byrne Northland Sauvignon Blanc   ★★★☆

Grown at Kerikeri, in the Bay of Islands, the 2016 vintage (★★★☆) is a mouthfilling, sweet-fruited wine, partly (30 per cent) fermented with indigenous yeasts in old French oak barrels. Full-bodied and fresh, it is ripely herbaceous, with tropical-fruit flavours, a very subtle seasoning of oak adding complexity, and a dry, crisp finish.

DRY $23 –V

Cable Bay Reserve Marlborough Sauvignon Blanc   (★★★★)

A complex style, the 2015 vintage (★★★★) was estate-grown in the Awatere Valley and fermented with indigenous yeasts in French oak barrels (15 per cent new). Mouthfilling, it has impressive weight and depth of ripe tropical-fruit flavours and a slightly creamy texture.

Vintage	15
WR	6
Drink	17-22

DRY $28 –V

Catalina Sounds Marlborough Sauvignon Blanc   ★★★★

The fleshy, generous 2016 vintage (★★★★) was estate-grown in the Waihopai Valley (50 per cent) and other sites in the Wairau Valley, and partly barrel-fermented. It's an aromatic, sweet-fruited wine, with a touch of complexity and good acidity and length.

 DRY $23 AV

Catalina Sounds Sound of White Marlborough Sauvignon Blanc   ★★★★☆

The 2015 vintage (★★★★☆) is a complex, youthful, estate-grown wine from the Waihopai Valley, hand-picked and barrel-fermented. Light lemon/green, it has mouthfilling body and concentrated, ripe grapefruit/lime flavours, seasoned with nutty oak. Tightly structured, it shows excellent vigour, depth and potential.

 DRY $31 –V

Cathedral Cove Marlborough Sauvignon Blanc   (★★☆)

The very low-priced 2017 vintage (★★☆) is a good buy. Light lemon/green, it's a crisp, medium-bodied wine with satisfying depth of melon, lime and green-capsicum flavours, fresh, lively and balanced for early enjoyment.

 DRY $10 V+

Caythorpe Family Estate Marlborough Sauvignon Blanc   ★★★★☆

Grown in the 'heart of the Wairau Plains', the 2016 vintage (★★★★) is full-bodied, with strong, ripe tropical-fruit flavours, a hint of spice, good acid spine and a dry (3.5 grams/litre of residual sugar), lengthy finish.

 DRY $20 V+

Church Road Grand Reserve Barrel Fermented
Hawke's Bay Sauvignon Blanc   ★★★★★

The impressive 2016 vintage (★★★★★) was estate-grown in the Redstone Vineyard, in the Bridge Pa Triangle, hand-picked and barrel-fermented with indigenous yeasts. Light lemon/green, it has a fragrant, ripely scented, slightly biscuity bouquet. Weighty and fleshy, with highly concentrated tropical-fruit flavours, finely integrated oak adding complexity, gentle acidity and a well-rounded finish, it's still youthful, but already delicious; best drinking mid-2018+.

DRY $44 AV

Church Road Hawke's Bay Sauvignon Blanc   ★★★★☆

Aiming for a style that is 'more refined and softer than a typical New Zealand Sauvignon Blanc', this wine is based principally on fruit from Pernod Ricard NZ's inland, elevated, cool site at Matapiro (300 metres above sea level); about 10 per cent of the blend in 2016 was estate-grown in the Redstone Vineyard, in the Bridge Pa Triangle. The 2016 vintage (★★★★☆) was matured for three months on its full yeast lees and partly (6 per cent) barrel-fermented. Highly aromatic, it is weighty, pure and punchy, with strong, ripe tropical-fruit flavours to the fore, slightly 'salty' and minerally touches adding complexity, and a long finish. Tasted in mid-2017, it's maturing gracefully; drink now to 2018.

Vintage	15	14	13	12	11	10
WR	7	7	7	5	6	7
Drink	17-19	17-18	P	P	P	P

DRY $20 V+

Church Road McDonald Series Hawke's Bay
Barrel Fermented Sauvignon Blanc   ★★★★

The restrained and youthful 2016 vintage (★★★★☆) was designed as a 'more complex style of Sauvignon Blanc without relying on new oak'. A single-vineyard wine, it was hand-harvested in the Bridge Pa Triangle and fermented with indigenous yeasts in French oak barrels. Light lemon/green, it is mouthfilling, fleshy and sweet-fruited, with generous, ripe tropical-fruit flavours to the fore, gentle acidity and a dry, finely textured finish. Best drinking 2019+.

DRY $27 –V

Churton Best End Marlborough Sauvignon Blanc   ★★★★★

This is Churton's 'single block, organic Sauvignon Blanc'. From a north-facing slope, 185 metres above sea level, in the Waihopai Valley, the 2015 vintage (★★★★★) was fermented and lees-aged for over a year in French oak puncheons. Still youthful, it is ripely fragrant, with intense grapefruit-like flavours, gently seasoned with oak, and a long, tightly structured finish. Full of personality, it's a very complex and age-worthy wine; open 2018+. (There is no 2016 or 2017.)

Vintage	13
WR	7
Drink	17-26

DRY $50 AV

Churton Marlborough Sauvignon Blanc   ★★★★★

This producer aims for a style that 'combines the renowned flavour and aromatic intensity of Marlborough fruit with the finesse and complexity of fine European wines'. Estate-grown on an elevated site in the Waihopai Valley, it is hand-harvested and a small part of the blend (15 per cent in 2016) is fermented and lees-aged in seasoned French oak puncheons. Certified organic, the 2016 vintage (★★★★★) is maturing very gracefully. Ripely scented and mouthfilling, it is fleshy, with grapefruit/lime flavours, showing excellent intensity and harmony, and a fully dry, lingering finish. A distinctive wine, tightly structured and harmonious, it's now breaking into full stride.

Vintage	16	15	14	13
WR	6	7	5	7
Drink	17-25	17-28	17-22	17-25

 DRY $27 V+

Clearview Te Awanga Hawke's Bay Sauvignon Blanc   ★★★☆

The 2016 vintage (★★★) is medium-bodied, with a fresh, limey bouquet, good depth of ripely herbaceous flavours and a well-rounded finish.

 DRY $19 V+

Clifford Bay Marlborough Sauvignon Blanc   ★★★

Bright, light lemon/green, the 2016 vintage (★★★) is fresh and vibrant, with good depth of tropical-fruit and herbaceous flavours, crisp and lively. Fine value.

DRY $15 V+

Clos Henri Marlborough Sauvignon Blanc   ★★★★★

The Clos Henri Vineyard near Renwick is owned by Henri Bourgeois, a leading, family-owned producer in the Loire Valley, which feels this wine expresses 'a unique terroir . . . and French winemaking approach'. A sophisticated and distinctive Sauvignon Blanc, in top years it's a joy to drink. Certified organic, the 2015 vintage (★★★★★) was hand-picked and mostly fermented and matured for eight months on its yeast lees in tanks; 15 per cent was fermented in old French oak barrels. A powerful, tightly structured wine, it is full-bodied and sweet-fruited, with good complexity and penetrating, vigorous, ripely herbaceous flavours that build to a bone-dry, lasting finish. Best drinking 2018+.

Vintage	15	14	13	12	11	10	09
WR	7	6	7	7	6	7	6
Drink	17-22	17-21	17-21	17-20	P	P	P

 DRY $33 AV

Clos Marguerite Marlborough Sauvignon Blanc   ★★★★★

Estate-grown and hand-picked in the Awatere Valley, the 2016 vintage (★★★★☆) is freshly scented, lively and mouthfilling. Most of the wine was lees-aged in tanks, but 12 per cent was barrel-fermented. Sweet-fruited, it has crisp, dry, ripely herbaceous flavours, showing a distinct touch of complexity, that build across the palate to a finely textured, slightly minerally, lingering finish.

 DRY $28 V+

Cloudy Bay Sauvignon Blanc ★★★★★

New Zealand's most internationally acclaimed wine is sought after from Sydney to New York and London. Its irresistibly aromatic and zesty style and intense flavours stem from 'the fruit characters that are in the grapes when they arrive at the winery'. It is sourced from company-owned and several long-term contract growers' vineyards in the Rapaura, Fairhall, Renwick and Brancott districts of the Wairau Valley, Marlborough. The juice is mostly cool-fermented with cultured and indigenous yeasts in stainless steel tanks and aged on its yeast lees, and a small percentage of the blend (4 per cent in 2017) is fermented at warmer temperatures in old French oak barriques and large oak vats. From a tough growing season, the 2017 vintage (★★★★☆) is scented, mouthfilling and tightly structured, with strong, vigorous passionfruit and lime flavours, woven with steely acidity, and obvious potential. Slightly austere in its infancy, it needs time; open mid-2018+.

Vintage	17	16	15
WR	6	6	7
Drink	17-19	17-18	17-18

DRY $37 AV

Cloudy Bay Te Koko – see the Branded and Other White Wines section

Coopers Creek Marlborough Sauvignon Blanc ★★★☆

The 2017 vintage (★★★) is a fresh, medium-bodied wine, strongly varietal, with crisp, limey, appley flavours, dry (3 grams/litre of residual sugar), tangy and tasty. The 2016 vintage (★★★☆) is aromatic, with good depth of ripe tropical-fruit flavours, fresh and finely balanced.

DRY $18 V+

Coopers Creek SV Dillons Point Marlborough Sauvignon Blanc ★★★★

Aromatic and mouthfilling, the 2016 vintage (★★★★) has generous, ripe melon, capsicum and lime flavours, a slightly 'salty' streak, and a dry (3 grams/litre of residual sugar), finely balanced finish.

DRY $23 AV

Crafters Union Elegance + Intensity Marlborough Sauvignon Blanc (★★★★)

Drinking well in late 2017, the 2016 vintage (★★★★) is weighty and ripely herbaceous, with strong melon/lime flavours and a dry, lingering finish. It's a quietly satisfying wine, with good richness through the palate. (From Constellation NZ.)

DRY $22 V+

Crowded House Marlborough Sauvignon Blanc ★★★☆

The 2016 vintage (★★★) is an easy-drinking wine, mouthfilling, with fresh, ripely herbaceous flavours and a crisp, dry finish.

DRY $20 AV

Dashwood Marlborough Sauvignon Blanc ★★★☆

Typically great value. Grown in the Wairau Valley and Awatere Valley, the 2016 vintage (★★★☆) is aromatic, fresh and lively, with appetisingly crisp tropical-fruit and herbaceous flavours, showing very good vigour and depth.

DRY $18 V+

Delegat Awatere Valley Sauvignon Blanc

Strongly aromatic, the 2017 vintage (★★★★) is an elegant, medium-bodied wine, with vibrant, pure melon and green-capsicum flavours, dry (3 grams/litre of residual sugar) and zingy.

DRY $20 V+

Delta Marlborough Sauvignon Blanc (★★★★☆)

The 2016 vintage (★★★★☆) offers top value. A single-vineyard wine, it was grown at Dillons Point, in the lower Wairau Valley, and handled without oak. Aromatic, it is vibrantly fruity, with excellent intensity of ripely herbaceous flavours. Tightly structured, with a slightly 'salty' streak and a lingering, dry finish (2.8 grams/litre of residual sugar), it's enjoyable from the start.

DRY $22 V+

Doctor's, The, Marlborough Sauvignon Blanc ★★★

A good example of the low-alcohol style, the 2017 vintage (★★★) is pale and fresh, with vibrant green-apple flavours, slightly sweet and tangy. It's a strongly varietal wine, light (9.5 per cent alcohol) and lively.

MED/DRY $22 –V

Dog Point Vineyard Marlborough Sauvignon Blanc ★★★★★

This wine offers a clear style contrast to Section 94, Dog Point's complex, barrel-aged Sauvignon Blanc (see the Branded and Other White Wines section). Hand-harvested at several sites in the Wairau Valley, it is lees-aged in tanks but handled without oak. The 2017 vintage (★★★★) is ripely scented, with slightly 'funky' aromas. Light lemon/green, it is a medium-bodied, vigorous wine, vibrantly fruity and tightly structured, with strong, crisp melon/lime flavours, a hint of passionfruit, a distinct touch of complexity and a dry, tangy finish. Best drinking mid-2018+. Certified organic.

Vintage	17	16	15	14	13	12
WR	4	7	7	6	7	5
Drink	17-21	17-21	17-20	17-18	17-19	P

DRY $26 V+

Drowsy Fish by Crown Range Cellar Nelson Sauvignon Blanc ★★★★

The punchy 2016 vintage (★★★★☆) was grown in the Moutere hills and tank-fermented. Bright, light lemon/green, it is a fresh, fragrant, medium-bodied wine, with very good intensity of crisp melon and green-capsicum flavours, lively, minerally, racy and long.

DRY $25 AV

Durvillea 'D' by Astrolabe Marlborough Sauvignon Blanc ★★★☆

Offering excellent value, the aromatic, lively 2016 vintage (★★★☆) was grown in the Wairau Valley, Awatere Valley, and further south, at Kekerengu. Partly barrel-fermented, it is fresh and mouthfilling, with strong, ripely herbaceous flavours, showing a touch of complexity, and a crisp, dry (1.2 grams/litre of residual sugar) finish.

DRY $15 V+

Elephant Hill Hawke's Bay Sauvignon Blanc   ★★★☆

From a coastal site at Te Awanga, the 2015 vintage (★★★☆) is a medium-bodied, slightly minerally wine with fresh acidity, lively passionfruit, apple and green-capsicum flavours, a touch of bottle-aged complexity, and an appetisingly crisp, dry finish.

DRY $22 AV

Eradus Awatere Valley Marlborough Sauvignon Blanc   ★★★☆

The 2017 vintage (★★★☆) is aromatic and strongly varietal, with freshly herbaceous melon, lime and green-capsicum flavours, crisp and punchy.

DRY $19 V+

Esk Valley Marlborough Sauvignon Blanc   ★★★★

The 2016 vintage (★★★★) was grown in the Wairau Valley (75 per cent) and Awatere Valley (25 per cent). Very fresh and punchy, it is a fully dry style (1.7 grams/litre of residual sugar), with ripely herbaceous flavours, finely balanced and rich.

DRY $20 V+

Fairbourne Marlborough Sauvignon Blanc   ★★★★☆

From elevated, north-facing slopes in the Wairau Valley, the classy 2016 vintage (★★★★★) of this single-vineyard wine is one of the best yet. Hand-picked and fermented to full dryness (1.2 grams/litre of residual sugar), it was mostly handled in tanks, but a small portion of the blend was French oak-fermented. Pale lemon/green, it is ripely scented and weighty, with fresh, concentrated, grapefruit/lime fruit characters, showing good complexity, and a well-rounded, long finish. A very harmonious wine, with layers of flavour, it's delicious now.

Vintage	16	15	14	13	12	11	10
WR	7	6	7	7	6	7	6
Drink	17-22	17-21	17-20	17-19	17-18	17-18	P

DRY $35 –V

Fairhall Downs Single Vineyard Marlborough Sauvignon Blanc   ★★★★

The 2016 vintage (★★★★) was estate-grown in the Brancott Valley. Richly scented, it is mouthfilling, with ripe tropical-fruit flavours, showing excellent depth, and a dry (3.3 grams/litre of residual sugar, finely balanced finish.

DRY $24 AV

Falconhead Marlborough Sauvignon Blanc   ★★★

The 2017 vintage (★★★) is an aromatic, lively wine with punchy tropical-fruit and herbaceous flavours, tangy acidity, and a green-edged finish. Enjoyable young, it's priced sharply.

DRY $16 V+

Folium Reserve Marlborough Sauvignon Blanc   ★★★★★

The impressive 2016 vintage (★★★★★) was hand-picked in the Brancott Valley and handled almost entirely in tanks; 5 per cent of the blend was barrel-fermented. Set for a long life, it is bright, light lemon/green, weighty, youthful and tightly structured, with concentrated, ripe flavours, firm acid spine and a dry (below 2 grams/litre of residual sugar), lasting finish. Showing obvious power and potential, it's best cellared to at least mid-2018+.

Vintage	16
WR	6
Drink	17-30

 DRY $33 AV

Folium Vineyard Marlborough Sauvignon Blanc   ★★★★☆

The impressive 2015 vintage (★★★★★) was hand-harvested in the Brancott Valley and handled entirely in tanks. Light lemon/green, it is mouthfilling and tightly structured, with rich, ripe tropical-fruit flavours, showing excellent vibrancy and depth, and a long, slightly racy finish.

 DRY $28 AV

Forrest Marlborough Sauvignon Blanc   ★★★★

The 2017 vintage (★★★☆) is a crisp, medium-bodied wine, freshly herbaceous, with green-apple, lime and capsicum flavours, some riper, tropical-fruit notes, and very good vigour and depth.

 DRY $22 V+

Framingham F-Series Marlborough Sauvignon Blanc   ★★★★★

Estate-grown, hand-picked and partly barrel-fermented, this is a consistently classy, age-worthy wine; the light yellow/green 2016 vintage (★★★★☆) is still unfolding. Weighty and fleshy, it has generous, ripe tropical-fruit flavours, well-integrated oak, good complexity and obvious potential; open mid-2018+. The 2015 vintage (★★★★★) is breaking into full stride now, with rich, ripe tropical-fruit flavours, a subtle seasoning of oak, and lovely complexity and depth.

 DRY $35 AV

Framingham Marlborough Sauvignon Blanc   ★★★★

Consistently impressive and fine value. Grown at two sites in the Wairau Valley, the 2016 vintage (★★★★) was mostly handled in tanks, but 10 per cent of the blend was barrel-fermented. Light lemon/green, it is freshly aromatic, with mouthfilling body, good intensity of ripe melon/lime flavours, a hint of capsicums, and a long, dry, lively finish. Showing good personality, it should be at its best during 2018.

Vintage	16	15	14	13	12
WR	6	6	6	6	6
Drink	17-19	17-18	P	P	P

DRY $21 V+

Fromm La Strada Marlborough Sauvignon Blanc ★★★★

After 16 vintages, the Fromm winery, renowned for Pinot Noir, finally produced its first Sauvignon Blanc in 2008 – mostly for export markets. Certified organic, the 2016 vintage (★★★★) was hand-picked and fermented to full dryness in tanks. Pale lemon/green, it is a tightly structured, aromatic, medium-bodied wine with punchy melon and green-capsicum flavours, a minerally streak and a tangy finish.

Vintage	16	15	14	13
WR	6	7	7	6
Drink	17-20	17-20	17-19	P

 DRY $28 –V

Giesen Marlborough Sauvignon Blanc ★★★☆

This huge-volume wine from Giesen enjoys major export success. Grown in estate-owned and contract growers' vineyards, mostly in the Wairau Valley, with a smaller portion from the Awatere Valley, it is typically medium to full-bodied, with ripely herbaceous flavours, showing very good freshness, vigour and depth.

Vintage	15
WR	4
Drink	P

 DRY $17 V+

Gladstone Vineyard Sauvignon Blanc ★★★★

The 2015 vintage (★★★★) was grown in the northern Wairarapa and 40 per cent barrel-fermented; the rest was handled in tanks. Made in a fully dry style (1.4 grams/litre of residual sugar), it is mouthfilling, with fresh, finely balanced acidity, concentrated, ripe tropical-fruit flavours and slightly toasty notes adding complexity.

 DRY $25 AV

Glazebrook Marlborough Sauvignon Blanc ★★★☆

Drinking well now, the 2016 vintage (★★★☆) is mouthfilling and sweet-fruited, with ripe passionfruit and lime flavours, showing very good depth, and a smooth finish. (From Ngatarawa.)

 DRY $20 AV

Gold River Central Otago Sauvignon Blanc (★★★)

Full of youthful impact, the 2017 vintage (★★★) was hand-harvested and tank-fermented. Mouthfilling, it is vibrant and tangy, with strong, herbaceous flavours, dry (3.8 grams/litre of residual sugar) and crisp. (From Gibbston Valley.)

 DRY $23 –V

Goldwater Wairau Valley Marlborough Sauvignon Blanc ★★★★

The 2016 vintage (★★★★) is a fresh, medium to full-bodied wine with ripe tropical-fruit flavours, woven with fresh acidity. Crisp and lively, it shows good intensity, with a dry finish.

DRY $21 V+

Graham Norton's Own Marlborough Sauvignon Blanc ★★★★

From 'chief winemaker Graham Norton', Invivo's 2017 vintage (★★★☆) is medium-bodied, with lively tropical-fruit and herbaceous flavours, a vague suggestion of sweetness (6.1 grams/litre of residual sugar), crisp acidity, and lots of smooth, easy-drinking appeal.

DRY $19 V+

Greenhough Hope Vineyard Nelson Sauvignon Blanc ★★★★☆

Certified organic, the 2016 vintage (★★★★☆) was estate-grown, hand-picked and fermented with indigenous yeasts in French oak barrels (20 per cent new). Wood-aged for eight months, it is light lemon/green, mouthfilling and complex, with youthful tropical-fruit flavours, a slightly herbaceous undercurrent, a creamy texture, and a long, dry finish. Drink now or cellar.

DRY $32 –V

Greenhough Nelson Sauvignon Blanc ★★★★

Certified organic, this consistently rewarding wine is mostly handled in tanks, but a significant portion (15 per cent of the blend in 2017) is fermented with indigenous yeasts and lees-aged in French oak casks. The 2017 vintage (★★★★) is aromatic and lively, with very good depth of tropical-fruit and herbaceous flavours, showing a distinct touch of complexity, and a dry, lingering finish.

DRY $22 V+

Greyrock Marlborough Sauvignon Blanc (★★)

Solid but plain, the 2016 vintage (★★) is a medium-bodied wine with crisp green-apple flavours and a smooth (4 grams/litre of residual sugar) finish. (From Sileni.)

DRY $17 –V

Greystone Sauvignon Blanc Barrel Fermented ★★★★☆

Offering fine value, the 2016 vintage (★★★★★) was mostly (80 per cent) fermented with indigenous yeasts in old French oak barrels, and lees-aged in wood for six months. Bright, light lemon/green, it is mouthfilling and dry, with concentrated, ripe tropical-fruit flavours, showing very good complexity, lots of youthful drive, and a long finish. Full of personality, it's a drink-now or cellaring proposition.

Vintage	16
WR	5
Drink	17-21

DRY $22 V+

Greywacke Marlborough Sauvignon Blanc ★★★★★

Grown in the central Wairau Valley and the Southern Valleys, the 2017 vintage (★★★★☆) was handled entirely in tanks (15 per cent of the blend was fermented with indigenous yeasts). Mouthfilling and punchy, it shows good weight and intensity, with crisp acidity woven through its vibrant melon, passionfruit and lime flavours, dry and lingering.

Vintage	17	16	15	14	13	12
WR	6	6	6	6	6	5
Drink	18-22	17-22	17-21	17-20	17-19	P

DRY $26 V+

Greywacke Marlborough Wild Sauvignon ★★★★★

This is a leading example of Marlborough Sauvignon Blanc from well outside the mainstream. Fermented with indigenous yeasts in mostly old French oak barriques (8 per cent new), and wood-matured for a year, the 2015 vintage (★★★★★) is an arresting wine, revealing lovely delicacy and depth. Bright, light lemon/green, it has a fragrant, complex, ripely scented bouquet. Full-bodied, it is very rich, vibrant and harmonious, with sweet-fruit delights, a very subtle seasoning of oak, and a tightly structured, dry, very persistent finish. Already delicious, it should be at its best 2018+.

Vintage	15	14	13	12	11	10	09
WR	6	6	6	5	6	6	5
Drink	18-25	17-24	17-23	17-22	17-21	17-20	18-19

DRY $37 AV

Grove Mill Wairau Valley Marlborough Sauvignon Blanc ★★★★

The 2016 vintage (★★★★) is a mouthfilling, dry wine with balanced acidity and generous, ripe tropical-fruit flavours that linger well. (Five per cent barrel-fermented.)

DRY $20 V+

Gunn Estate Reserve Marlborough Sauvignon Blanc ★★★

Offering good, easy drinking, the 2017 vintage (★★★) is a lively, medium-bodied wine, with fresh melon/lime flavours, a sliver of sweetness (5.2 grams/litre of residual sugar) and crisp acidity. Priced right.

Vintage	17
WR	5
Drink	17-19

MED/DRY $17 AV

Haha Marlborough Sauvignon Blanc ★★★☆

This is a consistently good buy. Grown in the Wairau and Waihopai valleys, the 2016 vintage (★★★★) was mostly handled in tanks; 3 per cent of the blend was barrel-fermented. Crisp and punchy, it's a ripely herbaceous wine, with very good intensity of passionfruit/lime flavours, crisp and dry (2 grams/litre of residual sugar). Fine value.

DRY $16 V+

Hans Herzog Marlborough Sauvignon Blanc Barrel Fermented Sur Lie ★★★★★

Far outside the mainstream regional style, the 2015 vintage (★★★★★) was estate-grown and hand-picked on the north side of the Wairau Valley, fermented with indigenous yeasts in French oak puncheons, and wood-aged for 15 months. Bright, light yellow/green, it is mouthfilling and ripely herbaceous, with generous, highly concentrated grapefruit, lime and slight capsicum flavours, a subtle seasoning of oak, and a dry, lasting finish. Drink now or cellar. Certified organic.

DRY $44 AV

Huia Marlborough Sauvignon Blanc ★★★★

The 2016 vintage (★★★★) was grown in the Wairau Valley and partly barrel-fermented. Medium to full-bodied, it has fresh tropical-fruit flavours, showing very good vibrancy and depth, balanced acidity and a dry (3.9 grams/litre of residual sugar) finish. Certified organic.

DRY $28 –V

Hunter's Kaho Roa Marlborough Sauvignon Blanc ★★★★

Based on the ripest, least-herbaceous grapes, this wine is estate-grown in stony vineyards at Rapaura, on the relatively warm, north side of the Wairau Valley. The classy 2016 vintage (★★★★☆) was fermented with indigenous yeasts in mostly seasoned French oak barrels (5 per cent new). A mouthfilling, subtle wine, it is youthful and sweet-fruited, with excellent depth and delicacy of flavour, a gentle seasoning of oak, and a crisp, dry (2.4 grams/litre of residual sugar), lengthy finish.

DRY $25 AV

Hunter's Marlborough Sauvignon Blanc ★★★☆

Hunter's fame rests on this dry wine, which has the intense aromas of cool-climate grapes, uncluttered by oak handling. The goal is 'a strong expression of Marlborough fruit – a bell-clear wine with a mix of tropical and searing gooseberry characters'. The grapes are sourced from numerous sites in the Wairau Valley, and to retain their fresh, vibrant characters they are processed quickly, with some use of indigenous yeasts and lees-aging. The wine is usually at its best between one and two years old. The 2017 vintage (★★★☆) is a fresh, medium-bodied, fully dry wine, highly aromatic, with vibrant melon, lime and capsicum flavours, crisp and punchy.

DRY $21 AV

Invivo Marlborough Sauvignon Blanc ★★★★

The 2017 vintage (★★★☆) is a fresh, crisp, medium-bodied wine, with good depth of lively melon, lime and capsicum flavours, dry (4.2 grams/litre of residual sugar) and finely balanced for easy drinking.

Vintage	17	16	15	14
WR	5	7	7	5
Drink	17-19	17-19	17-18	P

DRY $19 V+

Jackson Estate Stich Marlborough Sauvignon Blanc ★★★★★

Estate-grown at three sites in the Wairau and Waihopai valleys (including some vines over 25 years old), this is typically a lush, ripe and rounded wine with concentration and huge drinkability. It has excellent aging ability, and the latest releases are often outstanding. The impressive 2015 vintage (★★★★★) is highly aromatic, mouthfilling and sweet-fruited, with excellent intensity of melon, lime and green-capsicum flavours, finely balanced acidity, and a long, dry (2.1 grams/litre of residual sugar) finish, zingy and harmonious.

Vintage	15	14	13	12
WR	6	5	5	6
Drink	17-18	P-17	P	P

DRY $21 V+

Johanneshof Cellars Marlborough Sauvignon Blanc   ★★★

The easy-drinking 2016 vintage (★★★) is medium-bodied, with crisp, freshly herbaceous flavours, citrusy, appley and limey, and an off-dry (5.8 grams/litre of residual sugar), tangy finish.

MED/DRY $24 –V

Johner Estate Wairarapa Sauvignon Blanc   ★★★☆

The 2016 vintage (★★★★) is medium to full-bodied, with strong, lively tropical-fruit flavours, a herbaceous undercurrent, and a dry (4 grams/litre of residual sugar), appetisingly crisp finish. Good value.

Vintage	16	15	14	13
WR	6	5	6	6
Drink	17-18	P	P	P

DRY $20 AV

Jules Taylor Marlborough Sauvignon Blanc   ★★★★☆

Grown in the Wairau and Awatere valleys, the vibrant, punchy 2016 vintage (★★★★☆) was handled entirely in tanks and made in a fully dry (1.1 grams/litre of residual sugar) style. It is highly aromatic, with an array of melon, grapefruit, lime and green-capsicum flavours, in an intensely varietal style with pure, penetrating flavours.

Vintage	16
WR	5
Drink	17-18

DRY $24 V+

Jules Taylor OTQ Limited Release Single Vineyard Marlborough Sauvignon Blanc   ★★★★★

Made 'On The Quiet', the 2016 vintage (★★★★★) is a classy, distinctive, single-vineyard wine, grown at Dillons Point, in the lower Wairau Valley. Hand-picked and fermented with indigenous yeasts in French oak barrels, it was matured on its yeast lees in wood for nine months. Light lemon/green, it is ripely scented, weighty and fleshy, with concentrated tropical-fruit flavours, gently seasoned with nutty oak, excellent complexity and harmony, and a well-rounded, dry (1 gram/litre of residual sugar), very long finish. Best drinking mid-2018+.

Vintage	16	15
WR	7	6
Drink	17-22	17-20

DRY $32 AV

Kaimira Estate Brightwater Sauvignon Blanc   ★★★☆

Certified organic, the 2016 vintage (★★★★) was estate-grown in Nelson. Light lemon/green, it is mouthfilling, with crisp, ripe pineapple and lime flavours, youthful and generous, and a dry (4.2 grams/litre of residual sugar), finely balanced finish. Good drinking now to 2018.

DRY $21 AV

Kakapo Marlborough Sauvignon Blanc   (★★★★)

Pale and punchy, the 2016 vintage (★★★★) is a mouthfilling, clearly herbaceous style, with fresh, strong melon and green-capsicum flavours and a tight, zingy finish.

DRY $19 V+

Kim Crawford Marlborough Sauvignon Blanc   (★★★★)

Drinking well now, the 2016 vintage (★★★★) is a light lemon/green, ripely scented wine. Weighty, with strong, fresh passionfruit/lime characters, it's a full-flavoured wine with a well-rounded (4.2 grams/litre of residual sugar) finish. Ready; no rush.

Vintage	16
WR	6
Drink	17-18

DRY $17 V+

Kim Crawford Small Parcels Spitfire Marlborough Sauvignon Blanc   ★★★★

From a vineyard in the central Wairau Valley, the 2016 vintage (★★★★) is ripely scented, mouthfilling and fleshy, with generous passionfruit/lime flavours and a dry (2.7 grams/litre of residual sugar), well-rounded finish. It's drinking well now.

DRY $25 AV

Kina Beach Vineyard Nelson Sauvignon Blanc   (★★★★)

Still on sale, the 2015 vintage (★★★★) is mouthfilling, sweet-fruited and lively, with melon/lime flavours, a touch of bottle-aged complexity, and a dry (2 grams/litre of residual sugar) finish. Showing plenty of personality, it's probably at its peak.

Vintage	15
WR	7
Drink	17-22

DRY $20 V+

Konrad Single Vineyard Marlborough Sauvignon Blanc   ★★★★

Certified organic, the attractive 2016 vintage (★★★★) was estate-grown in the Waihopai Valley and mostly handled in tanks; 8 per cent of the blend was barrel-fermented. Fresh and lively, it is medium to full-bodied, with excellent vigour and depth of ripe melon/lime flavours, a touch of complexity, and a finely balanced, dry (4.5 grams/litre of residual sugar) finish. Drink now to 2018.

DRY $28 –V

Lake Chalice Marlborough Sauvignon Blanc   ★★★★

Aromatic, with plenty of youthful impact, the 2016 vintage (★★★★) is a mouthfilling, vibrantly fruity wine, grown in the lower Wairau Valley. It shows good intensity of melon and green-capsicum flavours, a slightly 'salty' streak, and a dry (4 grams/litre of residual sugar), appetisingly crisp finish.

DRY $20 V+

Lake Chalice The Raptor Marlborough Sauvignon Blanc   ★★★★

From sites at Dillons Point, in the lower Wairau Valley, the 2016 vintage (★★★★) is a fleshy, vibrantly fruity wine, with mouthfilling body, strong, ripe tropical-fruit flavours, hints of passionfruit and limes, and a dry, rounded finish.

DRY $25 AV

Lake Hayes Central Otago Sauvignon Blanc   ★★☆

The 2016 vintage (★★☆) is an easy-drinking, light-bodied wine with fresh, citrusy, appley flavours, dry (2 grams/litre of residual sugar) and crisp. (From Amisfield.)

DRY $20 –V

Lawson's Dry Hills Marlborough Sauvignon Blanc   ★★★★★

One of the region's best, widely available Sauvignon Blancs, this stylish wine is vibrant, intense and finely structured. The grapes are grown at several sites, mostly in the Southern Valleys, and to add a subtle extra dimension, part of the blend (7 per cent in 2017) is fermented with indigenous yeasts in old French oak barriques. The wine typically has strong impact in its youth, but also has a proven ability to age, acquiring toasty, minerally complexities. The 2017 vintage (★★★★) is a bright, light lemon/green, medium to full-bodied wine, fresh and vibrant, with good intensity of melon and green-capsicum flavours, a hint of passionfruit, a distinct touch of complexity, and a dry (2.8 grams/litre of residual sugar), lingering finish. Fine value.

Vintage	17	16	15
WR	5	6	7
Drink	18-20	17-20	17-20

DRY $20 V+

Lawson's Dry Hills Wairau Reserve Marlborough Sauvignon Blanc   ★★★★★

The impressive 2016 vintage (★★★★★), grown at two sites in the Wairau Valley, was fermented in tanks (85 per cent) and old French oak puncheons (15 per cent). Light lemon/green, it is fresh and mouthfilling, with rich tropical-fruit flavours, showing excellent delicacy and complexity, and a dry (3.8 grams/litre of residual sugar), lasting finish. Best drinking 2018+. The 2017 vintage (★★★★) was grown in the Waihopai (65 per cent), Awatere (20 per cent) and Wairau (15 per cent) valleys. Partly barrel-fermented, it is still very youthful, with mouthfilling body and punchy, tangy melon/lime flavours, showing very good vigour and complexity. Open mid-2018+.

Vintage	17	16	15
WR	5	7	7
Drink	18-21	17-20	17-20

DRY $25 V+

Leefield Station Marlborough Sauvignon Blanc   (★★★★☆)

From Marisco, the 2016 vintage (★★★★☆) is full-bodied, with rich, ripely herbaceous flavours, a hint of 'sweaty armpit', good acid spine and a long, dry finish.

DRY $22 V+

Left Field Nelson Sauvignon Blanc   ★★★☆

Offering good value, the 2017 vintage (★★★☆) is a vivacious, medium-bodied wine, with punchy, freshly herbaceous flavours and a dry (4 grams/litre of residual sugar), finely balanced finish. (From Te Awa.)

Vintage	17	16
WR	5	5
Drink	17-19	17-19

DRY $18 V+

Leveret Estate Marlborough Sauvignon Blanc   (★★★☆)

Full of youthful impact, the 2017 vintage (★★★☆) has fresh, strong melon and green-capsicum flavours to the fore, with a hint of passionfruit. A crisp, herbaceous style, it is full-bodied, with very good depth and vibrancy.

Vintage	17
WR	7
Drink	18-19

DRY $23 AV

Lime Rock Central Hawke's Bay Sauvignon Blanc   (★★★★)

Showing good personality, the 2016 vintage (★★★★) was mostly handled in tanks; 7 per cent of the blend was barrel-fermented. A pale, mouthfilling wine, it is lively, with melon/lime flavours, a minerally streak, and good intensity, building across the palate to a dry (4.7 grams/litre of residual sugar), crisp finish. Drink now to 2018.

Vintage	16
WR	6
Drink	18-20

DRY $20 V+

Linden Estate Hawke's Bay Sauvignon Blanc   (★★★)

Grown in the Esk Valley, the 2016 vintage (★★★) was fermented and lees-stirred in French oak barrels, and wood-aged for a year. Bright, light lemon/green, it is medium-bodied, with fresh, ripe tropical-fruit flavours, threaded with lively acidity, a touch of complexity, and a distinctly off-dry (6.6 grams/litre of residual sugar), tangy finish.

MED/DRY $20 –V

Loveblock Marlborough Sauvignon Blanc   ★★★★

Certified organic, the lively 2016 vintage (★★★★) was estate-grown in the lower Awatere Valley, and 7 per cent of the blend was aged for six months in old French oak barrels. The bouquet is fresh and ripely aromatic; the palate is mouthfilling, with good intensity of vibrant tropical-fruit and green-capsicum flavours, slightly leesy notes adding complexity, and a finely balanced, smooth (5 grams/litre of residual sugar), lingering finish. (Retasted in mid-2017, the 2013 vintage (★★★★) was still very lively, with strong, ripely herbaceous flavours and toasty, bottle-aged notes adding interest.)

Vintage	16
WR	5
Drink	17-21

DRY $25 AV

Luminary, The, Martinborough Sauvignon Blanc ★★★☆

From Palliser Estate, the easy-drinking 2016 vintage (★★★☆) has a fresh, fragrant, ripely herbaceous bouquet. Medium to full-bodied, it has generous melon/lime flavours, fresh acidity and a smooth finish. Priced sharply.

DRY $17 V+

Mahi Boundary Farm Sauvignon Blanc ★★★★☆

Grown on the lower slopes of the Wither Hills, the 2014 vintage (★★★★☆), still on sale, is a single-vineyard wine, hand-picked, fermented with indigenous yeasts and lees-aged for 10 months in French oak barriques. A complex, dry style (3.1 grams/litre of residual sugar), it is still fresh and vibrant, with lively acidity and very good intensity of tropical-fruit flavours.

Vintage	15	14	13	12
WR	6	6	6	6
Drink	17-22	17-21	17-21	17-20

DRY $29 AV

Mahi Marlborough Sauvignon Blanc ★★★★☆

The 2016 vintage (★★★★★) is the most impressive yet. Grown at six sites – principally at the western end of the Wairau Valley – it was mostly handled in tanks; 12 per cent of the blend was fermented with indigenous yeasts in old French oak barrels. Lees-aged for 10 months (longer than in the past), it is fully dry (less than 1 gram/litre of residual sugar), with moderate acidity, mouthfilling body, and excellent vigour, delicacy and depth. Freshly scented and sweet-fruited, with layers of flavour, it offers top value.

Vintage	16	15	14	13	12
WR	7	6	6	6	6
Drink	17-20	17-18	17-18	P	P

DRY $22 V+

Main Divide Marlborough Sauvignon Blanc (★★★★)

The 2016 vintage (★★★★) is mouthfilling, fleshy and dry, with ripe tropical-fruit characters to the fore. Fresh and punchy, with generous passionfruit/lime flavours, a hint of green capsicums, and a crisp, persistent finish, it offers good value. (From Pegasus Bay.)

Vintage	16
WR	7
Drink	17-20

DRY $21 V+

Maison Noire Hawke's Bay Sauvignon Blanc (★★★☆)

Drinking well now, the 2015 vintage (★★★☆) is a slightly minerally wine, blended with a 'touch of Viognier' and partly barrel-fermented. Medium to full-bodied, it is fresh, crisp, lively and dry, with melon/lime flavours, showing a touch of complexity. Priced right.

Vintage	15
WR	5
Drink	17-21

DRY $18 V+

Maison Noire Marlborough Sauvignon Blanc   (★★★)

The distinctive 2016 vintage (★★★) is a pale, medium-bodied wine, fermented and lees-aged in seasoned oak barrels. Still developing, it has ripe tropical-fruit flavours with slightly biscuity and creamy notes.

Vintage	16
WR	5
Drink	17-18

 DRY $18 AV

Man O' War Waiheke Island Sauvignon Blanc   ★★★☆

The light lemon/green 2016 vintage (★★★☆) was estate-grown, hand-picked, blended with a small portion of Sémillon, and partly barrel-fermented. A tangy, medium-bodied wine, it has strong melon and green-capsicum flavours, showing a touch of complexity, and a crisp, dry finish.

Vintage	16	15	14
WR	6	6	5
Drink	17-21	17-19	17-18

 DRY $22 AV

Map Maker Marlborough Sauvignon Blanc   ★★★☆

Priced right, the 2016 vintage (★★★☆) is a full-bodied, ripely herbaceous wine, grown at Rapaura. It offers good depth of passionfruit/lime flavours, fresh, finely balanced and smooth. (From Staete Landt.)

 DRY $18 V+

Margrain Martinborough Sauvignon Blanc   ★★★☆

This wine is made in an easy-drinking, off-dry style. The 2016 vintage (★★★☆) is fresh and lively, with strong melon, grapefruit and lime flavours, a sliver of sweetness (6 grams/litre of residual sugar) and appetising acidity.

Vintage	16	15
WR	6	6
Drink	17-20	17-20

MED/DRY $24 –V

Martinborough Vineyard Martinborough Sauvignon Blanc   ★★★★

The 2016 vintage (★★★★) was partly barrel-aged. It is fleshy and dry, with rich, ripe tropical-fruit flavours, gently seasoned with nutty oak, and good complexity.

 DRY $25 AV

Matakana Estate Marlborough Sauvignon Blanc   (★★★★)

Intensely varietal, the 2016 vintage (★★★★) has fresh, lively herbal aromas, leading into a medium-bodied wine with strong citrus-fruit, lime and green-capsicum flavours. Tightly structured, it builds across the palate to a crisp, dry, lingering finish.

 DRY $22 V+

Maui Marlborough Sauvignon Blanc   ★★★☆

The 2016 vintage (★★★☆) is a crisp, mouthfilling wine with good depth of fresh melon, lime and green-capsicum flavours, lively, tangy, and skilfully balanced for easy drinking. (From Tiki.)

DRY $19 V+

Mill Road Marlborough Sauvignon Blanc   (★★☆)

Looking for a low-priced, top-value Sauvignon Blanc? The 2016 vintage (★★☆) offers easy drinking. Fresh and medium-bodied, it is lively and ripely herbaceous, with decent depth of melon and green-capsicum flavours and a dry (3.3 grams/litre of residual sugar), smooth finish.

MED/DRY $10 V+

Mills Reef Estate Marlborough Sauvignon Blanc   ★★☆

The easy-drinking 2017 vintage (★★★) is fresh and vibrantly fruity, with good depth of melon and green-capsicum flavours, tangy acidity and a smooth finish. Enjoyable young.

Vintage	17	16	15
WR	5	7	7
Drink	17-18	17-18	P

DRY $19 –V

Mills Reef Reserve Hawke's Bay Sauvignon Blanc   ★★★☆

Grown in the inland, elevated Puketapu district, the 2016 vintage (★★★☆) is aromatic, fresh and lively, with good depth of melon/lime flavours, dry (2 grams/litre of residual sugar) and crisp. Enjoyable young. The light lemon/green 2017 vintage (★★★☆) has lots of youthful impact, in a medium-bodied style with strong, ripely herbaceous flavours, fresh and finely balanced.

Vintage	17	16
WR	5	7
Drink	17-19	17-18

DRY $23 –V

Misha's Vineyard The Starlet Central Otago Sauvignon Blanc   ★★★★

The 2015 vintage (★★★★), released in 2017, was estate-grown at Bendigo, in the Cromwell Basin. Hand-picked at over 24 brix, it was mostly handled in tanks, but 23 per cent of the blend was fermented with indigenous yeasts in seasoned French oak casks. Pale lemon/green, it is mouthfilling and smooth, with fresh, ripe tropical-fruit flavours, showing a distinct touch of complexity, balanced acidity, and a strong, dry (4 grams/litre of residual sugar) finish. Maturing gracefully, it's drinking well now.

Vintage	15	14	13	12	11
WR	6	6	7	7	6
Drink	17-18	17-20	17-19	17-18	P

DRY $27 –V

Mission Marlborough Sauvignon Blanc   ★★★☆

The 2017 vintage (★★★☆) was estate-grown in the Awatere Valley. Bright, light lemon/green, it has fresh, strong tropical-fruit and herbaceous flavours, basically dry (4.6 grams/litre of residual sugar), crisp and full of youthful vigour.

DRY $18 V+

Mission Vineyard Selection Marlborough Sauvignon Blanc ★★★★

The 2017 vintage (★★★★) was estate-grown in the Awatere Valley. Pale lemon/green, it is vibrant and punchy, with good intensity of tropical-fruit and herbaceous flavours, a slightly minerally streak, and a crisp, off-dry (6 grams/litre of residual sugar), tangy finish.

 MED/DRY $20 V+

Momo Organic Marlborough Sauvignon Blanc ★★★☆

Certified organic, the 2015 vintage (★★★☆) is enjoyable young. Full-bodied, it has ripe tropical-fruit flavours, crisp and generous, with a hint of honey. (From Seresin.)

 DRY $20 AV

Montana Reserve Marlborough Sauvignon Blanc (★★★☆)

The debut 2016 vintage (★★★☆) is an easy-drinking style, ready to roll. Ripely herbaceous aromas lead into a mouthfilling, weighty wine with generous tropical-fruit and herbaceous flavours, crisp acidity and a smooth finish.

 DRY $17 V+

Mount Brown Estates Grand Reserve Barrique
Ferment Waipara Valley Sauvignon Blanc ★★★★

The 2016 vintage (★★★★) is a pale lemon/green, medium-bodied wine, vibrantly fruity, with a distinct touch of complexity. Freshly aromatic, with gooseberry/lime flavours and gentle, biscuity, creamy notes adding complexity, it's a drink-now or cellaring proposition.

 DRY $20 V+

Vintage	16
WR	5
Drink	17-22

Mount Brown Waipara Valley Sauvignon Blanc ★★★

Mouthfilling and fleshy, the 2016 vintage (★★★) is a single-vineyard wine, with ripe passionfruit and lime flavours, showing satisfying depth, in a smooth (4 grams/litre of residual sugar), easy-drinking style. Priced sharply.

 DRY $16 V+

Mount Vernon Marlborough Sauvignon Blanc ★★★★

From Lawson's Dry Hills, the 2017 vintage (★★★★) is aromatic and lively, with a touch of complexity and melon and green-capsicum flavours, showing very good delicacy and length. Finely balanced, it's delicious from the start.

DRY $19 V+

Mountain Road Taranaki Sauvignon Blanc   ★★★☆

Grown at Kairau Lodge, north of New Plymouth, this rare wine is from vines planted in 2004. Designed to be enjoyed 'with cobbers', it is made with some use of barrel fermentation and lees-stirring. I tasted the 2014 to 2016 vintages together in November 2016. Maturing well, the 2014 (★★★☆) was fleshy, with good depth of ripe tropical-fruit flavours, showing bottle-aged complexity. The 2015 (★★★☆) was finely balanced, with strong, lively, ripely herbaceous flavours. The 2016 (★★★) was very fresh and youthful, with lively acidity and plenty of ripe, smooth flavour.

 DRY $20 AV

Moutere Hills Nelson Sauvignon Blanc   ★★★

The 2016 vintage (★★★★) is a punchy wine, grown at Hope, on the Waimea Plains. Light lemon/green, it is freshly scented and medium-bodied, with ripely herbaceous flavours, showing good vigour and intensity, and a crisp, dry (3 grams/litre of residual sugar) finish.

 DRY $21 –V

Mt Beautiful North Canterbury Sauvignon Blanc   ★★★★

Estate-grown at Cheviot, north of Waipara, the light lemon/green 2016 vintage (★★★★☆) is a sturdy, weighty wine, with excellent vigour and concentration of ripe passionfruit/lime flavours, finely balanced, dry, crisp and long. Drink now or cellar. Fine value.

Vintage	16	15
WR	6	6
Drink	17-19	17-18

 DRY $24 AV

Mt Difficulty Bannockburn Sauvignon Blanc   ★★★☆

The 2016 vintage (★★★☆) of this Central Otago wine is fresh, youthful and mouthfilling, with crisp, lively passionfruit/lime flavours, a touch of complexity, firm acid spine, and a tight finish. Drink now to 2018.

 DRY $23 –V

Mud House Marlborough Sauvignon Blanc   ★★★★

This is typically a lively, herbaceous wine, offering top value. The 2017 vintage (★★★☆) is fresh and medium-bodied, with good depth of pure, melon and green-capsicum flavours, finely balanced for early drinking (4 grams/litre of residual sugar).

 DRY $15 V+

Mud House Single Vineyard The Woolshed Marlborough Sauvignon Blanc   ★★★★

Estate-grown in the upper Wairau Valley, the 2017 vintage (★★★☆) is a dry (4 grams/litre of residual sugar), medium to full-bodied wine, with very good depth of vibrant melon and green-capsicum flavours, balanced for enjoyable, early drinking.

DRY $23 AV

Mud House Sub Region Series Rapaura Marlborough Sauvignon Blanc   (★★★☆)

The 2017 vintage (★★★☆) of this district wine was grown at Rapaura, on the north side of the Wairau Valley, and made in a fully dry (1.4 grams/litre of residual sugar) style. Pale lemon/green, it is fresh and medium-bodied, with punchy passionfruit/lime flavours and lots of youthful impact.

Music Bay Summer Marlborough Sauvignon Blanc   ★★★

Estate-grown in the Awatere Valley, the 2016 vintage (★★★☆) offers good value. A fresh, lively, medium-bodied wine, it has strong, ripely herbaceous flavours, slightly 'salty' notes adding interest, and an appetisingly crisp finish. (From O:TU.)

Nautilus Marlborough Sauvignon Blanc   ★★★★☆

This is typically a fragrant, sweet-fruited wine with mouthfilling body and crisp, concentrated flavours. The 2017 vintage (★★★★) is highly aromatic, with crisp, lively tropical fruit and herbaceous flavours, showing good intensity, and a dry, lingering finish.

Vintage	17	16	15	14	13
WR	7	7	7	7	7
Drink	17-20	17-19	17-18	P	P

Neudorf Nelson Sauvignon Blanc   ★★★★

Grown on the Waimea Plains, the 2016 vintage (★★★★) was mostly handled in tanks; 20 per cent of the blend was fermented and matured in old French oak barriques. Mouthfilling, it is fresh and sweet-fruited, with melon, grapefruit and lime flavours that build to a strong finish, appetisingly crisp and dry.

Nga Waka Martinborough Sauvignon Blanc   ★★★★

Still on sale, the 2015 vintage (★★★★) is a mouthfilling, dry wine, fermented in tanks (60 per cent) and seasoned oak barrels (40 per cent). Crisp and lively, it has strong tropical-fruit flavours, with a minerally streak and a persistent finish.

Vintage	15
WR	7
Drink	17-18

Nikau Point Nine Marlborough Sauvignon Blanc   (★★)

'Nine', in this case, refers to the wine's low (9 per cent) alcohol. The 2016 vintage (★★) is light-bodied and slightly rustic, with crisp, appley, green-edged flavours.

MED/DRY $12 AV

Nikau Point Reserve Marlborough Sauvignon Blanc ★★★

Priced sharply, the 2017 vintage (★★★) is a fresh, mouthfilling wine with ripe tropical-fruit flavours, smooth and finely balanced for easy drinking.

DRY $14 V+

Nikau Point Select Marlborough Sauvignon Blanc (★★★)

Enjoyable now, the 2016 vintage (★★★) is a softly mouthfilling, fleshy wine with ripe tropical-fruit flavours and a well-rounded finish. Good value.

DRY $12 V+

O:TU Blend 102 Marlborough Sauvignon Blanc (★★★★)

The highly attractive 2016 vintage (★★★★) is a single-vineyard wine, grown in the Awatere Valley. Aromatic, it is lively and finely textured, with good intensity of fresh, herbaceous flavours and a well-balanced, lengthy finish.

DRY $28 –V

O:TU Marlborough Sauvignon Blanc ★★★☆

Estate-grown in the Awatere Valley, the 2017 vintage (★★★☆) is a lively, medium-bodied wine with a freshly herbaceous bouquet. Enjoyable young, it is strongly varietal, with good depth of vibrant melon, lime and green-capsicum flavours, woven with crisp acidity.

DRY $23 –V

O:TU Single Vineyard Marlborough Sauvignon Blanc (★★★★☆)

Full of youthful impact, the 2016 vintage (★★★★☆) was grown in the Awatere Valley. Highly aromatic, it is a freshly herbaceous, intensely varietal wine, full-bodied, with strong melon, grapefruit and green-capsicum flavours, showing excellent vibrancy, delicacy and depth. Drink now to 2018.

DRY $29 AV

Ohinemuri Estate Marlborough Sauvignon Blanc (★★★★)

Drinking well now, the 2016 vintage (★★★★) is a ripely scented, weighty, punchy wine, strongly varietal, with good intensity of melon, passionfruit and green-capsicum flavours, lively and lingering.

DRY $24 AV

Old Coach Road Lighter Alcohol Nelson Sauvignon Blanc ★★☆

The 2017 vintage (★★) from Seifried is pale, light and crisp, with low alcohol (9.5 per cent), citrusy, appley, green-edged flavours, and a dry (4 grams/litre of residual sugar), tangy finish.

Vintage	17
WR	6
Drink	17-18

DRY $13 V+

Old Coach Road Nelson Sauvignon Blanc ★★★

This is Seifried Estate's lowest-tier Sauvignon, priced right and enjoyable young. The 2017 vintage (★★★) is crisp and lively, with melon, lime, green-capsicum and passionfruit flavours, showing good varietal character, and a dry (2 grams/litre of residual sugar) finish.

Vintage	17
WR	6
Drink	17-18

DRY $13 V+

Opawa Marlborough Sauvignon Blanc ★★★★

From Nautilus, the 2017 vintage (★★★☆) was grown in the Wairau Valley and mostly handled in tanks, but 5 per cent was fermented with indigenous yeasts in large oak cuves. Mouthfilling, it has very good body and depth, with ripely herbaceous flavours, a touch of complexity, and a crisp, dry (2 grams/litre of residual sugar), finely balanced finish. Enjoyable young.

DRY $22 V+

Overstone Marlborough Sauvignon Blanc (★★★)

The 2016 vintage (★★★) is fresh, lively and smooth, with good depth of ripely herbaceous flavours and a dry (4 grams/litre of residual sugar) finish. (From Sileni.)

DRY $16 V+

Oyster Bay Marlborough Sauvignon Blanc ★★★☆

Oyster Bay is a Delegat brand, focused mostly on Marlborough wines and enjoying huge success in global markets. Two-thirds estate-grown, this wine is grown at a multitude of sites around the Wairau (mostly) and Awatere valleys, handled entirely in stainless steel tanks, and made in a dry style with tropical-fruit and herbaceous flavours, crisp and punchy. The 2017 vintage (★★★☆) is an invitingly scented, medium-bodied wine, intensely varietal, with lively melon, lime and green-capsicum flavours, and a finely balanced, dry (4 grams/litre of residual sugar), appetisingly crisp finish.

DRY $20 AV

Pa Road Marlborough Sauvignon Blanc ★★★☆

The 2017 vintage (★★★☆) was estate-grown in the Wairau Valley (65 per cent) and Awatere Valley (35 per cent). Mouthfilling, it is fresh and lively, with crisp acidity and good depth of melon, lime and green-capsicum flavours, dry (4 grams/litre of residual sugar) and smooth. (From te Pa.)

DRY $18 V+

Paddy Borthwick Wairarapa Sauvignon Blanc ★★★☆

Grown at Gladstone, in the Wairarapa, the pale lemon/green 2017 vintage (★★★☆) is a single-vineyard wine. Medium to full-bodied, it is lively and strongly varietal, with tropical-fruit and herbaceous flavours, crisp and finely balanced.

DRY $22 AV

Palliser Estate Martinborough Sauvignon Blanc ★★★★★

At its best, this is a seductive wine, one of the best Sauvignons in the country. A distinctly cool-climate style, it offers an exquisite harmony of crisp acidity, mouthfilling body and fresh, penetrating fruit characters. The 2016 vintage (★★★★☆), grown at four sites, was fermented (partly with indigenous yeasts) and lees-aged for three months in tanks. Light lemon/green, it is fresh, mouthfilling and punchy, with youthful, ripe tropical-fruit flavours, leesy notes adding a touch of complexity, and a crisp and lively, lingering, basically dry (4 grams/litre of residual sugar) finish. Drink now to 2018.

Paper Nautilus, The, Marlborough Sauvignon Blanc ★★★★★

Named after a paper-thin shell, the 2016 vintage (★★★★★) was estate-grown, hand-picked and fermented in a single, seasoned French oak cuve. Made in a dry style (2 grams/litre of residual sugar), it is mouthfilling, weighty and sweet-fruited, with strong, youthful, ripely herbaceous flavours, showing good complexity, gentle acidity and a persistent, seamless finish. A distinctive, finely poised wine, it's well worth discovering. Best drinking mid-2018+.

DRY $35 AV

Pegasus Bay Sauvignon/Sémillon ★★★★★

At its best, this Waipara, North Canterbury wine is concentrated and complex, with loads of personality. From vines 30 years old, the highly impressive 2015 vintage (★★★★★) is a blend of Sauvignon Blanc (15 per cent fermented in new French oak barriques) and Sémillon (fermented in old French oak puncheons), matured for eight months on its yeast lees. The fragrant, complex bouquet leads into a sturdy, sweet-fruited wine, still very fresh and youthful, with deep, ripely herbaceous flavours, showing excellent complexity, and a fully dry (0.8 grams/litre of residual sugar), lasting finish. Best drinking 2018+.

Vintage	15	14
WR	6	6
Drink	17-27	17-25

DRY $31 AV

Pencarrow Martinborough Sauvignon Blanc ★★★★

Delicious young, the 2016 vintage (★★★★) from Palliser Estate has 'sweaty armpit' aromas, leading into a fresh, mouthfilling, vibrantly fruity wine. It has punchy, ripe passionfruit/lime flavours, showing excellent depth, and a dry, crisp finish.

DRY $22 V+

Peregrine Central Otago Sauvignon Blanc ★★★☆

Certified organic, the fresh, herbaceous 2017 vintage (★★★) was grown at Bendigo and Pisa, in the Cromwell Basin. Pale lemon/green, it is medium-bodied, with crisp, green-edged melon and green-capsicum flavours. The 2016 vintage (★★★☆) has strong, ripely herbaceous flavours, very crisp and lively.

DRY $27 –V

Peter Yealands Marlborough Sauvignon Blanc ★★★★

The 2016 vintage (★★★★) offers terrific value. Estate-grown in the Seaview Vineyard, in the Awatere Valley, it is a fresh, aromatic, mouthfilling wine, with strong, ripe tropical-fruit flavours, some grassy notes, lively acidity and a smooth, dry (3.7 grams/litre of residual sugar) finish.

Vintage	16	15	14
WR	7	7	7
Drink	17-18	P	P

DRY $15 V+

Peter Yealands Reserve Awatere Valley Marlborough Sauvignon Blanc ★★★★

Offering great value, the 2016 vintage (★★★★) is a classic Awatere Valley style. Medium to full-bodied, it has fresh, vibrant melon, lime and green-capsicum flavours, showing good intensity, a slightly minerally streak and a tangy, dry (3.6 grams/litre of residual sugar), persistent finish.

Vintage	16	15	14
WR	7	6	6
Drink	17-18	P	P

DRY $18 V+

Petit Clos by Clos Henri Marlborough Sauvignon Blanc ★★★★

Certified organic, the 2016 vintage (★★★★) is from young vines, estate-grown in the Wairau Valley. Tank-fermented and lees-aged, it is mouthfilling, fresh and sweet-fruited, with strong passionfruit/lime flavours, balanced acidity and a fully dry, lingering finish. Good value.

Vintage	16	15	14	13	12
WR	6	7	6	7	6
Drink	17-20	17-18	P	P	P

DRY $21 V+

Pruner's Reward, The, Waipara Sauvignon Blanc ★★★☆

From Bellbird Spring, the 2016 vintage (★★★★) was fermented in tanks (80 per cent) and old oak casks (20 per cent). The best yet, it is medium to full-bodied, fresh and lively, with very good vigour and depth of ripe tropical-fruit flavours, showing a touch of complexity, and a dry, crisp finish.

DRY $22 AV

Ra Nui Marlborough Sauvignon Blanc ★★★☆

Grown in the Wairau Valley and partly (5 per cent) barrel-fermented, the 2016 vintage (★★★☆) is mouthfilling and fleshy, with ripe tropical-fruit flavours, showing good depth, slightly yeasty notes adding complexity, and a well-rounded finish.

DRY $25 –V

Rapaura Springs Marlborough Sauvignon Blanc ★★★☆

Bargain-priced, the easy-drinking 2017 vintage (★★★☆) is fresh and lively, with melon and green-capsicum flavours, showing good depth, and a finely balanced, dry (3.3 grams/litre of residual sugar) finish.

Vintage	17	16	15	14	13
WR	5	7	7	6	7
Drink	17-20	17-19	17-18	17-18	P

DRY $17 V+

Rapaura Springs Reserve Marlborough Sauvignon Blanc ★★★★

Offering fine value, the 2017 vintage (★★★★) was grown in the Wairau Valley. Full-bodied, it has strong, ripe passionfruit/lime flavours, in a fleshy, dry style (3.5 grams/litre of residual sugar), vibrant, rich and well-rounded. It's already drinking well.

Vintage	17
WR	6
Drink	17-20

DRY $19 V+

Rapaura Springs Wairau Classic Marlborough Sauvignon Blanc (★★★★)

This sub-regional wine is sharply priced. The 2017 vintage (★★★★) is mouthfilling and youthful, with vibrant, ripe passionfruit/lime flavours, showing excellent delicacy and depth, good acid spine, and a dry (3.3 grams/litre of residual sugar), lingering finish.

DRY $19 V+

Renato Nelson Sauvignon Blanc ★★★★

The 2016 vintage (★★★★), grown on the Waimea Plains, is a very lively, full-bodied wine, with an aromatic, freshly herbaceous bouquet. Intensely varietal, it is finely balanced, with strong passionfruit and green-capsicum flavours, dry (3 grams/litre of residual sugar) and appetisingly crisp.

Vintage	16	15	14
WR	6	6	7
Drink	17-20	17-19	17-18

DRY $18 V+

Richmond Plains Nelson Sauvignon Blanc ★★★★

Certified organic, the 2016 vintage (★★★★) is a lively, aromatic, medium-bodied wine, with good intensity of melon, citrus and green-capsicum flavours, showing excellent varietal character and depth.

DRY $22 V+

Roaring Meg Central Otago Sauvignon Blanc ★★★☆

From Mt Difficulty, the 2017 vintage (★★★☆) is a light lemon/green, mouthfilling wine, with strong, freshly herbaceous flavours of melons, limes and green capsicums. Crisp and lively, it's already drinking well.

DRY $23 –V

Rock Ferry 3rd Rock Marlborough Sauvignon Blanc ★★★★☆

(This label recently replaced the former Rock Ferry Marlborough Sauvignon Blanc.) Still on sale, the stylish, tightly structured 2015 vintage (★★★★★) was estate-grown at Rapaura and mostly handled in tanks; 12 per cent of the blend was fermented with indigenous yeasts in seasoned oak casks. Ripely scented and weighty, it is vibrant and intense, with tropical-fruit flavours to the fore, showing excellent delicacy and depth, barrel-ferment complexity and a crisp, lasting finish. A fresh, concentrated, harmonious wine, it shows strong personality. Certified organic.

DRY $25 V+

Rockburn Central Otago Fumé Blanc ★★★★

Showing powerful personality, the 2015 vintage (★★★★☆) now on sale is a single-vineyard Sauvignon Blanc, estate-grown at Parkburn, in the Cromwell Basin. Fermented with indigenous yeasts in French oak barrels, it was wood-aged for the unusually long period of 18 months, and bottled without fining or filtration. Bright yellow/green, it is a full-bodied wine, with highly concentrated, lively tropical-fruit and herbaceous flavours, showing excellent complexity, and a lasting finish. Drinking well now, it's also well worth cellaring.

 DRY $40 –V

Rockburn Central Otago Sauvignon Blanc ★★★

Currently on sale, the 2015 vintage (★★★☆) was estate-grown in the Cromwell Basin and Gibbston, and partly fermented with indigenous yeasts in French oak barrels. Light yellow/green, it's a full-flavoured, clearly herbaceous wine, with good intensity of crisp, nettley flavours and some oak-derived complexity.

 DRY $27 –V

Rossendale Marlborough Sauvignon Blanc ★★☆

The low-priced 2016 vintage (★★☆) has freshly herbaceous aromas. Medium-bodied, it is lively, with melon, lime and capsicum flavours, green-edged and smooth.

 DRY $14 AV

Russian Jack Marlborough Sauvignon Blanc ★★★☆

Offering fine value, the 2017 vintage (★★★★) from Foley Family Wines is a fresh, crisp, medium-bodied wine, offering excellent depth of vibrant, ripely herbaceous flavours, smooth and lively.

 DRY $15 V+

Sacred Hill Marlborough Sauvignon Blanc ★★★☆

The latest release (★★★) is described on the back label as from 'the legendary 2017 vintage'. A medium-bodied wine, it is crisp and lively, with melon, capsicum and green-apple flavours, dry (3.9 grams/litre of residual sugar) and fresh.

Vintage	17	16
WR	5	6
Drink	17-19	17-18

DRY $17 V+

Sacred Hill Reserve Marlborough Sauvignon Blanc ★★★★

The 2017 vintage (★★★☆) was partly barrel-fermented. Aromatic, it is lively and green-edged, with good intensity of fresh, herbaceous flavours and a lengthy, dry (2.9 grams/litre of residual sugar) finish.

Vintage	16
WR	6
Drink	17-19

 DRY $25 AV

Saint Clair Barrique Marlborough Sauvignon Blanc

The 2015 vintage (★★★★) is a limited release (five barrels), fermented and lees-aged for 15 months in seasoned oak barriques. Fleshy and smoothly textured, it is mouthfilling, with ripe tropical-fruit flavours, slightly spicy and nutty, a strong seasoning of oak and obvious potential; open 2018+.

DRY $27 –V

Saint Clair James Sinclair Marlborough Sauvignon Blanc

The 2017 vintage (★★★★) was grown at Dillons Point, in the lower Wairau Valley. Bright, light lemon/green, it has a punchy bouquet, leading into a medium-bodied, vibrantly fruity wine. Slightly minerally and 'salty', it shows very good intensity, with a finely balanced, dry (4.3 grams/litre of residual sugar) finish.

DRY $25 –V

Saint Clair Marlborough Premium Sauvignon Blanc

The 2016 vintage (★★★) is floral, fresh and sweet-fruited, with hints of passionfruit and limes, a delicate creaminess on the palate and a well-rounded finish. However, it lacks the intensity of past vintages.

DRY $22 V+

Saint Clair Origin Marlborough Sauvignon Blanc

The debut 2017 vintage (★★★★) is from a 'selection of Saint Clair's highest quality vineyards', near the coast. Medium to full-bodied, it is fresh and lively, with ripe melon/lime flavours, showing very good depth, slightly 'salty' notes, and a finely balanced, dry (4.2 grams/litre of residual sugar), lingering finish.

DRY $22 V+

Saint Clair Pioneer Block 1 Foundation Marlborough Sauvignon Blanc

This single-vineyard Marlborough wine is grown east of Blenheim, at Dillons Point, in the lower Wairau Valley, at a site formerly the source of the Wairau Reserve Sauvignon Blanc. The 2016 vintage (★★★★) is weighty and sweet-fruited, with fresh, ripe tropical-fruit flavours, showing excellent depth, and a rounded, lengthy finish.

DRY $27 –V

Saint Clair Pioneer Block 18 Snap Block Marlborough Sauvignon Blanc ★★★★

Grown east of Blenheim, in the lower Wairau Valley, on a site originally used to grow Snap apples, the 2016 vintage (★★★★) is a refreshing, medium-bodied wine, pungently aromatic, with citrusy, limey, grassy flavours, showing excellent spine, delicacy and length.

DRY $27 –V

Saint Clair Pioneer Block 20 Cash Block Marlborough Sauvignon Blanc ★★★★☆

From vines close to the sea, at Dillons Point, in the lower Wairau Valley, the 2016 vintage (★★★★★) is an intensely aromatic, appetisingly crisp wine, packed with vibrant, herbaceous flavours. Very fresh and zingy, it has penetrating gooseberry, fresh-cut grass and green-capsicum characters, some riper fruit flavours, and excellent concentration.

DRY $27 AV

Saint Clair Pioneer Block 3 43 Degrees Marlborough Sauvignon Blanc   ★★★★☆

This Marlborough wine is grown at Dillons Point, in the lower Wairau Valley, at a site with rows 'running at an unusual angle of 43 degrees north-east to south-west', giving 'a slightly more herbaceous Sauvignon Blanc'. The 2016 vintage (★★★★) is aromatic and lively, with crisp, strongly varietal melon, lime and green-capsicum flavours, showing very good freshness, delicacy and length.

Saint Clair Vicar's Choice Marlborough Sauvignon Blanc   ★★★☆

Vicars, like many of us, will gladly worship a bargain – and this very easy-drinking wine delivers the goods. Drinking well from the start, the 2017 vintage (★★★☆) is a fresh, lively, medium-bodied wine, with ripely herbaceous flavours, finely balanced and showing very good depth.

Saint Clair Wairau Reserve Marlborough Sauvignon Blanc   ★★★★★

Marlborough's largest family-owned wine producer has an extensive array of Sauvignon Blancs. This is not the region's most complex Savvy, but in terms of sheer pungency, it's a star, having won countless gold medals and trophies since the first, 2001, vintage. Grown in the cooler, coastal end of the Wairau Valley and handled entirely in stainless steel tanks, it is typically supercharged, in an exuberantly fruity, very pure and zesty style. The 2016 vintage (★★★★★), grown at two neighbouring sites at Dillons Point, is an aromatic, mouthfilling, fleshy and sweet-fruited wine, with fresh, concentrated grapefruit/lime flavours, dry (3.1 grams/litre of residual sugar) and appetisingly crisp. Tightly structured and persistent, it should be in full stride 2018+.

Sanctuary Marlborough Sauvignon Blanc   ★★★

The easy-drinking 2016 vintage (★★★) is fresh and full-bodied, with ripe tropical-fruit flavours to the fore and a smooth finish. (From Foley Family Wines.)

DRY $15 V+

Satellite Marlborough Sauvignon Blanc   ★★★

From Spy Valley, the 2017 (★★☆), grown in the Wairau Valley, is a lesser vintage of this label. Smooth and medium-bodied, it has citrusy, appley flavours, with a dry (2.8 grams/litre of residual sugar), green-edged finish.

Vintage	17	16	15
WR	4	5	5
Drink	17-19	P	P

DRY $16 V+

Satyr by Sileni Marlborough Sauvignon Blanc   (★★★)

The easy-drinking 2016 vintage (★★★) is a fresh, medium-bodied wine with good depth of lively, ripely herbaceous flavours, balanced acidity, and a dry (4 grams/litre of residual sugar), smooth finish.

Seifried Nelson Sauvignon Blanc ★★★☆

Priced right, the 2017 vintage (★★★) has a herbaceous, strongly varietal bouquet. Full-bodied and tangy, it has melon, apple and green-capsicum flavours, fresh and strong, with a dry (2 grams/litre of residual sugar), crisp finish.

Vintage	17	16	15	14	13
WR	6	6	6	6	6
Drink	17-18	17-18	P	P	P

DRY $18 V+

Selaks Founders Limited Edition Marlborough Sauvignon Blanc ★★★★☆

Delicious now, the 2016 vintage (★★★★☆) is weighty, mouthfilling, ripe and smooth, with excellent delicacy and depth of melon, lime and green-capsicum flavours, a slightly 'salty' streak, and a dry, harmonious, persistent finish.

Vintage	16
WR	6
Drink	17-18

DRY $25 V+

Selaks Reserve Marlborough Sauvignon Blanc ★★★

Enjoyable young, the 2017 vintage (★★★) is medium-bodied, with fresh, herbaceous flavours, showing some tropical-fruit notes, good depth and a crisp, lively finish.

Vintage	17
WR	5
Drink	18-19

DRY $16 V+

Selaks The Taste Collection Marlborough Zesty Sauvignon Blanc (★★★★)

The debut 2016 vintage (★★★★) has a freshly scented, herbaceous bouquet. An intensely varietal wine, it is crisp and dry (2 grams/litre of residual sugar), with strong grapefruit and green-capsicum flavours, lively acidity and a tangy finish. Drink now to 2018.

Vintage	16
WR	6
Drink	17-18

DRY $22 V+

Seresin Marama Sauvignon Blanc ★★★★★

This multi-faceted style of Sauvignon Blanc is hand-picked from the oldest vines in the estate vineyard at Renwick, in Marlborough, fermented with indigenous yeasts in French oak barriques (7 per cent new in 2013), wood-matured for well over a year, and released after a long period of bottle aging. Pale yellow, the 2013 vintage (★★★★★) is fragrant and weighty, with rich, ripe, complex flavours of passionfruit and pineapple, enriched with biscuity oak. Slightly buttery, with a long, dry (2.9 grams/litre of residual sugar), harmonious finish, it's delicious now. Certified organic.

Vintage	13	12	11	10
WR	7	6	6	7
Drink	17-22	17-22	17-20	17-18

DRY $45 AV

Seresin Marlborough Sauvignon Blanc ★★★★★

This is one of the region's most sophisticated, subtle and satisfying Sauvignons. It's also one of the most important, given its widespread international distribution and certified BioGro status. The grapes are grown in the original estate vineyard near Renwick, and in the company's younger vineyards, especially Raupo Creek, on an elevated slope in the Omaka Valley. The wine (which includes 5 to 9 per cent Sémillon) is mostly fermented in tanks with indigenous yeasts, but 15 to 20 per cent of the blend is fermented and lees-aged in seasoned French oak casks. Full of personality, the lively 2015 vintage (★★★★☆) has an aromatic bouquet, with hints of melons, limes and nuts. Pale straw, it has strong, fully dry flavours (1.6 grams/litre of residual sugar), in a minerally style with good complexity and a lingering, slightly flinty finish.

DRY $25 V+

🍇🍇🍇

Seresin OSIP Organic Marlborough Sauvignon Blanc (★★★☆)

The debut 2015 vintage (★★★☆) was grown organically and biodynamically and made with no use of sulphur in the winery. The bouquet has no real delights, lacking the fresh, lifted aromatics typical of the variety and region, but the palate is interesting – full-bodied, dry and crisp, with very good weight and depth of ripe tropical-fruit flavours, a touch of complexity, and plenty of personality.

DRY $30 –V

Sherwood Estate Stoney Range Waipara Valley Sauvignon Blanc ★★★

Enjoyable young, the 2017 vintage (★★☆) is an easy-drinking, medium-bodied wine with citrusy, herbal flavours and a dry (1.5 grams/litre of residual sugar), smooth finish.

DRY $17 AV

Sileni Cellar Selection Hawke's Bay Sauvignon Blanc ★★★

The easy-drinking 2016 vintage (★★★) is fresh and light, with passionfruit-like aromas, moderate acidity, lively, ripely herbaceous flavours and a dry (4 grams/litre of residual sugar) finish.

DRY $20 –V

Sileni Cellar Selection Marlborough Sauvignon Blanc ★★★☆

Enjoyable young, the 2017 vintage (★★★) is a fresh, medium-bodied wine, dry (4 grams/litre of residual sugar) and crisp, with melon/lime flavours, showing good delicacy and vibrancy.

DRY $20 AV

Sileni Estate Selection Cape Hawke's Bay Sauvignon Blanc ★★★★

Drinking well now, the 2016 vintage (★★★★) is weighty and ripely flavoured , with bottle-aged notes adding complexity. It has citrus and tropical-fruit characters, in a northern style, with gentle acidity and a well-rounded, dry (2.3 grams/litre of residual sugar) finish.

DRY $25 AV

Vintage	16	15
WR	6	7
Drink	17-20	17-19

Sileni Estate Selection Straits Marlborough Sauvignon Blanc ★★★★

The 2017 vintage (★★★☆) is an aromatic, fresh, medium-bodied wine, with lively, citrusy, appley flavours, showing very good depth, and a dry (4 grams/litre of residual sugar) finish. Still very youthful, it's worth cellaring.

Vintage	16	15	14	13
WR	6	7	6	6
Drink	17-18	P	P	P

DRY $25 AV

Soho Stella Marlborough Sauvignon Blanc ★★★☆

'Inspired by eco conscious fashionistas', the punchy, appetisingly crisp 2016 vintage (★★★★) is unfolding well. A regional blend, it is mouthfilling and vibrantly fruity, with good intensity of melon and green-capsicum flavours, fresh, dry (2.7 grams/litre of residual sugar), lively and lingering.

Vintage	16	15
WR	6	5
Drink	17-18	P

DRY $25 –V

Southern Cross Marlborough Sauvignon Blanc (★★☆)

Ready now, the 2016 vintage (★★☆) is a light lemon/green, medium-bodied wine, with citrusy, herbal flavours, showing a touch of bottle-aged development. Crisp and dry, it's priced right.

DRY $13 V+

Southern Dawn Marlborough Sauvignon Blanc (★★☆)

Low-priced, the 2016 vintage (★★☆) is a fresh, smooth, medium-bodied wine, with slightly toasty, bottle-aged notes starting to emerge. An easy-drinking wine with gentle acidity, it's ready to roll.

DRY $13 V+

Spinyback Nelson Sauvignon Blanc ★★★☆

From Waimea Estates, this is typically a good buy. Grown at three sites on the Waimea Plains, the 2016 vintage (★★★) has a freshly herbaceous bouquet, leading into a strongly varietal wine with lively green-capsicum and lime flavours, punchy and crisp.

DRY $15 V+

Springs, The, South Island Sauvignon Blanc (★★★)

Priced sharply, the 2016 vintage (★★★), grown in Waipara, North Canterbury, is a medium-bodied wine with clearly herbaceous flavours, fresh and lively.

DRY $15 V+

Spy Valley Easy Tiger Marlborough Sauvignon Blanc

The 2016 vintage (★★★) is light-bodied, with green-edged flavours. Low in alcohol (9 per cent), it is tasty and dry (3.9 grams/litre of residual sugar), with a hint of passionfruit, firm acid spine, and a touch of complexity (from some barrel fermentation).

Vintage	16	15
WR	6	7
Drink	17-18	P

DRY $18 AV

Spy Valley Envoy Johnson Vineyard Marlborough Sauvignon Blanc ★★★★★

Estate-grown in the lower Waihopai Valley, the classy 2015 vintage (★★★★★) was hand-picked from vines over 20 years old and fermented and lees-aged in oak (mostly new) for almost a year. It is mouthfilling and sweet-fruited, with vibrant, ripe non-herbaceous flavours, crisp, intense, dry (2.9 grams/litre of residual sugar), tightly structured and long. Showing excellent complexity and harmony, it should be at its best 2018+.

Vintage	15	14	13	12	11	10
WR	7	7	7	6	5	6
Drink	17-23	17-20	17-19	P	P	P

DRY $32 AV

Spy Valley Marlborough Sauvignon Blanc ★★★☆

Typically a very good buy. The 2017 vintage (★★★) was partly barrel-fermented and made in a dry style (2.8 grams/litre of residual sugar). Fresh and crisp, it is medium-bodied, with grapefruit, lime and green-apple flavours, showing good depth, and a tangy finish.

Vintage	17	16	15	14	13
WR	5	7	6	7	7
Drink	17-19	17-18	P	P	P

DRY $18 V+

Staete Landt Annabel Marlborough Sauvignon Blanc ★★★★★

Estate-grown at Rapaura, on the relatively warm north side of the Wairau Valley, the ripely scented, richly flavoured 2016 vintage (★★★★★) is a classic district style. Handled in tanks and old oak vessels, it is fragrant, with fresh tropical-fruit aromas, mouthfilling body, strong, vibrant, passionfruit/lime flavours, lively acidity and a dry, persistent finish. Fine value.

DRY $22 V+

Stanley Estates Single Vineyard Awatere Valley Marlborough Sauvignon Blanc (★★★★☆)

Showing good vigour and intensity, the 2016 vintage (★★★★☆) is a lively, aromatic wine. Full-bodied and fresh, it has crisp passionfruit/lime flavours, slightly leesy notes adding complexity, and a dry (2.1 grams/litre of residual sugar), lingering finish.

DRY $23 V+

Vintage	16
WR	6
Drink	17-20

Starborough Family Estate Marlborough Sauvignon Blanc ★★★★

This label typically offers good value. Estate-grown, the 2017 vintage (★★★☆) is from two vineyards in the Awatere Valley and a third site in the Wairau Valley. Mouthfilling, it has fresh, vibrant melon/lime flavours, in a clearly herbaceous style, with a crisp, dry (3 grams/litre of residual sugar), lingering finish.

DRY $20 V+

Stoneburn Marlborough Sauvignon Blanc ★★★

Enjoyable young, the 2017 vintage (★★★) is a fresh, tightly structured wine, medium-bodied, with tropical-fruit and herbaceous flavours, crisp and dry. Finely balanced, it offers good drinking during 2018. (From Hunter's.)

DRY $19 AV

Stonecroft Hawke's Bay Sauvignon Blanc ★★★☆

The attractive 2016 vintage (★★★★) was fermented in a mix of tanks (90 per cent) and barrels (10 per cent). Mouthfilling, it has good concentration of ripe tropical-fruit flavours, with a touch of toasty oak adding complexity and a crisp, dryish (5 grams/litre of residual sugar) finish. Best drinking 2018+.

MED/DRY $22 AV

Stoneleigh Latitude Marlborough Sauvignon Blanc ★★★★

From 'vineyards on the Golden Mile' (Rapaura Road, along the north side of the Wairau Valley), the 2017 vintage (★★★★) shows excellent intensity and vigour. Bright, light lemon/green, it is ripely scented and full-bodied, with strong, lively melon/lime flavours and a crisp, dry, lingering finish.

DRY $23 AV

Stoneleigh Lighter Marlborough Sauvignon Blanc (★★☆)

Picked early and made in a low-alcohol style (9.6 per cent), the 2016 vintage (★★☆) is light and crisp, with citrusy, appley flavours, pleasant and smooth.

MED/DRY $17 –V

Stoneleigh Marlborough Sauvignon Blanc ★★★☆

From Pernod Ricard NZ, this typically satisfying wine flows from the stony, relatively warm Rapaura district of the Wairau Valley, which produces a ripe style of Sauvignon Blanc, yet retains good acidity and vigour. Over 300,000 cases are produced. The 2017 vintage (★★★☆) has lots of youthful impact, with mouthfilling body, fresh, crisp melon, green-capsicum and passionfruit flavours, and very good vigour and depth.

Vintage	16	15	14
WR	6	7	7
Drink	17-18	P	P

DRY $17 V+

Stoneleigh Rapaura Series Marlborough Sauvignon Blanc ★★★★☆

This richly flavoured wine is grown in the warm, shingly soils of the Rapaura district and briefly lees-aged, with regular stirring. The 2016 vintage (★★★★) is a single-vineyard wine, mouthfilling, ripe and rounded, with good weight and generous tropical-fruit flavours, fresh and sustained.

DRY $27 AV

Stoneleigh Wild Valley Marlborough Sauvignon Blanc ★★★☆

The 2016 vintage (★★★☆) was 'wild fermented by the micro-flora that occur naturally in the Rapaura environment' and partly barrel-fermented. Ripely scented, it is mouthfilling and sweet-fruited, with gentle acidity, tropical-fruit flavours, and slightly honeyed notes emerging with bottle age. Ready.

DRY $19 V+

Summerhouse Marlborough Sauvignon Blanc ★★★★☆

The 2017 vintage (★★★★☆) offers great value. Full-bodied and lively, it has penetrating, vibrant melon, lime and capsicum flavours, showing a distinct touch of complexity, and a finely balanced, dry (3.4 grams/litre of residual sugar), persistent finish.

DRY $19 V+

Vintage	17
WR	6
Drink	17-21

Te Kairanga Estate Martinborough Sauvignon Blanc ★★★★

The 2016 vintage (★★★★) is a partly barrel-fermented wine, aromatic, mouthfilling, vibrantly fruity and dry, with ripely herbaceous flavours, crisp and finely poised.

DRY $20 V+

Te Mania Nelson Sauvignon Blanc ★★★☆

Typically a good wine – full-flavoured, with tropical-fruit characters, nettley notes and appetising acidity. The 2016 vintage (★★★☆) is fresh and lively, in a medium to full-bodied style with crisp, ripely herbaceous flavours, showing good depth. Certified organic.

DRY $20 AV

Te Mata Cape Crest Sauvignon Blanc ★★★★★

This oak-aged Hawke's Bay label is impressive for its ripely herbal, complex, sustained flavours. Most of the grapes are hand-picked in the company's relatively warm Bullnose Vineyard, inland from Hastings (the rest is grown at Woodthorpe, in the Dartmoor Valley), and the blend includes small proportions of Sémillon (to add longevity) and Sauvignon Gris (which contributes weight and mouthfeel). The wine is fully fermented and lees-aged for eight months in French oak barriques (partly new). In a vertical tasting, the two to four-year-old wines look best – still fresh, but very harmonious. The very refined 2015 vintage (★★★★★) is a blend of Sauvignon Blanc (85 per cent), Sauvignon Gris (11 per cent) and Sémillon (4 per cent). Ripely scented, mouthfilling and sweet-fruited, it is very fresh, vibrant and youthful, with concentrated grapefruit, lime and passionfruit flavours, a subtle seasoning of oak, and a tight, dry, long finish. Best drinking 2018+.

Vintage	15	14
WR	7	7
Drink	17-27	17-19

DRY $30 AV

Te Mata Estate Vineyards Hawke's Bay Sauvignon Blanc ★★★☆

The 2016 vintage (★★★★) is a weighty, rounded wine, grown in the Bridge Pa Triangle and at the Woodthorpe Terraces Vineyard, in the Dartmoor Valley. Handled without oak, it is sweet-fruited, with ripe tropical-fruit flavours and a smooth finish. Instantly appealing.

DRY $20 AV

Te Pa Marlborough Sauvignon Blanc (★★★★)

The skilfully crafted 2016 vintage (★★★★) was estate-grown at two sites – the MacDonald Home Vineyard in the lower Wairau Valley (77 per cent), and in the Redwood Hills Vineyard, in the Awatere Valley (23 per cent). Tank-fermented, it is bright, light lemon/green, with a freshly herbaceous bouquet. Mouthfilling, it is vibrantly fruity, with incisive tropical-fruit and nettley flavours, showing excellent vigour and depth, and a crisp, dry (3.5 grams/litre of residual sugar) finish. Ready.

DRY $20 V+

Te Pa Oke Marlborough Sauvignon Blanc (★★★★☆)

Estate-grown in the lower Wairau Valley, the 2015 vintage (★★★★☆) was hand-picked and fermented with indigenous yeasts in French oak barrels. Bright, light lemon/green, it has a fragrant, slightly herbaceous, complex bouquet. Full-bodied and fresh, it's a clearly herbaceous style, with well-integrated oak, excellent depth, vigour and complexity, and a finely balanced, dry (2 grams/litre of residual sugar), lingering finish. Drink now.

DRY $25 AV

Ten Sisters Single Vineyard Marlborough Sauvignon Blanc ★★★★

Grown in the Southern Valleys, the 2016 vintage (★★★★) was matured on its yeast lees for four months. Mouthfilling and smooth, it is a ripely herbaceous style, with very good flavour depth, leesy notes adding a touch of complexity, and a slightly minerally, lingering finish.

DRY $20 V+

Thornbury Marlborough Sauvignon Blanc ★★★☆

Offering fine value, the 2017 vintage (★★★☆) was tank-ferrmented and lees-aged. Made in a dry style (3.6 grams/litre of residual sugar), it is an aromatic, medium-bodied wine, with fresh, lively, herbaceous flavours, crisp and punchy.

Vintage	17	16	15	14
WR	4	6	7	6
Drink	17-19	17-18	P	P

DRY $16 V+

Three Paddles Martinborough Sauvignon Blanc ★★★☆

From Nga Waka, the 2016 vintage (★★★☆) is a very fresh and lively, medium to full-bodied wine, with good depth of melon and green-capsicum flavours, dry and slightly minerally. Maturing well, it offers good drinking now to 2018.

Vintage	16	15	14	13
WR	6	7	7	7
Drink	17-19	17-18	P	P

DRY $18 V+

Tiki Marlborough Sauvignon Blanc ★★★☆

The 2016 vintage (★★★☆), grown in the Wairau Valley, is fresh and lively, with very good depth of melon, lime and capsicum flavours, and a finely balanced, smooth finish. Enjoyable from the start.

DRY $20 AV

Tiki Single Vineyard Marlborough Sauvignon Blanc ★★★★

Estate-grown in the upper Wairau Valley, the 2016 vintage (★★★★) is mouthfilling, fresh and vibrantly fruity, with strong tropical-fruit and herbaceous flavours, woven with appetising acidity, and a finely balanced, smooth finish.

DRY $23 AV

Toa Marlborough Sauvignon Blanc (★★★☆)

The 2016 vintage (★★★☆) was grown in the Wairau Valley. It is fleshy, ripe and rounded, with mouthfilling body, moderate acidity and very satisfying depth of ripe tropical-fruit flavours. Priced right.

DRY $19 V+

Tohu Mugwi Reserve Marlborough Sauvignon Blanc ★★★★☆

The 2015 vintage (★★★★) was estate-grown in the Awatere Valley and fermented with indigenous yeasts in old French oak barriques. Vibrant, with ripe-fruit flavours, slightly nutty notes adding complexity, and a bone-dry, lingering finish, it should be at its best during 2018.

DRY $30 –V

Tohu Single Vineyard Marlborough Sauvignon Blanc   ★★★★

This consistently enjoyable wine is estate-grown in the upper Awatere Valley. Delicious young, the 2016 vintage (★★★★) is strongly aromatic and full-bodied, with incisive, pure, ripely herbaceous flavours, dry (3.9 grams/litre of residual sugar), crisp and long.

`DRY $20 V+`

Toi Toi Marlborough Sauvignon Blanc   ★★★

Fresh and lively, the 2016 vintage (★★★☆) is a ripely herbaceous wine, with melon, passionfruit and lime flavours, showing very good delicacy and depth, and a smooth, dryish (5.1 grams/litre of residual sugar) finish, balanced for easy drinking.

`MED/DRY $18 AV`

Trinity Hill Hawke's Bay Sauvignon Blanc   ★★★

This wine is grown in coastal and inland vineyards. The 2016 vintage (★★★), handled in a mix of tanks (85 per cent) and barriques (15 per cent), is fresh, medium-bodied and sweet-fruited, with zesty peach, passionfruit and lime flavours and a dry (2.5 grams/litre of residual sugar) finish.

`DRY $20 –V`

Tupari Awatere Valley Marlborough Sauvignon Blanc   ★★★★

Estate-grown in the upper Awatere Valley, this single-vineyard wine is partly oak-aged. The 2016 vintage (★★★★) is attractively scented, with vibrant, punchy, ripely herbaceous flavours, dry (2 grams/litre of residual sugar) and lingering.

`DRY $23 AV`

Tupari Boulder Rows Awatere Valley Marlborough Sauvignon Blanc   ★★★★

Currently delicious, the 2015 vintage (★★★★☆) is a fully barrel-fermented wine. Highly aromatic, it has very good intensity of ripely herbaceous flavours, finely integrated oak adding complexity, and a tangy, dry (2 grams/litre of residual sugar), long finish.

`DRY $29 –V`

Twin Islands Marlborough Sauvignon Blanc   ★★★☆

Negociants' wine offers highly attractive, easy drinking. The 2017 vintage (★★★☆) is medium to full-bodied, fresh and tangy, with good depth of vibrant melon, lime and green-capsicum flavours, and a finely balanced, dry (3 grams/litre of residual sugar) finish.

`DRY $18 V+`

Two Rivers of Marlborough Altitude Sauvignon Blanc   ★★★★★

Instantly appealing, the 2016 vintage (★★★★★) is a single-vineyard wine, grown in the Southern Valleys, hand-harvested, and matured for 10 months in a concrete egg-shaped tank (40 per cent) and seasoned oak hogsheads (60 per cent). Weighty and fleshy, it has concentrated, ripe tropical-fruit flavours, a gentle seasoning of oak adding complexity, fresh, balanced acidity, and a finely textured, dry (1.5 grams/litre of residual sugar), very harmonious finish.

Vintage	16	15
WR	6	6
Drink	17-22	17-21

`DRY $36 AV`

Two Rivers of Marlborough Convergence Sauvignon Blanc   ★★★★☆

The 2017 vintage (★★★★) is from sites in the Awatere, Southern and Wairau valleys. Matured for three months on its yeast lees, it is mouthfilling and crisp, with citrusy, limey flavours, showing excellent freshness and delicacy, lively acidity, and a dry (3.4 grams/litre of residual sugar), lingering finish.

Vintage	17	16	15
WR	6	6	6
Drink	17-19	17-19	17-18

Urlar Gladstone Sauvignon Blanc   ★★★★

Drinking well now, the 2016 vintage (★★★★) was mostly tank-fermented; 7 per cent was fermented in old oak barrels. It's an aromatic, mouthfilling wine, vibrantly fruity, with good intensity of ripely herbaceous flavours and a finely balanced, dry (2.5 grams/litre of residual sugar) finish. Certified organic.

Urlar Select Parcels Gladstone Sauvignon Blanc   ★★★★

Still on sale, the 2014 vintage (★★★) was estate-grown in the northern Wairarapa, barrel-fermented, oak-aged for eight months, and given a full, softening malolactic fermentation. It's a weighty, fleshy wine, showing considerable complexity, but held back by a slight lack of freshness and vibrancy. Certified organic.

Vavasour Awatere Valley Marlborough Sauvignon Blanc   ★★★★

The 2016 vintage (★★★★★) is a classic Awatere Valley style. Highly aromatic and tightly structured, it has fresh, pure, citrusy, herbal flavours, threaded with mouth-watering acidity, a minerally streak and a lasting finish. Great value.

Vidal Marlborough Sauvignon Blanc   ★★★☆

The 2017 vintage (★★★☆) was grown in the Wairau Valley (mostly) and Awatere Valley. Handled entirely in tanks, it is a fresh, medium-bodied wine, with an aromatic bouquet and good depth of vibrant, ripely herbaceous flavours, dry (3.2 grams/litre of residual sugar) and finely balanced. Priced right.

DRY $16 V+

Vintage	17	16	15	14
WR	6	7	6	6
Drink	17-19	P	P	P

Vidal Reserve Marlborough Sauvignon Blanc ★★★★

Offering great value, the 2016 vintage (★★★★☆) was grown in the Wairau (75 per cent) and Awatere (25 per cent) valleys, tank-fermented and lees-aged. Delicious now, it is full-bodied and sweet-fruited, with strong, ripe tropical-fruit flavours, dry (3 grams/litre of residual sugar) and long.

Vintage	16	15
WR	7	7
Drink	17-18	P

 DRY $20 V+

Villa Maria Cellar Selection Marlborough Sauvignon Blanc ★★★★☆

An intensely flavoured wine, typically of a high standard, blended from Wairau Valley and Awatere Valley grapes, and fermented and lees-aged in tanks. The 2017 vintage (★★★★☆) is a highly aromatic, medium-bodied wine, with concentrated, vibrant tropical-fruit and herbaceous flavours, dry (3.7 grams/litre of residual sugar) and lasting.

Vintage	17	16	15
WR	6	6	6
Drink	17-19	17-19	17-18

 DRY $19 V+

Villa Maria Private Bin Marlborough Sauvignon Blanc ★★★★

This huge-volume label offers consistently good quality and value. The 2017 vintage (★★★★) was grown in the Wairau and Awatere valleys. It is highly aromatic, with a freshly herbaceous bouquet. A crisp, medium-bodied wine, it has strong tropical-fruit and herbaceous flavours, dry (4.2 grams/litre of residual sugar) and finely balanced, with lots of youthful impact.

Vintage	17	16	15	14
WR	5	6	6	6
Drink	17-19	17-19	P	P

 DRY $16 V+

Villa Maria Private Bin Organic Marlborough Sauvignon Blanc ★★★★

The 2017 vintage (★★★☆) is crisp and dry (3.8 grams/litre of residual sugar). Medium-bodied, it is lively, with very good depth of fresh, herbaceous flavours, appetising acidity and a finely balanced finish. Priced sharply.

Vintage	17	16	15
WR	6	6	6
Drink	17-19	17-19	P

 DRY $16 V+

Villa Maria Reserve Clifford Bay Sauvignon Blanc ★★★★★

Grown in the Awatere Valley (although the label refers only to 'Clifford Bay', into which the Awatere River empties), this is a very classy Marlborough wine. Seddon Vineyards and the Taylors Pass Vineyard – both managed but not owned by Villa Maria – are the key sources of fruit. Handled entirely in stainless steel tanks and aged on its light yeast lees for several months, the wine typically exhibits the leap-out-of-the-glass fragrance and zingy, explosive flavour of

Marlborough Sauvignon Blanc at its best. The 2017 vintage (★★★★☆) is a very elegant, vibrantly fruity wine, medium-bodied, with intense, pungently herbaceous flavours and a dry (2.8 grams/litre of residual sugar), lasting finish.

Vintage	17
WR	6
Drink	17-19

DRY $28 V+

Villa Maria Reserve Wairau Valley Sauvignon Blanc   ★★★★★

An authoritative wine, it is typically ripe and zingy, with impressive weight and length of flavour, and tends to be fuller in body, less herbaceous and rounder than its Clifford Bay stablemate (above). The contributing vineyards vary from vintage to vintage, but Peter and Deborah Jackson's warm, stony vineyard in the heart of the valley has long been a key source of grapes, and sometimes a small part of the blend is barrel-fermented, to enhance its complexity and texture. The 2016 vintage (★★★★★) is fragrant and lively, with slightly 'sweaty' tropical-fruit aromas leading into a mouthfilling wine (13.5 per cent alcohol) with concentrated, ripely herbaceous flavours and a dry (3.4 grams/litre of residual sugar), finely poised, rich finish. The 2017 vintage (★★★★☆) is intensely aromatic and medium-bodied, with incisive, ripely herbaceous flavours, lees-aging notes adding complexity, and a dry (3 grams/litre of residual sugar), long finish.

Vintage	17	16	15	14
WR	6	7	7	7
Drink	17-19	17-19	17-18	P

DRY $28 V+

Villa Maria Single Vineyard Taylors Pass Marlborough Sauvignon Blanc   ★★★★★

Taylors Pass Vineyard lies 100 metres above sea level in the Awatere Valley. This is typically a classic example of the sub-regional style – vibrant, punchy, minerally and herbal, with intense capsicum and 'tomato stalk' aromas and a long, dry, racy finish. The 2016 vintage (★★★★) is very fresh and lively, in a medium to full-bodied style with grapefruit and herbaceous flavours, showing excellent delicacy and depth, and a dry (2.6 grams/litre of residual sugar) finish.

DRY $30 AV

Waimea Nelson Sauvignon Blanc   ★★★★

Always a good buy. The 2016 vintage (★★★☆), estate-grown on the Waimea Plains, is a fresh, medium to full-bodied wine, clearly herbaceous, with crisp, slightly nettley flavours, lively and strong, and a basically dry (4.3 grams/litre of residual sugar) finish.

DRY $17 V+

Waipara Hills Marlborough Sauvignon Blanc ★★★★

Grown mostly (70 per cent) in the Awatere Valley, the 2016 vintage (★★★★) is a weighty, sweet-fruited wine with vibrant melon/lime flavours, woven with fresh, finely balanced acidity, and a dry finish. Ripely scented, it's a subtle, satisfying style of Sauvignon Blanc, drinking well young. The light lemon/green 2017 vintage (★★★☆) is a tangy, medium-bodied wine, with good depth of fresh tropical-fruit and herbaceous flavours, and a dry (4.2 grams/litre of residual sugar), crisp finish.

 DRY $22 V+

Wairau River Marlborough Sauvignon Blanc ★★★☆

The 2016 vintage (★★★★) is mouthfilling and vibrantly fruity, with good intensity of passionfruit/lime flavours, dry (1.9 grams/litre of residual sugar) and mouth-wateringly crisp. Enjoyable young.

Vintage	16	15	14
WR	6	7	6
Drink	17-18	P	P

 DRY $20 AV

Wairau River Reserve Marlborough Sauvignon Blanc ★★★★☆

The 2016 vintage (★★★★☆) is a single-vineyard wine, grown on the north side of the Wairau Valley. Weighty, it has concentrated, ripe tropical-fruit flavours, in a fresh, tightly structured, classic sub-regional style with balanced acidity and a long, dry (2.5 grams/litre of residual sugar) finish.

Vintage	16	15
WR	6	6
Drink	17-18	17-18

 DRY $30 –V

Walnut Block Collectables Marlborough Sauvignon Blanc ★★★☆

Certified organic, the 2016 vintage (★★★★) is a full-bodied, ripely flavoured wine, delicious young. Grown in the Wairau Valley, it has tropical-fruit characters to the fore, finely balanced, crisp, dry and strong.

 DRY $20 AV

Walnut Block Nutcracker Marlborough Sauvignon Blanc ★★★★☆

Certified organic, the fresh, youthful 2016 vintage (★★★★☆) was hand-picked and fermented with indigenous yeasts. Light yellow/green, it is mouthfilling and sweet-fruited, with generous, ripe tropical-fruit flavours, showing a touch of complexity, and a fully dry (1.3 grams/litre of residual sugar), appetisingly crisp finish. Best drinking 2018+.

Vintage	16	15	14
WR	6	7	5
Drink	17-20	17-20	17-18

 DRY $24 V+

Whitehaven Hidden Barrel Marlborough Sauvignon Blanc (★★★★)

Showing good complexity, the 2016 vintage (★★★★) was fermented with indigenous yeasts in seasoned French oak barrels. Bright, light lemon/green, it is mouthfilling, with vibrant, ripe fruit flavours, gently seasoned with oak, slightly 'funky' notes adding interest, moderate acidity and a smooth, dry finish. Drink now or cellar.

DRY $25 AV

Wild Grace Marlborough Sauvignon Blanc (★★★★)

Tasted in its infancy, the debut 2016 vintage (★★★★) was disappointing – mouthfilling and ripely flavoured, but disjointed. Retasted in October 2017, it is weighty and sweet-fruited, with strong tropical-fruit flavours, showing a touch of bottle-aged complexity, and a dry, rounded finish. (From Constellation NZ.)

DRY $27 –V

Wild Rock Marlborough Sauvignon Blanc (★★★★)

From Craggy Range, the 2016 vintage (★★★★) is a quietly satisfying wine, delicious young. Full-bodied, it is crisp and lively, in a highly drinkable, dry style (3 grams/litre of residual sugar), with melon, lime and capsicum flavours, showing very good vigour, purity, balance and depth.

DRY $19 V+

Wild South Marlborough Sauvignon Blanc ★★★☆

Zesty and finely balanced, the 2016 vintage (★★★☆) is a crisp, medium-bodied wine, strongly varietal, with vibrant melon, lime and green-capsicum flavours.

DRY $18 V+

Yealands Estate Single Vineyard Awatere Valley Marlborough Sauvignon Blanc ★★★★☆

Estate-grown at Seaview, in the lower Awatere Valley, the 2017 vintage (★★★★) is mouthfilling, with very good depth of fresh, youthful melon, lime and green-capsicum flavours. A dry style (3.4 grams/litre of residual sugar), it is appetisingly crisp, with leesy notes adding complexity and a lingering finish.

DRY $23 V+

Yealands Estate Winemakers Reserve Awatere Valley Marlborough Sauvignon Blanc ★★★★☆

The 2016 vintage (★★★★) was estate-grown and fermented in tanks and French oak puncheons. Aromatic and full-bodied, it is ripely herbaceous, with very good vigour and depth of melon and green-capsicum flavours, showing considerable complexity, in a clearly Awatere Valley style.

DRY $25 V+

Sauvignon Gris

Pernod Ricard NZ launched New Zealand's first commercial bottlings of an old French variety, Sauvignon Gris, from the 2009 vintage. Also known as Sauvignon Rosé – due to its pink skin – Sauvignon Gris typically produces less aromatic, but more substantial, wines than Sauvignon Blanc.

Sauvignon Gris is not a blend of Sauvignon Blanc and Pinot Gris (watch out for the confusing 'Sauvignon Blanc/Pinot Gris' under several brands); nor is it a new vine, bred by crossing those grapes. Sauvignon Gris is a variety in its own right.

In Bordeaux, Sauvignon Gris is commonly used as a minority partner in dry white blends dominated by Sauvignon Blanc, but in Chile – like New Zealand – producers are bottling and exporting Sauvignon Gris as a varietal wine. In Marlborough, where the majority of the vines are planted, Sauvignon Gris has proved to be fairly disease-resistant, ripening in the middle of the Sauvignon Blanc harvest. Of New Zealand's 104 hectares of bearing vines in 2018, 102 hectares are in Marlborough, with the rest in Hawke's Bay.

Brancott Estate Letter Series 'R' Sauvignon Gris ★★★★☆

The 2015 vintage (★★★★) is instantly appealing. Mouthfilling (14.5 per cent alcohol), it is very smooth, with fresh, ripely herbaceous aromas and flavours, stone-fruit notes, some oak-derived complexity, and lots of youthful impact.

MED/DRY $33 –V

Brancott Estate Marlborough Sauvignon Gris ★★★☆

The 2014 vintage (★★★☆) is full-bodied (14.5 per cent alcohol), fresh, crisp and lively, with ripely herbaceous flavours of melon, passionfruit and lime. An ideal, all-purpose, dryish wine with good acid spine, it shows very good vibrancy and depth.

MED/DRY $17 V+

Clearview Te Awanga Hawke's Bay Sauvignon Gris (★★★★)

The 2014 vintage (★★★★) is a generous, instantly appealing wine, estate-grown, hand-picked and fermented in old French oak casks. Weighty, sweet-fruited and well-rounded, it has vibrant, ripe stone-fruit flavours, a subtle seasoning of oak and a sustained finish.

DRY $21 V+

Villa Maria Cellar Selection Marlborough Sauvignon Gris (★★★★)

Aromatic, mouthfilling and dry (4 grams/litre of residual sugar), the 2015 vintage (★★★★) is a single-vineyard wine, grown in the Wairau Valley and mostly handled in tanks; a small part of the blend was barrel-fermented. Fruit-driven, it has a touch of complexity and strong, ripely herbaceous flavours, crisp and refreshing.

DRY $18 V+

Waimea Nelson Sauvignon Gris ★★★★

Enjoyable young, the 2015 vintage (★★★★) was estate-grown at Hope. Full-bodied and fleshy, it has strong, ripe tropical-fruit flavours to the fore, a herbal undercurrent, fresh acidity and a dryish (4.8 grams/litre of residual sugar), finely balanced finish.

DRY $23 AV

Sémillon

You'd never guess it from the tiny selection of labels on the shelves, but Sémillon is New Zealand's eighth most widely planted white-wine variety. The few winemakers who once played around with Sémillon could hardly give it away, so aggressively stemmy and spiky was its flavour. Now, there is a new breed of riper, richer, rounder Sémillons on the market – and they are ten times more enjoyable to drink.

The Sémillon variety is beset by a similar problem to Chenin Blanc. Despite being the foundation of outstanding white wines in Bordeaux and Australia, Sémillon is out of fashion in the rest of the world, and in New Zealand its potential is still largely untapped. The area of bearing Sémillon vines has contracted markedly between 2007 and 2018, from 230 to 48 hectares.

Sémillon is highly prized in Bordeaux, where as one of the two key varieties both in dry wines, most notably white Graves, and the inimitable sweet Sauternes, its high levels of alcohol and extract are perfect foils for Sauvignon Blanc's verdant aroma and tartness. With its propensity to rot 'nobly', Sémillon forms about 80 per cent of a classic Sauternes.

Cooler climates like those of New Zealand's South Island, however, bring out a grassy-green character in Sémillon which, coupled with its higher acidity in these regions, can give the variety strikingly Sauvignon-like characteristics.

Grown principally in Hawke's Bay, Gisborne and Marlborough, Sémillon is mostly used in New Zealand not as a varietal wine, but as a minor (and anonymous) partner in wines labelled Sauvignon Blanc, contributing complexity and aging potential. By curbing the variety's natural tendency to grow vigorously and crop bountifully, winemakers are now overcoming the aggressive cut-grass characters that in the past plagued the majority of New Zealand's unblended Sémillons. The spread of clones capable of giving riper fruit characters has also contributed to quality advances.

However, very few wineries in New Zealand are exploring Sémillon's potential to produce complex, long-lived dry whites.

Clearview Reserve Hawke's Bay Sémillon ★★★☆

The 2014 vintage (★★★☆) is a mouthfilling wine, hand-picked at Te Awanga and fermented and matured in American oak barriques (partly new). It's lively, with good depth of ripe-fruit flavours, a strong seasoning of biscuity oak, and considerable complexity.

DRY $27 –V

Man O' War South Three Sémillon (★★★☆)

Estate-grown on Waiheke Island and barrel-aged for nine months, the 2015 vintage (★★★☆) has a slightly nettley, nutty bouquet. Full-flavoured, it has moderately ripe flavours, showing good complexity, crisp acidity and a dry finish.

Vintage	15
WR	7
Drink	17-21

DRY $34 –V

Poverty Bay Young Vines Sémillon ★★★☆

Estate-grown in the Bridge Estate Vineyard at Matawhero, in Gisborne, the light yellow 2014 vintage (★★★☆) is mouthfilling and dry. It has ripe tropical-fruit flavours, showing good concentration, slightly buttery notes and considerable complexity. Ready.

DRY $30 –V

Verdelho

A Portuguese variety traditionally grown on the island of Madeira, Verdelho preserves its acidity well in hot regions, yielding enjoyably full-bodied, lively, lemony table wines in Australia. It is still extremely rare in New Zealand, with only 7 hectares of bearing Verdelho vines in 2018, mostly in Hawke's Bay and Auckland.

Esk Valley Gimblett Gravels Verdelho ★★★★

The 2016 vintage (★★★★) was hand-picked in the company's Omahu Gravels Vineyard and 40 per cent barrel-fermented. A dry style (2.5 grams/litre of residual sugar), it is mouthfilling and vibrantly fruity, with strong tropical-fruit flavours, woven with fresh acidity, and clear-cut varietal characteristics. The 2017 vintage (★★★★) was fermented in a 3:1 mix of tanks and barrels. Full-bodied and vibrantly fruity, it has fresh, strong tropical-fruit flavours, showing a touch of complexity, and a dry (3.3 grams/litre of residual sugar), appetisingly crisp finish.

Vintage	17	16	15	14	13	12	11	10
WR	5	7	7	7	7	7	7	6
Drink	17-19	17-19	17-18	P	P	P	P	P

 DRY $20 V+

Summerhouse Marlborough Verdelho ★★★★

Offering fine value, the 2016 vintage (★★★★) was fermented and matured for nine months in seasoned oak barriques. Bright, light lemon/green, it is weighty and vibrant, with fresh, ripe tropical-fruit flavours, a subtle seasoning of oak, balanced acidity, considerable complexity and a dry (1.7 grams/litre of residual sugar), lingering finish.

Vintage	16	15	14
WR	6	7	7
Drink	17-23	17-21	17-20

 DRY $19 V+

TW Verdelho (★★★★)

Drinking well now, the light yellow 2014 vintage (★★★★) was grown in Gisborne. Full-bodied and fleshy, it has strong, vibrant tropical-fruit flavours to the fore, slightly buttery notes, appetising acidity, and very good depth and complexity.

DRY $25 AV

Villa Maria Single Vineyard Ihumatao Vineyard Auckland Verdelho ★★★★★

Estate-grown at Mangere, in South Auckland, the organically certified 2014 vintage (★★★★★) is a notably varietal wine. Highly fragrant and mouthfilling, it has fresh, concentrated tropical-fruit flavours, with hints of pears and spices, and a long, dry finish.

Vintage	13	12	11	10
WR	7	6	6	6
Drink	P	P	P	P

 DRY $30 AV

Vermentino

Extremely rare in New Zealand, this aromatic variety is grown extensively on Sardinia and Corsica, and is also well known in north-west Italy and southern France. Often compared to Sauvignon Blanc, it yields dry, light-bodied wines, with peach, lemon and dried-herb flavours, woven with fresh acidity. According to New Zealand Winegrowers' *Vineyard Register Report 2015–2018*, only 0.1 hectares will be bearing in 2018, planted in Northland.

Doubtless Vermentino   ★★★☆

Grown at Doubtless Bay, in Northland, this is New Zealand's only example of a variety associated with coastal European wine regions. The 2016 vintage (★★★☆) is a freshly scented, medium-bodied wine, with strong, lively, peachy, slightly citrusy flavours, firm acid spine and a dry, persistent finish. A good food wine.

DRY $23 AV

Viognier

A classic grape of the Rhône Valley, in France, Viognier is renowned for its exotically perfumed, substantial, peach and apricot-flavoured dry whites. A delicious alternative to Chardonnay, Viognier (pronounced 'Vee-yon-yay') is an internationally modish variety, popping up with increasing frequency in shops and restaurants here.

Viognier accounts for only 0.3 per cent of the national vineyard, but the area of bearing vines has expanded from 15 hectares in 2002 to 125 hectares in 2018. Over 70 per cent of the vines are clustered in Hawke's Bay and Gisborne, with further significant plantings in Marlborough (14 per cent) and Auckland (7 per cent).

As in the Rhône, Viognier's flowering and fruit set have been highly variable here. The deeply coloured grapes go through bud-burst, flowering and 'veraison' (the start of the final stage of ripening) slightly behind Chardonnay and are harvested about the same time as Pinot Noir.

The wine is often fermented in seasoned oak barrels, yielding scented, substantial, richly alcoholic wines with gentle acidity and subtle flavours. If you enjoy mouthfilling, softly textured, dry or dryish white wines, but feel like a change from Chardonnay and Pinot Gris, try Viognier. You won't be disappointed.

Alpha Domus The Wingwalker Hawke's Bay Viognier ★★★★

The 2014 vintage (★★★★) was estate-grown in the Bridge Pa Triangle and barrel-fermented. Mouthfilling, fleshy and fully dry (1.4 grams/litre of residual sugar), it has concentrated, ripe, peachy, slightly spicy flavours, gently seasoned with oak, soft acidity, good complexity and a well-rounded finish. Delicious young.

DRY $26 –V

Ascension The Vestal Virgin Matakana Viognier ★★★☆

The 2014 vintage (★★★☆) was estate-grown at Matakana. It's a vibrantly fruity, attractively scented wine with good depth of stone-fruit and spice flavours, crisp and lively.

DRY $40 –V

Ash Ridge Premium Hawke's Bay Viognier ★★★★

The 2016 vintage (★★★★), grown inland at Mangatahi, was fermented and matured for 10 months in seasoned French oak barriques. Attractively scented, it is a medium to full-bodied wine, sweet-fruited and slightly oily-textured, with fresh, ripe peach, pear and lychee flavours, dry and harmonious.

DRY $30 –V

Askerne Hawke's Bay Viognier ★★★★

The 2015 vintage (★★★★) is a rich, weighty, complex wine, fully barrel-fermented (20 per cent new oak). It has a fragrant bouquet, with a slightly creamy texture and concentrated stone-fruit flavours, gently seasoned with toasty oak.

 DRY $22 V+

Babich Family Estates Fernhill Hawke's Bay Viognier ★★★☆

The 2014 vintage (★★★★) is an estate-grown wine, mouthfilling and dry, with generous, ripe peach, pear and spice flavours, gentle acidity, a slightly creamy texture, and very good delicacy and depth. It's drinking well now.

 DRY $25 –V

Black Barn Vineyards R & D Hawke's Bay 'Sur Lie' Viognier   (★★★★★)

The impressive 2015 vintage (★★★★★) is a single-vineyard wine, matured on its yeast lees and bottled straight from the barrel, without fining or filtering. A notably powerful and fleshy wine (14.5 per cent alcohol), it shows excellent complexity, with concentrated, ripe stone-fruit flavours, enriched with finely integrated oak, balanced acidity, and a finely textured, lasting finish. Still youthful, it should be long-lived.

Byrne Northland Waingaro Viognier   ★★★★

The 2016 vintage (★★★★), grown at Kerikeri, was fermented and matured in seasoned French oak barriques. Pale straw, it is full-bodied and soft, with generous, peachy, slightly toasty flavours, a creamy-smooth texture, and lots of drink-young appeal.

Cable Bay Waiheke Island Viognier   ★★★★

The 2015 vintage (★★★★) was hand-harvested and handled in French oak and acacia barriques. Fragrant, with a slightly buttery bouquet, it is mouthfilling, with ripe pear, stone-fruit and spice flavours, a creamy texture, a sliver of sweetness (5 grams/litre of residual sugar), and very good depth and harmony.

Vintage	15	14
WR	6	6
Drink	17-20	17-19

Churton Marlborough Viognier   ★★★★☆

The 2015 vintage (★★★★), estate-grown and hand-picked in the Waihopai Valley, was fermented and matured for 10 months in large, 600-litre French oak casks. Sturdy and fleshy, it is tightly structured, with lively acidity, fresh, strong, peachy, slightly spicy flavours, showing good complexity, and a fully dry finish. Well worth cellaring.

Vintage	14	13
WR	6	7
Drink	17-21	17-22

Clos de Ste Anne Viognier Les Arbres   ★★★★★

This biodynamically certified Gisborne wine from Millton shows impressive richness and complexity. Hill-grown, it is hand-harvested and fermented with indigenous yeasts in large, 600-litre oak barrels. The light lemon/green 2015 vintage (★★★★★) is instantly seductive. Weighty and fleshy, it is rich, sweet-fruited and soft, with generous, peachy flavours, a creamy texture, and a very harmonious, dry (4 grams/litre of residual sugar), lasting finish.

Coopers Creek Select Vineyards Cook County Gisborne Viognier   ★★★★

Creamy-textured, the 2016 vintage (★★★☆) is medium-bodied, with lychee, pear and apple flavours, showing a touch of complexity, and a finely balanced, dry (2 grams/litre of residual sugar) finish.

DRY $23 AV

De La Terre Reserve Hawke's Bay Viognier   ★★★★☆

The 2015 vintage (★★★★☆) was grown on limestone terraces at Havelock North, hand-picked, and fermented in seasoned French oak barriques. Bright, light lemon/green, it is fleshy, with rich stone-fruit flavours, showing good complexity, a slightly minerally thread, and a dry, lingering finish.

Vintage	15	14
WR	6	6
Drink	17-24	17-20

DRY $40 –V

De La Terre Ridgeline Hawke's Bay Viognier   ★★★★☆

Handled without oak, the refined 2016 vintage (★★★★☆) was estate-grown at Havelock North. Weighty, fresh and vibrant, it has concentrated, ripe stone-fruit flavours, slightly spicy and minerally, and a dry, long finish. Well worth discovering.

DRY $40 –V

Dry River Martinborough Viognier   ★★★★☆

The 2016 vintage (★★★★☆) is already delicious. Handled without oak, it is a fragrant, full-bodied, fleshy wine with rich, ripe, citrusy, peachy flavours, a sliver of sweetness (7 grams/litre of residual sugar) and a rounded finish. A youthful, vibrantly fruity, generous wine, it's a drink-now or cellaring proposition.

MED/DRY $55 –V

Falconhead Hawke's Bay Viognier   ★★★☆

The 2014 vintage (★★★★) offers top value. Barrel-fermented, it is fragrant, mouthfilling (14.5 per cent alcohol), sweet-fruited and smooth, with generous, peachy, slightly buttery and spicy flavours, soft acidity and a well-rounded finish. A good Chardonnay alternative.

MED/DRY $16 V+

Framingham F-Series Marlborough Viognier   ★★★★☆

Certified organic, the rare 2015 vintage (★★★★★) was hand-picked and partly barrel-fermented. It is mouthfilling (14.5 per cent alcohol), fleshy and harmonious, with concentrated, ripe, peachy flavours, a subtle seasoning of oak, a slightly oily texture and a dry, well-rounded finish. Delicious young.

DRY $35 –V

Gladstone Vineyard Viognier ★★★★

The 2016 vintage (★★★★) was hand-picked in the northern Wairarapa and mostly handled in tanks; 30 per cent of the blend was fermented in seasoned French oak barrels. Mouthfilling and smooth, it is sweet-fruited and fully dry (1.9 grams/litre of residual sugar), with very good depth of peachy, gently spicy flavours, a slightly creamy texture, and lots of drink-young appeal.

DRY $25 AV

Hans Herzog Marlborough Viognier ★★★★★

Certified organic, the 2014 vintage (★★★★) was hand-harvested from mature, estate-grown vines on the north side of the Wairau Valley, and fermented and matured for 18 months in French oak puncheons. Mouthfilling and dry, it is fleshy and well-rounded, with concentrated, citrusy, peachy, slightly spicy flavours, integrated oak, good complexity and a smooth finish. Best drinking 2018+.

DRY $44 AV

Hopesgrove Estate Single Vineyard Hawke's Bay Viognier (★★★★)

The 2014 vintage (★★★★) was estate-grown, hand-picked and fermented and matured in French oak casks (25 per cent new). It's a full-bodied, well-rounded wine with ripe stone-fruit flavours, seasoned with toasty oak, good concentration and a dry, finely textured finish.

DRY $30 –V

Kaimira Estate Brightwater Viognier (★★★★☆)

Certified organic, the impressive 2014 vintage (★★★★☆) was estate-grown, hand-picked and fermented in seasoned oak casks. It is fragrant, with concentrated stone-fruit flavours, finely integrated oak adding complexity, and a rich, dry (1.6 grams/litre of residual sugar) finish. Drink now or cellar. Fine value.

DRY $25 V+

Kainui Road Bay of Islands Viognier ★★☆

Hand-picked at Kerikeri, in Northland, the easy-drinking 2015 vintage (★★★☆) is mouthfilling and sweet-fruited, with vibrant, peachy, gently spicy flavours, showing good delicacy and moderate richness.

DRY $25 –V

La Collina Viognier ★★★★★

The classy 2014 vintage (★★★★★) from Bilancia, in Hawke's Bay, was fermented in very old French oak barriques. It is sturdy (14.5 per cent alcohol), with deep stone-fruit and spice flavours, a very subtle seasoning of oak, impressive complexity and a slightly creamy, long finish.

DRY $45 AV

Vintage	14
WR	7
Drink	17-20

Leveret Estate Hawke's Bay Viognier   (★★★★☆)

Offering fine value, the 2015 vintage (★★★★☆) was fermented and matured for a year in seasoned oak barrels. Bright, light yellow/green, it is floral, fleshy, sweet-fruited and soft, with mouthfilling body and vibrant, peachy flavours, a very subtle oak influence, and a dry, harmonious finish.

DRY $23 V+

Linden Estate Hawke's Bay Viognier   ★★★★

The 2014 vintage (★★★★) was grown in the Dartmoor Valley and fermented in tanks and barrels. It is full-bodied, with strong, peachy, slightly spicy flavours, creamy and buttery notes adding a touch of complexity, fresh acidity and a slightly off-dry (6 grams/litre of residual sugar), finely balanced finish. Ready.

MED/DRY $25 AV

Marsden Bay of Islands Viognier   ★★★☆

The mouthfilling 2015 vintage (★★★☆) was hand-picked and matured in seasoned oak barrels. It has ripe, peachy, slightly spicy flavours, in a vibrant, fruity style with a dry (3 grams/litre of residual sugar), seductively smooth finish.

Vintage	15
WR	6
Drink	P

DRY $27 –V

Millton Clos de Ste Anne Viognier Les Arbres – see Clos de Ste Anne Viognier Les Arbres

Millton Riverpoint Vineyard Gisborne Viognier   ★★★★☆

Maturing very gracefully, the 2015 vintage (★★★★☆) was hand-picked and fermented with indigenous yeasts in tanks and French oak hogsheads. Marsanne was added to the blend, for 'depth and richness', and a splash of Muscat, for a 'fruity lift'. Certified organic, it is fragrant and softly mouthfilling, with rich, ripe, peachy, spicy, slightly toasty flavours, showing very good complexity, gentle acidity, a slightly oily texture, and a dry (4 grams/litre of residual sugar) finish. Delicious now.

Vintage	15	14
WR	6	7
Drink	17-21	17-20

DRY $26 AV

Moutere Hills Nelson Viognier   (★★★☆)

Estate-grown in Nelson, the 2016 vintage (★★★☆) is a rare wine – only 23 cases were produced. Hand-picked and matured for 11 months in French oak barrels, it is pale gold, fleshy and soft, with very good depth of peachy, slightly honeyed flavours. Drink now to 2018.

DRY $44 –V

Obsidian Reserve Waiheke Island Viognier ★★★★

Hand-harvested at Onetangi, the 2015 vintage (★★★☆) is a bright lemon/green, youthful, vibrantly fruity wine. Mouthfilling, it has fresh, peachy, appley flavours, hints of apricot and spice, and drink-young appeal.

DRY $45 –V

Okahu Estate Viognier ★★★☆

Grown at Kaitaia, in Northland, and handled without oak, the 2014 vintage (★★★☆) is a weighty wine with ripe, peachy, slightly spicy flavours, showing good depth.

DRY $39 –V

Quarter Acre Hawke's Bay Viognier ★★★★

The 2014 vintage (★★★★☆) was hand-picked in the Bridge Pa Triangle and fermented with indigenous yeasts in French oak barriques. It is mouthfilling and sweet-fruited, with ripe stone-fruit flavours, well-integrated oak and a slightly oily texture. Strongly varietal and dry, it has lots of early-drinking appeal.

DRY $27 –V

Saint Clair Hawke's Bay Viognier ★★★☆

Maturing gracefully, the 2015 vintage (★★★★) was estate-grown in the Gimblett Gravels and tank-fermented. A mouthfilling, vibrantly fruity wine, it is creamy-textured, with fresh, peachy, slightly spicy flavours, lively, dry (2.8 grams/litre of residual sugar) and smooth.

DRY $21 AV

Sileni Estate Selection Hedonist Hawke's Bay Viognier (★★★★)

Currently delicious, the 2015 vintage (★★★★) was hand-picked at Te Awanga and fermented in seasoned oak casks. Mouthfilling and sweet-fruited, it has ripe stone-fruit and pear flavours, with a soft, dry (4.7 grams/litre of residual sugar), creamy-textured finish. Drink now to 2018.

Vintage	15
WR	6
Drink	17-22

DRY $25 AV

Staete Landt State of Surrender Marlborough Viognier ★★★★

Estate-grown at Rapaura, the 2014 vintage (★★★★) was hand-picked and matured on its yeast lees for eight months. Fleshy and soft, it is vibrantly fruity, with pure, ripe, peachy flavours, showing excellent depth, and a slightly oily texture.

Vintage	14	13	12
WR	6	6	6
Drink	17-20	17-19	17-18

DRY $39 –V

Stonecroft Gimblett Gravels Hawke's Bay Viognier   (★★★★)

Certified organic, the 2016 vintage (★★★★) was grown at Roys Hill, in the Gimblett Gravels, and fermented and matured for six months in seasoned French oak barrels. Light lemon/green, it is scented and smooth, with vibrant, youthful peach and pear flavours to the fore, a subtle seasoning of oak, and a softly textured, dryish finish. Instantly attractive, it should be at its best 2018+.

Vintage	16
WR	5
Drink	17-21

 MED/DRY $25 AV

Te Mata Zara Viognier   ★★★★★

This estate-grown wine is from Woodthorpe Terraces, on the south side of the Dartmoor Valley in Hawke's Bay. Hand-picked, it is partly fermented and lees-aged in seasoned French oak barrels. Already delicious, the 2016 vintage (★★★★★) is a bright, light lemon/green, sturdy and fleshy dry wine, with deep, well-ripened stone-fruit flavours, barrel-ferment complexity, gentle acidity and a seductively soft finish. It's ready to roll.

Vintage	16	15
WR	6	6
Drink	17-24	17-23

 DRY $27 V+

Tohu Single Vineyard Marlborough Viognier   (★★★☆)

The easy-drinking 2015 vintage (★★★☆) is a single-vineyard wine, grown in the upper Awatere Valley and partly barrel-fermented. Freshly scented, it is mouthfilling and slightly creamy, with strong, citrusy, appley flavours, gentle sweetness (10 grams/litre of residual sugar) and a smooth finish.

 MED/DRY $20 AV

Turanga Par Nature Viognier   (★★★★)

Estate-grown and hand-picked at Whitford, in Auckland, the attractive 2014 vintage (★★★★) is full-bodied, with fresh, vibrant stone-fruit flavours, showing very good ripeness and depth, a slightly oily texture, and a fully dry finish. Certified organic.

 DRY $25 AV

TW Viognier   (★★★☆)

Estate-grown in Gisborne, the 2016 vintage (★★★☆) is a bright, light lemon/green wine, fragrant, fresh and full-bodied. Vibrantly fruity, with pear and peach flavours, gentle acidity and a soft finish, it's enjoyable young.

 DRY $25 –V

Villa Maria Cellar Selection Gisborne Viognier   (★★★★)

Bargain-priced, the powerful 2015 vintage (★★★★) is sturdy (14.5 per cent alcohol) and fleshy, with strong, ripe, peachy, slightly biscuity flavours, a hint of honeysuckle, gentle acidity and a dry finish.

DRY $18 V+

Villa Maria Cellar Selection Hawke's Bay Viognier   ★★★★☆

The fine-value 2015 vintage (★★★★☆) was partly hand-picked and fermented with indigenous yeasts in tanks (40 per cent) and seasoned French oak barriques (60 per cent). Mouthfilling (14.5 per cent alcohol) and fleshy, it has fresh stone-fruit and spice flavours, showing excellent ripeness and richness, gentle acidity, and a fully dry (2 grams/litre of residual sugar) finish. The 2016 vintage (★★★★) was mostly (85 per cent) fermented and matured for eight months in French oak barriques (14 per cent new). It's a sturdy, fleshy, well-rounded wine, with vibrant, ripe tropical-fruit flavours, balanced acidity and a dry (2.5 grams/litre of residual sugar), smooth finish. Drink now or cellar.

Vintage	16	15	14	13
WR	6	7	7	7
Drink	17-20	17-20	17-19	P

 DRY $18 V+

Villa Maria Private Bin Gisborne Viognier   ★★★☆

Enjoyable young, the strongly varietal 2016 vintage (★★★★) has a fresh, peachy, slightly spicy bouquet, leading into a mouthfilling wine with strong, ripe stone-fruit flavours, gentle acidity, and a finely textured, dry (2.5 grams/litre of residual sugar) finish. Great value.

Vintage	16	15	14	13
WR	7	7	7	7
Drink	17-19	17-18	P	P

 DRY $15 V+

Waimarie Mangawhai Viognier   (★★★)

Ready now, the 2015 vintage (★★★) is a full-bodied, fleshy Auckland wine, handled entirely in stainless steel tanks. Pale straw, with a hint of development, it has strong stone-fruit flavours, a vague hint of honey, and a rounded, fully dry finish.

 DRY $25 –V

Waimea Nelson Viognier   ★★★★

The 2014 vintage (★★★★) was estate-grown on the Waimea Plains, hand-picked and tank-fermented. Scented and smooth, it is a fleshy, finely textured style with strong, peachy flavours to the fore, a slightly creamy texture and an off-dry (8 grams/litre of residual sugar) finish.

MED/DRY $23 AV

Wairau River Reserve Marlborough Viognier   ★★★★

The 2015 vintage (★★★★) was estate-grown on the banks of the Wairau River, and fermented and lees-aged for a year in seasoned French oak barrels. It is mouthfilling and vibrantly fruity, with rich, peachy flavours to the fore, a very subtle twist of oak adding complexity, and a smooth (4.9 grams/litre of residual sugar) finish.

Vintage	15	14	13	12	11
WR	6	7	7	6	6
Drink	17-20	17-18	P	P	P

 DRY $30 –V

Würzer

A German crossing of Gewürztraminer and Müller-Thurgau, Würzer is extremely rare in New Zealand, with 0.4 hectares of bearing vines in 2018, all in Nelson, where Seifried has 'a few rows' at its Redwood Valley Vineyard.

Seifried Nelson Würzer ★★★☆

Offering very easy drinking, the 2016 vintage (★★★) is fresh and full-bodied, with vibrant, citrusy, slightly appley and spicy flavours, a gentle splash of sweetness (11 grams/litre of residual sugar), and a refreshingly crisp finish.

MED/DRY $25 –V

Sweet White Wines

New Zealand's sweet white wines (often called dessert wines) are hardly taking the world by storm, with only about 10,000 cases exported each year. Yet around the country, winemakers work hard to produce some ravishingly beautiful, honey-sweet white wines that are worth discovering and can certainly hold their own internationally. New Zealand's most luscious, concentrated and honeyish sweet whites are made from grapes which have been shrivelled and dehydrated on the vines by 'noble rot', the dry form of the *Botrytis cinerea* mould. Misty mornings, followed by clear, fine days with light winds and low humidity, are ideal conditions for the spread of noble rot, but in New Zealand this favourable interplay of weather factors occurs irregularly.

Some enjoyable but rarely exciting dessert wines are made by the 'freeze-concentration' method, whereby a proportion of the natural water content in the grape juice is frozen out, leaving a sweet, concentrated juice to be fermented.

Marlborough has so far yielded a majority of the finest sweet whites. Most of the other wine regions, however, can also point to the successful production of botrytised sweet whites in favourable vintages.

Riesling has been the foundation of the majority of New Zealand's most opulent sweet whites, but Sauvignon Blanc, Sémillon, Gewürztraminer, Pinot Gris, Chenin Blanc, Viognier and Chardonnay have all yielded fine dessert styles. With their high levels of extract and firm acidity, most of these wines mature well for two to three years, although few are very long-lived.

Ake Ake La Douce (★★★)

The 2014 vintage (★★★) is a Northland blend of Pinot Gris (90 per cent) and Sauvignon Blanc (10 per cent). It is mouthfilling, with gentle sweetness (120 grams/litre of residual sugar) and good depth of ripe, peachy, slightly spicy flavours.

SW $25 (750ML) AV

Allan Scott Marlborough Late Harvest Riesling (★★★★★)

The luscious 2014 vintage (★★★★★) is golden, with rich honey and apricot scents and flavours. Delicious now, it harbours just 7.5 per cent alcohol, but is a highly botrytised, concentrated wine with abundant sweetness and good acid spine. Intense and oily, with lovely vibrancy, richness and harmony, it's a drink-now or cellaring proposition.

SW $28 (375ML) V+

Alpha Domus AD Noble Selection ★★★★★

A pale gold beauty, the botrytis-affected 2015 vintage (★★★★★) was made from Sémillon grapes, grown in the Bridge Pa Triangle and mostly harvested with soaring sugar contents (45 to 47 brix). French oak-aged, it is fresh and full-bodied (although only 10 per cent alcohol), with rich, ripe flavours, showing good complexity, plentiful sweetness (248 grams/litre of residual sugar), and an oily, honeyed richness.

SW $38 (375ML) AV

Alpha Domus The Pilot Leonarda Late Harvest   (★★★★)

Delicious now, the 2015 vintage (★★★★) is a blend of Sémillon and Viognier grapes, estate-grown in the Bridge Pa Triangle, Hawke's Bay, harvested at an average of 32 brix, and partly barrel-fermented. Pale gold, it is weighty, with rich stone-fruit and honey flavours, a slightly oily texture, and a sweet (121 grams/litre of residual sugar), finely balanced finish. Good value.

SW $20 (375ML) V+

Ara Select Block Limited Release Cut Cane Sauvignon Blanc   (★★★★☆)

Light gold, the refined 2014 vintage (★★★★☆) has an inviting, honeyed bouquet and ripe, peachy, nectareous flavours. Finely balanced, with abundant sweetness (200 grams/litre of residual sugar), it has excellent vibrancy and depth.

Vintage	14
WR	7
Drink	17-18

SW $30 (375ML) AV

Ash Ridge Premium Estate Late Harvest Chardonnay   (★★★☆)

Harvested at 32 brix in early April, three weeks after the main crop, but with very little botrytis, the 2015 vintage (★★★☆) has pure, vibrant, sweet (120 grams/litre of residual sugar), grapey flavours. Worth cellaring.

SW $25 (375ML) –V

Ataahua Waipara Late Harvest Gewürztraminer   (★★★★★)

The pale gold 2014 vintage (★★★★★) is packed with personality. From grapes hand-harvested in early winter and barrel-fermented with indigenous yeasts, it is perfumed and weighty, with sweet, concentrated stone-fruit and spice flavours, showing lovely complexity, richness and harmony. Drink now or cellar.

SW $26 (375ML) V+

Awatere River by Louis Vavasour Marlborough
Late Harvest Gewürztraminer   (★★★★★)

The golden, honey-sweet 2014 vintage (★★★★★) was picked in mid-May at over 40 brix, with an 'extensive' botrytis infection, and barrel-fermented. The bouquet is perfumed, honeyish and spicy; the palate is fresh and rich, with peach, apricot and spice flavours, good sugar/acid balance (213 grams/litre of residual sugar), and great drink-young appeal.

SW $40 (375ML) AV

Babich Family Estates Cowslip Valley Marlborough Noble Riesling   (★★★★☆)

A strong candidate for cellaring, the 2016 vintage (★★★★☆) was harvested at 32 brix, with a 70 per cent botrytis infection, and fermented in tanks (80 per cent) and new oak casks (20 per cent). Light yellow/green, it is mouthfilling (12 per cent alcohol) and sweet (101 grams/litre of residual sugar), with vibrant, pure, citrusy, gently honeyed flavours, showing lovely delicacy and harmony. Best drinking 2019+.

SW $35 (375ML) –V

Babich Family Estates Gimblett Gravels
Hawke's Bay Noble Gewürztraminer   (★★★★☆)

Showing strong personality, the 2014 vintage (★★★★☆) is an amber-hued, honeyed dessert wine, hand-harvested at 42 brix. Mouthfilling (14.5 per cent alcohol), with rich peach, spice and apricot flavours, it's a sweet but not super-sweet style (115 grams/litre of residual sugar) with a powerful botrytis influence.

SW $25 (375ML) V+

Beach House Hawke's Bay Noble Chardonnay   (★★★★)

Already delicious, the 2016 vintage (★★★★) is a single-vineyard wine, hand-harvested when the grapes were 'botrytis laden', and tank-fermented. Light gold, with a a slightly oily richness, it has concentrated peach, apricot and honey flavours, sweet (120 grams/litre of residual sugar) and smooth.

SW $20 (375ML) V+

Beach House Hawke's Bay Noble Sauvignon Blanc   (★★★★☆)

The impressive 2016 vintage (★★★★☆) is a single-vineyard wine, hand-picked at 35 brix, when the grapes were 'botrytis laden', and tank-fermented. Light gold, it is full-bodied, with deep, ripe, peach and passionfruit flavours, fresh and honeyed, abundant sweetness (126 grams/litre of residual sugar), balanced acidity and a long finish. Already delicious, it's also worth cellaring.

SW $35 (375ML) –V

Bellbird Spring Muté 'L'Alouette'   (★★★★)

The 2016 vintage (★★★★) was made from late-picked Sauvignon Blanc, estate-grown at Waipara, fermented in old barrels and fortified with the estate's own pot still brandy. Light lemon/green, it is weighty (17.5 per cent alcohol) and very harmonious, with gentle, pear-like flavours, showing good complexity. A quietly satisfying, rather than dramatic, moderately sweet wine (81 grams/litre of residual sugar), it's well worth trying.

SW $35 (375ML) –V

Bellbird Spring Muté 'Les Epices'   (★★★★★)

The delicious 2016 vintage (★★★★★) is a Waipara blend of Riesling, Gewürztraminer and Muscat, late-picked, fermented in old barrels and fortified with the estate's own pot still brandy. Light yellow, it's a distinctive wine, sturdy (17.5 per cent alcohol), rich and rounded, with pear, peach and spice flavours, sweet (85 grams/litre of residual sugar), complex and harmonious. It's already drinking well.

SW $35 (375ML) AV

Brancott Estate Letter Series 'B' Late Harvest Marlborough Sauvignon Blanc   ★★★★☆

The 2014 vintage (★★★★☆) has a gently honeyed, faintly herbal bouquet, leading into a luscious wine with rich passionfruit, ginger and apricot-like flavours, woven with fresh acidity, excellent drive and depth through the palate, and a long, sweet finish.

SW $36 (375ML) –V

Brookfields Indulgence Hawke's Bay Viognier   ★★★★☆

Already highly seductive, the 2017 vintage (★★★★☆) was made from botrytis-affected grapes, handled without oak. Pale gold, it is deliciously rich and sweet (over 250 grams/litre of residual sugar), with an oily texture and a strong surge of peach, apricot and honey flavours.

Vintage	17	16
WR	7	7
Drink	17-19	18-20

SW $25 (375ML) V+

Charcoal Gully Late Harvest Central Otago Gewürztraminer   (★★★★)

The 2014 vintage (★★★★) is a full-bodied, generous, gently sweet wine (57 grams/litre of residual sugar), hand-picked at 27 brix, six weeks after the normal harvest. Attractively scented, with ripe stone-fruit, lychee and spice flavours, concentrated and soft, it's drinking well now, developing bottle-aged complexity.

SW $28 (750ML) V+

Churton Marlborough Petit Manseng   ★★★★★

The lovely 2015 vintage (★★★★★) of this traditional variety of Jurancon, in south-west France, was estate-grown in the Waihopai Valley and fermented in seasoned oak barrels. Harvested by hand at 26.7 brix, it is a light yellow, invitingly scented, fresh, medium-bodied wine with peachy, slightly honeyed flavours, gentle sweetness (69 grams/litre of residual sugar), steely acidity, and excellent intensity and harmony. The 2016 vintage (★★★★★) reveals great personality. Light gold, it is slightly weightier than the 2015, with highly concentrated, honey-sweet flavours, threaded with appetising acidity, and lots of youthful vigour.

Vintage	16	15
WR	7	7
Drink	17-35	17-30

SW $50 (500ML) AV

Coopers Creek Coopers Gold   ★★★☆

The 2017 vintage (★★★) was made from Gisborne Chardonnay. Light lemon/green, it is fresh and smooth, with citrusy, peachy flavours, gentle sweetness and an easy-drinking charm. The 2016 vintage (★★★☆) is a lively, peachy, lemony wine, also made from Gisborne Chardonnay. Finely balanced, it has very good depth of flavour, sweet (100 grams/litre of residual sugar) and fresh.

SW $22 (375ML) AV

De La Terre Late Harvest Hawke's Bay Viognier   (★★★★)

The pale yellow 2015 vintage (★★★★) was estate-grown at Havelock North and handled without oak. A gently sweet style (55 grams/litre of residual sugar), it is finely balanced, with vibrant, peachy flavours, showing a touch of complexity, and very good ripeness and concentration.

Vintage	15
WR	5
Drink	17-18

SW $24 (375ML) V+

De La Terre Noble Hawke's Bay Viognier ★★★★☆

The delicious 2015 vintage (★★★★☆) was estate-grown at Havelock North and handled without oak. It is rich and rounded, with concentrated, peachy, slightly spicy and honeyed flavours, sweet (125 grams/litre of residual sugar), finely balanced and youthful. Bright, light lemon/green, the 2016 vintage (★★★★☆) is weighty and smooth, with ripe, peachy, slightly honeyed flavours, gentle sweetness (100 grams/litre of residual sugar), and a well-rounded, very harmonious finish. Delicious drinking now onwards.

Vintage	15
WR	6
Drink	17-20

 SW $34 (375ML) AV

Esk Valley Late Harvest Chenin Blanc ★★★★★

Well worth cellaring, the gold/amber 2016 vintage (★★★★☆) is from hand-picked, raisined grapes in the Joseph Soler Vineyard, near Hastings. Partly (25 per cent) barrel-fermented, it has fresh, concentrated, sweet (155 grams/litre of residual sugar) flavours of apricot and honey, firm acid spine, a slightly oily texture and excellent richness and harmony. Best drinking 2019+.

Vintage	16	15	14	13
WR	7	NM	NM	7
Drink	17-25	NM	NM	17-23

 SW $30 (375ML) V+

Felton Road Block 1 Central Otago Riesling ★★★★★

Estate-grown in The Elms Vineyard, from mature vines on a 'steeper slope' which yields 'riper fruit' without noble rot, this Bannockburn wine is made in a style 'similar to a late-harvest, Mosel spätlese'. The 2016 vintage (★★★★★) is delicious in its youth. Light (9 per cent alcohol) and lively, with rich, ripe, lemony, peachy, slightly spicy flavours, it has gentle sweetness (66.5 grams/litre of residual sugar), appetising acidity, and lovely depth and harmony.

Vintage	16	15	14	13
WR	7	7	6	7
Drink	17-41	17-40	17-28	17-28

 SW $43 (750ML) V+

Forrest Botrytised Marlborough Riesling ★★★★★

Already delicious, the 2016 vintage (★★★★☆) is bright, light lemon/green, with moderate alcohol (10.5 per cent) and rich peach, apricot and honey flavours, sweet (147 grams/litre of residual sugar), crisp and concentrated.

SW $28 (375ML) V+

Framingham F-Series Riesling Auslese ★★★★★

The 2015 vintage (★★★★★), handled in tanks (57 per cent) and old oak casks (43 per cent), is bright yellow/green, with a honeyed bouquet. Light (9 per cent alcohol) and rich, it has sweet (120 grams/litre of residual sugar), ripe, peachy, spicy flavours, honeyed and highly concentrated. The 2016 vintage (★★★★★) is light gold, vibrantly fruity and rich, with low alcohol (8.5 per cent), good acid spine, and concentrated, citrusy, honeyed flavours. Showing lovely freshness, depth and poise, it's already delicious, but very ageworthy.

Vintage	16	15
WR	7	7
Drink	17-21	17-20

 SW $45 (375ML) AV

Framingham F-Series Riesling Trockenbeerenauslese ★★★★★

Hand-harvested in Marlborough when all the berries were botrytis-affected and dried out, the memorable 2015 vintage (★★★★★) was handled in tanks (65 per cent) and old oak casks (35 per cent). Bright lemon/green, with advanced sweetness (260 grams/litre of residual sugar) and finely balanced acidity, it is vibrantly fruity, with concentrated lemon, apricot and honey flavours, showing lovely harmony, and a notably rich, lasting finish. The 2016 vintage (★★★★★) is a ravishing wine. Light gold, it is highly scented and vibrantly fruity, with bottomless depth of sweet, lemony, honeyed flavours, perfectly pitched acidity, a distinct hint of apricot and a very long finish. A memorable mouthful, it's a drink-now or cellaring proposition.

Vintage	16	15
WR	7	7
Drink	17-21	17-20

 SW $70 (375ML) AV

Framingham Noble Riesling ★★★★★

Delicious from the start, the 2017 vintage (★★★★★) is rich, sweet and vibrantly fruity. Bright, light lemon/green, it has fresh, concentrated lemon, apple and honey flavours, enriched but not swamped by botrytis, good acid spine and a very harmonious, lasting finish. Drink now or cellar.

SW $40 (375ML) AV

Framingham Select Marlborough Riesling ★★★★★

'Inspired by the German Spätlese style', the light lemon/green 2017 vintage (★★★★★) is light-bodied (9 per cent alcohol) and lemon-scented. Vibrantly fruity, it is gently sweet, with penetrating, citrusy, appley flavours, showing lovely purity, delicacy and harmony. A very ageworthy wine, it should break into full stride from 2020 onwards.

SW $35 (750ML) V+

Fromm Riesling Spätlese
★★★★☆

This vivacious Marlborough wine is made from the ripest hand-picked grapes with no botrytis infection, in an intense, low-alcohol style with plentiful sweetness (typically around 80 to 90 grams/litre of residual sugar). The 2014 vintage (★★★★★) is scented, light (7 per cent alcohol) and lively, with lovely poise and immediacy. It has pure, penetrating, lemony, appley flavours, good acid spine, delicious sugar/acid balance and a long, racy finish. Delicious young, it should mature well.

Vintage	14	13	12	11	10	09
WR	7	7	7	6	7	7
Drink	17-24	17-23	17-22	17-21	17-20	17-19

 SW $35 (750ML) V+

Gibbston Valley Late Harvest
★★★★

Grown at Bendigo, in Central Otago, the 2014 vintage (★★★☆) is not labelled by variety, but was blended from Riesling (70 per cent) and Pinot Blanc (30 per cent). It is light-bodied (8.5 per cent alcohol), with good depth of fresh, peachy, slightly spicy and honeyed flavours, sweet (138 grams/litre of residual sugar) and smooth.

Vintage	14	13
WR	7	6
Drink	17-25	17-25

SW $35 (375ML) –V

Giesen The Brothers Late Harvest Marlborough Sauvignon Blanc
★★★★★

The lovely 2014 vintage (★★★★★) is a single-vineyard, hand-picked wine. Golden, honeyed and rich, with an oily texture, it is highly concentrated, with peachy, unabashedly sweet flavours (252 grams/litre of residual sugar), balanced acidity, a strong botrytis influence, and lots of current-drinking appeal.

Vintage	14
WR	7
Drink	17-18

 SW $30 (375ML) V+

Greystone Brittle Star Waipara Valley Riesling
★★★★☆

The 2015 vintage (★★★★☆) was hand-picked at high natural sugar levels (26.9 to 30.6 brix), when 70 per cent of the bunches were botrytis-infected. Pale gold, with a gently honeyed bouquet, it is medium-bodied, with strong, ripe peach, apricot and marmalade flavours, a hint of honey, and a sweet (108 grams/litre of residual sugar), rounded finish. Delicious young, it's also worth cellaring.

Vintage	15
WR	6
Drink	17-25

SW $38 (750ML) V+

Hunter's Hukapapa Marlborough Riesling Dessert Wine
★★★☆

The 2014 vintage (★★★☆) is a freeze-concentrated wine. It has strong, lemony, slightly limey flavours, sweet (130 grams/litre of residual sugar) and crisp, showing very good depth and harmony. Drink now or cellar.

 SW $24 (375ML) AV

Jackson Estate Botrytis Marlborough Riesling   (★★★★★)

Estate-grown in the heart of the Wairau Valley, the 2014 vintage (★★★★★) is delicious now. Amber-hued, with a honeyed bouquet, it has concentrated, apricot-like flavours, abundant sweetness (260 grams/litre of residual sugar), good acid spine, and lovely richness and harmony.

SW $45 (375ML) AV

Johanneshof Noble Late Harvest Marlborough Riesling   (★★★★★)

Still on sale in 2017, the striking 2011 vintage (★★★★★) is amber-hued, with a honeyed, rich, complex bouquet and flavours. Probably at its peak, it has highly concentrated apricot and honey flavours, crisp, sweet (150 grams/litre of residual sugar) and finely poised. A very 'complete' wine.

SW $40 AV

Johner Estate Gladstone Noble Pinot Noir   ★★★

Estate-grown in the northern Wairarapa, the 2014 vintage (★★★☆) is a sweet (140 grams/litre of residual sugar), light pink/orange wine. Mouthfilling and smooth, it is slightly honeyed, with strawberry, peach and spice flavours, woven with fresh acidity, good depth, and lots of drink-young charm.

Vintage	14
WR	6
Drink	17-20

SW $22 (375ML) –V

Johner Estate Gladstone Noble Sauvignon Blanc   ★★★☆

Estate-grown in the northern Wairarapa, the 2016 vintage (★★★☆) is still youthful. Handled without oak, it has vibrant, ripe, peachy, vaguely honeyed flavours, gentle sweetness (140 grams/litre of residual sugar), crisp acidity and very good poise and depth.

Vintage	16
WR	6
Drink	17-22

SW $22 (375ML) AV

Johner Estate Wairarapa Noble Lynder Cabernet   (★★★☆)

The light red 2014 vintage (★★★☆) is mouthfilling (13.5 per cent alcohol), with raspberry/plum flavours, fresh, sweet (140 grams/litre of residual sugar) and strong. It's a distinctive wine, ready to roll.

Vintage	14
WR	5
Drink	17-20

SW $22 (375ML) AV

Jules Taylor Late Harvest Marlborough Sauvignon Blanc   ★★★★☆

The 2015 vintage (★★★★) was handled without oak. It has a gently honeyed bouquet, leading into a finely balanced wine with rich, ripe, peachy, non-herbaceous flavours, slightly honeyed and sweet (169 grams/litre of residual sugar). Drink now.

Vintage	15
WR	6
Drink	17-22

SW $35 (375ML) –V

Leveret Hawke's Bay Late Harvest (★★★★☆)

Currently delicious, the 2016 vintage (★★★★☆) is hard to beat as a sweet, drink-young charmer. Made from Viognier, it is a light yellow/green, fragrant wine, with vibrant, peachy, honeyed flavours, sweet (140 grams/litre of residual sugar), rich and oily-textured. Fine value.

Vintage	16
WR	6
Drink	18-23

SW $23 (375ML) V+

Leveret Reserve Hawke's Bay Late Harvest (★★★★★)

The classy 2016 vintage (★★★★★) is already difficult to resist. Made from Viognier, it is a golden, honey-sweet beauty (200 grams/litre of residual sugar), strongly botrytis-influenced, with lively acidity, an oily texture, and lush, peachy, honeyed flavours.

Vintage	16
WR	7
Drink	18-26

SW $30 V+

Lime Rock Central Hawke's Bay Late Harvest Sauvignon Blanc (★★★☆)

Bright, light lemon/green, the 2016 vintage (★★★☆) was estate-grown in Central Hawke's Bay and partly (29 per cent) barrel-fermented. Full-bodied, it is sweet but not super-sweet (109 grams/litre of residual sugar), with good weight and depth of well-ripened flavours, showing considerable complexity. Drink now or cellar.

Vintage	16
WR	7
Drink	18-30

SW $28 (375ML) –V

Loveblock Marlborough Noble Chenin Blanc (★★★★★)

Full of youthful vigour, but already delicious, the 2014 vintage (★★★★★) was estate-grown and hand-picked in the Awatere Valley at 42 brix, with 100 per cent botrytis infection. Light gold, deliciously peachy and honeyed, it has abundant sweetness (230 grams/litre of residual sugar), balanced by firm acidity, and a slightly oily, lasting finish.

SW $30 (500ML) V+

Loveblock Marlborough Sweet Moscato (★★★★)

Estate-grown in the Awatere Valley, the 2014 vintage (★★★★) is a full-bodied (13.5 per cent alcohol), sweet but not super-sweet wine, fortified with grain alcohol, 'in true Muscat de Beaumes-de-Venise style'. Light lemon/green, it is invitingly perfumed, with fresh, pure Muscat aromas and strong, vibrant peach, lemon, orange and grape flavours.

SW $30 (500ML) V+

Marsden Bay of Islands Late Harvest Muscat ★★★

Light and lively, the 2016 vintage (★★★) was made from grapes grown in Gisborne. Pale and soft, it has peachy, slightly limey, sweet flavours, showing good delicacy, purity and freshness.

SW $20 –V

Misha's Vineyard The Cadenza Late Harvest Gewürztraminer   ★★★★☆

The 2016 vintage (★★★★☆) was hand-harvested at Bendigo, in Central Otago, at 29.3 brix, with a 20 per cent botrytis infection, and handled without oak. Light lemon/green, it is richly scented, with deliciously ripe lychee and pear flavours, showing excellent delicacy, and a gently spicy, sweet (159 grams/litre of residual sugar) finish. Vibrantly fruity and harmonious, it's a drink-now or cellaring proposition.

Vintage	16	15	14
WR	7	7	6
Drink	17-24	17-23	17-22

 SW $32 (375ML) AV

Mission Estate Late Harvest   ★★★

The 2014 vintage (★★★☆), grown in Hawke's Bay and Gisborne, is a pale gold, sweetish Gewürztraminer, full-bodied, with good depth of ripe, gentle, moderately spicy flavours and an invitingly perfumed bouquet.

 SW $18 (375ML) AV

Mondillo Nina Late Harvest Riesling   ★★★★☆

Estate-grown at Bendigo, in Central Otago, the 2014 vintage (★★★★) has lemony, appley scents and flavours, a hint of honey, good acid spine, abundant sweetness (110 grams/litre of residual sugar), and a finely poised, lengthy finish.

Vintage	14	12	11
WR	7	7	7
Drink	17-20	17-19	17-18

 SW $35 (375ML) –V

Mt Difficulty Growers Series Silver Tussock Tinwald Burn Noble Riesling   (★★★★)

From a site at the head of Lake Dunstan, in the Cromwell Basin, the elegant 2016 vintage (★★★★) is a gently botrytised style. Light lemon/green, it has strong, youthful, lemony flavours, a hint of apricot, plentiful sweetness (137 grams/litre of residual sugar), good acid spine, and obvious potential for cellaring; best drinking 2019+.

 SW $27 (750ML) V+

Nevis Bluff Selection De Grains Noble Pinot Gris   ★★★★★

The 2015 vintage (★★★★★) is a truly memorable Central Otago wine. Bright, light yellow/green, it is enticingly scented, with lovely vibrancy and intensity of peach, pear and honey flavours. Unabashedly sweet (338 grams/litre of residual sugar), it is oily textured, with balanced acidity, and notable concentration and harmony. Drink now.

 SW $35 (375ML) AV

Ngatarawa Proprietors' Reserve Noble Riesling   (★★★★★)

The ravishing 2014 vintage (★★★★★) is from a Hawke's Bay producer with a decades-long commitment to dessert wines. Hand-picked in two passes through the vineyard, at 42 and 44 brix, it is golden and richly scented, with highly concentrated, sweet (204 grams/litre of residual sugar), peachy, citrusy, gently honeyed flavours, enriched but not swamped by botrytis. A very elegant wine, it's hard to resist.

SW $40 (375ML) AV

Northfield Late Harvest Frog Rock Vineyard
Waipara Valley Sauvignon Blanc/Sémillon

Showing some Sauternes-like characters, the 2010 vintage (★★★☆) is still on sale. Light gold, it is full-bodied, with ripely herbaceous, slightly honeyed flavours, showing very good complexity and depth. Ready; no rush.

SW $25 –V

Palliser Estate Martinborough Noble Riesling

Amber-hued, the 2015 vintage (★★★★★) has a fragrant, richly botrytised bouquet of apricots, figs and honey. It is a luscious, notably concentrated, honey-sweet wine with good acid spine, lovely harmony and powerful personality.

SW $30 V+

Pegasus Bay Aria Late Picked Riesling

From 'a great botrytis year', the 2014 vintage (★★★★☆) is a sweet but not super-sweet (86 grams/litre of residual sugar) wine from Waipara, in North Canterbury. Bright, light lemon/green, with a honeyed, complex bouquet, it is finely poised, with fresh, citrusy, peachy, honeyed flavours, concentrated and long. Drink now or cellar.

Vintage	14	13	12
WR	6	7	6
Drink	17-37	17-25	17-25

SW $39 (375ML) AV

Pegasus Bay Encore Noble Riesling

Grown at Waipara, in North Canterbury, this beauty is from hand-selected, botrytised bunches and berries, harvested late in the season in multiple passes through the vineyard. The 2016 vintage (★★★★★) is bright, light yellow/green, with a scented, honeyed bouquet. A very elegant, youthful wine, it has concentrated, citrusy, peachy, honeyed flavours, sweet (177 grams/litre of residual sugar), crisp, finely balanced and lasting. Drink now or cellar.

Vintage	16
WR	6
Drink	17-42

SW $40 (375ML) AV

Pegasus Bay Finale Noble Sémillon/Sauvignon Blanc Barrique Matured

The powerful 2014 vintage (★★★★★) is a striking Waipara, North Canterbury dessert wine, matured for two years in French oak barrels (50 per cent new). Gold/amber, it is full-bodied, with highly concentrated, peachy, honey-sweet flavours (186 grams/litre of residual sugar), fresh acidity, a rich, oily texture and excellent complexity. Drink now or cellar.

Vintage	14
WR	7
Drink	17-37

SW $40 (375ML) AV

Pegasus Bay Fortissimo Waipara Muscat   (★★★★★)

The very rare 2016 vintage (★★★★★) was estate-grown in North Canterbury. Modelled on Muscat Beaumes de Venise, a traditional fortified Muscat from the Rhône Valley, it is richly perfumed and full-bodied (17 per cent alcohol), with lovely, vibrant, pure lemon and orange flavours, deliciously sweet (142 grams/litre of residual sugar) and strong. Finely balanced, it's already delicious.

Vintage	16
WR	7
Drink	17-32

 SW $40 AV

Riverby Estate Marlborough Noble Riesling   ★★★★☆

Strongly botrytis-affected, the 2014 vintage (★★★★★) is liquid honey. Golden, with concentrated peach and apricot flavours, it has an oily texture, abundant sweetness (200 grams/litre of residual sugar) and good acid spine.

 SW $35 (375ML) –V

Rock Ferry Botrytised Riesling   ★★★★☆

Certified organic, the 2015 vintage (★★★★☆) was hand-picked at 33 brix in Marlborough and fermented with indigenous yeasts, partly in old oak casks. Light gold, with a hint of straw, it has an inviting, richly honeyed bouquet. Delicious from the start, it is full-bodied (13 per cent alcohol), lush and sweet (138 grams/litre of residual sugar), with peachy, honeyed flavours, gentle acidity, and excellent concentration and roundness.

 SW $35 (375ML) –V

Saint Clair Godfrey's Creek Reserve Noble Gewürztraminer   (★★★★)

Light gold, with a spicy, honeyed bouquet, the 2014 vintage (★★★★) is a single-vineyard Marlborough wine, hand-picked in the Wairau Valley. Delicious young, it is medium to full-bodied, in a vividly varietal style with abundant sweetness (161 grams/litre of residual sugar), gentle acidity and peachy, spicy flavours, rich and soft.

 SW $29 (375ML) AV

Saint Clair Godfrey's Creek Reserve Noble Pinot Gris   (★★★★)

The 2014 vintage (★★★★) is an amber-hued, single-vineyard Marlborough dessert wine, hand-picked and handled entirely in tanks. A strongly botrytised style, it is sweet but not super-sweet (97 grams/litre of residual sugar), with a nectareous bouquet, good acid spine and rich apricot and honey flavours.

SW $29 (375ML) AV

Seifried Winemaker's Collection Sweet Agnes Nelson Riesling ★★★★☆

Seifried's most celebrated wine. The 2016 vintage (★★★★★) is highly impressive, with a real sense of vigour and potential. Refined and tightly structured, it has concentrated peach and pear flavours, a hint of honey, abundant sweetness (175 grams/litre of residual sugar), and a crisp, lasting finish. The 2017 vintage (★★★★☆) is very tight and youthful. Bright, light yellow/green, it is fresh and vibrant, with rich, peachy, honeyed flavours, ample sweetness (153 grams/litre of residual sugar) and crisp, steely acidity. It needs time; open 2019+.

Vintage	17	16	15
WR	6	7	6
Drink	17-25	17-26	17-24

SW $25 (375ML) V+

Sileni Estate Selection Late Harvest Hawke's Bay Sémillon ★★★☆

The 2016 vintage (★★★★☆) is a weighty, 'Sauternes-style' wine, handled without oak. Bright yellow/green, it's already delicious, with rich, ripe, peachy, slightly spicy and honeyed flavours, sweet (76 grams/litre of residual sugar) and well-rounded. The 2015 vintage (★★★☆) is fragrant, with citrusy, peachy, slightly honeyed flavours, gentle sweetness (82 grams/litre of residual sugar), and bottle-aged notes adding complexity.

Vintage	16	15	14	13	12
WR	5	5	6	5	7
Drink	17-22	17-21	17-20	17-18	P

SW $20 (375ML) AV

Sileni Exceptional Vintage Marlborough Pourriture Noble ★★★★☆

The lovely 2014 vintage (★★★★★) is light gold, very honeyed and rich, with lush stone-fruit flavours, advanced sweetness (245 grams/litre of residual sugar), an oily texture and good acid spine. (Although not labelled by variety, it was made from botrytised Sauvignon Blanc grapes, picked in Marlborough at 46 brix.)

Vintage	14
WR	7
Drink	17-22

SW $32 (375ML) AV

Spy Valley Iced Marlborough Sauvignon Blanc ★★★★☆

The 2015 vintage (★★★★) was picked at 34 brix and fermented in tanks and barrels. It is fresh and sweet (157 grams/litre of residual sugar), with vibrant, citrusy, peachy flavours, balanced acidity, and a rich, harmonious finish. Delicious young.

Vintage	15	14
WR	6	6
Drink	17-20	17-19

SW $23 (375ML) V+

Staete Landt State of Love Marlborough Sweet Riesling (★★★★☆)

The 2014 vintage (★★★★☆) is amber-hued, with a honeyed bouquet. A richly botrytised style, it is sweet, with strong, peachy, honeyed flavours, good acid spine, an oily texture, lovely intensity, and plenty of drink-young appeal.

SW $29 (375ML) V+

Stonecroft Gimblett Gravels Hawke's Bay Late Harvest Gewürztraminer   (★★★★★)

The lovely 2016 vintage (★★★★★) is from two 'passes' through the vineyard, when 80 per cent of the grapes were botrytis-affected. Bright, light yellow/green, it is full-bodied and youthful, with ripe, peachy, spicy, gently honeyed flavours, in a sweet but not super-sweet style (80 grams/litre of residual sugar), with strong personality. It should be long-lived.

`SW $35 (375ML) AV`

Terra Sancta Late Harvest Bannockburn Central Otago Mysterious White   (★★★★★)

Currently delicious, the 2015 vintage (★★★★★) is a blend of Muscat, Gewürztraminer and Riesling, estate-grown at Bannockburn, harvested in June, and aged in old French oak barrels. Softly seductive, it is perfumed, with concentrated peach and orange flavours, a hint of honey, abundant sweetness (112 grams/litre of residual sugar), and lovely balance, roundness and richness.

Vintage	15
WR	6
Drink	18-28

`SW $37 (375ML) AV`

Tohu Raiha Reserve Limited Release Marlborough Noble Riesling   ★★★★☆

The 2014 vintage (★★★★☆) is an amber-hued, Awatere Valley wine, strongly botrytis-affected. It has a richly honeyed bouquet, moderate acidity, and vibrant peach, apricot and honey flavours, sweet (175 grams/litre of residual sugar) and concentrated.

`SW $28 (375ML) V+`

Toi Toi Late Harvest New Zealand Dessert Wine   (★★★)

The 2014 vintage (★★★) is a Waipara, North Canterbury Riesling. It is citrusy and sweet, with balanced acidity and slightly toasty, bottle-aged notes emerging. Ready.

`SW $18 AV`

Tupari Late Harvest Marlborough Riesling   (★★★★)

The 2014 vintage (★★★★) is a light gold, Awatere Valley wine with a honeyed bouquet and good intensity and drive on the palate. Fresh, sweet (120 grams/litre of residual sugar) and finely balanced, it has lemon, apricot, honey and marmalade flavours, showing a strong botrytis influence. Drink now or cellar.

`SW $29 (375ML) AV`

Urlar Noble Riesling   ★★★★☆

The 2016 vintage (★★★★☆) was estate-grown in the northern Wairarapa. Certified organic, it is delicious in its youth, with rich peach and slight apricot flavours, sweet (130 grams/litre of residual sugar), gently honeyed and very harmonious.

`SW $30 AV`

Valli Late Harvest Waitaki North Otago Riesling   ★★★★☆

The 2015 vintage (★★★★) is light-bodied (9 per cent alcohol) and still very youthful. Pale lemon/green, it has strong, gently sweet flavours, citrusy, appley, and woven with appetising acidity. Best drinking 2018+.

`SW $45 (750ML) V+`

Villa Maria Reserve Marlborough Noble Riesling Botrytis Selection   ★★★★★

One of New Zealand's top sweet wines on the show circuit. It is typically stunningly perfumed, weighty and oily, with intense, very sweet honey/citrus flavours and a lush, long finish. The grapes are grown mainly in the Fletcher Vineyard, in the centre of Marlborough's Wairau Plains, where trees create a 'humidity crib' around the vines and sprinklers along the vines' fruit zone create ideal conditions for the spread of noble rot. The 2015 vintage (★★★★★), hand-harvested in mid-May, is a pale gold wine, light (10 per cent alcohol), peachy, sweet (240 grams/litre of residual sugar), oily-textured and long, with instant appeal.

Vintage	15
WR	7
Drink	17-25

SW $37 (375ML) AV

Wairau River Botrytised Reserve Riesling   ★★★★☆

The 2016 vintage (★★★★☆) is a light gold, honeyed, low-alcohol (10 per cent) wine, with abundant sweetness (213 grams/litre of residual sugar). It has rich, vibrant, peachy flavours, hints of apricot and honey, and obvious potential; open 2018+.

Vintage	16	15
WR	6	6
Drink	17-20	17-18

SW $30 (375ML) AV

Whitehaven Marlborough Noble Riesling   ★★★★☆

The classy 2014 vintage (★★★★★) has a fragrant, honeyed bouquet. Concentrated and oily-textured, it is light-bodied (8.3 per cent alcohol), with a strong surge of rich peach and apricot flavours, sweet, crisp and very harmonious. Hard to resist.

SW $28 (375ML) V+

Wooing Tree Tickled Pink   ★★★★

The bright pink 2017 vintage (★★★★) was made from Pinot Noir, late-harvested at over 28 brix on 23 May in the Cromwell Basin, Central Otago. The fermentation, in tanks, was arrested when the wine had reached 10.5 per cent alcohol. Scented and light, it has vibrant strawberry and watermelon flavours, sweet (125 grams/litre of residual sugar), smooth and delicious from the start.

SW $38 (375ML) –V

Yealands Estate Single Vineyard Awatere Valley Noble Sauvignon Blanc   (★★★★)

The golden 2014 vintage (★★★★) was estate-grown at Seaview and handled without oak. From botrytised grapes, it is sweet (160 grams/litre of residual sugar), peachy and honeyed, very open and expressive, with fresh acidity, a slightly oily texture and loads of drink-young charm.

Vintage	14
WR	7
Drink	17-18

SW $23 (375ML) V+

Sparkling Wines

Fizz, bubbly, 'méthode traditionnelle', sparkling – whatever name you call it by (the word Champagne is reserved for the wines of that most famous of all wine regions), wine with bubbles in it is universally adored.

How good are Kiwi bubblies? Good enough for the industry to export over 120,000 cases in 2017, although that accounts for less than 1 per cent of New Zealand's overseas wine shipments.

The selection of New Zealand bubblies is not wide, but has been boosted in recent years by an influx of low-priced sparkling Sauvignon Blancs, sparkling Pinot Gris and the like. Most small wineries find the production of bottle-fermented sparkling wine too time-consuming and costly, and the domestic demand for premium bubbly is limited. The vast majority of purchases are under $15.

New Zealand's sparkling wines can be divided into two key classes. The bottom end of the market is dominated by extremely sweet, simple wines which acquire their bubbles by simply having carbon dioxide pumped into them. Upon pouring, the bubbles race out of the glass. A few other sparklings are made by the 'Charmat' method, which involves a secondary fermentation in a sealed tank.

At the middle and top end of the market are the much drier, bottle-fermented, 'méthode traditionnelle' (formerly 'méthode Champenoise', until the French got upset) labels, in which the wine undergoes its secondary, bubble-creating fermentation not in a tank but in the bottle, as in Champagne itself. Ultimately, the quality of any fine sparkling wine is a reflection both of the standard of its base wine and of its later period of maturation in the bottle in contact with its yeast lees. Only bottle-fermented sparkling wines possess the additional flavour richness and complexity derived from extended lees-aging.

Pinot Noir and Chardonnay, both varieties of key importance in Champagne, are also the foundation of New Zealand's top sparkling wines. Pinot Meunier, also extensively planted in Champagne, is still rare here, with 21 hectares of bearing vines in 2018.

Marlborough, with its cool nights preserving the grapes' fresh natural acidity, has emerged as the country's premier region for bottle-fermented sparkling wines (10 producers launched a promotional group, Méthode Marlborough, in 2013), but there are also some very stylish examples flowing from Central Otago.

The vast majority of sparkling wines are ready to drink when marketed, and need no extra maturation. A short spell in the cellar, however, can benefit the very best bottle-fermented sparklings.

Akarua Central Otago Brut NV ★★★★

This non-vintage wine (★★★★) is a blend of Pinot Noir (55–70 per cent) and Chardonnay (30–45 per cent), estate-grown at Bannockburn and disgorged after 18 months to two years on its yeast lees. The bouquet is typically fresh and yeasty; the palate is crisp and vigorous, with strong, lemony, appley, yeasty, slightly nutty flavours and a finely balanced finish.

MED/DRY $34 –V

Akarua Central Otago Rosé Brut NV ★★★★

This non-vintage wine (★★★★) is a pale pink, vivacious blend of Pinot Noir and Chardonnay, estate-grown at Bannockburn and disgorged after 18 months to two years on its yeast lees. It is typically crisp and dryish, with fresh, gentle strawberry and spice flavours, showing excellent complexity and length.

MED/DRY $37 –V

Akarua Central Otago Vintage Brut   ★★★★☆

The 2011 vintage (★★★★) is a pale, light and vivacious blend of Pinot Noir (61 per cent) and Chardonnay (39 per cent), estate-grown at Bannockburn and disgorged after a minimum of three years on its yeast lees. It has a yeasty bouquet and crisp, racy palate, showing good complexity.

MED/DRY $48 –V

Alpha Domus AD Cumulus Méthode Traditionnelle   (★★★★)

The 2015 vintage (★★★★) is a 'blanc de blancs' style, estate-grown and hand-picked in the Bridge Pa Triangle, Hawke's Bay. Partly barrel-fermented and closed with a crown seal, rather than a cork, it is light lemon/green, with a fragrant, citrusy, yeasty bouquet. Fresh, lemony, yeasty and dry (1 gram/litre of residual sugar), it is vivacious, with very good depth and complexity, and a smooth finish.

DRY $35 –V

Alpha Domus Beatrix Sparkling Rosé   (★★★★)

Well worth trying, this instantly attractive, non-vintage wine (★★★★), launched recently, is made from Merlot, estate-grown in the Bridge Pa Triangle, Hawke's Bay, and closed with a crown seal, rather than a cork. Pale pink, it is invitingly scented, crisp and vivacious, with dryish (5 grams/litre of residual sugar), strawberryish, slightly spicy and yeasty flavours, showing excellent delicacy and length.

MED/DRY $20 V+

Aotea Nelson Méthode Traditionnelle   (★★★★)

The non-vintage bubbly released in late 2016 (★★★★) was made from Chardonnay and Pinot Noir, harvested by hand in 2011 and disgorged after four years' maturation on its yeast lees. Scented and lively, it is citrusy and yeasty, with moderate acidity and a fully dry (1 gram/litre of residual sugar) but not austere, lingering finish. (From Seifried.)

DRY $39 –V

Aurum Blanc de Blancs Vintage   (★★★★☆)

Currently on sale, the 2008 vintage (★★★★☆) is a distinctive, bone-dry style from Central Otago Chardonnay, disgorged after six years of maturation on its yeast lees. Crisp and zesty, it has good intensity of lively, citrusy flavour, yeasty and toasty notes adding complexity, and excellent vigour and length.

Vintage	08
WR	6
Drink	17-20

DRY $45 –V

Brancott Estate New Zealand Brut Cuvée   ★★★☆

The non-vintage wine I tasted in late 2016 (★★★★) is a blend of Pinot Noir and Chardonnay. Pale straw, with a faintly pink hue, it is lively and smooth, with citrusy, peachy, biscuity flavours, showing good complexity, and a dryish, slightly creamy, very harmonious finish. Fine value.

MED/DRY $17 V+

Cecilia Brut NV   (★★★★)

The non-vintage wine I tasted in mid to late 2017 (★★★★) is a blend of Chardonnay (60 per cent) and Pinot Noir (40 per cent), grown in Marlborough and disgorged after three years of maturation on its yeast lees (the minimum for this label is 18 months). It's an elegant wine, with fresh, lively, citrusy flavours, showing considerable complexity, and a crisp, dryish finish. (From Allan Scott.)

MED/DRY $25 AV

Clos Henri La Chappelle Blanc de Noirs   (★★★★)

The non-vintage wine on sale in 2017 (★★★★) was made entirely from Pinot Noir, estate-grown in the Wairau Valley, Marlborough, bottle-fermented and disgorged after 'long' lees aging. Pale, crisp and lively, it's a dryish style (6 grams/litre of residual sugar), with citrusy, slightly appley, yeasty, lingering flavours and an invitingly scented bouquet.

MED/DRY $39 –V

Cloudy Bay Pelorus NV   ★★★★☆

Cloudy Bay's non-vintage Marlborough bubbly is a Chardonnay-dominant style, with 30 per cent Pinot Noir, grown in the Wairau Valley and hand-picked. The base wines are fermented and aged in tanks, large oak vats and small French oak barrels, and the bottle-fermented blend is matured for at least two years on its yeast lees, before it is disgorged. Refined, tightly structured and elegant, it typically has strong, citrusy, peachy, yeasty flavours, showing excellent depth and harmony. The sample I tasted in late 2017 (★★★★★) has a rich, citrusy, yeasty bouquet. A very harmonious, instantly attractive wine, it is fresh and lively, with strong, citrusy, yeasty flavours, showing excellent vigour, complexity and length.

MED/DRY $37 AV

Cloudy Bay Pelorus Rosé   (★★★★☆)

The non-vintage wine on sale in late 2017 (★★★★☆) is a blend of Pinot Noir (mostly) and Chardonnay, hand-picked in the Wairau Valley and disgorged after at least two years maturing on its yeast lees. Pink/pale red, it is mouthfilling, complex and smooth, with crisp, lively, strawberry and spice flavours and a dryish, long finish.

MED/DRY $40 –V

Daniel Le Brun Méthode Traditionnelle Brut NV   ★★★★☆

The Daniel Le Brun brand is owned by the beer giant Lion – which owns Wither Hills. A non-vintage blend of Chardonnay and Pinot Noir, grown in Marlborough, it is disgorged after at least two years on its yeast lees. Top batches are highly impressive – tight and rich, with lovely vibrancy and depth of citrusy, appley, peachy flavours, yeasty, bready notes adding real complexity, and a finely balanced, lasting finish.

MED/DRY $29 V+

De La Terre Blanc de Blancs Hawke's Bay Méthode Traditionnelle   (★★★★☆)

The light lemon/green 2014 vintage (★★★★☆), estate-grown at Havelock North, is an elegant, punchy wine, with crisp, incisive, lemony, yeasty flavours, dryish and long.

MED/DRY $55 –V

De La Terre Cuvée 11 Hawke's Bay Méthode Traditionnelle   (★★★★☆)

The stylish 2015 vintage (★★★★☆) was estate-grown at Havelock North. Invitingly scented and vivacious, it is appetisingly crisp, with citrusy, gently yeasty flavours, showing excellent intensity, good complexity and a lasting finish.

MED/DRY $40 –V

Deutz Marlborough Cuvée Blanc de Blancs   ★★★★★

New Zealand's most awarded bubbly on the show circuit. This Chardonnay-predominant blend is hand-harvested on the south side of the Wairau Valley, at Renwick Estate and in the Brancott Vineyard, and matured for up to three years on its yeast lees. It is typically a very classy wine with delicate, piercing, lemony, appley flavours, well-integrated yeastiness and a slightly creamy finish. The very elegant 2013 vintage (★★★★★) has a rich, citrusy, yeasty bouquet, leading into an intense, vibrant, tightly structured wine, yeasty, complex and long.

MED/DRY $33 V+

Deutz Marlborough Cuvée Brut NV   ★★★★

The marriage of Pernod Ricard NZ's fruit at Marlborough with the Champagne house of Deutz's 150 years of experience created an instant winner. Bottled-fermented and matured on its yeast lees for two to three years, this non-vintage wine has evolved over the past decade into a less overtly fruity, more delicate and flinty style. The Pinot Noir grapes are drawn principally from Kaituna Estate, on the north side of the Wairau Valley; the Chardonnay comes mostly from Renwick Estate, in the middle of the valley. Before being bottled, the base wine is lees-aged for up to three months and given a full malolactic fermentation. Reserve wines, a year or two older than the rest, are added to each batch, contributing consistency and complexity to the final blend. The wine I tasted in November 2016 (★★★★) was highly fragrant and vivacious, crisp and refreshing, with fresh, citrusy, gently yeasty flavours, showing excellent delicacy and length.

MED/DRY $27 AV

Deutz Marlborough Prestige Cuvée   ★★★★★

This is typically a very classy, Chardonnay-predominant style, disgorged after three years on its yeast lees. Light lemon/green, the lovely 2012 vintage (★★★★★) is finely scented, very elegant and rich, with intense, vibrant, citrusy, yeasty flavours.

MED/DRY $33 V+

Deutz Marlborough Cuvée Rosé   ★★★★

The 2014 vintage (★★★★), made predominantly from Pinot Noir, is pink-hued, with fresh, lively, berryish aromas and flavours, good delicacy and an off-dry, lingering finish.

MED/DRY $33 –V

Elstree Marlborough Cuveé Brut ★★★★

Still on sale, the 2010 vintage (★★★★☆) was made from hand-picked Chardonnay and Pinot Noir, and disgorged after three years on its yeast lees. Pale lemon/green, it is a drier style than most sparklings (5 grams/litre of residual sugar), lemon-scented, punchy and vivacious, with strong citrusy, toasty flavours, tight and lively.

Vintage	10	
WR	7	
Drink	P	MED/DRY $38 –V

En Rose ★★★★☆

This Martinborough sparkling is based entirely on Pinot Noir. The 2013 vintage (★★★★☆) is very pale pink, crisp, tight and dry (4 grams/litre of residual sugar), with strong peach, strawberry and spice flavours, showing good complexity, and a long finish. (From Margrain.)

Vintage	13	
WR	7	DRY $45 –V
Drink	17-20	

Forrest Brigid Méthode Traditionnelle Vintage Marlborough Brut (★★★★☆)

Currently on sale, the 2010 vintage (★★★★☆) is a blend of Chardonnay (70 per cent) and Pinot Noir (30 per cent), disgorged after three years maturing on its yeast lees. Light lemon/green, it has a complex, lively, citrusy, yeasty bouquet, leading into a tight, elegant, unusually dry wine (2 grams/litre of residual sugar), with lemony, slightly appley flavours, showing excellent intensity, vigour and complexity.

DRY $45 –V

Gibbston Valley Blanc de Blancs Méthode Traditionnelle (★★★★★)

Currently on sale, the classy 2011 vintage (★★★★★) was made from a base wine of barrel-fermented Central Otago Chardonnay. Bottle-fermented, it was matured on its yeast lees for four and a half years, then finally disgorged in September 2016. Made in an 'extra brut' style (6 grams/litre of residual sugar), it is very elegant, with crisp, citrusy, yeasty, slightly toasty flavours, showing notable delicacy, complexity and length.

MED/DRY $120 –V

Gibbston Valley Méthode Traditionnelle NV Extra Brut ★★★★★

The wine on sale in 2017 (★★★★★), from grapes hand-picked in Central Otago, was disgorged in August 2016, after 29 months on its yeast lees. Pale straw, with a fragrant, yeasty bouquet, it is complex and vivacious, with penetrating, crisp, lemony, appley flavours, yeasty and nutty, and a dryish (6 grams/litre of residual sugar), long finish. Showing lots of personality, it's well worth discovering.

MED/DRY $45 AV

Gibbston Valley Rosé Méthode Traditionnelle   (★★★★★)

Disgorged in September 2016, the distinctive 2011 vintage (★★★★★) currently on sale was made from barrel-fermented base wine, bottle-fermented and matured on its yeast lees for four and a half years. Pink-hued, with a hint of orange, it is a highly complex wine, with peach, strawberry and spice flavours, showing lovely depth, and a long, yeasty, dry (4 grams/litre of residual sugar), very harmonious finish. It's ready to roll.

DRY $120 –V

Giesen Classic Cuvée   (★★★)

The fresh, crisp and lively 2014 vintage (★★★) was made from Chardonnay, grown in the Wairau Valley, Marlborough. It's a stimulating apéritif, not complex, but citrusy and slightly sweet (16 grams/litre of residual sugar), in a very attractive, refreshing style.

MED $20 –V

Gold Digger Frizzante Naturally Sparkling Pinot Gris   (★★★☆)

Ensconced in a beer bottle with a crown seal, this non-vintage wine (★★★☆) is from Maori Point Vineyard, at Tarras, in Central Otago. Promoted as a 'prosecco style', it was made from grapes grown in 2016, tank-fermented, and bottled at Wanaka Beer Works. Pale, it is gently sparkling, light and lively, with citrusy, appley, slightly spicy and gingery flavours, and a slightly sweet (14 grams/litre of residual sugar), crisp finish. Ready to roll.

MED/DRY $11 (330ML) AV

Haha Brut Cuvée   (★★★)

The non-vintage (★★★) launched in 2016 was blended from Chardonnay and Pinot Noir. Pale lemon/green, it is fresh and lively, with good depth of citrusy, slightly peachy flavours, showing a touch of complexity, and a crisp, dryish (6.7 grams/litre of residual sugar) finish.

MED/DRY $22 –V

Hans Herzog Cuvée Thérèse Rosé Méthode Traditionnelle   ★★★★☆

This highly distinctive Marlborough wine is made occasionally. The 2011 vintage (★★★★) is a blend of Pinot Noir (80 per cent) and Chardonnay (20 per cent). The base wines were barrel-aged for eight months and then blended, before the wine was bottled for its lengthy maturation on yeast lees. It has a light red hue and cherryish, slightly nutty flavours, crisp and dry (4 grams/litre of residual sugar), with plenty of yeast-derived complexity. A distinctive style, it's a good food wine. Certified organic.

DRY $64 –V

Vintage	11
WR	7
Drink	17-18

Huia Blanc de Blancs   (★★★★★)

Certified organic, the classy 2010 vintage (★★★★★) was made from barrel-fermented Marlborough Chardonnay, disgorged after spending over five years maturing on its yeast lees. Very vigorous and yeasty, it is crisp and intense, with piercing, citrusy, complex flavours, tangy, dryish (6 grams/litre of residual sugar) and long.

MED/DRY $40 AV

Hunter's Miru Miru NV ★★★★

'Miru Miru' means 'Bubbles'. This wine is disgorged after a minimum of 18 months on its yeast lees (earlier than its Reserve stablemate, below), has a lower Pinot Noir content and a crisper finish. The non-vintage wine I tasted in late 2017 (★★★★☆) is a blend of Chardonnay, Pinot Noir and Pinot Meunier. Fragrant, it is vivacious, with rich, citrusy, yeasty flavours, showing very good complexity, and a dryish (7.5 grams/litre of residual sugar) finish.

 MED/DRY $29 AV

Hunter's Miru Miru Reserve ★★★★☆

This has long been one of Marlborough's best sparklings, full and lively, with loads of citrusy, yeasty, nutty flavour and a creamy, long finish. It is matured on its yeast lees for an average of three and a half years. The 2013 vintage (★★★★★) is a blend of Pinot Noir, Chardonnay and Pinot Meunier. It's a very elegant and tight-knit wine, with crisp, citrusy, yeasty flavours, a dry impression (6 grams/litre of residual sugar), and a very long, harmonious finish. Tasted in late 2017, the intense 2011 vintage (★★★★★) was at the peak of its powers.

 MED/DRY $50 –V

Hunter's Miru Miru Rosé NV (★★★★★)

The very classy, non-vintage wine currently on sale (★★★★★) is mostly from 2011 base wine, blended from Pinot Noir (55 per cent), Chardonnay (41 per cent) and Pinot Meunier (4 per cent), and was disgorged after three years on its yeast lees. Pink/pale orange, it is highly scented, vivacious, complex and smooth, with strawberry, peach and yeast flavours, and a long, dryish (7.5 grams/litre of residual sugar), very finely balanced finish. Well worth trying.

 MED/DRY $50 AV

Johanneshof Cellars Blanc de Blancs ★★★★☆

Released after a minimum of five years' maturation on its yeast lees, this wine, still on sale, is made from hand-picked, barrel-fermented Marlborough Chardonnay and Pinot Blanc. The 2008 vintage (★★★★) is a vivacious wine, crisp and lively, with citrusy, slightly appley, biscuity and nutty flavours, showing excellent depth, and a dryish, very smooth finish.

 MED/DRY $38 –V

Joiy (★★★)

This freshly scented, gently sparkling wine is made from Riesling and packaged in 250-ml bottles. The non-vintage wine I tasted in mid-2016 (★★★) was light (10 per cent alcohol) and lively, with strong, lemony, appley flavours. It offers crisp, slightly sweet, very easy drinking.

 MED $6 AV

Junction Persistence (★★★☆)

Made from Riesling, Flora and Gewürztraminer, the 2014 vintage (★★★☆) was grown in Central Hawke's Bay, barrel-fermented and oak-aged for nine months. It's a vivacious wine, fresh and lively, with crisp, dryish, citrusy, slightly limey and spicy flavours.

 MED/DRY $22 AV

June Nelson Méthode Traditionnelle   (★★★☆)

From Kaimira Estate, the 2009 vintage (★★★☆) is still on sale. A pale straw blend of Chardonnay (78 per cent) and Pinot Noir (22 per cent), it was grown at Brightwater and disgorged after six years aging on its yeast lees. The bouquet is citrusy; the palate is tightly structured, crisp and lemony, with considerable complexity and a dryish (6 grams/litre of residual sugar), smooth finish.

MED/DRY $39 –V

La Michelle   ★★★★

From Margrain, the 2013 vintage (★★★★) is a bottle-fermented bubbly, blended from Pinot Noir (66 per cent) and Chardonnay (34 per cent), grown in Martinborough and made in an unusually dry (4 grams/litre of residual sugar) but not austere style. Disgorged after 30 months on its yeast lees, it is pale, fresh and lively, with vibrant, citrusy, moderately yeasty flavours, in a youthful, very elegant style, showing good intensity.

DRY $45 –V

Vintage	13
WR	7
Drink	17-21

Leveret IQ 3 Méthode Traditionnelle   ★★★☆

The non-vintage wine (★★★) I tasted in late 2017 was made from Chardonnay grapes, grown in Hawke's Bay, and disgorged after a minimum of three years on its yeast lees. Bright, light yellow/green, it is moderately complex, with citrusy, slightly buttery and toasty flavours, and a dryish (7 grams/litre of residual sugar), smooth finish.

MED/DRY $25 –V

Leveret IQ Premium Brut NV   ★★★

This bottle-fermented Hawke's Bay blend of Pinot Noir, Chardonnay and Pinot Meunier is disgorged after a minimum of 18 months on its yeast lees. The wine I tasted in 2017 (★★★☆) is pale straw, fresh, crisp and lively, with a steady bead and very good depth of citrusy, peachy, gently yeasty and toasty flavours, showing good complexity and harmony.

MED/DRY $23 –V

Leveret IQ7 Méthode Traditionnelle   (★★★★)

The distinctive, non-vintage wine I tasted in late 2017 (★★★★) is a blend of Pinot Noir and Pinot Meunier, grown in Hawke's Bay and disgorged after seven years on its yeast lees. Straw-hued, with a fragrant, yeasty bouquet, it shows good complexity, with strong, peachy, toasty, very yeasty flavours, crisp, dryish (7 grams/litre of residual sugar) and lingering. Ready.

MED/DRY $30 –V

Leveret Mimi Méthode Traditionnelle   (★★★)

Skilfully balanced for easy drinking, the non-vintage wine on sale in 2017 (★★★) was disgorged after at least nine months on its yeast lees. Bright, light yellow, it is a slightly sweet style (16 grams/litre of residual sugar), with plenty of citrusy, peachy, crisp and lively flavour.

MED $17 AV

Leveret Mimi Méthode Traditionnelle Pink   (★★★☆)

Bargain-priced, the non-vintage wine on sale in 2017 (★★★☆) is a pink/pale red, lively wine, crisp and gently yeasty. It has fresh strawberry and spice flavours, a hint of apricot, gentle sweetness (14 grams/litre of residual sugar), and a finely balanced finish. Very easy to enjoy.

MED/DRY $17 V+

Lindauer Brut Cuvée NV   ★★★

Given its track record of very good quality, low price and huge volumes (batch variation is inevitable), this non-vintage bubbly has been a miracle of modern winemaking. Made from Pinot Noir and Chardonnay, grown in Gisborne and Hawke's Bay, it is matured for a year on its yeast lees, and blended with some reserve wine from past vintages. Fractionally sweet (12 grams/litre of residual sugar), it typically has good vigour and depth in a refined style, crisp and finely balanced, with lively, lemony, slightly nutty and yeasty flavours.

MED/DRY $10 V+

Lindauer Enlighten Moscato Rosé   (★★★☆)

'Enlighten' is – you guessed it – a range of light wines, and this charmer is just 8.5 per cent alcohol. Based on Muscat grapes, grown in Gisborne, it was blended with a splash of Pinotage (hence its enticing, pale pink hue). Deliciously light and lively, it is unabashedly sweet (60 grams/litre of residual sugar), but very crisp, fruity and well-balanced, in a simple but vivacious style that offers plenty of pleasure.

SW $13 V+

Lindauer Enlighten Sauvignon Blanc   (★★)

The non-vintage wine (★★) I tasted in 2016 was light (8.5 per cent alcohol), with herbaceous aromas and flavours, fresh and simple.

MED/DRY $13 –V

Lindauer Special Reserve Brut Cuveé   ★★★★

The non-vintage wine I tasted in 2016 (★★★★) is a blend of Pinot Noir (70 per cent) and Chardonnay (30 per cent), grown in Gisborne and Hawke's Bay. Disgorged after two years maturing on its yeast lees, with a portion of reserve wine added from previous vintages, it is pale pink, with a steady bead. Smooth, with strawberryish, yeasty flavours, fresh and crisp, it shows good complexity, with a finely balanced, lengthy finish. Great value on special at around $13.

MED/DRY $20 V+

Loveblock Marlborough Moscato Brut   (★★★☆)

Pale yellow, with a perfumed bouquet, the 2014 vintage (★★★☆) is an easy-drinking wine, estate-grown in the lower Awatere Valley. Crisp and lively, it has fresh peach and orange-like flavours, with a hint of Turkish delight and a dryish (7 grams/litre of residual sugar) finish.

MED/DRY $25 –V

Man O' War Tulia ★★★☆

Still on sale, the 2012 vintage (★★★☆) was made from Waiheke Island Chardonnay grapes, hand-harvested. The base wine was partly barrel-fermented and all barrel-aged, followed by secondary fermentation in the bottle and nine months' lees-aging. Tight and elegant, it is bone-dry, with vibrant, citrusy, appley flavours, showing moderate complexity, and a well-balanced, lengthy finish.

DRY $45 –V

Mansfield & Marsh Méthode Traditionnelle (★★★)

The very easy-drinking, non-vintage wine I tasted in late 2017 (★★★) was disgorged after at least nine months on its yeast lees. Fresh and lively, it is citrusy and gently yeasty, with a touch of complexity and a slightly sweet (8 grams/litre of residual sugar) finish.

MED/DRY $17 AV

Matahiwi Estate Hawke's Bay Blanc de Blancs (★★★)

The non-vintage wine (★★★) currently on sale was made from Chardonnay. Crisp and lively, it has citrusy, moderately yeasty flavours, with a slightly buttery finish.

MED/DRY $22 –V

Matahiwi Estate Wairarapa Cuvée (★★★)

This non-vintage wine is made from Pinot Gris. Showing clear-cut varietal characters, it has fresh lemon, pear and apple aromas and flavours, in a refreshing, crisp and vivacious style.

MED/DRY $22 –V

Nautilus Cuvée Marlborough ★★★★★

Recent releases of this non-vintage, bottle-fermented sparkling have generally revealed an intensity and refinement that positions the label among the finest in the country. Made with Pinot Noir (mostly) and Chardonnay, it is blended with older, reserve stocks held in old oak barriques and disgorged after a minimum of three years aging on its yeast lees. Lean and crisp, piercing and long, it's a beautifully tight, vivacious and refined wine, its Marlborough fruit characters enriched with intense, bready aromas and flavours. The sample I tasted in September 2017 (★★★★☆) was – as the back label indicates helpfully – bottled in September 2013 and disgorged in May 2017. A blend of Pinot Noir (71 per cent) and Chardonnay (29 per cent), it was blended with 7 per cent reserve stocks. Light lemon/green, it is very fresh and elegant, with vibrant, citrusy, slightly appley and nutty flavours, showing good intensity, and a dryish (6 grams/litre of residual sugar), crisp, tight-knit finish.

MED/DRY $39 AV

Nautilus Cuvée Marlborough Vintage Rosé ★★★★☆

The delicious 2014 vintage (★★★★★), made entirely from Pinot Noir, was bottle-fermented and disgorged after two years on its yeast lees in May 2017. Pink/pale orange, it is a rich, dryish style (6 grams/litre of residual sugar), with penetrating, strawberryish, yeasty flavours, a hint of apricots, and excellent freshness, complexity and harmony.

MED/DRY $49 –V

Nikau Point Gold Méthode Traditionnelle (★★★☆)

The attractive, non-vintage wine (★★★☆) I tasted in late 2017 is a blend of Chardonnay, Pinot Noir and Pinot Meunier. Bright yellow, it is lively and yeasty, with fresh, citrusy, slightly peachy flavours, showing a touch of complexity, and a slightly sweet (12 grams/litre of residual sugar), crisp, finely balanced finish. Good value.

MED/DRY $17 V+

No 1 Cuvée Marlborough Méthode Traditionnelle ★★★★☆

This is a non-vintage 'blanc de blancs', based entirely on Marlborough Chardonnay. Made by Daniel Le Brun (in his family company) and matured for two years on its yeast lees, it is typically a stylish wine, fresh-scented, with tight-knit, delicate flavours, citrusy, yeasty and biscuity, and a crisp, dryish finish. The wine I tasted in mid-2017 (★★★★☆) is punchy, crisp, citrusy and yeasty, with excellent vigour and length.

MED/DRY $40 –V

No 1 Cuvée Virginie ★★★★★

Currently on sale, the 2009 vintage (★★★★★) is very classy. A Marlborough blend of Chardonnay (80 per cent) and Pinot Noir (20 per cent), it was disgorged after more than four years on its yeast lees. Bright yellow, with an inviting, complex bouquet, it has vibrant, citrusy, yeasty flavours, showing notable intensity, vigour and harmony. A lovely mouthful.

MED/DRY $95 –V

No 1 Family Estate Assemblé (★★★★☆)

The non-vintage Marlborough wine I tasted in mid-2017 (★★★★☆) was disgorged after at least 18 months on its yeast lees. Very crisp and lively, it is tightly structured, with strong, vibrant, peachy, yeasty flavours, firm acidity and a lasting finish.

MED/DRY $33 AV

No 1 Rosé (★★★★☆)

The non-vintage wine I tasted in mid-2017 (★★★★☆) was made from Pinot Noir, estate-grown at Rapaura, in Marlborough. Disgorged after 20 months on its yeast lees, it is a light pink/orange, elegant, tightly structured wine, with strong, lively, plummy, yeasty flavours and a dryish, long finish.

MED/DRY $40 –V

Omaha Bay Vineyard FAB Matakana Sparkling Flora ★★☆

'FAB' stands for Flora Avec Bulles (Flora With Bubbles). An enjoyable summer sipper, the 2014 vintage (★★★) is a slightly sweet (15 grams/litre of residual sugar) style with fresh, vibrant fruit flavours to the fore, showing good harmony and depth.

MED $27 –V

Osawa Prestige Collection Méthode Traditionnelle NV   (★★★★)

This is a fragrant, complex Hawke's Bay blend of equal portions of Chardonnay and Pinot Noir, grown at Maraekakaho. Attractively scented, it has crisp, lively, citrusy, yeasty, slightly toasty flavours, showing good intensity.

MED/DRY $60 –V

Oyster Bay Sparkling Cuvée Brut   ★★★

Chardonnay-based, this Hawke's Bay wine is vivacious, with fresh, citrusy fruit flavours to the fore, crisp and slightly sweet. Made by the 'Charmat' method (where the secondary, bubble-inducing fermentation occurs in tanks, rather than the individual bottles), it is typically attractive, although not complex. The wine I tasted in late 2017 (★★★) has strong, crisp, lemony, slightly yeasty flavours.

MED/DRY $22 –V

Oyster Bay Sparkling Cuvée Rosé   ★★★☆

The non-vintage wine I tasted in late 2017 (★★★☆) was blended from Hawke's Bay Chardonnay (80 per cent) and Marlborough Pinot Noir (20 per cent). A lively, generous, dryish wine, it has peach, strawberry and spice flavours, fresh acidity and a finely balanced, smooth finish.

MED/DRY $22 AV

Palliser Estate Martinborough Méthode Traditionnelle   ★★★★☆

This is the sub-region's finest sparkling (although very few are produced). The 2013 vintage (★★★★☆), grown at three sites, is a blend of Chardonnay (56 per cent) and Pinot Noir (44 per cent), disgorged in December 2016 after maturing for 30 months on its yeast lees. Pale lemon/green, it is vivacious, with strong, vibrant, citrusy, gently yeasty and biscuity flavours, considerable complexity, balanced acidity and a dryish (7.6 grams/litre of residual sugar), very harmonious finish. An elegant, youthful wine, it should develop very gracefully.

MED/DRY $51 –V

Peregrine Central Otago Méthode Traditionnelle N/V   (★★★★☆)

Certified organic, the classy wine on sale in late 2017 (★★★★☆) is a blend of Pinot Noir and Chardonnay, estate-grown at Gibbston. Pale lemon/green, it is vivacious, with strong, citrusy, yeasty, slightly biscuity and buttery flavours, showing very good complexity, depth and harmony.

MED/DRY $50 –V

Peter Yealands Sparkling Marlborough Pinot Gris Blush   ★★★

This non-vintage wine is typically pink, fresh and lively, with good depth of peachy, slightly spicy flavours, a sliver of sweetness and balanced acidity. It's an attractive, very easy-drinking style.

MED/DRY $17 AV

Peter Yealands Sparkling Marlborough Sauvignon Blanc   ★★☆

This non-vintage wine typically has strongly herbaceous aromas, leading into a slightly sweet wine with fresh, crisp, direct, distinctly green-edged flavours.

MED/DRY $17 –V

Quartz Reef Méthode Traditionnelle [Vintage]   ★★★★★

Top vintages are outstanding, showing great vigour and complexity in a Champagne-like style, intense and highly refined. The 2010 (★★★★★) is a blend of Chardonnay (93 per cent) and Pinot Noir (7 per cent), estate-grown and hand-picked at Bendigo, in Central Otago, and disgorged after maturing for nearly four years on its yeast lees. Light straw, it is elegant and racy, with intense, citrusy, slightly peachy and nutty flavours that float very harmoniously to a lively, lasting finish.

Vintage	12
WR	7
Drink	17-19

MED/DRY $45 AV

Quartz Reef Méthode Traditionnelle Brut NV   ★★★★☆

This increasingly Champagne-like, non-vintage bubbly is estate-grown at Bendigo, in Central Otago, and lees-aged for at least two years. The batches vary in their varietal composition, but the release I tasted in September 2016 (★★★★) is a blend of Pinot Noir (64 per cent) and Chardonnay (36 per cent), disgorged from autumn 2016 onwards. Very faintly pink, with a steady bead, it floats smoothly across the palate, with lively, lemony, slightly appley flavours, and yeasty, biscuity notes adding complexity. Certified biodynamic.

MED/DRY $34 AV

Quartz Reef Méthode Traditionnelle Rosé   ★★★★☆

The lively, non-vintage wine (★★★★☆) I tasted in 2016 was estate-grown at Bendigo, in Central Otago. Made entirely from Pinot Noir and disgorged after at least two years on its yeast lees, it is bright, pale pink, vivacious and smooth, with dryish, strawberryish, slightly spicy, yeasty flavours, showing excellent complexity. Certified biodynamic.

MED/DRY $37 –V

Rock Ferry Brut NV   (★★★★★)

Full of personality, the generous, non-vintage (★★★★★) released in 2016 is a blend of Marlborough and Central Otago base wines, fermented initially in old oak and stainless steel barrels. Disgorged after three and a half years on its yeast lees, it is pale straw, with a fine, persistent bead. The bouquet is fragrant, yeasty and biscuity; the palate is rich, lively and appetisingly crisp, with strong, peachy, citrusy, biscuity, yeasty flavours, showing excellent complexity and richness, and a dryish (6 grams/litre of residual sugar), finely balanced finish.

MED/DRY $35 AV

Saint Clair Dawn

The vivacious 2012 vintage (★★★★★), released in 2016, is a top-flight debut. Full of personality, it is a blend of Marlborough Pinot Noir and Chardonnay, hand-picked, partly barrel-fermented, and disgorged after nearly three years aging on its yeast lees. Pale straw, it is fragrant, with fresh, crisp, toasty, yeasty flavours, showing excellent intensity and complexity, and a finely poised, dryish (6.5 grams/litre of residual sugar), lasting finish.

MED/DRY $45 AV

Saint Clair Vicar's Choice Marlborough Sauvignon Blanc Bubbles   ★★★

The 2016 vintage (★★★) is a fresh, crisp, lively, carbonated sparkling, from grapes grown in the Wairau Valley and Ure Valley. Aromatic and vivacious, with ripely herbaceous flavours, it tastes just like you would expect – Sauvignon Blanc with bubbles.

MED/DRY $19 AV

Satyr Sparkling Sauvignon Blanc

From Sileni, the non-vintage wine (★★☆) I tasted in late 2016 was grown in Hawke's Bay. Fresh and punchy, it has ripely herbaceous flavours, crisp, dryish (7.5 grams/litre of residual sugar) and direct.

MED/DRY $20 –V

Seresin Moana Blanc Marlborough Méthode Traditionnelle

The highly distinctive 2009 vintage (★★★★☆) is a bone-dry blend of Pinot Noir (59 per cent) and Chardonnay (41 per cent). Disgorged after three years on its yeast lees, it has a scented, lemony, yeasty, complex bouquet. Tightly structured, it is lively, with strong, crisp, citrusy, slightly toasty flavours, showing good complexity. Certified organic.

DRY $45 –V

Seresin Moana Rosé Marlborough Méthode Traditionnelle

Certified organic, the 2009 vintage (★★★★★) is a distinctive blend of Pinot Noir (62 per cent) and Chardonnay (38 per cent), oak-aged for two months and disgorged after three years on its yeast lees. Pale orange, it is crisp and dry (5.4 grams/litre of residual sugar), with rich, mature flavours of strawberries, oranges and spices, intense, yeasty and complex. Showing strong personality, it is an unusually complex, dry and persistent wine, worth discovering.

MED/DRY $45 AV

Sileni Art Deco Sparkling   ★★★

The non-vintage bubbly (★★★) released in early 2017 is a sparking Pinot Gris. Designed as a celebration of the city of Napier's Art Deco buildings, it is crisp and lively, with good depth of citrus-fruit and pear flavours, offering dryish, easy drinking.

MED/DRY $25 –V

Sileni Sparkling Cuvée Brut (★★★)

The non-vintage wine (★★★) I tasted in 2016 was grown in Hawke's Bay. Light lemon/green, it is lively and smooth, offering vibrantly fruity and fresh, very easy, slightly sweet (6 grams/litre of residual sugar) drinking.

MED/DRY $20 –V

Sileni Sparkling Cuvée Pinot Gris (★★★)

The easy-drinking, non-vintage wine (★★★) released in 2016 was grown in Hawke's Bay, briefly lees-aged and carbonated. Light lemon/green, it tastes like Pinot Gris with bubbles, in a simple but very lively style, with strong, peachy, slightly spicy flavours and a crisp, dryish (6.5 grams/litre of residual sugar) finish.

MED/DRY $19 AV

Sileni Sparkling Cuvée Rosé ★★☆

The non-vintage wine I tasted in early 2017 (★★★) is a carbonated Hawke's Bay bubbly, Chardonnay-based (90 per cent), with a splash of Merlot (10 per cent). Pink/pale red, it is crisp and lively, with berryish, slightly yeasty flavours, smooth and dryish (5.6 grams/litre of residual sugar).

MED/DRY $20 –V

Soljans Fusion Sparkling Muscat ★★★★☆

This 'Asti-style' bubbly has a long, proud history. The wine I tasted in late 2017 (★★★★☆), a multi-region blend, is highly perfumed, light-bodied and vivacious, with fresh, pure Muscat flavours of lemons and oranges, in a soft, sweetly seductive style. A great buy.

SW $15 V+

Soljans Legacy Méthode Traditionnelle ★★★★

Currently on sale, the 2012 vintage (★★★★☆) is a multi-region blend of Pinot Noir and Chardonnay. Bright lemon/green, it is rich, yeasty and smooth, with peachy, slightly toasty flavours, balanced acidity, and excellent vigour, complexity and harmony. Ready.

MED/DRY $29 AV

Spy Valley Echelon Marlborough Méthode Traditionnelle ★★★★

The 2011 vintage (★★★★☆) is an elegant blend of Pinot Noir (59 per cent) and Chardonnay (41 per cent), aged in old oak casks for a year before bottling and then disgorged after three and a half years maturing on its yeast lees. Tightly structured, it is very crisp and lively, with good intensity of citrusy, yeasty, slightly nutty flavours, unusually dry (2.8 grams/litre of residual sugar) and persistent.

Vintage	11	10	09	08
WR	5	7	7	6
Drink	17-20	P	P	P

DRY $37 –V

Thomas Waiheke Island Blanc De Gris

The delicious, although not complex, 2015 vintage (★★★★) is an estate-grown, hand-picked blend of Pinot Gris (83 per cent) and Flora (17 per cent). Bottled in early 2017, it was aged on its fine yeast lees in tanks for 18 months, then carbonated. Pale, with inviting, fresh, slightly appley aromas, it is crisp and very lively, with gentle sweetness (16 grams/litre of residual sugar), appetising acidity, and instant appeal.

MED $38 –V

Tohu Rewa Marlborough Blanc de Blancs

The 2013 vintage (★★★★) is a fresh, elegant sparkling, from Chardonnay grapes grown at Rapaura. Disgorged after 20 months on its yeast lees, it is refined and poised, with citrusy, appley, dry (4 grams/litre of residual sugar) flavours, slightly yeasty and nutty, and very good delicacy and length.

DRY $34 –V

Toi Toi Marlborough Sparkling Sauvignon Blanc

The non-vintage wine (★★☆) I tasted in 2016 was pale lemon/green, crisp and lively, in an aromatic, clearly herbaceous style with a sliver of sweetness and fresh, direct flavours.

MED/DRY $17 –V

Toi Toi New Zealand Sparkling Rosé

★★★

The non-vintage wine (★★★) I tasted in 2016 was bright pink/red, very fresh, crisp and lively, with berry and plum flavours, off-dry and vivacious.

MED $17 AV

Twin Islands Chardonnay/Pinot Noir Brut NV

'A great bottle to be seen with in some of the classiest bars and restaurants', Nautilus's sparkling is a bottle-fermented, non-vintage style. The batch I tasted in 2017 (★★★★) is a pale lemon/green, moderately complex wine, with crisp, citrusy, appley, dryish (10 grams/litre of residual sugar) flavours, showing very good vigour and intensity.

MED/DRY $25 AV

Rosé Wines

The number of rosé labels on the market has exploded recently, as drinkers discover that rosé is not an inherently inferior lolly water, but a worthwhile and delicious wine style in its own right. New Zealand rosé is even finding offshore markets and collecting overseas awards.

In Europe many pink or copper-coloured wines, such as the rosés of Provence, Anjou and Tavel, are produced from red-wine varieties. (Dark-skinned grapes are even used to make white wines: Champagne, heavily based on Pinot Meunier and Pinot Noir, is a classic case.) To make a rosé, after the grapes are crushed, the time the juice spends in contact with its skins is crucial; the longer the contact, the greater the diffusion of colour, tannin and flavour from the skins into the juice.

'Saignée' (bled) is a French term that is seen occasionally on rosé labels. A technique designed to produce a pink wine or a more concentrated red wine – or both – it involves running off or 'bleeding' free-run juice from crushed, dark-skinned grapes after a brief, pre-ferment maceration on skins. An alternative is to commence the fermentation as for a red wine, then after 12 or 24 hours, when its colour starts to deepen, drain part of the juice for rosé production and vinify the rest as a red wine.

Pinot Noir and Merlot are the grape varieties most commonly used in New Zealand to produce rosé wines. Regional differences are emerging. South Island and Wairarapa rosés, usually made from Pinot Noir, are typically fresh, slightly sweet and crisp, while those from the middle and upper North Island – Hawke's Bay, Gisborne and Auckland – tend to be Merlot-based, fuller-bodied and drier.

These are typically charming, 'now-or-never' wines, peaking in their first six to 18 months with seductive strawberry/raspberry-like fruit flavours. Freshness is the essence of the wines' appeal.

Alexander Raumati Martinborough Pinot Noir Rosé ★★★★

The 2016 vintage (★★★★) is a 'serious' but delicious wine, drinking well in late 2017. Made from estate-grown Pinot Noir, it is a bright pink, mouthfilling wine with strong, vibrant plum and red-berry flavours, hints of spices and apricots, and a fully dry finish.

DRY $24 AV

Allan Scott Marlborough Rosé ★★★☆

The 2016 vintage (★★★) has an appealing, bright pink hue. Fresh and lively, it is berryish and plummy, with slightly earthy notes, hints of strawberry and watermelon, and a dryish finish.

MED/DRY $18 V+

Alluviale Hawke's Bay Rosé (★★★★)

The 2016 vintage (★★★★) is a blend of Merlot (85 per cent) and Malbec (15 per cent), grown in the Bridge Pa Triangle and fermented in an old oak vat. Bright pink, it is full-bodied, dry (2 grams/litre of residual sugar) and smooth, with fresh, berryish, spicy flavours, showing good harmony. Delicious young.

DRY $24 AV

Alpha Domus The Heroines Hawke's Bay Rosé ★★★

The 2017 vintage (★★★), made from Merlot, is a single-vineyard wine, grown in the Bridge Pa Triangle. Pale pink, it is a fully dry style, light-bodied, with delicate strawberry, watermelon and spice flavours, fresh and smooth.

DRY $22 –V

Amisfield Central Otago Pinot Noir Rosé ★★★★

Estate-grown in the Cromwell Basin and fermented in tanks (mostly) and barrels, the highly attractive 2016 vintage (★★★★) is bright pink, with strong, vibrant strawberry and spice flavours, showing a distinct touch of complexity. Made in a basically dry style (4.6 grams/litre of residual sugar), it's a good food wine.

Aronui Single Vineyard Nelson Pinot Rosé ★★★☆

The 2016 vintage (★★★) was made from Pinot Noir, estate-grown at Upper Moutere. Salmon pink, it is full-bodied and smooth (12 grams/litre of residual sugar), with plummy, slightly spicy flavours, balanced acidity and good depth.

Ashwell Martinborough Rosé ★★★☆

The attractive, very easy-drinking 2017 vintage (★★★★) is bright pink, with a floral bouquet. Medium-bodied, it is vibrantly fruity, with ripe plum and red-berry flavours, fresh acidity and a dry finish.

DRY $20 AV

Astrolabe Vineyards Beacon Hill Vineyard Marlborough Pinot Rosé ★★★★

The distinctive 2016 vintage (★★★★) is a blend of Pinot Noir (75 per cent) and Pinot Gris (25 per cent), grown in the lower Waihopai Valley. Light pink, it is weighty and dry, with a gentle touch of tannin and strong peach, strawberry and spice flavours. It should be at its peak over the summer of 2017–18.

DRY $23 AV

Babich Marlborough Rosé ★★★☆

Pink/pale orange, the delicious 2016 vintage (★★★★) is a single-vineyard, Wairau Valley wine, matured on its yeast lees for four months in tanks. Made from Pinot Noir, it is full-bodied, with strawberry and spice flavours, a hint of apricot, and a long, dry finish.

DRY $20 AV

Bannock Brae Cathy's Rosé ★★★★

The very charming 2016 vintage (★★★★) is from Pinot Noir grapes grown at Bendigo, in Central Otago. Bright pink, it is floral, fresh and full-bodied, with strong berry, plum and spice flavours, a gentle splash of sweetness (6 grams/litre of residual sugar), balanced acidity and a smooth finish. Instantly attractive.

Beach House Gimblett Gravels Hawke's Bay Rosé (★★★★)

Delicious young, the 2017 vintage (★★★★) is bright pink, very fresh and lively. Medium-bodied, it is a dry style (3 grams/litre of residual sugar), wih vibrant strawberry, watermelon and spice flavours, finely balanced and lingering.

Bellbird Spring Pinot Noir Rosé   ★★★★

Grown at Waipara, the 2016 vintage (★★★★) was fermented in old oak casks. Pale pink/slight orange, it is full-bodied, with good depth of ripe, peachy and spicy flavours, showing a touch of complexity, and a dry, rounded finish. Drink this summer.

DRY $28 –V

Black Barn Hawke's Bay Rosé   ★★★★

Very pale pink, the 2017 vintage (★★★★) was made from estate-grown, hand-picked Merlot. Medium to full-bodied, it has fresh, strong strawberry and spice flavours, firm and dry. Delicious young.

DRY $23 AV

Black Cottage Marlborough Rosé   ★★★☆

The pale pink, medium-bodied 2016 vintage (★★★☆) is a dryish blend of Pinot Noir and Pinot Gris. Fresh and smooth, it has lively peach, watermelon, lychee and pear flavours, showing very good delicacy and harmony. (From Two Rivers of Marlborough.)

MED/DRY $18 V+

Black Ridge Central Otago Pinot Rosé   (★★★☆)

Bright pink, the 2017 vintage (★★★☆) is crisp and dryish (4 grams/litre of residual sugar), with mouthfilling body and an earthy streak running through its fresh strawberry, peach and spice flavours. Good drinking for the summer of 2017–18.

DRY $22 AV

Blackenbrook Nelson Pinot Rosé   ★★★★

The weighty 2017 vintage (★★★☆) was made from hand-picked Nelson Pinot Noir. Made in a fully dry style (2 grams/litre of residual sugar), it is a pink/pale red, mouthfilling wine, with fresh plum and red-berry flavours, showing good depth, and a smooth finish.

Vintage	17
WR	6
Drink	17-19

DRY $23 AV

Boulder Bay Rosé   (★★★☆)

The 2016 vintage (★★★☆) is a lively, pale pink Northland rosé, from Syrah grown on Moturoa Island, in the Bay of Islands. Floral, with fresh, vibrant watermelon and spice flavours, it has very good depth and a slightly sweet (6 grams/litre of residual sugar), finely balanced finish.

MED/DRY $25 –V

Brancott Estate Flight Rosé   ★★☆

Pale pink, the 2016 vintage (★★☆) is lively and light (9 per cent alcohol), with fresh, gentle, peachy flavours, hints of strawberries and spices, a sliver of sweetness, appetising acidity and a smooth finish.

MED/DRY $17 –V

Brightside Organic Blush   (★★★)

Certified organic, the 2016 vintage (★★★) is a pink/pale red, very easy-drinking Nelson wine. Fresh and vibrantly fruity, it has berryish, slightly spicy flavours and a slightly sweet (6 grams/litre of residual sugar), smooth finish. (From Kaimira Estate.)

$16 V+

Byrne Northland Rosé   ★★★★

Grown at Kerikeri, the very charming 2017 vintage (★★★★) was made from Syrah. Bright pink, it is mouthfilling, with strong, vibrant, berryish flavours and a dry, lingering finish. Good drinking for the summer of 2017–18.

DRY $22 V+

Church Road Hawke's Bay Rosé   ★★★★

The generous 2016 vintage (★★★★) is Merlot-based (86 per cent), with splashes of Syrah, Malbec and Cabernet Sauvignon. Bright pink, it is full-bodied, fragrant and fresh, with vibrant berry and spice flavours, a hint of watermelon, and a dryish (8 grams/litre of residual sugar), very harmonious finish.

MED/DRY $20 V+

Clearview Black Reef Blush   ★★★★

The 2016 vintage (★★★★) is an instantly appealing Hawke's Bay wine, with Chambourcin, a well-regarded French hybrid, contributing bright pink/pale red colour. Fleshy and vibrantly fruity, it has fresh, berryish, plummy flavours and a smooth, long finish.

MED/DRY $21 V+

Clos Marguerite Marlborough Rosé   (★★★★)

The fresh, characterful 2016 vintage (★★★★) was made from Pinot Noir, estate-grown in the Awatere Valley. Pink/orange, it has generous, strawberryish, slightly spicy and leesy flavours, with a touch of complexity and a dry, smooth finish.

DRY $26 –V

Coal Pit Central Otago Rosé   ★★★★☆

Full of personality, the classy 2016 vintage (★★★★★) is from Pinot Noir grapes, estate-grown at Gibbston. Pink-hued, it is attractively perfumed, full-bodied and vibrantly fruity, with strong, ripe flavours of watermelon, strawberries and spices, appetising acidity, and a dry (3 grams/litre of residual sugar), finely balanced, lasting finish. Delicious now.

DRY $27 AV

Coopers Creek Huapai Rosé   ★★★☆

The 2016 vintage (★★★★) is a bright pink, lively blend of Malbec (80 per cent) and Merlot (20 per cent). It has fresh watermelon, strawberry and spice flavours, showing excellent vibrancy, delicacy and length.

Vintage	15
WR	7
Drink	P

DRY $20 AV

Crafters Union Hawke's Bay Rosé (★★★☆)

Enjoyable from the start, the 2017 vintage (★★★☆) is freshly scented, with very good depth of vibrant plum, red-berry and spice flavours, finely balanced and smooth. (From Constellation NZ.)

Vintage	17	MED/DRY $22 AV
WR	6	
Drink	18-19	

Doctor's, The, Marlborough Rosé (★★★)

Light and lively, the 2017 vintage (★★★) is bright pink, with low alcohol (9.5 per cent). Offering very easy drinking, it is slightly sweet, with balanced acidity and fresh, delicate strawberry and spice flavours.

MED/DRY $22 –V

Elder, The, Martinborough Rosé ★★★★☆

Drinking well early, the 2017 vintage (★★★★) was made from Pinot Noir grapes, estate-grown at Te Muna. Full, bright pink, it is mouthfilling, with generous red-berry and spice flavours, a touch of tannin, and a lengthy, dry finish.

DRY $33 –V

Eradus Awatere Valley Single Vineyard Pinot Rosé (★★★)

Ready to roll, the 2016 vintage (★★★) is a pink/slight orange, medium-bodied wine, with good depth of peach, strawberry and spice flavours, and a smooth finish.

DRY $19 AV

Esk Valley Hawke's Bay Merlot Rosé ★★★★

For many years, this was New Zealand's most successful rosé on the show circuit. The 2016 vintage (★★★☆) is a bright, tasty, Merlot-based wine, vibrantly fruity, with red-berry, watermelon and spice flavours and a fresh, crisp, almost bone-dry (2.6 grams/litre of residual sugar) finish.

DRY $20 V+

Falconhead Hawke's Bay Rosé (★★☆)

Made in an off-dry style, the 2016 vintage (★★☆) is a pink/pale red wine, medium-bodied, with berryish, slightly sweet flavours, balanced acidity and a smooth finish. Ready.

MED/DRY $16 AV

Forrest Marlborough Rosé ★★★☆

The 2017 vintage (★★★☆) is a bright pink, floral, vibrantly fruity wine, with fresh red-berry and plum flavours, crisp and skilfully balanced for early consumption.

MED/DRY $22 AV

Fromm La Strada Marlborough Rosé   ★★★★

'A charming rosé with an air of sophistication', the 2016 vintage (★★★★) is based on Pinot Noir (85 per cent), blended with Malbec (13.5 per cent) and Syrah (1.5 per cent). Bright pink, it is floral, fresh and smooth, with balanced acidity, lively watermelon and spice flavours, a hint of apricot, and a fully dry finish. Certified organic.

DRY $23 AV

Georges Road Les Terrasses Waipara Rosé   ★★★★

The pale pink, freshly scented 2016 vintage (★★★★) was made from Syrah grapes, fermented with indigenous yeasts and lees-aged in tanks. Fresh and lively, it is medium-bodied, with watermelon and spice flavours, hints of berries and apricots, and a dry (2.5 grams/litre of residual sugar), mouth-wateringly crisp finish.

DRY $21 V+

Gibbston Valley GV Collection Central Otago Rosé   ★★★☆

The pale pink 2017 vintage (★★★☆) is fresh, crisp and slightly sweet (6 grams/litre of residual sugar). Medium-bodied, it has good depth of red-berry, plum and watermelon flavours, vibrant and youthful.

MED/DRY $28 –V

Giesen Hawke's Bay Rosé   (★★★☆)

The 2016 vintage (★★★☆) is a pale pink, Merlot-based wine, grown in the Bridge Pa Triangle. It has fresh, ripe peach, watermelon and spice flavours, showing good depth, and a dry (2.3 grams/litre of residual sugar) finish.

DRY $20 AV

Gladstone Vineyard Rosé   ★★★★

Grown in the northern Wairarapa, the 2016 vintage (★★★★☆) is a pale pink blend of Cabernet Franc (63 per cent), Merlot (19 per cent) and Pinot Noir (18 per cent), made in a dry (1.7 grams/litre of residual sugar) style. Ripely scented, it is softly mouthfilling, with generous, strawberryish, slightly spicy flavours, showing excellent vibrancy, delicacy, harmony and length.

DRY $25 AV

Graham Norton's Own Pink by Design Rosé   ★★★★

The vivacious 2017 vintage (★★★★) was made from Pinot Noir (mostly), Pinot Gris and Sauvignon Blanc, grown in Marlborough and Hawke's Bay. Fresh-scented, it is a vibrantly fruity, medium-bodied wine with gentle strawberry and spice flavours, slightly peachy notes, and a slightly sweet (7.5 grams/litre of residual sugar), finely balanced finish. Delicious young.

MED/DRY $19 V+

Greyrock Hawke's Bay Rosé   (★★★☆)

The attractive 2016 vintage (★★★☆) is bright pink, mouthfilling and smooth, with vibrant red-berry and spice flavours, showing good delicacy and harmony. A basically dry style (4 grams/litre of residual sugar), it's sharply priced. (From Sileni.)

DRY $17 V+

Haha Hawke's Bay Rosé (★★★)

The bright pink 2017 vintage (★★★) is a blend of Merlot (73 per cent) and Malbec (27 per cent). Medium-bodied, it is fresh and lively, with strawberry and peach flavours, balanced acidity and a smooth, dry (3 grams/litre of residual sugar) finish. Good value.

DRY $16 V+

Hunter's Pinot Noir Marlborough Rosé ★★★☆

Good summer sipping, the 2016 vintage (★★★☆) has a pale, delicate pink hue. Grown at Rapaura and made in a fully dry (1.1 grams/litre of residual sugar) style, it is medium-bodied, very fresh and vibrant, with gentle peach, strawberry and spice flavours, lively and refreshing.

DRY $20 AV

In The Pink Rosé (★★☆)

The pale 2016 vintage (★★☆) is a light, smooth blend of Pinot Noir and Sauvignon Blanc. It has gentle, ripe flavour of peaches and strawberries, with some greener, herbaceous notes, and moderate depth. Priced right.

MED/DRY $15 AV

Johanneshof Marlborough Pinot Noir Rosé Maybern Single Vineyard (★★★★★)

A 'serious' yet charming rosé, the bright pink/pale red 2016 vintage (★★★★★) is from a hillside vineyard at Koromiko. Full of personality, it is freshly scented, vibrantly fruity and smooth (7 grams/litre of residual sugar), with substantial body (14.5 per cent alcohol) and a lovely surge of plum, strawberry, cherry and spice flavours, strong and smooth.

MED/DRY $25 V+

Johner Estate Gladstone Pinot Noir Rosé ★★★★

The 2016 vintage (★★★★) is bright pink, appetisingly crisp and lively, with generous, plummy, berryish flavours and a slightly spicy, dryish (5 grams/litre of residual sugar) finish. Delicious young.

Vintage	16	15
WR	6	6
Drink	17-18	17-18

MED/DRY $20 V+

Jules Taylor Gisborne Rosé ★★★★

Merlot-based, the 2017 vintage (★★★★) is bright pink and mouthfilling, with very vibrant, strawberryish flavours, hints of peaches and spices, and a finely balanced, fully dry finish. Delicious young.

Vintage	17	16
WR	5	5
Drink	17-18	17-18

DRY $24 AV

Jules Taylor OTQ Single Vineyard Marlborough Rosé   (★★★★☆)

Strikingly packaged, the debut 2017 vintage (★★★★☆) was produced 'OTQ' (On The Quiet) from Pinot Noir. Scented, with a very inviting, pale pink hue, it is mouthfilling, vibrant and smooth, with an array of gentle fruit flavours – suggestive of strawberry, watermelon, peach, apricot – and a finely poised, dry (1.1 grams/litre of residual sugar), lingering finish. Already delicious, it should be at its best during 2018.

DRY $34 –V

Kim Crawford Hawke's Bay Rosé   (★★★☆)

Appealing from the start, the 2017 vintage (★★★☆) is pale pink, with fresh, gentle strawberry, spice and peach flavours, and a dryish (5.2 grams/litre of residual sugar), finely balanced, lingering finish. Fine value.

Vintage	17
WR	4
Drink	17-18

 MED/DRY $17 V+

Lake Chalice The Raptor Marlborough Rosé   (★★★★)

Bright, pale pink, the 2016 vintage (★★★★) was hand-harvested in the Wairau Valley. A very fresh and vibrant wine, it is medium-bodied, with watermelon and spice flavours, showing excellent delicacy and poise, and a dry (3.9 grams/litre of residual sugar), persistent finish.

DRY $25 AV

Lawson's Dry Hills Pinot Rosé   ★★★☆

The 2016 vintage (★★★☆) of this Marlborough wine was made from Pinot Noir. Salmon-pink, it is medium to full-bodied, with good depth of strawberry and spice flavours, and a dry (4 grams/litre of residual sugar) finish. Ready.

Vintage	16
WR	6
Drink	17-18

 DRY $20 AV

Left Field Hawke's Bay Rosé   ★★★☆

The 2016 vintage (★★★☆) is a blend of Pinotage (65 per cent), Arneis and Pinot Gris. Bright pink, it is a dryish style (5.9 grams/litre of residual sugar), full-bodied, with vibrant cherry/plum flavours and a smooth finish. (From Te Awa.)

Vintage	17	16
WR	6	6
Drink	18-19	17-19

 MED/DRY $18 V+

Lime Rock Central Hawke's Bay Pinot Rosé   (★★★★)

The attractive 2017 vintage (★★★★) was made from Pinot Noir, estate-grown in Central Hawke's Bay. Bright pink, it is mouthfilling, very fresh and vibrant, with good intensity of watermelon and strawberry flavours, hints of peaches and apricots, and a dryish (7 grams/litre of residual sugar), finely balanced finish.

 MED/DRY $22 V+

Linden Estate Hawke's Bay Rosé ★★★

Enjoyable young, the 2017 vintage (★★★) is a bright pink, gently sweet style (11.6 grams/litre of residual sugar). Medium-bodied, it has fresh, lively, berryish flavours, a confectionery note, and a smooth finish.

Vintage	17
WR	5
Drink	17-18

MED/DRY $20 –V

Mahana Pinot Noir Carbonique (★★★★★)

Full of personality, the 2016 vintage (★★★★★) is a top-flight rosé, grown in Nelson and fermented in old barrels. Pink/pale red, it is full-bodied, with concentrated, berryish flavours, vibrant, dry and very harmonious. Certifed organic. Well worth discovering.

DRY $35 AV

Maison Noire Hawke's Bay Rosé (★★☆)

Bright, pale pink, the 2017 vintage (★★☆) is a fresh, light-bodied wine with gentle watermelon, spice and peach flavours, crisp and dry.

Vintage	17
WR	6
Drink	17-18

DRY $21 –V

Man O'War Waiheke Island Pinque ★★★☆

The refreshing 2016 vintage (★★★☆) is a blend of equal portions of Syrah, Merlot and Malbec, estate-grown on Waiheke Island. Made in a fully dry style, it is pale pink and medium-bodied, with peach, spice and watermelon flavours, very fresh and crisp.

Vintage	16	15
WR	6	5
Drink	17-19	P

DRY $29 –V

Margrain Martinborough Pinot Rosé ★★★☆

The very easy-drinking 2017 vintage (★★★☆) was made from Pinot Noir. Bright pink, it is floral, with fresh, lively, red-berry and spice flavours, a hint of apricot, balanced acidity and a gently sweet (8 grams/litre of residual sugar), smooth finish.

Vintage	17	16
WR	6	7
Drink	17-19	17-18

Marsden Bay of Islands Rosé ★★★☆

Bright pink, the 2016 vintage (★★★☆) is a Merlot-based rosé, fresh, medium-bodied and smooth, with strawberry and peach flavours, a sliver of sweetness, and very good delicacy, depth and sheer drinkability.

Matakana Estate Marlborough Pinot Noir Rosé   (★★★★)

Drinking well in 2017, the 2016 vintage (★★★★) is an unoaked, dry wine with pink/faint orange colour. Full-bodied, it has strong strawberry, peach and spice flavours, a slightly creamy texture, and plenty of personality.

DRY $22 V+

Matawhero Single Vineyard Gisborne Pinot Rosé   ★★★☆

Released early – in June – the 2017 vintage (★★★☆) is an exuberantly fruity wine, made from Pinot Noir. Pale pink, it is freshly scented and mouthfilling, with gentle, vibrant, strawberryish flavours, hints of apricots and spices, fractional sweetness (4.3 grams/litre of residual sugar), moderate acidity and a seductively smooth finish.

DRY $23 –V

Mill Road Hawke's Bay Rosé   (★★)

Priced right, the 2016 vintage (★★) has pink, slightly developed colour. Medium-bodied, it has pleasant red-berry, plum and spice flavours, slightly sweet and smooth. Ready.

MED/DRY $10 AV

Mills Reef Reserve Gimblett Gravels Hawke's Bay Rosé   (★★★☆)

The debut 2016 vintage (★★★☆) is a single-vineyard wine, made from Merlot. Pale red, it is mouthfilling and fleshy, with fresh, ripe berry and plum flavours, generous, dry and smooth.

DRY $25 –V

Millton Te Arai Vineyard Rosé   ★★★★

Certified organic, the 2016 vintage (★★★★) is pale pink, mouthfilling and smooth, with fresh peach, spice and strawberry flavours, showing a touch of complexity, a sliver of sweetness and good personality.

Vintage	16
WR	6
Drink	17-18

MED/DRY $26 –V

Misha's Vineyard The Soloist Central Otago Pinot Rosé   (★★★★☆)

Instantly appealing, the debut 2016 vintage (★★★★☆) was made from Pinot Noir, estate-grown at Bendigo. Bright pink, it is invitingly scented and mouthfilling, with notably vibrant plum, spice and strawberry flavours, showing excellent delicacy and depth, and a very smooth, dry (4 grams/litre of residual sugar) finish.

DRY $27 AV

Mission Hawke's Bay Rosé   ★★★☆

The charming 2017 vintage (★★★☆) is bright pink/pale red, with good body and vibrant, plummy, berryish flavours, showing very good delicacy and depth. A dryish, harmonious wine, it's drinking well from the start.

MED/DRY $18 V+

Mission Vineyard Selection Hawke's Bay Rosé   (★★★)

The 2016 vintage (★★★) is Merlot-based (77 per cent), with minor portions of Cabernet Franc, Cabernet Sauvignon and Syrah. Bright, light pink, it is lively, with fresh, gentle berry and spice flavours, a hint of herbs, and a smooth, dryish (6 grams/litre of residual sugar) finish.

MED/DRY $20 –V

Mud House Sub Region Series Burleigh Marlborough Pinot Noir   (★★★☆)

The debut 2016 vintage (★★★☆) is fresh, light and lively, with strawberry, peach and spice flavours, showing very good delicacy and depth, and a medium-dry (8 grams/litre of residual sugar), appetisingly crisp finish.

MED/DRY $20 AV

Neudorf Nelson Pinot Rosé   ★★★★☆

The 2016 vintage (★★★★) was hand-picked at Upper Moutere and mostly handled in tanks; 10 per cent was handled in old barriques. Pale pink, it is mouthfilling and smooth, with gentle watermelon and spice flavours, showing a touch of complexity, a hint of apricot and a dry finish.

DRY $25 V+

Nevis Bluff Central Otago Pinot Noir Rosé   ★★★☆

The 2016 vintage (★★★★) was made from Pinot Noir grapes, estate-grown in the Cromwell Basin. Pink/very pale red, it is mouthfilling, lively and dry (3 grams/litre of residual sugar), with vibrant strawberry and watermelon flavours, woven with fresh acidity, and very good depth, delicacy and vigour.

DRY $30 –V

Nga Waka Martinborough Rosé   (★★★☆)

From Pinot Noir grapes, the debut 2016 vintage (★★★☆) has a bright pink, pale red hue. Fresh and vibrantly fruity, it offers very good depth of plummy, slightly cherryish flavours, threaded with lively acidity, and a dry finish.

Vintage	16
WR	6
Drink	17-18

DRY $25 –V

Nikau Point Select Hawke's Bay Rosé   (★★☆)

The very smooth, easy-drinking 2016 vintage (★★☆) is a slightly sweet style, with pink, slightly developed colour. Medium-bodied, it is peachy and berryish, with a soft finish.

MED/DRY $12 V+

O:TU Hawke's Bay Merlot Rosé   (★★★)

Bright pink, the easy-drinking 2017 vintage (★★★) is a fresh, lively, medium-bodied wine, buoyantly fruity, with plum and red-berry flavours, a sliver of sweetness, and lots of drink-young charm. Enjoy this summer.

MED/DRY $23 –V

Obsidian Waiheke Island Estate Rosé ★★★★

Bright pink, with an inviting, floral bouquet, the 2017 vintage (★★★★) is a hand-picked, Merlot-based wine. Vibrantly fruity, it has good body, fresh plum, strawberry and spice flavours, balanced acidity and a long, dry finish.

DRY $27 –V

Opawa Marlborough Rosé ★★★★

Grown at Rapaura, in the Wairau Valley, the 2017 vintage (★★★★) was hand-harvested and handled in tanks (mostly) and old barrels. Pale pink, it is very fresh, delicate and vibrant, with watermelon and spice flavours, a hint of apricot, and a dryish (5 grams/litre of residual sugar), lingering finish. Delicious from the start.

MED/DRY $22 V+

Oyster Bay Marlborough Rosé ★★★★☆

The impressive 2017 vintage (★★★★☆) was made from Pinot Noir, grown in the Brancott and Renwick districts, in the Wairau Valley. Showing strong personality, it is pale pink, with an encitingly scented bouquet. Full-bodied and fleshy, it has strong, vibrant red-berry and plum flavours, a gentle touch of tannin, and a lasting, dry (3 grams/litre of residual sugar) finish. Fine value.

DRY $20 V+

Pa Road Marlborough Rosé ★★★☆

Pale pink, the 2017 vintage (★★★☆) is a fresh, medium to full-bodied wine, with good depth of gently sweet peach, spice and slight apricot flavours, balanced for easy drinking. (From Te Pa.)

MED/DRY $17 V+

Palliser Estate Martinborough Rosé ★★★☆

The fresh, lively 2016 vintage (★★★☆) is Pinot Noir-based, with bright pink/pale red colour. It has red-berry, strawberry and spice flavours, showing very good depth, vibrancy and harmony, and an off-dry (6 grams/litre of residual sugar) finish.

MED/DRY $26 –V

Peacock Sky Waiheke Island Rosé ★★☆

The 2016 vintage (★★) is an estate-grown blend of Merlot (70 per cent), Cabernet Sauvignon (20 per cent) and Cabernet Franc (10 per cent). Smooth, berryish, spicy and dry, it has developed colour and shows a slight lack of freshness and vibrancy. Drink up.

DRY $29 –V

Peregrine Central Otago Pinot Noir Rosé (★★★★)

Certified organic, the instantly attractive 2017 vintage (★★★★) was estate-grown at Bendigo. Bright, pale pink, it is attractively scented, with very good depth of vibrant peach, spice and slight apricot flavours and a smooth, dryish finish. Already delicious.

MED/DRY $27 –V

Postage Stamp Wines View East Vineyard Genevieve Rosé   (★★★★☆)

The instantly attractive 2016 vintage (★★★★☆) was made from Syrah grapes, grown on Waiheke Island. Bright pink, it is mouthfilling and lively, with strong, vibrant peach, watermelon and spice flavours, a hint of apricot, and a finely balanced, dry, persistent finish. A top debut.

DRY $25 V+

Puriri Hills Clevedon Rosé   (★★★★)

Freshly scented, the 2016 vintage (★★★★) was made predominantly from Merlot (90 per cent), with splashes of Malbec and Cabernet Sauvignon. Medium-bodied, it has strong strawberry and spice flavours, hints of peaches and apricots, balanced acidity and a dry (4 grams/litre of residual sugar), smooth finish.

DRY $28 –V

Rapaura Springs Reserve Marlborough Pinot Rosé   ★★★★

Delicious young, the 2017 vintage (★★★★) is a bright, light pink wine with a fresh, floral bouquet. Medium-bodied, it has lively watermelon, spice and peach flavours, with a finely balanced, slightly sweet (6 grams/litre of residual sugar), crisp finish.

Vintage	16
WR	6
Drink	17-18

 MED/DRY $19 V+

Redmetal Vineyards Hawke's Bay Cabernet Franc Rosé   ★★★

Grown in the Bridge Pa Triangle, the 2016 vintage (★★★☆) is a pale pink wine, based on Cabernet Franc. Full-bodied (14 per cent alcohol), it is fleshy, with generous, peachy, slightly spicy flavours and a smooth, dry (4 grams/litre of residual sugar) finish. Ready to roll.

 DRY $19 AV

Rockburn Central Otago Stolen Kiss   ★★★

The 2017 vintage (★★★) of this easy-drinking, 'sweetly frivolous' wine is made from Pinot Noir. Pale pink, it is fresh, lively and gently sweet (15 grams/litre of residual sugar), with delicate watermelon and spice flavours, crisp acidity and a smooth finish.

MED/DRY $30 –V

Ruru Central Otago Rosé   ★★★★

From Immigrant's Vineyard, at Alexandra, the 2017 vintage (★★★★) is Pinot Noir-based. Pale pink, it is scented and dryish (5 grams/litre of residual sugar), with vibrant strawberry, watermelon, spice and peach flavours, showing very good delicacy and harmony. Drink now to 2018.

MED/DRY $22 V+

Sacred Hill Hawke's Bay Rosé   (★★★★)

Offering excellent value, the debut 2017 vintage (★★★★), made with a small proportion of barrel fermentation, is instantly appealing. Bright, light pink, it is fresh and medium-bodied, with vibrant watermelon, peach and spice flavours, and a finely balanced, dryish (5 grams/litre of residual sugar) finish.

 MED/DRY $17 V+

Saint Clair Marlborough Pinot Gris Rosé   ★★★★

The 2016 vintage (★★★★) is a pale pink blend of Pinot Gris (mostly) and Pinot Noir. Mouthfilling, it is vibrantly fruity, with fresh, subtle, peachy, gently spicy flavours, showing very good delicacy and depth, and a dry (3.9 grams/litre of residual sugar), lingering finish.

 DRY $22 V+

Schubert Rosé   (★★★★)

Grown in the Wairarapa, the fresh, attractive 2016 vintage (★★★★) was made from Pinot Noir. Pale pink, it's a mouthfilling wine, with strong, vibrant strawberry and spice flavours, and a fully dry finish. Certified organic.

 DRY $27 –V

Selaks Reserve Hawke's Bay Rosé   (★★★☆)

The attractive, very easy-drinking 2017 vintage (★★★☆) is bright, light pink, fresh and mouthfilling, with good depth of plum, spice and watermelon flavours, lively, slightly sweet and smooth. Good value.

Vintage	17
WR	6
Drink	17-18

 MED/DRY $16 V+

Sileni Cellar Selection Hawke's Bay Cabernet Franc Rosé   ★★★☆

Pink/pale red, the lively 2016 vintage (★★★☆) is a mouthfilling wine, grown in the Bridge Pa Triangle (60 per cent) and the Dartmoor Valley (40 per cent). It has fresh, plummy, slightly spicy flavours, showing good depth, and a dryish finish. The 2017 vintage (★★★☆) is a pale pink, medium-bodied wine, with fresh, lively watermelon, peach and spice flavours, showing good depth, and a finely balanced, smooth (5.1 grams/litre of residual sugar) finish.

MED/DRY $20 AV

Sileni Estate Selection Hawke's Bay Ridge Pinot Noir Rosé   ★★★★☆

Delicious from the start, the 2016 vintage (★★★★★) is made from Pinot Noir, grown at Mangatahi and Te Awanga. Bright pink, it is very attractively scented, mouthfilling and smooth, with strong, fresh strawberry, peach and spice flavours and a finely balanced, dry (3.6 grams/litre of residual sugar) finish. The 2017 vintage (★★★★☆) is pale pink, mouthfilling and vibrantly fruity, with excellent weight and depth of peach, apricot, watermelon and spice flavours, dry and lingering.

 DRY $25 V+

Spy Valley Marlborough Pinot Noir Rosé ★★★☆

The pale pink 2016 vintage (★★★☆) was made from hand-picked Pinot Noir grapes, with some use of barrel fermentation. It has fresh watermelon, peach and spice flavours, crisp and dry (2.7 grams/litre of residual sugar), showing very good depth.

Vintage	16	15	14	13
WR	6	7	7	6
Drink	17-18	P	P	P

DRY $23 –V

Stables Reserve Hawke's Bay Rosé (★★★☆)

The pink/pale red 2016 vintage (★★★☆) is a blend of Merlot (92.5 per cent) and Pinot Noir (7.5 per cent). Full-bodied, dry and smooth, it has strong, vibrant red-berry flavours, balanced acidity, and very good freshness and immediacy.

DRY $19 V+

Stonecroft Gimblett Gravels Hawke's Bay Rosé (★★★☆)

Offering very easy drinking, the debut 2016 vintage (★★★☆) was grown at Fernhill. Light pink, it is medium-bodied, with good depth of fresh, lively, plummy flavours and a smooth (6 grams/litre of residual sugar), harmonious finish.

MED/DRY $22 AV

Stoneleigh Latitude Marlborough Rosé ★★★★

The fragrant, lively 2016 vintage (★★★★) is an inviting, light pink rosé, grown at Rapaura, in the Wairau Valley, and mostly fermented in large French oak cuves. It has fresh, strong peach, strawberry and spice flavours, finely balanced, dryish (4.9 grams/litre of residual sugar) and lingering.

DRY $23 AV

Stoneleigh Lighter Marlborough Rosé (★★☆)

From early-picked grapes, the 2016 vintage (★★☆) is a very pale pink, light-bodied wine (9.9 per cent alcohol), with vibrant, peachy flavours and a crisp, slightly sweet finish.

MED/DRY $17 –V

Stoneleigh Marlborough Pinot Noir Rosé ★★★☆

The very easy-drinking 2016 vintage (★★★☆) is a bright pink, fresh-scented, full-bodied wine, with good depth of vibrant strawberry, peach and spice flavours and a dry (4 grams/litre of residual sugar), smooth finish. Fine value.

MED/DRY $17 V+

Summerhouse Marlborough Pinot Rosé ★★★★

The 2017 vintage (★★★★) is labelled 'Pinot', rather than Pinot Noir, suggesting the inclusion of Pinot Gris. Pale pink, it is fresh-scented, with vibrant watermelon and peach flavours, dryish (6 grams/litre of residual sugar), crisp, lively and lingering. Fine value.

MED/DRY $19 V+

Tatty Bogler Central Otago Rosé   (★★★★)

Maturing very gracefully, the 2016 vintage (★★★★) is a pale pink, mouthfilling wine, fresh and crisp, with lively strawberry and spice flavours. A basically dry style (4.5 grams/litre of residual sugar), it is finely balanced, with a lingering finish. (From Forrest.)

DRY $25 AV

Te Mania Nelson Pinot Noir Rosé   ★★★☆

Certified organic, the 2016 vintage (★★★) is a pink-hued, dryish style (5 grams/litre of residual sugar), with red-berry, peach and spice flavours, fresh and smooth.

MED/DRY $22 AV

Te Pa Marlborough Pinot Noir Rosé   (★★★★)

Drinking well in 2017, the 2016 vintage (★★★★) is a blend of Pinot Noir (90 per cent) and Pinot Gris (10 per cent), grown at three sites at Rapaura, west of Renwick and in the upper Wairau Valley. Bright pink, it has strawberry, watermelon and spice flavours, woven with lively acidity, slight sweetness (5 grams/litre of residual sugar), and very good freshness, vigour and depth.

MED/DRY $20 V+

Terra Sancta Bannockburn Central Otago Pinot Noir Rosé   ★★★★★

From one vintage to the next, this is one of the country's leading rosés. Bursting with freshness, the 2017 vintage (★★★★★) was mostly handled in tanks; a small part of the blend was fermented and aged in old French oak casks. Bright pink, it is highly scented and vivacious, with mouthfilling body, an array of plum, red-berry, strawberry, watermelon and spice flavours, showing lovely depth and harmony, and a dry (4.3 grams/litre of residual sugar) finish. Great drinking for the summer of 2017–18.

Vintage	17
WR	7
Drink	18-20

DRY $28 V+

Terrace Edge Waipara Valley Rosé   (★★★★★)

Sturdy and rich, the 2016 vintage (★★★★★) is a classy, distinctive wine, made from co-fermented Pinot Noir (80 per cent) and Syrah (20 per cent). Light pink, it is deliciously fragrant, full-bodied and soft, with generous strawberry and spice flavours, hints of peach and apricot, and a fresh, smooth (4.5 grams/litre of residual sugar) finish. A highly satisfying wine, it's certified organic.

Vintage	16
WR	7
Drink	17-20

DRY $22 V+

Thomas Waiheke Island Field Blend Rosé   (★★★★☆)

Currently delicious, the 2016 vintage (★★★★☆) was blended in the vineyard (hence the term 'field blend') from Syrah (46 per cent), Chardonnay (31 per cent), Riesling (13 per cent), Flora (8 per cent) and Pinot Gris (2 per cent). Estate-grown and hand-picked, it was tank-fermented to dryness and matured for six months on its yeast lees. A rare wine (only 592 bottles were produced), it is salmon pink and weighty, with mouthfilling body, vibrant strawberry, red-berry and spice flavours, a distinct hint of apricot, and a very harmonious, well-rounded finish. Drink now and during the summer of 2017–18.

DRY $38 –V

Ti Point Ruby Hawke's Bay Rosé   (★★★☆)

Light pink, the 2016 vintage (★★★☆) is Merlot-based. Made in a crisp, dry style, it has gentle peach, watermelon and spice flavours, showing good delicacy and depth.

DRY $23 –V

Ti Point Tess Hawke's Bay White Merlot   (★★☆)

A rosé in all but name, the 2016 vintage (★★☆) is a pale pink wine, made entirely from Merlot. Medium-bodied, it has fresh watermelon and spice flavours, dry and slightly earthy, but lacks a bit of charm and fragrance.

DRY $23 –V

Tiki Estate Marlborough Pinot Noir Rosé   ★★★★

The 2016 vintage (★★★☆) is bright pink, mouthfilling and smooth, with cherryish flavours, a gentle splash of sweetness, balanced acidity and good vigour and freshness.

MED/DRY $23 AV

Tohu Nelson Pinot Rosé   (★★★)

Estate-grown at Upper Moutere, the 2016 vintage (★★★) is a basically dry style (3 grams/litre of residual sugar). Medium-bodied, it is lively, with balanced acidity and fresh peach, strawberry and spice flavours.

DRY $22 –V

Tono Hawke's Bay Rosado   (★★★★)

Instantly likeable, the 2016 vintage (★★★★) was made mostly from Tempranillo and Syrah (with 5 per cent Muscat), grown at Havelock North and Bridge Pa. Bright pink, it is aromatic and lively, with a sliver of sweetness (6 grams/litre of residual sugar), appetising acidity and plenty of fresh, strawberryish, peachy flavour. (From Ant McKenzie Wines.)

MED/DRY $19 V+

Tupari Awatere Valley Pink Pukeko Rosé   (★★★★)

The pale pink 2017 vintage (★★★★) is a vibrantly fruity, medium-bodied blend of Pinot Noir (80 per cent) and Pinot Gris (20 per cent). It has strawberry, watermelon and spice flavours, very fresh and lively, and an appetisingly crisp, dry (3.5 grams/litre of residual sugar) finish.

DRY $20 V+

Two Rivers of Marlborough Isle of Beauty Rosé   ★★★★

Grown in the Southern Valleys, the very youthful 2017 vintage (★★★★) is a single-vineyard wine, made from Pinot Noir. Pale pink, it is medium-bodied, with fresh, lively strawberry, spice and peach flavours, crisp, delicate and dry (2.4 grams/litre of residual sugar). Best drinking 2018+.

Vintage	16
WR	6
Drink	P

Villa Maria Cellar Selection Pinot Noir Marlborough Rosé   (★★★★☆)

Instantly appealing, the debut 2017 vintage (★★★★☆) is bright pink, with good intensity of vibrant watermelon and strawberry flavours, mouth-wateringly crisp, dry (3.1 grams/litre of residual sugar), racy and long.

Villa Maria Private Bin Hawke's Bay Rosé   ★★★☆

The 2017 vintage (★★★★) is a bright pink, off-dry style (5.5 grams/litre of residual sugar), made principally from Merlot. Vibrantly fruity, with strawberry and spice flavours, showing excellent delicacy and freshness, and a smooth finish, it's already delicious. Fine value.

MED/DRY $16 V+

Vintage	17	16	15	14
WR	7	7	6	6
Drink	17-19	17-18	P	P

Villa Maria Private Bin Lighter Hawke's Bay Rosé   ★★★

Looking for 'a quality wine with less calories'? This light-bodied rosé is blended from varieties such as Pinot Noir, Arneis and Merlot. Bright pink, the 2017 vintage (★★★) is vibrantly fruity, with moderate alcohol (10 per cent), fresh, lively, gentle, strawberryish flavours and a slightly sweet (6.5 grams/litre of residual sugar) finish.

MED/DRY $16 V+

Vintage	17	16	15
WR	6	6	6
Drink	17-18	P	P

Waimea Nelson Pinot Rosé   ★★★

The pale pink 2016 vintage (★★★) is light-bodied and lively, with fresh watermelon and spice flavours, a hint of peach, and a slightly sweet (7.8 grams/litre of residual sugar), crisp finish.

Wairau River Marlborough Rosé   ★★★☆

The delicious 2016 vintage (★★★★) is pale pink, with strawberry, watermelon and spice flavours, showing excellent vibrancy and depth, and a slightly sweet (7.9 grams/litre of residual sugar), smooth finish.

Vintage	16	15	14	13
WR	6	7	7	4
Drink	17-18	P	P	P

 MED/DRY $20 AV

West Brook Crackling Pinot Noir Rosé   (★★★)

Revealing 'a tickle of effervescence' (gentle bubbles), the 2017 vintage (★★★) is a bright, light pink, freshly scented wine. Crisp, light and lively, with delicate strawberry and watermelon flavours, and a dry finish, it offers enjoyable, easy drinking for the summer of 2017–18.

 DRY $20 –V

Whitehaven Marlborough Pinot Rosé   ★★★★

The delicious 2016 vintage (★★★★☆) is bright, light pink. Fragrant and full-bodied, it is vibrantly fruity, with fresh, delicate, strawberryish, spicy, slightly peachy flavours, and a very finely balanced, dry (3.8 grams/litre of residual sugar) finish.

 DRY $23 AV

Wild Grace Central Otago Pinot Noir Rosé   ★★★★

The attractive 2017 vintage (★★★★) is already drinking well. Light pink, it is very fresh and mouthfilling, with strong fruit flavours of red berry, peach and watermelon, a touch of tannin, and a crisp, dry finish. (From Constellation NZ.)

 DRY $27 –V

Wooing Tree Central Otago Rosé   ★★★★

From estate-grown Pinot Noir grapes, hand-picked in the Cromwell Basin, the 2017 vintage (★★★★) is a bright pink, scented, dry wine (2.9 grams/litre of residual sugar). Fresh and vibrantly fruity, it has lively berry, watermelon and spice flavours, finely balanced and lingering.

 DRY $27 –V

Yealands Estate Single Vineyard Awatere Valley Pinot Noir Rosé   ★★★☆

The 2017 vintage (★★★☆) was estate-grown in the Seaview Vineyard and fermented in tanks and old French oak barrels. Pale pink/orange, it is a 'serious' style of rosé, medium-bodied, lively and dry, with peachy, spicy flavours that linger well.

DRY $23 –V

Red Wines

Barbera

One of Italy's most widely planted red-wine varieties – particularly in Piedmont, in the north-west – Barbera is known for its generous yields of robust, full-coloured reds, typically with lively acidity. Although increasingly popular in California, it is extremely rare in New Zealand and is not listed separately in New Zealand Winegrowers' *Vineyard Register Report 2015-2018*.

De La Terre Hawke's Bay Barbera ★★★★

The 2014 vintage (★★★★) was hand-picked at Havelock North and matured for 18 months in seasoned French oak barriques. Full and fairly youthful in colour, it is mouthfilling, with concentrated, ripe, plummy, gently spicy flavours, firm tannins beneath, and good complexity. Best drinking 2018+.

DRY $40 –V

Vintage	14	13
WR	6	5
Drink	17-20	17-18

Branded and Other Red Wines

Most New Zealand red wines carry a varietal label, such as Pinot Noir, Syrah, Merlot or Cabernet Sauvignon (or blends of the last two). Those not labelled prominently by their principal grape varieties – often prestigious wines such as Esk Valley The Terraces or Destiny Bay Magna Praemia – can be found here.

Although not varietally labelled, these wines are mostly of high quality and sometimes outstanding.

Alpha Domus AD The Aviator ★★★★★

Estate-grown in the Bridge Pa Triangle, this is a blend of classic Bordeaux varieties. The outstanding 2015 vintage (★★★★★) is a marriage of Cabernet Sauvignon (50 per cent), Cabernet Franc (22 percent), Merlot (21 percent) and Malbec (7 per cent). Matured in French oak barriques (46 per cent new), it is deeply coloured, with a fragrant, very refined bouquet. Full-bodied, it is youthful, with concentrated, deliciously ripe blackcurrant, plum and spice flavours, excellent complexity and a long finish. A very elegant, rich wine, showing lovely delicacy and depth, it's already very approachable, but likely to be at its best 2020+.

Vintage	15	**DRY $98 AV**
WR	7	
Drink	18-25	

Alpha Domus The Navigator ★★★★☆

The deeply coloured, generous 2014 vintage (★★★★☆) is a blend of Merlot (46 per cent), Malbec (24 per cent), Cabernet Sauvignon (16 per cent) and Cabernet Franc (14 per cent), estate-grown in the Bridge Pa Triangle, Hawke's Bay, and matured in seasoned oak barrels (mostly French). Full-bodied, it has fresh, strong, well-ripened blackcurrant, plum and spice flavours, hints of nuts, leather and coffee, excellent complexity and good tannin backbone. A 'full-on' style, with a slightly sweet oak influence, it's still unfolding, but already drinking well.

Vintage	14	**DRY $32 AV**
WR	7	
Drink	17-22	

Ash Ridge Hawke's Bay Reserve The Blend ★★★★☆

Grown in the Bridge Pa Triangle, the 2015 vintage (★★★★) was blended from five varieties, mostly Merlot and Cabernet Sauvignon, and matured in French and American oak casks. Full-coloured, with a youthful, slightly spicy bouquet, it is a medium to full-bodied style, with strong, vibrant, plummy, spicy flavours, showing good complexity. Best drinking 2019+. (This label will be replaced by a top Cabernet Sauvignon/Merlot.)

DRY $45 –V

Ata Rangi Martinborough Célèbre ★★★★☆

Pronounced 'say-lebr', this is a blend of Merlot, Syrah and Cabernet Sauvignon. It typically has impressive weight and depth of plummy, spicy flavours in a complex style that matures well. The impressive 2014 vintage (★★★★☆) is a blend of Merlot (55 per cent), Syrah (35 per cent) and Cabernet Sauvignon (10 per cent). An elegant, notably drinkable red, it is fragrant and full-coloured, with strong, fresh, well-ripened berry, plum and spice flavours, to which the Syrah makes a noticeable, but not pungent, contribution. A distinctive wine, complex and harmonious, it is already delicious, but should be at its best 2018+.

Vintage	14	13	12	11	10	09	08	07	06
WR	7	7	NM	6	NM	6	7	7	7
Drink	17-26	17-25	NM	17-20	NM	17-20	17-20	17-19	17-18

DRY $40 –V

Babich The Patriarch ★★★★★

This is promoted as Babich's greatest red, regardless of the variety or region of origin, but all vintages have been grown in the company's shingly Irongate Vineyard in Gimblett Road, Hawke's Bay (in other words, they have been Cabernet/Merlots, rather than Pinot Noirs from further south). It is typically a dark, ripe and complex, deliciously rich red. The very classy 2015 vintage (★★★★★) is a boldly coloured, youthful blend of Cabernet Sauvignon (51 per cent), Merlot (27 per cent) and Malbec (22 per cent), matured for 15 months in French oak barriques. Highly fragrant, it has concentrated, ripe blackcurrant, plum, spice and nut flavours, complex, savoury, finely textured and sustained. A very refined, harmonious wine, it's well worth cellaring to at least 2020+.

Vintage	15	14	13	12	11	10	09	08
WR	7	7	7	5	5	7	7	5
Drink	17-25	17-25	17-25	17-21	17-20	17-22	17-21	17-18

DRY $70 AV

Cable Bay Five Hills (★★★★)

The 2014 vintage (★★★★) is a Waiheke Island blend of Malbec (63 per cent), Merlot (25 per cent) and Cabernet Sauvignon (12 per cent), hand-picked at several sites and matured in French and Hungarian oak casks (30 per cent new). Fresh plum and spice aromas lead into a mouthfilling, vibrantly fruity red with generous, youthful plum and blackcurrant flavours, gentle tannins, and a long, spicy, smooth finish.

Vintage	14
WR	6
Drink	17-25

DRY $48 –V

Church Road Tom ★★★★★

Pernod Ricard NZ's top Hawke's Bay red honours pioneer winemaker Tom McDonald, the driving force behind New Zealand's first prestige red, McWilliam's Cabernet Sauvignon. The early vintages in the mid-1990s were Cabernet Sauvignon-predominant, but since 1998 Merlot has emerged as an equally crucial part of the recipe. Typically not a blockbuster but a wine of great finesse, it is savoury, complex and more akin to a quality Bordeaux than other New World reds. Released in 2017, the 2014 vintage (★★★★★) is a dark blend of Merlot (62 per cent), estate-grown in the Gimblett Gravels, and Cabernet Sauvignon (38 per cent), estate-grown in the Redstone Vineyard, in the Bridge Pa Triangle. Harvested at 23.8 to 25.3 brix and matured for 20 months in French oak barriques (74 per cent new), it was bottled unfined and unfiltered. Weighty (15 per cent alcohol), it is notably rich and sweet-fruited, with dense blackcurrant, plum and spice flavours, hints of liquorice and nuts, fine-grained tannins, and great potential; best drinking 2024+. (The 2015 vintage will be Cabernet Sauvignon-predominant.)

Vintage	14	13	12	11	10	09	08	07	06	05
WR	7	7	NM	NM	NM	7	NM	7	NM	7
Drink	20-30	20-29	NM	NM	NM	17-25	NM	17-22	NM	17-20

DRY $200 –V

Clearview Enigma ★★★★☆

Entirely estate-grown at Te Awanga, the classy 2015 vintage (★★★★★) is a fragrant, dark blend of Merlot (75 per cent), Malbec (16.5 per cent) and Cabernet Franc (8.5 per cent), matured for 17 months in French oak casks (33 per cent new). Already inviting, it is deeply coloured and sturdy, with fresh, concentrated, youthful blackcurrant, plum and spice flavours, hints of coffee and dark chocolate, nutty, savoury notes adding complexity, and a finely poised, lasting finish. Best drinking 2019+.

Vintage	15
WR	7
Drink	19-25

 DRY $55 –V

Clearview Old Olive Block ★★★★★

This Hawke's Bay red is named after the estate vineyard at Te Awanga, which has a very old olive tree in the centre. It is grown there and in the Gimblett Gravels. The 2015 vintage (★★★★☆) is a dark, purple-flushed blend of Cabernet Sauvignon (69 per cent), Malbec (19 per cent) and Cabernet Franc (12 per cent), matured for 17 months in French oak casks (25 per cent new). The bouquet is fragrant, savoury and slightly herbal; the palate is concentrated and supple, with fresh acidity woven through very youthful blackcurrant, plum, herb and spice flavours, showing good complexity. Well worth cellaring.

Vintage	15
WR	6
Drink	20-25

 DRY $36 V+

Clearview The Basket Press ★★★★★

The distinguished 2013 vintage (★★★★★) is a youthful blend of 35 per cent Cabernet Sauvignon, grown in the Gimblett Gravels, with coastal Te Awanga fruit: Merlot (30 per cent), Cabernet Franc (30 per cent) and Malbec (5 per cent). Hand-picked and matured for over two years in all-new French oak barriques, it is deeply coloured, with dense, pure blackcurrant, plum and spice flavours that build to a lasting, finely poised finish. Weighty and highly concentrated, with a backbone of ripe, supple tannins, it has lapped up the new oak influence, creating a savoury, multi-faceted red. Already delicious, it should flourish for a decade -- or longer.

Vintage	13
WR	7
Drink	17-25

DRY $165 –V

Coopers Creek Four Daughters ★★★

The 2013 vintage (★★★) is a Hawke's Bay blend of roughly equal portions of Malbec, Cabernet Franc, Syrah and Merlot. Fullish in colour, it has ripe, moderately rich berry and spice flavours, a smooth finish and a fragrant bouquet.

DRY $18 AV

Craggy Range Aroha
★★★★★

The distinguished 2015 vintage (★★★★★) is a single-vineyard Pinot Noir, estate-grown at Te Muna, on the edge of Martinborough. Hand-picked at 24.2 brix, it was fermented with indigenous yeasts and matured for nine months in French oak barriques (30 per cent new). Deep ruby, it has a highly fragrant, very savoury bouquet. Mouthfilling, it has deep, ripe cherry, plum, spice and nut flavours, showing excellent complexity, good tannin backbone, and a long, very harmonious finish. Already delicious, it should be at its best 2019+.

Vintage	15	14	13	12	11	10	09	08	07
WR	7	7	7	7	7	NM	6	7	7
Drink	17-26	17-25	17-25	17-24	17-23	NM	17-20	17-21	17-18

DRY $120 –V

Craggy Range Le Sol
★★★★★

This famous Syrah impresses with its lovely fragrance and finesse. Estate-grown in the Gimblett Gravels of Hawke's Bay, the densely packed 2015 vintage (★★★★★) was hand-picked at 23.9 brix and matured for 17 months in French oak barriques (30 per cent new). The colour is deep and purple-flushed; the bouquet is floral and peppery. Still very youthful, it is mouthfilling but not heavy, with arrestingly concentrated blackcurrant, plum, spice and black-pepper flavours, and a finely textured, lasting finish. Already approachable, it should be at its best 2022+.

Vintage	15	14	13	12	11	10	09	08	07	06
WR	7	7	7	NM	7	7	7	7	7	6
Drink	17-30	17-30	17-30	NM	17-25	17-27	17-26	17-23	17-22	17-20

DRY $120 AV

Craggy Range Sophia
★★★★★

This is Craggy Range's premier Merlot-based red. The very stylish 2015 vintage (★★★★★) is a Gimblett Gravels, Hawke's Bay blend of Merlot (73 per cent), Cabernet Sauvignon (14 per cent) and Cabernet Franc (13 per cent), hand-picked at 23.9 brix and matured for 19 months in French oak barriques (45 per cent new). Deep and youthful in colour, it is mouthfilling and vibrantly fruity, with concentrated, ripe blackcurrant, plum and spice flavours, seasoned with quality oak, very fine-grained tannins, and a finely poised finish. Approachable in its youth, it should be at its best 2020+.

Vintage	15	14	13	12	11	10	09	08	07	06
WR	7	7	7	NM	7	7	7	7	7	7
Drink	17-30	17-30	17-30	NM	17-25	17-27	17-26	17-23	17-27	17-26

DRY $95 AV

Craggy Range Te Kahu
★★★★

Estate-grown in the Gimblett Gravels, the 2014 vintage (★★★★) of this Hawke's Bay red is Merlot-based (68 per cent), with smaller portions of Cabernet Sauvignon (18 per cent), Malbec (8 per cent) and Cabernet Franc (6 per cent). Matured for 17 months in oak barriques (28 per cent new), it is deeply coloured and full-bodied, with youthful, well-ripened blackcurrant, plum and spice flavours, showing good concentration and complexity, and a fairly firm finish. Well worth cellaring to 2018+.

Vintage	14	13	12	11	10	09	08	07	06
WR	7	7	NM	5	6	6	6	7	6
Drink	17-23	17-23	NM	17-18	17-20	17-18	P	17-22	17-20

DRY $32 –V

Crazy by Nature Gisborne Cosmo Red   ★★★☆

Certified organic, the 2014 vintage (★★★★) from Millton is a blend of Malbec, Syrah and Viognier, matured for 11 months in American oak barrels. Full-coloured, it is mouthfilling, with strong berry, plum and spice flavours, good tannin backbone, and a tight, lingering finish.

Vintage	14
WR	5
Drink	17-20

 DRY $26 –V

Crossroads Hawke's Bay Talisman   ★★★★★

A blend of several red varieties whose identities the winery long delighted in concealing (I saw Malbec and Syrah as prime suspects), Talisman was at first estate-grown in the Origin Vineyard at Fernhill, in Hawke's Bay, and has recently also included grapes from sites in the Gimblett Gravels (a spy tells me that the key 'mystery' varieties are in fact Tannat and Petite Syrah). The 2014 vintage (★★★★★) has bold, inky-red colour. Sturdy and rich, it is a powerful, very youthful red, with dense plum, spice, liquorice and dark chocolate flavours, buried tannins and a smooth, long finish.

Vintage	14	13	12	11	10	09	08
WR	7	7	5	5	7	6	6
Drink	17-25	17-23	17-23	17-22	17-22	17-20	P

 DRY $56 AV

Destiny Bay Destinae   ★★★★★

The 2013 vintage (★★★★★) is a perfect introduction to the Destiny Bay range. Estate-grown on Waiheke Island, it is a blend of Cabernet Sauvignon (38 per cent), Merlot (36 per cent), Cabernet Franc (12 per cent), Malbec (8 per cent) and Petit Verdot (6 per cent), harvested at 24 to 25.6 brix and matured in a 50:50 split of French and American oak casks (40 per cent new). A distinguished but already very approachable red, it is deeply coloured, fleshy, rich and softly textured, with blackcurrant, plum, dried-herb and spice flavours, showing excellent concentration, complexity and harmony. Best drinking 2018+. ($60 to Patron Club members.)

DRY $125 –V

Destiny Bay Magna Praemia   ★★★★★

The powerful, lush 2013 vintage (★★★★★), harvested at 24 to 25.6 brix, is a blend of Cabernet Sauvignon (71 per cent) and Merlot (16 per cent), with minor portions of Cabernet Franc, Petit Verdot and Malbec. Matured for up to 15 months in an even split of French and American oak casks (60 per cent new), it is dark and full-bodied (14.5 per cent alcohol), with deliciously dense, ripe blackcurrant, plum and spice flavours, fine-grained tannins, excellent complexity and a lasting finish. A classy, youthful, savoury, highly concentrated red, it's already approachable, but likely to be long-lived; best drinking 2020+. ($195 to Patron Club members.)

 DRY $355 –V

Destiny Bay Mystae ★★★★★

The 2013 vintage (★★★★★) of this Waiheke Island blend is Cabernet Sauvignon-based (52 per cent), with Merlot (25 per cent), Cabernet Franc (9 per cent), Malbec (8 per cent) and Petit Verdot (6 per cent). Harvested at 24 to 25.6 brix, it was matured in an even split of French and American oak casks (60 per cent new). Dark and youthful in colour, it is a powerful red (14.5 per cent alcohol), fleshy and rich, sweet-fruited and lush, with concentrated blackcurrant and spice flavours, a hint of sweet oak, and fine-grained tannins. A very age-worthy wine, it should be at its best 2020+. ($85 to Patron Club members.)

DRY $155 –V

Elephant Hill Hawke's Bay Le Phant Rouge ★★★★

The 2015 vintage (★★★★) is a deeply coloured, Merlot-based red (70 per cent), with minor portions of Cabernet Sauvignon, Syrah, Malbec and Cabernet Franc. Hand-picked in the Gimblett Gravels, at Te Awanga and in the Bridge Pa Triangle, it was oak-aged for a year. Fragrant and fresh, with generous, ripe blackcurrant, plum and spice flavours, tinged with sweet oak, it has a solid foundation of tannin, and nutty, savoury notes adding complexity. Enjoyable young, it's also well worth cellaring.

DRY $24 V+

Elephant Hill Hieronymus (★★★★★)

The dense, flowing 2013 vintage (★★★★★) is a blend of Cabernet Sauvignon, Malbec and Merlot, grown in the Gimblett Gravels and the Bridge Pa Triangle, and matured for 17 months in French oak casks (80 per cent new). Dark and purple-flushed, it is mouthfilling, with ripe sweet-fruit characters and highly concentrated plum, spice, blackcurrant and coffee flavours. Lush and approachable in its youth, it should flourish for a decade; open 2017+.

DRY $95 –V

Esk Valley Heipipi The Terraces ★★★★★

Grown on the steep, terraced, north-facing hillside flanking the winery at Bay View, in Hawke's Bay, this is a strikingly bold, dark wine with bottomless depth of blackcurrant, plum and strongly spicy flavour. Malbec (43 per cent of the vines) and Merlot (35 per cent) are typically the major ingredients, supplemented by Cabernet Franc; the Malbec gives 'perfume, spice, tannin and brilliant colour'. Yields in the 1-hectare vineyard are very low, and the wine is matured for 17 to 22 months in mostly new French oak barriques. 'En primeur' (payment at a reduced price of $99, in advance of delivery) has been the best way to buy. It typically matures well, developing a beautiful fragrance and spicy, Rhône-like complexity. The powerful 2015 vintage (★★★★★) is a densely coloured blend of Malbec, Merlot and Cabernet Franc. Robust (14.5 per cent alcohol), It has highly concentrated, ripe, berryish, spicy flavours, notably deep and smooth-flowing, with a finely textured, harmonious, resounding finish. A very 'complete' wine, it's already delicious, but should flourish with cellaring.

Vintage	15	14	13	12	11	10	09	08	07	06
WR	7	7	7	NM	NM	NM	7	NM	NM	7
Drink	17-30	17-30	17-35	NM	NM	NM	17-25	NM	NM	17-20

DRY $135 AV

Frenchmans Hill Estate Waiheke Island Blood Creek 8   ★★★★★

The fragrant, highly concentrated 2014 vintage (★★★★★) is a blend of eight varieties – principally Cabernet Sauvignon (36 per cent), Merlot (17 per cent) and Petit Verdot (15 per cent), plus smaller portions of Cabernet Franc, Tannat, Syrah, Viognier and Koler. Matured for 16 months in all-new French oak barriques, it is dark, fresh and full-bodied, with dense, ripe blackcurrant, plum and spice flavours, good tannin backbone, and impressive power through the palate. Still very youthful, it should be at its best from 2021 onwards. The 2013 vintage (★★★★★) is also highly impressive. Matured for 16 months in new French oak barriques, it has dark, youthful colour. A lovely rich and supple red, it is muscular, with generous, ripe blackcurrant/spice flavours, showing excellent complexity, real power through the palate and obvious potential; best drinking 2020+.

DRY $125 –V

Gillman   ★★★★★

This rare Matakana red is blended from Cabernet Franc, Merlot and Malbec, French oak-aged. Tasted in 2016, the 2010 vintage (★★★★★) is a powerful, sweet-fruited, complex blend of Cabernet Franc (65 per cent), Merlot (31 per cent) and Malbec (4 per cent), matured for two years in French oak barrels (50 per cent new). Deeply coloured, with a fragrant, spicy, complex bouquet, it is sturdy, with generous, ripe plum, spice and nut flavours, in a savoury, very Bordeaux-like style, rich and rounded. The slightly lighter 2011 (★★★★) is medium to full-bodied, with a fragrant, spicy bouquet and strong, vibrant blackcurrant, plum and spice flavours; it's drinking well now. The 2012 vintage (★★★★★) is very elegant, with a cedary bouquet, deep, ripe blackcurrant, plum, spice and nut flavours, fine-grained tannins, and a lengthy, silky-smooth finish. These are classy wines, worth discovering.

Vintage	12	11	10	09	08	07	06
WR	6	6	7	6	7	7	6
Drink	17-24	17-23	17-30	17-22	17-24	17-20	17-18

DRY $70 AV

Heron's Flight Amphora   (★★★★★)

The classy and distinctive, strikingly packaged 2015 vintage (★★★★★) was made from Sangiovese, estate-grown at Matakana. Made in a 500-litre clay amphora, it spent six months on its skins and a further six months in the amphora before bottling (Heron's Flight reports that terracotta, being porous, allows the wine to develop, without – unlike oak – imparting a direct flavour impact). Deep and bright in colour, it is powerful and sweet-fruited, with highly concentrated blackcurrant and plum flavours, buried tannins, and lovely ripeness, drive and harmony. Already delicious, it also should be long-lived.

DRY $120 AV

Kaimira Estate Brightwater Hui Whero   ★★★☆

Certified organic, the youthful 2016 vintage (★★★☆) is a Nelson 'blend of classic varieties', matured for 10 months in oak casks (15 per cent new). Full-coloured, with a spicy bouquet, it is a medium-bodied, vibrantly fruity, slightly Syrah-like red, fresh, plummy and distinctly peppery, with lively acidity and very good flavour depth.

Vintage	16
WR	6
Drink	18-26

DRY $28 –V

Linden Estate Reserve Dam Block ★★★★

Scented and savoury, the stylish 2015 vintage (★★★★☆) is Merlot-based (64 per cent), with smaller portions of Cabernet Sauvignon (20 per cent), Cabernet Franc (15 per cent) and Malbec (1 per cent). Estate-grown in the Esk Valley of Hawke's Bay and French oak-matured for over a year, it is full-coloured, with well-ripened blackcurrant, plum and spice flavours, gentle tannins, good harmony and a lingering finish. Best drinking 2020+.

DRY $40 –V

Little Brother (★★★☆)

The attractive, easy-drinking 2016 vintage (★★★☆) was grown at two sites in Kerikeri, Northland. Syrah is the principal variety, 'spiked with Viognier and a touch of Chambourcin'. Matured in old oak barriques, it is full-coloured, mouthfilling and smooth, in a vibrantly fruity style with fresh, ripe, plummy, juicy flavours to the fore. A good summer red. (From Byrne.)

DRY $19 V+

Man O' War Ironclad ★★★★☆

Launched from 2008, this powerful red, grown at the eastern end of Waiheke Island, is typically a blend of Cabernet Franc and Merlot, with minor portions of Cabernet Sauvignon, Petit Verdot and Malbec. From a very cool, late-ripening season, the 2012 vintage (★★★★☆), matured in French oak casks (40 per cent new), is deeply coloured, powerful, generous and sweet-fruited, with blackcurrant, herb and nut flavours, showing excellent concentration and potential. The 2011 (★★★★), from a wet growing season, is slightly leaner, but tight and elegant, with excellent depth.

Vintage	12	11
WR	5	4
Drink	17-25	17-23

DRY $50 –V

Man O' War Warspite ★★★★☆

The 2013 vintage (★★★★☆) is a classy, generous blend of Cabernet Franc (60 per cent), Merlot (30 per cent) and Malbec (10 per cent), grown on Ponui Island, near Waiheke Island. Hand-harvested at 24.1–26.5 brix and matured for two years in French oak casks (42 per cent new), it is a deeply coloured, robust red (15 per cent alcohol), fragrant, sweet-fruited and supple, with generous red-berry, plum, herb and nut flavours, good complexity and gentle tannins. Highly enjoyable now, it should be at its best 2018+. The 2014 vintage (★★★★) is also a Ponui Island blend of Cabernet Franc, Merlot and Malbec, matured in French oak casks (45 per cent new). Deeply c oloured, with slightly herbal aromas, it is a powerful, sturdy (15 per cent alcohol) red, with generous plum, spice and herb flavours, seasoned with nutty oak, good complexity and a well-rounded finish. Drink now or cellar.

Vintage	14
WR	5
Drink	17-20

DRY $46 –V

Marsden Bay of Islands Cavalli   ★★★

The easy-drinking 2014 vintage (★★★) is a Northland blend of Pinotage, Chambourcin and Merlot. Matured for nine months in French oak casks (20 per cent new), it is full-coloured, mouthfilling and smooth, with ripe, berryish, plummy, gently spicy flavours, a touch of complexity and good depth.

Vintage	14
WR	6
Drink	P

 DRY $25 –V

Messenger   ★★★★★

After the lovely debut 2008 (★★★★★), Messenger is established as one of Auckland's greatest reds. It is estate-grown at Stillwater, north of the city. French oak-matured for two years, the 2013 vintage (★★★★☆) is a blend of Merlot, Cabernet Franc and Malbec. Dense and inky in colour, it's a robust (14.8 per cent alcohol), almost super-charged red, very sweet-fruited, with highly concentrated plum, spice and slight liquorice flavours. Notable for its power and richness, rather than finesse, it is full of personality.

 DRY $85 AV

Mills Reef Elspeth One   (★★★★★)

The 2013 vintage (★★★★★) is the first for many years. Likely to be long-lived, it is a Gimblett Gravels, Hawke's Bay blend of estate-grown Syrah (41 per cent), Cabernet Franc (23 per cent), Merlot (18 per cent) and Cabernet Sauvignon (18 per cent), matured for 20 months in French oak casks (35 per cent new). Full-coloured, it has deep, youthful, plummy, spicy flavours – in which the Syrah makes its presence well felt – finely balanced tannins, excellent complexity, and a long, very persistent finish. Best drinking 2020+.

 DRY $150 –V

Mission Jewelstone Gimblett Gravels Antoine   ★★★★★

Named after pioneer winemaker Father Antoine Gavin, the 2014 vintage (★★★★★) is a dark, powerful blend of Merlot (75 per cent), Cabernet Sauvignon (20 per cent) and Cabernet Franc (5 per cent), grown in the Gimblett Gravels, Hawke's Bay, and matured for 18 months in French oak casks (60 per cent new). Still very youthful, it is a fresh, mouthfilling, firmly structured red, with concentrated, ripe blackcurrant, plum and spice flavours, complex and savoury, and buried tannins. A classic, 'claret style' red, it should be at its best 2020+.

Vintage	14	13
WR	7	6
Drink	17-30	17-25

DRY $50 AV

Mokoroa ★★★☆

From Puriri Hills, the 2016 vintage (★★★☆) was estate-grown at Clevedon, in South Auckland. Promoted as 'a good lunchtime wine', It is a blend of Merlot (71 per cent), Cabernet Sauvignon (15 per cent), Cabernet Franc (8 per cent), Carménère (5 per cent) and Malbec (1 per cent). Deep ruby, it is a medium-bodied red with vibrant, berryish, plummy flavours, slightly earthy and savoury notes adding complexity, and a smooth, very harmonious finish. Best drinking during 2018.

Vintage	11
WR	6
Drink	17-18

DRY $30 –V

Moutere Hills Nelson Rumer (★★★☆)

Enjoyable young, the 2016 vintage (★★★☆) is a blend of Syrah, Merlot and Cabernet Sauvignon, hand-picked and matured for 10 months in French and American oak casks. Full-coloured, it is mouthfilling, fresh and smooth, with plum and blackcurrant flavours, a hint of herbs, fresh acidity and very good depth.

DRY $55 –V

Mudbrick Vineyard Velvet ★★★★★

The 2013 vintage (★★★★★) is a secret blend, for when 'it is important to make a good impression'. Estate-grown on Waiheke Island (in the Mudbrick and Shepherds Point vineyards), and matured in French oak casks (40 per cent new), it is deep and youthful in colour, with very ripe blackcurrant-like aromas. Finely poised and highly concentrated, it has cassis, plum, spice and nut flavours, a hint of dark chocolate, impressive density and complexity, and firm but not grippy tannins. It should flourish for a decade.

Vintage	13
WR	7
Drink	17-25

DRY $140 –V

Newton Forrest Estate Cornerstone ★★★★★

Grown in the Cornerstone Vineyard, on the corner of Gimblett Road and State Highway 50 – where the first vines were planted in 1989 – this is a distinguished Hawke's Bay blend of Cabernet Sauvignon, Merlot and Malbec, matured in French (principally) and American oak barriques. The 2014 vintage (★★★★☆) is deeply coloured, mouthfilling and supple, with ripe blackcurrant, plum, spice and liquorice flavours, showing excellent complexity and depth. The highly refined 2015 vintage (★★★★★) is dark, full-bodied and tightly structured, with concentrated, ripe blackcurrant, plum and spice flavours, complex and savoury, fine-grained tannins, and a very harmonious finish. Already delicious, it's well worth cellaring.

DRY $60 AV

Obsidian Reserve The Obsidian   ★★★★★

The Obsidian Vineyard at Onetangi produces one of the most stylish Waiheke Island reds. Blended from classic Bordeaux red varieties – Cabernet Franc, Merlot, Cabernet Sauvignon, Petit Verdot and Malbec – it is matured in French oak barriques. The 2013 vintage (★★★★★) has deep, moderately youthful colour. Fleshy and generous, it has dense blackcurrant, herb, spice and nut flavours, savoury notes adding complexity, and good tannin backbone. Still unfolding, it's full of potential; open 2018+. The 2014 vintage (★★★★★) has deep, youthful colour. Fragrant and supple, it has deep blackcurrant, plum, herb and spice flavours, showing excellent complexity, fine-grained tannins, and a rich, harmonious finish. A graceful wine, it's already delicious, but well worth cellaring.

Vintage	14	13	12	11	10	09	08	07	06	05	DRY $68 AV
WR	7	7	6	6	7	6	7	5	NM	7	
Drink	17-24	17-23	17-20	17-18	17-20	17-18	17-20	17-19	NM	P	

Obsidian Waiheke Island Reserve The Mayor   ★★★★☆

The elegant 2013 vintage (★★★★☆) is a blend dominated by Cabernet Franc, with smaller proportions of Petit Verdot and Malbec. Deeply coloured, it is fragrant, fresh and vibrantly fruity, with strong blackcurrant, plum and herb flavours, supple, finely textured and lingering. Best drinking mid-2018+.

Vintage	13	12	11	DRY $45 –V
WR	7	5	6	
Drink	17-21	17-20	17-18	

Obsidian Waiheke Island Vitreous   (★★★★)

Grown at Onetangi, the debut 2015 vintage (★★★★) is a blend of Cabernet Sauvignon (28 per cent), Merlot (25 per cent), Cabernet Franc (23 per cent), Petit Verdot (19 per cent) and Malbec (5 per cent). Matured in French oak casks (20 per cent new), it is full-coloured, mouthfilling and smooth, with fresh, generous, slightly spicy and herbal flavours, nutty and savoury. Showing good complexity, it should be at its best mid-2018+.

DRY $32 –V

Ohinemuri Kaipaki Reserve Taniwha   (★★★)

The 2014 vintage (★★★) was grown at Kaipaki, between Hamilton and Cambridge, in the Waikato. A blend of Cabernet Franc (55 per cent), Pinotage (27 per cent) and Merlot (18 per cent), oak-aged for a year, it is full-coloured, with a slightly leafy bouquet, mouthfilling body and strong red-berry, plum and herb flavours, fresh and firm. Ready.

Vintage	14	DRY $30 –V
WR	6	
Drink	17-20	

Paritua 21:12   ★★★★☆

The 2013 vintage (★★★★★) is a blend of Cabernet Sauvignon, Merlot, Cabernet Franc and Malbec, estate-grown in the Bridge Pa Triangle, Hawke's Bay. A very powerful (15 per cent alcohol) red, it was matured for 18 months in oak casks (60 per cent new). Densely coloured, it is purple-flushed, with fresh, concentrated, very ripe blackcurrant, plum, spice and coffee flavours, and fine-grained tannins. Still youthful, it should be at its best 2018+.

Vintage	13
WR	7
Drink	17-25

 DRY $100 –V

Paritua Hawke's Bay Red   ★★★★☆

The 2013 vintage (★★★★☆) is a blend of Merlot, Cabernet Sauvignon, Cabernet Franc and Malbec, matured for 14 months in French oak casks (50 per cent new). Dark and youthful in colour, it is powerful (14.5 per cent alcohol), with dense blackcurrant, plum and spice flavours, a hint of coffee, integrated oak, and finely balanced tannins. It should be long-lived.

Vintage	13
WR	7
Drink	17-25

 DRY $40 –V

Paroa Bay Bay of Islands CMC   ★★★★

The 2014 vintage (★★★☆) is a full-bodied, slightly earthy Northland blend of Cabernet Franc (72 per cent), Cabernet Sauvignon (23 per cent) and Malbec (5 per cent). It has generous red-berry, spice and oak flavours, showing some complexity and aging potential.

 DRY $45 –V

Pask Small Batch Gimblett Gravels Trilliant   (★★★★)

The debut 2014 vintage (★★★★) is a Merlot-based blend, with smaller amounts of Cabernet Sauvignon and Malbec, matured for 20 months in French and American oak casks (55 per cent new). Deeply coloured, with a fragrant, spicy bouquet, it is mouthfilling, with generous, ripe, plummy, spicy flavours, showing good complexity, finely balanced tannins and lots of drink-young appeal. Best drinking 2018+.

Vintage	14
WR	6
Drink	17-22

DRY $35 –V

Passage Rock Waiheke Island Magnus   ★★★★★

The delicious 2013 vintage (★★★★★) is a blend of Syrah, Cabernet Sauvignon, Merlot, Malbec and Petit Verdot, grown on Waiheke Island. Deeply coloured, it is sturdy (14.5 per cent alcohol) and still youthful, with concentrated, vibrant plum, blackcurrant and spice flavours, fine-grained tannins, and excellent ripeness, complexity and harmony. Drink now or cellar.

 DRY $70 AV

Peacock Sky Le Côté de la Colline ★★★

The 2013 vintage (★★★☆) is a firmly structured Waiheke Island blend of Cabernet Sauvignon (63 per cent), Cabernet Franc (26 per cent) and Malbec (11 per cent). It has strong, ripe blackcurrant, plum and spice flavours, with hints of herbs, and good cellaring potential.

DRY $42 –V

Pegasus Bay Maestro ★★★★

The youthful 2015 vintage (★★★★) is a Waipara, North Canterbury blend of Merlot, Cabernet Sauvignon and Malbec, barrel-aged for two years (50 per cent new). Densely coloured, it is mouthfilling and vibrantly fruity, with very generous, berryish flavours, showing good but not great complexity, gentle tannins and a smooth finish. Worth cellaring.

Vintage	15
WR	6
Drink	18-28

DRY $50 –V

Puriri Hills Estate ★★★★☆

Estate-grown at Clevedon, in South Auckland, this is a stylish, Merlot-based blend. The 2010 vintage (★★★★★) is a beauty – dark, fleshy and silky, with lovely ripeness and mouthfeel. From a warm but damp growing season, the 2011 vintage (★★★★) is a blend of Merlot (50 per cent), Carménère (29 per cent), Cabernet Franc (14 per cent) and Malbec (7 per cent). Originally intended to be marketed as Puriri Hills Reserve, it was declassified to the Estate label. Mouthfilling, with fullish, fairly mature colour, it is leathery, nutty and savoury, with hints of herbs and spices, fresh acidity and very good complexity. It's probably at its peak; drink now to 2018.

Vintage	11	10	09	08	07	06	05
WR	6	7	6	7	6	4	7
Drink	17-19	17-27	17-22	17-25	17-20	P	17-20

DRY $40 –V

Puriri Hills Pope (★★★★★)

Named after Ivan Pope, who planted and tended the vines at this Clevedon, South Auckland vineyard. The 2010 vintage (★★★★★), a blend of Merlot (54 per cent), Cabernet Franc (25 per cent), Carménère (17 per cent) and Malbec (4 per cent), was matured for nearly two years in French oak casks (75 per cent new). Outstandingly lush and complex, with ripe, supple tannins and very deep plum, spice, herb and slight liquorice flavours, it shows great potential. Full of youthful promise, the 2013 vintage (★★★★★) is a classy blend of Merlot (70 per cent), Cabernet Franc (10 per cent), Carménère (10 per cent), Cabernet Sauvignon (5 per cent) and Malbec (5 per cent), matured in French oak casks (100 per cent new). Deeply coloured, it has a fragrant, youthful, berryish, spicy bouquet, leading into a full-bodied, already very approachable wine, with densely packed, complex plum, blackcurrant and spice flavours, firm, savoury and persistent. Best drinking 2020+.

DRY $120 –V

Puriri Hills Reserve

A regional classic. Estate-grown at Clevedon, in South Auckland, it is blended from varying proportions of Merlot (principally), Cabernet Franc, Carménère, Cabernet Sauvignon and Malbec, and typically matured for two years in French oak barriques (a high percentage new). In a vertical tasting of the 2008 to 2014 vintages (there is no 2011), held in December 2016, the 2008 vintage (★★★★) was in brilliant form – memorably fragrant, rich and complex. Other stars were the very generous, 'complete' 2010 vintage (★★★★★), and the highly refined, beautifully rich, finely textured 2013 vintage (★★★★★).

Vintage	10	09	08	07	06	05	04
WR	7	6	7	NM	6	7	7
Drink	17-27	17-23	17-25	NM	17-20	17-20	17-20

DRY $70 AV

Ransom Mahurangi ★★★☆

The full-coloured 2013 vintage (★★★☆), estate-grown north of Auckland, was blended mostly from Syrah, with smaller portions of Cabernet Sauvignon and Cabernet Franc. Barrel-aged for 20 months, it is medium-bodied, with fresh, spicy aromas and flavours, hints of plums and herbs, some savoury complexity, gentle tannins and good harmony. Drink now or cellar.

DRY $27 –V

Runner Duck Passion (★★★★)

The 2013 vintage (★★★★), grown at Matakana, was made solely from Syrah. Full and bright in colour, it is floral and supple, with vibrant plum and spice flavours, showing excellent depth, savoury notes adding complexity, and good potential.

DRY $40 –V

Sacred Hill Brokenstone

Merlot-based, this is a typically outstanding Hawke's Bay red from the Gimblett Gravels (principally the company's Deerstalkers Vineyard). The highly attractive 2015 vintage (★★★★★), matured for 19 months in French oak casks (22 per cent new), is Merlot-dominant (87 per cent), with minor portions of Malbec (4 per cent), Syrah (4 per cent), Cabernet Sauvignon (3 per cent) and Cabernet Franc (2 per cent). Full-coloured, it is vibrantly fruity, with concentrated, ripe, plummy, spicy flavours, well-integrated oak, savoury notes adding complexity, and supple tannins. Already delicious, it should be at its best 2020+.

Vintage	15	14	13	12	11	10	09	08	07
WR	7	7	7	NM	6	7	7	6	7
Drink	18-30	17-26	17-23	NM	17-18	17-20	17-18	P	P

DRY $50 AV

Sacred Hill Helmsman   ★★★★★

This is a classy, single-vineyard Gimblett Gravels red from Hawke's Bay. The powerful 2015 vintage (★★★★★), blended from Cabernet Sauvignon (76 per cent), Merlot (19 per cent) and Cabernet Franc (5 per cent), was hand-picked and matured for 20 months in French oak barriques (50 per cent new). A classic, youthful, Cabernet-based red, it is fragrant and deeply coloured, with highly concentrated blackcurrant, plum and herb flavours, seasoned with nutty oak. Dense and firmly structured, it's a stylish, very age-worthy wine, likely to be at its best 2022+.

Vintage	15	14	13	12	11	10	09
WR	7	7	7	NM	6	7	7
Drink	18-30	18-29	17-28	NM	17-24	17-25	17-20

DRY $85 AV

Schubert Wairarapa Con Brio   (★★★★)

Barrel-matured for several years, the 2013 vintage (★★★★) is a Martinborough blend of Syrah and Merlot, with a splash of Pinot Noir. The colour shows some maturity; the palate is firm and savoury, with very good depth of ripe, spicy, slightly nutty flavour.

DRY $45 –V

Sileni Estate Selection Hawke's Bay Ruber   ★★★★☆

The debut 2014 vintage (★★★★☆) is a classy blend of Cabernet Franc, Merlot and Syrah, grown in the Bridge Pa Triangle. It was matured for 14 months in French oak barriques (40 per cent new), then aged for a further five months in one-year-old barrels. Full-coloured, it has fragrant red-berry and spice aromas, leading into a mouthfilling, still youthful wine, with generous berry, plum and spice flavours, complex, savoury and finely structured. The 2015 vintage (★★★★) is full-coloured and mouthfilling, with generous plum, spice and liquorice flavours, fresh acidity and a fairly firm finish. An 'upfront' style, it's a drink-now or cellaring proposition.

Vintage	15	14
WR	6	7
Drink	17-24	17-24

DRY $33 AV

Soho Blue Blood Zabeel Reserve   ★★★★★

The powerful 2015 vintage (★★★★★) is a distinctive Waiheke Island blend of Syrah (51 per cent), Petit Verdot (35 per cent) and Malbec (14 per cent), estate-grown at Onetangi and matured for nine months in French oak casks (75 per cent new). Deeply coloured, with a fragrant, spicy bouquet, it's a 'full-on', bold style, weighty and fruit-packed, with fresh, highly concentrated, still very youthful plum, spice and blackcurrant flavours, rich, savoury and long. It's crying out for time; open 2020+.

DRY $99 AV

Soho Revolver   ★★★★

Estate-grown at Onetangi, on Waiheke Island, the 2015 vintage (★★★☆) is a blend of Merlot (44 per cent), Malbec (27 per cent), Cabernet Franc (20 per cent) and Cabernet Sauvignon (9 per cent). French and American oak-aged, it is fragrant and lively, with moderately rich, berryish, spicy flavours, fresh acidity and gentle tannins.

 DRY $38 AV

Vintage	15	14	13	12	11	10	09
WR	6	5	7	6	NM	7	7
Drink	17-23	17-22	17-20	17-18	NM	17-18	P

St Nesbit   ★★★★☆

This South Auckland red is estate-grown at Karaka, on a southern arm of the Manukau Harbour. It enjoyed a high profile for its Bordeaux-style reds from 1984 to 1991, but following replanting, production ceased for a decade. I tasted the 2007, 2008 and 2009 vintages in mid-2015. The 2009 (★★★★) is a blend of Merlot (70 per cent), Cabernet Franc (20 per cent) and Petit Verdot (10 per cent), matured in French and American oak casks. An elegant rather than powerful red, it showed considerable maturity, with a savoury, leathery, nutty complexity, a hint of herbs, and lots of current-drinking appeal. The powerful 2008 (★★★★★) was dark, sturdy, fleshy and rich, with concentrated plum, blackcurrant, spice and nut flavours, a hint of dark chocolate, and obvious potential. My pick was the seductive 2007 (★★★★★), a very fragrant, complex red with rich blackcurrant, plum, spice and herb flavours, supple, generous and lingering.

 DRY $75 –V

Stonyridge Larose   ★★★★★

Typically a stunning Waiheke Island wine. Dark and seductively perfumed, with smashing fruit flavours, at its best it is a magnificently concentrated red that matures superbly for a decade or longer, acquiring great complexity. The vines – Cabernet Sauvignon, Merlot, Cabernet Franc, Malbec and Petit Verdot – are grown in free-draining clay soils on a north-facing slope, a kilometre from the sea at Onetangi, and are very low-yielding (4 tonnes/hectare). The wine is matured for a year in French (80–90 per cent) and American oak barriques (half new, half one year old), and is sold largely on an 'en primeur' basis, whereby the customers, in return for paying for their wine about nine months in advance of its delivery, secure a substantial price reduction. The 2015 vintage (★★★★★) is a classic young claret-style red, dense but not tough, with power through the palate and obvious potential. Dark and purple-flushed, it is sturdy, rich and supple, with very ripe blackcurrant, plum and spice flavours, showing lovely freshness, harmony and length. Needing five years to unfold, it should mature gracefully for decades.

 DRY $280 –V

Vintage	13	12	11	10	09	08	07	06	05
WR	7	6	5	7	6	7	5	7	7
Drink	23-33	18-25	17-23	20-30	18-25	18-28	17-20	P	17-22

Tantalus Waiheke Island Ecluse Reserve (★★★)

The 2014 vintage (★★★), blended from Cabernet Sauvignon, Merlot, Cabernet Franc and Malbec, was grown at Onetangi and matured for 11 months in French oak barriques. Full and moderately youthful in colour, with an earthy bouquet, it is a mouthfilling red, revealing a slight lack of delicacy and finesse, but also good depth of blackcurrant and spice flavours, showing considerable complexity.

Vintage	14
WR	6
Drink	17-26

DRY $65 –V

Tantalus Waiheke Island Evoque Reserve (★★★★☆)

The 2014 vintage (★★★★☆), grown at Onetangi, is a blend of Merlot, Malbec, Cabernet Sauvignon and Cabernet Franc, matured for 11 months in French oak barriques. Deeply coloured, it is mouthfilling and sweet-fruited, with generous, plummy, gently spicy flavours, finely integrated oak, slightly earthy and savoury notes adding complexity, and a well-structured finish. Showing good potential, it should be at its best 2018+.

Vintage	14
WR	6
Drink	17-26

DRY $60 –V

Te Mata Coleraine ★★★★★

Breed, rather than brute power, is the hallmark of Coleraine (correctly pronounced Cole-raine rather than Coler-aine), which since its first vintage in 1982 has carved out an illustrious reputation among New Zealand's claret-style reds. In all vintages since 2007, Cabernet Sauvignon has been the predominant variety. At its best, it is a magical Hawke's Bay wine, with a depth, complexity and subtlety on the level of a top-class Bordeaux. The grapes are grown in the Havelock North hills, in the company's warm, north-facing Buck and 1892 vineyards, and the wine is matured for 17 to 20 months in French oak barriques, predominantly new. The lovely, highly fragrant 2015 vintage (★★★★★) is a blend of Cabernet Sauvignon (54 per cent), Merlot (36 per cent) and Cabernet Franc (10 per cent). A typically refined, authoritative wine, it is deep and very youthful in colour, with highly concentrated, ripe blackcurrant, plum and spice flavours, showing notable density, poise, structure and complexity. Revealing obvious potential for long-term cellaring, it's best cellared until at least 2022.

Vintage	15	14	13	12	11	10	09	08	07	06
WR	7	7	7	NM	7	7	7	7	7	7
Drink	19-30	18-28	17-33	NM	17-23	17-22	17-21	17-20	17-27	17-26

DRY $115 AV

Te Motu

This Waiheke Island red is grown at Onetangi, over the fence from Stonyridge. Compared to its neighbour, it has typically been less opulent than Larose, in a more earthy, slightly leafy style. Cabernet Sauvignon-predominant, the 2008 vintage (★★★★☆) has dark, mature colour. Rich and savoury, it has blackcurrant, herb and nut flavours, showing excellent depth and complexity. The 2012 vintage (★★★★☆) is full-coloured and mouthfilling, with youthful, vibrant red-berry and spice flavours, showing excellent depth, and a firm finish. Best drinking 2019+.

DRY $90 –V

Te Motu Kokoro

Launched from 2012 (★★★★☆), this red is a major change in style for the long-established Waiheke Island producer – it's a lot more vibrant and youthful than past releases. Grown at Onetangi, the 2013 vintage (★★★★☆) was blended from Merlot (principally), with smaller amounts of Cabernet Sauvignon, Cabernet Franc, Malbec and Syrah. Dark and mouthfilling, it has fresh blackcurrant/plum flavours, ripe and generous, savoury notes adding complexity, good tannin backbone, and obvious potential.

DRY $75 –V

Te Motu Tipua

'Within any vintage, there is always a varietal that transcends', according to the back label on this Waiheke Island red. The 2008 (★★★★★) was a powerful Syrah, but the 2013 vintage (★★★★★) is one of New Zealand's best-yet Cabernet Francs. Grown at Onetangi and matured for 20 months in French oak casks (30 per cent new), it has fragrant red-berry and spice aromas. A lovely, mouthfilling, silky-textured red, it is sweet-fruited, with youthful, ripe berry, spice and nut flavours, oak complexity, and excellent depth and harmony. Best drinking 2018+.

DRY $115 AV

Te Whau The Point ★★★★★

This classy Waiheke Island red flows from a steeply sloping vineyard at Putiki Bay. The outstanding 2014 vintage (★★★★★) was blended from Cabernet Sauvignon (50 per cent), Merlot (31 per cent), Cabernet Franc (12 per cent), Malbec (5 per cent) and Petit Verdot (2 per cent), matured in French oak casks for 18 months. Deeply coloured and ripely fragrant, it is a powerful, weighty red, dense and savoury, with concentrated blackcurrant, plum and spice flavours, seasoned with nutty oak, and good tannin backbone. A top vintage that reminded me of a fine Pauillac, it should be long-lived, but is already a delicious mouthful.

Vintage	14	13	12	11	10	09	08	07	06	05
WR	7	7	6	NM	7	7	7	7	6	7
Drink	18-26	17-25	17-20	NM	17-25	17-18	17-22	17-24	P	17-20

DRY $75 AV

Tincan Cult Crimson NZ NaturalWine (★★★)

The ruby-hued, slightly hazy 2016 vintage (★★★) was handled without sulphur dioxide, and bottled without fining or filtering. A blend of Pinot Noir (65 per cent), Syrah (25 per cent) and Pinot Gris (10 per cent), it is medium-bodied, with ripe, berryish flavours, hints of plums and spices, fresh acidity, gentle tannins and good depth.

DRY $29 –V

Trinity Hill Gimblett Gravels The Gimblett   ★★★★★

The very elegant 2015 vintage (★★★★★) is a Hawke's Bay blend of Cabernet Sauvignon (42 per cent), Cabernet Franc (31 per cent) and Merlot (23 per cent), with splashes of Malbec and Petit Verdot. Matured for 16 months in French oak casks (35 per cent new), it has dark, youthful colour. Mouthfilling, it's a 'serious' but delicious red, with deep, blackcurrant-like flavours, gently seasoned with nutty oak, fine-grained tannins, excellent complexity, and lovely poise and harmony. Offering fine value, it's well worth cellaring to 2020+.

Vintage	15	14	13	12	11	10	09	08	07	06
WR	6	6	7	4	5	6	7	5	6	6
Drink	17-27	17-25	17-25	17-25	17-25	17-20	17-30	17-20	17-22	17-18

DRY $35 V+

Trinity Hill Hawke's Bay The Trinity   ★★★☆

The 2014 vintage (★★★☆) is a blend of Merlot (55 per cent), Tempranillo (17 per cent), 'Cabernets' (13 per cent), Malbec (8 per cent), and Syrah (7 per cent). Designed for early consumption, it is full-coloured, with generous, ripe berry and plum flavours, fresh and smooth, in a very fruit-driven style.

Vintage	14	13	12
WR	6	6	4
Drink	17-18	17-18	P

DRY $22 AV

TW Makauri   (★★★☆)

Grown in Gisborne, the 2014 vintage (★★★☆) is a blend of Malbec and Merlot. Full-coloured, it is fresh and mouthfilling, with youthful, plummy, spicy flavours, oak complexity and good depth. It's still developing; best drinking mid-2018+.

DRY $27 –V

Villa Maria Ngakirikiri The Gravels   (★★★★★)

The debut 2013 vintage (★★★★★) is promoted as the company's 'icon' Bordeaux-style red. From vines planted in the Gimblett Gravels between 1998 and 2000, it is Cabernet Sauvignon-based (97 per cent), with a splash of Merlot (3 per cent). Matured for 18 months in French oak barrels (52 per cent new), it is densely coloured, with substantial body (14 per cent alcohol) and bold, still extremely youthful, blackcurrant and plum-evoking flavours, showing lovely richness, purity and complexity. It should flourish for decades; open 2020 onwards.

Vintage	13
WR	7
Drink	20-30

DRY $130 AV

Waimea Nelson Trev's Red   ★★★

Enjoyable young, the 2015 vintage (★★★) is a blend of co-fermented Cabernet Franc, Syrah and Viognier. Fullish in colour, with fresh berry and spice aromas, it is medium-bodied, with berryish, plummy, slightly spicy flavours, a touch of complexity and a smooth finish.

DRY $23 –V

Cabernet Franc

New Zealand's sixth most widely planted red-wine variety, Cabernet Franc is probably a mutation of Cabernet Sauvignon, the much higher-profile variety with which it is so often blended. Jancis Robinson's phrase, 'a sort of claret Beaujolais', aptly sums up the nature of this versatile and underrated red-wine grape.

As a minority ingredient in the recipe of many of New Zealand's top reds, Cabernet Franc lends a delicious softness and concentrated fruitiness to its blends with Cabernet Sauvignon and Merlot. However, admirers of Château Cheval Blanc, the illustrious St Émilion (which is two-thirds planted in Cabernet Franc), have long appreciated that Cabernet Franc need not always be Cabernet Sauvignon's bridesmaid, but can yield fine red wines in its own right. The supple, fruity wines of Chinon and Bourgueil, in the Loire Valley, have also proved Cabernet Franc's ability to produce highly attractive, soft light reds.

According to the latest national vineyard survey, the bearing area of Cabernet Franc will be 109 hectares in 2018 – well below the 213 hectares in 2004. Over 70 per cent of the vines are clustered in Hawke's Bay and most of the rest are in Auckland. As a varietal red, Cabernet Franc is lower in tannin and acid than Cabernet Sauvignon; or as Michael Brajkovich, of Kumeu River, has put it: 'more approachable and easy'.

Beach House Gimblett Gravels Hawke's Bay Cabernet Franc ★★★★☆

The youthful 2014 vintage (★★★★☆) was grown in The Track Vineyard, in Mere Road, hand-picked at 25 brix and matured for a year in French oak barrels (30 per cent new). Deeply coloured, it is fragrant, fresh, weighty and concentrated, with vibrant, rich plum, spice and slight herb flavours, oak complexity and obvious potential; best drinking 2018+.

 DRY $30 AV

Black Estate Home North Canterbury Cabernet Franc (★★★★)

The charming, youthful 2015 vintage (★★★★) was handled without sulphur dioxide. Estate-grown at Waipara, it was hand-picked, aged in a 2:1 mix of old barriques and stainless steel tanks, and bottled unfined and unfiltered. Deep ruby, it is floral, medium-bodied, vibrantly fruity and supple, with ripe plum and red-berry flavours, very gentle tannins, and lots of drink-young appeal.

DRY $45 –V

Boneline, The, Waipara Cabernet Franc ★★★★

From 'some of the oldest and most southerly Cabernet Franc vines in New Zealand', the 2016 vintage (★★★★☆) is of eye-catching quality. The colour is deep and youthful; the palate is sturdy and vibrant, with deep, ripe blackcurrant, plum and spice flavours, gentle tannins, and a seductively rich, smooth finish. This ranks among the South Island's best-yet Cabernet Francs.

 DRY $30 –V

Clearview Reserve Hawke's Bay Cabernet Franc ★★★★★

From mature vines, around 30 years old, the 2015 vintage (★★★★★) was estate-grown at Te Awanga and matured for 17 months in barrels (30 per cent new). Deep and youthful in colour, it is floral and rich, with fresh, dense blackcurrant, plum and spice flavours, hints of herbs and dark chocolate, and a very harmonious, finely textured, lasting finish. Best drinking 2019+.

 DRY $45 AV

Lime Rock Central Hawke's Bay Cabernet Franc ★★★★

The highly attractive 2015 vintage (★★★★☆) was estate-grown, hand-picked and matured in seasoned French oak barriques. Full and bright in colour, it is fresh, fragrant and full-bodied, with strong, ripe berry, plum and spice flavours, showing excellent complexity. A savoury, finely structured red, it should be at its best 2019+. The youthful 2016 vintage (★★★★) is medium to full-bodied, with fresh, vibrant plum, spice and herb flavours, oak complexity, gentle tannins and a lingering finish.

Vintage	16	15
WR	7	7
Drink	18-23	18-22

DRY $28 AV

Maison Noire Hawke's Bay Cabernet Franc (★★★★)

Grown on north-facing hills near Maraekakaho, the 2014 vintage (★★★★) was hand-picked and matured for 20 months in French oak barrels (20 per cent new). A medium-bodied, 'feminine' style of red, it has fresh acidity, with attractive blackcurrant, red-berry, plum and spice flavours, a hint of herbs, savoury notes adding complexity, gentle tannins and a smooth finish. Drink now or cellar.

Vintage	14
WR	6
Drink	17-20

DRY $25 AV

Mission Hawke's Bay Reserve Cabernet Franc ★★★★☆

The powerful 2014 vintage (★★★★☆) was grown in the Bridge Pa Triangle and matured for a year in French oak barrels. Deep and youthful in colour, it is sturdy (14.5 per cent alcohol) and concentrated, with very ripe plum, nut and slight liquorice flavours, seductively smooth and rich. Drink now or cellar.

Vintage	14	13
WR	7	6
Drink	17-25	17-25

DRY $29 V+

Peacock Sky Waiheke Island Pure Franc (★★★☆)

Fullish in colour, the 2014 vintage (★★★☆) is a fresh, smooth wine, like a very light Bordeaux, with youthful berry, plum, spice and herb flavours, savoury notes adding complexity, and some elegance.

DRY $40 –V

Pyramid Valley Vineyards Growers Collection Howell Family Vineyard Hawke's Bay Cabernet Franc ★★★★

The 2013 vintage (★★★★) was hand-picked in the Bridge Pa Triangle and matured for 15 months in seasoned French oak barrels. Deep and fairly youthful in colour, it is mouthfilling and sweet-fruited, with good concentration of fresh, vibrant blackcurrant, plum and spice flavours.

DRY $52 –V

Sileni Cellar Selection Hawke's Bay Cabernet Franc ★★★

The clearly varietal 2014 vintage (★★★☆) was matured for nine months in French and American oak casks (20 per cent new). Full and youthful in colour, with fresh spice and herb aromas, it is mouthfilling (14.5 per cent alcohol), with vibrant plum, herb and spice flavours, gentle tannins and a very smooth finish.

DRY $24 AV

Vintage	14	13
WR	7	6
Drink	17-22	17-19

Sileni Estate Selection Pacemaker Hawke's Bay Cabernet Franc ★★★★

Grown in the Bridge Pa Triangle, the 2014 vintage (★★★★) was matured for 14 months in a 2:1 mix of French and American oak barriques (30 per cent new). Full-coloured, it is mouthfilling (14.5 per cent alcohol) and smooth, with fresh, generous red-berry, plum and slight herb flavours, oak-derived complexity and a finely balanced finish. Drink now or cellar.

DRY $37 –V

Vintage	14
WR	7
Drink	17-24

Thomas Cabernet Franc/Merlot ★★★★☆

The 2014 vintage (★★★★☆) is a blend of Cabernet Franc (48 per cent) and Merlot (45 per cent), with splashes of Syrah (4 per cent) and Cabernet Sauvignon (3 per cent). Hand-harvested at Onetangi, on Waiheke Island, it was matured for 15 months in French oak barriques (26 per cent new). Full-coloured, it is mouthfilling, fresh and smooth, with strong, ripe plum, red-berry and spice flavours, seasoned with nutty oak. An elegant red, youthful and supple, it should be at its best 2019+. (From Batch Winery.)

DRY $46 –V

Cabernet Sauvignon and Cabernet-predominant blends

Cabernet Sauvignon has proved a tough nut to crack in New Zealand. Mid-priced models were – until recently – usually of lower quality than a comparable offering from Australia, where the relative warmth suits the late-ripening Cabernet Sauvignon variety. Yet a top New Zealand Cabernet-based red from a favourable vintage can hold its own in illustrious company and the overall standard of today's middle-tier, $20 bottlings is far higher than many wine lovers realise – which makes for some great bargains.

Cabernet Sauvignon was widely planted here in the nineteenth century. The modern resurgence of interest in the great Bordeaux variety was led by Tom McDonald, the legendary Hawke's Bay winemaker, whose string of elegant (though, by today's standards, light) Cabernet Sauvignons under the McWilliam's label, from the much-acclaimed 1965 vintage to the gold medal-winning 1975, proved beyond all doubt that fine-quality red wines could be produced in New Zealand.

During the 1970s and 1980s, Cabernet Sauvignon ruled the red-wine roost in New Zealand. Since then, as winemakers – especially in the South Island, but also Hawke's Bay – searched for red-wine varieties that would ripen more fully and consistently in our relatively cool grape-growing climate than Cabernet Sauvignon, it has been pushed out of the limelight by Merlot, Pinot Noir and Syrah. Between 2003 and 2018, the country's total area of bearing Cabernet Sauvignon vines will contract from 741 to 280 hectares. Growers with suitably warm sites have often retained faith in Cabernet Sauvignon, but others have moved on to less challenging varieties.

Over 85 per cent of the country's Cabernet Sauvignon vines are clustered in Hawke's Bay, and Auckland also has significant plantings. In the South Island, Cabernet-based reds have typically lacked warmth and richness. This magnificent but late-ripening variety's future in New Zealand clearly lies in the warmer vineyard sites of the north.

What is the flavour of Cabernet Sauvignon? When newly fermented a herbal character is common, intertwined with blackcurrant-like fruit aromas. New oak flavours, firm acidity and taut tannins are other hallmarks of young, fine Cabernet Sauvignon. With maturity the flavour loses its aggression and the wine develops roundness and complexity, with assorted cigar-box, minty and floral scents emerging. It is unwise to broach a Cabernet Sauvignon-based red with any pretensions to quality at less than three years old; at about five years old the rewards of cellaring really start to flow.

Ashwell Martinborough Cabernet Sauvignon ★★★

French oak-aged, the fresh 2013 vintage (★★★) has full, youthful colour. It shows a slight lack of ripeness and richness, but is vibrantly fruity, with blackcurrant, plum and spice flavours, and a smooth finish. Drink now or cellar.

Vintage	13
WR	5
Drink	17-23

DRY $28 –V

Awaroa Cabernet/Merlot/Malbec ★★★★

The dark, youthful 2014 vintage (★★★★) was hand-picked on Waiheke Island and matured for a year in seasoned French oak barriques. The bouquet is fresh and fragrant; the palate is mouthfilling, with generous, ripe blackcurrant, plum, herb and spice flavours, showing good density and complexity.

Vintage	14
WR	6
Drink	18-25

DRY $38 –V

Awaroa Requiem Waiheke Island Cabernet/Merlot/Malbec ★★★★☆

The fragrant, full-coloured 2015 vintage (★★★★★) is a classy blend of Cabernet Sauvignon (60 per cent), Merlot (25 per cent) and Malbec (15 per cent), estate-grown, hand-picked and matured in French oak barriques (100 per cent new). Dark, concentrated and sweet-fruited, it has very generous blackcurrant, plum and spice flavours, fine-grained tannins, and obvious cellaring potential; best drinking 2020+.

Vintage	15	14
WR	7	7
Drink	20-25	20-25

DRY $65 –V

Awaroa The Dan Cabernet/Syrah/Malbec (★★★★☆)

Matured for a year in all-new French oak barriques, the 2015 vintage (★★★★☆) is robust (14.8 per cent alcohol) and sweet-fruited, with concentrated blackcurrant, plum, spice and nut flavours, oak complexity and a finely textured finish.

DRY $65 –V

Babich Irongate Gimblett Gravels Hawke's Bay Cabernet/Merlot/Franc ★★★★★

Grown in the Irongate Vineyard and aged in French oak barriques (typically 35 per cent new), this elegant, complex, firmly structured red is designed for cellaring. Still very youthful, the refined 2015 vintage (★★★★☆) is a blend of Cabernet Sauvignon (51 per cent), Merlot (30 per cent) and Cabernet Franc (19 per cent). Deeply coloured, with a fragrant, savoury bouquet, it is mouthfilling, with deep, ripe blackcurrant, plum and spice flavours, showing good complexity, fine-grained tannins, and a long future ahead; open 2020+.

Vintage	15	14	13	12	11	10	09	08
WR	6	7	7	5	4	7	7	5
Drink	17-25	17-25	17-25	17-22	17-20	17-22	17-21	P

DRY $37 V+

Babich Limited Edition 100 Years Cabernet Sauvignon (★★★★★)

Launched in 2016 – a century after Babich's first vintage in 1916 – the rare 2013 vintage (★★★★★) was not shown to critics. Estate-grown in the Gimblett Gravels, Hawke's Bay, and French oak-aged, it is deeply coloured and weighty, sweet-fruited and savoury, with youthful, complex flavours of blackcurrant, plums and spices, and a tight, exceptionally long finish.

DRY $399 –V

Babich The Patriarch – see the Branded and Other Red Wines section

Beach House Hawke's Bay Gimblett Gravels Cabernet/Malbec ★★★★☆

The 2014 vintage (★★★★☆) is a single-vineyard red, blended from Cabernet Sauvignon (55 per cent), Malbec (35 per cent) and Cabernet Franc (10 per cent), and matured for a year in French oak casks (18 per cent new). It has deep, purple-flushed colour, mouthfilling body and strong, fresh blackcurrant, plum, spice and dark chocolate flavours, rich, ripe and firmly structured. Still very youthful, it should be at its best 2019+.

DRY $30 AV

Bespoke Mills Reef Gimblett Gravels Hawke's Bay Cabernet Sauvignon /Cabernet Franc

(★★★★☆)

The debut 2015 vintage (★★★★☆) is a blend of Cabernet Sauvignon (63 per cent) and Cabernet Franc (37 per cent), harvested from 20-year-old vines in Mere Road and matured for over a year in a 2:1 mix of French and American oak casks (39 per cent new). Full-coloured, it is fresh, mouthfilling and vibrantly fruity, with ripe blackcurrant, plum and spice flavours, oak-derived complexity and finely balanced tannins. Already drinking well, it should be in peak form from 2019 onwards.

DRY $40 –V

Bridge Estate Heritage Vines Cabernet/Merlot

★★★★

The distinctive 2014 vintage (★★★★☆) is from vines planted at Matawhero, Gisborne, in 1985. Merlot-based (43 per cent), with lesser amounts of Cabernet Sauvignon, Cabernet Franc and Malbec, it was matured in seasoned and rejuvenated French oak casks. Full and fairly youthful in colour, it has strong, ripe berry and spice flavours, with nutty and savoury notes, and good tannin backbone. A classy, subtle wine with good complexity, it's drinking well already, but likely to be at its best 2018+.

$42 –V

Brookfields Ohiti Estate Cabernet Sauvignon

★★★☆

Hawke's Bay winemaker Peter Robertson believes the warm, shingly Ohiti Estate, inland from Fernhill, produces 'sound Cabernet Sauvignon year after year – which is a major challenge to any vineyard'. The easy-drinking 2015 vintage (★★★☆) was matured in seasoned French and American oak casks. Full-coloured, it is mouthfilling, with generous berry, plum and spice flavours, tinged with sweet oak, and a smooth finish.

Vintage	15
WR	7
Drink	18-21

DRY $20 AV

Brookfields Reserve Vintage Cabernet/Merlot

★★★★★

Brookfields' top red is one of the most powerful, long-lived reds in Hawke's Bay. At its best, it is a thrilling wine – robust, tannin-laden and overflowing with very rich cassis, plum and mint flavours. The grapes are sourced from the Lyons family's sloping, north-facing vineyard at Bridge Pa, and the wine is matured a year in predominantly new French oak barriques. The 2015 vintage (★★★★☆) is deeply coloured, fragrant and rich, with mouthfilling body, concentrated blackcurrant, plum, spice and nut flavours, oak complexity and fine-grained tannins. Still youthful, it should be at its best 2019+.

Vintage	15	14	13	12	11	10	09	08	07	06
WR	7	7	7	NM	NM	NM	7	NM	7	7
Drink	20-26	19-25	18-25	NM	NM	NM	17-20	NM	17-19	P

DRY $60 AV

Church Road Cabernet/Merlot – see Church Road Merlot/Cabernet Sauvignon

Church Road Grand Reserve Hawke's Bay Cabernet Sauvignon/Merlot   (★★★★★)

Still youthful, the 2013 vintage (★★★★★) is a powerful, concentrated blend of Cabernet Sauvignon (56 per cent) and Merlot (44 per cent), estate-grown in Redstone Vineyard, in the Bridge Pa Triangle, French oak-aged for 18 months, and bottled unfined and unfiltered. Bold and youthful in colour, it is sturdy (14.5 per cent alcohol), with dense, ripe blackcurrant, plum and spice flavours, a hint of minty, oak complexity and firm tannins. A very age-worthy wine, it should be at its best 2018+.

DRY $45 AV

Church Road McDonald Series Hawke's Bay Cabernet Sauvignon   ★★★★★

This consistently impressive red is grown principally in the company's Redstone Vineyard, in the Bridge Pa Triangle, and matured in French and Hungarian oak barrels (30–35 per cent new). Lovely young, the deeply coloured 2014 vintage (★★★★★) was bottled unfined and unfiltered. It is sturdy (14.5 per cent alcohol), with vibrant, pure blackcurrant, plum and spice flavours, showing excellent ripeness and concentration, a seasoning of nutty oak, fine-grained tannins and obvious potential. A top buy.

DRY $27 V+

Collaboration Argent Cabernet Sauvignon   ★★★★☆

The distinctive, skilfully crafted 2013 vintage (★★★★★) is the finest yet. Hand-harvested at 'select vineyard sites' in Hawke's Bay and matured in French oak barrels (25 per cent new), it is deeply coloured, with a ripely fragrant bouquet. A refined, mouthfilling, generous red, it is a pure expression of Cabernet Sauvignon, with strong, vibrant blackcurrant, plum and spice flavours, fine-grained tannins, and excellent length.

DRY $40 –V

Collaboration Impression Cabernet/Cabernet Franc/Merlot   (★★★★)

Enjoyable now but worth cellaring, the 2014 vintage (★★★★) is a Hawke's Bay blend, matured for 16 months in seasoned French oak barrels, and bottled unfined and unfiltered. Full-coloured, it is mouthfilling, with generous, plummy, berryish, slightly earthy and nutty flavours, showing good freshness and complexity, and a well-rounded finish.

DRY $28 AV

Coopers Creek Reserve Hawke's Bay Cabernet Sauvignon   (★★★★★)

The outstanding 2013 vintage (★★★★★) has bold, dense colour. A powerful red, it was grown in the Gimblett Gravels and matured for a year in French oak casks (33 per cent new). Silky-textured, with concentrated blackcurrant, plum and spice flavours, showing beautiful ripeness and richness, it's a very harmonious wine, likely to be long-lived. It should be at its best 2018+.

DRY $57 AV

Coopers Creek Select Vineyards Gimblett Gravels
Hawke's Bay Cabernet/Merlot   ★★★★

The 2015 vintage (★★★★☆) is a full-coloured blend of Cabernet Sauvignon (53 per cent) and Merlot (47 per cent), grown in the Gimblett Gravels and barrel-aged for a year. Mouthfilling, it is still very youthful, with excellent depth of blackcurrant, plum and spice flavours, a vague hint of herbs, earthy notes adding complexity and good tannin backbone. Best drinking 2019+.

Vintage	15
WR	7
Drink	17-22

DRY $28 AV

Coopers Creek Select Vineyards Hawke's Bay Cabernet Sauvignon   (★★★★☆)

Offering fine value, the 2014 vintage (★★★★☆) was grown in the Gimblett Gravels and matured for 11 months in French oak casks (33 per cent new). Deeply coloured, it is mouthfilling, with generous, youthful, well-ripened blackcurrant and plum flavours, a hint of liquorice, and good tannin backbone. Already drinking well, it also shows excellent vigour and potential.

DRY $25 V+

Cornerstone Cabernet/Merlot/Malbec – see Newton Forrest Estate
Cornerstone in the Branded and Other Red Wines section

Crossroads Winemakers Collection Hawke's Bay Cabernet/Merlot   ★★★★☆

The 2013 vintage (★★★★★) was grown at two sites and barrel-aged. Deep and youthful in colour, it's a powerful young red with concentrated blackcurrant, plum and spice flavours, a hint of herbs, oak complexity, good tannin backbone, and excellent vigour and depth. Well worth cellaring.

Vintage	13	12
WR	7	5
Drink	17-23	17-23

DRY $40 –V

Dunleavy, The Strip Waiheke Island Cabernet/Merlot   ★★★★☆

Although made in a 'forward, fruit-driven style', the 2013 vintage (★★★★☆) was barrel-matured for 10 months. Deeply coloured, it is mouthfilling and smooth-flowing, with excellent depth of fresh blackcurrant, plum, herb and spice flavours. Enjoyable young, with savoury, earthy notes adding real complexity, it's a very harmonious wine; drink now or cellar.

DRY $45 –V

Johner Estate Wairarapa Cabernet/Merlot/Malbec

The 2013 vintage (★★★★), matured in French oak barrels (25 per cent new), is full-coloured, rich and vibrantly fruity, with strong plum and spice flavours, a gentle seasoning of oak, and gentle tannins. Drink now or cellar.

DRY $40 –V

Vintage	13
WR	6
Drink	17-20

Kidnapper Cliffs Gimblett Gravels Hawke's Bay
Cabernet Sauvignon/Merlot (★★★★★)

From Te Awa, the estate-grown 2013 vintage (★★★★★) was hand-harvested from vines averaging 25 years old and matured for 21 months in French oak barriques (35 per cent new). A blend of Cabernet Sauvignon (73 per cent), Merlot (24 per cent) and Cabernet Franc (3 per cent), it is full-coloured and ripely scented, with mouthfilling body and very generous blackcurrant, plum, spice and nut flavours. Delicious now, but also age-worthy, it's a very finely textured red, savoury, complex and smooth, with strong personality.

DRY $65 AV

Mahurangi River Cabernet Sauvignon/Merlot/Malbec (★★★★)

The full-coloured 2014 vintage (★★★★) is a savoury Matakana red, Cabernet Sauvignon-based (67 per cent), with equal parts of Merlot and Malbec, matured for over a year in French and American oak casks (30 per cent new). It has fresh, concentrated blackcurrant, plum, herb and spice flavours, showing good complexity.

DRY $29 AV

Maison Noire Hawke's Bay Cabernet Sauvignon (★★★★☆)

Already enjoyable, the 2015 vintage (★★★★☆) was grown in the Gimblett Gravels and matured for 16 months in barrels (35 per cent new). Full-coloured, with a fragrant, spicy bouquet, it is mouthfilling, with generous, ripe plum and spice flavours, finely integrated oak, savoury, earthy notes adding complexity, and gentle tannins. A very harmonious red, highly approachable in its youth, it also shows good potential and should be at its best 2019+. Priced sharply.

DRY $25 V+

Vintage	15
WR	5
Drink	17-22

Maison Noire Hawke's Bay Cabernet/Merlot (★★★☆)

A fresh, medium-bodied red, the 2016 vintage (★★★☆) was matured for a year in French oak barrels (25 per cent new). Enjoyable young, it is vibrantly fruity, with plummy, berryish, slightly spicy flavours, showing some savoury complexity, and a smooth finish.

DRY $25 –V

Vintage	16
WR	5
Drink	17-20

Mills Reef Elspeth Gimblett Gravels Hawke's Bay Cabernet Sauvignon   ★★★★★

The 2015 vintage (★★★★☆) was hand-picked from estate-grown, 20-year-old vines, including a small proportion of Cabernet Franc, and matured for over a year in a mix of American (63 per cent) and French (37 per cent) oak barrels (40 per cent new). Full-coloured, it is mouthfilling, with youthful, vibrant blackcurrant, red-berry, plum and spice flavours, showing excellent depth, good complexity and a firm backbone of tannin. Best drinking 2019+.

Vintage	15	14	13	12	11	10	09	08	07	06	DRY $40 AV
WR	7	7	7	NM	7	7	7	NM	7	7	
Drink	17-25	17-24	17-25	NM	17-18	17-18	17-18	NM	17-18	P	

Mills Reef Elspeth Gimblett Gravels Hawke's Bay Cabernet/Merlot   ★★★★★

Grown and hand-picked at the company's close-planted Mere Road site, this is a consistently impressive red. The 2013 vintage (★★★★☆) is a blend of Cabernet Sauvignon (79 per cent), Merlot (14.5 per cent) and Cabernet Franc (6.5 per cent), matured for 16 months in French (principally) and American oak barrels (40 per cent new). Deep and youthful in colour, it is mouthfilling and very age-worthy, with concentrated, ripe plum, spice and blackcurrant flavours, seasoned with slightly sweet oak, and a firmly structured finish. Best drinking 2018+.

Vintage	13	12	11	10	09	08	07	06	05	DRY $49 AV
WR	7	NM	7	7	7	NM	7	7	7	
Drink	17-25	NM	17-18	17-20	17-18	NM	P	P	P	

Mills Reef Elspeth Trust Vineyard Gimblett Gravels
Hawke's Bay Cabernet Sauvignon   ★★★★☆

The 2013 vintage (★★★★☆), the first release of this label since 2010, was estate-grown in the Trust Vineyard, in Mere Road, and matured for 15 months in French (80 per cent) and American (20 per cent) oak casks (33 per cent new). Deeply coloured, it is generous and smooth, with gentle tannins and fresh, concentrated, plummy, spicy flavours, seasoned with sweet oak. Already highly approachable, it should be at its best 2018+.

Vintage	13	12	11	10	09	08	07	06	DRY $50 –V
WR	7	NM	NM	7	7	NM	7	6	
Drink	17-25	NM	NM	17-18	17-18	NM	P	P	

Mills Reef Reserve Gimblett Gravels Hawke's Bay Cabernet/Merlot   ★★★★

The 2014 vintage (★★★★) was grown in the Gimblett Gravels and matured for a year in French (56 per cent) and American oak hogsheads (30 per cent new). Deeply coloured, it is mouthfilling, with blackcurrant, plum and spice flavours, generous, vibrant, youthful and smooth. Best drinking 2018+.

Vintage	14	13	12	DRY $25 AV
WR	6	7	6	
Drink	17-20	17-19	P	

Mission Gimblett Gravels Barrique Reserve Cabernet Sauvignon ★★★★☆

Offering top value, the 2015 vintage (★★★★☆) was matured for a year in French oak barrels. Dark and youthful in colour, it is fragrant, with concentrated, ripe, blackcurrant-like flavours to the fore, hints of plums, spices and nuts, and a firm, lingering finish. A complex, finely structured red, with good cellaring potential; best drinking 2018+.

Vintage	15	14	13
WR	6	5	7
Drink	17-23	17-22	17-25

DRY $29 V+

Mission Gimblett Gravels Barrique Reserve Cabernet/Merlot ★★★★☆

The impressive, well-priced 2015 vintage (★★★★☆) is a deeply coloured blend of Cabernet Sauvignon (67 per cent) and Merlot (33 per cent), matured for 18 months in French oak barriques (27 per cent new). Deeply coloured, it is fragrant and firm, with mouthfilling body, concentrated blackcurrant, plum and spice flavours, and a subtle seasoning of oak adding complexity. A finely structured, very age-worthy red, it should be at its best 2020+. Still youthful, the 2014 vintage (★★★★☆) is full-coloured, weighty and generous, with concentrated, ripe blackcurrant, plum and spice flavours, finely integrated oak and a firm, long finish.

Vintage	13
WR	7
Drink	17-25

DRY $29 V+

Mission Hawke's Bay Cabernet Sauvignon ★★★

The 2014 vintage (★★★) is a 'lightly oaked' red, full-coloured, fresh and vibrantly fruity, with satisfying depth of blackcurrant and spice flavours, ripe and smooth. Enjoyable young.

DRY $18 AV

Osawa Prestige Collection Hawke's Bay Cabernet Sauvignon/Merlot (★★★★)

The 2013 vintage (★★★★) is a concentrated, ripe, slightly earthy, 50:50 blend of Cabernet Sauvignon and Merlot, grown at Maraekakaho. It has some slightly herby, gamey notes, in a fleshy, rich and complex style.

DRY $60 –V

Pask Declaration Gimblett Gravels Hawke's Bay Cabernet/Merlot/Malbec ★★★★☆

The 2014 vintage (★★★★☆) was matured for two years in French and American oak puncheons (100 per cent new). Full-coloured, it shows good concentration, with fresh, ripe blackcurrant, plum and spice flavours, complex and savoury, and fine-grained tannins. Well worth cellaring, it should be at its best 2019 onwards.

Vintage	14	13	12	11	10	09	08	07	06
WR	7	7	NM	NM	6	6	NM	7	6
Drink	17-25	17-25	NM	NM	17-20	17-19	NM	17-18	P

DRY $50 –V

Pask Gimblett Road Cabernet/Merlot/Malbec ★★★★

The attractive 2013 vintage (★★★★) was estate-grown in the Gimblett Gravels and matured for 14 months in French and American oak casks (20 per cent new). A blend of Cabernet Sauvignon (76 per cent), Merlot (14 per cent) and Malbec (10 per cent), it has full, youthful colour. Mouthfilling and supple, it offers ripe blackcurrant, herb, plum and spice flavours, gently seasoned with oak, in a finely balanced, vibrantly fruity style, for drinking now or cellaring. The 2014 vintage (★★★★) is deeply coloured, full-bodied and smooth, with generous blackcurrant, plum and spice flavours, nutty, savoury notes adding complexity, and a very harmonious finish. Drink now or cellar. Fine value.

Vintage	14	13
WR	7	7
Drink	17-21	17-20

DRY $22 V+

Pask Small Batch Cabernet Sauvignon ★★★★

Estate-grown in the Gimblett Gravels, Hawke's Bay, the 2014 vintage (★★★★) was matured for 17 months in French and American oak casks (20 per cent new). Full-coloured, it is ripe and savoury, with concentrated blackcurrant, plum and spice flavours, a hint of herbs, good complexity and a finely poised finish.

Vintage	14	13
WR	6	7
Drink	17-20	17-20

DRY $29 AV

Passage Rock Reserve Waiheke Island Cabernet Sauvignon/Merlot ★★★★☆

The 2013 vintage (★★★★☆) is a blend of Cabernet Sauvignon (85 per cent), Merlot (10 per cent) and Malbec (5 per cent), matured in oak barriques for 15 months. Deep and youthful in colour, it is sturdy, fragrant and supple, with rich, ripe blackcurrant, plum, herb and spice flavours. Already highly enjoyable, it should be at its best 2018+. The 2014 vintage (★★★★) is dark, mouthfilling, generous and savoury, with a slightly green thread, but also good concentration and complexity.

DRY $45 –V

Peacock Sky Waiheke Island Cabernet Sauvignon ★★★☆

Medium to full-bodied, the 2014 vintage (★★★☆) is a blend of Cabernet Sauvignon (85 per cent), Cabernet Franc (10 per cent) and Malbec (5 per cent), French oak-aged for over a year. Deeply coloured, it is fresh, with plummy, spicy, slightly herbal flavours, in a clearly varietal style with good but not great depth.

DRY $40 –V

Riverview Hawke's Bay Cabernet Sauvignon /Merlot (★★★)

Still on sale, the 2010 vintage (★★★) was barrel-aged for two years. It has fullish, mature colour, a herbal bouquet and a smooth, full-bodied palate with blackcurrant, plum and herb flavours, showing some complexity. Ready.

DRY $25 –V

Saint Clair James Sinclair Gimblett Gravels Hawke's Bay Cabernet/Merlot   (★★★☆)

A drink-now or cellaring propositon, the 2014 vintage (★★★☆) is a full-coloured blend of Cabernet Sauvignon (84 per cent) and Merlot (16 per cent), estate-grown in the Plateau Vineyard and partly American oak-aged. It is mouthfilling, with very good depth of blackcurrant, herb and red-berry flavours, in a generous, vibrantly fruity style, with gentle tannins.

DRY $25 –V

Saint Clair Pioneer Block 17 Plateau Gimblett Gravels Cabernet/Merlot   ★★★★

The 2015 vintage (★★★★☆) is an estate-grown, deeply coloured blend of Cabernet Sauvignon (78 per cent) and Merlot (22 per cent), matured for 11 months in French oak casks (55 per cent new). Vibrantly fruity, it is generous and supple, with fresh, strong blackcurrant, plum, herb and spice flavours, that have easily lapped up the new oak influence. Enjoyable in its youth, it should reward cellaring to 2019+.

DRY $38 –V

Squawking Magpie SQM Gimblett Gravels Cabernets/Merlot   ★★★★★

The 2013 vintage (★★★★★), French oak-matured, is deeply coloured and fleshy, with rich, youthful blackcurrant, plum, herb and spice flavours, supple tannins, and excellent texture and harmony. The 2014 vintage (★★★★★) is dark and refined, in a Bordeaux-like style, with concentrated, ripe blackcurrant, plum, spice and nut flavours. Still youthful, it's crying out for cellaring; best drinking 2020+.

Vintage	14	13
WR	7	7
Drink	17-30	17-35

DRY $79 AV

Stolen Heart, The, Hawke's Bay Cabernet Sauvignon/Merlot   (★★★★☆)

Certified organic, the 2014 vintage (★★★★☆) was grown in the Gimblett Gravels and matured for a year in French oak casks (30 per cent new). Deep and youthful in colour, it is medium-bodied and savoury, in a distinctly Bordeaux-like style with fresh, ripe blackcurrant, plum, spice and herb flavours, seasoned with nutty oak, good complexity, firm tannins and obvious cellaring potential. Best drinking 2019+. (From Crown Range Cellar.)

DRY $50 –V

Stonecroft Gimblett Gravels Hawke's Bay Cabernet Sauvignon   ★★★★☆

Just starting to unfold, the classy 2015 vintage (★★★★★) is an unblended Cabernet Sauvignon, estate-grown in Mere Road and matured for 18 months in French oak barrels (15 per cent new). The colour is dark and youthful; the palate is mouthfilling, concentrated and supple, with fresh, deep blackcurrant, plum and spice flavours, seasoned with nutty oak, good tannin backbone, and obvious potential for long-term cellaring. Open 2020+.

Vintage	15	14
WR	7	7
Drink	19-28	19-26

DRY $47 –V

Te Mata Awatea Cabernets/Merlot   ★★★★★

Positioned below its Coleraine stablemate in Te Mata's hierarchy of Hawke's Bay, claret-style reds, since 1995 Awatea has been grown at Havelock North and in the Bullnose Vineyard, inland from Hastings. A blend of Cabernet Sauvignon, Merlot and Cabernet Franc – with a splash of Petit Verdot in most years since 2001 – it is hand-harvested and matured for 15 to 18 months in French oak barriques (partly new). Compared to Coleraine, in its youth Awatea is more seductive, more perfumed, and tastes more of sweet, ripe fruit, but it is more forward and slightly less concentrated. The wine can mature gracefully for many years, but is also typically delicious in its youth. The classy 2015 vintage (★★★★★) is a blend of Cabernet Sauvignon (46 per cent), Merlot (43 per cent) and Cabernet Franc (11 per cent). Already highly approachable, it is full-coloured, with a fragrant bouquet, mouthfilling body and rich blackcurrant, plum, herb and spice flavours. A classic claret-style red, warm and savoury, it's likely to be at its best 2020 onwards. Fine value.

Vintage	15	14	13	12	11	10	09	08	07
WR	7	6	7	6	7	7	7	7	7
Drink	17-25	17-25	17-23	17-19	17-19	17-18	P	P	17-20

DRY $35 V+

Te Mata Coleraine – see the Branded and Other Red Wines section

Thomas Waiheke Island Cabernet Sauvignon   (★★★★☆)

Grown at Onetangi, the youthful 2014 vintage (★★★★☆) is based entirely on Cabernet Sauvignon, hand-picked and matured for 15 months in French oak barriqes (43 per cent new). Full-coloured, it has a fragrant, fresh, slightly herbal bouquet, leading into a mouthfilling wine with rich plum, spice, herb and nut flavours, finely poised, complex and lingering. An elegant, savoury red, it should be at its best 2020+.

DRY $56 –V

Unison Selection Gimblett Gravels Cabernet Sauvignon/Merlot   ★★★★☆

The 2012 (★★★★★) is one of the best reds from a cool, wet growing season in Hawke's Bay. A blend of Cabernet Sauvignon (86 per cent) and Merlot (14 per cent), it was estate-grown and matured for 20 months in French oak barrels (33 per cent new). Full-coloured, it is mouthfilling, with ripe blackcurrant, plum and nutty oak flavours, in a sturdy and savoury, slightly earthy, firmly structured style that reminded me of a good St Estèphe. It's built to last.

DRY $60 –V

Vidal Legacy Gimblett Gravels Hawke's Bay Cabernet Sauvignon   (★★★★★)

The highly impressive 2014 vintage (★★★★★) is an unblended Cabernet Sauvignon, estate-grown in the Omahu Gravels Vineyard and matured for 20 months in French oak barriques (50 per cent new). Invitingly dark and fragrant, it is fleshy and concentrated, with dense, ripe blackcurrant, plum, spice and nut flavours, hints of dark chocolate and herbs, well-integrated oak adding complexity, and fine-grained tannins. A classic – and classy – young Cabernet Sauvignon, it should flourish for decades. (There is no 2015.)

Vintage	14
WR	7
Drink	18-28

DRY $70 AV

Vidal Legacy Gimblett Gravels Hawke's Bay Cabernet Sauvignon/Merlot ★★★★★

Retasted in mid-2017, the graceful, still-youthful 2013 vintage (★★★★★) is a blend of Cabernet Sauvignon (80 per cent) and Merlot (20 per cent), matured for 19 months in French oak barriques (50 per cent new). Deeply coloured, it is mouthfilling, with a savoury, nutty complexity and strong, ripe blackcurrant, plum and spice flavours that build across the palate to a smooth, lasting finish. An elegant, very age-worthy red, it should be at its best 2020+.

Vintage	13	12	11	10	09
WR	7	NM	NM	7	7
Drink	18-30	NM	NM	17-19	17-20

 DRY $70 AV

Villa Maria Library Release Gimblett Gravels
Hawke's Bay Cabernet Sauvignon (★★★★★)

Released in 2017, the 2009 vintage (★★★★★) is a still-youthful red, to savour over the next decade. Matured for 20 months in French oak barriques (67 per cent new), it has deep, moderately youthful colour, rich, ripe, blackcurrant-like flavours to the fore, hints of plums and spices, and savoury, nutty notes adding complexity. An elegant, tightly structured, classic Cabernet Sauvignon, it's set for the long haul.

Vintage	09
WR	7
Drink	17-24

 DRY $70 AV

Villa Maria Reserve Gimblett Gravels Hawke's Bay
Cabernet Sauvignon/Merlot ★★★★★

The 2014 vintage (★★★★★) is a dark, dense blend of Cabernet Sauvignon (75 per cent) and Merlot (25 per cent), matured for 18 months in French oak barriques (40 per cent new). Highly concentrated, with pure blackcurrant, plum and spice flavours, showing lovely weight, ripeness and structure, it's full of cellaring potential. The 2015 vintage (★★★★★) is a blend of Cabernet Sauvignon (70 per cent) and Merlot (30 per cent), matured for 18 months in French oak barriques (34 per cent new). Boldly coloured, it is still very youthful, with concentrated, ripe blackcurrant, plum and spice flavours, seasoned with quality oak, impressive complexity and a finely textured, lasting finish. A very elegant, 'seamless' wine, it's best cellared to 2020+.

Vintage	15	14	13	12	10	09	08	07	06	05
WR	7	7	7	6	7	6	6	7	7	6
Drink	18-25	18-25	18-25	17-22	17-25	17-22	17-18	17-22	17-19	17-20

 DRY $50 AV

Villa Maria Reserve Library Release Gimblett Gravels
Hawke's Bay Cabernet Sauvignon/Merlot   (★★★★★)

Released in 2017, the very elegant, still age-worthy 2009 vintage (★★★★★) is a blend of Cabernet Sauvignon (55 per cent) and Merlot (45 per cent), matured for 20 months in French oak barrels (70 per cent new). Delicious now, it has deep, fairly youthful colour, beautifully ripe, still fresh blackcurrant/plum flavours, and spicy, leathery notes adding complexity. Notably rich and savoury, it is developing superbly, but the best is yet to come; open 2020+. (Note: most 'Library Release' reds have been – and in future will be – labelled as a stand-alone range, without the 'Reserve' designation.)

DRY $70 AV

Waimarie Muriwai Valley Cabernet Sauvignon   (★★★☆)

Drinking well now, the 2013 vintage (★★★☆) was grown in the Muriwai Valley, West Auckland, and matured for 12 months in one-year-old French oak barriques. Lightish in colour, with a hint of development, it's a characterful red, with an earthy streak running through its plummy, spicy, slightly herbal flavours, which show very good depth.

DRY $40 –V

Carménère

Ransom, at Matakana, in 2007 released New Zealand's first Carménère. Now virtually extinct in France, Carménère was once widely grown in Bordeaux and still is in Chile, where, until the 1990s, it was often mistaken for Merlot. In Italy it was long thought to be Cabernet Franc.

In 1988, viticulturist Alan Clarke imported Cabernet Franc cuttings here from Italy. Planted by Robin Ransom in 1997, the grapes ripened about the same time as the rest of his Cabernet Franc, but the look of the fruit and the taste of the wine were 'totally different'. So Ransom arranged DNA testing at the University of Adelaide. The result? His Cabernet Franc vines are in fact Carménère.

Only 1 hectare of Carménère has been recorded in New Zealand, and the variety is not listed separately in New Zealand Winegrowers' *Vineyard Register Report 2015-2018*.

Ransom Carménère   ★★★☆

Estate-grown at Mahurangi, north of Auckland, the 2013 vintage (★★★☆) is deeply coloured, with a fresh, slightly herbal bouquet. Mouthfilling, it shows good density, with vibrant plum and herb flavours, a hint of nuts, and fine-grained tannins. Drink now or cellar.

DRY $29 –V

Chambourcin

Chambourcin is one of the more highly rated French hybrids, well known in Muscadet for its good disease-resistance and bold, crimson hue. Rare in New Zealand (with 3 hectares of bearing vines in 2018), it is most often found as a varietal red in Northland.

Byrne Northland Chambourcin
★★★★☆

The 2015 vintage (★★★★★) established Byrne as the region's finest producer of Chambourcin. Fragrant, boldly coloured, mouthfilling and exuberantly fruity, it's delicious young. The 2016 vintage (★★★★), matured in old oak barriques, is full-coloured, with fresh, berryish, spicy aromas and flavours. Vibrantly fruity, with the slightly rustic note typical of the variety, gentle tannins and a lingering finish, it's a highly attractive, drink-young style.

DRY $21 V+

Mahinepua Bay Chambourcin
(★★★★)

Estate-grown in Northland at a coastal site well north of the Bay of Islands, the 2014 vintage (★★★★) is a sturdy, boldly coloured red, fresh and fruit-packed, with generous plum and spice flavours, showing good vigour and concentration.

DRY $28 –V

Marsden Bay of Islands Chambourcin
★★★★

Top vintages of this Northland red are generous, deeply coloured and crammed with flavour. The 2014 vintage (★★★★) was matured for 16 months in American oak casks (20 per cent new). Densely coloured and perfumed, it is weighty, with rich plum/spice flavours, fresh acidity, gentle tannins and a seductively smooth finish.

Vintage	14	13	12	11	10
WR	6	6	4	5	7
Drink	17-20	P	P	P	P

DRY $28 –V

Okahu Chambourcin
★★★☆

The easy-drinking 2014 vintage (★★★☆) is a Northland red, grown at Kaitaia. Full-coloured, it is weighty and vibrantly fruity, with youthful, ripe, berryish, plummy flavours, showing good freshness, harmony and depth.

DRY $49 –V

Dolcetto

Grown in the north of Italy, where it produces purple-flushed, fruity, supple reds, usually enjoyed young, Dolcetto is extremely rare in New Zealand. Only 2 hectares of bearing vines have been recorded in New Zealand, mostly in Auckland, and the variety is not listed separately in New Zealand Winegrowers' *Vineyard Register Report 2015-2018*.

Hitchen Road Dolcetto ★★★☆

Grown at Pokeno, in North Waikato, the 2014 vintage (★★★★) was barrel-matured for 10 months. The colour is full and bright; the palate is mouthfilling, with ripe berry and spice flavours, earthy, savoury notes adding complexity, fine-grained tannins, and a persistent finish. Enjoyable young, it's also worth cellaring.

DRY $18 V+

Gamay Noir

Gamay Noir is single-handedly responsible for the seductively scented and soft red wines of Beaujolais. The grape is still very rare in New Zealand, with 7 hectares of bearing vines in 2018, almost all in Hawke's Bay. In the Omaka Springs Vineyard in Marlborough, Gamay ripened later than Cabernet Sauvignon (itself an end-of-season ripener), with higher levels of acidity than in Beaujolais, but at Te Mata's Woodthorpe Terraces Vineyard in Hawke's Bay, the crop is harvested as early as mid-March.

Te Mata Estate Vineyards Hawke's Bay Gamay Noir ★★★★

The summery 2016 vintage (★★★★) was matured for two months in seasoned French oak barrels. Bright ruby, it is floral, berryish and supple, with fresh, vibrant, plummy, spicy flavours and very gentle tannins. Very much in the Beaujolais mould, it's delicious young.

Vintage	16
WR	6
Drink	17-19

DRY $20 V+

Grenache

Grenache, one of the world's most extensively planted grape varieties, thrives in the hot, dry vineyards of Spain and southern France. It is also yielding exciting wines in Australia, especially from old, unirrigated, bush-pruned vines, but is exceedingly rare in New Zealand, with a total producing area in 2018 of 1 hectare, all in Hawke's Bay.

Villa Maria Cellar Selection Gimblett Gravels Hawke's Bay Grenache ★★★★

The instantly attractive 2014 vintage (★★★★) is the fourth of what will be a regular release of this very late-ripening variety. From 16-year-old vines in the company's Ngakirikiri Vineyard, it was hand-picked and matured for 11 months in French oak barrels of varying sizes (30 per cent new). Full-coloured and mouthfilling (14.5 per cent alcohol), with strong, vibrant plum/spice flavours, showing some smoky, savoury complexity, and a tight, finely textured finish, it's worth cellaring. (There is no 2015, but the label returns from the 2016 vintage.)

Vintage	16	15	14	13	12	11	10
WR	6	NM	7	6	NM	6	7
Drink	17-23	NM	17-22	17-19	NM	P	P

DRY $25 AV

Lagrein

Cultivated traditionally in the vineyards of Trentino-Alto Adige, in north-east Italy, Lagrein yields deeply coloured, slightly astringent reds with fresh acidity and plum/cherry flavours, firm and strong. The area of bearing vines in New Zealand will leap from 2 hectares in 2015 to 11 hectares in 2018, mostly in Hawke's Bay (6 hectares), but also in Nelson and Marlborough.

Coopers Creek SV Single Barrel Gisborne Lagrein (★★★★)

Still very youthful, the 2014 vintage (★★★★) was matured for 14 months in a seasoned oak cask. Full-coloured, it is medium-bodied, with fresh, berryish, spicy aromas, good concentration of berry, plum and spice flavours, showing some savoury complexity, and a firm finish. Best drinking mid-2018+.

DRY $28 –V

Stanley Estates Awatere Valley Marlborough Lagrein ★★★★

The lively 2015 vintage (★★★☆) was estate-grown, hand-picked and matured for 10 months in French oak casks (24 per cent new). Deeply coloured, it is youthful, mouthfilling and vibrantly fruity, with strong, plummy, spicy flavours, showing considerable complexity, and a lingering finish. Best drinking 2018+.

Vintage	15
WR	6
Drink	17-25

DRY $28 –V

Malbec

With a rise from 25 hectares of bearing vines in 1998 to 132 hectares in 2018, this old Bordeaux variety is starting to make its presence felt in New Zealand, where over 75 per cent of all plantings are clustered in Hawke's Bay (most of the rest are in Auckland). It is often used as a blending variety, adding brilliant colour and rich, sweet-fruit flavours to its blends with Merlot, Cabernet Sauvignon and Cabernet Franc. Numerous unblended Malbecs have also been released recently, possessing loads of flavour and often the slight rusticity typical of the variety (or at least some of the clones established here).

Ash Ridge Premium Estate Hawke's Bay Malbec (★★★★)

Grown in the Bridge Pa Triangle and barrel-aged, the 2014 vintage (★★★★) is delicious young. A fruit-driven style with a gentle seasoning of oak, it is full-coloured, with gentle tannins and fresh, concentrated plum and spice flavours that avoid the rusticity often found in New Zealand Malbec. Drink now or cellar.

DRY $26 AV

Brookfields Hawke's Bay Sun Dried Malbec ★★★★☆

Labelled as 'Malbec on steroids', the very youthful 2016 vintage (★★★★) was made from grapes sun-dried to concentrate their sugars and flavours, then matured for a year in French and American oak casks. Full-coloured, it is fragrant and mouthfilling, with strong, fresh plum/spice aromas and flavours, a hint of liquorice, and a lingering finish. Best drinking 2019+.

Vintage	16	15	14	13
WR	7	7	7	7
Drink	17-21	19-24	18-25	17-23

DRY $25 V+

Clearview Two Pinnacles Reserve Hawke's Bay Malbec ★★★★

The 2015 vintage (★★★★☆) is a boldly coloured red, estate-grown on the coast, at Te Awanga, and matured for 17 months in oak barrels (14 per cent new). Gutsy and fruit-packed, it's a 'full-on' style, with strong, fresh plum, spice and blackcurrant flavours, showing good ripeness, tannin backbone, and obvious cellaring potential; open 2019+.

DRY $26 AV

Coopers Creek Gisborne Malbec (★★★☆)

The 2015 vintage (★★★☆) was matured for a year in seasoned oak barrels. Full and bright in colour, it is a medium-bodied, vibrantly fruity red with good depth of plummy, spicy flavours, fresh and firm. Best drinking mid-2018+.

Vintage	13
WR	7
Drink	17-20

DRY $18 V+

Esk Valley The Hillside Malbec/Merlot/Cabernet Franc (★★★★★)

The 2010 vintage (★★★★★) was bottle-aged for five years, before being released in late 2016. Estate-grown at The Terraces Vineyard in Bay View, Hawke's Bay, it is a blend of Malbec (58 per cent), Merlot (26 per cent) and Cabernet Franc (16 per cent), matured for 16 months in French oak barriques (100 per cent new). Deep and still youthful in colour, it is full-bodied, smooth and savoury, with delicious blackcurrant, plum, spice and nut flavours, a hint of liquorice, and excellent concentration, complexity and personality. Best drinking 2018+.

DRY $70 AV

Fromm Malbec Fromm Vineyard ★★★★☆

Estate-grown in Marlborough and matured for 18 months in French oak casks, this wine is recommended by winemaker Hätsch Kalberer for drinking with 'a large piece of wild venison'. The 2013 vintage (★★★★☆) is rare – just three barrels were made. The colour is dense; the palate is sturdy and highly concentrated, with strong, plummy, spicy flavours, well-integrated oak, and a fresh, firm finish. It's a very age-worthy red.

Vintage	13	12	11	10	09	08	07	06	05	DRY $54 –V
WR	7	7	6	7	6	6	7	6	6	
Drink	17-28	17-28	17-26	17-27	17-23	17-22	17-24	17-21	17-20	

Kaipara Estate Malbec (★★★)

The 2014 vintage (★★★), estate-grown in Auckland, is deeply coloured, sturdy and smooth, with a vague suggestion of sweetness amid its strong berry, spice and liquorice flavours.

DRY $30 –V

Man O' War Death Valley Malbec (★★★★★)

The delicious 2014 vintage (★★★★★) was estate-grown on Waiheke Island. It was almost entirely (95 per cent) matured for 22 months in French oak (15 per cent new); the rest was handled in seasoned American oak. Deeply coloured, it is fragrant and mouthfilling, with dense, ripe blackcurrant, plum and spice flavours, hints of coffee and liquorice, and a finely textured, smooth finish. A classy young red, it should be long-lived, but is already hard to resist.

Vintage	14	DRY $34 V+
WR	6	
Drink	17-21	

Matua Single Vineyard Hawke's Bay Malbec (★★★★★)

The fruit-drenched 2013 vintage (★★★★★) is a densely coloured, single-vineyard red, hand-picked in the Matheson Vineyard, in the Bridge Pa Triangle, and French oak-aged. Purple/black, it is powerful, with highly concentrated blackcurrant, plum and spice flavours, gentle tannins and a finely textured, very smooth finish. Best drinking 2018+.

DRY $58 AV

Mission Reserve Hawke's Bay Malbec ★★★★★

The 2013 vintage (★★★★★), grown in the Bridge Pa Triangle and matured in French oak barrels (10 per cent new), has deep, purple-flushed colour. An elegant, very age-worthy wine, it is full-bodied (14 per cent alcohol), with youthful, concentrated blackcurrant, plum and spice flavours, finely textured, harmonious and long.

Vintage	13	DRY $29 V+
WR	5	
Drink	17-22	

One Off Hawke's Bay Malbec   (★★★★)

The partly barrel-matured 2014 vintage (★★★★) is deeply coloured, rich and smooth. Full-bodied, with fresh, strong plum/spice flavours and finely balanced tannins, it's enjoyable young, but also worth cellaring. (From Rod McDonald.)

DRY $30 –V

Peacock Sky Waiheke Island Pure Malbec   ★★★☆

Matured for over a year in French oak barrels, the 2014 vintage (★★★★) is a deeply coloured, fruity red, medium to full-bodied, with strong, lively plum and spice flavours, slightly earthy notes adding complexity, and a fairly firm finish. Best drinking 2018+.

DRY $40 –V

Pegasus Bay Malbec   (★★★★☆)

The debut 2014 vintage (★★★★☆) was estate-grown at Waipara, in North Canterbury, and matured for two years in oak barrels (30 per cent new). Fragrant and robust, it has full, youthful colour and highly concentrated plum, spice and liquorice flavours, good complexity and a firm finish. Drink now or cellar.

Vintage	14
WR	5
Drink	17-27

DRY $35 AV

Reserve Road Hawke's Bay Malbec/Merlot/Cabernet   (★★★☆)

The 2015 vintage (★★★☆) is a full-coloured, mouthfilling red, vibrantly fruity, with a touch of complexity and fresh, generous, plummy, slightly herbal flavours. (From Otuwhero.)

DRY $37 –V

Saint Clair James Sinclair Gimblett Gravels Hawke's Bay Malbec   (★★★★)

The dark, purple-flushed 2014 vintage (★★★★) was estate-grown in the Plateau Vineyard and French oak-aged. Mouthfilling, it has strong, plummy flavours, showing some savoury complexity, and gentle tannins, in a seductively rich, smooth style.

DRY $25 AV

Saint Clair Pioneer Block 17 Plateau Gimblett Gravels Hawke's Bay Malbec   ★★★★

The smooth, easy-drinking 2015 vintage (★★★★) was estate-grown and French oak-aged. Full-coloured, with fresh, berryish, plummy flavours, some earthy notes, gentle tannins and good depth, it's a drink-now or cellaring proposition.

DRY $38 –V

Stonyridge Luna Negra Waiheke Island Hillside Malbec ★★★★★

Promoted as 'like going on an energetic dance with a Cuban beauty queen', this bold, classy red is estate-grown in the Vina del Mar Vineyard at Onetangi and matured in American oak barriques. The 2015 vintage (★★★★★) has dense, inky, purple-flushed colour. A powerful, sturdy wine, it has concentrated, well-ripened blackcurrant and plum flavours, in a structured, age-worthy style, already delicious, but likely to be at its best 2020+.

DRY $95 –V

Te Aotea Vineyard South Kaipara Malbec ★★★★☆

Delicious now, but still youthful, the 2014 vintage (★★★★☆) was matured for 16 months in new American and seasoned French oak barrels. Full-coloured, it is mouthfilling, with strong, ripe berry, plum and spice flavours, a hint of liquorice, good complexity and a finely balanced, long finish. Also youthful, the 2013 vintage (★★★★) is dark, berryish and rich, with fresh acidity, good tannin backbone and a long future ahead.

DRY $60 –V

Tironui Estate Hawke's Bay Malbec/Merlot/Cabernet ★★★★☆

From an elevated site at Taradale, this single-vineyard red has strong personality. The 2014 vintage (★★★★☆) is a blend of Malbec (66 per cent), Merlot (25 per cent) and 'Cabernet' (9 per cent). Matured for a year in French oak barrels (20 per cent new), it is densely coloured, with a plummy, spicy bouquet. Full-bodied and fruit-packed, it is concentrated and finely textured, with fresh, ripe flavours, well-integrated oak, fine-grained tannins, and excellent balance, richness and flow. Drink now or cellar.

DRY $35 AV

Villa Maria Reserve Gimblett Gravels Hawke's Bay Malbec ★★★★★

The dark, rich 2013 vintage (★★★★★) was matured for 18 months in French oak barriques (60 per cent new). It is concentrated, with beautifully ripe plum, dark chocolate and liquorice flavours, fairly firm tannins and a lasting finish. Very age-worthy.

Vintage	13
WR	7
Drink	18-25

DRY $60 AV

West Brook Waimauku Malbec (★★★★☆)

Maturing gracefully, the 2014 vintage (★★★★☆) was estate-grown in West Auckland and fully barrel-aged (20 per cent new). The colour is dark and purple-flushed; the palate is fresh, smooth and full-bodied, with deep blackcurrant, plum, spice and nut flavours, oak complexity, gentle tannins and a rich, finely balanced finish. Best drinking mid-2018+.

Vintage	14
WR	4
Drink	17-21

DRY $30 AV

Marzemino

Once famous, but today rare, Marzemino is cultivated in northern Italy, where it typically yields light, plummy reds. Established in New Zealand in 1995, Marzemino has been made commercially by Pernod Ricard NZ under the Church Road brand since 2005, but is not listed separately in New Zealand Winegrowers' *Vineyard Register Report 2015-2018*.

Church Road McDonald Series Hawke's Bay Marzemino ★★★★

Grown in the company's Redstone Vineyard, in the Bridge Pa Triangle, this rare wine is matured in French oak barriques. The 2015 vintage (★★★★☆) is dark and purple-flushed. Still unfolding, it is buoyantly fruity, with fresh berry, plum and spice flavours, showing excellent ripeness and density, gentle tannins and obvious potential; open mid-2018+.

DRY $28 AV

Merlot

Pinot Noir is New Zealand's red-wine calling card on the world stage, but our Merlots are also proving competitive. Interest in this most extensively cultivated red-wine grape in Bordeaux is especially strong in Hawke's Bay. Everywhere in Bordeaux – the world's greatest red-wine region – except in the Médoc and Graves districts, the internationally higher-profile Cabernet Sauvignon variety plays second fiddle to Merlot. The elegant, fleshy wines of Pomerol and St Émilion bear delicious testimony to Merlot's capacity to produce great, yet relatively early-maturing, reds.

In New Zealand, after initial preoccupation with the more austere and slowly evolving Cabernet Sauvignon, the rich, rounded flavours and (more practically) earlier-ripening ability of Merlot are now fully appreciated. Poor set can be a major drawback with the older clones, reducing yields, but Merlot ripens ahead of Cabernet Sauvignon, a major asset in cooler wine regions, especially in vineyards with colder clay soils. Merlot grapes are typically lower in tannin and higher in sugar than Cabernet Sauvignon's; its wines are thus silkier and a shade stronger in alcohol.

Hawke's Bay has over 85 per cent of New Zealand's bearing Merlot vines in 2018; the rest are clustered in Gisborne, Auckland and Marlborough. The country's fifth most widely planted variety, Merlot covers over four times the area of Cabernet Sauvignon. Between 2003 and 2018, the total area of bearing Merlot vines barely changed, from 1249 to 1327 hectares, but in top vintages, such as 2010, 2013 and 2014, the wines offer terrific value.

Merlot's key role in New Zealand was traditionally that of a minority blending variety, bringing a soft, mouthfilling richness and floral, plummy fruitiness to its marriages with the predominant Cabernet Sauvignon. Now, with a host of straight Merlots and Merlot-predominant blends on the market, this aristocratic grape is fully recognised as a top-flight wine in its own right.

Alexander Martinborough Merlot ★★★★

Still very youthful, the 2015 vintage (★★★★) is a sturdy wine (14.5 per cent alcohol), estate-grown, hand-picked and matured for 16 months in seasoned French and American oak barriques. Full-coloured, it has fresh, concentrated blackcurrant, plum and spice flavours, showing excellent cellaring potential. The 2016 vintage (★★★★) was matured in French oak barriques (33 per cent new). Deeply coloured, it is fragrant, with deep, vibrant, plummy flavours, woven with fresh acidity, and a rich, smooth finish. Best drinking 2019+.

Vintage	16	15
WR	7	6
Drink	20-25	17-24

DRY $29 AV

Allan Scott Hawke's Bay Merlot (★★★☆)

The 2015 vintage (★★★☆) from this Marlborough-based producer is deeply coloured and mouthfilling, with generous, plummy, spicy, slightly herbal flavours. Gently oaked, with good tannin support, it's an age-worthy wine, likely to be at its best 2018+.

DRY $26 –V

Alluviale Hawke's Bay Merlot/Cabernet Sauvignon   (★★★★☆)

The instantly appealing 2015 vintage (★★★★☆) is a blend of Merlot (76 per cent), Cabernet Sauvignon (14 per cent) and Cabernet Franc (10 per cent), matured for 15 months in French oak barrels (25 per cent new), and bottled unfined and unfiltered. The colour is deep and purple-flushed; the palate is mouthfilling and fruit-packed, with generous plum/spice flavours, a subtle seasoning of oak, and fine-grained tannins.

DRY $32 AV

Alpha Domus The Foxmoth Hawke's Bay Merlot   (★★★☆)

Partly barrel-aged, the 2014 vintage (★★★☆) has full, slightly mature colour. Mouthfilling and smooth, it has very good depth of plummy, slightly nutty flavours, in an attractive, drink-young style. (Retasted in mid-2017, it's maturing solidly and will probably be at its best now to 2018.)

DRY $25 –V

Alpha Domus The Pilot Merlot/Cabernet   ★★★☆

The 2014 vintage (★★★☆), a single-vineyard red, estate-grown in the Bridge Pa Triangle of Hawke's Bay, was mostly (80 per cent) matured in seasoned French oak barrels. Fullish and slightly developed in colour, it is mouthfilling, with very good depth of ripe plum, berry and spice flavours, showing some complexity. It's drinking well now.

DRY $19 V+

Ash Ridge Estate Hawke's Bay Merlot   ★★★★

A consistently good buy. The 2016 vintage (★★★★), grown in the Bridge Pa Triangle, was matured in seasoned French (mostly) and American oak casks. Full-coloured, it is mouthfilling and vibrantly fruity, with very good depth of plum/spice flavours, finely integrated oak adding complexity, and ripe, supple tannins. Offering fine value, it should be at its best 2019+.

DRY $20 V+

Askerne Hawke's Bay Merlot/Cabernet Franc/Cabernet Sauvignon/Malbec   ★★★

The 2015 vintage (★★★☆) is a deeply coloured, supple, drink-young blend of Merlot (65 per cent) with Cabernet Franc, Cabernet Sauvignon, Malbec and Petit Verdot, barrel-aged for 10 months. It has strong plum and spice flavours, showing some savoury complexity.

DRY $22 –V

Ataahua Waipara Merlot   ★★★☆

Delicious young, the 2014 vintage (★★★★) of this estate-grown red was matured for a year in seasoned French oak casks. Fragrant and full-coloured, it is mouthfilling, with fine-grained tannins and a strong surge of fresh plum/blackcurrant flavours.

DRY $30 –V

Awaroa Waiheke Island Merlot/Malbec   ★★★★

The 2015 vintage (★★★★) is deep and youthful in colour. A weighty, fleshy red, it has concentrated flavours, complex and savoury, and good tannin backbone. Worth cellaring.

DRY $38 –V

Babich Hawke's Bay Merlot/Cabernet ★★★

Grown in the Gimblett Gravels and the Bridge Pa Triangle, the 2015 vintage (★★★) was blended with a small amount of Malbec. It is a medium-bodied, ruby-hued blend with good depth of plum, spice and herb flavours, and lots of early-drinking appeal.

 DRY $22 –V

Babich Winemakers Reserve Hawke's Bay Merlot ★★★★

Estate-grown in Gimblett Road, in the heart of the Gimblett Gravels, and matured for 14 months in French oak casks (25 per cent new), the youthful 2014 vintage (★★★★☆) is clearly from a top season. Deeply coloured and mouthfilling, it has strong blackcurrant, plum and spice flavours, hints of dark chocolate and nuts, and excellent ripeness, concentration and complexity. Showing obvious potential, it should be at its best 2018+.

Vintage	14	13	12	11	10
WR	7	7	5	5	6
Drink	17-22	17-22	17-20	17-19	P

 DRY $30 –V

Beach House Reserve Gimblett Gravels Hawke's Bay Merlot ★★★★☆

Still unfolding, the 2014 vintage (★★★★☆) is a single-vineyard red, grown in Mere Road and matured for a year in French oak casks (25 per cent new). Full-coloured, it is mouthfilling and fruit-packed, with strong, ripe, plummy, spicy flavours, integrated oak, good tannin backbone and obvious potential; best drinking 2019+. Fine value.

 DRY $25 V+

Black Barn Vineyards Hawke's Bay Merlot/Cabernet Franc ★★★★

Estate-grown and hand-picked at Havelock North, the 2014 vintage (★★★★☆) is densely coloured and savoury, with a complex, leathery bouquet. A full-bodied, powerful red with concentrated blackcurrant and plum flavours, hints of nutty oak, and ripe, supple tannins, it should be at its best 2018+.

 DRY $33 –V

Brancott Estate Hawke's Bay Merlot ★★★☆

Enjoyable young, the 2015 vintage (★★★☆) is full-coloured, with very good body and depth of ripe, plummy, spicy flavours, a hint of dark chocolate, a touch of complexity and a smooth finish. A generous, 'fruit-driven' style, it offers fine value.

 DRY $17 V+

Brookfields Burnfoot Hawke's Bay Merlot ★★★★

Typically great value. The 2015 vintage (★★★☆), grown in the Tuki Tuki Valley, was matured for a year in seasoned French and American oak casks. A mouthfilling red with fullish, youthful colour, it is vibrantly fruity, with fresh acidity and strong, plummy, slightly herbal flavours, gently seasoned with oak. Best drinking mid-2018+.

Vintage	15
WR	7
Drink	17-21

DRY $20 V+

Brookfields Highland Hawke's Bay Merlot/Cabernet ★★★★☆

The very youthful 2015 vintage (★★★★☆) is a blend of Merlot and Cabernet Sauvignon, matured for a year in new and one-year-old French and American oak casks. Deeply coloured, with plenty of personality, it has mouthfilling body and rich, vibrant plum, cassis and spice flavours, with a hint of coffee. Complex and savoury, it's still a baby; open 2019+.

Vintage	15	14
WR	7	7
Drink	20-26	18-25

Cathedral Cove Hawke's Bay Merlot/Cabernet (★★☆)

A decent quaffer, the 2013 vintage (★★☆) is mouthfilling, with full, slightly developed colour and fresh, smooth blackcurrant, plum and distinctly herbal flavours. It's a bit lacking in richness, ripeness and complexity, but a good buy at this price.

DRY $10 V+

Church Road Hawke's Bay Merlot/Cabernet Sauvignon ★★★★

This full-flavoured, Bordeaux-like red from Pernod Ricard NZ can offer wonderful value. Merlot-based, it is typically estate-grown in the Redstone Vineyard, in the Bridge Pa Triangle, and matured in French and Hungarian oak barrels. The 2015 vintage (★★★★) is a blend of Merlot (74 per cent) and Cabernet Sauvignon (26 per cent), oak-aged for a year. Dark and purple-flushed, it's a fresh, 'fruit-driven' style, with substantial body, very generous, ripe blackcurrant/plum flavours, gentle tannins and excellent depth. It's already delicious.

DRY $20 V+

Church Road McDonald Series Hawke's Bay Merlot ★★★★★

Estate-grown in the Gimblett Vineyard, in the Gimblett Gravels (75 per cent), and the Redstone Vineyard, in the Bridge Pa Triangle (25 per cent), the 2014 vintage (★★★★☆) was matured for 20 months in French and Hungarian oak barrels (39 per cent new), and bottled unfined and unfiltered. A powerful, very ripe-tasting, sturdy red, it is deep and youthful in colour. Fragrant, rich and supple, it has very generous plum/spice flavours, hints of liquorice and nuts, well-integrated oak and gentle tannins. Best drinking 2019+.

DRY $27 V+

Clearview Cape Kidnappers Hawke's Bay Merlot ★★★★

The generous 2015 vintage (★★★★) is a finely textured, age-worthy, Merlot-based red, with 10 per cent Malbec in the blend. Grown at Te Awanga and matured in one to four-year-old oak, it is deeply coloured and weighty, with strong, ripe blackcurrant, plum and spice flavours, a hint of fruit cake, cedary oak in evidence, and good richness and roundness.

DRY $21 V+

Collaboration Ceresia Merlot/Cabernet Franc   ★★★★★

Hand-picked at 'ideal sites' in Hawke's Bay, the 2014 vintage (★★★★☆) is a blend of Merlot (80 per cent) and Cabernet Franc (20 per cent), matured for two years in French oak barrels (25 per cent new). Full-coloured, it is youthful, but already drinking well, with mouthfilling body, vibrant, ripe blackcurrant and plum flavours, showing good concentration, well-integrated oak, finely balanced tannins and excellent potential; best drinking 2019+.

DRY $45 AV

Collaboration Impression Merlot/Cabernet/Cabernet Franc   (★★★★)

Already drinking well, the 2015 vintage (★★★★) is a blend of Merlot (55 per cent), Cabernet Sauvignon (25 per cent) and Cabernet Franc (20 per cent). Matured for 18 months in seasoned French oak barrels, and bottled unfined and unfiltered, it is full-coloured and mouthfilling, with ripe berry, plum and spice flavours, showing good complexity, and gentle tannins. Still youthful, it should be at its best 2019+.

DRY $28 AV

Coopers Creek Select Vineyards Gravels & Metals
Hawke's Bay Merlot/Malbec   ★★★★

The attractive 2015 vintage (★★★★☆) is a blend of Gimblett Gravels Merlot and Malbec grown in the Bridge Pa Triangle, matured for 14 months in French oak casks (10 per cent new). Full-coloured, with a fresh, plummy bouquet, it is a mouthfilling, elegant, tightly structured red, with very generous, ripe blackcurrant, plum and dark chocolate flavours, gently seasoned with oak, and a lasting finish. Best drinking 2019+.

DRY $25 AV

Craggy Range Gimblett Gravels Hawke's Bay Merlot   ★★★★☆

The very age-worthy 2014 vintage (★★★★☆) is a blend of Merlot (88 per cent) and Cabernet Franc (12 per cent), matured for 17 months in oak barriques (27 per cent new). Full-coloured, it is mouthfilling, with ripe, plummy, spicy flavours, gentle tannins, and excellent complexity and concentration. A generous, well-structured red with obvious potential, it should be at its best 2018+.

DRY $32 AV

Delegat Crownthorpe Terraces Merlot   ★★★★

Bargain-priced, the 2016 vintage (★★★★) was estate-grown in the company's cool, elevated, inland vineyard at Crownthorpe, in Hawke's Bay, and a 'large portion' was matured for 11 months in French oak barriques. Deeply coloured, with a fragrant bouquet of berries and herbs, it is mouthfilling, vibrantly fruity and supple, with generous, plummy flavours, fine-grained tannins, and loads of drink-young appeal.

DRY $20 V+

Eaton Marlborough Merlot/Malbec/Cabernet   (★★★★☆)

The 2014 vintage (★★★★☆) is rare – only 540 bottles were produced. Grown in the Eaton Family Vineyard, in the Omaka Valley, it is a blend of Merlot (85 per cent), Malbec (10 per cent) and Cabernet Sauvignon (5 per cent), fermented with indigenous yeasts, matured for a year in French oak barrels, and bottled unfined and unfiltered. Dark and youthful in colour, it is a powerful red with concentrated, ripe plum, blackcurrant, spice and nut flavours, fine-grained tannins, and strong personality. Well worth cellaring, it should be at its best 2020+.

Vintage	14
WR	5
Drink	17-24

DRY $48 –V

Elephant Hill Hawke's Bay Merlot/Malbec   ★★★★☆

The 2015 vintage (★★★★☆) is a deeply coloured blend of Merlot and Malbec, estate-grown and hand-picked in the Gimblett Gravels and the Bridge Pa Triangle. Matured in French oak casks, it is a full-bodied, generous red with concentrated, ripe plum, red-berry and spice flavours, gently seasoned with oak, hints of dark chocolate and liquorice, and excellent harmony and potential.

Vintage	15
WR	6
Drink	17-25

DRY $34 AV

Elephant Hill Reserve Hawke's Bay Merlot/Malbec/Cabernet Sauvignon   ★★★★★

The powerful, finely textured, harmonious 2014 vintage (★★★★★) was hand-picked in the company's vineyards in the Gimblett Gravels and Bridge Pa Triangle, and matured for 19 months in French oak casks (40 per cent new). The colour is dark and youthful; the palate is sturdy and sweet-fruited, with dense plum, spice and nut flavours, hints of blackcurrants and dark chocolate, and a long, supple finish. A generous red, it's already enjoyable, but likely to be at its best 2018+.

Vintage	14
WR	6
Drink	17-25

DRY $49 AV

Esk Valley Gimblett Gravels Merlot/Cabernet Sauvignon/Malbec   ★★★★

Offering great value, the 2016 vintage (★★★★) is a blend of Merlot (44 per cent), Cabernet Sauvignon (30 per cent), Malbec (22 per cent) and Cabernet Franc (4 per cent), matured for a year in French oak barriques (15 per cent new). Deeply coloured, it is mouthfilling, with strong, fresh plum, red-berry and spice flavours, showing good complexity, and a well-rounded finish. Drink now or cellar.

Vintage	16	15	14	13	12	11
WR	6	6	7	7	6	5
Drink	17-22	17-21	17-21	17-20	P	P

DRY $20 V+

Esk Valley Winemakers Reserve Merlot/Malbec/Cabernet Franc ★★★★★

This powerful, classy wine is typically one of Hawke's Bay's greatest reds (it is always Merlot-based, but the proportions of minor varieties vary). Grown in the company's Ngakirikiri Vineyard and the Cornerstone Vineyard, both in the Gimblett Gravels, it is matured for up to 20 months in French oak barriques (40 per cent new in 2014). The 2014 vintage (★★★★☆) is a concentrated blend of Merlot (54 per cent) with Malbec (31 per cent), Cabernet Franc (10 per cent) and Cabernet Sauvignon (5 per cent). Very full-bodied, with a strong surge of ripe dark berry and plum flavours, it has savoury notes adding complexity, supple tannins, and a rich, rounded finish. (There is no 2015.)

Vintage	15	14	13	12	11	10	09	08	07	06
WR	NM	7	7	NM	7	7	7	NM	7	7
Drink	NM	17-30	17-30	NM	17-25	17-25	17-25	NM	17-25	17-20

 DRY $60 AV

Falconhead Hawke's Bay Merlot/Cabernet ★★★☆

Priced sharply, the 2014 vintage (★★★☆) is a smooth, full-coloured red, made in a fresh, fruit-driven style (40 per cent of the blend was barrel-aged). It has generous, ripe red-berry and spice flavours, with hints of herbs and dark chocolate. Showing very good depth, it's drinking well now.

Vintage	14	13
WR	7	7
Drink	17-20	17-20

DRY $16 V+

Giesen Hawke's Bay Merlot   (★★★☆)

Drinking well young, the 2015 vintage (★★★☆) is full-coloured, fresh, vibrantly fruity and smooth, with ripe plum and spice flavours, gently seasoned with oak, fine-grained tannins, and very good balance and depth.

Vintage	15
WR	4
Drink	17-18

DRY $17 V+

Giesen The Brothers Hawke's Bay Merlot   (★★★★)

The 2014 vintage (★★★★) is a single-vineyard red, grown in the Bridge Pa Triangle and matured for 13 months in French oak barrels (new and one year old). Deeply coloured, with spicy oak aromas, it is medium to full-bodied, with gentle tannins and strong, ripe plum and spice flavours. A youthful, age-worthy wine, it should be at its best 2018+.

Vintage	14
WR	6
Drink	17-19

DRY $33 –V

Glazebrook Regional Reserve Hawke's Bay Merlot/Cabernet   (★★★☆)

From Ngatarawa, the 2014 vintage (★★★☆) is a deeply coloured, mouthfilling red with strong plum, spice, herb and blackcurrant flavours. Slightly earthy, it is a firmly structured, age-worthy wine, likely to be at its best mid-2018+.

DRY $25 –V

Gold Star Merlot/Malbec X   (★★☆)

From Pukeora Estate, in Central Hawke's Bay, the 2010 vintage (★★☆) has lightish, moderately youthful colour and decent depth of slightly leafy flavour.

DRY $20 –V

Greyrock Hawke's Bay Merlot   (★★☆)

From Sileni, the very easy-drinking 2014 vintage (★★☆) is a 'lightly oaked' style. Full and youthful in colour, it is a very fruit-driven style, with mouthfilling body and plummy, slightly herbal flavours, fresh and smooth.

DRY $17 –V

Gunn Estate Reserve Hawke's Bay Merlot/Cabernet   ★★★☆

The 2016 vintage (★★★☆) is a very fruit-driven style, but was French oak-aged for a year. It has full, bright, very youthful colour. Fresh and full-bodied, it has very good depth of plum and blackcurrant-like flavours, gentle tannins, and lots of drink-young appeal.

Vintage	16	15
WR	6	6
Drink	17-22	17-20

DRY $17 V+

Haha Hawke's Bay Merlot   ★★★☆

Offering fine value, the 2016 vintage (★★★☆) is deep ruby, mouthfilling and supple. Made in a 'fruit-driven' style, it's a very harmonious wine, with good depth of fresh, ripe plum and red-berry flavours, showing a touch of complexity, and plenty of drink-young charm.

DRY $17 V+

Hans Herzog Spirit of Marlborough Merlot/Cabernet   ★★★★★

Who says you can't make outstanding claret-style reds in the South Island? Estate-grown on the banks of the Wairau River, matured for at least two years in new and one-year-old French oak barriques, and then bottle-aged for several years, this is typically a densely coloured wine with a classy fragrance, substantial body and notably concentrated blackcurrant, plum, herb and spice flavours. The powerful 2007 vintage (★★★★★) has deep, moderately mature colour. A highly concentrated, still fairly youthful red, it has dense plum, blackcurrant and dried-herb flavours, showing excellent complexity, richness and harmony. Set for a very long life, it's a drink-now or cellaring proposition. The 2008 vintage (★★★★☆) also has deep, fairly mature colour. Fragrant and fleshy, it is sturdy, with concentrated, ripe blackcurrant, plum, spice and nut flavours, and a hint of liquorice. Showing excellent ripeness, it's drinking well now.

Vintage	08	07
WR	6	7
Drink	17-21	17-22

DRY $69 AV

Hunter's Marlborough Merlot

Grown in the Wairau Valley, the 2013 vintage (★★★) is a single-vineyard red, hand-picked from 20-year-old vines, fermented with indigenous yeasts, and matured for 18 months in French oak barrels (30 per cent new). Lightish in colour, it is medium-bodied, with blackcurrant, plum and herb flavours, vibrant and smooth. Offering fresh, easy drinking, it's enjoyable now.

DRY $25 –V

Karikari Estate Calypso Merlot

Estate-grown in Northland, the 2014 vintage (★★★☆) is fullish in colour, mouthfilling and smooth, with good depth of ripe, berryish, plummy, spicy, nutty flavours, showing a touch of complexity, and gentle tannins. It's drinking well now.

DRY $29 –V

Kim Crawford Reserve Hawke's Bay Merlot

The generous, mouthfilling 2014 vintage (★★★☆) was partly barrel-aged. Full-coloured, it has strong, plummy flavours to the fore, with hints of spices and dried herbs, a gentle seasoning of oak, and good harmony. Drink now or cellar.

DRY $17 AV

Kumeu River Melba's Vineyard Merlot

Estate-grown at Kumeu, in West Auckland, and barrel-aged for a year, the 2013 vintage (★★★★) is deeply coloured. An elegant rather than powerful red, it is sweet-fruited, with youthful, vibrant, plummy flavours, showing some savoury complexity, and a finely poised finish. Best drinking 2018+. (Bottled under screwcap and opened in 2016, the 2000 vintage, a Merlot/Malbec, was impressive – highly concentrated, spicy and leathery.)

DRY $30 –V

Kumeu Village Merlot

Priced sharply, the 2014 vintage (★★☆) has fullish colour. Fresh and vibrantly fruity, with plummy flavours, it's an easy-drinking quaffer, enjoyable young. ($11 in six-bottle packs ex-winery.)

DRY $14 V+

Left Field Hawke's Bay Merlot

Drinking well now, the sharply priced 2015 vintage (★★★★) is an estate-grown, Gimblett Gravels blend of Merlot with small portions of Cabernet Sauvignon and Cabernet Franc, matured for 20 months in French oak casks (15 per cent new). Full-coloured, it is vibrantly fruity, with strong, ripe, plummy, spicy flavours, showing some savoury complexity, and a well-rounded finish. (From Te Awa.)

Vintage	15	14
WR	6	5
Drink	17-20	17-20

DRY $19 V+

Leveret Estate Hawke's Bay Merlot/Cabernet ★★★☆

Barrel-aged for a year (20 per cent new), the good-value 2014 vintage (★★★★) is a deeply coloured blend, with generous plum, spice and nut flavours. Showing good concentration, ripe, supple tannins and a well-rounded finish, it's a drink-now or cellaring proposition.

Vintage	14	13
WR	7	7
Drink	17-20	17-20

DRY $23 AV

Leveret Estate Reserve Hawke's Bay Merlot Cabernet ★★★★

Probably at its peak, the 2009 vintage (★★★☆), still on sale, is generous, savoury, slightly herbal, nutty and smooth. The 2014 vintage (★★★★) was matured for a year in barrels (20 per cent new). Fragrant and deeply coloured, it is fresh and sweet-fruited, with concentrated blackcurrant, plum, spice and dried-herb flavours, and gentle tannins. It's already drinking well.

Vintage	14	13	09
WR	6	7	5
Drink	18-24	18-25	18-20

DRY $30 –V

Lime Rock Central Hawke's Bay Merlot (★★★★)

Maturing gracefully, the 2013 vintage (★★★★) was grown in Central Hawke's Bay, hand-harvested and matured in seasoned French oak casks. An attractive red, it is fragrant, full-coloured and mouthfilling, with very good depth of ripe, plummy, spicy flavours, nutty and leathery notes adding complexity, and supple tannins. Drink now or cellar.

Vintage	13
WR	6
Drink	18-21

DRY $24 V+

Linden Estate Reserve Hawke's Bay Merlot ★★★★

Estate-grown and hand-picked in the Esk Valley, the age-worthy 2015 vintage (★★★★) was matured in French oak casks. Full-coloured, it is mouthfilling and savoury, with youthful plum/spice flavours, hints of nuts and liquorice, good concentration and a firm finish. Best drinking 2019+.

Vintage	15
WR	5
Drink	17-25

DRY $38 –V

Mahurangi River Winery Merlot/Cabernet Sauvignon/Malbec ★★★★

The 2014 vintage (★★★★), grown at Matakana, is a blend of Merlot (54 per cent), Cabernet Sauvignon (31 per cent) and Malbec (15 per cent), matured for 14 months in French and American oak barrels (50 per cent new). Deeply coloured, with fresh plum/spice aromas, it is weighty and generous, with ripe blackcurrant, plum, herb and spice flavours, savoury notes adding complexity, finely integrated oak and obvious cellaring potential.

DRY $29 AV

Main Divide Waipara Valley Merlot/Cabernet   ★★★☆

The 2014 vintage (★★★☆) from Pegasus Bay was fermented with indigenous yeasts and matured for a year in French oak barriques (two years old). Fullish in colour, it is mouthfilling and supple, with blackcurrant, plum and nut flavours, showing very good depth, ripeness and harmony. Drinking well now, it's priced right.

Vintage	14
WR	5
Drink	17-21

DRY $21 AV

Man O' War Merlot/Cabernet/Malbec/Petit Verdot   ★★★★

The attractive 2014 vintage (★★★★) is a blend of Merlot (50 per cent), Cabernet Franc (20 per cent), Malbec (15 per cent), Petit Verdot (10 per cent) and Cabernet Sauvignon (5 per cent), matured in seasoned French oak casks. Deeply coloured, it's a fruit-driven wine with fresh, generous red-berry, plum, herb and spice flavours, showing a touch of complexity, and smooth, ripe tannins. Best drinking 2018+.

Vintage	14
WR	7
Drink	17-20

DRY $29 AV

Marsden Bay of Islands The Winemaker's Daughter Merlot   ★★★☆

The deeply coloured 2014 vintage (★★★☆) was grown at Kerikeri, matured for a year in French oak casks (30 per cent new), and bottled without fining or filtering. Fragrant and supple, it is fresh and vibrantly fruity, in a moderately complex style, with plum/spice flavours, ripe and generous. Best drinking 2018+.

Vintage	14	13
WR	6	5
Drink	17-20	17-19

DRY $30 –V

Matua Single Vineyard Hawke's Bay Merlot/Malbec   ★★★★☆

The dark, purple-flushed 2014 vintage (★★★★★) is a classy, fruit-packed blend from the Matheson Vineyard, in the Bridge Pa Triangle. Hand-picked and matured in French (mostly) and American oak barrels, it is powerful, with concentrated, very ripe plum/spice flavours, a hint of dark chocolate, gentle tannins and a rich, finely textured finish.

DRY $58 –V

Milcrest Estate Nelson Merlot   (★★★☆)

The 2014 vintage (★★★☆) is a single-vineyard red, matured for 10 months in French oak barrels. Medium to full-bodied, with good colour depth, it is vibrantly fruity, with strong plum/spice flavours, a hint of herbs, fresh acidity and considerable complexity.

DRY $34 –V

Mill Road Hawke's Bay Merlot/Cabernet Sauvignon   (★★)

A gutsy quaffer, priced right, the 2013 vintage (★★) is sturdy and smooth, with fullish, slightly developed colour and decent depth of berry, plum and herb flavours. Ready.

DRY $10 V+

Mills Reef Elspeth Gimblett Gravels Hawke's Bay Merlot   ★★★★☆

The 2013 vintage (★★★★☆) was grown in the company's Mere Road Vineyard and matured for 17 months in French oak barrels (28 per cent new). Deep and youthful in colour, it is floral, rich and smooth, with a smoky oak influence and concentrated, ripe plum/spice flavours, savoury and finely textured. Best drinking 2018+.

Vintage	13	12	11	10	09	08	07	06
WR	7	NM	NM	7	7	NM	7	7
Drink	17-25	NM	NM	17-18	17-18	NM	17-18	P

DRY $49 –V

Mills Reef Estate Hawke's Bay Merlot/Cabernet   ★★★

The 2014 vintage (★★★) was matured for nine months in French and American oak casks. Full-coloured, it is mouthfilling and smooth (5 grams/litre of residual sugar), with plum, blackcurrant and spice flavours, showing some complexity. It's drinking well young.

Vintage	15	14	13
WR	7	6	7
Drink	17-20	17-18	17-19

MED/DRY $19 AV

Mills Reef Reserve Gimblett Gravels Hawke's Bay Merlot   ★★★☆

The attractive 2015 vintage (★★★★) is a single-vineyard red, estate-grown in Mere Road and matured for over a year in French and American oak hogsheads (31 per cent new). Full-coloured, it is mouthfilling and savoury, with youthful, ripe plum/spice flavours, nutty oak adding complexity, gentle tannins, and very good vigour and depth. An age-worthy wine, it should be at its best mid-2018+.

Vintage	15	14	13	12
WR	7	6	7	6
Drink	17-21	17-20	17-19	P

DRY $25 –V

Mills Reef Reserve Gimblett Gravels Hawke's Bay Merlot/Malbec   ★★★☆

The easy-drinking 2015 vintage (★★★☆) is a blend of Merlot (55 per cent) and Malbec (45 per cent), matured for 13 months in French (70 per cent) and American (30 per cent) oak barrels. Full-coloured, it is mouthfilling and vibrantly fruity, with very good depth of plum, spice and blackcurrant flavours, a hint of sweet oak, and a smooth finish.

Vintage	15	14	13	12	11	10
WR	7	7	7	6	7	7
Drink	17-21	17-20	17-19	P	P	P

DRY $25 –V

Mission Gimblett Gravels Barrique Reserve Merlot   ★★★★

The 2015 vintage (★★★★☆) is a generous, single-vineyard red from the Gimblett Gravels, matured for a year in French oak barriques. Deep and bright in colour, it is fragrant and supple, with concentrated blackcurrant and plum flavours, nutty, savoury elements adding complexity, and obvious cellaring potential; open 2019+.

Vintage	14	13	12	11	10	09	08
WR	7	7	5	5	6	6	5
Drink	17-25	17-25	17-18	17-18	17-18	P	P

 DRY $29 AV

Mission Hawke's Bay Merlot   ★★★

The 'lightly oaked' 2014 vintage (★★★☆) offers fine value. Full-coloured and mouthfilling, it has generous, ripe blackcurrant and plum flavours, gentle tannins and a seductively smooth finish. Drink now onwards.

 DRY $18 AV

Mission Hawke's Bay Merlot/Cabernet Sauvignon   ★★★

The 2015 vintage (★★★) is full-coloured, with a fresh, slightly leafy bouquet. Mouthfilling, it is vibrantly fruity, with berryish, plummy, slightly herbal flavours, showing good depth, gentle tannins and a well-rounded finish. Drink young.

 DRY $18 AV

Mission Vineyard Selection Hawke's Bay Merlot   ★★★☆

The youthful 2015 vintage (★★★★) was mostly matured for over a year in French oak casks. Deeply coloured, it is full-bodied and smooth, with strong blackcurrant and plum flavours, a hint of herbs, and very good vigour and depth. Best drinking mid-2018+.

 DRY $20 AV

Moana Park Hawke's Bay Merlot/Malbec   ★★★☆

The 2014 vintage (★★★★) is a powerful, bold Gimblett Gravels blend of Merlot (80 per cent), Malbec (15 per cent) and Cabernet Franc (5 per cent), matured for a year in French oak barriques (30 per cent new). It has concentrated plum, spice and herb flavours, with smooth tannins. Sharply priced.

Vintage	14	13
WR	6	5
Drink	17-21	17-20

DRY $20 AV

Monarch Estate Vineyard Matakana Merlot   (★★★☆)

The 2014 vintage (★★★☆) was matured in French and American oak barrels (45 per cent new). Full-coloured, it is mouthfilling and vibrant, with fresh, ripe, moderately concentrated, plummy flavours, an earthy streak, and drink-young appeal.

 DRY $28 –V

Montana Winemakers' Series Hawke's Bay Merlot ★★★

From Pernod Ricard NZ, the 2015 vintage (★★★☆) is deeply coloured and mouthfilling, with generous plum and spice flavours. Priced sharply.

DRY $15 V+

Moutere Hills Nelson Merlot (★★★☆)

Estate-grown at Upper Moutere, the 2016 vintage (★★★☆) is a single-vineyard red, hand-harvested from 23-year-old vines and matured for 10 months in French oak casks. Made in a 'fruit-driven' style, it is fresh and youthful, with good depth of plummy, berryish, gently spicy flavours, lively acidity and some cellaring potential; open mid-2018+.

DRY $32 –V

Moutere Hills Sarau Reserve Nelson Merlot (★★★☆)

The fragrant 2015 vintage (★★★☆) is a single-vineyard red, estate-grown at Upper Moutere, hand-picked and matured in French oak barriques. Full-coloured, it has lively acidity and very good depth of fresh blackcurrant, plum and spice flavours, but slightly lacks the warmth and roundness of Merlots grown further north.

DRY $55 –V

Music Bay Winter Hawke's Bay Merlot/Cabernet/Malbec (★★★☆)

Enjoyable young, the generous 2016 vintage (★★★☆) is a fresh, mouthfilling red with full, bright, youthful colour. It has very good depth of ripe, plummy, spicy flavours, with gentle tannins and lots of upfront appeal. (From Otuwhero.)

DRY $20 AV

Ngatarawa Proprietors' Reserve Hawke's Bay Merlot/Cabernet (★★★★★)

Grown in the Bridge Pa Triangle and the Gimblett Gravels, the 2013 vintage (★★★★★) is a memorable wine, in the classic Bordeaux style. Dark, with a fragrant, spicy, complex bouquet, it is rich and sweet-fruited, with highly concentrated blackcurrant, plum and spice flavours, a hint of dark chocolate, fine-grained tannins and obvious cellaring potential. It should flourish for a decade.

DRY $40 AV

Ngatarawa Stables Reserve Hawke's Bay Merlot ★★★

The 2015 vintage (★★★) is a full-coloured, berryish, slightly herbal red with plenty of flavour and a moderately firm finish.

DRY $19 AV

Nikau Point Reserve Hawke's Bay Merlot ★★

The very smooth, mouthfilling 2014 vintage (★★) was partly barrel-aged. Fullish and slightly developed in colour, it's an easy-drinking, plummy red, with hints of spices and herbs, and moderate length.

DRY $14 –V

Nikau Point Reserve Hawke's Bay Merlot/Cabernet   ★★☆

The 2013 vintage (★★☆), partly barrel-aged, has fullish, fairly mature colour. Fresh and smooth, it offers decent depth of plum and slight herbal flavours. Priced right.

DRY $14 AV

Obsidian Estate Waiheke Island Merlot/Cabernets/Petit Verdot   (★★★☆)

The 2014 vintage (★★★☆) is fresh, vibrantly fruity and flavoursome, with a herbal thread. Full-coloured, with a slightly leafy bouquet, it is plummy and spicy, with some nutty, savoury complexity, very good depth, and moderate tannins. Enjoyable young.

DRY $29 –V

Old Coach Road Nelson New Zealand Merlot   (★★)

Priced right, the 2013 vintage (★★) was matured for 10 months in French and American oak. Lightish in colour, it is a solid quaffer, with fresh plum and herb flavours. (From Seifried.)

Vintage	13	DRY $13 AV
WR	5	
Drink	17-18	

Old Coach Road Nelson New Zealand Merlot/Malbec/Cabernet Franc   (★★)

The French oak-aged 2014 vintage (★★) is lightish in colour, with fresh plum, spice and herb flavours. A pleasant quaffer, it's best drunk young.

Vintage	14	DRY $13 AV
WR	5	
Drink	17-18	

Omaka Springs Marlborough Merlot   ★★☆

Estate-grown in the Omaka Valley and American oak-aged, the 2014 vintage (★★★) is drinking well now. Lightish in colour, with a hint of maturity, it is medium to full-bodied, with a slightly herbal bouquet leading into a fresh, fruity, smooth red with plum, herb and spice flavours, seasoned with nutty oak, moderate tannins and some complexity.

DRY $23 –V

Oyster Bay Hawke's Bay Merlot   ★★★★

From Delegat, this red accounts for a huge slice of New Zealand's exports of 'Bordeaux-style' wines (Merlot and/or Cabernet Sauvignon). Winemaker Michael Ivicevich aims for a wine with 'sweet fruit and silky tannins. The trick is – not too much oak.' It is typically fragrant and mouthfilling, with strong blackcurrant, herb and dark chocolate flavours, supple tannins, and plenty of drink-young appeal. The 2015 vintage (★★★★) was grown in the Gimblett Gravels, elsewhere on the Heretaunga Plains and at Crownthorpe, and 'a large portion' of the blend was matured for 11 months in French oak barriques. Deeply coloured, it is generous and supple, with good concentration of fresh, vibrant, plummy flavours, gentle tannins and excellent ripeness, depth and charm. The 2016 vintage (★★★★) is fragrant and full-coloured, very fresh and vibrant, with strong, plummy flavours, a hint of herbs, and loads of drink-young appeal.

DRY $20 V+

Pask Declaration Hawke's Bay Merlot ★★★★☆

Estate-grown in the Gimblett Gravels and matured for 21 months in French oak barrels (90 per cent new), the 2014 vintage (★★★★☆) is deeply coloured, mouthfilling, rich and smooth. Finely poised, with good varietal character, it has strong, youthful plum and spice flavours, showing very good complexity, and a finely balanced finish. Best drinking 2018+.

Vintage	14	13
WR	6	7
Drink	18-25	17-25

 DRY $50 –V

Pask Gimblett Gravels Merlot ★★★☆

The 2014 vintage (★★★☆) was matured for over a year in French and American oak barrels (8 per cent new). Deep ruby, it is mouthfilling and vibrantly fruity, with ripe, plummy, slightly spicy flavours, a gentle seasoning of oak, and drink-young appeal.

Vintage	14
WR	6
Drink	17-24

 DRY $22 AV

Peacock Sky Waiheke Island Merlot/Malbec ★★★★

Showing good potential, the 2014 vintage (★★★★) is a 3:1 blend of Merlot and Malbec, French oak-aged for over a year. Deeply coloured, it has fresh, smooth, ripe blackcurrant, plum and spice flavours, gently seasoned with oak, and firm tannins.

DRY $40 –V

Peacock Sky Waiheke Island Pure Merlot ★★★☆

The sturdy 2014 vintage (★★★☆) was matured for over a year in French oak barrels. Full-coloured, it has strong, ripe, plummy, slightly spicy and nutty flavours, and a firm backbone of tannin.

DRY $40 –V

Pegasus Bay Waipara Valley Merlot/Cabernet ★★★★

The 2013 vintage (★★★★☆) is the best since 2010 (★★★★☆). Blended principally from Merlot, Cabernet Sauvignon and Cabernet Franc, with a splash of Malbec, it was matured for two years in French oak barriques (20 per cent new). Deeply coloured, it is youthful, with strong, vibrant blackcurrant, plum and spice flavours, finely integrated oak, ripe, supple tannins, and excellent depth, complexity and harmony. Best drinking 2018+.

Vintage	13	12	11	10
WR	7	6	6	7
Drink	17-24	17-22	17-21	17-21

 DRY $31 –V

Redmetal Vineyards Hawke's Bay Merlot/Cabernet Franc   ★★★☆

The 2014 vintage (★★★★) is a good buy. Grown in the Bridge Pa Triangle, it was matured in a 50:50 split of tanks and barrels. Deeply coloured, it is mouthfilling, with generous, ripe plum, spice and dark chocolate flavours, savoury notes adding complexity, and a finely textured finish. Delicious from the start.

Vintage	15
WR	5
Drink	17-20

 DRY $18 V+

Redmetal Vineyards Resolution Hawke's Bay Merlot   (★★★★☆)

The powerful 2013 vintage (★★★★☆) was grown in the Bridge Pa Triangle and matured for 14 months in French (85 per cent) and American (15 per cent) oak barrels (30 per cent new). Dark, it is mouthfilling, rich, fruit-packed and supple, with strong berry, plum and spice flavours. Fleshy, sweet-fruited and generous, it should be at its best 2018+.

Vintage	13
WR	6
Drink	17-25

 DRY $60 –V

Regent of Tantallon, The, Hawke's Bay Merlot/Cabernet Limited Edition   ★★★★

From The Wine Portfolio (formerly owner of Morton Estate), the 2013 vintage (★★★★☆) was barrel-aged for two years. Full and still fairly youthful in colour, with a fragrant, fresh bouquet, it is a refined, mouthfilling red, with deep, vibrant blackcurrant/plum flavours, silky tannins, and lots of current-drinking appeal.

DRY $40 –V

Renato Estate Nelson Merlot   ★★★☆

From mature, very low-cropped (3 tonnes/ha) vines at Kina, the 2014 vintage (★★★★) is a full-bodied and generous red, drinking well now. Matured in one to two-year-old French oak barriques, it is deeply coloured, with ripe, plummy, spicy flavours, a hint of herbs, gentle tannins, savoury notes adding complexity, and excellent depth and harmony.

Vintage	14	13	12
WR	6	5	6
Drink	17-19	17-19	17-18

DRY $25 –V

Sacred Hill Brokenstone Merlot – see Sacred Hill Brokenstone in the Branded and Other Red Wines section

Sacred Hill Halo Hawke's Bay Merlot/Cabernet Sauvignon ★★★★

The 2014 vintage (★★★★), blended from Merlot (88 per cent) and Cabernet Sauvignon (12 per cent), was hand-picked in the Gimblett Gravels and matured for 18 months in French oak barrels (10 per cent new). It is deeply coloured and mouthfilling, with strong plum, blackcurrant and spice flavours, a subtle seasoning of oak and ripe, supple tannins.

Vintage	14	13	12	11
WR	6	7	6	6
Drink	17-20	17-18	P	P

DRY $28 AV

Sacred Hill Hawke's Bay Merlot/Cabernet Sauvignon ★★★☆

The good-value 2016 vintage (★★★☆) was French oak-matured for 10 months. A 'fruit-driven' style, it is full-coloured, with mouthfilling body and strong, berryish, slightly herbal flavours, fresh and smooth. Best drinking 2018+.

Vintage	16	15
WR	6	6
Drink	17-22	17-20

DRY $17 V+

Sacred Hill Reserve Hawke's Bay Merlot/Cabernet Sauvignon ★★★☆

Delicious young, the 2016 vintage (★★★★) was French oak-aged for a year. Full, bright and very youthful in colour, it is rich and flowing, with generous, plummy flavours, hints of herbs, spices and nuts, and fine-grained tannins. Best drinking mid-2018+.

Vintage	16
WR	6
Drink	17-26

DRY $25 –V

Saint Clair Hawke's Bay Merlot ★★★★

The 2014 vintage (★★★★) is a floral, deeply coloured, single-vineyard Gimblett Gravels red, American oak-matured. Mouthfilling, it has ripe blackcurrant, plum and spice flavours, showing some savoury complexity, and soft tannins.

DRY $25 AV

Saint Clair Pioneer Block 17 Plateau Block Hawke's Bay Merlot ★★★★

The deeply coloured 2015 vintage (★★★★) was estate-grown in the Gimblett Gravels and matured in American oak casks. It is mouthfilling, very fresh and smooth, with strong, ripe, plummy, slightly spicy and nutty flavours, and gentle tannins. Delicious young.

DRY $38 –V

Selaks Founders Limited Edition Hawke's Bay Merlot/Cabernet ★★★★

The estate-grown, barrel-matured 2015 vintage (★★★★) is a powerful red, already drinking well. Mouthfilling, it has rich, ripe berry and plum flavours, hints of herbs, spices and liquorice, a slightly nutty oak influence, and a smooth finish. Drink now or cellar.

Vintage	15
WR	5
Drink	18-21

DRY $25 AV

Selaks Reserve Hawke's Bay Merlot/Cabernet ★★★

Priced right, the 2016 vintage (★★★) is enjoyable young. Mouthfilling, with fullish, youthful colour, it is vibrantly fruity, with satisfying depth of plummy, berryish flavours, hints of spices and herbs, and a well-rounded finish.

Vintage	16
WR	5
Drink	18-19

DRY $16 V+

Sileni Cellar Selection Hawke's Bay Merlot ★★★☆

Enjoyable young, the 2016 vintage (★★★☆) is a lightly oaked, 'fruit-driven' red. Floral, it is medium-bodied, with bright, youthful colour, fresh, generous plum and spice flavours, and gentle tannins. Best drinking 2018+.

Vintage	16	15	14	13
WR	6	7	7	6
Drink	18-23	17-23	17-22	17-19

DRY $20 AV

Sileni Estate Selection Cut Cane Hawke's Bay Merlot ★★★★★

The 2015 vintage (★★★★) is a powerful red (15 per cent alcohol), matured for 16 months in a mix of French and American oak barriques (40 per cent new). Grown in the Bridge Pa Triangle, it is a single-vineyard wine. The crops were thinned to one bunch per shoot, before 'at optimal ripeness, the canes were cut, allowing the fruit on the vine to shrivel, concentrating the juice within'. Forward in its appeal, but still youthful, it is deeply colourful and robust, with gentle tannins, strong, ripe plum and spice flavours, hints of coffee and liquorice, and a seasoning of sweet oak. Best drinking 2018+.

Vintage	15	14	13
WR	7	7	7
Drink	17-26	17-26	17-23

DRY $40 AV

Sileni Estate Selection Triangle Hawke's Bay Merlot ★★★★☆

The 2015 vintage (★★★★☆) was estate-grown in the Bridge Pa Triangle and matured for 18 months in French oak barriques (20 per cent new). Deep and youthful in colour, it is sturdy and fleshy, with deep, plummy flavours, hints of herbs and spices, fine-grained tannins, and a rich, harmonious finish. Drink now or cellar.

Vintage	15	14	13	12	11	10	09	08
WR	6	7	7	5	6	6	7	6
Drink	17-24	17-24	17-23	17-18	P	P	P	P

DRY $33 AV

Sileni Exceptional Vintage Hawke's Bay Merlot ★★★★☆

The 2014 vintage (★★★★☆), estate-grown in the Bridge Pa Triangle, was matured for 14 months in French oak barriques (50 per cent new). A powerful, strapping red (15 per cent alcohol), it is deeply coloured and jam-packed with ripe plum, spice and liquorice flavours. Still youthful, it's a super-charged style that will appeal strongly to fans of 'big reds'.

Vintage	14	13
WR	7	7
Drink	17-25	17-25

DRY $70 –V

Soljans Tribute Hawke's Bay Merlot/Malbec ★★★☆

The attractive 2015 vintage (★★★★) was matured in French oak barriques (new and seasoned). Full-coloured, it is mouthfilling, sweet-fruited and smooth, with excellent depth of plum, blackcurrant and spice flavours, skilfully balanced for early enjoyment.

Vintage	15
WR	7
Drink	17-22

DRY $40 –V

Spy Valley Single Vineyard Marlborough Merlot/Malbec ★★★★

The 2014 vintage (★★★★) is a full-coloured blend of Merlot and Malbec, matured for 18 months in French oak barrels (29 per cent new). Deeply coloured, with a fresh, plummy, spicy bouquet, it is mouthfilling and vibrantly fruity, with good density of ripe plum, berry and spice flavours, fine-grained tannins, and good aging potential.

Vintage	14	13	12	11	10
WR	6	5	6	7	7
Drink	17-21	17-18	17-18	17-18	P

DRY $23 V+

Stables Reserve Hawke's Bay Merlot (★★★☆)

Priced sharply, the 2015 vintage (★★★☆) was grown in the Bridge Pa Triangle (80 per cent) and in the Gimblett Gravels (20 per cent), and fermented 'with', rather than 'in', oak (meaning not barrel-aged). Full-coloured, it is a mouthfilling, fresh, smooth red, with generous red-berry, plum and spice flavours, slightly savoury notes adding complexity, and lots of drink-young appeal. (From Ngatarawa.)

DRY $19 V+

Stolen Heart Merlot/Malbec (★★★★☆)

Densely packed and youthful, the 2014 vintage (★★★★☆) is a Gimblett Gravels, Hawke's Bay blend of Merlot (78 per cent) and Malbec (16 per cent), with splashes of Cabernet Franc (3 per cent) and Syrah (3 per cent). Deeply coloured, it is fresh and full-bodied, with vibrant, plummy, spicy flavours, finely integrated oak, good tannin backbone, and excellent ripeness and depth. Best drinking 2018+. (From Crown Range Cellar.)

DRY $50 –V

Stolen Heart Merlot/Malbec/Cabernet Franc   (★★★★★)

The impressive 2013 vintage (★★★★★) was grown in the Gimblett Gravels, Hawke's Bay. A stylish wine, still fresh and youthful, it is deeply coloured, with an invitingly fragrant bouquet. Displaying rich berry, plum, blackcurrant and spice flavours, with well-integrated oak and fine-grained tannins, it is complex and supple, with excellent cellaring potential; open 2018+. (From Crown Range Cellar.)

DRY $50 AV

Stonecroft Ruhanui Gimblett Gravels Hawke's Bay
Merlot/Cabernet Sauvignon   ★★★★☆

Certified organic, the 2015 vintage (★★★★☆) is a blend of Merlot (55 per cent) and Cabernet Sauvignon (45 per cent), estate-grown at Roys Hill and matured for 18 months in French oak barriques (15 per cent new). Still a baby, it is deeply coloured, with mouthfilling body, fresh acidity and strong, vibrant plum, spice, blackcurrant and nut flavours, showing excellent complexity and harmony. Best drinking 2020+.

Vintage	15	14	13
WR	6	7	7
Drink	19-26	19-26	18-25

DRY $35 AV

Stoneleigh Latitude Marlborough Merlot   ★★★☆

The debut 2014 vintage (★★★☆) was grown in the relatively warm Rapaura district, on the north side of the Wairau Valley, and matured for nine months in French and Hungarian oak barrels. Full-coloured, it is mouthfilling, with very good depth of fresh blackcurrant, plum, dried-herb and spice flavours, finely balanced tannins, moderate complexity and lots of drink-young charm. The 2015 vintage (★★★★) is a deeply coloured, fleshy wine, with rich, plummy flavours, a hint of herbs, savoury notes adding complexity, and a firmly structured finish.

DRY $22 AV

Stoneleigh Marlborough Merlot   ★★★☆

The 2015 vintage (★★★☆) from Pernod Ricard NZ is deeply coloured, with mouthfilling body, good depth of plummy, spicy flavours, showing some savoury complexity, and a finely balanced, smooth finish. Fine value.

DRY $17 V+

Tantalus Estate Waiheke Island Merlot/Cabernet Franc   (★★★★)

Grown at Onetangi, the 2014 vintage (★★★★) was matured for nine months in French and American oak casks. Full-coloured, it is mouthfilling, with generous, ripe, spicy, slightly earthy flavours, showing good freshness and complexity, underlying tannins, and lots of current-drinking appeal.

Vintage	14
WR	6
Drink	17-20

DRY $38 –V

Te Awa Single Estate Hawke's Bay Merlot/Cabernet Sauvignon ★★★★☆

The 2015 vintage (★★★★☆) is a dark, fruit-packed blend of Merlot (70 per cent), Cabernet Sauvignon (18 per cent) and Malbec (12 per cent), hand-picked and matured for 20 months in French oak casks (40 per cent new). It has a fragrant, berryish bouquet, leading into a mouthfilling, supple wine with concentrated, plummy flavours, hints of spices, herbs and chocolate, finely integrated oak and a rich, very harmonious finish. Best drinking 2019+.

Vintage	14	13
WR	7	7
Drink	17-24	17-23

 DRY $30 AV

Te Mata Estate Vineyards Merlot/Cabernets ★★★★

The highly attractive 2015 vintage (★★★★) is a blend of Merlot (55 per cent), Cabernet Sauvignon (25 per cent), Cabernet Franc (16 per cent) and Petit Verdot (4 per cent), matured for eight months in French oak barrels (partly new). Fragrant and deeply coloured, it is concentrated, with generous, vibrant plum, berry and spice flavours, in a fruit-driven style, delicious young.

Vintage	15
WR	6
Drink	17-23

 DRY $20 V+

Theory & Practice Hawke's Bay Merlot (★★★★)

Enjoyable young, the 2015 vintage (★★★★) is a blend of Merlot (91 per cent) and Cabernet Franc (9 per cent), hand-picked, fermented with indigenous yeasts and matured for a year in French oak casks (40 per cent new). Full-coloured, it is mouthfilling (14.5 per cent alcohol) and supple, with vibrant, ripe, plummy flavours, fresh and generous, and a well-rounded finish. Priced right.

 DRY $22 V+

Thornbury Hawke's Bay Merlot ★★★☆

The great-value 2016 vintage (★★★☆), grown mostly in the Gimblett Gravels, was blended with Cabernet Franc (10 per cent) and matured for 11 months in tanks with French and Hungarian oak staves. Deeply coloured, it is full-bodied, with very good depth of fresh, ripe, plummy, spicy flavours and a silky-smooth finish. (From Villa Maria.)

Vintage	16	15	14	13	12	11	10
WR	5	5	6	7	4	5	6
Drink	17-21	17-20	17-19	17-18	P	P	P

 DRY $14 V+

Tohu Hawke's Bay Merlot (★★★☆)

The easy-drinking but not simple 2014 vintage (★★★☆) was hand-picked and matured in old French oak barriques. Full-coloured, it is mouthfilling, with moderately concentrated, ripe plum/spice flavours, showing some savoury complexity, finely balanced tannins, and lots of current-drinking appeal.

DRY $22 AV

Toi Toi Gisborne Merlot ★★★

Enjoyable young, the 2014 vintage (★★★) has fullish colour. Mouthfilling, it has plummy, spicy, slightly earthy flavours, in a fruit-driven style with good depth.

DRY $18 AV

Trinity Hill Hawke's Bay Merlot ★★★★

This delicious, drink-young red is grown in the Gimblett Gravels and Bridge Pa Triangle. The 2015 vintage (★★★★) is full-coloured and mouthfilling, with strong plum/spice flavours, hints of liquorice and dark chocolate, some savoury complexity, and fine-grained tannins. Showing good ripeness, texture and density, it's a finely crafted red, likely to be at its best 2018+.

DRY $22 V+

Turanga Creek Notre Terroir Merlot/Malbec (★★★★)

Certified organic, the 2014 vintage (★★★★) is a barrel-aged blend of Merlot (40 per cent), Malbec (40 per cent) and Cabernet Franc (20 per cent), estate-grown at Clevedon, in South Auckland. Showing good personality, it is savoury, generous and firm, with the warm, earthy notes typical of Auckland reds. Drink now or cellar.

DRY $32 –V

TW Merlot (★★★)

Estate-grown in Gisborne, the 2015 vintage (★★★) is medium-bodied, with firm, plummy, slightly spicy flavours and some savoury, nutty notes adding complexity.

DRY $20 –V

Vidal Hawke's Bay Merlot/Cabernet Sauvignon ★★★☆

Already drinking well, the good-value 2016 vintage (★★★☆) is a fresh, vibrant blend of Merlot (69 per cent), Cabernet Sauvignon (26 per cent) and Malbec (5 per cent), partly barrel-matured. Full-coloured, it is mouthfilling, with plummy, slightly spicy flavours, showing very good depth, ripeness and roundness.

Vintage	16	15
WR	6	6
Drink	17-21	17-20

DRY $16 V+

Vidal Reserve Gimblett Gravels Merlot/Cabernet Sauvignon ★★★★☆

A consistently great buy. Already delicious, but still unfolding, the 2015 vintage (★★★★☆) is a blend of Merlot (75 per cent), Cabernet Sauvignon (18 per cent) and Malbec (7 per cent), matured for 16 months in French oak casks (24 per cent new). Deeply coloured, it is mouthfilling, vibrantly fruity and supple, with excellent density of ripe, plummy, spicy flavours and a long, finely poised finish. A refined, savoury, age-worthy red, it should be at its best 2019+.

Vintage	15	14	13	12	11	10
WR	7	7	7	5	6	7
Drink	17-23	17-23	17-22	17-18	P	P

DRY $20 V+

Villa Maria Cellar Selection Hawke's Bay Merlot/Cabernet Sauvignon   ★★★★

Sharply priced, the 2015 vintage (★★★★) is a blend of Merlot (65 per cent), Cabernet Sauvignon (28 per cent) and Malbec (7 per cent), matured for 18 months in oak casks (18 per cent new). Instantly attractive, it is mouthfilling, with very good depth of ripe red-berry, plum and spice flavours, showing good complexity, and a smooth finish. Best drinking 2019+.

Vintage	15	14	13	12	11	10	09
WR	6	7	7	6	6	7	7
Drink	17-23	17-22	17-22	17-19	P	P	P

DRY $19 V+

Villa Maria Cellar Selection Hawke's Bay Organic Merlot   ★★★★

The good-value 2016 vintage (★★★★) was grown in the Joseph Soler Vineyard and matured for 17 months in oak barriques (20 per cent new). It's a full-bodied, vibrant red with excellent depth of plum/spice flavours, rich and smooth.

Vintage	15	14	13
WR	6	6	7
Drink	17-22	17-20	17-20

DRY $19 V+

Villa Maria Library Release Gimblett Gravels
Merlot/Cabernet Sauvignon   (★★★★★)

Released in 2017, the 2010 vintage (★★★★★) is a classy, very refined blend of Merlot (62 per cent) and Cabernet Sauvignon (38 per cent), matured in French oak barriques (60 per cent new) for 18 months. It has deep, still youthful colour. Currently delicious, but still unfolding, it has concentrated, beautifully ripe blackcurrant and spice flavours, showing good, savoury complexity, and fine-grained tannins. Built to last, it should be at its best 2018+.

Vintage	10
WR	7
Drink	17-22

DRY $70 AV

Villa Maria Private Bin Hawke's Bay Merlot   ★★★☆

The 2016 vintage (★★★☆) is an easy-drinking, full-bodied red with good depth of vibrant, ripe red-berry and plum flavours, fresh and silky-smooth.

Vintage	16	15	14	13
WR	7	7	7	6
Drink	17-21	17-20	17-19	17-18

DRY $16 V+

Villa Maria Private Bin Hawke's Bay Merlot/Cabernet Sauvignon ★★★☆

Drinking well now, the 2015 vintage (★★★☆) is a blend of Merlot (50 per cent), Cabernet Sauvignon (40 per cent), and minor portions of Syrah and Cabernet Franc. Partly barrel-aged, it is mouthfilling and full-coloured, with vibrant, plummy, slightly herbal flavours, generous and smooth.

Vintage	15	14	13	12	11
WR	6	7	7	5	6
Drink	17-20	17-18	17-18	P	P

DRY $16 V+

Villa Maria Reserve Gimblett Gravels Hawke's Bay Merlot ★★★★★

This consistently outstanding wine is grown at company-owned vineyards in the Gimblett Gravels and matured for 17 to 20 months in French oak barriques (28 per cent new in 2015). The 2015 vintage (★★★★★) is built for cellaring. Dark and rich, it is full-bodied and impressively concentrated, with dense, ripe plum, red-berry and spice flavours, youthful, complex and savoury, very fine-grained tannins and obvious potential; best drinking 2020+.

Vintage	15	14	13
WR	7	7	7
Drink	18-25	19-26	17-23

DRY $50 AV

🍇🍇🍇

Villa Maria Single Vineyard Braided Gravels Hawke's Bay Merlot (★★★★★)

Certified organic, the outstanding 2013 vintage (★★★★★) was grown in the Gimblett Gravels and matured for 17 months in French oak barriques (35 per cent new). Bold, bright and youthful in colour, it has rich, ripe plum/spice flavours, with fine-grained tannins. A powerful, dense red, it is sweet-fruited, soft and long.

Vintage	13
WR	7
Drink	17-23

DRY $60 AV

Wairau River Marlborough Merlot (★★★)

The 2014 vintage (★★★) was matured in French and American oak casks (30 per cent new). Fullish in colour, it is mouthfilling, with fresh plum and spice flavours, showing a touch of complexity, gentle tannins and drink-young appeal.

Vintage	14
WR	6
Drink	17-20

DRY $20 –V

Montepulciano

Montepulciano is widely planted across central Italy, yielding deeply coloured, ripe wines with good levels of alcohol, extract and flavour. In the Abruzzi, it is the foundation of the often superb-value Montepulciano d'Abruzzo, and in the Marches it is the key ingredient in the noble Rosso Conero.

In New Zealand, Montepulciano is a rarity and there has been confusion between the Montepulciano and Sangiovese varieties. Some wines may have been incorrectly labelled. According to the latest national vineyard survey, between 2005 and 2018, New Zealand's area of bearing Montepulciano vines will expand slightly from 6 to 9 hectares (mostly in Auckland, Hawke's Bay, Nelson and Marlborough).

Beach House Hawke's Bay Montepulciano ★★★★

The fragrant, rich and age-worthy 2014 vintage (★★★★☆) is a single-vineyard red, estate-grown in the Gimblett Gravels and matured for a year in French oak casks (20 per cent new). Boldly coloured, it is mouthfilling, with vibrant, concentrated plum and spice flavours, oak complexity and a firm finish. Still youthful, it should break into full stride 2019+.

DRY $30 –V

Blackenbrook Family Reserve Nelson Montepulciano (★★★★)

Showing good personality, the 2016 vintage (★★★★) was matured for a year in seasoned French oak barriques. Full-coloured, it is mouthfilling, with strong, fresh plum and spice flavours, earthy, savoury notes adding complexity, and finely balanced tannins. Drink now or cellar.

Vintage	16
WR	7
Drink	18-25

DRY $39 –V

Blackenbrook Nelson Montepulciano ★★★☆

The 2014 vintage (★★★☆) was matured for a year in seasoned French oak barriques. It has full, bright colour, with a slightly herbal bouquet, and strong plum, berry and spice flavours, showing some savoury complexity. A youthful, finely balanced wine, it should be at its best 2018+.

Vintage	15	14
WR	7	7
Drink	17-25	17-20

DRY $33 –V

Coopers Creek SV Guido In Velvet Pants Huapai Montepulciano ★★★★

Estate-grown at Huapai, in West Auckland, the 2014 vintage (★★★★) was matured for a year in seasoned oak barrels. Deep and youthful in colour, it is mouthfilling and vibrantly fruity, with concentrated blackcurrant, plum and spice flavours, showing good complexity, and fine-grained tannins. The 2015 vintage (★★★★) is fragrant and full-coloured, with concentrated plum, berry and spice flavours and a firm, lengthy finish. Best drinking mid-2018+.

Vintage	15	14	13
WR	6	6	6
Drink	18-20	18-19	17-18

DRY $28 AV

De La Terre Hawke's Bay Montepulciano ★★★★★

The classy, youthful 2015 vintage (★★★★☆) is rare, but well worth tracking down. Hand-harvested at Havelock North and matured for 16 months in French oak barriques (50 per cent new), it's a worthy follow-up to the delicious 2014 vintage (★★★★★). Deeply coloured, it is concentrated and vibrantly fruity, with generous plum, spice and slight liquorice flavours, oak complexity, and a moderately firm, long finish. Open 2019+.

Vintage	15	14	13
WR	6	7	6
Drink	17-27	17-25	17-28

 DRY $45 AV

Hans Herzog Marlborough Montepulciano ★★★★★

This powerful, classy, estate-grown red is typically overflowing with ripe sweet-fruit flavours. The 2013 vintage (★★★★★) was hand-picked on the north side of the Wairau Valley, fermented with indigenous yeasts, matured for two and a half years in French oak barriques (partly new), and bottled unfined and unfiltered. Dark and purple-flushed, it is still youthful, with inviting red-berry and spice aromas. Mouthfilling, it is a rich, complex, age-worthy wine, with an array of ripe plum, berry, spice, nut and dark chocolate flavours, and good tannin backbone. It should flourish for a decade; open 2018+. Certified organic.

Vintage	13
WR	7
Drink	17-23

 DRY $64 AV

Obsidian Estate Waiheke Island Montepulciano ★★★★

The 2015 vintage (★★★★) is the first to be labelled as 'Estate'. Full-coloured, it is sturdy (14.5 per cent alcohol) and vibrantly fruity, with strong, ripe plum, blackcurrant and spice flavours, slightly earthy notes adding complexity, and gentle tannins. Delicious young, it's also worth cellaring. The 2016 vintage (★★★★) has a fragrant, fresh, spicy bouquet, leading into a mouthfilling, youthful red with deep, plummy, spicy flavours, showing good complexity, and a firm finish. Best drinking 2019+.

 DRY $38 –V

Trinity Hill Gimblett Gravels Montepulciano (★★★★☆)

The 2014 vintage (★★★★☆) is impressive. Dark and youthful in colour, it is mouthfilling and supple, with deep, ripe blackcurrant, plum and spice flavours, showing excellent texture and richness. A generous, sweet-fruited Hawke's Bay wine, partly barrel-aged, it's a drink-now or cellaring proposition.

DRY $35 AV

Nebbiolo

Nebbiolo is the foundation of Piedmont's most majestic red wines – Barolo, Barbaresco and Gattinara – renowned for their complex leather and tar flavours, powerful tannins and great longevity. In New Zealand, only 1 hectare of vines will be bearing in 2018, mostly in Central Otago, Marlborough and Auckland.

Hans Herzog Marlborough Nebbiolo ★★★★☆

Estate-grown on the north side of the Wairau Valley, the very rare 2011 vintage (★★★★☆) was matured for two years in French oak barriques (100 per cent new). Full-coloured, it has vibrant, deep plum, spice and blackcurrant flavours, hints of tar and liquorice, savoury notes adding complexity, and a sustained finish. Certified organic.

DRY $115 –V

Vintage	11
WR	7
Drink	17-26

Pinot Noir

New Zealand Pinot Noir enjoys strong overseas demand and there are now countless Pinot Noir labels, as producers launch second and even third-tier labels, as well as single-vineyard bottlings (and others under 'buyer's own' and export-only brands you and I have never heard of). The wines are enjoying notable success in international competitions, but you need to be aware that most of the world's elite Pinot Noir producers, especially in Burgundy, do not enter. Between 2000 and 2018, New Zealand's area of bearing Pinot Noir vines is expanding from 1126 hectares to 5768 hectares, makng it the country's most widely planted red-wine variety (far ahead of Merlot, with 1327 hectares). Pinot Noir is the princely grape variety of red Burgundy. Cheaper wines typically display light, raspberry-evoking flavours, but great Pinot Noir has substance, suppleness and a gorgeous spread of flavours: cherries, fruit cake, spice and plums.

Pinot Noir is now New Zealand's most internationally acclaimed red-wine style. Well over 45 per cent of the country's total Pinot Noir plantings are in Marlborough, and the variety is also well established in Otago (27 per cent), Wairarapa (9 per cent), Canterbury (7 per cent), Hawke's Bay and Nelson.

Yet Pinot Noir is a frustrating variety to grow. Because it buds early, it is vulnerable to spring frosts; its compact bunches are also very prone to rot. One crucial advantage is that it ripens early, well ahead of Cabernet Sauvignon. Low cropping and the selection of superior clones are essential aspects of the production of fine wine.

Martinborough (initially) and Central Otago have enjoyed the highest profile for Pinot Noir over the past 30 years. As their output of Pinot Noir has expanded, average prices have fallen, reflecting the arrival of a tidal wave of 'entry-level' (drink-young) wines.

Of the other small regions, Nelson and Canterbury (especially Waipara) are also enjoying success. Marlborough's potential for the production of outstanding – but still widely underrated – Pinot Noir, in sufficient volumes to supply the burgeoning international demand, has also been tapped.

12,000 Miles Gladstone Pinot Noir   ★★★☆

Enjoyable young, the 2014 vintage (★★★☆) is a ruby-hued, floral red, grown in the northern Wairarapa. Fresh and smooth, with a touch of complexity, it's a mouthfilling, 'fruit-driven' style with vibrant, plummy, slightly spicy flavours, generous, ripe and well-rounded. (From Gladstone Vineyard.)

DRY $25 AV

---

8 Ranges Tussock Ridge Central Otago Pinot Noir   ★★★☆

Estate-grown at Alexandra, the elegant 2014 vintage (★★★★) was matured for 10 months in French oak casks (30 per cent new). Deep ruby, it is fresh, ripe, plummy and spicy, with savoury, earthy notes adding complexity. Best drinking 2018+.

DRY $36 –V

Akarua Bannockburn Central Otago Pinot Noir   ★★★★★

Estate-grown, harvested from mature vines and matured in French oak barriques, the 2014 vintage (★★★★★) is deep ruby, with an enticingly fragrant bouquet. Generous, vibrantly fruity and supple, it has concentrated, well-ripened cherry, plum, spice and dried-herb flavours, showing excellent complexity, and a finely poised, lasting finish. Delicious young, it should be at its best 2018+.

Vintage	14	13	12	11	10	09
WR	7	7	7	7	7	7
Drink	17-24	17-23	17-22	17-20	17-18	17-18

DRY $42 V+

Akarua Rua Central Otago Pinot Noir ★★★★

For a third-tier label, this regional blend can be remarkably good. Matured for six months in French oak barriques (10 per cent new), the highly attractive 2015 vintage (★★★★) was grown at three company-owned sites, two at Bannockburn. Delicious in its youth, it is floral, sweet-fruited and supple, with strong, plummy, cherryish, slightly nutty flavours, showing good complexity. More subtle and savoury than you'd expect at this price, it offers fine value.

DRY $28 V+

Akarua The Siren Bannockburn Central Otago Pinot Noir ★★★★★

The second, 2013 vintage (★★★★★) of Akarua's top Pinot Noir was estate-grown and selected from 13 barrels out of 650. Deeply coloured, it has a highly perfumed, savoury bouquet. Powerful and densely packed, it is very sweet-fruited and finely textured, with concentrated, vibrant cherry, plum and spice flavours, fresh acidity and silky tannins. Already delicious, it should be long-lived; best drinking 2018+.

Vintage	13	12
WR	7	7
Drink	20-24	19-23

 DRY $100 –V

Akitu A1 Central Otago Pinot Noir ★★★★☆

Estate-grown by Hawkesbury Estates at Mt Barker, in the Wanaka sub-region, the 2015 vintage (★★★★☆) is a youthful, bright ruby-hued red, matured for 10 months in French oak barrels (25 per cent new). Fresh and finely textured, it is savoury and supple, with concentrated, ripe cherry, plum and spice flavours, showing good complexity. Well worth cellaring, it should break into full stride 2018+.

 DRY $59 –V

Akitu A2 Central Otago Pinot Noir ★★★★

Grown at Mt Barker, in the Wanaka sub-region, the skilfully crafted 2015 vintage (★★★★) is enjoyable from the start. Matured for 10 months in French oak barrels (13 per cent new), it has a scented, savoury bouquet, leading into an elegant wine with ripe cherry, plum and spice flavours, showing very good delicacy, complexity and depth. (From Hawkesbury Estates.)

 DRY $40 –V

Alex K Big Backyard Central Otago Pinot Noir (★★★)

The 2015 vintage (★★★) is a fresh, medium-bodied, distinctly spicy blend of Alexandra and Bendigo fruit, bottled unfined and unfiltered. Bright ruby, it has red-berry, spice and dried-herb flavours, showing some savoury, smoky complexity, gentle acidity and a moderately firm finish.

DRY $28 –V

Alex Ridgeback Central Otago Pinot Noir (★★★☆)

The 2014 vintage (★★★☆) is a ruby-hued, full-bodied Alexandra red with very good depth of vibrant, ripe, plummy, spicy flavours and a smooth finish. A gently oaked style, it shows some complexity. (From Greylands Ridge.)

 DRY $25 AV

Alexander Dusty Road Martinborough Pinot Noir ★★★★

Designed for early drinking, this second-tier red consistently offers great value. The 2016 vintage (★★★★) is a single-vineyard wine, hand-picked and matured for 11 months in French oak barriques (17 per cent new). Deep and youthful in colour, it is mouthfilling and fruit-packed, with well-integrated oak and generous cherry, plum and spice flavours. The 2015 vintage (★★★★) is scented, full-flavoured and smooth; the 2014 vintage (★★★★) is full-bodied, rich and rounded, with considerable complexity. Overall, these are more concentrated Pinot Noirs than most in the sub-$30 category.

Vintage	16	15	14
WR	6	6	6
Drink	18-22	17-21	17-20

DRY $26 V+

Alexander Martinborough Pinot Noir ★★★★★

Offering top value, the highly fragrant 2015 vintage (★★★★★) was estate-grown in Martinborough, hand-picked and matured for 11 months in French oak barriques (20 per cent new). Deep ruby, it is mouthfilling, with concentrated, ripe cherry, plum, spice and nut flavours, showing excellent complexity, and a lasting, finely textured finish. Delicious now, it should be at its best 2019+. The 2016 vintage (★★★★☆) is deeply coloured and full-bodied, with youthful, rich plum, cherry and spice flavours, fine-grained tannins and obvious potential; open 2020+. The savoury 2014 vintage (★★★★★), tasted in mid-2017, is delicious now, with ripe, plummy, spicy, slightly nutty flavours, showing excellent depth and complexity.

Vintage	16	15	14
WR	7	7	7
Drink	20-24	18-23	18-22

DRY $38 V+

Alexandra Wine Company Alex Gold Central Otago Pinot Noir ★★★★

Delicious young, the 2014 vintage (★★★★) was matured in French oak casks (31 per cent new). Bright ruby, it is finely scented, in an elegant, supple style with cherry, plum and spice flavours, fresh and strong. Instantly likeable.

DRY $30 AV

Alexandra Wine Company Davishon Central Otago Pinot Noir ★★★★

The 2015 vintage (★★★☆) is a full ruby, mouthfilling red with fresh plum and spice flavours, showing a gentle oak influence, good tannin support, and some savoury complexity. Best drinking 2018+.

DRY $36 AV

Allan Scott Eli Marlborough Pinot Noir (★★★★☆)

Just one barrel was made of the debut 2015 vintage (★★★★☆), grown in The Hounds Vineyard. Deep ruby, it is very fragrant and sweet-fruited, with rich, vibrant fruit flavours, very gentle tannins and loads of drink-young charm.

DRY $150 –V

Allan Scott Generations Marlborough Pinot Noir   (★★★☆)

Enjoyable young, the 2015 vintage (★★★☆) is a single-vineyard red, hand-picked and matured for 16 months in new French oak puncheons. Bright ruby, it is floral and supple, with attractive, berryish, slightly nutty flavours, showing some complexity. Best drinking 2018+.

 DRY $36 –V

Allan Scott Marlborough Pinot Noir   (★★★☆)

The 2014 vintage (★★★☆) was matured in French oak casks (20 per cent new). Bright ruby, it is a medium to full-bodied, sweet-fruited wine with cherry, plum and spice flavours, a hint of herbs, considerable complexity and a fairly firm finish. Best drinking 2018+.

 DRY $26 AV

Amisfield Central Otago Pinot Noir   ★★★★★

Estate-grown at Pisa, in the Cromwell Basin, the 2014 vintage (★★★★☆) is from vines planted from 1999 to 2007. Hand-picked at 23 to 25 brix, fermented with indigenous yeasts and matured for 10 months in French oak barriques (23 per cent new), it is deep ruby and floral, mouthfilling and sweet-fruited, with generous, cherryish, plummy flavours, savoury notes adding compexity, good harmony and a rounded finish. Already delicious.

 DRY $50 AV

Amisfield RKV Reserve Central Otago Pinot Noir   ★★★★★

Estate-grown at Pisa, in the Cromwell Basin, the youthful 2013 vintage (★★★★★) was harvested at 24 to 25 brix from selected blocks, fermented with indigenous yeasts, and matured for 18 months in French oak casks (35 per cent new). Deep ruby, with a fragrant, very savoury bouquet, it is ripe and supple, with highly complex plum, cherry, spice and nut flavours, fine-grained tannins, and obvious potential; open 2018+.

 DRY $120 –V

Anchorage Family Estate Nelson Pinot Noir   ★★☆

The 2014 vintage (★★★) is a light ruby, medium-bodied, fruity style with plum and spice flavours, fresh and lively, and a tight finish.

 DRY $21 –V

Anna's Way Marlborough Pinot Noir   (★★★★)

Full of drink-young charm, the 2016 vintage (★★★★) was grown in the Awatere and Wairau valleys, and barrel-aged. Bright ruby, it is fragrant, fresh, sweet-fruited and vibrantly fruity, with strong, cherryish, plummy flavours, finely integrated oak and gentle tannins. Already delicious, it's well worth cellaring. (From Awatere River Wine Co.)

 DRY $25 V+

Ant Moore Signature Series Marlborough Pinot Noir   (★★★☆)

Certified organic, the 2014 vintage (★★★☆) was grown in the Wairau Valley. Ruby-hued, it is mouthfilling, with satisfying depth of plum, cherry and spice flavours, a hint of herbs, balanced tannins and good complexity.

DRY $27 AV

Ara Single Estate Marlborough Pinot Noir   ★★★★

The good-value 2014 vintage (★★★★) was estate-grown in the Waihopai Valley. Bright ruby, it is mouthfilling, sweet-fruited and supple, with cherry, plum and spice flavours, showing very good depth, complexity and harmony. Best drinking 2018+.

Vintage	14
WR	5
Drink	17-18

DRY $25 V+

Aravin Central Otago Pinot Noir   ★★★★

Grown at Alexandra and barrel-aged, the 2014 vintage (★★★★) is bright ruby, floral and supple, with very good depth of ripe plum/spice flavours, finely integrated oak and gentle tannins. An elegant rather than powerful wine, it's drinking well now.

DRY $32 AV

Aronui Single Vineyard Nelson Pinot Noir   ★★★☆

From Kono (which also owns the Tohu brand), the 2014 vintage (★★★☆) was estate-grown at Upper Moutere, hand-picked and French oak-aged. Deep ruby, it is mouthfilling, sweet-fruited and supple, with cherry, plum and spice flavours, in a moderately complex style, enjoyable young.

DRY $28 AV

Ashwell Martinborough Pinot Noir   ★★★☆

Still on sale, the 2010 vintage (★★★☆) was matured in French oak casks (50 per cent new). Mature in colour, it is mellow, slightly herbal, very nutty and savoury. Ready.

Vintage	10
WR	5
Drink	17-20

DRY $45 –V

Ashwell Reserve Martinborough Pinot Noir   ★★★★

Still on sale, the 2009 vintage (★★★★) was matured in French oak casks. Fragrant, with mature colour, it is still drinking well, with generous, ripe, plummy, spicy flavours, hints of herbs, leather and nuts, good complexity, and a well-rounded finish. Ready.

Vintage	09
WR	6
Drink	17-20

DRY $45 –V

Askerne Hawke's Bay Pinot Noir

(★★★)

The ruby-hued 2015 vintage (★★☆) was matured for 10 months in barrels (25 per cent new). Maturing well, it is full-bodied, with cherry, plum, spice and herb flavours, developing considerable complexity. Drink now or cellar.

DRY $22 AV

Astrolabe Province Marlborough Pinot Noir

★★★★

The classy 2015 vintage (★★★★☆) was grown at five sites, from the lower Waihopai Valley to Kekerengu, hand-picked, fermented with indigenous yeasts and matured for 10 months in French oak barriques. Deeply coloured, it is mouthfilling and concentrated, with youthful, deep plum, cherry, spice and dried-herb flavours, finely balanced tannins, and good cellaring potential. Best drinking 2019+.

DRY $32 AV

Astrolabe Vineyards Wrekin Vineyard Pinot Noir

(★★★★☆)

Still developing, the 2014 vintage (★★★★☆) was hand-harvested in the upper Brancott Valley of Marlborough, fermented with indigenous yeasts, matured for 18 months in French oak barrels (33 per cent new), and bottled unfined and unfiltered. Deep and youthful in colour, it is weighty (14.5 per cent alcohol), with fresh, ripe plum and spice flavours, showing excellent depth and harmony. Best drinking mid-2018 onwards.

DRY $40 AV

Ata Rangi Crimson Martinborough Pinot Noir

★★★★☆

This second-tier label is 'a vibrant expression of younger' vines and made for relatively early drinking – but the majority of the vines are still 10 to 20 years old. Hand-harvested at Martinborough, fermented with indigenous yeasts and matured in French oak casks (20 per cent new), the 2016 vintage (★★★★☆) is full of youthful promise. Deep ruby, it is mouthfilling and boldly fruity, with strong, ripe cherry, plum and spice flavours, showing good vigour and complexity, savoury notes adding complexity, and a well-rounded finish. Best drinking 2019+.

DRY $36 V+

Ata Rangi Martinborough Pinot Noir

★★★★★

One of the greatest of all New Zealand wines, this Martinborough red is powerfully built and concentrated, yet seductively fragrant and supple. 'Intense, opulent fruit with power beneath' is founder Clive Paton's goal. 'Complexity comes with time.' The grapes are drawn from numerous sites, including the estate vineyard, planted in 1980, and the vines, up to 37 years old, have a very low average yield of 4.5 tonnes of grapes per hectare. The wine is fermented with indigenous yeasts and maturation is for 11 months in French oak barriques (35 per cent new in 2015). From a dry, low-yielding season, the classy 2015 vintage (★★★★★) is deeply coloured, mouthfilling and savoury, with highly concentrated, ripe cherry, plum and spice flavours, hints of dried herbs and nuts, excellent complexity and a finely poised, lasting finish. Still youthful, it shows obvious potential; best drinking 2020+.

Vintage	15	14	13	12	11	10	09	08
WR	7	7	7	7	7	7	7	7
Drink	17-27	17-26	17-25	17-24	17-23	17-22	17-21	17-20

DRY $75 AV

Ataahua Waipara Pinot Noir ★★★★

Still on sale, the 2013 vintage (★★★★) is an elegant, ruby-hued wine, hand-picked, fermented with indigenous yeasts and matured for a year in seasoned French oak barrels. Mouthfilling and supple, with ripe cherry, plum and spice flavours, a gentle seasoning of nutty oak, and a finely poised, lingering finish, it is vibrantly fruity, with good harmony. Drink now or cellar.

Vintage	13	12	11	10
WR	7	6	7	6
Drink	17-20	17-18	17-20	P

DRY $37 AV

Auntsfield Road Ridge Southern Valleys Marlborough Pinot Noir ★★★★

Still on sale, the 2012 vintage (★★★★) of this single-block, estate-grown red was matured for 10 months in French oak casks (33 per cent new). Sturdy, with fullish, slightly developed colour, it's a firm, concentrated style of Pinot Noir, with strong, slightly earthy, spicy flavours, a hint of herbs, and good, savoury complexity.

Vintage	12
WR	5
Drink	17-22

DRY $59 –V

Auntsfield Single Vineyard Southern Valleys Marlborough Pinot Noir ★★★★★

Grown on north-facing slopes at Auntsfield, on the south side of the Wairau Valley, the 2014 vintage (★★★★★) is impressive. Matured for 10 months in French oak casks (31 per cent new), it is deeply coloured, mouthfilling, warm and concentrated, with very ripe plum, cherry and spice flavours, nutty and savoury, good tannin backbone and strong personality. Best drinking 2018+.

Vintage	14	13	12	11	10	09	08
WR	7	7	7	6	7	6	5
Drink	17-23	17-23	17-22	17-20	P	P	P

DRY $40 V+

Aurum Central Otago Pinot Noir ★★★★☆

Estate-grown at Lowburn, in the Cromwell Basin, and matured for 12 months in French oak casks, the 2016 vintage (★★★★☆) was hand-picked, fermented with indigenous yeasts, and bottled unfined and unfiltered. Instantly appealing, it is sweet-fruited, generous, savoury and supple, with youthful cherry, plum and spice flavours, showing good complexity, and fine-grained tannins. Best drinking mid-2018+. Certified organic.

DRY $38 AV

Aurum Madeleine Central Otago Pinot Noir ★★★★☆

Named after the winemaker's daughter, the rare 2015 vintage (★★★★☆) was estate-grown at Lowburn, hand-picked, fermented with indigenous yeasts, and matured for a year in French oak casks. Mouthfilling and very savoury, it is complex, with generous spicy, nutty flavours, already very open and expressive, and a moderately firm finish. Drink now or cellar. Certified organic.

DRY $85 –V

Aurum Mathilde Central Otago Pinot Noir ★★★★☆

Estate-grown at Lowburn, in the Cromwell Basin, the full, bright ruby 2014 vintage (★★★★★) was fermented with indigenous yeasts, matured for a year in French oak casks, and bottled unfined and unfiltered. Mouthfilling and sweet-fruited, it has concentrated, very ripe cherry, plum and spice flavours, good tannin backbone, and loads of current-drinking appeal. Certified organic.

DRY $55 –V

Awatere River by Louis Vavasour Marlborough Pinot Noir ★★★☆

The 2016 vintage (★★★☆) was grown at three sites and matured for 10 months in French oak barriques (25 per cent new). Full, bright ruby, it is floral, mouthfilling and supple, with ripe cherry, plum and spice flavours, and lots of drink-young charm. Best drinking mid-2018+. The 2015 vintage (★★★☆) is full-coloured, with a freshly scented, slightly leafy bouquet, very good depth of cherry, plum, spice and herb flavours, and a smooth finish.

Vintage	16	15
WR	7	7
Drink	17-26	17-25

DRY $31 –V

Babich Black Label Marlborough Pinot Noir ★★★★

Designed for sale principally in restaurants, the 2016 vintage (★★★★) was mostly estate-grown in the Waihopai Valley, and barrel-matured for 10 months. Deep ruby, it is fragrant, mouthfilling and supple, with strong, ripe cherry, plum, spice, herb and nut flavours, earthy notes adding complexity, and lots of current-drinking appeal.

DRY $25 V+

Babich Family Estates Headwaters Organic Pinot Noir ★★★★

Certified organic, the deep ruby 2015 vintage (★★★★) is a single-vineyard Marlborough red, matured for seven months in French oak barriques (30 per cent new). Still youthful, it has deep, plummy, slightly nutty flavours, complex and savoury, and obvious cellaring potential. Best drinking mid-2018+.

DRY $37 AV

Babich Marlborough Pinot Noir ★★★

The 2016 vintage (★★★☆), partly barrique-aged, is fragrant, full-bodied and supple, with good depth of ripe, cherryish, plummy flavours, skilfully balanced for early enjoyment.

DRY $22 AV

Babich Winemakers' Reserve Marlborough Pinot Noir ★★★★

The 2014 vintage (★★★★☆) is the best yet. Estate-grown in the Waihopai Valley, it was matured for 10 months in barrels (35 per cent new). Deeply coloured and fleshy, it is generous, with substantial body, concentrated, ripe, plummy, spicy flavours, nutty, savoury, earthy notes adding complexity, and good tannin backbone. A wine of strong personality, it's a drink-now or cellaring proposition.

Vintage	14	13	12	11	10
WR	7	7	7	7	7
Drink	17-20	17-19	17-18	P	P

DRY $35 AV

Bald Hills 3 Acres Central Otago Pinot Noir   ★★★★

The youthful 2016 vintage (★★★★) was estate-grown at Bannockburn and matured for a year in French oak barriques (31 per cent new). Full, bright ruby, it is mouthfilling and vibrantly fruity, with fresh cherry, plum and spice flavours, well-integrated oak, and very good complexity and depth. Best drinking 2019+.

DRY $35 AV

Bald Hills Bannockburn Single Vineyard Central Otago Pinot Noir   ★★★★☆

A proven performer in the cellar. The 2015 vintage (★★★★☆) is a floral, finely textured red, estate-grown and matured in French oak barriques (30 per cent new). Full, bright ruby, it has cherry, plum, spice and dried-herb flavours, showing very good complexity. Already delicious, it's also well worth cellaring. The 2014 vintage (★★★★☆) is a stylish, deeply coloured red, mouthfilling and still youthful, with strong cherry, plum and spice flavours, integrated oak, and fine-grained tannins. Vibrantly fruity and concentrated, with good harmony, it has excellent cellaring potential. The 2013 vintage (★★★★☆) is also still unfolding, with deep, bright colour, mouthfilling body, and fresh, strong cherry, plum and spice flavours. Set for a long life, it should be at its best 2019+.

Vintage	15	14	13
WR	6	5	4
Drink	17-25	17-20	17-19

DRY $46 –V

Ballasalla Central Otago Pinot Noir   ★★★★☆

From Folding Hill, at Bendigo, the 2016 vintage (★★★★☆) is a youthful, single-vineyard red, matured for 10 months in French oak barriques (20 per cent new). Full, bright ruby, it is mouthfilling, sweet-fruited, savoury and smooth, with ripe cherry, plum and spice flavours, a subtle seasoning of oak, and a silky-textured, very harmonious finish. Best drinking 2019+. Good value.

Vintage	16
WR	7
Drink	17-22

DRY $32 V+

Bannock Brae Central Otago Pinot Noir   ★★★★★

Top vintages of this single-vineyard Bannockburn red are outstanding. The classy 2014 vintage (★★★★★) was matured for 10 months in French oak casks (35 per cent new), and bottled unfined and unfiltered. Deep ruby, with an enticingly fragrant bouquet, it is full-bodied, with a sense of youthful vigour and concentrated, vibrant cherry, plum and spice flavours, showing excellent complexity and harmony. Best drinking 2018+.

Vintage	14	13	12	11	10	09	08
WR	7	7	NM	7	6	7	5
Drink	17-25	17-25	NM	17-25	17-24	P	P

DRY $60 AV

Bannock Brae Goldfields Central Otago Pinot Noir   ★★★★

This is typically a 'feminine', very graceful, supple wine. The 2015 vintage (★★★★), grown at Bannockburn and Bendigo, was matured in French oak barrels (15 per cent new). Bright ruby, it is mouthfilling, scented, savoury and silky, with ripe plum, cherry and spice flavours, showing very good complexity and length. Priced right, it's well worth cellaring, but already delicious.

Vintage	15	14	13	12	11	10	09	08
WR	6	7	6	7	6	7	7	5
Drink	17-23	17-23	17-22	17-22	17-19	17-20	P	P

 DRY $30 AV

Bel Echo by Clos Henri Marlborough Pinot Noir   ★★★★

The 2015 vintage (★★★★) was estate-grown on the stonier, less clay-bound soils at Clos Henri, in the Wairau Valley, and matured in large oak vats (40 per cent) and old French barrels (60 per cent). Deep ruby, it is mouthfilling and savoury, with good concentration of youthful plum, cherry and spice flavours. Best drinking 2019+. Certified organic.

Vintage	15	14	13	12
WR	6	6	6	6
Drink	17-22	17-20	17-19	17-18

 DRY $32 AV

Bellbird Spring River Terrace Waipara Pinot Noir   ★★★☆

Still on sale, the 2012 vintage (★★★☆), matured for a year in French oak casks (15 per cent new), has full, slightly developed colour, mouthfilling body, and very good depth of cherry and plum flavours, soft and harmonious, with considerable complexity. Ready.

Vintage	12	11
WR	6	6
Drink	17-19	17-18

 DRY $37 –V

Bird Big Barrel Marlborough Pinot Noir   ★★★☆

The floral, supple 2014 vintage (★★★☆) is a single-vineyard wine, grown at Rapaura and fermented and matured for 10 months in large, 900-litre barrels. Ruby-hued, it is mouthfilling, with ripe, plummy, slightly nutty flavours, showing considerable complexity and good harmony.

 DRY $35 –V

Black Cottage Reserve Central Otago Pinot Noir   ★★★☆

Enjoyable young, the partly barrel-aged 2015 vintage (★★★☆) is bright ruby, mouthfilling and smooth, with ripe cherry, plum and spice flavours, showing some savoury complexity.

DRY $25 AV

Black Estate Damsteep North Canterbury Pinot Noir   ★★★★☆

The impressive 2015 vintage (★★★★★) was estate-grown at Omihi, in the Damsteep Vineyard, planted in 1999. Fermented with indigenous yeasts, it was matured for a year in seasoned French oak barrels, and bottled unfined and unfiltered. Deep ruby, it is mouthfilling and supple, with generous, ripe cherry, plum and spice flavours that build well across the palate, slightly earthy notes adding complexity, a subtle seasoning of oak, and excellent depth and harmony. Showing obvious cellaring potential, it should be at its best 2019 onwards.

 DRY $45 –V

Black Estate Home North Canterbury Pinot Noir   ★★★★☆

The 2015 vintage (★★★★☆) was grown in the home vineyard at Omihi, planted in 1994. Hand-picked, it was fermented with indigenous yeasts, matured for a year in seasoned French oak barriques, and bottled unfined and unfiltered. Deep ruby, it is mouthfilling, savoury and supple, with concentrated, ripe, plummy, spicy flavours, showing good structure, density and complexity. Still youthful, it has obvious cellaring potential.

 DRY $45 –V

Black Estate Netherwood North Canterbury Pinot Noir   ★★★★☆

From the first hill-grown vineyard in North Canterbury, the 2015 vintage (★★★★☆) was hand-harvested from ungrafted, unirrigated vines. Fermented with indigenous yeasts, matured for a year in seasoned oak barrels, and bottled unfined and unfiltered, it is a ruby-hued, medium-bodied wine, with very youthful, cherryish, plummy flavours, savoury notes adding complexity, fresh acidity, and a finely poised finish. Best drinking 2019+.

 DRY $60 –V

Black Quail Estate Central Otago Pinot Noir   ★★★★

The youthful, graceful 2015 vintage (★★★★) is a single-vineyard red, grown at Bannockburn. Ruby-hued, it is mouthfilling and supple, with very good depth of vibrant cherry, plum and spice flavours, and savoury notes adding complexity. Best drinking 2018+.

 DRY $39 AV

Black Ridge Central Otago Pinot Noir   (★★★★)

Currently on sale, the 2013 vintage (★★★★) was estate-grown at Alexandra, hand-harvested and matured for a year in seasoned French oak barrels. Ruby-hued, with a hint of maturity, it is mouthfilling, savoury and smooth, with very satisfying depth of cherry, plum and spice flavours, fresh acidity and good complexity. Drink now to 2019.

Vintage	13
WR	5
Drink	17-25

DRY $35 AV

Black Stilt Waitaki Valley Pinot Noir   ★★★

Grown in the Waitaki Valley, North Otago, and barrel-matured, the 2014 vintage (★★★☆) shows signs of early development, with mature colour. Mouthfilling, it has strong plum, spice and nut flavours, slightly leafy notes, fresh acidity and some savoury complexity. Drink now to 2018.

 DRY $39 –V

Blackenbrook Family Reserve Nelson Pinot Noir ★★★★☆

The 2015 vintage (★★★★) was estate-grown, hand-picked and matured for a year in French oak barriques (23 per cent new). Deeply coloured, it is mouthfilling and supple, with generous, very ripe plum, spice and slight liquorice flavours. Fruit-packed, with some savoury complexity, it's an unabashedly bold style of Pinot Noir, already enjoyable but well worth cellaring.

Vintage	15	14
WR	6	7
Drink	17-26	17-25

 DRY $38 V+

Blind River Awatere Valley Marlborough Pinot Noir ★★★☆

Estate-grown in the Awatere Valley, the 2015 vintage (★★★★) was matured for 10 months in French oak casks (25 per cent new). Full ruby, with a hint of development, it has a scented, savoury bouquet. Drinking well now, it has fresh cherry, plum and spice flavours, a hint of herbs, finely balanced tannins and very good complexity.

Vintage	15
WR	7
Drink	17-23

 DRY $35 –V

Boneline (The) Waipara Pinot Noir ★★★★☆

From 'venerable, old vines', the classy 2014 vintage (★★★★★) was hand-picked and matured for a year in French oak casks. A beautiful wine in its youth, it is deep ruby, rich and poised, with fresh acidity, concentrated plum/spice flavours and ripe, silky tannins. Well worth cellaring.

 DRY $40 AV

Boundary Vineyards Kings Road Waipara Pinot Noir ★★★

Offering great value, the 2015 vintage (★★★☆) from Pernod Ricard NZ is bright ruby, mouthfilling and supple, with very good depth of plummy, spicy flavour, showing a touch of complexity. Enjoyable young.

 DRY $20 AV

Brancott Estate Letter Series 'T' Marlborough Pinot Noir ★★★★

The 2015 vintage (★★★★☆), still youthful, is a classy, vibrantly fruity red, well worth cellaring to 2018+. Bright ruby, with a fragrant, ripe, cherryish bouquet, it is full-bodied and supple, with strong, ripe cherry and plum flavours, savoury notes adding complexity, and a persistent finish.

DRY $33 AV

Brancott Estate Living Land Series Marlborough Pinot Noir ★★★

The 2014 vintage (★★★☆) is ruby-hued, mouthfilling and supple, with moderately concentrated red-berry, strawberry and spice flavours, gentle tannins and good harmony. Certified organic.

 DRY $20 AV

Brancott Estate Terroir Series Awatere Valley Marlborough Pinot Noir   ★★★

The 2016 vintage (★★★) is a youthful, ruby-hued red, medium-bodied, with ripe, moderately concentrated plum/spice flavours and savoury notes adding a distinct touch of complexity. Best drinking 2018+.

 DRY $20 AV

Brennan B2 Central Otago Pinot Noir   ★★★☆

Estate-grown at Gibbston, the deep ruby 2014 vintage (★★★★) has a fragrant bouquet of plums and dried herbs. It is full-bodied and supple, with generous, ripe fruit flavours, a gentle seasoning of French oak (27 per cent new) adding complexity, and a well-rounded finish. Drink now or cellar.

 DRY $31 –V

Brightside Organic New Zealand Pinot Noir   ★★★

Certified organic, the youthful 2016 vintage (★★★) was grown in Nelson. Ruby-hued, fragrant and vibrantly fruity, it has plum and red-berry flavours, with a seasoning of French oak adding complexity, and good depth. Best drinking mid-2018+. (From Kaimira Estate.)

 DRY $19 AV

Brightwater Vineyards Lord Rutherford Nelson Pinot Noir   ★★★★

The 2014 vintage (★★★★☆) was estate-grown, fermented with indigenous yeasts, and matured for 16 months in French oak barriques (25 per cent new). Bright ruby, it is fragrant, vibrant, savoury and supple, with strong, ripe cherry, plum and nutty oak flavours, showing good complexity, fine-grained tannins, and obvious potential. Best drinking 2018+.

 DRY $40 –V

Brightwater Vineyards Nelson Pinot Noir   ★★★★☆

The classy 2015 vintage (★★★★☆) was grown at Hope and matured for 11 months in French oak casks (20 per cent new). Finely poised, it is attractively scented and ruby-hued, with youthful strawberry, spice and slight herb flavours, savoury notes adding complexity, and excellent vigour, harmony and depth. Best drinking 2019+.

Vintage	15	14	13	12	11	10
WR	6	7	6	6	7	6
Drink	17-20	17-19	17-18	P	P	P

 DRY $35 V+

Bronte Nelson Pinot Noir   ★★★☆

From Rimu Grove, the 2015 vintage (★★★★) was estate-grown and matured for 11 months in French oak casks. Deeply coloured, it is fragrant and full-bodied, with gentle tannins, fresh plum, cherry and spice flavours, showing very good ripeness and depth, and some savoury complexity. Delicious young.

Vintage	15
WR	7
Drink	17-26

DRY $24 V+

Burn Cottage Burn Cottage Vineyard Central Otago Pinot Noir ★★★★★

Estate-grown in the Cromwell Basin, the 2015 vintage (★★★★★) was hand-harvested and matured in French oak barriques (19 per cent new). A very 'complete' wine, it is full-coloured, mouthfilling, ripe and supple, with deep cherry, plum, herb, spice and nut flavours, gentle acidity, and a very savoury, complex, harmonious finish. Drink now or cellar.

Vintage	15	14	13	12	11	10	09
WR	6	7	7	7	6	6	6
Drink	17-25	17-25	17-25	17-21	17-19	17-19	17-19

 DRY $65 AV

Burn Cottage Moonlight Race Central Otago Pinot Noir ★★★★★

The classy 2015 vintage (★★★★★) was grown at three sites (including Burn Cottage Vineyard) in the Cromwell Basin, fermented with indigenous yeasts and matured in French oak casks (25 per cent new). Full-coloured, it is mouthfilling and savoury, with deep, ripe plum/spice flavours, good tannin support, and excellent complexity and harmony. Already 'open' and expressive, but well worth cellaring, it should break into full stride 2019+.

 DRY $45 AV

Burn Cottage Valli Vineyard Gibbston Central Otago Pinot Noir ★★★★★

Since the debut 2014 vintage (★★★★★), Burn Cottage, based in the Cromwell Basin, has drawn grapes from the more elevated Valli Vineyard, at Gibbston (for their reverse swap, see Valli Burn Cottage Vineyard Central Otago Pinot Noir). Matured in French oak barriques (25 per cent new), the 2015 vintage (★★★★★) is rich and finely textured. From 16-year-old vines, it is deeply coloured, fragrant, mouthfilling, savoury and supple, with generous, ripe cherry, plum, herb and spice flavours, seasoned with nutty oak (French, 25 per cent new), gentle acidity, and loads of current-drinking appeal. Open now to 2020.

 DRY $65 AV

Cable Bay Awatere Valley Marlborough Pinot Noir (★★★)

The pale ruby 2014 vintage (★★★) is an estate-grown red, matured in tanks and barrels. A light style, it has ripe, cherryish, savoury, slightly nutty flavours, showing a touch of complexity, and good tannin support. Enjoyable now.

Vintage	14
WR	5
Drink	17-20

DRY $28 –V

Camshorn Waipara Pinot Noir ★★★☆

From Pernod Ricard NZ, the 2015 vintage (★★★☆) is deep ruby, mouthfilling and rounded, with moderately rich strawberry and spice flavours, showing some savoury complexity. Delicious young.

 DRY $23 V+

Carrick Bannockburn Central Otago Pinot Noir   ★★★★★

A regional classic. Certified organic, the 2015 vintage (★★★★☆) was matured for a year in French oak barrels (20 per cent new). A finely textured, savoury red, it is full-bodied, with fresh, ripe cherry, plum, spice, dried-herb and nut flavours, revealing good complexity, and obvious cellaring potential; open 2019+.

DRY $45 AV

Carrick Excelsior Central Otago Pinot Noir   ★★★★★

From mature, estate-grown vines at Bannockburn, the 2014 vintage (★★★★★) is a full-coloured, powerful but approachable wine, barrel-aged, with substantial body, fresh, deep cherry, plum and spice flavours, nutty oak adding complexity, fine-grained tannins and a lasting finish. Best drinking 2020+.

DRY $85 AV

Carrick Unravelled Central Otago Pinot Noir   ★★★★

Designed to be 'easy-drinking, laidback', the 2016 vintage (★★★★) was matured for 11 months in French oak casks (15 per cent new). It has a fragrant, spicy, inviting bouquet. Fresh and supple, with cherry, plum and spice flavours, woven with lively acidity, it is vividly varietal, with considerable complexity and the structure to age well. Open mid 2018+. Certified organic.

DRY $27 V+

Catalina Sounds Marlborough Pinot Noir   ★★★☆

Delicious young, the 2014 vintage (★★★★) is a generous, supple red, from sites in the Omaka Valley and Waihopai Valley. Deep ruby, with fresh, strong, berryish aromas, it is sweet-fruited, with good concentration, finely integrated oak and a well-rounded, rich finish.

DRY $29 AV

Catalina Sounds Sound of White Marlborough Pinot Noir   (★★★★)

The fragrant, deeply coloured 2015 vintage (★★★★) was estate-grown in the Southern Valleys. It has rich, cherryish, plummy flavours, seasoned with smoky, spicy oak (French, 40 per cent new), and a hint of liquorice. A youthful, structured wine, it's well worth cellaring.

DRY $45 −V

Ceres Composition Bannockburn Central Otago Pinot Noir   ★★★★☆

The highly attractive 2015 vintage (★★★★☆) was grown in the neighbouring Inlet (70 per cent) and Black Rabbit (30 per cent) vineyards, and matured for a year in French oak casks (28 per cent new). Bright ruby, it is fragrant, mouthfilling, sweet-fruited and savoury, with generous, youthful plum/spice flavours, showing excellent complexity, good tannin backbone and a rich, well-rounded finish. A very age-worthy red, it should be at its best 2019+.

DRY $40 AV

Charcoal Gully Sally's Pinch Central Otago Pinot Noir   ★★★★

The deeply coloured 2014 vintage (★★★★) is a single-vineyard red, hand-picked at Pisa, in the Cromwell Basin, and matured for 10 months in French oak casks (32 per cent new). Fragrant, mouthfilling and sweet-fruited, it's still youthful, with fresh, generous, well-ripened cherry, plum and spice flavours and a firm finish. Best drinking mid-2018+.

Vintage	14	13
WR	7	5
Drink	17-27	17-24

DRY $32 AV

Chard Farm Mason Vineyard Central Otago Pinot Noir   (★★★★)

Still youthful, the 2014 vintage (★★★★) was grown at Parkburn, in the Cromwell Basin, and matured in French oak barrels (20 per cent new). Ruby-hued, it is fragrant, mouthfilling and smooth, with fresh, delicate cherry, plum and spice flavours, gently seasoned with nutty oak, and good complexity. Best drinking mid-2019+.

Vintage	14
WR	6
Drink	17-22

DRY $69 –V

Chard Farm Mata-Au Central Otago Pinot Noir   ★★★★

Pronounced 'Martar-O', Chard Farm's 'signature' red is estate-grown in the Lowburn and Parkburn districts, in the Cromwell Basin, and barrel-aged. Bright ruby, the 2015 vintage (★★★★) is ripely scented, mouthfilling and supple, with gentle cherry, plum, spice and nut flavours, savoury and finely textured. Delicious young.

Vintage	15	14
WR	5	6
Drink	17-22	17-22

DRY $45 –V

Chard Farm River Run Central Otago Pinot Noir   ★★★☆

This 'fruit-driven' style slides down very easily. The highly attractive 2015 vintage (★★★★) was hand-harvested in the Cromwell Basin (Lowburn, Parkburn) and at Gibbston, and barrel-aged (15 per cent new). Ruby-hued, it is floral and sweet-fruited, with mouthfilling body and ripe, delicate cherry, plum and spice flavours, slightly nutty, finely poised and lively. A subtle, satisfying red, it's drinking well now, but should also age well.

Vintage	15
WR	5
Drink	17-22

DRY $33 –V

Chard Farm The Tiger Lowburn Central Otago Pinot Noir ★★★★☆

This single-vineyard red is estate-grown in the Cromwell Basin. The 2014 vintage (★★★★☆) is still youthful. Ruby-hued, it is a very elegant, silky-textured wine, with concentrated cherry, plum and spice flavours, showing excellent delicacy and complexity. A very harmonious wine, with good potential, it should be at its best 2019+.

Vintage	14
WR	6
Drink	17-22

 DRY $69 –V

Chard Farm The Viper Parkburn Central Otago Pinot Noir ★★★★

A single-vineyard red, grown in the Cromwell Basin, the 2014 vintage (★★★★) was barrel-matured (20 per cent new). Ruby-hued, it is mouthfilling, savoury and supple, with gentle cherry, plum, spice and nut flavours that linger well. Showing good complexity, it's a 'feminine' style, for drinking now to 2020.

Vintage	14
WR	6
Drink	17-22

 DRY $69 –V

Cherry Orchard, The, Bannockburn Single Vineyard Central Otago Pinot Noir (★★★★)

Estate-grown and matured for 10 months in old oak barrels, the 2013 vintage (★★★★), still on sale in 2017, is an elegant, 'feminine' style, maturing gracefully. Plummy and cherryish, with fresh acidity, it is a strongly varietal, medium-bodied, supple red, with savoury notes adding complexity. Drink now to 2019.

 DRY $28 V+

China Girl by Crown Range Cellar Central Otago Pinot Noir ★★★★☆

The powerful 2016 vintage (★★★★★) was hand-picked on Chinaman's Terrace, at Bendigo, and matured for a year in French oak casks (30 per cent new). Deep ruby, it is fragrant, mouthfilling and vibrantly fruity, with ripe plum and spice flavours, showing excellent concentration, fresh acidity, good complexity and a lasting finish. Still very youthful, it's a savoury, well-structured red with obvious potential; open 2020+.

DRY $65 –V

Churton Marlborough Pinot Noir ★★★★☆

Estate-grown at an elevated site in the Waihopai Valley, hand-picked, fermented with indigenous yeasts and matured in French oak barriques, this is 'a delicate, refined' Pinot Noir, according to winemaker Sam Weaver. The 2015 vintage (★★★★☆), barrel-aged for 18 months, is ruby-hued, with a fragrant, savoury, complex bouquet. Mouthfilling, it has strong, vibrant plum, cherry, herb and nut flavours, showing excellent complexity and harmony, and the structure to mature well. Best drinking 2019+. Certified organic.

Vintage	15	14	13	12	11	10	09
WR	6	NM	7	5	6	7	6
Drink	18-27	NM	17-28	17-22	17-25	17-27	17-20

 DRY $45 –V

Churton The Abyss Marlborough Pinot Noir ★★★★★

The 2013 vintage (★★★★★) was estate-grown on an elevated site in the Waihopai Valley, on a north-east-facing clay slope which catches the early morning sun. Hand-picked from vines planted in 1999, fermented with indigenous yeasts and matured for 18 months in French oak casks (30 per cent new), it is deeply coloured and highly fragrant, with rich plum/spice flavours, earthy notes adding complexity, firm tannins and obvious potential. Best drinking 2018+. Certified organic. (Not made since 2013, but further vintages are planned.)

Vintage	17	16	15	14	13	12	11	10	09	08	DRY $75 AV
WR	NM	NM	NM	NM	7	NM	NM	7	NM	6	
Drink	NM	NM	NM	NM	20-30	NM	NM	17-22	NM	17-20	

Circuit North Canterbury Pinot Noir (★★★★)

From three sites at Waipara, including Black Estate, the debut 2014 vintage (★★★★) was hand-picked from 15 to 27-year-old vines, matured for a year in seasoned French oak barrels, and bottled without fining or filtration. Full ruby, it is mouthfilling and supple, with ripe plum/spice flavours and earthy, savoury notes adding considerable complexity. A very distinctive, youthful wine, it should be at its best 2018+. (From Black Estate.)

DRY $28 V+

Clark Estate Marlborough Pinot Noir (★★★☆)

The 2014 vintage (★★★☆) is a single-vineyard, Awatere Valley red, matured in seasoned oak casks. Ruby-hued, it is mouthfilling, fresh and supple, with youthful, ripe, vibrantly fruity flavours of cherries and plums, gently seasoned with oak.

Vintage	14	DRY $24 V+
WR	6	
Drink	17-19	

Clevedon Hills Pinot Noir ★★★★

Estate-grown at Clevedon, in South Auckland, this wine has plenty of personality and is of superior quality to most Pinot Noirs from the upper North Island. The 2014 vintage (★★★☆) is ruby-hued, with ripe, moderately concentrated, cherryish, slightly nutty flavours, showing some savoury complexity. A very harmonious and finely textured red, it's a drink-now or cellaring proposition.

DRY $40 –V

Clifford Bay Marlborough Pinot Noir ★★★

Attractive young, the 2015 vintage (★★★☆) has full, bright ruby colour. Vibrantly fruity, it has good depth of youthful, plummy, spicy flavours, with slightly toasty and savoury notes adding complexity, and a well-rounded finish. Drink now or cellar.

Vintage	15	14	DRY $20 AV
WR	7	7	
Drink	17-19	17-18	

Clos de Ste Anne Naboth's Vineyard Pinot Noir ★★★★

This Gisborne red from Millton is one of this country's northernmost quality Pinot Noirs. Grown at the hillside Clos de Ste Anne site at Manutuke, it is hand-harvested from vines up to 25 years old, fermented with indigenous yeasts, barrique-aged, and bottled without fining or filtering. Certified biodynamic, the 2015 vintage (★★★★) is ruby-hued, fragrant, mouthfilling and savoury, with ripe, strawberryish, spicy, nutty flavours, gentle acidity, and good complexity and harmony. Drink now or cellar.

DRY $60 –V

Clos Henri Marlborough Pinot Noir ★★★★☆

From Henri Bourgeois, a top Loire Valley producer with a site near Renwick, the 2013 vintage (★★★★☆) – still on sale in 2017 – was hand-picked from eight to 13-year-old vines, fermented in large oak vats, and matured for a year in French oak casks (25 per cent new). Full ruby, it is a complex style, firm and savoury, with good concentration of ripe plum, cherry and spice flavours, and the backbone to age well. Certified organic.

Vintage	13	12	11	10	09	08	07
WR	6	6	6	7	6	6	6
Drink	17-22	17-21	17-20	17-18	P	P	P

DRY $44 AV

Clos Marguerite Marlborough Pinot Noir (★★★☆)

Still on sale, the 2012 vintage (★★★☆) is drinking well now. A single-vineyard, Awatere Valley red, it was hand-harvested and barrel-aged for a year. Ruby-hued, with a hint of maturity, it has a fragrant, slightly leafy bouquet. Mouthfilling and supple, with plum and dried-herb flavours, it shows very good depth and complexity.

DRY $46 –V

Cloudy Bay New Zealand Pinot Noir ★★★★☆

Consistently classy. Grown at sites on the cooler, more clay-influenced south side of the Wairau Valley, the 2015 vintage (★★★★☆) was matured for a year in French oak barriques (35 per cent new). A fragrant, deep ruby red, it is mouthfilling, fresh and youthful, with concentrated, ripe, plummy, spicy, nutty flavours, showing good complexity, fine-grained tannins, and the structure to mature well. Best drinking 2019+.

Vintage	15	14	13	12	11	10	09
WR	7	7	7	7	6	7	6
Drink	17-21	17-21	17-20	17-19	17-19	P	P

DRY $42 AV

Cloudy Bay Te Wahi Central Otago Pinot Noir ★★★★★

The debut 2010 vintage (★★★★★) marked Cloudy Bay's first foray beyond the Marlborough region. The 2015 vintage (★★★★★) of Te Wahi ('The Place') was estate-grown in the Calvert Vineyard at Bannockburn and Northburn Vineyard, on the east bank of Lake Dunstan. Fermented with indigenous yeasts, it was matured for a year in French oak barriques (35 per cent new). Deep ruby, it is a powerful, sturdy, complex red, still very youthful, with concentrated, well-ripened cherry, plum and spice flavours, nutty and savoury, good tannin backbone, and obvious cellaring potential; best drinking 2019+.

Vintage	15	14
WR	7	7
Drink	17-25	17-24

DRY $105 –V

Coal Pit Tiwha Central Otago Pinot Noir ★★★★☆

Already delicious, the 2015 vintage (★★★★☆) is a very finely textured red, estate-grown and hand-harvested at Gibbston, over 400 metres above sea level, and matured in French oak casks (40 per cent new). Deep ruby, with a fragrant, fresh, slightly herbal bouquet, it is mouthfilling and supple, with concentrated plum, herb and spice flavours, savoury notes adding complexity, and excellent harmony. Still youthful, it should be at its best 2019+.

Vintage	15	14	13	12	11	10	09
WR	6	7	7	6	5	7	7
Drink	17-22	17-22	17-21	17-20	17-18	17-18	P

DRY $45 –V

Coopers Creek Hawke's Bay Pinot Noir ★★★☆

Offering good value, the 2016 vintage (★★★☆) was given 'minimal' exposure to oak. Bright ruby, it has good varietal character, with satisfying depth of cherryish, plummy flavours, a hint of herbs, a touch of complexity and a well-rounded finish. Drink now onwards.

DRY $18 V+

Coopers Creek Marlborough Pinot Noir ★★★

Offering good value, the 2014 vintage (★★★☆) is fresh and finely balanced, with vibrant, ripe red-fruit and spice flavours, showing a touch of complexity.

DRY $20 AV

Coopers Creek Select Vineyards Razorback Central Otago Pinot Noir ★★★

The easy-drinking 2015 vintage (★★★) was matured for seven months in French oak casks (20 per cent new). Bright ruby, it is mouthfilling and sweet-fruited, with lively cherry, plum and red-berry flavours, fresh acidity and a smooth finish.

DRY $28 –V

Coopers Creek SV Gibsons Run Marlborough Pinot Noir ★★★☆

Deep ruby, the 2014 vintage (★★★☆) has a fragrant, plummy, spicy bouquet, strong cherry, plum, dried-herb and spice flavours, and good texture and harmony.

Vintage	14	13
WR	6	6
Drink	17-19	17-18

DRY $25 AV

Crab Farm Winery Reserve Hawke's Bay Pinot Noir   (★★★☆)

The 2014 vintage (★★★☆) was matured for a year in French oak casks. Full-coloured, it's a slightly gutsy, very ripe style with strong plum, spice and slight liquorice flavours, and a firm tannin backbone.

Crafters Union Depth & Finesse Central Otago Pinot Noir   (★★★☆)

Enjoyable young, but also worth cellaring, the youthful 2016 vintage (★★★☆) was oak-aged. Deep ruby, it is fragrant and vibrantly fruity, with generous, cherryish, plummy flavours, moderate complexity and a well-rounded finish. Best drinking 2019+. (From Constellation NZ.)

Vintage	16
WR	5
Drink	18-19

Craggy Range Te Muna Road Vineyard Martinborough Pinot Noir   ★★★★★

The 2013 vintage (★★★★☆) was estate-grown, hand-picked at 24.3 brix, fermented with indigenous yeasts and matured for 10 months in French oak barriques (25 per cent new). Bright ruby, it is floral, sweet-fruited, savoury and supple, with strong cherry, plum and spice flavours, showing good complexity, fine-grained tannins and a well-rounded finish. Drink now or cellar.

Vintage	13	12	11	10	09	08
WR	7	6	6	7	6	7
Drink	17-21	17-19	17-18	17-18	P	P

Crossings, The, Marlborough Pinot Noir   ★★★☆

The 2014 vintage (★★★☆) is a ruby-hued, finely balanced Awatere Valley red, matured for seven months in French oak barriques (20 per cent new). Mouthfilling and supple, it has very good depth of plum, cherry and spice flavours, showing some savoury complexity.

Vintage	14
WR	7
Drink	17-19

Crossroads Milestone Series Marlborough Pinot Noir   ★★★☆

Drinking well from the start, the 2014 vintage (★★★☆) is bright ruby, full-bodied and smooth, with very good depth of ripe berry and plum flavours, gentle tannins and a touch of complexity.

Vintage	14
WR	6
Drink	17-23

DRY $22 V+

Crowded House Marlborough Pinot Noir ★★★☆

The 2014 vintage (★★★☆) is an attractive, drink-young style, ruby-hued, vibrant and supple, with moderately concentrated, ripe plum and dried-herb flavours, showing good freshness, delicacy and harmony.

DRY $23 V+

Crown Range Cellar Signature Selection Grant Taylor Central Otago Pinot Noir ★★★★★

The 2016 vintage (★★★★★) is very rare – only 100 cases were produced. Grown in the Gibbston sub-region, it was crafted by pioneer Central Otago winemaker Grant Taylor (owner of the Valli brand). Matured for a year in French oak casks (30 per cent new), it is a very refined and graceful red, ruby-hued, with an enticingly scented bouquet. Mouthfilling and supple, with ripe cherry, plum and spice flavours, fresh acidity and finely integrated oak, it's a very youthful, 'feminine' style of Pinot Noir, well worth cellaring to 2020+.

Vintage	16	15	14
WR	6	6	6
Drink	18-26	18-25	17-24

DRY $150 –V

Darling, The, Marlborough Pinot Noir (★★★★)

Certified organic, the 2014 vintage (★★★★) is a ruby-hued, mouthfilling, supple red, with moderately rich, well-ripened cherry, plum, spice and nut flavours. Savoury and finely textured, with good complexity, it's a drink-now or cellaring proposition.

DRY $33 AV

Dashwood Marlborough Pinot Noir ★★★

Enjoyable young, the 2015 vintage (★★★☆) is bright ruby, mouthfilling and smooth, with very good depth of vibrant cherry, plum and spice flavours. Priced sharply, it should be at its best 2018+.

Vintage	15	14	13	12
WR	6	7	6	6
Drink	17-19	17-18	P	P

DRY $20 AV

Davishon Central Otago Pinot Noir ★★★

The bright ruby 2015 vintage (★★★) was grown at Alexandra and matured in French oak barriques (25 per cent new). It has good depth of fresh plum, herb and spice flavours, oak complexity and a fairly firm finish.

DRY $35 –V

Delegat Awatere Valley Pinot Noir ★★★★

Offering great value – as in previous years – the 2016 vintage (★★★★) was estate-grown in Marlborough and matured for a year in French oak barriques (new and one year old). Deep ruby, it is mouthfilling and fleshy, with fresh, ripe, cherryish, plummy, slightly nutty flavours, showing excellent depth, and a well-rounded finish. Already delicious.

DRY $26 V+

Delta Hatters Hill Marlborough Pinot Noir ★★★★

The graceful 2015 vintage (★★★★☆) was grown in the Wairau Valley and French oak-matured. Deep ruby, it is fragrant, generous and supple, with strong, ripe cherry, plum, spice and dried-herb flavours, nutty and savoury notes adding complexity, and obvious potential. Best drinking 2018+.

DRY $34 AV

Delta Marlborough Pinot Noir ★★★★

Estate-grown in Delta Farm Vineyard, on the south side of the Wairau Valley, the 2015 vintage (★★★★) was matured in seasoned French oak casks. Fragrant and fruit-packed, with generous, ripe cherry/plum flavours to the fore, a subtle oak influence, and fine-grained tannins, it's delicious young, but should be at its best 2018+. Priced sharply.

DRY $24 V+

Devil's Staircase Central Otago Pinot Noir ★★★☆

From Rockburn, this is a drink-young style, handled without barrel aging. The 2017 vintage (★★★☆) is ruby-hued, fragrant, fruity and supple, with strong cherry and plum flavours, vibrant and smooth. Delicious young, it should be at its best mid-2018+.

DRY $29 AV

Devotus Reserve Single Vineyard Pinot Noir ★★★★★

The refined, debut 2014 vintage (★★★★★), grown on the Martinborough Terrace, was harvested from 28-year-old vines, established by Dry River. Matured for 11 months in French oak barriques (25 per cent new), it is deep and youthful in colour, scented, rich and supple. A lovely young red, with plum, cherry and spice flavours, integrated oak, and a flowing, finely textured finish, it's already delicious, but well worth cellaring. The 2015 vintage (★★★★★) is a very powerful, bold style of Pinot Noir, deeply coloured and sweet-fruited, with highly concentrated plum and spice flavours, a hint of liquorice, and obvious potential; best drinking 2020+.

DRY $62 AV

Devotus Single Vineyard Pinot Noir ★★★★☆

From vines planted at Martinborough in 1986, the 2014 vintage (★★★★☆) was matured for 11 months in French oak barriques, and bottled unfined and unfiltered. Richly coloured, it is mouthfilling, sturdy and sweet-fruited, with generous plum/spice flavours, gentle tannins and good, savoury complexity. Already drinking well, it should be at its best 2018+. The generous 2015 vintage (★★★★☆) is a deep ruby, fleshy wine with concentrated plum, spice and slight herb flavours, gentle acidity and good, savoury complexity. Best drinking 2018+.

Vintage	14
WR	4
Drink	17-20

DRY $38 V+

Discovery Point Martinborough Pinot Noir (★★★★)

From wine distributor Steve Bennett, the 2014 vintage (★★★★) is from 'mature' vines and was aged for nine months in French oak barriques (one to two years old). Ruby-hued, with a hint of development, it is fragrant and mouthfilling, with ripe plum/spice flavours, nutty and savoury, and fairly firm tannins. Showing good personality, it offers fine value. Drink now to 2018.

Vintage	14
WR	6
Drink	17-20

DRY $25 V+

Distant Land Reserve Central Otago Pinot Noir (★★★)

The 2014 vintage (★★★) is a moderately concentrated blend of Alexandra and Gibbston fruit, matured for a year in French oak barrels (50 per cent new). Fullish in colour, it has plum, spice and herb flavours, showing a touch of complexity, and soft tannins.

DRY $38 –V

Doctors Flat Central Otago Pinot Noir ★★★★★

The classy 2014 vintage (★★★★★) is a single-vineyard red, grown at Bannockburn, matured for a year in French oak barrels (25 per cent new), and bottled without fining or filtering. Deep ruby, it is mouthfilling, rich and savoury, with deep, ripe plum/spice flavours, showing excellent complexity, and fine-grained tannins. Very generous and savoury, it's approachable now, but likely to be at its best 2018+.

Vintage	14	13
WR	7	6
Drink	17-22	17-21

DRY $47 AV

Dog Point Vineyard Marlborough Pinot Noir ★★★★★

This classy, finely structured red is estate-grown on the south side of the Wairau Valley and matured for 18 months in French oak barriques (35 per cent new in 2015). The impressive 2015 vintage (★★★★★) is deeply coloured, with a fragrant bouquet of berries, dried herbs and spices. Mouthfilling and sweet-fruited, it has concentrated, youthful, plummy, spicy flavours, showing excellent complexity, and a rich, finely textured, very long finish. Already delicious, it's a very age-worthy, savoury and supple red, well worth cellaring to 2020+.

Vintage	15	14	13	12	11	10	09	08
WR	6	7	7	7	5	7	6	6
Drink	17-25	17-25	17-25	17-24	17-19	17-22	17-18	17-20

DRY $46 AV

Domain Road Vineyard Central Otago Pinot Noir ★★★★☆

Built to last, the 2013 vintage (★★★★☆) of this single-vineyard, Bannockburn red was matured for nine months in French oak barriques. It's a tightly structured wine with full, fairly youthful colour and a fragrant bouquet, suggestive of spices and dried herbs. Concentrated, it has plummy, nutty flavours, complex and savoury, and a persistent finish.

Vintage	13	12	11	10	09	08
WR	7	5	6	7	7	6
Drink	17-20	17-19	17-18	17-18	P	P

 DRY $40 AV

Domaine Rewa Central Otago Pinot Noir ★★★★☆

Showing excellent potential, the 2014 vintage (★★★★☆) was hand-picked in the Epicurious Vineyard, in the Cromwell Basin. Matured for 10 months in French oak barriques (33 per cent new), it is mouthfilling and youthful, with very generous, vibrant, cherryish, plummy flavours, savoury, nutty and complex. Best drinking 2019+.

 DRY $40 AV

Domaine-Thomson Rows 1–37 Single Clone Central Otago Pinot Noir (★★★★★)

Certified organic, the 2014 vintage (★★★★★) was estate-grown at Lowburn. Selected from a 0.8-hectare block of clone 777 vines, planted in 2000, it was matured for 10 months in French oak barrrels (25 per cent new). Deep and still youthful in colour, it is full-bodied, with generous, ripe cherry, plum and spice flavours, showing excellent complexity. A very savoury wine with good tannin backbone, it's still unfolding and likely to be long-lived; open 2019+.

 DRY $68 AV

Dry River Martinborough Pinot Noir ★★★★★

Dark and densely flavoured, this Martinborough red ranks among New Zealand's greatest Pinot Noirs. It is grown in three company-owned vineyards – Dry River Estate, Craighall and Lovat – on the Martinborough Terrace, and most of the vines are over 20 years old. Matured for a year in French oak hogsheads (20–30 per cent new), it is a slower-developing wine than other New Zealand Pinot Noirs, but matures superbly. Revealing great density, the deeply coloured 2015 vintage (★★★★★) is mouthfilling, with highly concentrated, plummy, gently spicy flavours, well-integrated oak (20 per cent new), and fine-grained tannins. Almost supercharged with flavour, it should flourish for a decade; open 2019+.

Vintage	15	14	13	12	11	10	09
WR	7	7	7	6	7	7	7
Drink	18-28	17-27	17-27	17-25	17-25	17-24	17-23

DRY $95 AV

Durvillea by Astrolabe Marlborough Pinot Noir (★★★☆)

Offering very good value, the 2016 vintage (★★★☆) was mostly hand-picked and partly barrel-aged. Bright ruby, it is mouthfilling and smooth, with ripe cherry, plum and spice flavours, showing very good depth, and slightly nutty, savoury notes adding complexity. Already drinking well, it's also worth cellaring.

DRY $20 V+

Earth's End Central Otago Pinot Noir   (★★★★)

From Mount Edward, the 2014 vintage (★★★★) is an excellent drink-young style – deep ruby, with generous, ripe, plummy, spicy flavours, slightly earthy notes adding complexity, gentle tannnins and good harmony.

DRY $29 V+

Elder, The, Martinborough Pinot Noir   ★★★★★

Fragrant and supple, the 2014 vintage (★★★★★) was grown in the Hanson Vineyard, at Te Muna, and matured in French oak casks (13 per cent new). Deep ruby, it is mouthfilling and savoury, with a strong surge of well-ripened plum, cherry and spice flavours, showing good complexity, and a rich, finely textured finish. Retasted in mid to late 2017, it's still youthful. Maturing very gracefully, it looks set for a long life.

DRY $65 –V

Elephant Hill Central Otago Pinot Noir   ★★★★

The 2014 vintage (★★★★) from this Hawke's Bay-based winery was matured for 10 months in French oak casks (25 per cent new). It is mouthfilling and vibrantly fruity, with bright, deep ruby colour and strong, plummy, slightly spicy flavours, finely textured and harmonious. Best drinking 2018+.

DRY $34 AV

Ellero Pisa Terrace Central Otago Pinot Noir   ★★★★

Certified organic, the 2014 vintage (★★★★) is one of the finest yet. Estate-grown and matured in French oak casks (20 per cent new), it is a rich, silky-smooth red, with deep plum and spice flavours, an earthy streak and good complexity. Highly approachable, it's a drink-now or cellaring proposition.

DRY $40 –V

Eon of Bendigo Central Otago Pinot Noir   ★★★★☆

From Accolade Wines, based in South Australia (formerly BRL Hardy), the 2012 vintage (★★★★) is sturdy, with full, fairly youthful colour. Fleshy, it is a powerful wine, with rich flavours, hints of prunes and liquorice, savoury notes adding complexity and a firmly structured finish. The 2013 vintage (★★★★) is mouthfilling, generous and sweet-fruited, with ripe cherry, plum and spice flavours, fresh and firm. The 2014 vintage (★★★★★) is the best yet – fragrant and silky-textured, in a highly refined style with concentrated, plummy, spicy flavours, already delicious, but likely to be at its best 2018+. (All vintages tasted in late 2016.)

DRY $45 –V

Eradus Awatere Valley Single Vineyard Marlborough Pinot Noir   ★★★

Ruby-hued, fresh and smooth, the 2016 vintage (★★★☆) is a medium to full-bodied, sweet-fruited, finely textured red, with ripe cherry and plum flavours, gentle tannins, and lots of drink-young charm. Best drinking mid-2018+.

DRY $22 AV

Esk Valley Marlborough Pinot Noir   ★★★★

The 2015 vintage (★★★★) was hand-harvested in the Awatere Valley and Southern Valleys, and matured for 11 months in French oak barriques (13 per cent new). Delicious from the start, it is mouthfilling and savoury, with gentle tannins and strong cherry, plum and spice flavours, showing good complexity.

Vintage	15	14	13	12	11	10
WR	7	6	6	7	7	7
Drink	17-19	17-18	P	P	P	P

 DRY $27 V+

Explorer Central Otago Pinot Noir   ★★★★

The generous, youthful 2016 vintage (★★★★) is from 13-year-old Domaine-Thomson vines, at Lowburn, in the Cromwell Basin. Barrel-aged for 10 months (20 per cent new), it is deep ruby, mouthfilling and fruit-packed, with fresh, ripe cherry, plum and spice flavours, savoury notes adding complexity, and good tannin support. Best drinking 2019+.

 DRY $29 AV

Fairhall Downs Single Vineyard Marlborough Pinot Noir   (★★★☆)

Enjoyable young, the 2016 vintage (★★★☆) was hand-harvested in the Brancott Valley and French oak-aged. Light ruby, it is a graceful wine, floral and supple, with moderately rich, well-ripened strawberry and spice flavours, a gentle seasoning of nutty oak adding complexity, and a well-rounded finish. Drink now or cellar.

 DRY $35 –V

Falconhead Marlborough Pinot Noir   ★★★

The easy-drinking 2016 vintage (★★★) is a light ruby red, medium-bodied, with good depth of fresh, cherryish, plummy, slightly spicy flavours and a smooth finish. Partly barrel-aged, it should be at its best mid-2018+.

 DRY $17 V+

Fancrest Estate Waipara Valley Pinot Noir   ★★★☆

Certified organic, matured in old oak casks, and bottled without fining or filtering, the 2014 vintage (★★★☆) is an 'honest and authentic, artisan Pinot Noir', matured with 'exceptionally low sulphite levels'. It has developed colour, fresh acidity, and good depth of firm berry, spice and herb flavours, showing considerable complexity. Retasted in mid to late 2017, it looks fully developed.

 DRY $45 –V

Felton Road Bannockburn Central Otago Pinot Noir   ★★★★★

The Bannockburn winery's 'standard' Pinot Noir is a distinguished wine, blended from its four sites in the district. Matured in French oak casks (25 per cent new in 2016), it is fermented with indigenous yeasts and bottled without fining or filtering. From a warm, early-ripening season, the 2016 vintage (★★★★★) is a bright ruby, enticingly perfumed wine, very savoury and supple. Delicious young, it is sweet-fruited, with vibrant cherry, plum and spice flavours, velvety tannins, and excellent complexity and harmony. Don't expect a 'fruit bomb' – it's a refined, age-worthy red, with charm and potential.

Vintage	16	15	14	13	12	11	10	09	08	07
WR	7	7	7	7	7	7	7	7	7	7
Drink	17-27	17-26	17-25	17-24	17-26	17-23	17-22	17-21	17-20	17-18

DRY $66 AV

Felton Road Block 3 Central Otago Pinot Noir ★★★★★

Grown at Bannockburn, on a north-facing slope 270 metres above sea level, this is a majestic Central Otago wine, among the finest Pinot Noirs in the country. The mature vines are cultivated in front of the winery, in a section of the vineyard where the clay content is relatively high, giving 'dried herbs and ripe fruit characters'. The wine is matured for about a year in Burgundy oak barrels (35 per cent new in 2016), and bottled without fining or filtration. The ruby-hued, very floral 2016 vintage (★★★★★) is mouthfilling, complex and silky-textured. Sweet-fruited, with cherry, plum, dried-herb and nut flavours, it is very savoury and seductive, with gentle tannins and lots of drink-young appeal. Best drinking 2019+.

Vintage	16	15	14	13	12	11	10	09	08	07
WR	7	7	7	7	7	7	7	7	7	7
Drink	17-32	17-31	17-30	17-24	17-26	17-23	17-22	17-21	17-20	17-18

DRY $105 AV

Felton Road Block 5 Pinot Noir ★★★★★

This is winemaker Blair Walter's favourite Felton Road red. Grown in a 'special' block of The Elms Vineyard at Bannockburn, in Central Otago, it is matured for a year in French oak barriques (33 per cent new in 2015), and bottled unfined and unfiltered. The 2015 vintage (★★★★★) is a deep ruby, powerful, generous wine, full-bodied and savoury, with concentrated, finely structured cherry, spice and nut flavours, good tannin backbone, and excellent complexity and harmony.

Vintage	15	14	13	12	11	10	09	08	07	06
WR	7	7	7	7	7	7	7	7	7	6
Drink	17-31	17-30	17-27	17-26	17-23	17-22	17-21	17-20	17-18	P

DRY $98 AV

Felton Road Calvert Pinot Noir ★★★★★

Grown in the Calvert Vineyard at Bannockburn, matured in French oak barriques (30 per cent new in 2015), and bottled unfined and unfiltered, the 2015 vintage (★★★★★) is a deep ruby, very elegant, rich but not heavy wine. A lovely young red, it has fresh, concentrated berry and spice flavours, very complex, savoury, harmonious and long. Best drinking 2018+.

Vintage	15	14	13	12	11	10	09	08	07	06
WR	7	7	7	7	7	7	7	7	7	6
Drink	17-31	17-28	17-24	17-26	17-23	17-22	17-21	17-20	17-18	P

DRY $72 AV

Felton Road Cornish Point Pinot Noir ★★★★★

From the company-owned Cornish Point Vineyard at the eastern end of Bannockburn, 6 kilometres from the winery, this is always one of my favourite Felton Road reds. From a warm, early-ripening season, the 2016 vintage (★★★★★) was matured for 13 months in French oak barriques (25 per cent new), and bottled without fining or filtering. Bright ruby, it is highly perfumed. Full of personality, it is very savoury and supple, with ripe plum, spice, dried-herb and nut flavours, gentle tannins and lovely complexity and harmony. Delicious young, it's a drink-now or cellaring proposition.

Vintage	16	15	14	13	12	11	10
WR	7	7	7	7	7	7	7
Drink	17-30	17-29	17-28	17-24	17-26	17-23	17-22

 DRY $78 AV

Fifth Bridge Central Otago Pinot Noir ★★★★

Delicious young, the floral, supple 2014 vintage (★★★★☆) was French oak-aged for nine months. Deep ruby, it is full-bodied, savoury and generous, with strong, ripe cherry, plum and spice flavours, fine-grained tannins and good complexity. Great value. (From Ceres Wines.)

 DRY $28 V+

Fifth Innings, The, Marlborough Pinot Noir (★★★★)

The sturdy 2014 vintage (★★★★) was estate-grown at Rapaura, fermented with indigenous yeasts and matured for over a year in French oak puncheons. Deep ruby, it is fleshy, with strong, ripe, plummy, spicy, nutty flavours, a hint of coffee, and good tannin backbone. Best drinking 2017+. (From Misty Cove.)

 DRY $70 –V

Folding Hill Bendigo Central Otago Pinot Noir ★★★★★

The classy, elegant 2015 vintage (★★★★★) was matured for 10 months in French oak barriques (25 per cent new), and bottled unfined and unfiltered. Full of personality, it is deep ruby, fragrant, full-bodied and youthful, with strong, ripe plum/spice flavours, a hint of dried herbs, fine-grained tannins, and excellent complexity, harmony and length. Best drinking 2020+.

Vintage	15
WR	7
Drink	17-27

 DRY $45 AV

Folding Hill Orchard Block Bendigo Central Otago Pinot Noir ★★★★☆

The 2014 vintage (★★★★★) is a very refined, 'complete' wine. Estate-grown and hand-picked, it was fermented with indigenous yeasts, matured for 20 months in French oak barrels, and bottled unfined and unfiltered. Full and fairly youthful in colour, it is highly fragrant, mouthfilling and sweet-fruited, with layers of cherry, plum, spice and nut flavours. An elegant, complex wine, still unfolding, it should be long-lived; best drinking 2019+.

Vintage	14
WR	7
Drink	17-27

DRY $55 –V

Folium Marlborough Pinot Noir ★★★★☆

The 2016 vintage (★★★★) was grown in the Brancott Valley and matured for 11 months in French oak casks (10 per cent new). Full ruby, it is mouthfilling, with very youthful, ripe cherry, plum and spice flavours, fresh acidity, and considerable complexity. Still a baby, it's best cellared to 2019+. The 2015 vintage (★★★★☆) is deep ruby, with substantial body and well-ripened flavours, showing excellent depth, vigour, structure and complexity.

Vintage	16
WR	5
Drink	17-25

DRY $31 V+

Folium Reserve Marlborough Pinot Noir ★★★★★

The classy 2015 vintage (★★★★★) of this Brancott Valley red was hand-harvested and matured for 18 months in French oak casks (40 per cent new). Deeply coloured, it is mouthfilling, with very generous, ripe cherry, plum and spice flavours, slightly earthy, savoury and complex, good tannin support, and excellent potential. Best drinking 2019+.

Vintage	15
WR	6
Drink	20-30

DRY $41 V+

Forrest Marlborough Pinot Noir ★★★☆

The 2015 vintage (★★★☆) is a bright ruby, full-bodied, sweet-fruited red, with very good depth of plummy, berryish flavours, in a moderately complex style, enjoyable from now on. The 2014 vintage (★★★☆), tasted in mid to late 2017, is similar – mouthfilling, with spicy, savoury notes, a hint of dried herbs, and good complexity and depth.

DRY $30 –V

Framingham F-Series Marlborough Pinot Noir ★★★★☆

The very refined, silky-textured 2015 vintage (★★★★★) was grown on the south side of the Wairau Valley, hand-picked and barrel-aged for 16 months. Full, bright ruby, it is mouthfilling, with ripe cherry, plum and spice flavours, showing excellent complexity and harmony. A supple, seamless red, it should be at its best mid-2018+.

DRY $40 AV

Framingham Marlborough Pinot Noir ★★★★

This wine is 'feminine', says winemaker Andrew Hedley, meaning it is elegant, rather than powerful. The 2014 vintage (★★★★), matured for 10 months in French oak casks (20 per cent new), is ruby-hued, mouthfilling and savoury, with ripe plum, cherry and spice flavours, a subtle seasoning of oak, and gentle tannins. A very harmonious wine, showing good complexity, it's already delicious. The 2015 vintage (★★★★) was grown on gravel and clay sites. A refined, supple wine, with ripe cherry, plum and spice flavours, it shows excellent depth and complexity, with lots of drink-young appeal.

Vintage	15	14
WR	7	6
Drink	17-21	17-20

DRY $30 AV

Fromm Churton Vineyard Marlborough Pinot Noir   (★★★★★)

The debut 2015 vintage (★★★★★) is extremely rare – only 300 bottles (one barrel) were made. Grown organically in the Churton Vineyard, in the Waihopai Valley, it was fermented with indigenous yeasts, oak-matured for 16 months, and bottled unfined and unfiltered. Deep ruby, with a fragrant, savoury bouquet, it has highly concentrated, well-ripened cherry, plum, dried-herb and spice flavours, showing impressive complexity, good tannin backbone and obvious potential; best drinking 2019+.

DRY $55 AV

Fromm Clayvin Vineyard Pinot Noir   ★★★★★

This acclaimed Marlborough red is grown and hand-picked at the hillside Clayvin Vineyard in the Brancott Valley, fermented with indigenous yeasts, matured in French oak barriques, and bottled without fining or filtering. In its youth, it is more floral and charming than its Fromm Vineyard stablemate. Certified organic, the youthful 2015 vintage (★★★★★) is extremely rare – only two barrels (600 bottles) were produced. Deeply coloured, it's a wine of real beauty, rich and supple, with searching cherry, plum and spice flavours, fine-grained tannins, and a strong sense of youthful vigour. Best drinking 2020+.

Vintage	15	14	13	12	11	10	09	08	07	06
WR	7	6	7	7	7	7	7	6	7	7
Drink	17-27	17-25	17-25	17-26	17-23	17-24	17-24	17-18	17-19	P

DRY $85 AV

Fromm Cuvée 'H' Marlborough Pinot Noir   (★★★★★)

Certified organic, the debut 2015 vintage (★★★★★) is labelled in honour of Hätsch Kalberer, Fromm's winemaker since the first vintage in 1992. A multi-site blend, it was hand-picked, fermented with indigenous yeasts, matured for well over a year in French oak casks (10 per cent new), and bottled unfined and unfiltered. A sturdy, dense wine, it is very age-worthy, with concentrated, ripe cherry, plum and spice flavours, showing excellent complexity, real power and depth through the palate, buried tannins and obvious potential. Best drinking 2020+.

DRY $65 AV

Fromm Fromm Vineyard Pinot Noir   ★★★★★

Winemaker Hätsch Kalberer describes this Marlborough red as 'not a typical New World style, but the truest expression of terroir you could find'. In the Fromm Vineyard near Renwick, in the heart of the Wairau Valley, many clones of Pinot Noir are close-planted on a flat site with alluvial topsoils overlying layers of clay and free-draining gravels. The wine is fermented with indigenous yeasts, matured for 18 months in Burgundy oak barrels (10 per cent new in 2015), and bottled unfined and unfiltered. Certified organic, the powerful 2015 vintage (★★★★★) is sturdy and firm, with highly concentrated cherry, plum and spice flavours, ripe, savoury, complex and long. A 'masculine', very age-worthy style of Pinot Noir, it should be at its best 2020+.

Vintage	15	14	13	12	11	10	09	08	07	06
WR	7	6	7	7	6	7	7	NM	7	6
Drink	17-27	17-26	17-26	17-25	17-22	17-23	17-22	NM	17-21	P

DRY $85 –V

Fromm La Strada Marlborough Pinot Noir ★★★★☆

This wine is made to be ready for drinking upon release, by 'steering the fermentation towards more fruit expression and moderate tannins and structure'. Certified organic, the 2015 vintage (★★★★☆) is a multi-site blend, from 14 to 25-year-old vines in the Wairau, Brancott and Waihopai valleys. Full-coloured, it is mouthfilling and youthful, with concentrated, ripe plum/spice flavours, showing good complexity, and gentle tannins, in a 'serious' but approachable style. An excellent introduction to the Fromm range of Pinot Noirs, it should be at its best 2019+.

Vintage	15	14	13	12	11	10	09	08
WR	7	6	7	7	6	7	7	7
Drink	17-22	17-21	17-20	17-19	17-18	17-18	P	P

DRY $40 AV

Fromm Quarters Vineyard Marlborough Pinot Noir (★★★★★)

Certified organic, the rare 2015 vintage (★★★★★) was hand-harvested in the lower Brancott Valley, fermented with indigenous yeasts, and matured in a single French oak barrique (yielding a total production of 300 bottles). Deep ruby, it is fragrant, concentrated and savoury, with very generous, ripe cherry, plum and spice flavours, fresh acidity and a finely textured, very harmonious finish. Already delicious, it's a top debut. Best drinking 2019+.

Vintage	15
WR	7
Drink	17-25

DRY $55 AV

Georges Road Williams Hill Waipara Pinot Noir ★★★★

The deeply coloured 2014 vintage (★★★★☆) is a single-vineyard red, hand-picked on the eastern slopes of the Waipara Valley and matured for over a year in French oak casks (20 per cent new). Still youthful, it is mouthfilling and fruit-packed, with concentrated, ripe, plummy, spicy flavours, a hint of dried herbs, fine-grained tannins and obvious potential. Best drinking 2018+.

DRY $34 AV

Gibbston Valley Central Otago Pinot Noir ★★★★☆

The powerful 2014 vintage (★★★★☆), blended from Bendigo (90 per cent) and Gibbston (10 per cent) grapes, was matured in French oak casks (20 per cent new). Boldly coloured, it is floral, mouthfilling (14 per cent alcohol) and supple, with plum, spice, dried-herb and cherry flavours, showing excellent ripeness and depth, finely integrated oak and good complexity. Approachable from the start, it should reward cellaring for several years. (This label has been replaced from the 2015 vintage by the GV Collection Pinot Noir – see below.)

Vintage	14	13	12	11	10	09
WR	7	7	7	7	7	7
Drink	17-21	17-20	17-20	P	17-18	P

DRY $45 –V

Gibbston Valley China Terrace Bendigo Central Otago Pinot Noir ★★★★★

Estate-grown at altitude (320 metres above sea level) in the China Terrace Vineyard, at Bendigo, the 2016 vintage (★★★★☆) was hand-picked and matured for 11 months in French oak casks (23 per cent new). Deep and youthful in colour, it is a mouthfilling, smooth red, with concentrated, ripe cherry, plum and spice flavours, finely integrated oak, and impressive richness and complexity. Still very youthful, it's well worth cellaring; open 2020+.

Vintage	16	15	14	13	12	11	10	09
WR	6	7	7	7	7	7	7	6
Drink	17-27	17-27	17-26	17-25	17-23	17-22	17-20	P

 DRY $65 AV

Gibbston Valley Glenlee Central Otago Pinot Noir ★★★★☆

A single-vineyard red, grown at Gibbston, the classy 2016 vintage (★★★★★) was hand-picked, fermented with indigenous yeasts and matured in French oak barriques (26 per cent new). Deep ruby, it is fragrant and finely textured, with rich, ripe, vibrant cherry, plum and spice flavours, oak complexity and obvious potential. A very elegant, 'feminine' style of Pinot Noir, it's well worth cellaring to 2020+.

Vintage	16	15	14	13	12	11
WR	6	NM	7	7	7	7
Drink	17-25	NM	17-24	17-20	17-23	17-22

 DRY $65 –V

Gibbston Valley Gold River Central Otago Pinot Noir ★★★☆

This is the winery's 'lighter' red, for 'immediate enjoyment'. Already delicious, the 2016 vintage (★★★★) was grown at Gibbston (50 per cent) and Bendigo (50 per cent), hand-picked and barrel-aged for 10 months. Deep ruby, it is mouthfilling and exuberantly fruity, with strong, fresh, ripe, plummy, spicy flavours, showing considerable complexity, fine-grained tannins, and loads of drink-young charm.

 DRY $23 V+

Gibbston Valley GV Collection Central Otago Pinot Noir ★★★★★

This replaces the former 'Gibbston Valley Central Otago Pinot Noir' label. The classy, debut 2015 vintage (★★★★★) was mostly grown at Bendigo (95 per cent); the rest came from Gibbston. Hand-picked and matured for 10 months in French oak casks (20 per cent new), it is full-coloured, mouthfilling, savoury and supple, with lovely poise, texture and depth. Already delicious, it has ripe cherry, plum, dried-herb and spice flavours, showing excellent complexity and harmony. The 2016 vintage (★★★★☆) was grown at Bendigo (95 per cent) and Gibbston (5 per cent), hand-picked and matured for 10 months in French oak casks (20 per cent new). Bright ruby, it is mouthfilling, with strong, vibrant, ripe cherry, plum and spice flavours, showing excellent complexity and harmony. Already delicious, it should be at its best 2019+.

DRY $46 AV

Gibbston Valley Le Maitre Gibbston Central Otago Pinot Noir ★★★★★

Grown in the Home Block at Gibbston, where the oldest vines were planted in 1983, the outstanding 2016 vintage (★★★★★), certified organic, was matured for 11 months in French oak casks (30 per cent new). Deep and youthful in colour, it is mouthfilling, rich and silky-textured, with dense, ripe, plummy, spicy flavours, a hint of dark chocolate, buried tannins and savoury, nutty notes adding complexity. An authoritative, youthful but already approachable wine, it's very age-worthy and should break into full stride 2020+.

Vintage	16	15	14	13	12	11
WR	7	7	7	7	7	7
Drink	17-27	17-26	17-25	17-20	17-23	17-22

 DRY $100 AV

Gibbston Valley Reserve Central Otago Pinot Noir ★★★★★

At its best, this Central Otago red is mouthfilling and savoury, with superb concentration of sweet-tasting, plummy fruit and lovely harmony. The grapes have been drawn from various sub-regions and vineyards over the years and yields have been very low (under 5 tonnes/hectare). The 2015 vintage (★★★★★) was grown at Bendigo and matured for 11 months in French oak barriques (33 per cent new). Deep and youthful in colour, it is powerful, ripe and concentrated, with dense, vibrant plum, spice and nut flavours, earthy notes adding complexity, and obvious potential. Best drinking 2020+. The 2016 vintage (★★★★★) was also grown at Bendigo. Deeply coloured, it is powerful and sturdy (14.5 per cent alcohol), with lovely depth of fresh, plummy, spicy flavours, oak complexity, supple, ripe tannins and a resounding finish. Still very youthful, it's best cellared to at least 2020.

Vintage	16	15
WR	7	7
Drink	19-26	18-25

 DRY $120 AV

Gibbston Valley School House Central Otago Pinot Noir ★★★★★

This consistently classy red is estate-grown in the late-ripening School House Vineyard, at Bendigo, an extremely elevated site (up to 420 metres above sea level). The 2016 vintage (★★★★★) was hand-picked and matured for 11 months in French oak casks (28 per cent new). Deeply coloured, it is fragrant, rich and vibrantly fruity, with deep, ripe plum and spice flavours, a hint of liquorice, and savoury, nutty notes adding complexity. Highly concentrated, with a lasting finish, it' s already delicious, but well worth cellaring to at least mid-2019.

Vintage	16	15	14	13	12	11	10	09
WR	7	7	7	7	7	7	7	7
Drink	17-27	17-37	17-26	17-25	17-23	17-22	17-20	P

 DRY $65 AV

Giesen Marlborough Pinot Noir ★★★☆

The 2014 vintage (★★★☆), grown at multiple sites and oak-aged, is a deep ruby, fairly firm red, with a touch of complexity and cherry, plum and spice flavours, showing very good depth.

Vintage	14
WR	5
Drink	P

DRY $26 AV

Gladstone Vineyard Pinot Noir ★★★★

Estate-grown and hand-harvested in the northern Wairarapa, and matured in French oak casks, the 2015 vintage (★★★★) is bright ruby, fragrant and full-bodied. It has rich, ripe flavours of plums, dried herbs and spices, earthy notes adding complexity, and gentle tannins. Best drinking mid-2018+.

Vintage	15	14	13	12	11	10
WR	6	7	6	NM	5	6
Drink	17-23	17-23	17-22	NM	17-20	17-20

DRY $39 AV

Glasnevin Limited Release Waipara Valley Pinot Noir ★★★★☆

The classy, top-value 2015 vintage (★★★★★) was hand-picked, fermented with indigenous yeasts and matured for 18 months in French oak barriques (40 per cent new). Bright ruby, it is very attractively perfumed, mouthfilling, rich and supple, with deliciously concentrated, ripe fruit flavours, oak complexity and impressive harmony. The 2016 vintage (★★★★), matured for 14 months in seasoned French oak barriques, is freshly scented, sturdy and vibrantly fruity, with strong, ripe, spicy flavours, hints of raisins and liquorice, and good tannin backbone.

Vintage	16	15
WR	6	6
Drink	17-27	17-24

DRY $35 V+

Goldwater Marlborough Pinot Noir ★★★☆

The 2015 vintage (★★★☆) is a boldly fruity, sweet-fruited red with strong red-berry and plum flavours, showing a touch of complexity, and a smooth finish. Enjoyable young.

DRY $23 V+

Grasshopper Rock Earnscleugh Vineyard Central Otago Pinot Noir ★★★★★

Estate-grown in Alexandra, this is typically a wonderful buy. From vines planted in 2003, the 2016 vintage (★★★★★) was fermented partly with indigenous yeasts and matured for 10 months in French oak barriques (29 per cent new). Bright ruby, with a richly perfumed bouquet, it is mouthfilling, with concentrated cherry, plum, spice and nut flavours, complex and savoury. Already delicious, it's also well worth cellaring; open 2019+.

Vintage	16	15	14	13	12	11
WR	7	7	7	6	7	7
Drink	18-23	18-22	17-21	17-20	17-21	17-20

DRY $35 V+

Grava Martinborough Pinot Noir (★★★☆)

The 2015 vintage (★★★☆) was grown at a site south of Martinborough township, formerly Hudson Vineyard. Matured for 10 months in oak barrels (10 per cent new), it was bottled unfined and unfiltered. Light ruby, it is a supple, medium-bodied red with fresh, moderately concentrated cherry/plum flavours. Showing some savoury complexity, it's still youthful; best drinking 2018+.

DRY $45 –V

Greenhough Hope Vineyard Nelson Pinot Noir   ★★★★★

One of Nelson's greatest reds, at its best powerful, rich and long-lived. It is estate-grown and hand-picked on an elevated terrace of the south-eastern Waimea Plains, where the vines, planted in gravelly loam clays, have an average age of 20 years. Yields are very low – 4 to 5 tonnes of grapes per hectare – and the wine is matured for at least a year in French oak barriques (13 per cent new in 2015). Certified organic, the 2015 vintage (★★★★★) was bottled unfined and unfiltered. Deep ruby, it has a fragrant, complex bouquet of strawberries and spices. Mouthfilling, it is a powerful yet elegant, sweet-fruited wine, with deep, youthful plum, spice and nut flavours, firm, savoury and lingering. Very age-worthy, it's well worth cellaring to 2019+.

Vintage	15	14	13	12	11	10	09	08
WR	6	7	NM	NM	6	7	6	6
Drink	17-23	17-22	NM	NM	17-18	17-20	17-16	P

 DRY $46 AV

Greenhough Nelson Pinot Noir   ★★★★

Offering great value, the 2015 vintage (★★★★☆) was hand-picked in the Home and Morison vineyards at Hope, and matured for a year in French oak barriques and puncheons (32 per cent new). Full, bright ruby, with a fragrant, ripe bouquet, it is full-bodied and sweet-fruited, with generous plum, cherry, spice and nut flavours, showing excellent complexity and harmony. Already delicious, it should be at its best 2019+. (From grapes certified organic or in transition to organic status.)

Vintage	15	14	13	12	11	10	09
WR	6	7	6	6	6	6	6
Drink	17-21	17-20	17-19	17-18	P	P	P

 DRY $30 AV

Greylands Ridge Central Otago Pinot Noir   ★★★★

Grown at Alexandra, this single-vineyard red is matured in seasoned French oak casks. The 2014 vintage (★★★★) is a youthful, mouthfilling, full-coloured red with strong, ripe cherry, plum and spice flavours, integrated oak and supple tannins. A stylish, generous wine, it's well worth cellaring.

Vintage	14	13
WR	6	7
Drink	17-19	17-20

 DRY $35 AV

Greyrock Hawke's Bay Pinot Noir   (★★☆)

From Sileni, the 2015 vintage (★★☆) is ruby-hued, with a hint of development. Mouthfilling, fruity and smooth, it's a 'lightly oaked' style, with plum/spice flavours and gentle tannins. Easy, early drinking.

DRY $17 AV

Greystone Thomas Brothers Waipara Valley Pinot Noir   ★★★★★

The 2015 vintage (★★★★★), grown in the steep Brothers Block, was hand-picked at over 24 brix, fermented with indigenous yeasts, matured for 15 months in French oak barriques (70 per cent new), and bottled without fining or filtering. Deep and youthful in colour, it is invitingly fragrant, with mouthfilling body and highly concentrated, beautifully ripe flavours of plums, cherries and spices. A notably rich, sweet-fruited and supple red, showing lovely depth, poise and complexity, it's still very youthful; best drinking 2019+.

Vintage	15
WR	6
Drink	17-30

 DRY $99 AV

Greystone Waipara Valley Pinot Noir   ★★★★★

The delicious 2015 vintage (★★★★★) was matured in French oak barriques (25 per cent new). Deep and youthful in colour, it is highly fragrant, mouthfilling and supple, with rich, ripe cherry, plum and spice flavours, finely structured and long. A classy, age-worthy wine, it should be at its best 2018+.

Vintage	16	15
WR	6	7
Drink	17-28	17-30

 DRY $42 V+

Greywacke Marlborough Pinot Noir   ★★★★★

Grown at elevated sites in the Southern Valleys, hand-harvested and matured for 18 months in French oak barriques (40 per cent new), the 2014 vintage (★★★★★) is deep ruby and richly fragrant, with mouthfilling body and strong, plummy, spicy flavours. Still youthful, it is concentrated, very sweet-fruited and savoury, with buried tannins and impressive richness, complexity and harmony. Best drinking 2018+. The 2015 vintage (★★★★★) is similar – deeply coloured, rich, sweet-fruited and smooth, with bold plum, spice and nut flavours, showing good complexity, and the structure to age well. Best dnnking 2019+.

Vintage	15	14	13	12	11	10	09
WR	6	6	6	5	6	6	5
Drink	18-23	17-22	17-21	17-20	17-20	17-18	17-18

 DRY $47 AV

Grove Mill Marlborough Pinot Noir   ★★★☆

The 2014 vintage (★★★☆) was grown in the Wairau Valley and matured in French oak casks (25 per cent new). Bright ruby, it is mouthfilling, fresh and smooth, with plum, spice and herb flavours, showing a touch of complexity.

Vintage	14	13
WR	7	7
Drink	17-20	17-19

DRY $25 AV

Gunn Estate Reserve Marlborough Pinot Noir ★★★☆

As a low-priced, drink-young style, the 2016 vintage (★★★☆) is hard to beat. Partly barrel-aged, it is bright ruby, mouthfilling and supple, with fresh, ripe cherry and plum flavours to the fore, gentle tannins and slightly savoury notes adding complexity. Great value from Sacred Hill.

Vintage	16	15
WR	5	6
Drink	17-20	17-18

DRY $17 V+

Haha Marlborough Pinot Noir ★★★

Priced right, the 2016 vintage (★★★) is a ruby-hued, medium to full-bodied red, with cherry/plum flavours, fresh and youthful. Sweet-fruited, with a touch of complexity and gentle tannins, it has lots of drink-young appeal, and should be at its best mid-2018+.

DRY $20 AV

Haha Reserve Marlborough Pinot Noir ★★★☆

Enjoyable young, the 2016 vintage (★★★☆) was estate-grown and hand-harvested in the Awatere Valley, and matured in French oak barrels. Ruby-hued, it is mouthfilling, sweet-fruited and supple, with ripe cherry, plum and spice flavours, gentle tannins and considerable complexity. Drink now or cellar.

DRY $28 AV

Hans Herzog Marlborough Pinot Noir ★★★★★

Still on sale, the 2011 vintage (★★★★) was estate-grown on the north side of the Wairau Valley, fermented with indigenous yeasts, matured for 18 months in French oak barriques, and bottled unfined and unfiltered. Ruby-hued, with moderately youthful colour, it is mouthfilling, with concentrated, ripe plum/spice flavours, slightly earthy notes adding complexity, gentle tannins, and a rounded finish. Drinking well now, it's certified organic.

Vintage	11	10	09	08
WR	7	7	7	7
Drink	17-21	17-20	17-19	17-20

DRY $49 AV

Hawkshead Bannockburn Central Otago Pinot Noir ★★★★

The 2014 vintage (★★★★☆) is a single-vineyard red, matured in French oak casks (30 per cent new). Full, bright ruby, it is mouthfilling, ripe and savoury, with good concentration of plummy, spicy, slightly nutty flavours, gentle tannins and obvious potential. A very harmonious wine, it should be at its best 2018+.

DRY $49 –V

Hawkshead Central Otago Pinot Noir ★★★☆

The 2014 vintage (★★★★) of this regional blend was matured in French oak barriques (20 per cent new). Bright ruby, it is a generous, savoury red with strong, ripe, plummy, spicy flavours, showing good complexity. Best drinking 2018+.

DRY $40 –V

Huia Marlborough Pinot Noir ★★★★

Certified organic, the 2014 vintage (★★★★) was hand-picked, fermented with indigenous yeasts and matured for a year in French oak barrels. Drinking well now, it is fragrant and full-coloured, with vibrant, plummy, spicy flavours, showing excellent depth and complexity.

 DRY $39 AV

Hunky Dory Marlborough Pinot Noir ★★★☆

From Huia, the 2014 vintage (★★★☆) is deeply coloured, with mouthfilling body and strong, ripe plum/spice flavours, slightly earthy and firm. Certified organic.

DRY $25 AV

Hunter's Marlborough Pinot Noir ★★★

Typically a supple, charming red. The 2014 vintage (★★★☆) was estate-grown at Rapaura and in the Omaka Valley, fermented with indigenous yeasts and matured for 11 months in French oak casks (20 per cent new). Ruby-hued, it is fragrant and supple, with ripe cherry, plum and spice flavours, showing some savoury, nutty complexity. Drinking well now, it's still developing and should be at its best 2018+.

 DRY $29 –V

Impromptu by Misha's Vineyard Central Otago Pinot Noir ★★★★

This red is made principally for sale by the glass in restaurants and bars. Estate-grown at Bendigo, the 2014 vintage (★★★★), released in 2017, was fermented with indigenous yeasts and matured in French oak hogsheads (18 per cent new). Full, bright ruby, it is mouthfilling and savoury, with well-ripened plum, cherry, spice and nut flavours, a hint of mint chocolate, and very satisfying complexity, harmony and depth. Drink now onwards.

Vintage	14	13	12	11	10
WR	6	6	7	5	7
Drink	17-22	17-21	17-20	17-18	P

 DRY $30 AV

Invivo Central Otago Pinot Noir ★★★★

The 2016 vintage (★★★★) was grown in the Cromwell Basin and Gibbston sub-regions, and barrel-aged. Bright ruby, it is fragrant and mouthfilling, with generous, ripe plum and spice flavours, nutty and savoury notes adding complexity, and good tannin support. Best drinking mid-2018+.

DRY $35 AV

Invivo Michelle's Central Otago Pinot Noir ★★★★★

Delicious young, but also age-worthy, the powerful 2016 vintage (★★★★★) is rare – only five barrels were made. Grown at Bannockburn, it is deeply coloured, sturdy (14.5 per cent alcohol) and sweet-fruited, with concentrated, youthful plum, spice and nut flavours, showing excellent complexity.

Vintage	16	15	14
WR	7	7	7
Drink	17-25	17-24	17-23

 DRY $40 V+

Isabel Marlborough Pinot Noir

(★★★)

The 2015 vintage (★★★) was estate-grown in the Wairau Valley. Light ruby, with a fragrant bouquet, it is a 'fruit-driven' style, not complex, but offering plenty of youthful, plummy, spicy flavour, with a hint of tamarillo. Best drinking mid-2018+.

DRY $32 –V

Jackson Estate Homestead Marlborough Pinot Noir

★★★☆

Partly barrel-aged, the 2014 vintage (★★★☆) was estate-grown in the Gum Emperor Vineyard in the Waihopai Valley. Bright ruby, it is full-bodied, vibrantly fruity and smooth, with plummy, slightly spicy flavours, showing a touch of complexity, and lots of drink-young charm. Priced right.

DRY $24 V+

Vintage	14	13
WR	6	6
Drink	17-18	P

Jackson Estate Vintage Widow Marlborough Pinot Noir

★★★★

The finely balanced 2014 vintage (★★★★) was estate-grown in the Waihopai Valley, hand-picked and matured for 10 months in French oak casks. Full ruby, it is mouthfilling, with good concentration of ripe cherry, plum and spice flavours, and nutty, savoury notes adding complexity. Drinking well now, it's also worth cellaring.

DRY $36 AV

Vintage	14	13	12
WR	6	6	6
Drink	17-21	17-20	17-19

Johanneshof Maybern Single Vineyard Reserve Marlborough Pinot Noir

★★★☆

Estate-grown on a steep (30 degrees), north-facing slope at Koromiko, between Picton and Blenheim, the 2014 vintage (★★★☆) of this distinctive wine was hand-harvested, fermented with indigenous yeasts and barrel-aged. Ruby-hued, it is mouthfilling and savoury, with slightly 'green' tannins, but very satisfying depth of cherry, spice and herb flavours, showing good complexity.

DRY $43 –V

Johner Estate Gladstone Pinot Noir

★★★★

Estate-grown in the northern Wairarapa, matured for a year in French oak barrels (25 per cent new), and bottled unfined and unfiltered, the 2014 vintage (★★★★☆) is a powerful, deeply coloured red. It is sturdy (14.5 per cent alcohol) and sweet-fruited, with concentrated plum, spice and dried-herb flavours, and fine-grained tannins. Drink now or cellar. Good value.

DRY $36 AV

Vintage	14
WR	7
Drink	17-22

Johner Estate Gladstone Reserve Pinot Noir ★★★★☆

The powerful, full-bodied 2014 vintage (★★★★★) is a single-vineyard, estate-grown Wairarapa red, hand-picked from the oldest vines and matured for a year in French oak casks (75 per cent new). Bold and youthful in colour, it is very rich, ripe and supple, with dense plum, spice and dried-herb flavours, showing excellent complexity and harmony, and a deliciously smooth finish. A classy young red, it should be long-lived.

Vintage	14
WR	7
Drink	17-25

 DRY $60 –V

Johner Estate Moonlight Wairarapa Pinot Noir ★★★☆

Offering good value, the 2014 vintage (★★★) was matured for a year in seasoned oak barrels. Deep ruby, it is mouthfilling and savoury, with generous, ripe plum, spice and dried-herb flavours, showing good complexity, and a fairly firm finish.

Vintage	14	13
WR	6	7
Drink	17-20	17-18

 DRY $26 AV

Judge Rock Alexandra Central Otago Pinot Noir ★★★★☆

This single-vineyard red is estate-grown at Alexandra and French oak-matured. The 2015 vintage (★★★★☆) is ruby-hued, with mouthfilling body, fresh acidity, generous cherry, plum, dried-herb and spice flavours, and fine-grained tannins. An age-worthy wine, it's likely to be at its best 2018+.

 DRY $40 AV

Jules Taylor Marlborough Pinot Noir ★★★★

The 2016 vintage (★★★★) was grown in the Southern Valleys and matured in French oak barrels (15 per cent new). Full, bright ruby, it is mouthfilling, with concentrated, very vibrant plum and cherry flavours, well-integrated oak adding complexity, and smooth tannins. Full of youthful vigour, it should mature gracefully; open mid-2018+.

Vintage	16	15	14
WR	6	6	6
Drink	17-21	17-20	17-20

DRY $35 AV

Jules Taylor OTQ Limited Release Single Vineyard Marlborough Pinot Noir

★★★★☆

Made 'On The Quiet', the 2016 vintage (★★★★☆) was grown in the Meadowbank Vineyard, on the south side of the Wairau Valley, and barrel-matured for 10 months (33 per cent new). A powerful, fruit-packed red, it is deeply coloured and full-bodied, with impressive depth of ripe, plummy, slightly spicy flavours, well-integrated oak and fine-grained tannins. Still very youthful, it should flourish with cellaring; open 2019+.

Vintage	16	15
WR	6	6
Drink	17-22	17-20

DRY $45 –V

Junction Possession Central Hawke's Bay Pinot Noir (★★★)

Grown on the Takapau Plains, the 2014 vintage (★★★) was hand-picked and matured for 18 months in French oak casks (30 per cent new). Ruby-hued, with distinctly spicy, slightly herbal aromas and flavours, it is moderately concentrated, with some complexity. Still youthful, it should be at its best 2018+.

DRY $27 –V

Kaimira Estate Brightwater Vintner's Selection Pinot Noir ★★★

Certified organic, the 2016 vintage (★★★) was grown in Nelson and matured for 10 months in French oak barrels (29 per cent new). Ruby-hued, with a hint of development, it is mouthfilling, with satisfying depth of plum, tamarillo, spice and dried-herb flavours, showing some complexity, and a firm finish. Best drinking mid-2018+.

DRY $28 –V

Vintage	16	15	14
WR	5	7	6
Drink	18-26	17-21	17-19

Kalex Central Otago Pinot Noir ★★★★

The highly attractive 2014 vintage (★★★★☆) was hand-harvested, French oak-matured, and bottled unfined and unfiltered. Deep ruby, it is savoury and supple, sweet-fruited and silky, with concentrated cherry, plum and spice flavours, good complexity, and a finely textured, long finish. Drink now or cellar.

DRY $40 –V

Kim Crawford Marlborough/Central Otago Pinot Noir ★★★☆

The highly approachable, light ruby 2015 vintage (★★★☆) is a blend of Marlborough and Central Otago grapes, partly barrel-aged. Mouthfilling and smooth, it has good depth of ripe cherry and spice flavours, a touch of complexity, gentle tannins, and lots of drink-young charm.

DRY $24 V+

Kim Crawford Small Parcels Rise & Shine Central Otago Pinot Noir (★★★★)

Still developing, the 2014 vintage (★★★★) was matured in French oak casks (30 per cent new). Full ruby, it is mouthfilling and smooth, with very good weight and depth of ripe, plummy, slightly savoury and nutty flavours, showing considerable complexity. Finely textured, it should be at its best mid-2018+.

DRY $30 AV

Vintage	14
WR	4
Drink	17-19

Kina Beach Vineyard Nelson Pinot Noir   (★★☆)

The easy-drinking 2015 vintage (★★☆) is a single-vineyard red, barrel-aged for a year and bottled unfined and unfiltered. It has light, slightly developed colour, a slightly leafy bouquet, and a herbal thread running through its cherryish, plummy flavours. Fruity and smooth, it's ready to roll.

Vintage	15
WR	7
Drink	17-20

DRY $29 –V

Kina Beach Vineyard Reserve Pinot Noir   (★★★★)

Still on sale, the 2012 vintage (★★★★) was estate-grown on the Nelson coastline and matured for 11 months in French oak casks. Deep and mature in colour, it is mouthfilling, with strong cherry, plum, spice and dried-herb flavours, showing good complexity. Savoury, with plenty of personality, it's probably at its peak.

Vintage	12
WR	4
Drink	17-22

DRY $40 –V

Kiritea Martinborough Pinot Noir   (★★★★★)

Offering irresistible value, the 2014 vintage (★★★★★) is the second-tier label of Te Hera Estate. Deep ruby, it is seductively rich and supple, with concentrated ripe-fruit flavours, hints of cherries, dried herbs and mushrooms, excellent weight and harmony, and a welcoming fragrance.

DRY $25 V+

Koha Marlborough Pinot Noir   (★★★★)

Offering great value, the 2015 vintage (★★★★) is fragrant, with strong cherry, plum and spice flavours, slightly nutty and savoury. An age-worthy red, it should be at its best mid-2018+. (From te Pa.)

DRY $19 V+

Konrad Marlborough Pinot Noir   ★★★☆

Certified organic, the 2016 vintage (★★★☆) is a single-vineyard red, estate-grown in the Waihopai Valley and matured in French oak barriques (partly new). Deep ruby, it is sweet-fruited, with strong, vibrant, plummy flavours to the fore, moderate complexity, and some potential. Still very youthful, it should be at its best 2019+.

DRY $30 –V

Kumeu River Hunting Hill Pinot Noir   ★★★★

Grown on the slopes above Mate's Vineyard, directly over the road from the winery at Kumeu, the 2014 vintage (★★★★) is a top example of Pinot Noir from the Auckland region. Deep ruby, it is fresh, vibrant and sweet-fruited, with mouthfilling body and concentrated cherry, plum and spice flavours. An elegant, savoury, finely structured wine, it should be at its best 2018+.

DRY $50 –V

Kumeu Village Pinot Noir

Estate-grown by Kumeu River, in West Auckland, the 2015 vintage (★★☆) was hand-picked and fermented with indigenous yeasts. Ruby-hued, it's a light, supple, easy-drinking red, with gentle tannins and fresh berry/plum flavours. Priced right.

DRY $18 AV

Kuru Kuru Central Otago Pinot Noir

The impressive 2015 vintage (★★★★☆), grown at Bendigo, was matured in French oak casks (33 per cent new). Deep ruby, it is ripely scented, sturdy and sweet-fruited, with generous cherry, plum and spice flavours, a hint of liquorice, well-integrated oak, good complexity and a rich, finely balanced finish. Still youthful, it should be at its best 2019+. The 2016 vintage (★★★★☆) should also age gracefully. Full ruby, it is mouthfilling, with strong, ripe cherry, plum, spice and nut flavours, savoury and complex, and a smooth, sustained finish. (From Tarras Wines.)

DRY $40 AV

Lake Chalice Marlborough Pinot Noir

Enjoyable young, the 2016 vintage (★★★☆) was grown in the Eyrie Vineyard, in the Southern Valleys. Bright ruby, it is mouthfilling, sweet-fruited, vibrant and smooth, with gentle tannins and ripe cherry, plum and spice flavours, showing very good depth.

DRY $20 V+

Lake Chalice The Raptor Marlborough Pinot Noir

Finely textured, with good complexity, the 2015 vintage (★★★★) is an estate-grown red, hand-picked from 15-year-old vines in the lower Waihopai Valley. Bright ruby, it is full-bodied and savoury, with ripe cherry, plum and spice flavours, fresh acidity, excellent depth and considerable potential; open 2018+.

DRY $35 AV

Lake Hayes Central Otago Pinot Noir

From Amisfield, the 2014 vintage (★★★★) was estate-grown at Pisa and partly barrel-aged. Deep and bright in colour, it is mouthfilling and vibrantly fruity, with plum/spice flavours showing excellent ripeness and depth. A generous, savoury wine, it's drinking well now.

DRY $30 –V

Last Shepherd, The, Central Otago Pinot Noir ★★★☆

Floral and supple, the 2016 vintage (★★★☆) is a drink-young charmer. Bright ruby, it has good depth of vibrant cherry, plum, herb and spice flavours, a touch of complexity and gentle tannins. (From Pernod Ricard NZ.)

DRY $25 AV

Lawson's Dry Hills Marlborough Pinot Noir ★★★☆

The 2015 vintage (★★★) is a single-vineyard red, matured for 10 months in seasoned French oak barrels. Ruby-hued, it is full-bodied, with ripe cherry, plum and spice flavours, some rustic, earthy notes, considerable complexity, and a fairly firm finish.

Vintage	15
WR	7
Drink	17-18

 DRY $25 AV

Lawson's Dry Hills Reserve Marlborough Pinot Noir ★★★★☆

Offering fine value, the deeply coloured 2015 vintage (★★★★☆) was grown at two sites in the Waihopai Valley and matured for 10 months in French oak barriques (25 per cent new). Mouthfilling, it is youthful and fruit-packed, with ripe cherry, plum and spice flavours, showing excellent concentration, texture and complexity. Best drinking mid-2018+.

Vintage	15	14	13	12
WR	7	6	7	7
Drink	17-25	17-20	17-19	17-18

 DRY $30 V+

Lawson's Dry Hills The Pioneer Marlborough Pinot Noir ★★★★☆

The 2014 vintage (★★★★☆) was grown in the Waihopai Valley and French oak-matured for over a year. Deep ruby, it is mouthfilling, sweet-fruited and savoury, with concentrated, youthful cherry, plum and spice flavours. Still unfolding, it should be at its best mid-2018+.

Vintage	14	13	12
WR	7	7	7
Drink	17-25	17-25	17-20

 DRY $38 V+

Left Field Nelson Pinot Noir ★★★☆

Offering fine value, the 2016 vintage (★★★☆) was grown in Nelson, fermented with indigenous yeasts and matured for 10 months in French oak barrels (75 per cent) and tanks (25 per cent). Ruby-hued, it is medium-bodied, with good depth of vibrant cherry/plum flavours, funky notes adding a touch of complexity and a well-rounded finish. Enjoyable young. (From Te Awa.)

Vintage	16	15
WR	5	5
Drink	17-19	17-19

 DRY $18 V+

Leveret Estate Marlborough Pinot Noir ★★★

The 2014 vintage (★★★☆) was matured for a year in seasoned oak barrels. Retasted in 2017, it is sturdy, with full, fairly youthful colour and generous, ripe plum/spice flavours. Showing considerable complexity, it's probably at its peak.

Vintage	14	13
WR	5	6
Drink	17-20	17-18

DRY $25 –V

Leveret Estate Reserve Hawke's Bay Pinot Noir   ★★★☆

Deeply coloured, the 2014 vintage (★★★★) was matured for a year in French oak barrels (20 per cent new). It is a fleshy red, maturing gracefully, with strong, plummy, spicy, slightly cherryish flavours, nutty oak and balanced tannins. Drink now or cellar.

Vintage	14	13
WR	7	7
Drink	18-24	17-18

DRY $31 –V

Lime Rock Central Hawke's Bay Pinot Noir   ★★★★

I tasted the 2013 to 2016 vintages in mid to late 2017. Matured in French oak barriques (20 to 40 per cent new), the wines are all drinking well, in an elegant, mid-weight style with vivid varietal characteristics and proven aging ability. The 2016 vintage (★★★★) is ruby-hued and sweet-fruited, with youthful, vibrant cherry, plum and spice flavours, some funky notes adding complexity, and a long finish. Well worth cellaring, it should be at its best 2019+. The 2015 vintage (★★★★) is ruby-hued, savoury, ripe and supple, with very good complexity; drink now or cellar.

Vintage	16	15	14	13
WR	7	6	7	7
Drink	18-30	17-20	17-24	17-24

DRY $42 –V

Lime Rock White Knuckle Hill Central Hawke's Bay Pinot Noir   ★★★★☆

Showing plenty of personality, the 2013 vintage (★★★★☆) was matured in French oak barriques (20 per cent new). Ruby-hued, with a hint of maturity, it is very savoury, with mouthfilling body, dense, ripe cherry, plum and spice flavours, good tannin support, and excellent complexity and length. Best drinking mid-2018+.

Vintage	13
WR	7
Drink	17-30

DRY $59 –V

Little Black Shag Nelson Pinot Noir   (★★☆)

Low-priced, the 2014 vintage (★★☆) has light, fairly mature colour. Light-bodied, it has fresh acidity and spicy, slightly herbal and nutty flavours. Ready.

DRY $14 V+

Loveblock Central Otago Pinot Noir   ★★★★

Still on sale, the 2013 vintage (★★★★) is a bright ruby, single-vineyard red with a fresh bouquet, showing good complexity. Sweet-fruited, it has vibrant cherry, plum and spice flavours, showing good vigour and potential. Best drinking 2018+.

Vintage	14	13	12
WR	7	6	6
Drink	17-22	17-21	17-20

DRY $37 AV

Lowburn Ferry Home Block Central Otago Pinot Noir ★★★★★

This single-vineyard red is estate-grown and hand-picked at Lowburn, in the Cromwell Basin. The elegant 2016 vintage (★★★★☆) was matured for 10 months in French oak barriques (27 per cent new). Deep ruby, it is mouthfilling and concentrated, with very vibrant, youthful cherry, plum and spice flavours, well-integrated oak, fresh acidity and a supple, long finish. Best drinking 2019+.

Vintage	16	15	14	13	12
WR	7	7	7	7	7
Drink	18-23	18-22	17-21	17-20	17-20

DRY $55 AV

Lowburn Ferry Skeleton Creek Central Otago Pinot Noir ★★★★

The 2014 vintage (★★★★) was grown at two nearby sites in the Cromwell Basin, including the estate vineyard at Lowburn (55 per cent). Hand-picked and matured for 10 months in French oak barriques (26 per cent new), it is deeply coloured, mouthfilling and supple, with fresh plum/spice flavours, integrated oak and good concentration. Approachable young, it should be at its best 2018+.

Vintage	14	13
WR	7	7
Drink	17-19	17-18

DRY $45 –V

Lowburn Ferry The Ferryman Reserve Pinot Noir ★★★★★

Estate-grown in the Home Block at Lowburn, in Central Otago, this is the producer's flagship red, made only in top vintages. Hand-harvested at over 24 brix and matured for over a year in French oak barriques (33 per cent new), the 2014 vintage (★★★★★) is deeply coloured and mouthfilling, with dense, ripe, plummy, spicy, nutty flavours, very savoury and complex. It should flourish with cellaring; open 2018+.

DRY $85 AV

Luminary, The, Martinborough Pinot Noir ★★★★

From Palliser Estate, the 2014 vintage (★★★★) is a great buy (especially on special in supermarkets). Estate-grown, fermented with indigenous yeasts and matured for a year in French oak (20 per cent new), it rivals the quality of many producers' $30-plus Pinot Noirs. Full ruby, it is mouthfilling and savoury, with generous cherry, plum, spice and nut flavours, showing good complexity, and gentle tannins. Drink now or cellar.

DRY $22 V+

Ma Maison Martinborough Cuvée Two Richards Pinot Noir (★★★★★)

Named after two family members, the 2014 vintage (★★★★★) is a rare wine – only 822 bottles were produced. Bottled unfined and unfiltered, it has full, moderately youthful colour. A powerful (14.5 per cent alcohol), fleshy red, it is highly fragrant, with a strong surge of ripe cherry, spice and dried-herb flavours, showing excellent concentration and complexity. Best drinking 2019+.

DRY $108 –V

Ma Maison Martinborough Pinot Noir   ★★★★☆

Estate-grown at Martinborough, barrel-matured, and bottled without fining or filtering, the 2015 vintage (★★★★★) is a very elegant red, already drinking well. Full ruby, it is highly fragrant, mouthfilling and supple, with concentrated, ripe plum/spice flavours, finely balanced acidity and a lasting finish. Drink now or cellar.

`DRY $45 –V`

Mahana Pinot Noir   (★★★★☆)

Certified organic, the 2014 vintage (★★★★☆) was estate-grown in Nelson, matured for a year in French oak casks (25 per cent new), and bottled unfined and unfiltered. Ruby-hued, it is mouthfilling and savoury, with generous, ripe cherry and spice flavours, a hint of dried herbs, excellent complexity, and a long, finely balanced finish. An age-worthy red, it should be at its best mid-2018+.

`DRY $39 V+`

Mahi Byrne Marlborough Pinot Noir   (★★★★)

Still on sale, the 2013 vintage (★★★★) is a single-vineyard red, hand-picked at Conders Bend, in the Wairau Valley, and matured for 11 months in French oak barriques. Ruby-hued, with a hint of development, it is ripe and savoury, with cherry and spice flavours, showing good complexity.

Vintage	13
WR	7
Drink	17-24

`DRY $45 –V`

Mahi Marlborough Pinot Noir   ★★★★

The excellent 2015 vintage (★★★★☆) was hand-harvested at three sites (mostly the Twin Valleys Vineyard at Renwick), fermented with indigenous yeasts and matured for 18 months in French oak barrels. Deep ruby, it is fragrant, mouthfilling, savoury and supple, with generous, ripe, plummy flavours, hints of herbs, spices and nuts, and very good complexity and harmony. It's still youthful; drink now or cellar.

Vintage	15	14	13	12
WR	6	6	6	6
Drink	17-23	17-20	17-20	17-18

`DRY $34 AV`

Main Divide North Canterbury Pinot Noir   ★★★★

A consistently rewarding, drink-young style from Pegasus Bay. The 2014 vintage (★★★★) was grown at Waipara. Matured for 18 months in French oak barriques (20 per cent new), it is deep ruby, full-bodied and fresh, with strong, plummy, spicy flavours, savoury notes adding complexity, and a finely textured, persistent finish. Still youthful, it's an age-worthy red, offering great value.

Vintage	14	13	12	11	10	09
WR	6	7	7	5	7	7
Drink	17-23	17-23	17-20	17-18	17-20	17-18

`DRY $25 V+`

Main Divide Tehau Reserve Waipara Valley Pinot Noir   ★★★★

The attractive 2014 vintage (★★★★) was fermented with indigenous yeasts and matured for 18 months in French oak barriques (30 per cent new). Deep ruby, it is mouthfilling, with generous, plummy, spicy flavours and ripe, supple tannins. It's already drinking well. (From Pegasus Bay.)

Vintage	14
WR	6
Drink	17-24

 DRY $33 AV

Maori Point Central Otago Pinot Noir   ★★★★

Retasted in 2017, the 2014 vintage (★★★★) of this single-vineyard wine, grown at Tarras, in the Cromwell Basin, was matured in French oak barrels (20 per cent new), and bottled unfined and unfiltered. Sturdy, sweet-fruited, savoury and smooth, it is ruby-hued, with ripe cherry, plum, spice and nut flavours, showing good complexity. Drink now or cellar.

DRY $39 AV

Maori Point Reserve Central Otago Pinot Noir   (★★★★★)

The fragrant, silky-textured 2014 vintage (★★★★★) was estate-grown at Tarras, in the Cromwell Basin. Barrel-selected, it is a very harmonious, 'complete' red, already delicious, with deep, ripe plum, cherry and nut flavours, savoury and lingering. Drink now or cellar.

 DRY $64 AV

Map Maker Marlborough Pinot Noir   ★★★☆

From Staete Landt, the 2015 vintage (★★★☆) was estate-grown and hand-picked at Rapaura, and matured for 14 months in French oak barriques (10 per cent new). Bright ruby, it is mouthfilling, with fresh, ripe, plummy, spicy flavours, a subtle seasoning of oak adding complexity, and a well-rounded finish. Drink now or cellar.

 DRY $26 AV

Margrain Home Block Martinborough Pinot Noir   ★★★★

The youthful 2015 vintage (★★★★☆) was harvested from mature vines and matured for 18 months in French oak barriques (25 per cent new). Deep ruby, it is mouthfilling and supple, with strong, ripe plum and spice flavours, a hint of liquorice, savoury, nutty notes adding complexity, and good structure and aging potential. Best drinking 2019+.

Vintage	13
WR	7
Drink	17-27

 DRY $45 –V

Margrain Reserve Martinborough Pinot Noir   ★★★★☆

The classy 2015 vintage (★★★★★) is a single-vineyard wine, matured for 18 months in French oak barriques (30 per cent new). A powerful young red, it is deep ruby, with mouthfilling body, strong, very ripe plum/spice flavours, a hint of liquorice, fairly firm tannins and a lasting finish. Best drinking 2019+.

Vintage	15
WR	7
Drink	17-28

 DRY $65 –V

Margrain River's Edge Martinborough Pinot Noir ★★★☆

Designed for early drinking, this wine is 'barrel selected for its smoothness and charm'. The 2014 vintage (★★★☆), matured for a year in seasoned oak casks, then six months in tanks before bottling, is light ruby, mouthfilling, savoury and supple, with ripe cherry, plum and spice flavours, a touch of tannin, and considerable complexity. Ready.

 DRY $26 AV

Vintage	14	13
WR	6	6
Drink	17-22	17-20

Martinborough Vineyard Home Block Pinot Noir ★★★★☆

The 2014 vintage (★★★★☆) is deep ruby, with generous cherry, plum and spice flavours, vibrant and youthful. Savoury and slightly nutty, with good complexity, it's well worth cellaring; open 2018+.

 DRY $68 –V

Martinborough Vineyard Marie Zelie Reserve Pinot Noir ★★★★★

The intriguing 2013 vintage (★★★★★) is the first since 2010. Hand-picked from the oldest vines and matured in French oak barriques, it is all about refinement, rather than sheer power. Light ruby in hue, it is very finely perfumed, with cherry, red-berry and nut flavours, highly complex, very savoury and harmonious. Still youthful, it's a gentle, persuasive, persistent wine, likely to be at its best 2018+.

 DRY $225 –V

Martinborough Vineyard Te Tera Pinot Noir ★★★★

Te Tera ('The Other') is made for early drinking, compared to its stablemates. The 2015 vintage (★★★★) is ruby-hued, very fresh and lively, with generous, youthful cherry, plum and spice flavours, finely integrated oak and gentle tannins.

 DRY $30 AV

Matahiwi Estate Wairarapa Pinot Noir ★★★☆

The finely poised 2015 vintage (★★★★) is already highly enjoyable, but well worth cellaring. Deep ruby, it is mouthfilling and smooth, with fresh acidity, a subtle seasoning of oak, and strong, ripe plum and spice flavours. Priced right.

 DRY $29 AV

Matakana Estate Marlborough Pinot Noir (★★★☆)

The 2015 vintage (★★★☆) is drinking well now. Mouthfilling, with fullish, slightly developed colour, it has plenty of plummy, spicy, slightly leafy and nutty flavour, woven with fresh acidity, and some savoury complexity.

DRY $24 V+

Matt Connell Bendigo Single Vineyard Central Otago Pinot Noir   (★★★★★)

The powerful 2016 vintage (★★★★★) was hand-picked and matured for 10 months in French oak barriques (one-third new). It's a rare wine – only 822 bottles were produced. 'Serious' but very approachable in its youth, it is powerful and fleshy, with very generous, ripe plum/spice flavours, finely integrated oak, excellent complexity, and the structure to mature well. Still youthful, it should be at its best 2019+.

DRY $67 AV

Matua Single Vineyard Central Otago Pinot Noir   ★★★★☆

Grown at Bannockburn, the elegant 2014 vintage (★★★★☆) was hand-harvested and matured for 14 months in French oak barrels (38 per cent new). Deep ruby, it is floral, sweet-fruited and supple, with rich, vibrant cherry and plum flavours, a subtle seasoning of oak adding complexity, and gentle tannins. A youthful, 'feminine' style, it should be at its best 2018+.

DRY $58 –V

Maude Central Otago Pinot Noir   ★★★★☆

The 2015 vintage (★★★★☆) is a floral, finely textured wine, harvested from sites including the home vineyard at Wanaka, and matured for a year in French oak barriques (30 per cent new). Instantly appealing, it is sweet-fruited, with concentrated cherry, plum and spice flavours, well-integrated oak, supple tannins and a long, harmonious finish. Fine value.

Vintage	15	14	13	12	11	10	09	08
WR	6	7	6	6	5	6	5	4
Drink	17-22	17-22	17-22	17-22	17-18	17-20	17-18	P

DRY $32 V+

Maude Mt Maude Vineyard Wanaka Reserve Central Otago Pinot Noir   ★★★★★

Estate-grown at Wanaka, this wine is hand-picked from vines planted in 1994. The 2015 vintage (★★★★☆) was matured for 16 months in French oak casks (40 per cent new). Ruby-hued, it is floral, savoury and complex, with strawberry and spice flavours, hints of dried herbs and nuts, and a fairly firm finish. A distinctive, very age-worthy red, with some ethereal notes, it should be at its best 2019+.

Vintage	15	14	13	12	11	10	09
WR	6	7	6	6	5	6	6
Drink	17-22	17-24	17-22	17-20	17-18	17-20	17-20

DRY $62 AV

Milcrest Estate Nelson Pinot Noir   ★★★

The 2014 vintage (★★) was French oak-aged for 10 months. Light and slightly developed in colour, it is sturdy (14.5 per cent alcohol), with moderate depth of plum/spice flavours, showing a slight lack of freshness. Drink young.

DRY $29 –V

Mill Road New Zealand Pinot Noir

A good-value quaffer, the 2014 vintage (★★☆) is a ruby-hued, mouthfilling, gutsy red, with plenty of ripe, plummy, spicy flavour and a fairly firm finish. It's only moderately 'varietal', but look at the price!

DRY $11 V+

Mills Reef Reserve Marlborough Pinot Noir ★★★

The 2015 vintage (★★★☆) was grown in the Wairau Valley and French oak-aged. Ruby-hued, it is a fruit-driven style, plummy, ripe and smooth, with good flavour depth, a touch of complexity, and lots of drink-young appeal.

DRY $25 –V

Vintage	15	14	13	12
WR	7	6	7	6
Drink	17-20	17-18	P	P

Millton La Cote Gisborne Pinot Noir ★★★★

Certified organic, the thought-provoking 2015 vintage (★★★★☆) was hill-grown, hand-picked, fermented in small wooden French cuves, and bottled unfiltered. Mouthfilling and savoury, with ripe cherry, plum and spice flavours, it is youthful and complex, with excellent harmony and potential; open 2018+. Certified organic.

DRY $30 AV

Vintage	15	14
WR	6	6
Drink	17-20	17-19

Miner's Daughter, The, Reserve McAndrews Reach
North Canterbury Pinot Noir ★★★

The 2014 vintage (★★★) is bright ruby, with mouthfilling body, ripe plum and spice flavours, showing a touch of complexity, and a very smooth finish.

DRY $17 V+

Vintage	14
WR	5
Drink	17-18

Misha's Vineyard The High Note Central Otago Pinot Noir ★★★★☆

Released in 2017, the 2013 vintage (★★★★☆) is an elegant wine, still unfolding. Estate-grown at Bendigo, in the Cromwell Basin, it was harvested at 23.7 to 25.4 brix, fermented with indigenous yeasts and matured in French oak hogsheads (31 per cent new). Full, bright ruby, it is mouthfilling, savoury and complex, with youthful, ripe cherry, plum and spice flavours, balanced acidity, good tannin backbone, and plenty of cellaring potential; best drinking 2019+.

DRY $45 –V

Misha's Vineyard Verismo Central Otago Pinot Noir   ★★★★☆

This 'reserve style' is oak-aged longer, with greater exposure to new oak, than its High Note stablemate. Still on sale, the refined 2011 vintage (★★★★☆) was matured in French oak hogsheads (43 per cent new) and not bottled until December 2012. A generous, silky red, it has lightish colour, with plum, spice and nut flavours, showing excellent complexity and harmony.

Vintage	11	10	09	08
WR	6	7	6	6
Drink	17-22	17-22	17-19	17-20

DRY $63 –V

Mission Martinborough Barrique Reserve Pinot Noir   ★★★★

The 2015 vintage (★★★★☆) is a single-vineyard red, matured for a year in French oak barriques. Full-coloured, it is mouthfilling, with generous, ripe cherry, plum and spice flavours, complex and savoury, and a firm, lingering finish. Still youthful, it's well worth cellaring to 2018+. The 2014 vintage (★★★★) is a very ripe style, with substantial body (15 per cent alcohol). It has full, moderately youthful colour, concentrated cherry and spice flavours, a hint of liquorice, and a fairly firm finish.

Vintage	15	14
WR	7	6
Drink	18-27	17-27

DRY $29 V+

Mission Vineyard Selection Martinborough Pinot Noir   (★★★)

Grown at two sites, in Te Muna and Lake Ferry Road, the 2014 vintage (★★★) was gently oak-aged. Enjoyable early, it is full-bodied (14.5 per cent alcohol), with fresh cherry, plum and spice flavours, a hint of herbs, and good depth.

DRY $20 AV

Misty Cove Signature Marlborough Pinot Noir   ★★★☆

Estate-grown and hand-harvested at Rapaura, in the Wairau Valley, and barrel-matured, the 2014 vintage (★★★☆) only has the word 'Signature' on the back label. Light ruby, it is a savoury, oak-influenced style with ripe cherry, plum and spice flavours, showing some nutty complexity, balanced tannins, and drink-young appeal.

DRY $30 –V

Momo Marlborough Organic Pinot Noir   ★★★☆

Described by Seresin as its 'village wine', the organically certified 2015 vintage (★★★★) offers excellent value. Estate-grown and hand-picked, it was fermented with indigenous yeasts and matured for a year in French oak barriques. Ruby-hued, it is mouthfilling, with youthful, plummy, spicy, slightly nutty flavours, showing considerable complexity, and a fairly firm finish. A more savoury, 'serious' wine than most sub-$25 Pinot Noirs, it should be at its best 2018+.

DRY $24 AV

Mondillo Bella Central Otago Pinot Noir

The 2013 vintage (★★★★★) is not to be missed . . . but it will be by the vast majority of Pinot Noir fans, since there are just 840 bottles. A selection of three 'exceptional' barrels out of 65, it was estate-grown at Bendigo and matured for 22 months in one-year-old French oak casks. Deeply coloured, with a seductively perfumed, complex bouquet, it is generous, sweet-fruited and finely textured, with deep, vibrant cherry, plum and spice flavours, deliciously savoury, silky and 'complete'. A memorable debut.

Vintage	13
WR	7
Drink	17-22

DRY $85 AV

Mondillo Central Otago Pinot Noir   ★★★★★

Estate-grown at Bendigo, in the Cromwell Basin, the 2015 vintage (★★★★☆) was matured for a year in French oak casks (30 per cent new). Deep ruby, it is sturdy (14.5 per cent alcohol), vibrant and supple, with fresh, concentrated, plummy, spicy flavours, slightly earthy and nutty notes adding complexity, and a well-rounded, harmonious finish. Still youthful, it should be at its best 2018+.

Vintage	15	14	13	12	11	10
WR	7	7	7	7	6	7
Drink	17-22	17-22	17-22	17-20	17-18	17-18

DRY $45 AV

Motueka Vineyards Nelson Pinot Noir   (★★☆)

Floral and ruby-hued, the 2014 vintage (★★☆) is fresh and light, with berryish, slightly herbal and spicy flavours, balanced for easy drinking. Priced right. (From Anchorage.)

DRY $18 AV

Mount Brown Estates Grand Reserve North Canterbury Pinot Noir   ★★★★

The generous, well-rounded 2016 vintage (★★★★) was matured for 10 months in French oak barriques (25 per cent new). Deep ruby, with a slightly earthy bouquet, it is full-bodied, fresh and sweet-fruited, with strong cherry, plum and spice flavours, showing considerable complexity, and silky tannins. Already enjoyable, it should be in full stride from mid-2018 onwards.

DRY $30 AV

Mount Brown Estates Waipara Valley Pinot Noir   ★★★

The 2016 vintage (★★★☆) was matured for nine months in French oak barrels (22 per cent new). Ruby-hued, with good depth of vibrant, smooth plum and dried-herb flavours, gently seasoned with oak, it is slightly earthy, with a touch of complexity and lots of drink-young charm.

Vintage	16
WR	6
Drink	17-22

DRY $22 AV

Mount Riley Marlborough Pinot Noir   ★★★☆

The 2014 vintage (★★★) was grown in the Wairau Valley and matured for nine months in French oak barriques. Ruby-hued, it is mouthfilling and smooth, with fresh, ripe, plummy, berryish flavours to the fore, hints of dried herbs and spices, and gentle tannins. A drink-young charmer.

Vintage	14	13
WR	6	6
Drink	17-19	17-18

 DRY $20 V+

Mount Riley Seventeen Valley Marlborough Pinot Noir   ★★★★

The savoury 2014 vintage (★★★☆) was matured for 10 months in French oak barrels (partly new). Deep ruby, it is fresh and youthful, with generous cherry/plum flavours, an earthy streak, and a tight finish. It needs time; open 2018+.

Vintage	14	13
WR	6	6
Drink	17-23	17-22

 DRY $39 AV

Mountain Road Taranaki Pinot Noir   ★★★☆

From vines planted in 2004 at Kairau Lodge, north of New Plymouth, this is a rare red, worth discovering. The light ruby 2015 vintage (★★★☆) is full-bodied and supple, with good ripeness, texture and complexity. Best drinking 2018+.

 DRY $30 –V

Moutere Hills Nelson Pinot Noir   ★★★★

The fragrant, youthful 2015 vintage (★★★★) was estate-grown at Upper Moutere and barrel-matured for 11 months. Full ruby, it is mouthfilling and sweet-fruited, with finely balanced plum/spice flavours, complex and savoury, and obvious potential; best drinking 2018+. The 2016 vintage (★★★★) was also barrel-aged for 11 months. Ripely scented, it is elegant and supple, with fresh plum/spice flavours, savoury notes adding complexity, and lots of drink-young appeal.

DRY $32 AV

Moutere Hills Sarau Reserve Nelson Pinot Noir   (★★★★☆)

Likely to be long-lived, the 2014 vintage (★★★★☆) is a concentrated, estate-grown red, hand-harvested from 17-year-old vines at Upper Moutere. Full and bright in colour, it is mouthfilling and very savoury, with deep, ripe cherry, plum, spice and nutty oak flavours, showing good complexity, moderately firm tannins and good potential. Best drinking 2018+.

 DRY $55 –V

Mt Beautiful North Canterbury Pinot Noir ★★★☆

Maturing gracefully, the 2015 vintage (★★★★) was estate-grown at Cheviot, north of Waipara, and matured for a year in French oak barriques. Full-coloured, it is sturdy, with good weight and strong, ripe cherry, plum and spice flavours, slightly nutty and savoury. Developing good complexity, it should be at its best mid-2018+.

 DRY $33 –V

Vintage	15
WR	7
Drink	17-22

Mt Difficulty Bannockburn Central Otago Pinot Noir ★★★★☆

This popular red is grown at Bannockburn, in the Cromwell Basin. Matured for a year in French oak casks (30 per cent new), the 2014 vintage (★★★★☆) is deep ruby, mouthfilling and supple, with concentrated cherry, plum and spice flavours, gentle tannins, and excellent complexity and harmony. The 2015 vintage (★★★★★) is instantly appealing. Fragrant, mouthfilling and sweet-fruited, it is bright ruby, with rich cherry, plum and spice flavours, nutty, savoury notes adding complexity, good tannin support, and lovely balance and depth. Drink now or cellar.

 DRY $47 –V

Vintage	15	14	13
WR	6	6	6
Drink	17-27	17-26	17-25

Mt Difficulty Growers Series Chinamans Terrace Bendigo Pinot Noir (★★★★★)

The highly refined 2015 vintage (★★★★★) was barrel-matured for 16 months. Deep ruby, it is savoury, ripe and supple, with rich cherry, plum and spice flavours, showing excellent complexity, and a finely textured, long, very harmonious finish. Still very youthful, it's well worth cellaring to 2019+.

 DRY $75 AV

Mt Difficulty Growers Series Packspur Vineyard Pinot Noir ★★★★

The 2015 vintage (★★★★☆) is a single-vineyard Central Otago wine, grown at Lowburn. Matured for 16 months in French oak casks, it is deep ruby, fragrant, full-bodied and supple, with ripe cherry, plum and spice flavours, showing excellent depth and complexity. Full of potential, it's best cellared to at least mid-2018+.

 DRY $75 –V

Vintage	15
WR	6
Drink	17-27

Mud House Central Otago Pinot Noir ★★★★

Estate-grown at Bendigo, in the Claim 431 Vineyard, and matured in tanks and barrels, the 2014 vintage (★★★★) is a fragrant, full-coloured red, mouthfilling and sweet-fruited, with rich plum and spice flavours and supple tannins. Delicious drinking now onwards.

DRY $25 V+

Mud House Estate Claim 431 Vineyard Central Otago Pinot Noir   ★★★★☆

Already drinking well, the 2015 vintage (★★★★☆) was estate-grown at Bendigo, hand-picked and matured for a year in French oak barriques (25 per cent new). Deep ruby, it is fleshy, full-flavoured and finely textured. Showing good complexity, it has vibrant, ripe, cherryish, spicy flavours, excellent harmony, and a savoury, lingering finish. Full of personality, it's a drink-now or cellaring proposition. Fine value.

DRY $33 V+

Mud House Single Vineyard Dambuster Marlborough Pinot Noir   (★★★★)

The debut 2014 vintage (★★★★) is the first single-vineyard red from the company's Woolshed Vineyard, in the upper Wairau Valley. Matured for a year in French oak barrels (25 per cent new), it is ruby-hued, full-bodied and silky-textured, with fresh cherry/plum fruit flavours to the fore, a gentle seasoning of oak adding complexity, and good vigour and harmony. Best drinking 2018+.

DRY $40 –V

Mud House Sub Region Series The Narrows Marlborough Pinot Noir   (★★★☆)

Enjoyable young, the charming 2015 vintage (★★★☆) was grown in the upper Wairau Valley. Bright ruby, it is a fresh, vibrant, sweet-fruited wine, with very good depth of red-berry and plum flavours, and savoury notes adding a touch of complexity.

DRY $20 V+

Muddy Water Hare's Breath Waipara Pinot Noir   ★★★★☆

From 'a block on limestone slopes at the back of the property', the 2012 vintage (★★★★☆), still on sale, was hand-picked, fermented with indigenous yeasts, matured for 16 months in French oak barrels (40 per cent new), and bottled unfined and unfiltered. Certified organic, it is full-coloured and mouthfilling, in a refined, very graceful and distinctly savoury style. Finely textured, it has deep cherry and plum flavours, showing excellent complexity and harmony.

Vintage	12
WR	6
Drink	17-26

DRY $61 –V

Muddy Water Waipara Pinot Noir   ★★★★☆

Estate-grown and hand-harvested, the 2015 vintage (★★★★☆) was matured in French oak casks (25 per cent new). Still youthful, it is deeply coloured, sweet-fruited and supple, with mouthfilling body, a rich surge of cherry, spice and nut flavours, fine-grained tannins, and obvious potential. Open 2018 onwards.

Vintage	15
WR	6
Drink	17-30

DRY $42 AV

Murdoch James Blue Rock Martinborough Pinot Noir ★★★★

Estate-grown south of the township, the 2014 vintage (★★★★) was hand-picked and matured in French oak barrels. Delicious young, but also worth cellaring, it is bright ruby, floral and supple, with ripe cherry, plum and spice flavours, gentle tannins, good complexity and a smooth, harmonious finish.

DRY $50 –V

Nanny Goat Vineyard Central Otago Pinot Noir ★★★★☆

The attractive 2015 vintage (★★★★☆) is a generous, deep ruby red with vibrant, ripe plum, cherry and spice flavours, showing excellent depth and complexity. A refined wine, it is weighty and harmonious, with fine-grained tannins and good aging potential.

 DRY $36 V+

Nautilus Awatere River Vineyard Marlborough Pinot Noir (★★★★★)

Grown in the upper Awatere Valley, the debut 2014 vintage (★★★★★) is a single-vineyard red, matured in French oak casks (33 per cent new). Full ruby, it is very finely textured, with rich, vibrant plum, spice and dried-herb flavours, gentle tannins and a long finish. Already lovely, but also age-worthy, with a sense of youthful drive, it should be at its best 2018+.

DRY $70 AV

Nautilus Clay Hills Vineyard Marlborough Pinot Noir ★★★★☆

The 2015 vintage (★★★★☆) is a single-vineyard red, grown in the Southern Valleys and matured in French oak casks (33 per cent new). Full, bright ruby, with a slightly earthy bouquet, it is mouthfilling, supple and vibrantly fruity, with strong, ripe cherry, plum and spice flavours, and finely integrated oak adding complexity. Drink now or cellar.

 DRY $70 –V

Nautilus Four Barriques Marlborough Pinot Noir ★★★★★

The beautiful 2013 vintage (★★★★★) is rare – four out of over 120 barrels. Matured for 18 months in French oak barrels (50 per cent new), it has deep, fairly youthful colour. Very fragrant and sweet-fruited, it has rich cherry, plum, spice and dried-herb flavours, finely textured and seamless. Drink now or cellar.

Vintage	13	12	11	10	09
WR	7	7	NM	7	7
Drink	17-23	17-20	NM	17-20	17-18

DRY $85 AV

Nautilus Southern Valleys Marlborough Pinot Noir ★★★★☆

(This label has replaced the former Nautilus Marlborough Pinot Noir.) The 2015 vintage (★★★★☆) was matured in French oak casks (30 per cent new). Deep ruby, with a slightly earthy bouquet, it is mouthfilling, sweet-fruited and supple, with generous cherry, plum and spice flavours, showing very good complexity. It's already drinking well.

 DRY $42 AV

Vintage	15	14
WR	7	7
Drink	17-23	17-22

Neudorf Moutere Pinot Noir ★★★★★

Typically a very classy Nelson red. It is hand-picked from 'older vines' at Upper Moutere, fermented with indigenous yeasts, matured for 10 to 12 months in French oak barriques (18 per cent new in 2015), and usually bottled without fining or filtering. The impressive 2015 vintage (★★★★★) is deep ruby, mouthfilling and savoury, with dense, ripe plum and spice flavours, showing excellent complexity and harmony. It should be long-lived; best drinking 2020+.

Vintage	15	14	13	12	11	10
WR	7	6	6	7	6	7
Drink	19-22	17-21	17-20	17-23	17-18	17-18

DRY $59 AV

Neudorf Tom's Block Nelson Pinot Noir ★★★★

This regional blend can offer fine value. The 2015 vintage (★★★★☆) was hand-harvested at three Moutere sites (including the Home Block), matured in French oak barriques (22 per cent new), and bottled without fining or filtration. Still unfolding, it is a deep ruby, mouthfilling red, savoury and smooth, with ripe plum, cherry and spice flavours, seasoned with nutty oak, and excellent depth and complexity. Best drinking mid-2018+.

Vintage	15	14	13	12	11	10
WR	7	6	6	7	6	7
Drink	17-22	17-21	17-20	17-19	P	P

DRY $33 AV

Nevis Bluff Central Otago Pinot Noir ★★★

Currently on sale, the 2012 vintage (★★★☆) was matured for 10 months in French oak casks (20 per cent new). Ready for drinking, it has mature colour, mouthfilling body and spicy, nutty, slightly herbal flavours, showing considerable complexity.

Vintage	12	11	10
WR	6	5	6
Drink	17-22	17-18	17-18

DRY $48 –V

Nevis Bluff Reserve Central Otago Pinot Noir ★★★★

The 2014 vintage (★★★★) was matured for a year in French oak casks (35 per cent new). Ruby-hued, with some development showing, it is fragrant and full-bodied, with strong cherry, plum, spice and herb flavours, and nutty oak adding complexity. Best drinking mid-2018+.

Vintage	14
WR	6
Drink	17-22

DRY $85 –V

Nga Waka Martinborough Lease Block Pinot Noir

Still very youthful, the 2015 vintage (★★★★★) is a single-vineyard red, from vines planted in 1999. Matured for a year in French oak casks (40 per cent new), it is deeply coloured, mouthfilling, weighty and sweet-fruited, with concentrated, ripe cherry, plum and spice flavours, fine-grained tannins, and excellent complexity. A powerful Pinot Noir in the classic Martinborough style, it should be at its best 2019+.

Vintage	15	14	13
WR	6	7	7
Drink	17-24	17-23	17-18

DRY $50 AV

Nga Waka Martinborough Pinot Noir

The highly attractive 2016 vintage (★★★★☆) was matured for a year in French oak casks (30 per cent new). Deep ruby, it is floral, mouthfilling, sweet-fruited and savoury, with cherry, plum and spice flavours, showing excellent depth and harmony. Drink now or cellar.

Vintage	16	15	14	13
WR	6	6	7	7
Drink	18-25	17-24	17-23	P

DRY $40 –V

Ngatarawa Stables Reserve Hawke's Bay Pinot Noir

A drink-young style. The 2014 vintage (★★☆) is light ruby, floral and supple, with cherry, plum and dried-herb flavours, gentle tannins and a smooth finish.

Vintage	14
WR	6
Drink	17-20

DRY $20 –V

Nikau Point Reserve Marlborough Pinot Noir ★★★

Priced sharply, the 2016 vintage (★★★) was partly (40 per cent) barrel-aged. Bright ruby, it is fresh, vibrantly fruity and supple, with ripe, plummy, slightly spicy flavours. A drink-young charmer.

DRY $14 V+

Nor'Wester by Greystone North Canterbury Pinot Noir

The debut 2015 vintage (★★★★☆) offers fine value. Not estate-grown, it was hand-picked at Omihi at 24 brix, fermented with indigenous yeasts and matured for 16 months in French oak barrels (30 per cent new). Deep ruby, it is fragrant, mouthfilling, supple and savoury, in an instantly appealing, sweet-fruited style with generous cherry, plum, spice and nut flavours, showing excellent complexity and harmony. Drink now or cellar.

DRY $33 V+

Odyssey Marlborough Pinot Noir   ★★★★

Certified organic, the 2015 vintage (★★★★) was estate-grown in the Brancott Valley and matured in French oak barriques (30 per cent new). Full-coloured, it is mouthfilling, with excellent depth of youthful, ripe cherry, plum and spice flavours, showing good complexity, and a backbone of fine-grained tannins. A very age-worthy red, likely to be at its best from 2019 onwards, it's priced sharply.

DRY $26 V+

Odyssey Reserve Iliad Marlborough Pinot Noir   (★★★★☆)

The 2014 vintage (★★★★☆) is an impressive debut. Certified organic, it was estate-grown in the Brancott Valley, hand-picked and matured in French oak casks (27 per cent new). A powerful, sweet-fruited and generous wine, it has deep, youthful plum and spice flavours, good complexity and a finely textured, lasting finish. Already delicious, it should be at its best 2018+.

Vintage	14
WR	6
Drink	17-20

DRY $42 AV

Old Coach Road Nelson Pinot Noir   ★★☆

From Seifried, the 2014 vintage (★★☆) was matured for a year in French oak barriques (partly new). Light ruby, it is fresh and light, with strawberry and spice flavours, a hint of herbs, gentle tannins and drink-young appeal. Priced right.

DRY $16 AV

Omeo Hidden Valley Central Otago Pinot Noir   (★★★★)

Still unfolding, the 2014 vintage (★★★★) was grown at Alexandra and matured for 10 months in seasoned French oak casks. Ruby-hued, it is fragrant and savoury, with moderately concentrated, ripe cherry, plum, spice and nut flavours, a hint of dried herbs, good complexity, and a fairly firm finish. Best drinking 2019–20.

Vintage	14
WR	6
Drink	17-21

DRY $30 AV

Omihi Hills Limestone Ridge Pinot Noir   ★★★★

The great-value 2014 vintage (★★★★) was grown at Waipara and handled in seasoned oak. 'Made to be enjoyed in its youth', it is bright ruby, with mouthfilling body, strong, plummy, spicy flavours, balanced tannins and good complexity. Well worth cellaring, it's a great buy.

Vintage	14	13
WR	5	7
Drink	17-18	17-19

DRY $20 V+

Opawa Marlborough Pinot Noir   ★★★☆

From Nautilus, the 2016 vintage (★★★☆) was harvested from mature vines grown on the Wairau Valley floor, fermented with indigenous yeasts and fully barrel-aged (10 per cent new). Bright ruby, with a slightly earthy bouquet, it is mouthfilling and smooth, with good depth of ripe cherry, plum and spice flavours, moderate complexity, some funky notes adding interest, and lots of drink-young appeal. Best drinking mid-2018+.

DRY $28 AV

Osawa Winemaker's Collection Hawke's Bay Pinot Noir   (★★★★☆)

Delicious now, the 2014 vintage (★★★★☆) was matured in French oak casks (90 per cent new). Full-bodied and fleshy, it has concentrated cherry, plum and spice flavours, showing good complexity, and velvety tannins.

DRY $85 –V

Ostler Blue House Vines Waitaki Valley Pinot Noir   ★★★★

Part of Ostler's 'grower selection' (it is not estate-grown), the 2015 vintage (★★★★) was matured for 10 months in old French oak barriques. Ruby-hued, it is a graceful red, vibrant and supple, with fresh cherry and plum flavours, gently seasoned with oak, and very good depth and harmony. Best drinking mid-2018+.

DRY $30 AV

Ostler Caroline's Waitaki Valley Pinot Noir   ★★★★☆

Estate-grown in North Otago, the 2015 vintage (★★★★☆) was matured in French oak casks (20 per cent new). Still youthful, it is a deep ruby, mouthfilling red, firmly structured, with concentrated plum/spice flavours, savoury and complex. Best drinking 2019+.

DRY $59 –V

Overstone Hawke's Bay Pinot Noir   ★★★

From Sileni, the 2015 vintage (★★★) is light ruby, mouthfilling and sweet-fruited, with gentle tannins, slightly savoury notes and plenty of flavour. Fine value.

DRY $13 V+

Oyster Bay Marlborough Pinot Noir   ★★★☆

The 2016 vintage (★★★☆) was grown in the Wairau and Awatere valleys, and partly barrel-matured. Bright ruby, it is already drinking well, with fresh, ripe, slightly savoury and nutty flavours, generous and well-rounded.

DRY $25 AV

Pa Road Marlborough Pinot Noir   ★★★☆

Grown in the Southern Valleys, the 2015 vintage (★★★☆) was partly barrel-aged. Ruby-hued, it is fresh and full-bodied, with very good depth of plummy, spicy, slightly herbal flavours, moderate complexity and fine-grained tannins. Great value. The 2016 vintage (★★★☆) is similar – light ruby, fresh and supple, with mouthfilling body and ripe cherry/plum flavours, delicious young. (From te Pa.)

DRY $18 V+

Paddy Borthwick Falloon Block New Zealand Pinot Noir   ★★★★

Offering fine value, the 2016 vintage (★★★★) is a single-vineyard red, grown in the Wairarapa. Bright ruby, it is fresh, mouthfilling and lively, with ripe cherry, plum and spice flavours, nutty, savoury notes adding complexity, and good potential. Best drinking 2019+.

DRY $26 V+

Paddy Borthwick Left Hand New Zealand Pinot Noir   ★★★★

Estate-grown in the Wairarapa, this rare wine (70 cases per year) gives left-handed winemaker Braden Crosby the chance to express his 'logical, precise' approach. The 2014 vintage (★★★★) is an elegant red, mouthfilling and savoury, with vibrant plum and dried-herb flavours, generous and supple. The 2013 vintage (★★★★☆) has deep, fairly youthful colour. Mouthfilling and sweet-fruited, it is plummy, spicy and savoury, with fairly firm tannins, and very good concentration and complexity. Best drinking 2018+.

DRY $50 –V

Paddy Borthwick New Zealand Pinot Noir   ★★★★

Grown in the Wairarapa, the 2016 vintage (★★★★☆) is a single-vineyard red, deeply coloured and mouthfilling. A powerful wine, it has highly concentrated, ripe plum and dried-herb flavours, well-integrated oak, and the structure to mature well. Still very youthful, it's best cellared to 2019+.

DRY $34 AV

Paddy Borthwick Right Hand New Zealand Pinot Noir   ★★★★☆

Estate-grown, this is a rare wine (only 70 cases per year), made by Wairarapa winemaker Paddy Borthwick, an 'intuitive, impulsive', right-handed vigneron. The 2014 vintage (★★★★☆) is powerful, with concentrated, ripe, savoury, nutty flavours, youthful, complex and well-rounded. The 2013 vintage (★★★★★) is delicious now, but also worth cellaring. Deep ruby, it is mouthfilling, with strong cherry, plum, dried-herb and spice flavours, showing excellent complexity and harmony, good tannin backbone, and an invitingly fragrant bouquet.

DRY $50 –V

Palliser Estate Martinborough Pinot Noir   ★★★★★

This is typically an enticingly perfumed, notably elegant and harmonious red. The 2015 vintage (★★★★☆) was harvested at four sites from five to 18-year-old vines, fermented with indigenous yeasts and matured for a year in French oak casks (25 per cent new). Ruby-hued, it is youthful and savoury, with mouthfilling body, strong, ripe cherry, plum, spice and nut flavours, showing very good complexity, and fine-grained tannins. Best drinking mid-2018+.

DRY $57 AV

Paua Marlborough Pinot Noir ★★★

From Highfield, the 2014 vintage (★★★) was French oak-aged for 10 months. Enjoyable young, it has lightish, moderately youthful colour, mouthfilling body and ripe cherry, plum, spice and herb flavours, showing a touch of complexity.

Vintage	14
WR	6
Drink	P

 DRY $25 –V

Paul Henry's Own Central Otago Pinot Noir ★★★★

From Invivo, the softly mouthfilling 2016 vintage (★★★★) was grown at four sites. Floral, with berry and dried-herb aromas, it is deep ruby, full-bodied and smooth, in a sweet-fruited style with generous cherry, plum and spice flavours, gentle tannins and loads of drink-young appeal. Best drinking 2018–19.

 DRY $30 AV

Pegasus Bay Aged Release Pinot Noir (★★★★☆)

Re-released in August 2017, the 2007 vintage (★★★★☆) is the first of a planned annual release of 10-year-old wines from this top, long-established Waipara producer. Deep ruby, with mature edges, it is mouthfilling and smooth, with generous, mellow flavours, plummy, spicy, nutty and slightly herbal, and good complexity. It's probably at its peak.

 DRY $65 –V

Pegasus Bay Prima Donna Pinot Noir ★★★★★

For its top Waipara red, Pegasus Bay wants 'a heavenly voice, a shapely body and a velvety nose'. Based on the oldest vines, it is matured for 15 to 18 months in French oak barriques (50 per cent new). The 2013 vintage (★★★★★) is very refined. Deep and fairly youthful in colour, it is ripely scented, mouthfilling, sweet-fruited and supple, with lovely depth of plummy, spicy flavours, velvety tannins, and notable complexity and harmony. A rich, very graceful wine, it will be long-lived.

Vintage	13	12	11	10	09	08	07	06
WR	6	7	6	7	7	NM	NM	7
Drink	18-28	17-28	17-23	17-25	P	NM	NM	17-18

 DRY $95 AV

Pegasus Bay Waipara Valley Pinot Noir ★★★★★

This is one of North Canterbury's greatest Pinot Noirs, typically very rich in body and flavour. Many of the vines are over 25 years old and the wine is matured for 18 months in French oak barriques (about 40 per cent new). The 2014 vintage (★★★★★) is fragrant, with deep, youthful colour. Already delicious, it is weighty, with concentrated, very ripe plum and spice flavours, a vague hint of liquorice, and a well-rounded, lasting finish. Drink now or cellar.

Vintage	14	13	12	11	10	09	08
WR	6	6	7	6	6	6	6
Drink	17-26	17-29	17-28	17-23	17-20	17-18	P

 DRY $50 AV

Pencarrow Martinborough Pinot Noir ★★★★

This is Palliser Estate's second-tier label, but in most years it is impressive and offers good value. Already drinking well, the 2015 vintage (★★★★) was grown at six sites, fermented with indigenous yeasts and matured for 11 months in French oak casks (27 per cent new). Bright ruby, it is mouthfilling, very harmonious and smooth, with very satisfying depth of cherry, plum, spice and nut flavours, in the classic, well-ripened, savoury regional style.

 DRY $29 V+

People's, The, Central Otago Pinot Noir ★★★

From Constellation NZ, the 2014 vintage (★★★) has lightish, moderately youthful colour. A mouthfilling red, grown at Alexandra, it is enjoyable young, with satisfying depth of plummy, spicy flavour, showing some toasty, savoury complexity, and a smooth finish.

 DRY $24 AV

Peregrine Central Otago Pinot Noir ★★★★★

Outstanding in top seasons, this classic red is grown mostly in the Cromwell Basin, but also at Gibbston. The 2015 vintage (★★★★★) is a blend of Bendigo, Pisa and Gibbston grapes. Full, bright ruby, with a fragrant, savoury bouquet, it is generous, complex and supple, with ripe, youthful cherry, plum, spice and dried-herb flavours, concentrated and finely textured, and some earthy, 'funky' notes adding interest. Still youthful, it's already delicious.

 DRY $45 AV

Peter Yealands Marlborough Pinot Noir ★★★

The 2014 vintage (★★★) was made for early consumption; 'a portion of the parcels spent some time in third-year French oak barrels'. Ruby-hued, it is vibrant, with lively plum and dried-herb flavours, showing good vigour and depth.

Vintage	14	13
WR	7	7
Drink	17-18	P

 DRY $18 V+

Peter Yealands Reserve Awatere Valley Marlborough Pinot Noir ★★★☆

The 2016 vintage (★★★☆) is drinking well from the start. Partly barrel-aged, it is ruby-hued, fresh and softly mouthfilling, with vibrant red-berry, spice and dried-herb flavours, a touch of complexity, and a well-rounded finish.

 DRY $22 V+

Petit Clos by Clos Henri Marlborough Pinot Noir ★★★☆

Based on young vines, estate-grown and hand-harvested in the Wairau Valley, the 2016 vintage (★★★☆) was matured in large (7500-litre) French oak vats. Ruby-hued, it is a slightly earthy and savoury wine, with mouthfilling body and ripe plum, cherry and spice flavours, showing good depth. Drink now or cellar. Certified organic.

Vintage	16
WR	6
Drink	17-20

 DRY $26 AV

Pied Stilt Nelson Pinot Noir

The 2014 vintage (★★★) is a single-vineyard red. Ruby-hued, it is mouthfilling and supple, with cherry, plum, spice and herb flavours, showing a touch of complexity. Enjoyable young.

DRY $25 –V

Pisa Range Estate Black Poplar Block Pinot Noir

Estate-grown at Pisa Flats, north of Cromwell, in Central Otago, this classy, enticingly scented wine is well worth discovering. The 2014 vintage (★★★★★) was picked from the oldest vines and matured for a year in French oak barriques (33 per cent new). Deeply coloured, it is weighty and highly concentrated, with deep, ripe, youthful plum and spice flavours, showing excellent complexity, good tannin backbone, and obvious cellaring potential; open 2018+.

Vintage	14	13	12	11	10	09	08
WR	6	7	6	NM	6	7	7
Drink	17-26	17-25	17-23	NM	17-23	17-18	P

DRY $56 AV

Pisa Range Estate Run 245 Central Otago Pinot Noir

The 2014 vintage (★★★★) was hand-harvested from 'younger' vines (averaging over 10 years old) and matured in French oak barriques. It's a mouthfilling, generous red, full-coloured, with rich, ripe, plummy, spicy, youthful flavours, showing some savoury complexity, finely balanced tannins and good harmony.

Vintage	14
WR	7
Drink	17-18

DRY $32 AV

Prophet's Rock Home Vineyard Central Otago Pinot Noir

This consistently rewarding red is estate-grown at a high-altitude site at Bendigo, in the Cromwell Basin. Barrel-aged for 17 months (35 per cent new oak) and bottled unfiltered, the classy 2014 vintage (★★★★★) has full, fairly youthful colour. Mouthfilling, it is notably savoury and complex, with ripe plum, spice and nut flavours, concentrated, silky-textured and sustained. Already drinking well, it's well worth cellaring to 2019+.

Vintage	14	13
WR	7	7
Drink	17-28	17-26

DRY $66 AV

Prophet's Rock Infusion Central Otago Pinot Noir

The softly seductive 2016 vintage (★★★★) was estate-grown at Bendigo. All freshness and suppleness, it was 'made without the normal extraction from the grape skins during fermentation. Instead, the wine was fermented using indigenous wild yeast in old barrels, after being pressed and removed from its skins.' Veering in style towards rosé or Beaujolais, it's full of personality, with vibrant, ripe, gentle, cherryish flavours, full of drink-young charm.

Vintage	16
WR	6
Drink	17-20

DRY $36 AV

Pruner's Reward, The, Waipara Valley Pinot Noir ★★★

From Bellbird Spring, the 2014 vintage (★★★) was matured for a year in French oak casks (15 per cent new). Ruby-hued, with some development, it is medium-bodied, with cherry, plum, herb and nut flavours, showing some complexity. Drink now to 2018.

 DRY $27 –V

Quartz Reef Bendigo Estate Pinot Noir ★★★★★

This black-label red is estate-grown on a steep, warm, north-facing site at Bendigo, in Central Otago. The 2015 vintage (★★★★★) was matured for 15 months in French oak barriques. Deep and youthful in colour, it is mouthfilling and sweet-fruited, with strong cherry, plum and spice flavours, a hint of liquorice, and a long, harmonious finish. Very savoury, complex and rounded, it's a drink-now or cellaring proposition.

Vintage	15	14	13	12	11	10	09	08
WR	7	7	7	7	6	6	NM	7
Drink	17-22	17-22	17-20	17-19	17-18	P	NM	P

 DRY $79 AV

Quartz Reef Bendigo Estate Single Vineyard Central Otago Pinot Noir ★★★★★

Certified biodynamic, the classy 2016 vintage (★★★★★) was estate-grown at Bendigo, hand-picked and matured for a year in French oak barriques. Full, bright ruby, it is fragrant and mouthfilling, savoury and supple, with deep cherry, plum, spice and nut flavours, showing excellent complexity. A very harmonious and 'complete' wine, it's already delicious, but also age-worthy.

Vintage	16	15	14	13	12	11	10
WR	6	6	7	7	7	6	6
Drink	17-21	17-22	17-20	17-19	17-18	P	P

 DRY $49 AV

Rapaura Springs Marlborough Pinot Noir ★★★

The 2015 vintage (★★★) is ruby-hued and sweet-fruited, with plummy, spicy flavours, showing a touch of complexity, and a well-rounded finish. Enjoyable young.

Vintage	15	14	13	12
WR	6	6	6	5
Drink	17-21	17-20	17-19	P

 DRY $25 –V

Rapaura Springs Reserve Central Otago Pinot Noir ★★★☆

The 2016 vintage (★★★☆), partly barrel-aged for nine months, is a deep ruby, boldly fruity red. Mouthfilling, it has fresh, strong plum, cherry and spice flavours, in a moderately complex style, likely to be at its best mid-2018+.

Vintage	16	15	14	13	12	11
WR	6	7	5	7	6	6
Drink	17-23	17-22	17-20	17-20	17-20	P

 DRY $29 AV

Rapaura Springs Reserve Marlborough Pinot Noir ★★★☆

The 2016 vintage (★★★☆) was partly barrel-aged for nine months. Bright ruby, with a slightly earthy bouquet, it is mouthfilling, with youthful cherry and plum flavours, showing some savoury complexity, in a fresh, lively style with very good depth.

Vintage	16	15
WR	7	7
Drink	17-25	17-22

 DRY $29 AV

RD Central Otago Pinot Noir (★★★☆)

The 2014 vintage (★★★☆) is a bargain-priced, attractive Bannockburn red with good depth of plum, spice and dried-herb flavours in a floral, easy-drinking style.

 DRY $22 V+

Renato Nelson Pinot Noir ★★★☆

The 2016 vintage (★★★☆) was hand-picked at Kina and matured for 10 months in French oak barriques (20 per cent new). Already enjoyable, it's a slightly earthy red, full-bodied, with cherry, plum, spice and nut flavours, showing considerable complexity, and supple tannins. Drink now or cellar.

Vintage	16	15	14	13	12	11	10
WR	5	NM	7	5	7	6	5
Drink	18-22	NM	17-21	17-19	17-20	P	P

DRY $25 AV

Rendition Central Otago Pinot Noir (★★★★☆)

Delicious young, the debut 2016 vintage (★★★★☆) from Matt Connell offers an enticing blend of richness and early approachability. Hand-picked at Bendigo and Lowburn, it was matured for 10 months in French oak barriques (25 per cent new). Deeply coloured, it is mouthfilling, sweet-fruited and vibrantly fruity, with very generous, plummy, slightly spicy flavours, savoury notes adding complexity and a silky-smooth finish.

 DRY $44 AV

Ribbonwood Marlborough Pinot Noir ★★★

The 2014 vintage (★★★) is light ruby, mouthfilling and supple, with satisfying depth of ripe plum, strawberry and spice flavours, showing a touch of complexity. Enjoyable young. (From Framingham.)

DRY $25 –V

Richmond Plains Nelson Pinot Noir ★★★☆

Certified biodynamic, the 2015 vintage (★★★★) was matured in French oak casks (22 per cent new). Bright ruby, it has concentrated, ripe plum and spice flavours, showing some oak complexity, and a lingering finish. Best drinking 2018+.

 DRY $29 AV

Rimu Grove Nelson Pinot Noir   ★★★★☆

Estate-grown near Mapua, on the Nelson coast, this is typically a rich wine with plenty of
personality. The 2015 vintage (★★★★☆), French oak-matured, is a deep ruby, mouthfilling
red, with generous plum, spice and dried-herb flavours, showing excellent density and
complexity. Drinking well now, it should be at its best 2019+.

Vintage	15	14	13	12	11	10	09	08
WR	7	7	7	7	7	7	6	6
Drink	18-30	17-30	17-30	17-30	17-27	17-25	17-23	17-22

DRY $39 V+

Rimu Grove Synergy Nelson Pinot Noir   (★★★★★)

The powerful 2015 vintage (★★★★★) was estate-grown at Moutere and French oak-matured.
Deep and bright in colour, it is rich and complex, with concentrated, very ripe plum/spice
flavours, hints of herbs and nuts, silky-smooth tannins, and great depth through the palate.
Drink now or cellar.

Vintage	15
WR	7
Drink	18-35

DRY $98 –V

Rippon 'Rippon' Mature Vine Central Otago Pinot Noir   ★★★★★

This Lake Wanaka red has a long, proud history. Estate-grown but not a single-block wine
– winemaker Nick Mills views it as 'the farm voice' – it is typically a very elegant, 'feminine'
style, rather than a blockbuster. Hand-picked from ungrafted vines planted between 1985 and
1991, the 2013 vintage (★★★★★) was matured in French oak barrels (30 per cent new), and
bottled unfined and unfiltered. Rich and fairly youthful in colour, it is highly scented and very
savoury, with dense plum/spice flavours, a sense of youthful vigour, and a fairly firm finish.
Best drinking 2019+.

Vintage	13
WR	7
Drink	17-23

DRY $59 AV

Riverby Estate Marlborough Pinot Noir   ★★★☆

This single-vineyard red is grown in the heart of the Wairau Valley and French oak-aged. The
2015 vintage (★★★★) is bright ruby, mouthfilling, sweet-fruited and smooth, with ripe cherry,
plum and spice flavours, well-integrated oak, and lots of drink-young appeal.

DRY $27 AV

Riverby Estate Reserve Marlborough Pinot Noir   ★★★☆

The 2014 vintage (★★★★) of this single-vineyard, Rapaura red was hand-picked and barrel-
aged. Ruby-hued, it is mouthfilling, with concentrated cherry, plum, spice and nut flavours,
ripe and savoury, showing good complexity. The 2013 vintage (★★★☆) is probably at its peak,
with good body and plenty of flavour, ripe and rounded.

DRY $35 –V

Roaring Meg Central Otago Pinot Noir ★★★☆

From Mt Difficulty, the 2015 vintage (★★★☆) of this highly popular red was hand-picked and matured for nine months in French oak casks. Bright ruby, it is an attractively perfumed, sweet-fruited wine, medium to full-bodied, with good depth of plum and spice flavours, ripe and seductively smooth. Best drinking now to 2018.

 DRY $30 –V

Rock Ferry 3rd Rock Central Otago Pinot Noir ★★★★★

Estate-grown at a high-altitude site at Bendigo, in the Cromwell Basin, the 2014 vintage (★★★★★) was matured in French oak barriques. Deep and youthful in colour, it is mouthfilling, with rich, vibrant cherry, plum and dried-herb flavours, showing excellent complexity, and a fairly firm finish. Powerful, with strong personality, it's well worth cellaring. Certified organic.

 DRY $45 AV

Rock Ferry Trig Hill Vineyard Pinot Noir ★★★★★

The lovely 2013 vintage (★★★★★) was estate-grown, 400 metres above sea level, at Bendigo, in Central Otago. Hand-picked, it was fermented with indigenous yeasts, matured for 20 months in French oak barriques and puncheons (30 per cent new), and bottled unfined and unfiltered. Deep and bright in colour, it is finely scented and supple, with deep, ripe plum/spice flavours, hints of dried herbs and nuts, excellent complexity, and a long, tightly structured finish. Drink now or cellar. Certified organic.

 DRY $65 AV

Rockburn Central Otago Pinot Noir ★★★★★

This consistently stylish blend of Cromwell Basin (mostly) and Gibbston grapes typically has concentrated cherry, plum and dried-herb flavours, silky-textured and perfumed. The 2015 vintage (★★★★☆) was grown at Parkburn (86 per cent) and Gibbston (14 per cent), and matured for 10 months in French oak casks (35 per cent new). Floral and finely textured, it is a mouthfilling, supple and fruit-packed wine. Deep ruby, with strong cherry, plum and herb flavours, it is very harmonious, with drink-young appeal, but also good cellaring potential. The 2016 vintage (★★★★☆) is full-coloured and fragrant, with mouthfilling body and generous, vibrant cherry, plum and spice flavours, ripe and rounded. Delicious from the start.

Vintage	16	15	14	13	12	11	10	09
WR	7	6	7	7	6	6	7	7
Drink	17-27	17-26	17-24	17-23	17-22	17-20	17-20	17-18

DRY $45 AV

Rockburn Nine Barrels Central Otago Pinot Noir (★★★★★)

The very classy 2015 vintage (★★★★★) is a single-vineyard red, grown at Parkburn, in the Cromwell Basin. Based entirely on the 10/5 clone, it was fermented with indigenous yeasts and matured for 16 months in French oak casks (33 per cent new). Full, bright ruby, it is mouthfilling, savoury and supple, with generous, ripe cherry, plum and spice flavours, showing lovely depth, complexity and harmony. Finely textured, it's a very 'complete' wine, already drinking well.

Vintage	15
WR	7
Drink	17-30

 DRY $95 AV

Rockburn Seven Barrels Central Otago Pinot Noir   (★★★★★)

The notably graceful, silky-textured 2016 vintage (★★★★★) is a single-vineyard red, grown in the Gibbston Back Road Vineyard, barrel-matured (43 per cent new), and bottled without fining or filtering. Deep and youthful in colour, it is fragrant and full-bodied, with very generous, well-ripened plum and spice flavours, a hint of dried herbs, a seasoning of nutty oak, and excellent complexity and length. Very savoury and supple, it's already delicious, but well worth cellaring to 2020+.

Vintage	16
WR	7
Drink	17-32

DRY $95 AV

Rockburn The Art Central Otago Pinot Noir   (★★★★★)

Distinctive and thought-provoking, the 2016 vintage (★★★★★) is a single-vineyard red, grown at Bannockburn and matured for 10 months in French oak casks (43 per cent new), followed by 'extended aging in old barrels'. Full-coloured, with some development showing, it is highly fragrant and very savoury, in an elegant style with fresh acidity, a hint of herbs, excellent complexity and a very long, finely textured finish. It's already delicious.

Vintage	16
WR	7
Drink	18-30

DRY $99 AV

Rocky Point Central Otago Pinot Noir   ★★★★

From Prophet's Rock, the 2016 vintage (★★★★) was hand-picked at Bendigo, fermented with indigenous yeasts and matured for 10 months in French oak casks (15 per cent new). Deeply coloured, it is fresh, mouthfilling and supple, with generous, ripe, plummy, gently spicy flavours, savoury notes adding complexity and a well-rounded, very harmonious finish. Best drinking mid-2018+.

Vintage	16
WR	7
Drink	17-26

DRY $30 AV

Rod McDonald One Off Martinborough Pinot Noir   (★★★★)

The 2014 vintage (★★★★) was grown at Te Muna and matured in French oak barriques (10 per cent new). Deep ruby, it is fragrant, with good weight and depth of cherryish, plummy, spicy, slightly nutty flavours. Savoury and supple, it shows good complexity. Ready.

DRY $32 AV

Rossendale Canterbury Pinot Noir   (★★★)

Ruby-hued, the 2015 vintage (★★★) is a fresh, medium-bodied red, vibrantly fruity, with plummy, slightly spicy and toasty flavours and gentle tannins. An attractive, drink-young style, it's priced sharply.

DRY $16 V+

Rossendale Marlborough Pinot Noir (★★☆)

Priced right, the 2016 vintage (★★☆) is light ruby, with a slightly earthy bouquet. Fresh, berryish and spicy, with hints of herbs and nuts, and a smooth finish, it's a drink-young style.

DRY $16 AV

Ruru Central Otago Pinot Noir ★★★☆

From Immigrant's Vineyard, at Alexandra, the 2015 vintage (★★★☆) was French oak-aged for 10 months. Full ruby, it is mouthfilling, with very good depth of ripe plum and spice flavours, earthy, savoury notes and a moderately firm finish. The 2016 vintage (★★★☆) was also matured in French oak (20 per cent new) for 10 months. Bright ruby, it is mouthfilling, with plenty of plummy, spicy flavour, fairly firm tannins, and some cellaring potential; open mid-2018+.

Vintage	16	15
WR	5	5
Drink	18-26	17-22

DRY $26 AV

Russian Jack Martinborough Pinot Noir ★★★☆

From Martinborough Vineyard, the 2014 vintage (★★★) was partly barrel-aged. Light ruby, it is moderately concentrated, with ripe plum and spice flavours, a hint of dried herbs, gentle tannins and a touch of complexity.

DRY $20 V+

Sacred Hill Halo Marlborough Pinot Noir ★★★★

The 2015 vintage (★★★★) is a deep ruby, generous, supple red, hand-picked in the Omaka Valley and matured for eight months in French oak barrels (25 per cent new). It has good concentration of plummy, cherryish flavours, a sense of youthful vigour, and fine-grained tannins. Best drinking 2018+.

Vintage	15
WR	6
Drink	17-18

DRY $28 AV

Sacred Hill Marlborough Pinot Noir ★★★

Forward in its appeal, the 2016 vintage (★★★) is a ruby-hued, mouthfilling and supple red with gentle tannins, a touch of complexity, and fresh, ripe cherry, plum and spice flavours to the fore. Partly barrel-aged, it's priced right.

Vintage	16	15
WR	5	6
Drink	17-19	17-18

DRY $18 V+

Sacred Hill Reserve Marlborough Pinot Noir   (★★★☆)

The 2014 vintage (★★★☆) was matured for six months in French oak barrels. Ruby-hued, it is mouthfilling and supple, with vibrant plum, cherry, spice and dried-herb flavours, showing good freshness, vigour and depth, and some complexity. Enjoyable young.

Vintage	14	
WR	5	**DRY $25 AV**
Drink	17-19	

Saint Clair James Sinclair Marlborough Pinot Noir   ★★★☆

Grown in the Southern Valleys, the 2015 vintage (★★★★) is a deep ruby, full-bodied, sweet-fruited red, with strong, ripe cherry, plum and spice flavours, a hint of dried herbs, and good complexity. It's still youthful; drink now or cellar.

DRY $28 AV

Saint Clair Marlborough Pinot Noir   ★★★☆

The 2016 vintage (★★★☆), grown in the Southern Valleys, is a bright ruby, mouthfilling, supple red, with ripe cherry, plum and spice flavours, showing some nutty, savoury complexity. A very harmonious wine, it's already drinking well.

DRY $26 AV

Saint Clair Omaka Reserve Marlborough Pinot Noir   ★★★★☆

This is Saint Clair's top Pinot Noir, but understanding where the grapes were grown can be a challenge. Despite the prominence of 'Omaka' (a prestigious district for Pinot Noir, on the south side of the Wairau Valley) on its front label, past vintages have been grown in the Ure Valley, the Waihopai Valley, and 'carefully selected vineyards'. The 2016 vintage (★★★★☆) is a single-vineyard wine, grown in the Delta district of the Southern Valleys, and was matured for 10 months in French oak barriques (32 per cent new). Deeply coloured, it is mouthfilling, ripe and savoury, with strong, fresh cherry, plum and spice flavours, slightly earthy notes adding complexity, and a finely balanced, smooth finish.

DRY $44 AV

Saint Clair Pioneer Block 10 Twin Hills Omaka Valley Marlborough Pinot Noir   ★★★★

The 2016 vintage (★★★★) is an Omaka Valley red, matured in French oak barriques. Enjoyable young, it is bright ruby, full-bodied and smooth, with fresh, ripe cherry, plum and dried-herb flavours, nutty and savoury notes adding complexity, gentle tannins and a silky-smooth, persistent finish.

DRY $38 AV

Saint Clair Pioneer Block 14 Doctor's Creek Marlborough Pinot Noir   ★★★★☆

Estate-grown in the lower Omaka Valley and matured in French oak barriques, the instantly attractive 2016 vintage (★★★★☆) is deep ruby, sweet-fruited and softly textured, with concentrated, ripe plum, spice and nut flavours, a hint of liquorice, and a well-rounded finish. Already delicious, it's worth cellaring to 2019+.

DRY $38 V+

Saint Clair Pioneer Block 15 Strip Block Marlborough Pinot Noir   ★★★★☆

Grown in the lower reaches of the Waihopai Valley, the 2016 vintage (★★★★) was matured in French oak barriques. Deep ruby, it is mouthfilling and supple, with strong, vibrant cherry/plum flavours, nutty, savoury elements adding complexity, gentle tannins, and plenty of drink-young appeal. Best drinking 2019+.

DRY $38 V+

Saint Clair Pioneer Block 16 Awatere Pinot Noir   ★★★★

Showing good personality, the 2014 vintage (★★★★) is a sweet-fruited red with a smoky, savoury, oak-influenced bouquet. Matured in French oak barriques (38 per cent new), it is mouthfilling and supple, with strong plum, spice and dried-herb flavours, and some 'funky' notes adding complexity.

DRY $38 AV

Saint Clair Pioneer Block 22 Barn Block Marlborough Pinot Noir   ★★★★☆

Grown on the southern edge of the Wairau Valley, and matured in French oak barriques, the 2015 vintage (★★★★☆) is a deep ruby, generous, finely textured red, with concentrated cherry, plum and spice flavours, ripe and supple, and a seasoning of smoky, savoury oak adding complexity. Well worth cellaring.

DRY $38 V+

Saint Clair Pioneer Block 23 Master Block Marlborough Pinot Noir   ★★★★

The ruby-hued 2015 vintage (★★★☆) was grown in Benmorven Road, just west of Blenheim, and matured for 10 months in French oak barriques (40 per cent new). It has rich, ripe flavours, seasoned with toasty oak, some earthy complexity, and a finely textured finish.

DRY $38 AV

Saint Clair Pioneer Block 5 Bull Block Omaka Valley Marlborough Pinot Noir   ★★★★

Grown in clay soils on the south side of the Omaka Valley, the ruby-hued 2014 vintage (★★★★) was barrel-aged for 10 months. Floral and mouthfilling, it is sweet-fruited and finely textured, with cherryish, plummy flavours, a subtle seasoning of oak, and considerable complexity. Best drinking 2018+.

DRY $38 AV

Saint Clair Vicar's Choice Marlborough Pinot Noir   ★★★

Designed as Saint Clair's 'entry-level' Pinot Noir, the 2014 vintage (★★★) is an easy-drinking style, ruby-hued, with plum, cherry and spice flavours, a hint of herbs, a gentle seasoning of oak and a well-rounded finish.

DRY $23 AV

Sanctuary Marlborough Pinot Noir   ★★★☆

Offering good value, the 2015 vintage (★★★☆) is ruby-hued, mouthfilling and supple, in a vibrantly fruity style with generous, ripe, plummy, spicy flavours. Delicious young.

DRY $20 V+

Satellite Marlborough Pinot Noir   ★★★

From Spy Valley, the 2014 vintage (★★★) was hand-picked and barrel-aged. An easy-drinking red, it is ruby-hued, mouthfilling, sweet-fruited and smooth, with ripe cherry and plum flavours, a touch of complexity and gentle tannins. Drink now.

DRY $23 AV

Satyr Foothills Hawke's Bay Pinot Noir   ★★★★

The 2015 vintage (★★★★) was grown at coastal and elevated, inland sites, and matured in French oak barrels (20 per cent new). Full ruby, it is very vibrant and supple, with a strong surge of fresh cherry, plum and spice flavours, and gentle tannins. A graceful red with youthful vigour, it should be at its best 2018+. (From Sileni.)

DRY $34 AV

Satyr Hawke's Bay Pinot Noir   ★★☆

Ruby-hued, the 2015 vintage (★★☆) is a fruit-driven style with vibrant, ripe cherry/plum flavours, a hint of herbs, fresh acidity and a smooth finish. (From Sileni.)

DRY $20 –V

Schubert Marion's Vineyard Pinot Noir   ★★★★☆

Estate-grown at Gladstone, in the northern Wairarapa, the 2014 vintage (★★★★☆) was matured in French oak barriques. Ruby-hued, it is attractively scented, with strong, ripe cherry and spice flavours, hints of dried herbs and nuts, and excellent complexity. A very savoury, firmly structured red, it's well worth cellaring.

DRY $48 –V

Scott Base Central Otago Pinot Noir   ★★★☆

Estate-grown in the Cromwell Basin, the 2016 vintage (★★★) was matured in French oak casks. Enjoyable young, it's a fragrant, savoury and supple wine with ripe, strawberryish, spicy flavours, fine-grained tannins, good complexity, and lots of drink-young appeal. (From Allan Scott.)

DRY $40 –V

Seifried Nelson Pinot Noir   ★★★

Matured for 15 months in French oak barriques (new to three years old), the 2015 vintage (★★★☆) is drinking well in its youth. Full ruby, it is mouthfilling and savoury, with plummy, spicy flavours, showing very good complexity and depth. Fine value.

Vintage	15	14	13	12	11
WR	7	5	6	6	6
Drink	17-21	17-22	17-21	17-20	P

DRY $18 V+

Selaks Founders Limited Edition Central Otago Pinot Noir ★★★★

The 2015 vintage (★★★★) is deep ruby, with a hint of development. Full-bodied, it has generous, ripe cherry, spice and nut flavours, showing good complexity, and a moderately firm finish. A savoury, concentrated red, it's drinking well now.

Vintage	15
WR	6
Drink	17-20

DRY $40 –V

Selaks Reserve South Island Pinot Noir (★★☆)

Priced right, the easy-drinking, light ruby 2016 vintage (★★☆) is mouthfilling and smooth, with gentle, ripe, cherryish, slightly nutty flavours, showing a touch of complexity, and a well-rounded finish. Ready.

Vintage	16
WR	5
Drink	18-19

DRY $16 AV

Selaks The Taste Collection Marlborough Velvety Pinot Noir (★★★☆)

The attractive 2016 vintage (★★★☆) was partly barrel-aged. Ruby-hued, it is mouthfilling, vibrantly fruity and smooth, with ripe, plummy, spicy, slightly toasty flavours, showing some savoury complexity, and fine-grained tannins. Best drinking mid-2018+.

Vintage	16
WR	6
Drink	18-21

DRY $22 V+

Seresin Leah Pinot Noir ★★★★☆

Unlike the single-vineyard reds, this wine is estate-grown at three sites – mostly the Raupo Creek Vineyard, in the Omaka Valley – and is less new oak-influenced. The 2014 vintage (★★★★) was hand-picked, fermented with indigenous yeasts, matured for 11 months in French oak barriques (10 per cent new), and bottled without filtering. Light ruby, it is savoury and firm, with youthful plum, spice and dried-herb flavours, showing good concentration and complexity. Best drinking 2018+. Certified organic.

DRY $35 V+

Seresin Marlborough Pinot Noir (★★★★)

The 2014 vintage (★★★★) was estate-grown and hand-picked at three sites – mostly Raupo Creek Vineyard, in the Omaka Valley – fermented with indigenous yeasts, and matured for 11 months in seasoned French oak barriques. Ruby-hued and savoury, it is drinking well now, with ripe cherry and spice flavours, moderately firm tannins and very good complexity. Certified organic.

DRY $30 AV

Seresin Noa Marlborough Pinot Noir   ★★★★

Estate-grown in the company's original vineyard at Renwick, in the Wairau Valley, the 2013 vintage (★★★★☆), still on sale, is certified organic. Hand-picked, it was fermented with indigenous yeasts, matured for 18 months in French oak barriques (20 per cent new), and bottled unfined and unfiltered. Full-coloured, it is mouthfilling and savoury, with concentrated plum, cherry and spice flavours, a hint of herbs and a firmly structured finish. Best drinking 2018+.

DRY $95 –V

Seresin OSIP Marlborough Pinot Noir   (★★★★)

The debut 2014 vintage (★★★★) was grown organically and biodynamically and made with no use of sulphur in the winery. Full-coloured, fragrant and fruity, it is mouthfilling, with generous, ripe plum, cherry and spice flavours, showing good freshness, and earthy, savoury notes adding complexity. (Tasted side by side with its OSIP Sauvignon Blanc 2015 stablemate, I preferred the more attractively scented red.) Drink now or cellar.

DRY $42 –V

Seresin Rachel Marlborough Pinot Noir   ★★★★☆

From three company-owned vineyards (mostly the Raupo Creek Vineyard, in the Omaka Valley), the 2013 vintage (★★★★★), still on sale, is certified organic. Hand-picked and fermented with indigenous yeasts, it was matured for a year in French oak barriques (20 per cent new), barrel-selected, then barrel-aged for a further six months. Bottled unfined and unfiltered, it is deep ruby, mouthfilling and very savoury, with generous, ripe cherry, plum, spice and nut flavours, a hint of herbs, and excellent concentration and complexity. Best drinking 2019+.

DRY $57 –V

Seresin Raupo Creek Marlborough Pinot Noir   ★★★★★

Certified organic, the 2013 vintage (★★★★★), still on sale, is from clay slopes in the Omaka Valley. Estate-grown and hand-picked, it was fermented with indigenous yeasts, matured for 18 months in French oak barriques (20 per cent new), and bottled unfined and unfiltered. Deep ruby, it is fragrant, savoury and generous, with strong, youthful, plummy, spicy, slightly nutty flavours, showing good complexity, and a firm, sustained finish. Best drinking 2018+.

DRY $65 AV

Seresin Sun & Moon Marlborough Pinot Noir   ★★★★★

This rare wine is 'the purest expression of Pinot Noir we can make'. Certified organic, the 2013 vintage (★★★★★) was estate-grown and hand-picked in the Raupo Creek Vineyard, in the Omaka Valley, fermented with indigenous yeasts, matured for 17 months in French oak barriques (14 per cent new), and bottled unfined and unfiltered. Deep ruby, with a hint of development, it is highly fragrant, mouthfilling and very savoury, with concentrated, plummy, spicy flavours, showing excellent complexity, and good tannin backbone. A powerful, still youthful wine, it should be long-lived; open 2019+.

DRY $125 –V

Seresin Tatou Marlborough Pinot Noir ★★★★

Grown in deep gravels at the upper end of the Wairau Valley, the 2013 vintage (★★★★), still on sale, was hand-harvested, fermented with indigenous yeasts, matured for 18 months in French oak barriques (20 per cent new), and bottled unfined and unfiltered. Bright ruby, fresh and lively, it has concentrated, ripe, plummy, spicy, nutty flavours, good complexity, and a firm tannin grip. Still youthful, it should be at its best 2019+. Certified organic.

DRY $63 –V

Shelter Bay Marlborough Pinot Noir (★★★★)

The 2014 vintage (★★★★) is a deeply coloured, generous red with concentrated, youthful, plummy flavours and a tight, firm finish. Great value from Jackson Estate.

DRY $20 V+

Sherwood Estate Stoney Range New Zealand Pinot Noir (★★★☆)

Offering fine value, the 2015 vintage (★★★☆) is a blend of Waipara and Marlborough grapes, oak-matured for four months. Full-coloured, it is mouthfilling and supple, with generous, well-ripened dark berry, plum and spice flavours, gentle tannins, and loads of drink-young appeal.

DRY $19 V+

Sherwood Estate Waipara Valley Pinot Noir (★★★☆)

Barrel-aged for nine months, the 2014 vintage (★★★☆) is ruby-hued, with very good depth of fresh berry and spice flavours, gently seasoned with oak, gentle tannins, and a touch of complexity. It's drinking well now.

DRY $25 AV

Sileni Cellar Selection Hawke's Bay Pinot Noir ★★★

Top vintages offer lots of drink-young charm. The light ruby 2016 vintage (★★☆) is an easy-drinking red, medium-bodied, with decent depth of fresh, ripe cherry and spice flavours, and a smooth finish.

DRY $20 AV

Vintage	16	15	14	13
WR	6	7	7	6
Drink	18-21	17-21	17-20	17-18

Sileni Estate Selection Plateau Hawke's Bay Pinot Noir ★★★★

The graceful 2015 vintage (★★★★) was grown at two sites – mostly the elevated, inland Plateau Vineyard, at Mangatahi, but also at Parkhill, near the coast. Matured for nine months in French oak casks (25 per cent new), it is deep ruby and vibrantly fruity, with generous, youthful plum, cherry and spice flavours, a subtle seasoning of oak, gentle tannins, and lots of drink-young appeal. The 2016 vintage (★★★★) is already drinking well. Full ruby, it is mouthfilling and sweet-fruited, with strong, vibrant, cherryish, plummy flavours, showing good complexity, and gentle tannins. Best drinking 2019+.

DRY $33 AV

Vintage	16	15	14	13	12	11	10
WR	6	7	7	7	5	4	NM
Drink	17-24	17-23	17-22	17-20	P	P	NM

Sileni Estate Selection Springstone Hawke's Bay Pinot Noir   ★★★★

The highly attractive 2015 vintage (★★★★) was grown in the inland, elevated Mangatahi district and matured in mostly seasoned French oak barrels (5 per cent new). Full-bodied (14.5 per cent alcohol), it is ruby-hued, with strong, vibrant, cherryish, plummy flavours, gently seasoned with oak, and a smooth, well-rounded finish. A graceful, finely poised wine with good varietal character, it should be at its best 2018+. The 2016 vintage (★★★★☆), matured for 16 months in seasoned oak barriques, is very refined. Fragrant, mouthfilling and savoury, it is bright ruby, with strong, vibrant cherry, plum and spice flavours, showing excellent complexity, and a finely poised, long finish. Still youthful, it should break into full stride 2019+.

Vintage	16	15
WR	6	7
Drink	17-25	17-25

DRY $35 AV

Sileni Exceptional Vintage Hawke's Bay Pinot Noir   ★★★★☆

Is this the finest Pinot Noir in Hawke's Bay? The 2015 vintage (★★★★☆) was estate-grown at Mangatahi and matured for nine months in French oak barriques (20 per cent new). Bright ruby, it is very elegant and supple, with a savoury bouquet and powerful, ripe, concentrated, complex flavours. Crying out for cellaring, it should be at its best 2018+.

Vintage	15	14	13	11	10	09
WR	7	7	7	NM	NM	6
Drink	17-25	17-24	17-21	NM	NM	P

DRY $70 –V

Sileni Parkhill Hawke's Bay Pinot Noir   ★★★★

Full ruby, the 2014 vintage (★★★★) was grown in Sileni's coolest vineyard, a coastal site at Haumoana. Matured for nine months in French oak casks (20 per cent new), it is mouthfilling and savoury, with fresh, generous, plummy, spicy flavours, fine-grained tannins, and good complexity.

Vintage	15	14	13
WR	NM	7	6
Drink	NM	17-21	17-19

DRY $32 AV

Snapper Rock Marlborough Pinot Noir   (★★☆)

The easy-drinking 2014 vintage (★★☆) is light ruby, with gentle, berryish, plummy flavours, showing a touch of complexity, and a well-rounded finish. Priced right.

DRY $17 AV

Snow Bird South Island Pinot Noir   (★★★☆)

Drinking well already, the 2016 vintage (★★★☆) was grown in both the Waitaki Valley of North Otago and the Waipara Valley of North Canterbury, and matured in old oak casks. Full ruby, it is mouthfilling, with good depth of ripe plum and spice flavours, a hint of tamarillo, fresh acidity and considerable complexity. Best drinking mid-2018+. (From Ostler.)

DRY $25 AV

Soderberg Home Block Single Vineyard Marlborough Pinot Noir ★★★★

This rare wine flows from a tiny, 1-hectare vineyard at the base of the Wither Hills that previously supplied the grapes for Koru. The 2014 vintage (★★★★) was matured in French oak casks (25 per cent new). Full ruby, it is mouthfilling, smooth and very ripe-tasting, with plum, spice and slight liquorice flavours, slightly earthy, youthful and complex. Drink now or cellar. Certified organic.

Vintage	14	13	12	11	10
WR	7	NM	7	6	7
Drink	17-20	NM	17-18	P	P

DRY $34 AV

Soho Havana Marlborough Pinot Noir ★★★★☆

The 2015 vintage (★★★★☆) is a single-vineyard red, hand-harvested in the Southern Valleys and matured in French oak barrels (25 per cent new). An elegant, age-worthy wine, it is full-coloured, mouthfilling and generous, with ripe sweet-fruit characters. Tightly structured, it is finely balanced, with rich, youthful plum/spice flavours, a hint of dried herbs, and good complexity. Best drinking 2018+.

DRY $38 V+

Soho Marlborough Pinot Noir ★★★☆

The 2014 vintage (★★★) is light ruby, with slightly herbal aromas. Mouthfilling and smooth, it has gentle tannins and berry, plum, spice and herb flavours, showing a touch of earthy, nutty complexity.

DRY $27 AV

Soho McQueen Central Otago Pinot Noir ★★★★☆

The 2015 vintage (★★★★☆) was grown at Bendigo (50 per cent), Gibbston (35 per cent) and Bannockburn (15 per cent). Matured for a year in French oak casks, it is a fragrant, deep ruby wine with mouthfilling body, concentrated, ripe, plummy, spicy flavours, showing good complexity, fine-grained tannins and obvious potential. Even better, the powerful 2016 vintage (★★★★★) is deeply coloured, weighty and concentrated. It has dense, ripe plum and spice flavours, a hint of liquorice, nutty, savoury notes adding complexity, and good tannin support. A youthful, very age-worthy red, it should be at its best 2020+.

DRY $50 –V

Southern Dawn Marlborough Pinot Noir (★★☆)

Ready to roll, the 2013 vintage (★★☆) has light, mature colour, mouthfilling body and smooth, ripe flavours, plummy, slightly nutty and leathery. Priced sharply.

DRY $14 V+

Spencer Hill Coastal Ridge Pinot Noir (★★★☆)

Estate-grown at Upper Moutere, the 2015 vintage (★★★☆) was harvested from 26-year-old vines. Deep ruby, it is ripely scented and sweet-fruited, with cherry, plum and spice flavours, showing moderate complexity, gentle tannins and very good depth.

DRY $35 –V

Spencer Hill The Wild One Pinot Noir   (★★★★)

Retasted in August 2017, the age-worthy 2015 vintage (★★★★) was estate-grown at Upper Moutere, in Nelson, harvested from 26-year-old vines, and French and American oak-aged. Full ruby, it is a weighty style of Pinot Noir, with an array of strong cherry, plum, spice and herb flavours, showing good complexity, an earthy streak and a smooth, generous finish. Best drinking mid-2018+.

 DRY $35 AV

Spinyback Nelson Pinot Noir   ★★★

From Waimea Estates, the 2014 vintage (★★★) was grown on the Waimea Plains. Bright ruby, it is a full-bodied, fruit-driven style, with plenty of plummy, berryish flavour, fresh and smooth.

 DRY $17 V+

Spy Valley Envoy Johnson Vineyard Waihopai Valley Marlborough Pinot Noir   ★★★★☆

The 2015 vintage (★★★★★) was estate-grown in the Waihopai Valley, hand-harvested and French oak-aged for 16 months. Deep, bright ruby, it is mouthfilling, with dense, ripe plum and spice flavours, still very youthful, good tannin backbone, a savoury, nutty complexity, and a long finish. A powerful wine, it should be long-lived; open 2020+.

Vintage	15	14	13	12	11	10	09	08
WR	6	6	NM	7	7	6	6	6
Drink	17-23	17-20	NM	17-18	P	P	P	P

DRY $55 –V

Spy Valley Envoy Outpost Vineyard Omaka Valley Marlborough Pinot Noir   ★★★★★

From hill-grown vines in the Omaka Valley, the classy 2015 vintage (★★★★★) was hand-picked, fermented with indigenous yeasts and matured for 16 months in French oak casks. Deep and youthful in colour, it is mouthfilling, sweet-fruited and concentrated, with ripe cherry, plum, spice and nut flavours, complex and savoury, that build to a smooth, lasting finish. Already delicious, it's a classy, finely structured red that will mature gracefully; open 2019+.

Vintage	15	14	13	12	11	10
WR	6	6	6	7	6	6
Drink	18-25	17-20	17-19	17-18	17-18	P

DRY $55 AV

Spy Valley Southern Valleys Marlborough Pinot Noir   ★★★★

Offering good value, the 2015 vintage (★★★★☆) was grown in the Southern Valleys and barrel-aged for nearly a year. Deep ruby, it is still youthful, with mouthfilling body, fresh, generous plum/spice flavours, showing good complexity, and the structure to mature well. Showing impressive density and vigour, it should be at its best 2019+.

Vintage	15	14	13	12	11	10
WR	6	6	6	6	6	6
Drink	17-23	17-20	P	P	P	P

 DRY $32 AV

Stables Reserve Hawke's Bay Pinot Noir (★★★)

A drink-young charmer, the 2016 vintage (★★★) is a bright ruby, mouthfilling red, vibrantly fruity and smooth, with fresh, generous cherry/plum flavours and very gentle tannins. Priced right.

DRY $19 AV

Staete Landt State of Grace Marlborough Pinot Noir (★★★★)

The very harmonious 2015 vintage (★★★★) was hand-picked at Rapaura, on the north side of the Wairau Valley, and matured for 18 months in French oak barriques (25 per cent new). Ruby-hued, it is mouthfilling, sweet-fruited and supple, with vibrant, ripe cherry and plum flavours, seasoned with nutty oak, balanced acidity and gentle tannins. Best drinking 2018+.

DRY $35 AV

Stanley Estates Block 8 Awatere Valley Marlborough Pinot Noir ★★★☆

The 2015 vintage (★★★★) was estate-grown, hand-picked and matured for 10 months in French oak barrels (25 per cent new). Drinking well now, but still developing, it is deep ruby, fragrant and supple, with strong, plummy, spicy, slightly nutty flavours, smooth and lingering.

Vintage	15
WR	6
Drink	17-24

DRY $28 AV

Stoneburn Marlborough Pinot Noir ★★☆

From Hunter's, the 2014 vintage (★★☆) is ruby-hued, fresh, vibrantly fruity and supple, with berry/plum flavours and a smooth finish. Enjoyable young.

DRY $18 AV

Stoneleigh Latitude Marlborough Pinot Noir ★★★☆

Celebrating the 'Golden Mile' along Rapaura Road, on the stony north side of the Wairau Valley, the 2015 vintage (★★★☆) is deep ruby, mouthfilling and well-rounded, with generous, ripe plum and spice flavours, showing some savoury complexity.

DRY $23 V+

Stoneleigh Marlborough Pinot Noir ★★☆

From Pernod Ricard NZ, this red is grown on the relatively warm north side of the Wairau Valley. The 2016 vintage (★★☆) is ruby-hued and vibrantly fruity, with ripe cherry and red-berry flavours, a hint of dried herbs, and a smooth finish. An easy-drinking style, it's priced right.

DRY $17 AV

Stoneleigh Rapaura Series Marlborough Pinot Noir ★★★★

The 2015 vintage (★★★★) is a deep ruby, fragrant, generous red, named after the Rapaura series of soils, rather than the district in the Wairau Valley. Vibrantly fruity, with ripe plum, cherry and spice flavours, showing good complexity and harmony, it's a very harmonious wine, likely to be at its best 2018+.

DRY $27 V+

Stoneleigh Wild Valley Marlborough Pinot Noir   (★★★)

The ruby-hued 2015 vintage (★★★) was grown at Rapaura, on the northern side of the Wairau Valley, and fermented with indigenous (wild) yeasts (hence the 'Wild' Valley). Buoyantly fruity, with a floral bouquet, it is a sweet-fruited wine with satisfying depth of berryish, plummy flavours, fresh and smooth. A drink-young charmer.

DRY $19 AV

Stoney Range Reserve Waipara Valley Pinot Noir   (★★★)

Enjoyable young, the 2016 vintage (★★★) is fresh and vibrantly fruity. Briefly oak-aged, it is ruby-hued, with gentle, ripe plum and cherry flavours, a hint of herbs, and a smooth finish. (From Sherwood.)

DRY $19 AV

Stonyridge Fallen Angel Central Otago Pinot Noir   (★★★★)

Worth cellaring, the 2014 vintage (★★★★) is richly coloured and mouthfilling. Matured in French oak casks (30 per cent new), it is fruit-packed, with strong, ripe plum, cherry and spice flavours, fresh and youthful. Open 2018+.

DRY $55 –V

Summerhouse Central Otago Pinot Noir   (★★★☆)

The 2015 vintage (★★★☆) is a bright ruby, vibrantly fruity and supple blend of grapes grown at Alexandra and in the Cromwell Basin. Matured in French and American oak barriques, it is medium to full-bodied, with fresh plum, herb and spice flavours, showing good depth, oak-derived complexity and a smooth finish.

Vintage	15
WR	7
Drink	17-21

DRY $29 AV

Summerhouse Marlborough Pinot Noir   ★★★☆

Grown in the Southern Valleys, the 2016 vintage (★★★☆) was matured in new and seasoned oak barriques. Full ruby, it is an aromatic, juicy, very 'fruit-driven' style, with strong, vibrant, plummy and berryish flavours to the fore, youthful and well-rounded. Best drinking mid-2018+.

Vintage	16	15	14
WR	7	7	7
Drink	17-25	17-21	17-22

DRY $29 AV

Super Nanny Central Otago Pinot Noir   ★★★★

The sturdy, full-flavoured 2015 vintage (★★★★) was grown at Bannockburn and Pisa, barrel-aged (40 per cent new) and bottled unfined and unfiltered. Still youthful, it is concentrated and savoury, with strong strawberry, spice and dried-herb flavours, oak complexity and the structure to age well.

DRY $49 –V

Surveyor Thomson Single Vineyard Central Otago Pinot Noir ★★★★

From Domaine-Thomson, at Lowburn, the 2013 vintage (★★★★☆) is still youthful. Matured for 10 months in French oak barrels (25 per cent new), it is bright ruby, with a fragrant bouquet of spices and dried herbs, showing good complexity. It is elegant and savoury, with vibrant plum, spice, herb and nut flavours, generous and harmonious. Best drinking 2019+.

DRY $44 –V

Vintage	13	12	11	10
WR	6	7	6	7
Drink	17-22	17-20	17-21	17-19

Tarras Vineyards Central Otago Pinot Noir ★★★★

The 2014 vintage (★★★★) is a deeply coloured, rich blend of grapes from Bendigo (The Canyon Vineyard), other parts of the Cromwell Basin and Alexandra. It has strong plum and spice flavours, with ripe, supple tannins, oak complexity and a persistent finish.

DRY $39 AV

Tarras Vineyards The Canyon Single Vineyard Central Otago Pinot Noir ★★★★★

The powerful 2014 vintage (★★★★★) of this Bendigo red was matured in French oak barrels (33 per cent new). Deep and youthful in colour, it is sturdy (14.5 per cent alcohol), with concentrated, very ripe cherry, plum and spice flavours, a hint of liquorice, and lovely depth and harmony. A bold, age-worthy red, it should be at its best from 2019 onwards. The 2016 vintage (★★★★★) is similar. Richly coloured, it is mouthfilling, with lush, well-ripened cherry, plum and slight liquorice flavours, nutty, savoury notes adding complexity, fine-grained tannins, and excellent depth and harmony. Already delicious, it's well worth cellaring.

DRY $60 AV

Tatty Bogler Central Otago Pinot Noir ★★★★☆

Still youthful, the 2014 vintage (★★★★☆) was estate-grown at Bannockburn, in the Cromwell Basin, and matured in French oak barriques. Bright ruby, it is fragrant, with rich cherry, plum, spice and dried-herb flavours, showing excellent vigour and complexity, and good tannin backbone. The 2015 vintage (★★★★) is bright ruby, fresh, youthful and supple, with cherry, plum and dried-herb flavours, and nutty, savoury notes adding complexity. An elegant red, woven with fresh acidity, it's well worth cellaring. (From Forrest.)

DRY $35 V+

Te Amo Central Otago Pinot Noir (★★★★)

The lively 2015 vintage (★★★★) is deep ruby, with strong, vibrant plum and dried-herb flavours, hints of nuts and spices, fresh acidity, and good complexity and harmony. Full of youthful drive, it's best cellared to mid-2018+.

DRY $45 –V

Te Kairanga John Martin Martinborough Pinot Noir ★★★★☆

The powerful 2014 vintage (★★★★★) is a classic regional style, based on the 'best vineyard parcels'. Matured for a year in French oak barriques, it's a very harmonious wine, deep ruby, mouthfilling, fleshy and savoury, with highly concentrated plum, cherry and spice flavours, showing lovely ripeness, texture and complexity. Well worth cellaring. The youthful 2015 vintage (★★★★) is a deep ruby, mouthfilling, savoury red with strong plum/spice flavours, good complexity, a hint of dried herbs and a fairly firm finish.

Vintage	15	14	13
WR	7	7	7
Drink	17-25	17-25	17-24

DRY $45 –V

Te Kairanga Martinborough Pinot Noir ★★★★

The refined 2015 vintage (★★★★☆) is instantly appealing. Deep ruby, it is mouthfilling, ripe and supple, with generous plum/spice flavours, gentle tannins, and good complexity. Skilfully crafted, it is beautifully poised; drink now or cellar. Fine value.

Vintage	15	14	13
WR	7	7	7
Drink	17-21	17-20	17-19

DRY $28 V+

Te Kairanga Runholder Martinborough Pinot Noir ★★★★☆

This is the middle-tier label. The 2015 vintage (★★★★☆) was estate-grown and matured for 10 months in French oak barriques (25 per cent new). Delicious drinking from now onwards, it is full ruby, mouthfilling and well-rounded, with very generous, ripe cherry and spice flavours, harmonious, silky-textured and savoury. Fine value.

Vintage	15	14	13
WR	7	7	7
Drink	17-22	17-22	17-22

DRY $29 V+

Te Mania Nelson Pinot Noir ★★★

The 2015 vintage (★★★☆) was mostly barrel-aged. Still youthful, it is bright ruby, with mouthfilling body (14.5 per cent alcohol) and vibrant, plummy fruit flavours to the fore, fresh, ripe and generous. Best drinking 2018+.

DRY $25 –V

Te Mania Reserve Nelson Pinot Noir ★★★★

Certified organic, the age-worthy 2014 vintage (★★★★) was hand-picked and matured for 10 months in French oak barrels (20 per cent new). Full ruby, it is sturdy (14.5 per cent alcohol), with strong, plummy, spicy, slightly toasty flavours, oak complexity and a fairly firm finish. Best drinking 2018+.

DRY $36 AV

Te Pa Marlborough Pinot Noir (★★★★)

Still unfolding, the 2015 vintage (★★★★) was hand-picked at two sites on the south side of the Wairau Valley, fermented with indigenous yeasts and matured for 10 months in French oak barrels (20 per cent new). Ruby-hued, it is fresh and spicy, with dried-herb notes, nutty, savoury notes adding complexity and moderately firm tannins. Enjoyable young, it should be at its best 2018+.

 DRY $30 AV

Ten Sisters Marlborough Pinot Noir (★★★)

The 2014 vintage (★★★), from distributor Sanz Global, is enjoyable now. Light ruby, mellow and moderately concentrated, it is mouthfilling, with raspberry, strawberry and spice flavours, showing some savoury complexity.

 DRY $29 –V

Terra Sancta Estate Bannockburn Central Otago Pinot Noir ★★★★☆

The 2015 vintage (★★★★) was estate-grown at Bannockburn and matured in French oak barrels (10 per cent new). Bright ruby, it is a graceful, savoury, supple red, with ripe cherry, plum, spice and nut flavours, showing good complexity, and a finely textured, harmonious finish. Drink now or cellar.

Vintage	15	14	13
WR	7	7	6
Drink	18-26	17-22	17-20

 DRY $50 –V

Terra Sancta Jackson's Block Bannockburn Central Otago Pinot Noir ★★★★★

The classy, finely textured 2015 vintage (★★★★★) was matured in French oak barriques (25 per cent new). Bright ruby, it is very fragrant, savoury and supple, with cherry, plum, spice, dried-herb and nut flavours, showing excellent delicacy, depth and complexity. Conveying a strong sense of youthful potential, it's well worth cellaring to 2018 onwards.

Vintage	15	14	13	12	11
WR	6	6	5	7	7
Drink	17-25	17-24	17-20	17-24	17-20

 DRY $50 AV

Terra Sancta Mysterious Diggings Bannockburn Central Otago Pinot Noir ★★★★

Estate-grown, the 2016 vintage (★★★★) was matured in seasoned French oak barrels. Full ruby, it is fragrant and expressive, with ripe strawberry and spice flavours, showing very good complexity, velvety tannins, and lots of drink-young appeal. Fine value.

Vintage	16	15	14	13	12
WR	7	6	6	6	7
Drink	18-23	17-19	17-18	P	P

 DRY $27 V+

Terra Sancta Shingle Beach Bannockburn Central Otago Pinot Noir   ★★★★☆

From a block of mature, close-planted vines, the 2015 vintage (★★★★★) was matured in French oak barriques and puncheons (20 per cent new). Full-coloured, it's a generous, sweet-fruited and savoury red, already drinking well, with cherryish, spicy flavours, showing excellent complexity and harmony.

Vintage	15	14	13	12
WR	7	6	7	7
Drink	18-26	17-24	17-23	17-22

 DRY $50 –V

Terra Sancta Slapjack Block Bannockburn Pinot Noir   ★★★★☆

From the oldest vines in Bannockburn, planted in 1991, and matured in French oak barriques (25 per cent new), the beautiful 2014 vintage (★★★★★) is a deep ruby, deliciously fragrant and savoury wine, full-bodied, concentrated and harmonious. Still youthful, it has deep, ripe plum/spice flavours, showing excellent complexity, and a finely textured, lingering finish. The 2015 vintage (★★★☆) is a different style. Matured in French oak barrels (25 per cent new), it has bold, bright colour, substantial body and powerful, fresh fruit flavours, but is slightly disjointed in its youth, suggesting it needs more time. At this stage, it is less savoury and complex than past vintages, but well worth cellaring; open 2020+.

Vintage	15	14	13	12	11
WR	7	7	6	7	7
Drink	18-30	17-25	17-24	17-24	17-25

 DRY $88 –V

Terrace Edge Waipara Valley Pinot Noir   ★★★★

A consistently attractive red. The 2015 vintage (★★★★) was hand-harvested, fermented with indigenous yeasts and matured for a year in French oak casks (25 per cent new). Full ruby, it is mouthfilling and sweet-fruited, with fresh, generous cherry, plum and spice flavours, gentle tannins, savoury notes adding complexity, and very good depth and harmony. Best drinking 2018 onwards.

Vintage	15
WR	7
Drink	17-25

 DRY $32 AV

TerraVin Marlborough Pinot Noir   ★★★★

I tasted the 2011 to 2013 vintages together in mid-2016. The 2013 (★★★★) is the finest. Grown in the Southern Valleys (70 per cent in the Calrossie Vineyard, in the southern Wither Hills), it was matured in French oak barriques for over a year, and bottled unfined and unfiltered. Mouthfilling and savoury, it has fresh, ripe cherry, plum and spice flavours, showing good complexity, and finely balanced tannins. Drink now or cellar. The 2012 (★★★☆) is probably at its peak, with good depth, delicacy and complexity, but slightly leafy notes detracting. The 2011 (★★★☆) has a mature ruby colour, with an earthy streak and good depth of moderately ripe cherry, spice and nut flavours.

Vintage	13	12	11
WR	7	5	6
Drink	17-20	17-18	17-18

DRY $38 AV

Thistle Ridge Waipara Pinot Noir

The 2014 vintage (★★★☆) from Greystone offers great value. Full-bodied, generous and smooth, it is bright ruby, with good depth of cherry, plum, dried-herb and spice flavours. Softly textured, with some complexity, it's enjoyable now.

DRY $22 V+

Thornbury Central Otago Pinot Noir ★★★★

Offering fine value, the 2016 vintage (★★★★) was grown at Bannockburn, hand-harvested and matured for 11 months in French oak barriques (22 per cent new). Delicious young, it's a very harmonious wine, with good depth of ripe, cherryish, plummy, spicy flavours, savoury notes adding complexity, gentle tannins and a seductively smooth finish.

Vintage	16
WR	6
Drink	17-21

DRY $25 V+

Three Paddles Martinborough Pinot Noir ★★★★

From Nga Waka, this second-tier red is a rewarding, drink-young style. The 2015 vintage (★★★☆) was matured for a year in French oak barrels (20 per cent new). Full ruby, with a hint of development, it is mouthfilling and smooth, with good depth of ripe cherry, plum and spice flavours, and gentle tannins. It's drinking well now. The 2016 vintage (★★★★) is delicious young. Also French oak-aged for a year (20 per cent new), it is bright ruby, mouthfilling, sweet-fruited and smooth, with generous, ripe flavours, showing good complexity. Best drinking 2019+.

Vintage	16	15	14	13
WR	6	6	7	7
Drink	17-22	17-22	17-21	17-20

DRY $28 V+

Tiki Koro Central Otago Pinot Noir ★★★☆

Drinking well now, the 2014 vintage (★★★★) was grown at Wanaka and matured for 14 months in French oak casks. Rich and finely balanced, it is mouthfilling and full-coloured, with cherry, plum, dried-herb and spice flavours, well-integrated oak and a floral bouquet.

DRY $33 –V

Tiki Marlborough Pinot Noir ★★★

The 2015 vintage (★★☆), lightly oaked, is a ruby-hued, vibrantly fruity red, with plummy, berryish flavours, offering pleasant, easy drinking.

DRY $23 AV

Tinpot Hut Marlborough Pinot Noir ★★★

The 2014 vintage (★★★☆) is a blend of grapes estate-grown at Blind River, supplemented by fruit from the Wairau Valley. A mouthfilling, full-coloured red with very good depth of ripe plum/spice flavours, considerable complexity and fine-grained tannins, it's a skilfully crafted wine, enjoyable now.

DRY $25 –V

Tohu Awatere Valley Marlborough Pinot Noir   ★★★☆

The 2015 vintage (★★★★), grown in the upper Awatere Valley and French oak-aged, is deeply coloured and mouthfilling, with strong plum and spice flavours in an exuberantly fruity style, showing good concentration and some complexity. Best drinking 2018+.

DRY $28 AV

Toi Toi Central Otago Reserve Pinot Noir   ★★★☆

The 2014 vintage (★★★☆) is a single-vineyard, Lowburn (Cromwell Basin) red. Deep ruby, it is mouthfilling and sweet-fruited, with cherryish, plummy, moderately complex flavours, showing good vibrancy and vigour, and a smooth finish. Best drinking 2018+.

Vintage	14
WR	7
Drink	17-22

DRY $40 –V

Toi Toi Clutha Central Otago Pinot Noir   ★★★☆

Priced right, the 2015 vintage (★★★☆) is a youthful, ruby-hued red, fragrant, mouthfilling and supple, with fresh, ripe plum, red-berry and spice flavours, showing very good depth. Enjoyable young, it should be at its best 2018+.

DRY $27 AV

Totara Marlborough Pinot Noir   ★★☆

The 2014 vintage (★★★) is a ruby-hued, fruit-driven style with vibrant, plummy, slightly spicy flavours to the fore, fresh acidity and gentle tannins.

DRY $26 –V

Trinity Hill Hawke's Bay Pinot Noir   ★★★

The 2015 vintage (★★★) is an easy-drinking, vibrantly fruity red with good depth of cherry, plum, spice and herb flavours, fresh and smooth.

DRY $22 AV

Triplebank Awatere Valley Marlborough Pinot Noir   ★★★☆

Offering very good value, the 2015 vintage (★★★☆) is full-bodied, with fresh, moderately concentrated strawberry, spice, dried-herb and nut flavours, showing a touch of complexity, and a smooth finish. (From Pernod Ricard NZ.)

DRY $20 AV

Tupari Awatere Valley Marlborough Pinot Noir   ★★★☆

The 2014 vintage (★★★☆) is a single-vineyard red, matured in French oak casks (30 per cent new). Ruby-hued, with a hint of development, it is medium to full-bodied, with savoury, nutty flavours, showing good depth and complexity, and a well-rounded finish. Ready.

DRY $35 –V

Two Degrees Central Otago Pinot Noir   ★★★★☆

Grown at Queensberry, in the Cromwell Basin, on a site with a 'gentle two-degree slope', and matured in French oak casks, the highly attractive 2015 vintage (★★★★☆) is fragrant and supple, with ripe cherry, plum, spice and dried-herb flavours, gentle tannins, and savoury, nutty notes adding complexity. A graceful, finely textured wine, it should be at its best 2018+.

Vintage	15	14	13
WR	7	6	6
Drink	17-23	17-20	17-22

 DRY $39 V+

Two Paddocks Central Otago Pinot Noir   ★★★★★

The 2014 vintage (★★★★★) is the best yet. Grown in the company's vineyards at Bannockburn (49 per cent), Alexandra (32 per cent) and Gibbston (19 per cent), and matured in French oak casks, it is deep ruby, very fragrant and supple. A generous, savoury, complex red, it is intensely varietal, with strong, ripe cherry, plum and dried-herb flavours, finely structured and age-worthy.

 DRY $55 AV

Two Paddocks Picnic Central Otago Pinot Noir   ★★★☆

Promoted as 'the people's Pinot', the 2014 vintage (★★★☆) of this drink-young red was hand-harvested and French oak-aged. Bright ruby, it is mouthfilling, with gentle tannins and good depth of cherry, plum, spice and herb flavours, fresh and smooth.

 DRY $30 –V

Two Paddocks Proprietor's Reserve The First Paddock
Central Otago Pinot Noir   ★★★★☆

The 2015 vintage (★★★★☆), estate-grown at Gibbston, was harvested from vines planted in 1993 and matured for 14 months in French oak barrels (30 per cent new). Ruby-hued, with a fragrant bouquet of herbs and spices, it is medium-bodied, with strong, vibrant cherry, spice, dried-herb and nut flavours, showing good complexity. A very youthful, 'feminine' style, with fresh acidity and obvious potential, it's best cellared to 2019+.

 DRY $80 –V

Two Paddocks Proprietor's Reserve The Fusilier
Bannockburn Vineyard Pinot Noir   ★★★★★

The second, 2015 vintage (★★★★★) was estate-grown at Bannockburn, at the western end of Felton Road. Hand-picked, it was fermented with indigenous yeasts and matured in French oak barriques (33 per cent new). Deep ruby, with a hint of development, it is savoury and complex, with good weight, fresh acidity and concentrated, ripe, cherryish, plummy, nutty flavours that linger well. Sweet-fruited and supple, it's already delicious, but well worth cellaring to 2019+.

DRY $80 AV

Two Paddocks Proprietor's The Last Chance
Earnscleugh Vineyard Pinot Noir   ★★★★★

Estate-grown at Alexandra, in 'possibly the world's most southerly vineyard', the 2015 vintage (★★★★★) was hand-harvested, fermented with indigenous yeasts and matured in French oak barriques (one-third new). Invitingly perfumed, it is bright ruby, with mouthfilling body and an array of fresh, strong cherry, plum and spice flavours, seasoned with nutty oak. Still youthful, it's a vibrantly fruity, finely balanced, complex and age-worthy red, likely to be at its best 2019+.

DRY $80 AV

Two Rivers Altitude Marlborough Pinot Noir   ★★★★☆

Grown at two sites, in the Awatere Valley and upper Wairau Valley, the 2014 vintage (★★★★☆) was hand-picked, matured for 11 months in French oak barrels (40 per cent new), and bottled unfined and unfiltered. Deeply coloured, it is mouthfilling, very savoury and generous, with concentrated, ripe, plummy, spicy flavours, showing excellent complexity. Drink now onwards.

Vintage	14
WR	6
Drink	17-21

DRY $50 –V

Two Rivers of Marlborough Tributary Pinot Noir   ★★★★

The 2015 vintage (★★★★) is a regional blend, hand-picked and matured for 11 months in French oak barrels (25 per cent new). Full ruby, it is mouthfilling, savoury and fresh, with vibrant plum, cherry, herb and spice flavours, showing good complexity. Still youthful, it's worth cellaring.

Vintage	15
WR	6
Drink	17-20

DRY $36 AV

Two Sisters Central Otago Pinot Noir   ★★★★

The 2015 vintage (★★★★) is a single-vineyard wine from Lowburn, in the Cromwell Basin. Hand-harvested, fermented with indigenous yeasts and matured in French oak casks (30 per cent new), it is ruby-hued, scented and supple, with gentle tannins and ripe, cherryish, plummy, slightly nutty flavours, showing good complexity and harmony. Best drinking 2018+.

DRY $50 –V

Two Tails Marlborough Pinot Noir   ★★★☆

The 2015 vintage (★★★☆) was grown in the Wairau Valley. Ruby-hued, it's attractive young, with gentle, ripe cherry and spice flavours, showing a touch of savoury, nutty complexity, and a finely balanced, smooth finish.

DRY $23 V+

Urlar Gladstone Pinot Noir ★★★★

This wine is estate-grown in the northern Wairarapa. The 2014 vintage (★★★★) is savoury, full-coloured and mouthfilling, with concentrated plum, spice and dried-herb flavours, fairly firm tannins, and good complexity. Still youthful, it should be at its best 2018+. Certified organic.

Valli Bannockburn Vineyard Central Otago Pinot Noir ★★★★★

Showing obvious potential, the 2015 vintage (★★★★★) is a sturdy, concentrated red, matured for a year in French oak casks (30 per cent new), and bottled unfined and unfiltered. Deep ruby, it is generous and savoury, with fine-grained tannins, layers of ripe, plummy, spicy, nutty flavours, and impressive complexity and depth. The very graceful 2016 vintage (★★★★★) is powerful but refined, with mouthfilling body, generous, ripe cherry, plum and spice flavours, finely integrated oak, and a finely balanced, long finish. Best drinking 2020+.

Vintage	16	15	14	13	12	11	10
WR	7	6	7	7	7	6	6
Drink	18-28	17-27	17-26	17-26	17-25	17-24	17-23

Valli Bendigo Vineyard Central Otago Pinot Noir ★★★★★

The bold, deeply coloured, sweet-fruited 2015 vintage (★★★★★) is still youthful. Matured for a year in French oak casks (35 per cent new), and bottled unfined and unfiltered, it is rich and fruit-packed, plummy and spicy, showing excellent concentration, structure and complexity. The 2016 vintage (★★★★★) has a sense of hidden depths. Very youthful, it's a 'big' style of Pinot Noir, boldly coloured and sturdy, with dense, plummy, spicy flavours, firm tannins, and a long life ahead. Best drinking 2020+.

Vintage	16	15	14	13	12	11	10
WR	7	6	7	7	7	5	6
Drink	18-26	17-25	17-25	17-25	17-24	17-23	17-23

Valli Burn Cottage Vineyard Central Otago Pinot Noir ★★★★★

The 2016 vintage (★★★★★) is part of a collaboration between Valli and Burn Cottage, involving access to each other's grapes to explore key aspects of terroir. From vines planted in 2008 near Lowburn, it was matured in French oak barriques, and bottled unfined and unfiltered. Full, bright ruby, it is savoury and silky, with concentrated, ripe sweet-fruit flavours, well-integrated oak, spicy, nutty notes adding complexity, and gentle tannins. Perfumed and finely textured, it's a richly varietal, beautifully balanced wine, best cellared to 2019+.

DRY $65 AV

Valli Gibbston Vineyard Otago Pinot Noir ★★★★★

The deliciously rich and graceful 2015 vintage (★★★★★) was matured for a year in French oak casks (33 per cent new), and bottled unfined and unfiltered. Deep ruby, it is full-bodied and supple, with fresh acidity and concentrated, vibrant cherry, plum and spice flavours, showing excellent complexity and harmony. The refined 2016 vintage (★★★★★) is highly scented, mouthfilling and smooth, with very youthful, rich, vibrant, plummy, cherryish flavours, well-integrated oak, fresh acidity, and loads of potential; best drinking 2020+.

Vintage	16	15	14	13	12	11	10	09
WR	7	7	7	7	6	7	7	7
Drink	18-25	17-24	17-25	17-25	17-23	17-24	17-23	17-18

DRY $65 AV

Valli Waitaki Vineyard Otago Pinot Noir ★★★★☆

Floral and ruby-hued, the 2015 vintage (★★★★☆) is a very refined red, matured for almost a year in French oak casks (30 per cent new), and bottled unfined and unfiltered. Attractively perfumed, it is cherryish, spicy and nutty, with fresh acidity, a vague hint of herbs, gentle tannins and a sense of youthful drive. Already very approachable, it's a drink-now or cellaring proposition. Weighty and supple, the classy 2016 vintage (★★★★★) is one of the Waitaki Valley's most satisfying reds yet. Deep ruby, it is floral, with mouthfilling body, generous, very vibrant cherry, plum, dried-herb and spice flavours, fresh acidity and velvety tannins. Still youthful, it is already very open and expressive.

Vintage	16	15	14	13	12	11	10
WR	7	6	7	7	7	5	6
Drink	18-26	17-25	17-25	17-25	17-25	17-23	17-23

DRY $65 –V

Vavasour Awatere Valley Marlborough Pinot Noir ★★★★

The youthful 2014 vintage (★★★★) is deep ruby, with a fragrant, plummy, spicy bouquet. Sweet-fruited and supple, it has cherry, plum, spice and dried-herb flavours, with nutty, savoury notes adding complexity, and a finely poised finish. Best drinking 2018+.

DRY $31 AV

Vavasour Felix's Vineyard Awatere Valley Marlborough Pinot Noir ★★★★☆

The elegant 2015 vintage (★★★★☆) is fresh, tightly structured and youthful. Deep ruby, it has generous plum, cherry and spice flavours with fine-grained tannins and a sustained finish.

DRY $41 AV

Vidal Reserve Marlborough Pinot Noir ★★★★

Offering top value, the elegant 2016 vintage (★★★★) was grown in the Wairau Valley (87 per cent) and Awatere Valley (13 per cent), and matured for 10 months in French oak barriques (15 per cent new). Bright ruby, it is mouthfilling, with vibrant cherry, plum and spice flavours, showing very good depth, nutty, savoury notes adding complexity, and a seductively smooth finish. Drink now or cellar.

Vintage	16	15	14	13
WR	6	7	6	7
Drink	17-21	17-20	17-19	17-18

DRY $26 V+

Villa Maria Cellar Selection Marlborough Pinot Noir   ★★★★

Typically delightful, this is one of New Zealand's best-value Pinot Noirs. The 2016 vintage
(★★★★) was grown in the Wairau and Awatere valleys, and matured for 10 months in French
oak barriques (15 per cent new). Mouthfilling, it is vibrantly fruity, with strong cherry, plum
and spice flavours, showing good complexity, and a finely balanced, smooth finish. Drink now
or cellar.

DRY $26 V+

Vintage	16
WR	6
Drink	17-20

Villa Maria Cellar Selection Organic Marlborough Pinot Noir   ★★★★

The 2015 vintage (★★★★) was matured in French oak barriques (10 per cent new). Deep ruby,
it is fresh and vibrantly fruity, with strong, plummy, gently spicy flavours, savoury notes adding
complexity, and a smooth, harmonious finish.

DRY $26 V+

Vintage	15	14
WR	6	6
Drink	17-20	17-20

Villa Maria Private Bin Marlborough Pinot Noir   ★★★☆

Offering fine value, the 2016 vintage (★★★☆) was grown in the Wairau and Awatere valleys,
and partly barrel-aged. Enjoyable young, it is bright ruby, with mouthfilling body, good depth
of ripe cherry, plum and spice flavours, showing a touch of complexity, and a dry, smooth finish.

DRY $20 V+

Vintage	16	15	14	13	12	11	10
WR	5	5	6	6	6	6	6
Drink	17-20	17-20	17-20	17-18	17-18	P	P

Villa Maria Reserve Marlborough Pinot Noir   ★★★★★

Launched from 2000, this label swiftly won recognition as one of the region's boldest, lushest
reds. Grown in the Awatere Valley and the Southern Valleys, it is hand-picked, matured in
French oak barriques (30 per cent new in 2015), and bottled with minimal fining and filtration.
The 2015 vintage (★★★★☆) was almost entirely (97 per cent) grown in the Awatere Valley
(principally Taylors Pass Vineyard). Still youthful, it is mouthfilling, savoury, ripe and well-
rounded, with generous cherry, plum and spice flavours, showing good complexity, gentle
tannins, and obvious potential; best drinking 2019+.

DRY $50 AV

Vintage	15	14	13	12	11	10	09
WR	7	7	7	7	7	7	7
Drink	17-22	17-22	17-20	17-22	17-19	17-19	17-18

Villa Maria Single Vineyard Attorney Organic Marlborough Pinot Noir   ★★★★☆

Grown in the Southern Valleys, the 2015 vintage (★★★★☆) was hand-harvested and matured in French oak barriques (11 per cent new). Bright ruby, it is ripe and savoury, with strong, vibrant cherry, plum and spice flavours, an earthy streak adding complexity, and a long, smooth finish. An elegant, youthful wine, it's well worth cellaring; open mid-2018+.

Vintage	15	14
WR	7	7
Drink	17-22	17-22

DRY $56 –V

Villa Maria Single Vineyard Seddon Marlborough Pinot Noir   ★★★★★

From an Awatere Valley site even further inland and higher than its stablemate (below), the very classy 2015 vintage (★★★★★) was hand-picked, fermented with indigenous yeasts, and matured for 14 months in French oak barriques (23 per cent new). A lovely young wine, it is rich and silky-textured, with deep cherry, plum and dried-herb flavours, complex, harmonious and lasting. Drink now or cellar.

Vintage	15	14	13	12	11	10	09	08
WR	7	7	7	7	7	7	7	NM
Drink	17-23	17-22	17-20	17-22	17-19	17-19	P	NM

DRY $55 AV

Villa Maria Single Vineyard Southern Clays Marlborough Pinot Noir   ★★★★★

Hand-picked from north-facing slopes of the Rutherford Vineyard, on the south side of the Wairau Valley, the 2015 vintage (★★★★★) was matured for 14 months in French oak barriques (33 per cent new). Already delicious, it is full-bodied, with concentrated, ripe, plummy, spicy flavours, complex, savoury, finely textured and seamless.

Vintage	15	14	13	12	11	10	09
WR	7	7	7	7	7	7	7
Drink	17-23	17-22	17-20	17-22	17-19	17-19	17-18

DRY $55 AV

Villa Maria Single Vineyard Taylors Pass Marlborough Pinot Noir   ★★★★★

Estate-grown in the upper Awatere Valley, the elegant 2015 vintage (★★★★☆) was hand-picked and matured for 14 months in French oak barriques (25 per cent new). Fresh and vibrantly fruity, it has generous, youthful cherry, plum and spice flavours, woven with lively acidity, finely integrated oak adding complexity, and obvious cellaring potential; open 2019+.

Vintage	15	14	13	12	11	10
WR	7	7	7	7	7	7
Drink	17-23	17-22	17-20	17-22	17-18	P

DRY $55 AV

Vista Nelson Pinot Noir   (★★★)

Grown at Kina, the 2014 vintage (★★★) was matured for 11 months in French oak casks (40 per cent new). It's an upfront style, with strong, ripe, spicy fruit flavours to the fore, and some smoky, savoury notes.

DRY $25 –V

Waimea Nelson Pinot Noir   ★★★☆

The 2015 vintage (★★★☆) was estate-grown at five sites on the Waimea Plains and barrel-aged for 10 months. Still youthful, it is ruby-hued and mouthfilling, with good depth of cherry, plum and spice flavours, hints of tamarillo and dried herbs, and some savoury complexity. Best drinking 2018+.

DRY $25 AV

Waipara Hills Waipara Valley Pinot Noir   ★★★☆

The 2015 vintage (★★★☆) is a youthful, ruby-hued wine, partly barrel-matured. Fragrant, with a plummy, spicy bouquet, it is mouthfilling, with vibrant fruit flavours, showing very good depth, a touch of complexity and gentle tannins. Best drinking 2018+.

DRY $22 V+

Waipara Springs Reserve Premo Pinot Noir   ★★★★

Drinking well now, the 2014 vintage (★★★★) is a mouthfilling, savoury red with strong, ripe flavours, showing good harmony and complexity.

DRY $32 AV

Waipara Springs Waipara Pinot Noir   ★★★

The 2015 vintage (★★★☆) is a medium-bodied red, fresh and flavoursome, with some savoury complexity and plenty of drink-now appeal.

DRY $22 AV

Wairau River Marlborough Pinot Noir   ★★★☆

Estate-grown on the north side of the Wairau Valley, the 2015 vintage (★★★☆) was matured for 10 months in French oak barriques. Full ruby, it is mouthfilling and smooth, with vibrant plum and spice flavours, showing some savoury complexity, and very good depth. Best drinking 2018+.

Vintage	15	14
WR	6	6
Drink	17-20	17-20

DRY $25 AV

Wairau River Reserve Marlborough Pinot Noir   ★★★★

Estate-grown at Rapaura, the 2015 vintage (★★★★) was matured in French oak casks and bottled unfined and unfiltered. Deeply coloured, it is mouthfilling, with concentrated, ripe plum and spice flavours, showing good complexity. A youthful, savoury, well-structured wine, it's worth cellaring; open 2018+.

Vintage	15	14
WR	6	7
Drink	17-22	17-23

DRY $40 –V

Walnut Block Collectables Marlborough Pinot Noir   ★★★

The 2015 vintage (★★★☆) is a weighty and sweet-fruited, ruby-hued red, full-bodied, with ripe cherry, plum and spice flavours, showing considerable complexity, and a smooth finish. Certified organic.

DRY $29 –V

Walnut Block Nutcracker Marlborough Pinot Noir   ★★★★

Certified organic, the 2015 vintage (★★★★) is still unfolding. Hand-picked, it was fermented with indigenous yeasts, matured for a year in oak barrels (25 per cent new), and bottled unfiltered. Freshly scented, it is full-bodied and supple, with strong, youthful cherry and plum flavours, oak complexity and obvious potential; open mid-2018+.

Vintage	15	14	13
WR	6	7	6
Drink	17-22	17-25	17-24

DRY $40 –V

Ward Valley Estate Mt Victoria Block Pinot Noir   (★★★☆)

The 2014 vintage (★★★☆) was grown in Marlborough. Lightish in colour, with a hint of development, it is moderately concentrated, with strawberryish, nutty flavours, showing some savoury, mushroomy complexity, gentle tannins and good harmony. Drink now.

DRY $25 AV

Westbrook Marlborough Pinot Noir   (★★★★)

Still on sale, the 2013 vintage (★★★★) was hand-harvested and matured in French oak barrels (25 per cent new). Maturing gracefully, it is full-coloured, with ripe plum, cherry and spice flavours, fresh and strong, and nutty, savoury notes adding complexity. Best drinking 2018+.

Vintage	13
WR	5
Drink	17-20

DRY $29 V+

Wild Earth Central Otago Pinot Noir   ★★★★

Still youthful, the 2014 vintage (★★★★) is a generous red, hand-harvested at Bannockburn and matured for a year in French oak barriques (29 per cent new). Bright ruby, it is fragrant and sturdy, with fresh acidity woven through its vibrant cherry, plum and spice flavours, supple and strong.

DRY $42 –V

Wild Earth Reserve Earth & Sky Pinot Noir   (★★★★)

Still on sale, the 2012 vintage (★★★★) of this Bannockburn red is ruby-hued, with a hint of development. French oak-aged for well over a year, it is fragrant and finely textured, with cherryish, plummy flavours, very gentle tannins, and loads of current-drinking appeal.

DRY $65 –V

Wild Earth Special Edition Central Otago Pinot Noir

Still youthful, the 2014 vintage (★★★★☆) is a selection of two clones revealing notable individuality (clones 5 and 115), grown at Bannockburn and matured for about eight months in French oak barriques (24 per cent new). Full, bright ruby, it is finely scented and vibrantly fruity, with strong cherry, plum and spice flavours, fine-grained tannins and obvious potential. Best drinking 2019+.

DRY $65 –V

Wild Grace Central Otago Pinot Noir

Launched from the 2015 vintage (★★★☆), this is an easy-drinking red, full ruby, mouthfilling and supple, with generous, ripe cherry, plum, spice and nut flavours. Moderately complex, it should be at its best 2018+. (From Constellation NZ.)

DRY $27 AV

Wild South Marlborough Pinot Noir ★★★

From Sacred Hill, the 2015 vintage (★★★) was partly barrel-aged. Ruby-hued, it is an attractive, drink-young charmer. Mouthfilling, it is vibrantly fruity, with cherryish, plummy, slightly spicy flavours and an ultra-smooth finish. Priced right.

DRY $18 V+

Wooing Tree Beetle Juice Central Otago Pinot Noir ★★★★

This single-vineyard Cromwell red is hand-picked and matured for eight or nine months in French oak casks (34 per cent new in 2016). The 2016 vintage (★★★★) is bright ruby, floral, mouthfilling and smooth, with vibrant cherry, plum, spice and dried-herb flavours, showing good complexity and harmony. Enjoyable from the start.

DRY $28 V+

Wooing Tree Central Otago Pinot Noir ★★★★★

This single-vineyard Cromwell red is typically classy. The 2016 vintage (★★★★☆) was hand-picked and matured for 10 months in French oak casks. Deep ruby, it is mouthfilling and still very youthful, with vibrant plum, cherry, spice and nut flavours, showing excellent concentration and complexity, and a poised, finely structured finish. Best drinking 2019+.

DRY $48 AV

Wooing Tree Sandstorm Reserve Single Vineyard Central Otago Pinot Noir ★★★★★

Estate-grown at Cromwell, this wine is hand-picked from especially low-yielding vines. Matured for a year in French oak casks (33 per cent new), the 2015 vintage (★★★★☆) is deep ruby, floral, weighty, sweet-fruited and supple. Still youthful, it has strong, cherryish, plummy flavours, complex and savoury, and gentle tannins. Best drinking mid-2018+.

DRY $85 –V

Yealands Estate Land Made Marlborough Pinot Noir ★★★

The 2014 vintage (★★★) is bright ruby, mouthfilling and smooth, with ripe plum and spice flavours, a touch of savoury complexity, and good depth. Drink now.

Vintage	14	13
WR	7	7
Drink	17-18	P

Yealands Estate Single Vineyard Awatere Valley Marlborough Pinot Noir ★★★★

Estate-grown in the vast, coastal Seaview Vineyard, the 2016 vintage (★★★★) was matured for nine months in large French oak cuves and barriques. Full, bright ruby, it is mouthfilling and sweet-fruited, with strong, vibrant plum/spice flavours, hints of tamarillo and herbs, and gentle acidity. Still youthful, it's a finely balanced, generous red, already enjoyable, but also worth cellaring. Good value.

Vintage	16	15	14
WR	6	7	7
Drink	17-22	17-20	17-19

Yealands Estate Winemaker's Reserve Awatere Valley Marlborough Pinot Noir ★★★★☆

Already delicious, the softly seductive 2016 vintage (★★★★☆) was estate-grown, hand-picked, and matured for a year in seasoned French oak barriques. Bright ruby, it is full-bodied and smooth, with strong, ripe cherry, plum and spice flavours, savoury notes adding complexity, very gentle tannins, and loads of drink-young appeal.

Vintage	16
WR	5
Drink	17-20

Yealands Estate Winemaker's Reserve Gibbston Central Otago Pinot Noir ★★★★☆

The 2016 vintage (★★★★☆) was grown at Gibbston and matured for a year in French oak barriques (30 per cent new). Full and youthful in colour, it is fragrant and mouthfilling, with vibrant, ripe flavours of cherries, plums and dried herbs, integrated oak, and a long, well-rounded finish. Best drinking 2019+.

Zephyr Marlborough Pinot Noir ★★★★

The 2014 vintage (★★★★) is a sweet-fruited, savoury red, grown in the Southern Valleys and matured for 10 months in French oak casks (15 per cent new). Ruby-hued, it is floral and supple, with ripe cherry and spice flavours, showing good complexity, and a lingering finish.

DRY $32 AV

Pinotage

Popular in New Zealand in the 1960s and 1970s, Pinotage is today overshadowed by more glamorous varieties, with just 28 hectares of bearing vines in 2018. Pinotage now ranks as the country's seventh most extensively planted red-wine variety, well behind Cabernet Franc, ranked sixth, and fifth-placed Malbec.

Pinotage is a cross of the great Burgundian grape, Pinot Noir, and Cinsaut, a heavy-cropping variety popular in the south of France. Cinsaut's typically 'meaty, chunky sort of flavour' (in Jancis Robinson's words) is also characteristic of Pinotage. Valued for its reasonably early-ripening and disease-resistant qualities, and good yields, its plantings are mostly in Gisborne (32 per cent), Marlborough (21 per cent) and Auckland (21 per cent), with smaller pockets in Hawke's Bay and Northland.

A well-made Pinotage displays a slightly gamey bouquet and a smooth, berryish, peppery palate that can be reminiscent of a southern Rhône. It matures swiftly and usually peaks within two or three years of the vintage.

Karikari Estate Pinotage ★★★★

Estate-grown on the Karikari Peninsula, in the Far North, the 2014 vintage (★★★★) is full-coloured and mouthfilling, with generous, ripe, plummy, spicy flavours and the earthy streak typical of Pinotage. Concentrated and firmly structured, it should be at its best 2018+.

DRY $48 –V

Linden Estate Hawke's Bay Pinotage (★★★★)

The fresh, age-worthy 2016 vintage (★★★★) was estate-grown and hand-picked in the Esk Valley. Full-coloured, it is mouthfilling and savoury, with ripe, plummy, spicy flavours, showing good complexity. Best drinking mid-2018+.

DRY $25 AV

Marsden Bay of Islands Pinotage ★★★☆

The deeply coloured, generous 2015 vintage (★★★☆) was hand-harvested from 25-year-old vines in Northland and oak-aged for a year. It has ripe, plummy, spicy, slightly gamey flavours, seasoned with sweet oak, in a soft, very drinkable style.

Vintage	15	14	13
WR	5	6	6
Drink	17-18	P	P

DRY $28 –V

NTN Jubilee Reserve Pinotage (★★★★☆)

'NTN' is Nick Nobilo, who in the 1970s was a key pioneer of Pinotage in New Zealand. Released in January 2016, the 2007 vintage (★★★★☆) is a 'once-only' wine, harvested in Gisborne at 24 brix and aged for two years in French and American oak barriques. Deep and mature in colour, with the gamey, 'wild' bouquet typical of Pinotage, it is powerful, fleshy, rich and smooth, with generous, savoury, spicy, earthy flavours. Full of personality, it's currently at the peak of its powers, and certainly proves Pinotage's ability to mature for a decade.

DRY $70 –V

Sangiovese

Sangiovese, Italy's most extensively planted red-wine variety, is a rarity in New Zealand. Cultivated as a workhorse grape throughout central Italy, in Tuscany it is the foundation of such famous reds as Chianti and Brunello di Montalcino. Here, Sangiovese has sometimes been confused with Montepulciano and its plantings are not expanding. Only 8 hectares of Sangiovese vines will be bearing in 2018, mostly in Auckland and Hawke's Bay.

Heron's Flight Matakana Sangiovese ★★★★☆

North of Auckland, David Hoskins and Mary Evans specialise in traditional Italian grape varieties. The 2013 vintage (★★★★☆), from vines averaging 15 years old, was matured for six months in French oak barriques (20 per cent new). The colour is bold, youthful and purple-flushed; the palate is powerful, with mouthfilling body, balanced acidity and rich, plummy, spicy flavours, showing good complexity.

DRY $60 –V

St Laurent

This Austrian variety is known for its deeply coloured, silky-smooth reds. It buds early, so is prone to frost damage, but ripens well ahead of Pinot Noir. Judge Rock imported the vine in 2001, but St Laurent is still extremely rare in New Zealand, with just 1.4 hectares of bearing vines in 2018, clustered in Waipara, Otago and Marlborough.

Hans Herzog Marlborough St Laurent ★★★★

Certified organic, the 2012 vintage (★★★★☆) was matured for 30 months in French oak barriques. Full and bright in colour, it is weighty and supple, with vibrant plum, spice, herb and dark chocolate flavours, showing excellent density and complexity. Drink now or cellar.

Vintage	12	11
WR	7	7
Drink	17-22	17-19

DRY $64 –V

Judge Rock Central Otago St Laurent (★★★)

The 2012 vintage (★★★) is a fresh, brightly coloured, light to medium-bodied red (11.2 per cent alcohol). Still youthful, it is moderately ripe-tasting, with plenty of plummy, berryish flavour, threaded with lively acidity.

DRY $35 –V

Syrah

Hawke's Bay and the upper North Island (especially Waiheke Island) have a hot, new-ish red-wine variety, attracting growing international acclaim. The classic 'Syrah' of the Rhône Valley, in France, and Australian 'Shiraz' are in fact the same variety. On the rocky, baking slopes of the upper Rhône Valley, and in several Australian states, this noble grape yields red wines renowned for their outstanding depth of cassis, plum and black-pepper flavours.

Syrah was well known in New Zealand a century ago. Government viticulturist S.F. Anderson wrote in 1917 that Shiraz was being 'grown in nearly all our vineyards [but] the trouble with this variety has been an unevenness in ripening its fruit'. For today's winemakers, the problem has not changed: Syrah has never favoured a too-cool growing environment (wines that are not fully ripe show distinct tomato or tamarillo characters). It needs sites that are relatively hot during the day and retain the heat at night, achieving ripeness in Hawke's Bay late in the season, at about the same time as Cabernet Sauvignon. To curb its natural vigour, stony, dry, low-fertility sites or warm hillside sites are crucial.

Four hundred and fifty hectares of Syrah will be bearing in 2018 – a steep rise from 62 hectares in 2000. Syrah is now New Zealand's third most widely planted red-wine variety, behind Pinot Noir and Merlot, but well ahead of Cabernet Sauvignon, Malbec and Cabernet Franc. Over 75 per cent of the vines are in Hawke's Bay, with most of the rest in Auckland and Northland (although there are pockets as far south as Central Otago).

Syrah's potential in this country's warmer vineyard sites is finally being tapped. The top wines possess rich, vibrant blackcurrant, plum and black-pepper flavours, with an enticingly floral bouquet, and are winning growing international applause.

Could Syrah replace Bordeaux-style Merlot and Cabernet Sauvignon-based blends over the next decade or two as the principal red-wine style from Hawke's Bay and the upper North Island? Don't rule it out.

Ake Ake Northland Syrah   ★★★

The 2014 vintage (★★★☆) was matured in tanks and seasoned American oak casks. The colour is dense and inky; the palate is mouthfilling and vibrantly fruity, with strong, plummy, spicy flavours, a restrained oak influence, fresh acidity and gentle tannins. Worth cellaring.

Vintage	14
WR	5
Drink	17-18

DRY $25 –V

Alpha Domus The Barnstormer Hawke's Bay Syrah   ★★★★

Matured for a year in predominantly French oak barriques, the 2016 vintage (★★★★) was designed as a 'fruit-driven' style. Full-coloured, it is fragrant, mouthfilling and vibrantly fruity, with generous plum, spice and black-pepper flavours to the fore, well-integrated oak and considerable complexity. Still youthful, it's well worth cellaring to at least mid-2018+.

Vintage	16	15
WR	5	6
Drink	17-21	17-21

DRY $35 –V

Anchorage Family Estate Nelson Syrah   (★★★)

Enjoyable young, the 2015 vintage (★★★) has a Pinot Noir-ish charm. Wood-aged for six months, it is a full-coloured, medium-bodied red with good depth of fresh, ripe, plummy and spicy flavours, gentle tannins and a smooth, slightly peppery finish. Priced right.

DRY $18 AV

Ash Ridge Doppio Chave Syrah   (★★★★★)

The impressive 2014 vintage (★★★★★) is based solely on the Chave clone of Syrah. Estate-grown in the Bridge Pa Triangle, Hawke's Bay, it was barrel-aged for 20 months, and bottled unfined and unfiltered. Deep and youthful in colour, it is powerful, savoury and supple, with concentrated, plummy, spicy flavours, showing excellent ripeness, depth and complexity. (Sold only in a two-pack, including the Doppio MS Syrah 2014, for $150.)

 DRY $75 AV

Ash Ridge Doppio MS Syrah   (★★★★☆)

The elegant 2014 vintage (★★★★☆) is based solely on the MS (Mass Selection) clone of Syrah. Like its Doppio stablemate (see above), it was estate-grown in the Bridge Pa Triangle, Hawke's Bay, barrel-aged for 20 months, and bottled unfined and unfiltered. The colour is full and bright; the palate is fresh and generous, with concentrated, vibrant, strongly varietal plum and black-pepper flavours, lively and lingering. (Sold only in a two-pack, including the Doppio Chave Syrah 2014, for $150.)

 DRY $75 –V

Ash Ridge Estate Hawke's Bay Syrah   ★★★☆

The 2016 vintage (★★★☆), estate-grown in the Bridge Pa Triangle, is this fast-emerging producer's top-selling wine. Matured in French and American oak barrels (mostly seasoned), it is a full-coloured, medium-bodied red, with fresh, youthful, plummy, spicy flavours, gentle tannins, and very good balance and depth. Priced right.

Vintage	16	15	14	13	12	11	10	09
WR	6	6	7	7	6	6	7	7
Drink	17-19	17-20	17-21	17-20	17-18	17-18	P	P

 DRY $20 AV

Ash Ridge Premium Estate Hawke's Bay Syrah   ★★★★☆

The stylish 2015 vintage (★★★★☆) was matured in predominantly French oak casks (25 per cent new). Deeply coloured, it has an invitingly floral, spicy bouquet, leading into a medium to full-bodied red with concentrated, youthful, plummy, spicy flavours, good complexity and a supple, lingering finish. Best drinking 2018+.

 DRY $30 AV

Ash Ridge Vintners Reserve Hawke's Bay Syrah   ★★★★☆

The very stylish 2015 vintage (★★★★★) was estate-grown in the Bridge Pa Triangle, matured in French (mostly) and American oak casks (20 per cent new), and bottled unfined and unfiltered. Full-coloured, it is mouthfilling and concentrated, with deep plum/spice flavours, hints of liquorice and dark chocolate, savoury notes adding complexity, and a finely textured, lasting finish. A classy young red with obvious potential, it should be at its best 2020+.

DRY $50 –V

Awaroa Melba Peach Waiheke Island Syrah ★★★★★

Still youthful, the 2015 vintage (★★★★☆) is a concentrated, finely textured Waiheke Island red. Well worth cellaring, it has rich blackberry, spice, liquorice and toasty oak flavours, fine-grained tannins, and excellent balance and length. (In a vertical tasting held in late 2016, the 2014 (★★★★★), 2013 (★★★★★) and 2010 (★★★★★) vintages showed notable ripeness and density.)

Vintage	15	14	13	12	11	10
WR	6	7	7	5	NM	7
Drink	18-22	18-22	17-21	17-18	NM	17-24

DRY $65 AV

Awaroa The Dan Syrah/Cabernet/Malbec (★★★★★)

Deeply coloured and fragrant, the 2014 vintage (★★★★★) is Awaroa's first reserve blend of Syrah (65 per cent) and Cabernet Sauvignon (23 per cent), with a splash of Malbec (12 per cent). Matured in all-new French oak barriques, it is powerful, with concentrated, ripe plum, blackcurrant and spice flavours, and fine, silky tannins. Currently delicious.

Vintage	14
WR	7
Drink	19-23

DRY $65 –V

Awaroa Waiheke Island Syrah ★★★★

The full-coloured 2015 vintage (★★★☆) is a medium to full-bodied red with fresh, plummy, spicy flavours, hints of tamarillos, olives and herbs, a gentle seasoning of toasty oak, fine-grained tannins and a very smooth finish.

Vintage	14
WR	6
Drink	17-20

DRY $38 –V

Babich Hawke's Bay Syrah ★★★

The 2016 vintage (★★★) was briefly oak-matured. Ruby-hued, with a floral, peppery bouquet, it is medium-bodied, with vibrant plum and black-pepper flavours, gentle tannins and a well-rounded finish. Best drinking mid-2018+.

DRY $22 –V

Babich Winemakers Reserve Hawke's Bay Syrah ★★★★☆

Likely to be long-lived, the 2015 vintage (★★★★☆) is a concentrated, firmly structured, single-vineyard red, estate-grown in the Bridge Pa Triangle and matured for a year in French oak barrels (25 per cent new). Dark, with a fragrant bouquet of violets, oak complexity and rich plum, blackcurrant, spice and slight liquorice flavours, it's well worth cellaring.

DRY $35 AV

Beach House Gimblett Gravels Hawke's Bay Syrah ★★★★

Still unfolding, the 2015 vintage (★★★★☆) is a single-vineyard red, matured for a year in French oak casks (25 per cent new). It has a floral, peppery bouquet, leading into a mouthfilling, savoury wine with youthful, fresh plum, spice and black-pepper flavours, oak complexity, excellent intensity and the structure to mature well. Open 2019+.

 DRY $30 –V

Bell Bird Bay Reserve Hawke's Bay Syrah (★★★☆)

Grown in the Bridge Pa Triangle, the 2014 vintage (★★★☆) was matured in French oak barriques. Full-coloured, it is mouthfilling and savoury, with strong, spicy, slightly toasty flavours, woven with fresh acidity. Drink now to 2018. (From Alpha Domus.)

 DRY $28 –V

Boundary Vineyards Farm Lane Hawke's Bay Syrah ★★★★

From Pernod Ricard NZ, the 2015 vintage (★★★★) was estate-grown in the Bridge Pa Triangle. Delicious young, it is deeply coloured, with strong plum, spice and black-pepper flavours, savoury notes adding complexity, and good ripeness and harmony.

DRY $20 V+

Brookfields Back Block Hawke's Bay Syrah ★★★☆

Matured in seasoned French and American oak casks, the youthful 2016 vintage (★★★☆) is a full-coloured, mouthfilling red with very good depth of plum, spice and black-pepper flavours, showing considerable complexity. Already enjoyable, it should be at its best 2019+.

Vintage	16	15
WR	7	7
Drink	18-23	18-22

DRY $20 AV

Brookfields Hillside Syrah ★★★★★

This distinguished red is grown on a sheltered, north-facing slope between Maraekakaho and Bridge Pa, in Hawke's Bay (described by winemaker Peter Robertson as 'surreal – a chosen site'). The 2015 vintage (★★★★★), matured in new French (mostly) and American oak casks, is deeply coloured, fragrant and concentrated, with deep, ripe blackcurrant, spice, plum and black-pepper flavours, a hint of liquorice, and lovely density and smoothness. Best drinking 2018+.

Vintage	15	14	13
WR	7	7	7
Drink	20-26	18-25	18-23

 DRY $45 AV

Byrne Puketotara Northland Syrah (★★★☆)

The 2015 vintage (★★★☆) was grown in the Fat Pig Vineyard and matured in old French oak casks. Full and bright in colour, it has a spicy bouquet, leading into a medium-bodied red with fresh, strong, plummy, nutty, distinctly peppery flavours, showing considerable complexity.

 DRY $24 AV

Byrne Te Puna Northland Syrah   (★★★★★)

From a coastal site, overlooking Te Puna Inlet, the impressive 2015 vintage (★★★★★) was matured in French oak casks (50 per cent new) and bottled unfiltered. Deeply coloured, it has a fragrant, plummy, spicy, nutty bouquet. Sturdy (14.5 per cent alcohol), it is powerful, sweet-fruited and concentrated, with a strong surge of fresh, ripe plum, pepper and liquorice flavours. An arresting wine, it should be long-lived.

DRY $42 AV

Byrne Waingaro Northland Syrah   (★★★★★)

Offering fine value, the 2015 vintage (★★★★★) is a single-vineyard red, blended with Viognier (4 per cent) and matured in French oak barriques (one-third new). Full-coloured, it is perfumed, weighty and savoury, with excellent depth of blackcurrant, plum, liquorice and spice flavours, seasoned with toasty oak, and ripe, supple tannins. Full of personality, it's well worth cellaring.

DRY $32 AV

Cable Bay Reserve Waiheke Island Syrah   (★★★★)

The 2015 vintage (★★★★) was co-fermented with Viognier and matured for 18 months in a one-year-old French oak puncheon. Full-coloured, with a fresh, strong, peppery bouquet, it is a medium to full-bodied, vibrantly fruity wine, with very good depth of plummy, peppery flavours, a gentle seasoning of oak, and gentle tannins. Enjoyable young, it's worth cellaring and should break into full stride 2019+.

Vintage	15
WR	6
Drink	17-37

DRY $95 –V

Cable Bay Waiheke Island Syrah   ★★★★

The 2015 vintage (★★★★) is a single-vineyard red, hand-harvested and matured for 16 months in French oak barrels. Full and youthful in colour, it is a medium to full-bodied style with good density of ripe plum and spice flavours, savoury notes adding complexity, and good potential. Best drinking mid-2018+.

Vintage	15	14	13	12	11	10	09
WR	6	5	6	6	5	7	7
Drink	17-37	17-22	17-23	17-20	17-18	17-20	P

DRY $48 –V

Cathedral Cove Hawke's Bay Syrah   (★★★)

Priced very sharply, the 2013 vintage (★★★) is a full-coloured, mouthfilling, clearly varietal red with peppery aromas, fresh acidity, plenty of flavour and a smooth finish.

DRY $10 V+

Church Road Grand Reserve Hawke's Bay Syrah ★★★★★

Full of potential, the 2015 vintage (★★★★★) is a rich, sturdy red, grown in the Bridge Pa Triangle and the Gimblett Gravels, matured for 17 months in French (mostly) and Hungarian oak barriques (34 per cent new), and bottled unfiltered. Powerful yet elegant, it is still very youthful, with dense plum and black-pepper flavours, finely integrated oak, good tannin backbone and a highly fragrant, spicy bouquet.

Church Road Hawke's Bay Syrah ★★★★

The 2015 vintage (★★★★) is a great buy. Estate-grown in the Bridge Pa Triangle (70 per cent) and the Gimblett Gravels (30 per cent), it was matured for 18 months in French and Hungarian oak vessels (30 per cent new). Purple-flushed, with a floral, slightly peppery bouquet, it is softly mouthfilling, with generous plum and spice flavours, hints of liquorice, dark chocolate and nuts, very gentle tannins and considerable complexity. If you enjoy Pinot Noir, try this highly approachable red. Fine value.

Church Road McDonald Series Hawke's Bay Syrah ★★★★★

The bargain-priced 2015 vintage (★★★★☆) was estate-grown in the Bridge Pa Triangle (54 per cent) and the Gimblett Gravels (46 per cent). Matured for 19 months in French and Hungarian oak casks (15 per cent new), it is densely coloured and fragrant, with mouthfilling body and deep, youthful plum, spice and black-pepper flavours. Finely textured, it shows excellent concentration and cellaring potential; best drinking 2019+.

Church Road Tom Syrah ★★★★★

Syrah is the latest addition to Church Road's elite Tom selection. The second, 2014 vintage (★★★★★) was mostly estate-grown in the Redstone Vineyard, in the Bridge Pa Triangle, Hawke's Bay; 16 per cent was grown in the Gimblett Gravels. Harvested at 24 to 25.7 brix, and matured for 22 months in French oak barriques (54 per cent new), it is already delicious. A densely coloured, robust wine (15 per cent alcohol), it has lush, concentrated, very ripe blackcurrant, plum and spice flavours, hints of dark chocolate, black pepper and liquorice, and lovely fragrance and harmony.

Clayvin Single Vineyard Selection Marlborough Syrah   (★★★★☆)

From Giesen, the elegant 2013 vintage (★★★★☆) is still unfolding. Grown in the elevated Clayvin Vineyard, on the south side of the Wairau Valley, it is a full-coloured, medium to full-bodied red with concentrated, ripe plum/spice flavours, vibrant and youthful, and very good complexity. Best drinking 2018+.

Vintage	13
WR	6
Drink	17-22

 DRY $70 –V

Clearview Cape Kidnappers Hawke's Bay Syrah   ★★★★

Delicious young, the 2016 vintage (★★★★) is a full-coloured red, grown at Te Awanga and matured for eight months in French oak casks (10 per cent new). The bouquet is floral, plummy and spicy; the palate is mouthfilling, vibrantly fruity and supple, with ripe plum, spice and black-pepper flavours, finely integrated oak, savoury notes adding complexity, and a finely textured, very harmonious finish. Best drinking mid-2018+.

 DRY $27 AV

Clearview Reserve Hawke's Bay Syrah   ★★★★☆

Already delicious, the 2016 vintage (★★★★☆) was grown at Te Awanga, whole bunch-fermented and matured for 14 months in seasoned French oak puncheons. Deep ruby, with a floral, plummy, spicy bouquet, it is mouthfilling, vibrantly fruity and supple, with fresh, concentrated flavours and a finely textured, lasting finish. Best drinking 2019+.

 DRY $38 AV

Clevedon Hills Syrah   ★★★★☆

Estate-grown at Clevedon, in South Auckland, the 2014 vintage (★★★★) is deeply coloured, mouthfilling, rich and supple, with vibrant plum, spice and black-pepper flavours, gently seasoned with oak, and a finely textured, harmonious finish. Well worth cellaring.

 DRY $45 –V

Clos de Ste Anne The Crucible Syrah   ★★★★★

The 2015 vintage (★★★★★) is impressive. Grown biodynamically in Millton's elevated Clos de Ste Anne Vineyard in Gisborne, it was hand-harvested, co-fermented with Viognier (5 per cent), and matured in large, seasoned French oak casks. Deeply coloured, it is floral and full-bodied, with plum, spice and black-pepper flavours, hints of earth and dark chocolate, and notable depth, complexity and harmony. A very distinctive red, it's already delicious.

DRY $75 AV

Coopers Creek Hawke's Bay Syrah   ★★★☆

The 2014 vintage (★★★☆) has full, bright, youthful colour. Full-bodied, it's an exuberantly fruity red with very good depth of spicy, distinctly plummy flavour. Drink now to 2019.

Vintage	14	13
WR	7	7
Drink	18-20	18-19

 DRY $22 AV

Coopers Creek Reserve Hawke's Bay Syrah ★★★★★

The 2013 vintage (★★★★★) is a bold, rich red, dark and strongly varietal, with dense blackcurrant, plum and black-pepper flavours. A powerful, youthful wine with ripe tannins, it has impressive concentration and length.

Vintage	13
WR	7
Drink	18-24

DRY $57 AV

Coopers Creek SV Chalk Ridge Hawke's Bay Syrah ★★★★☆

The classy 2015 vintage (★★★★☆) is a single-vineyard red, offering fine value. Floral and deeply coloured, it is still youthful, with excellent density of plummy, spicy, peppery, distinctly varietal flavours and a long, finely textured finish. Full-bodied, it's a very age-worthy wine, likely to be at its best 2019+.

Vintage	15	14	13
WR	6	7	7
Drink	17-21	17-21	17-20

DRY $28 V+

Coopers Creek SV Gimblett Gravels Hawke's Bay Syrah (★★★★★)

Highly expressive in its youth, but very age-worthy, the 2014 vintage (★★★★★) is a dark, fragrant blend (2 per cent Viognier), matured in French oak casks (20 per cent new). Concentrated, sweet-fruited and finely structured, it is rich, ripe and smooth, with hints of liquorice. Great value.

Vintage	14	13
WR	7	6
Drink	18-22	18-20

DRY $28 V+

Couper's Shed Hawke's Bay Syrah ★★★☆

The strongly varietal 2015 vintage (★★★★) is deeply coloured, mouthfilling and supple, with excellent depth of plum/spice flavours, showing some savoury complexity. Delicious young, it offers fine value. (From Pernod Ricard NZ.)

DRY $23 AV

Craft Farm Lyons Vineyard Hawke's Bay Syrah (★★★★☆)

From an elevated site, overlooking Bridge Pa, the graceful 2014 vintage (★★★★☆) was hand-picked from young vines, matured for 14 months in French oak barrels (50 per cent new), and bottled unfined and unfiltered. Floral, deeply coloured, sweet-fruited and supple, it is still youthful, with mouthfilling body, concentrated, ripe plum/spice flavours, and gentle tannins. It shows obvious cellaring potential; open 2018+.

DRY $45 –V

Craggy Range Gimblett Gravels Vineyard Hawke's Bay Syrah ★★★★★

This label is overshadowed by the reputation of its stablemate, Le Sol, but proves the power, structure and finesse that can be achieved with Syrah grown in the Gimblett Gravels of Hawke's Bay. The outstanding, age-worthy 2014 vintage (★★★★) was hand-harvested at 23.7 brix and matured for 16 months in French oak barriques (26 per cent new). Dark and purple-flushed, it is mouthfilling, with concentrated, ripe plum and black-pepper flavours, a hint of dark chocolate, and a long, spicy finish. Densely packed and still youthful, it should hit full stride 2019+.

DRY $36 V+

Craggy Range Le Sol Syrah – see Craggy Range Le Sol in the Branded and Other Red Wines section

Crossroads Talisman Gimblett Gravels Syrah ★★★★★

The floral, graceful, very finely textured 2014 vintage (★★★★★) was estate-grown in The Elms Vineyard, matured for 14 months in French oak barriques (40 per cent new), and then aged for another four months in old barrels. Deeply coloured, with rich, ripe blackcurrant and spice flavours, hints of dark chocolate and liquorice, and a long, slightly peppery finish, it's already delicous, but should be at its best 2019+.

Vintage	14	13
WR	7	7
Drink	17-29	17-23

DRY $45 AV

Crossroads Winemakers Collection Gimblett Gravels Hawke's Bay Syrah ★★★★☆

The sturdy, youthful, clearly varietal 2014 vintage (★★★★☆) was estate-grown and hand-harvested in The Elms Vineyard, and matured for 14 months in French oak barriques (20 per cent new). It has concentrated plum and spice flavours, seasoned with nutty oak, earthy notes adding complexity, and good tannin backbone. Best drinking 2018+.

DRY $40 –V

Cypress Hawke's Bay Syrah ★★★☆

Estate-grown at the base of Roys Hill, hand-picked and matured for eight months in seasoned oak barrels, the 2014 vintage (★★★★) is sweet-fruited, with strong plum/spice flavours, showing very good depth, complexity and harmony.

DRY $26 –V

Cypress Terraces Hawke's Bay Syrah ★★★★

Estate-grown at an elevated, terraced site on Roys Hill, in the Gimblett Gravels, the 2013 vintage (★★★★☆) was matured for 20 months in French oak casks. It's a very savoury, complex wine with strong plum and spice flavours, a hint of liquorice, and fine-grained tannins.

DRY $42 –V

De La Terre Hawke's Bay Syrah ★★★★

The 2014 vintage (★★★★) was estate-grown at Havelock North and matured for over a year in French oak barriques (20 per cent new). Floral, with a slightly peppery fragrance, it is mouthfilling, with generous, vibrant, plummy, spicy flavours, oak complexity, and deep, youthful colour. Drink now or cellar.

Vintage	14	13
WR	6	6
Drink	17-20	17-20

 DRY $30 –V

De La Terre Reserve Hawke's Bay Syrah ★★★★☆

The classy 2015 vintage (★★★★☆), estate-grown at Havelock North, was matured for 16 months in French oak barrriques (50 per cent new). A very graceful, youthful red, it is full-coloured and mouthfilling, with fresh, concentrated plum and black-pepper flavours, well-integrated oak, fine-grained tannins and a long, spicy finish. Best drinking 2020+.

Vintage	15	14	13
WR	6	7	6
Drink	17-27	17-25	17-25

 DRY $45 –V

Dry River Lovat Vineyard Martinborough Syrah ★★★★☆

The 2013 vintage (★★★★☆) is labelled 'Amaranth', meaning it is recommended for long-term cellaring. Deep and youthful in colour, it is medium-bodied (12 per cent alcohol), floral and supple, with rich plum, spice and pepper flavours, tightly structured and smooth-flowing. Still youthful, it should be at its best 2018+.

Vintage	13	12	11	10	09	08	07	06	05
WR	7	NM	6	6	7	7	6	7	7
Drink	17-29	NM	17-26	17-20	17-23	17-22	17-21	17-20	P

 DRY $64 –V

Dunleavy The Grafter Single Vineyard Syrah (★★★★)

The 2015 vintage (★★★★) is a full-coloured Waiheke Island red, French oak-aged. Firm and spicy, it is strongly flavoured, with good complexity and obvious cellaring potential.

 DRY $40 –V

Easthope Moteo Hawke's Bay Syrah (★★★★☆)

The 2014 vintage (★★★★☆) was matured in thick concrete, egg-shaped tanks, and bottled without fining or filtration. Deeply coloured, it is mouthfilling and savoury, with concentrated, ripe plum/spice flavours, fine-grained tannins and good harmony. Drink now or cellar.

DRY $45 –V

Elephant Hill Airavata Hawke's Bay Syrah   (★★★★★)

Promoted as 'our flagship Syrah', the lovely 2013 vintage (★★★★★) was estate-grown in the Gimblett Gravels and at Te Awanga, and matured for 17 months in French oak casks (60 per cent new). Rich and youthful in colour, it is deliciously rich, supple and harmonious, with deep plum, spice and black-pepper flavours, complex, savoury and smooth-flowing. Combining power and elegance, it's a notably 'complete' wine, likely to be at its best 2020+.

DRY $105 AV

Elephant Hill Gimblett Vineyard Hawke's Bay Syrah   (★★★★★)

Tasted in early 2017, the debut 2013 vintage (★★★★★) is a classy, still very youthful, single-vineyard red, estate-grown in the Gimblett Gravels and matured for 16 months in French oak casks (35 per cent new). Fragrant, with deep, purple-flushed colour, it is rich and smooth, with concentrated blackcurrant, plum and spice flavours and a silky-textured, long, very harmonious finish. Sure to be long-lived, it should be at its best 2020+.

DRY $75 AV

Elephant Hill Hawke's Bay Syrah   ★★★★☆

The youthful 2015 vintage (★★★★☆) was grown in the Gimblett Gravels, at Te Awanga and in the Bridge Pa Triangle, blended with Viognier (1 per cent), and matured for 13 months in French oak casks (30 per cent new). Deeply coloured, it is fragrant and full-bodied, with deep, ripe plum and black-pepper flavours, fresh and supple, and a long, spicy finish. Finely structured, with good density, it should be at its best 2019+.

Vintage	15
WR	6
Drink	17-25

DRY $34 AV

Elephant Hill Reserve Hawke's Bay Syrah   ★★★★★

The stylish, finely poised 2014 vintage (★★★★★) was hand-picked in the Gimblett Gravels, at Te Awanga and in the Bridge Pa Triangle, and matured for 19 months in French oak casks (35 per cent new). Dark and purple-flushed, it is densely packed, with ripe, youthful plum and spice flavours, a hint of liquorice, good tannin backbone, excellent complexity, and a long future ahead. Best drinking 2019+.

DRY $49 AV

Esk Valley Gimblett Gravels Hawke's Bay Syrah   ★★★★☆

Offering fine value, the 2015 vintage (★★★★☆) was matured for 17 months in French oak barrels (15 per cent new). Already delicious, it is deeply coloured and fragrant, with vibrant plum and black-pepper flavours, showing excellent ripeness and richness, and a long, supple finish.

DRY $25 V+

Vintage	15	14	13	12	11	10	09
WR	7	6	6	6	5	6	6
Drink	17-22	17-20	17-20	17-19	P	17-18	P

Esk Valley Winemakers Reserve Gimblett Gravels Hawke's Bay Syrah   ★★★★★

Densely coloured, the powerful 2014 vintage (★★★★★) was grown in the Cornerstone Vineyard and matured for 16 months in French oak barriques (55 per cent new). A floral, vibrantly fruity red, it is sturdy (14.5 per cent alcohol), with highly concentrated, ripe plum, blackcurrant and spice flavours and a lush, smooth finish. Already delicious, it should be at its best 2019+.

Vintage	14	13	12	11	10	09	08	07
WR	7	6	NM	NM	7	7	NM	7
Drink	17-22	17-20	NM	NM	17-20	17-20	NM	17-18

DRY $60 AV

Expatrius Waiheke Island Syrah   ★★★★★

Grown on an 'elevated coastal headland', the 2013 vintage (★★★★★) was matured in new French oak barrels for 15 months. Deep and bright in colour, it is sturdy (14 per cent alcohol), youthful and very finely textured, with generous, ripe, plummy, gently spicy flavours, fine-grained tannins and obvious potential. Showing great harmony, it's already delicious, but should be at its best 2018 onwards.

DRY $85 –V

Falconhead Hawke's Bay Syrah   ★★★☆

Offering great value, the 2014 vintage (★★★☆) is a finely balanced Syrah that includes a splash of Viognier (4.5 per cent). Full and bright in colour, it is mouthfilling and smooth, with plum/spice flavours, a hint of dark chocolate, gentle tannins, and some savoury complexity. Ready.

Vintage	14	13
WR	7	7
Drink	17-20	17-20

DRY $16 V+

Frenchmans Hill Estate Waiheke Island Rock Earth Syrah   ★★★★★

The densely coloured 2014 vintage (★★★★★) was estate-grown in The 8 Vineyard and matured for 16 months in French oak barriques (60 per cent new). Still a baby, it is powerful and highly concentrated, with a firm backbone of tannin and bold blackcurrant, plum and spice flavours. Showing obvious potential, it should be at its best 2022+.

DRY $125 AV

Fromm La Strada Marlborough Syrah   ★★★★

A cool-climate, 'fruit-driven' style – with style. The 2015 vintage (★★★★☆), which includes a splash of Viognier, is certified organic. From various sites, including Fromm Vineyard and Clayvin Vineyard, it was hand-picked and matured in barriques and puncheons. Deeply coloured, with a fragrant, fresh, peppery bouquet, it is mouthfilling and firmly structured, with deep plum, spice and pepper flavours, oak complexity, and excellent potential for cellaring.

Vintage	15	14	13	12	11	10
WR	7	7	7	7	7	7
Drink	17-22	17-21	17-21	17-20	17-20	17-19

DRY $40 –V

Fromm Syrah Fromm Vineyard   ★★★★☆

Estate-grown in the Wairau Valley, Marlborough, and co-fermented with a splash of Viognier (3 per cent), the very impressive 2015 vintage (★★★★★) is a rare red (only four barrels were produced). Certified organic, it was harvested from vines averaging over 20 years old. Deep and youthful in colour, it is mouthfilling and highly concentrated, with plum, spice and black-pepper flavours, ripe, dense and complex, that build to a finely textured, powerful finish. It should be very long-lived; drink 2020 onwards.

Goldie Reserve Waiheke Island Syrah   (★★★★☆)

The powerful 2014 vintage (★★★★☆) is dark and fragrant, with lush, youthful plum/spice flavours, seasoned with nutty oak, and good tannin backbone. Well worth cellaring.

Hopesgrove Estate Single Vineyard Hawke's Bay Syrah   ★★★★☆

Estate-grown and hand-picked, the 2013 vintage (★★★★☆) was matured in French oak casks (40 per cent new). Dark and youthful, it is mouthfilling and strongly varietal, with rich, plummy, peppery flavours, showing good complexity, and a finely textured, harmonious finish. Best drinking 2018+.

Vintage	13	12	11
WR	6	NM	4
Drink	17-25	NM	17-19

Karikari Estate Syrah   ★★★★

Showing what can be achieved with Syrah in the warmth of the Far North, the powerful 2013 vintage (★★★★☆) was estate-grown on the Karikari Peninsula. The colour is deep, with a hint of development; the palate is sturdy and well-rounded, with very generous, plummy, spicy, nutty flavours, ripe tannins and a fragrant, slightly peppery bouquet. Concentrated, with earthy notes adding complexity, it's maturing well.

DRY $55 –V

Kidnapper Cliffs Gimblett Gravels Hawke's Bay Syrah   (★★★★★)

From Te Awa, the 2013 vintage (★★★★★), released in 2017, is a classy, youthful red, estate-grown, hand-picked, fermented with indigenous yeasts and matured for 20 months in French oak hogsheads (35 per cent new). Deeply coloured, with a highly fragrant bouquet, it is mouthfilling, with deep, ripe plum, spice and black-pepper flavours, fine-grained tannins and excellent complexity. Still unfolding, it's a savoury, very harmonious and age-worthy red; best drinking 2019+.

DRY $70 AV

La Collina Syrah ★★★★★

La Collina ('The Hill') is grown at Bilancia's steep, early-ripening site on the northern slopes of Roys Hill, overlooking the Gimblett Gravels, Hawke's Bay, co-fermented with Viognier skins (but not their juice, giving a tiny Viognier component in the final blend), and matured for 20 to 24 months in 85 per cent new (but 'low-impact') French oak barriques. A majestic red, it ranks among the country's very finest Syrahs. The 2014 vintage (★★★★★) is perfumed and weighty, but not heavy, with dark, youthful colour. Showing strong personality, it combines power and elegance, with plum, spice, liquorice and black-pepper flavours, refined tannins, and excellent complexity and depth. The 2015 vintage (★★★★★) is full-coloured, with a floral, complex bouquet. Still very youthful, it is savoury, with strong, ripe, plummy, spicy flavours, fine-grained tannins and a lasting finish. Open 2020+.

Vintage	15	14	13	12	11	10
WR	7	7	7	NM	NM	7
Drink	18-28	17-27	17-30	NM	NM	17-28

DRY $120 AV

Landing [The] Bay of Islands Syrah ★★★★☆

The stylish 2013 vintage (★★★★☆) was grown at the Mountain Landing Vineyard, in Northland, and matured for 18 months in French oak barriques (30 per cent new). The colour is deep and still youthful; the palate is powerful, sweet-fruited and concentrated, with dense, ripe, plummy, spicy flavours, showing good structure and complexity. Maturing well, it's likely to be at its best 2018+. The generous, weighty 2015 vintage (★★★★) is full-coloured, with strong, ripe red-berry and spice flavours, oak complexity, and a silky-smooth finish.

DRY $38 AV

Left Field Hawke's Bay Syrah ★★★☆

The 2015 vintage (★★★★) is delicious young. Matured in French oak casks (10 per cent new), it's a generous, mouthfilling wine, with ripe plum, spice and black-pepper flavours, gentle tannins, good complexity and a well-rounded finish. (From Te Awa, owned by Villa Maria.)

Vintage	15	14
WR	5	5
Drink	17-21	17-20

DRY $25 –V

Leveret Estate Hawke's Bay Syrah ★★★☆

Barrel-aged for a year, the 2014 vintage (★★★☆) is a fruit-driven style, blended from Syrah (95 per cent) and Viognier (5 per cent). Full-coloured and supple, with vibrant plum and black-pepper flavours, fresh and generous, it's delicious young.

Vintage	14	13
WR	6	7
Drink	18-22	17-20

DRY $23 AV

Leveret Estate Reserve Hawke's Bay Syrah ★★★★

Drinking well now, the 2014 vintage (★★★★), blended with Viognier (5 per cent), was matured in French oak casks (20 per cent new). Full-coloured, it is sturdy and generous, with ripe plum/spice flavours, savoury notes adding complexity, good backbone and excellent depth. Ready, but no rush.

DRY $30 –V

Vintage	14	13
WR	6	7
Drink	18-22	18-22

Linden Estate Hawke's Bay Syrah ★★★☆

Worth cellaring, the 2015 vintage (★★★☆) was French oak-matured for 18 months. Full-coloured, it is a fresh, medium to full-bodied red, with very good depth of plummy, spicy flavour, a hint of liquorice, considerable complexity and good tannin support.

DRY $30 –V

Vintage	15
WR	5
Drink	17-25

Linden Estate Hawke's Bay Syrah/Cabernet Sauvignon/Merlot/Malbec (★★★★)

Already drinking well, the 2015 vintage (★★★★) was estate-grown in the Esk Valley, hand-picked and matured for a year in French oak barriques. A full-coloured blend of Syrah (41 per cent), Cabernet Sauvignon (32 per cent), Merlot (18 per cent) and Malbec (9 per cent), it is fragrant, full-bodied and smooth, with an array of blackcurrant, plum, spice and black-pepper flavours, gentle tannins, and very good depth and complexity. Drink now or cellar.

DRY $35 –V

Linden Estate Reserve Hawke's Bay Syrah (★★★★)

Very age-worthy, the youthful 2015 vintage (★★★★) was estate-grown in the Esk Valley, hand-picked and matured in French oak barrels. Deeply coloured, with a fresh, spicy bouquet, it is full-bodied, with strong, ripe plum, spice and black-pepper flavours, nutty, savoury notes adding complexity, and good tannin backbone. Best drinking 2019+.

DRY $48 –V

Vintage	15
WR	7
Drink	17-25

Mahinepua Bay Shiraz (★★★★)

From a coastal site in Northland – well north of the Bay of Islands – the deeply coloured 2014 vintage (★★★★) is maturing gracefully. Labelled Shiraz (a synonym for Syrah, used far more frequently in Australia), it has good weight, concentrated, spicy flavours, hints of olives and liquorice, toasty, savoury notes adding complexity, and a smooth, lengthy finish.

DRY $30 –V

Maison Noire Hawke's Bay Syrah ★★★★

Grown in the Gimblett Gravels, the deeply coloured 2015 vintage (★★★★) was matured for 16 months in French oak barrels (30 per cent new). Floral, mouthfilling and supple, it has good concentration of plum and black-pepper flavours, fresh but not high acidity, and gentle tannins. Still very youthful, it's well worth cellaring to 2019+. The 2016 vintage (★★★☆) was matured for a year in French oak barrels (20 per cent new). Fullish in colour, with a peppery bouquet, it is medium-bodied, with good depth of fresh plum and black-pepper flavours, earthy, savoury notes adding complexity, and a distinctly spicy finish.

Vintage	16	15
WR	5	5
Drink	18-21	17-21

 DRY $25 AV

Man O' War Waiheke Island Bellerophon Syrah/Viognier ★★★★☆

Designed as an alternative to Man O' War's more 'robust' Dreadnought Syrah, this is intended to be 'more feminine, savoury, funky', with 3 per cent Viognier included in the blend and limited use of new oak (25 per cent in 2014). The 2014 vintage (★★★★☆) is full-coloured, fragrant and supple, with strong, vibrant, plummy, spicy flavours, showing excellent complexity. Best drinking 2018+.

Vintage	14
WR	7
Drink	17-21

 DRY $59 –V

Man O' War Waiheke Island Dreadnought Syrah ★★★★★

Estate-grown at the eastern end of the island, the 2014 vintage (★★★★★) was matured in French oak casks (30 per cent new). Bold and youthful in colour, it is a classy, highly concentrated, well-structured red, with dense, ripe blackcurrant, plum and spice flavours, a hint of liquorice and fine-grained tannins. It should be long-lived; open 2019+.

Vintage	14
WR	6
Drink	17-21

 DRY $52 AV

Marsden Bay of Islands Vigot Syrah ★★★★

The 2014 vintage (★★★★☆) is a deeply coloured Northland red, matured for a year in French oak casks (30 per cent new). Mouthfilling and firmly structured, it is concentrated, with ripe plum and spice flavours, seasoned with nutty oak, and excellent complexity and density. Well worth cellaring.

Vintage	14	13
WR	6	6
Drink	17-20	17-19

DRY $40 –V

Martinborough Vineyard Limited Edition Martinborough Syrah/Viognier   ★★★☆

The floral 2014 vintage (★★★☆) includes a splash of Viognier. The colour is full and youthful; the palate is supple and graceful, with plum, spice and black-pepper flavours, showing some savoury complexity, and a Pinot Noir-ish texture. A graceful rather than powerful style, it should be at its best 2018+.

DRY $48 –V

Matua Single Vineyard Hawke's Bay Syrah   ★★★★★

The instantly attractive 2014 vintage (★★★★★) was estate-grown in the Matheson Vineyard, in the Bridge Pa Triangle, hand-picked and matured in French (mostly) and American oak barrels. Deeply coloured, it is mouthfilling, with fresh, concentrated, plummy, peppery flavours, ripe and generous, savoury notes adding complexity, and a very finely textured, smooth finish. Best drinking 2018+.

DRY $58 AV

Mills Reef Elspeth Gimblett Gravels Hawke's Bay Syrah   ★★★★★

In top vintages, this is one of Hawke's Bay's greatest Syrahs. The 2013 vintage (★★★★★), hand-picked in the company's Mere Road and Trust Block vineyards, was matured for 17 months in French oak hogsheads (46 per cent new). Deeply coloured, it is deliciously fragrant and supple, with fresh, concentrated plum and black-pepper flavours and a sustained, spicy finish. Rich, finely textured and very harmonious, it's already drinking well, but should be at its best 2018+.

Vintage	13	12	11	10	09
WR	7	NM	7	7	7
Drink	17-25	NM	17-18	17-18	17-18

DRY $49 AV

Mills Reef Elspeth Trust Vineyard Gimblett Gravels Hawke's Bay Syrah   ★★★★

The 2013 vintage (★★★★☆) was grown principally (87 per cent) in the company's Trust Vineyard and matured for 15 months in French (80 per cent) and American (20 per cent) oak hogsheads (41 per cent new). Full-coloured, it is floral, vibrantly fruity and supple, with strong, ripe plum and black-pepper flavours and a softly textured finish. A refined rather than powerful red, it's already delicious. (Note: the name 'Trust Vineyard' appears only on the back label.)

Vintage	13	12	11	10	09
WR	7	NM	7	7	7
Drink	17-25	NM	P	17-18	17-18

DRY $49 –V

Mills Reef Estate Hawke's Bay Syrah   ★★☆

Made 'for immediate enjoyment', the 2016 vintage (★★☆) is a single-vineyard red, matured for six months in seasoned French and American oak barrels. Ruby-hued, with a floral bouquet, it has fresh, gentle plum and spice flavours, in a light, easy-drinking style.

DRY $19 –V

Mills Reef Reserve Hawke's Bay Syrah ★★★☆

The 2016 vintage (★★★☆) was grown at two sites, one in the Gimblett Gravels, and matured for nine months in a combination of French (52 per cent) and American (48 per cent) oak casks (32 per cent new). Full-coloured, it is a fresh, medium to full-bodied red, vibrantly fruity and smooth. A strongly varietal wine, with good depth of plummy, peppery flavours, showing some complexity, it should be at its best from mid-2018 onwards.

Vintage	16	15	14	13	12	11	10
WR	6	7	7	7	6	7	7
Drink	17-21	17-21	17-20	17-19	P	P	P

DRY $25 –V

Mission Barrique Reserve Gimblett Gravels Syrah ★★★★

The 2016 vintage (★★★★) was estate-grown in Hawke's Bay and matured in French oak casks. Full-coloured, it is mouthfilling and savoury, with concentrated, ripe plum, spice and black-pepper flavours, good tannin support, and excellent complexity and depth. Youthful, but approachable, it's well worth cellaring to 2019+.

Vintage	15
WR	5
Drink	17-22

DRY $29 AV

Mission Hawke's Bay Syrah ★★★

The 2016 vintage (★★★) is fresh, plummy and smooth, in a medium-bodied style, with hints of spices and tamarillos, good depth and plenty of drink-young charm.

DRY $18 AV

Mission Huchet Gimblett Gravels Syrah ★★★★★

Named in honour of nineteenth-century winemaker Cyprian Huchet, the 2013 vintage (★★★★★) is a powerful red with a fragrant, spicy bouquet. Estate-grown in Mere Road, in the Gimblett Gravels, and French oak-matured for 18 months (33 per cent new), it is deeply coloured, with a fragrant, spicy bouquet. Still youthful, it is mouthfilling, with richly varietal, concentrated blackcurrant, plum and spice flavours, fine-grained tannins, and a very harmonious finish. An elegant red with a long future, it should be at its best 2018+.

Vintage	13	12	11	10	09	08	07
WR	7	NM	NM	6	NM	NM	6
Drink	17-25	NM	NM	17-23	NM	NM	17-20

DRY $130 –V

Mission Jewelstone Hawke's Bay Syrah ★★★★★

The distinguished 2015 vintage (★★★★★) was estate-grown in the Gimblett Gravels and matured in French oak casks (new and seasoned). Dark and fragrant, it is notably concentrated, with dense, ripe blackcurrant, plum, spice and black-pepper flavours, seasoned with toasty oak. Showing lovely fruit sweetness, it's already delicious, but full of potential; open 2020+.

Vintage	15	14	13
WR	7	7	7
Drink	17-30	17-30	17-30

DRY $45 AV

Mission Vineyard Selection Hawke's Bay Syrah ★★★☆

The elegant, deeply coloured 2016 vintage (★★★★) was predominantly estate-grown in the Gimblett Gravels and mostly (90 per cent) barrel-matured. Full-coloured, it is a fragrant, medium to full-bodied wine, fresh and vibrantly fruity, with strong plum, spice and black-pepper flavours, oak complexity, supple tannins, and lots of drink-young appeal.

 DRY $20 AV

Moutere Hills Nelson Syrah (★★★☆)

The youthful 2016 vintage (★★★☆) was estate-grown, hand-picked and matured for 10 months in French and American oak casks. Full-coloured, it is mouthfilling and supple, with fresh acidity and vibrant plum and slight tamarillo flavours, showing very good delicacy and depth. Best drinking mid-2018+.

 DRY $35 –V

Murdoch James Martinborough Blue Rock Syrah ★★★☆

Worth cellaring, the 2014 vintage (★★★☆) is a medium-bodied style, bright ruby, fruity and supple. Estate-grown in the Blue Rock Vineyard, it is a tightly structured, distinctly cool-climate red, with very good depth of fresh, plummy, spicy, peppery flavours.

 DRY $50 –V

Nanny Goat Vineyard Central Otago Syrah ★★★☆

The 2015 vintage (★★★☆) is full-coloured, with an attractively scented bouquet. It has gentle tannins and ripe, plummy, spicy, slightly peppery flavours, showing very good balance and depth. Best drinking 2018+.

 DRY $36 –V

Ngatarawa Proprietors' Reserve Hawke's Bay Syrah (★★★★★)

The 2013 vintage (★★★★★) is a refined wine, grown in the Bridge Pa Triangle. Dark and mouthfilling, with rich, vibrant plum and black-pepper flavours, good density, a nutty oak complexity, and a long, firm, spicy finish, it's a strongly varietal red, likely to be at its best from 2018 onwards.

DRY $40 AV

Ngatarawa Stables Reserve Hawke's Bay Syrah ★★★

The 2015 vintage (★★★) is deep ruby, with plummy, spicy flavours, showing some earthy, gamey notes.

Vintage	15	14	13
WR	6	5	7
Drink	17-20	17-20	P

DRY $20 –V

Nikau Point Reserve Hawke's Bay Syrah ★★☆

A solid quaffer, the 2014 vintage (★★☆) was partly (40 per cent) barrel-aged. Fullish in colour, it is fruity and smooth, with plum and slight tamarillo flavours, showing decent depth. Drink now to 2018.

DRY $14 AV

Obsidian Estate Waiheke Island Syrah ★★★☆

The 2015 vintage (★★★☆) is an easy-drinking red, full-coloured, with a peppery, slightly earthy bouquet. It has generous plum, spice and dried-herb flavours, gently seasoned with toasty oak, and a smooth finish. The 2016 vintage (★★★☆) is floral and supple, with plum and slight tamarillo flavours, gentle tannins, good depth and lots of drink-young appeal.

DRY $38 –V

Obsidian Reserve Waiheke Island Syrah ★★★★★

Currently delicious, the impressive, boldly coloured 2014 vintage (★★★★★) was matured for a year in French oak casks. A fragrant, powerful, sweet-fruited red, it has commanding mouthfeel (14.5 per cent alcohol), with dense, ripe plum, liquorice and spice flavours, and a well-rounded finish. Full of personality, it's a drink-now or cellaring proposition. The 2015 vintage (★★★★☆) was matured for a year in French oak barriques (40 per cent new). Deeply coloured, it is fragrant, with generous, youthful plum, spice and slight tamarillo flavours, fine-grained tannins, savoury notes adding complexity, and very good potential; best drinking 2019+.

Vintage	15	14	13	12
WR	5	6	7	5
Drink	17-23	17-23	17-23	17-20

DRY $63 AV

Okahu Estate Syrah ★★★★

The 2014 vintage (★★★★) of this Northland red is generous and savoury, with fine-grained tannins, good weight and strong, ripe plum/spice flavours.

DRY $59 –V

Paroa Bay Bay of Islands Syrah ★★★☆

The 2014 vintage (★★★) is a deeply coloured Bay of Islands, Northland red with a perfumed, spicy bouquet. It has red-berry, spice and toasty oak flavours (French, new), with a firmly structured finish.

DRY $40 –V

Pask Declaration Hawke's Bay Syrah ★★★★☆

Estate-grown in Gimblett Road and matured in predominantly new French oak casks, the 2014 vintage (★★★★★) is maturing very gracefully. Deeply coloured, it is fragrant and mouthfilling, with concentrated plum, spice and nut flavours, complex and finely textured, that build across the palate to a lasting finish. Best drinking 2020+.

Vintage	14
WR	7
Drink	17-30

DRY $50 –V

Pask Gimblett Road Hawke's Bay Syrah   ★★★☆

Estate-grown, the 2016 vintage (★★★☆) was matured for a year in seasoned French oak casks. A medium-bodied style, it has fresh, ripe plum, spice and black-pepper flavours, showing considerable complexity, and a smooth finish. Already enjoyable, it should be at its best from mid-2018 onwards.

Vintage	16
WR	5
Drink	18-26

DRY $22 AV

Passage Rock Reserve Waiheke Island Syrah   ★★★★★

Waiheke's most awarded wine of the past decade is partly estate-grown at Te Matuku Bay, on the south side of the island, supplemented by fruit from Oneroa. Matured in American and French oak barriques, mostly new, it is typically a powerful, opulent red, rich and well-rounded. The 2014 vintage (★★★★★) is still youthful. Dark, full-bodied and sweet-fruited, with vibrant blackcurrant, plum and spice flavours, it is notably concentrated, but also supple and fragrant. Best drinking 2018+.

DRY $55 AV

Passage Rock Waiheke Island Syrah   ★★★★★

This Waiheke Island red is consistently rewarding. Partly estate-grown and fully matured for a year in American (mostly) and French oak barriques (30 per cent new), the 2014 vintage (★★★★☆) is deeply coloured, mouthfilling, fresh and supple. A generous, strongly varietal red, it is sturdy, with ripe, plummy, spicy flavours, showing excellent concentration and complexity, and good cellaring potential.

DRY $35 V+

Pont, Le, Grand Vin Rouge Syrah   (★★★★☆)

The 2014 vintage (★★★★☆) is a top Gisborne-grown red. Hand-picked at Patutahi, blended with a small portion of Merlot and French oak-matured for 30 months, it is full-coloured, fresh and mouthfilling, with generous, plummy, spicy flavours, good vigour, savoury notes adding complexity, and a firm backbone of tannin. It should be long-lived.

DRY $36 AV

Rangatira Reserve Gimblett Gravels Syrah   (★★★★☆)

The 2015 vintage (★★★★☆) is a single-vineyard red, matured for 18 months in French oak barriques (30 per cent new). It's a youthful, mouthfilling, full-coloured red, with generous, ripe plum, spice and slight liquorice flavours, a hint of herbs, oak complexity, fine-grained tannins and a long finish. Best drinking 2019+. (From Ka Tahi.)

DRY $30 AV

Redmetal Vineyards Basket Press Hawke's Bay Syrah ★★★★☆

Estate-grown in the Bridge Pa Triangle, the 2015 vintage (★★★★☆) was barrel-aged for 10 months (25 per cent new) and blended with 12 per cent Merlot for 'fruit and supple tannin structure'. Deep and youthful in colour, it is weighty (14.5 per cent alcohol), with concentrated, vibrant, well-ripened plum and black-pepper flavours, seasoned with nutty oak, and a rich, smooth finish. Already delicious, it's an age-worthy red, likely to be at its best 2019+.

Vintage	15	14	13
WR	6	5	5
Drink	18-25	17-23	17-20

 DRY $37 AV

Redmetal Vineyards Hawke's Bay Syrah ★★★☆

The fresh, lively 2016 vintage (★★★☆) is a single-vineyard red, blended with Merlot (5 per cent) and lightly oak-influenced. A medium-bodied style, it is vibrantly fruity and smooth, with plummy, spicy flavours, showing some complexity, gentle tannins, and lots of drink-young appeal.

Vintage	16
WR	6
Drink	17-23

 DRY $22 AV

Sacred Hill Deerstalkers Hawke's Bay Syrah ★★★★★

Estate-grown and hand-picked in the Gimblett Gravels, fermented with indigenous yeasts and matured for 16 months in French oak barriques and puncheons (35 per cent new), the 2015 vintage (★★★★★) is deeply coloured, with a scented, distinctly peppery bouquet. Mouthfilling, it has fresh, concentrated flavours of plums, spices and nuts, with supple tannins and a long, finely textured finish. Highly approachable in its youth, it's also well worth cellaring; best drinking 2020+.

Vintage	15	14	13	12	11	10	09	08
WR	7	7	7	6	NM	7	7	6
Drink	18-30	17-24	17-22	17-20	NM	17-19	17-18	P

DRY $60 AV

Sacred Hill Halo Hawke's Bay Syrah ★★★☆

The 2014 vintage (★★★★) was hand-picked and matured for a year in French oak barrels (20 per cent new). A mouthfilling, generous wine, it has concentrated plum, pepper and spice flavours, in a clearly varietal style, with gentle tannins and lots of drink-young appeal.

Vintage	14	13	12
WR	6	7	6
Drink	17-20	17-18	P

DRY $30 –V

Sacred Hill Reserve Hawke's Bay Syrah ★★★☆

A 'fruit-driven' style, the 2015 vintage (★★★) was matured for eight months in seasoned French barrels. Ruby-hued, it is peppery and slightly herbal, in a smooth, vibrantly fruity style, offering easy, early drinking. The 2016 vintage (★★★☆) was French oak-aged for eight months. Full-coloured, it is mouthfilling, with generous plum, spice and slight tamarillo flavours, showing considerable complexity, and gentle tannins. Best drinking mid-2018+.

Vintage	16	15
WR	5	6
Drink	18-19	17-18

DRY $30 –V

Saint Clair Gimblett Gravels Hawke's Bay Syrah ★★★☆

The 2016 vintage (★★★☆) is finely balanced for early consumption, but also worth cellaring. An estate-grown, single-vineyard red, partly barrel-aged, it is a medium to full-bodied style, with vibrant plum and spice flavours, a hint of tamarillo, youthful vigour and very good depth. Best drinking 2019+.

DRY $27 –V

Saint Clair James Sinclair Gimblett Gravels Hawke's Bay Syrah (★★★☆)

Partly oak-aged, the 2014 vintage (★★★☆) is a deeply coloured red, estate-grown in the Plateau Vineyard. Medium to full-bodied, it is strongly varietal, with plum, spice and black-pepper aromas and flavours, fresh, vibrant and smooth. Best drinking 2018+.

DRY $25 –V

Saint Clair Pioneer Block 17 Plateau Block
Gimblett Gravels Hawke's Bay Syrah ★★★★

The 2015 vintage (★★★★) was matured for 11 months in French oak casks (partly new). A fresh, rich, youthful red, it is deeply coloured and mouthfilling, with ripe plum, spice and liquorice flavours that linger well.

DRY $38 –V

Satyr Hawke's Bay Syrah ★★★

From Sileni, the 2015 vintage (★★★) is a medium-bodied, smooth red with fullish colour and good depth of fresh, spicy flavours, showing a touch of complexity. Best drinking 2018+.

DRY $20 –V

Seifried Nelson Syrah ★★★

Grown at Brightwater, on the Waimea Plains, the 2015 vintage (★★☆) was matured for 15 months in new one and two-year-old barriques. Lightish in colour, it is mouthfilling, with moderately ripe, spicy, slightly herbal and nutty flavours, showing a touch of complexity, and a smooth finish.

Vintage	15
WR	5
Drink	17-20

DRY $20 –V

Sileni Cellar Selection Hawke's Bay Syrah ★★★

Enjoyable young, the 2016 vintage (★★★) is a very lightly oaked wine, ruby-hued, floral and supple, in a medium-bodied, slightly savoury style with fresh plum and black-pepper flavours to the fore.

Vintage	16	15	14	13
WR	6	7	6	6
Drink	17-22	17-21	17-20	17-19

 DRY $20 –V

Sileni Estate Selection Peak Hawke's Bay Syrah ★★★★

Deeply coloured, the 2015 vintage (★★★★) was grown in the Bridge Pa Triangle and matured for nine months in French oak casks (12 per cent new). It has a fragrant, fresh, spicy bouquet, leading into a full-bodied, strongly varietal wine, with good complexity and excellent depth of plum, spice and black-pepper flavours. Best drinking 2018+. Maturing well, the 2014 vintage (★★★★) is mouthfilling and smooth, ripe and savoury, with gentle tannins and strong, plummy, spicy flavours, showing good complexity and harmony.

Vintage	15	14	13
WR	7	6	7
Drink	17-23	17-22	17-23

 DRY $33 –V

Sileni Exceptional Vintage Hawke's Bay Syrah (★★★★★)

The delicious 2013 vintage (★★★★★) was matured for 10 months in French oak casks (60 per cent new). Dark and mouthfilling, with sweet-fruit characters and concentrated blackcurrant, plum, spice and liquorice flavours, it's an impressively weighty and complex red, finely textured and long.

Vintage	13
WR	7
Drink	17-23

 DRY $70 –V

Soho Valentina Waiheke Island Syrah ★★★★☆

Estate-grown at Onetangi, the 2015 vintage (★★★★☆) is a dark, weighty, single-vineyard red, matured in French and American oak barriques (14 per cent new). Fragrant and full-bodied, it has rich, strongly varietal blackberry, plum and spice flavours, showing good complexity, and a lingering finish.

 DRY $38 AV

Soljans Barrique Reserve Hawke's Bay Syrah ★★★★

Drinking well now, the 2014 vintage (★★★★) was matured in new and seasoned French oak barriques. Fullish in colour, it is mouthfilling, with strong plum and spice flavours, hints of liquorice and herbs, and well-integrated oak adding complexity.

Vintage	14
WR	7
Drink	17-25

DRY $26 AV

Spy Valley Marlborough Syrah ★★★★

Maturing gracefully, the 2014 vintage (★★★★) was barrel-aged for 20 months. Deep ruby, it is medium to full-bodied, with good density of ripe plum/spice flavours, seasoned with nutty oak, considerable complexity and a fairly firm finish. Best drinking mid-2018+.

Vintage	14	13	12	11	10	09
WR	6	5	7	6	6	5
Drink	17-19	17-18	17-18	P	P	P

DRY $35 –V

Squawking Magpie Gimblett Gravels Stoned Crow Syrah ★★★★☆

The 2014 vintage (★★★★★) is an estate-grown, single-vineyard red, matured for 20 months in French oak casks (partly new). Dark and youthful in colour, it is fragrant and rich, with concentrated, ripe plum and spice flavours, seasoned with nutty oak, excellent complexity and a finely textured, long finish. A classy young red, it's already enjoyable, but should be at its best 2018+.

Vintage	14	13
WR	7	7
Drink	17-35	17-35

DRY $50 –V

Squawking Magpie The Chatterer Gimblett Gravels Hawke's Bay Syrah ★★★★

Still youthful, the 2014 vintage (★★★★) of this barrel-aged red is deeply coloured, with a fragrant, spicy bouquet. A strongly varietal wine, it is mouthfilling, with vibrant plum and black-pepper flavours, showing excellent ripeness, depth and harmony.

Vintage	14
WR	6
Drink	17-25

DRY $25 AV

Stolen Heart, The, Hawke's Bay Syrah (★★★★)

Still on sale, the 2013 vintage (★★★★) is a medium-bodied red, grown in the Gimblett Gravels and matured for a year in French oak casks (30 per cent new). Full-coloured, with fresh, peppery aromas, it is still youthful, with excellent depth of plummy, spicy, slightly nutty flavours, oak complexity and firm tannins. Best drinking 2018+. (From Crown Range Cellar.)

DRY $50 –V

Stonecroft Crofters Gimblett Gravels Hawke's Bay Syrah (★★★☆)

Certified organic, the 2016 vintage (★★★☆) was estate-grown at Fernhill and partly barrel-aged. Full-coloured, with a fresh, peppery bouquet, it is medium-bodied, vibrantly fruity and smooth, with plum, spice and black-pepper flavours, gentle tannins and lots of drink-young charm.

DRY $22 AV

Stonecroft Gimblett Gravels Hawke's Bay Reserve Syrah   ★★★★★

Certified organic, the very youthful 2015 vintage (★★★★★) was harvested from estate-grown vines, including the region's first Syrah plantings in 1984. Matured for 18 months in French oak casks (60 per cent new), it is dark and fragrant, with rich, ripe blackcurrant, plum, spice and liquorice flavours, showing excellent concentration and complexity, fine-grained tannins and a lasting finish. Open 2019+.

Vintage	15	14	13	12	11	10	09
WR	7	7	7	6	NM	7	6
Drink	19-27	19-26	18-25	17-24	NM	17-23	17-22

 DRY $65 AV

Stonecroft Gimblett Gravels Hawke's Bay Serine Syrah   ★★★★

Certified organic, the elegant 2015 vintage (★★★★☆) was estate-grown at Mere Road and Roys Hill, fermented with indigenous yeasts and matured for 18 months in French oak barriques (35 per cent new). Full and youthful in colour, it has a fragrant, plummy, distinctly peppery bouquet. Mouthfilling and supple, it has strong, plummy, spicy flavours, showing good concentration and complexity, and a long finish. Already enjoyable, it should be at its best 2019+.

Vintage	15	14	13	12	11	10	09
WR	7	6	7	5	NM	7	7
Drink	17-23	17-21	17-21	17-20	NM	17-18	P

 DRY $31 –V

Stonecroft Gimblett Gravels Hawke's Bay Undressed Syrah   (★★★★☆)

The tautly structured, 'preservative free' 2015 vintage (★★★★☆) was handled without sulphur dioxide. Certified organic, it's a single-vineyard wine, matured for 16 months in French oak barrels (35 per cent new). Deeply coloured, with a fragrant, peppery, earthy bouquet, it is notably concentrated, with dense plum and black-pepper flavours, firm, chewy tannins, and loads of personality. It looks age-worthy and needs time to soften; open 2019+.

 DRY $31 AV

Stonecroft The Original Gimblett Gravels Hawke's Bay Syrah   (★★★★★)

Still youthful, the 2014 vintage (★★★★★) is rare – fewer than 300 bottles were produced. Hand-harvested from the original vines, planted in Mere Road in 1984, it was matured for 18 months in a single, new French oak barrique. Deeply coloured, it is mouthfilling, with dense, vibrant blackcurrant, plum and black-pepper flavours, firm and savoury. Built for a long life, it's well worth cellaring to 2019+.

Vintage	14
WR	7
Drink	19-26

DRY $100 AV

Stonyridge Faithful Waiheke Island Syrah   (★★★★)

Designed for early consumption, the 2015 vintage (★★★★) was matured in French oak casks (20 per cent new). Deeply coloured, it has a spicy, slightly earthy bouquet, leading into a full-bodied, sturdy wine with good concentration of fresh, ripe, plummy, spicy flavours.

 DRY $35 –V

Stonyridge Pilgrim Waiheke Island Syrah/Mourvedre/Viognier/Grenache   ★★★★★

This distinguished Rhône-style blend is estate-grown at Onetangi and matured for a year in French oak barriques (30 per cent new in 2015). The 2015 vintage (★★★★★) is delicious in its youth, but also well worth cellaring. Deeply coloured, it is sturdy (14.5 per cent alcohol), vibrantly fruity and supple, with dense plum and spice flavours, complex and savoury, and ripe, supple tannins. Very finely textured and harmonious, it's already highly approachable, but should be at its best 2020+.

Vintage	15
WR	7
Drink	17-25

 DRY $95 AV

Summerhouse Marlborough Syrah   ★★★☆

The easy-drinking 2016 vintage (★★★☆) was matured for 10 months in French oak barriques, seasoned and new. Full-coloured, it is mouthfilling, with generous plum, berry, herb and tamarillo flavours, showing considerable complexity. Drink now or cellar.

Vintage	16	15
WR	6	7
Drink	17-25	17-26

 DRY $29 –V

Tantalus Voilé Reserve Waiheke Island Syrah   (★★★★☆)

Showing plenty of personality, the 2014 vintage (★★★★☆) was estate-grown and hand-picked at Onetangi and matured for 11 months in French oak barriques. Deep and youthful in colour, it is mouthfilling, with strong, ripe, plummy, spicy flavours, good tannin backbone, and an earthy, savoury, nutty complexity. Already drinking well, it should be at its best 2018+.

Vintage	14
WR	6
Drink	17-26

 DRY $60 –V

Te Awa Single Estate Hawke's Bay Syrah   ★★★★

The elegant 2014 vintage (★★★★) was matured in French oak casks (35 per cent new). Floral and fruit-packed, it has deep, bright colour and a strong surge of fresh, plummy, peppery, slightly nutty flavours, smooth and long. Best drinking 2018+.

Vintage	14	13
WR	7	7
Drink	17-24	17-23

 DRY $30 –V

Te Awanga Estate Hawke's Bay Syrah   ★★★★

Grown inland from Hastings, the 2014 vintage (★★★☆) was matured for 16 months in French oak barrels. Full ruby, it is floral and supple, in a medium-bodied style, with vibrant, ripe, moderately concentrated plum/spice flavours, and lots of drink-young charm.

DRY $28 AV

Te Mata Estate Bullnose Syrah   ★★★★★

Grown in the Bullnose and Isosceles vineyards, in the Bridge Pa Triangle inland from Hastings, in Hawke's Bay, this classy red is hand-picked and matured for 15 to 16 months in French oak barriques (about 35 per cent new). Unlike its Estate Vineyards stablemate (below), it is not blended with Viognier, and the vines for the Bullnose label are cropped lower. Fragrant and deeply coloured, the 2015 vintage (★★★★★) is a graceful, tightly structured red, with rich, youthful plum/spice flavours, a hint of dark chocolate, savoury notes adding complexity, and obvious potential; open 2019+.

Vintage	15	14	13	12	11	10	09	08	07	06
WR	7	7	7	7	6	7	7	7	7	7
Drink	17-25	17-24	17-23	17-21	17-19	17-19	17-19	P	P	P

 DRY $49 AV

Te Mata Estate Vineyards Hawke's Bay Syrah   ★★★★

The 2015 vintage (★★★★) is delicious young. Estate-grown in the Dartmoor Valley and Bridge Pa Triangle, it was blended with a splash of Viognier (2 per cent) and French oak-matured for seven months. Full-coloured, it is freshly scented, with strong plum, spice and black-pepper flavours, gentle tannins, and savoury notes adding complexity. Fine value.

Vintage	15
WR	6
Drink	17-23

DRY $20 V+

Te Whau Vineyard Waiheke Island Syrah   ★★★★☆

This wine is hand-picked from hill-grown vines, fermented with indigenous yeasts and matured for over a year in French oak barrels (partly new). The distinctive 2014 vintage (★★★★★) is full-coloured, fragrant and very finely textured. The bouquet is fragrant, ripe and spicy; the palate possesses a strong sense of youthful vigour, with strong, ripe plum, blackcurrant and nut flavours, very harmonious and lasting. Drink now onwards.

Vintage	14	13	12	11	10	09	08	07
WR	7	7	7	NM	7	7	7	7
Drink	17-24	17-23	17-25	NM	P	P	P	P

DRY $110 –V

Terrace Edge Waipara Valley Syrah   ★★★★

Grown on a '45-degree north facing "roasted slope"' and matured for over a year in French oak (25 per cent new), the 2016 vintage (★★★★) has a fragrant, peppery, slightly herbal bouquet. Sturdy (14.5 per cent alcohol) and generous, it has strong, spicy flavours, hints of herbs, liquorice and nuts, and lots of drink-young appeal.

Vintage	16	15
WR	7	7
Drink	17-25	17-26

DRY $32 –V

Theory & Practice Hawke's Bay Syrah ★★★☆

Delicious now, the 2014 vintage (★★★★) was grown in the Bridge Pa Triangle, hand-harvested, fermented with indigenous yeasts and matured for 20 months in French oak barrels (19 per cent new). Full-coloured, it is mouthfilling, fresh and supple, with plenty of vibrant, plummy, spicy flavour, gentle tannins and a Pinot Noir-like texture and charm.

 DRY $22 AV

Tohu Hawke's Bay Syrah ★★★

The ruby-hued, easy-drinking 2014 vintage (★★★) was matured for over a year in old French oak barriques. It shows good depth of plummy, spicy flavours, with savoury notes adding a touch of complexity and gentle tannins. Drink now to 2018.

 DRY $28 –V

Trinity Hill Gimblett Gravels Syrah ★★★★★

Estate-grown and matured for 14 months in French oak barriques and 5000-litre ovals (new and old), the 2015 vintage (★★★★☆) is deeply coloured, mouthfilling and supple. Weighty, it has concentrated, plummy, spicy flavours, hints of herbs and tamarillos, and impressive complexity and harmony. Drink now onwards.

Vintage	15	14	13	12	11	10	09	08
WR	6	7	6	5	5	7	7	5
Drink	17-25	17-25	17-25	17-18	17-18	17-20	17-20	P

 DRY $35 V+

Trinity Hill Hawke's Bay Syrah ★★★★

The 2016 vintage (★★★☆) was 'made to be enjoyed while young'. A fresh, medium-bodied red, grown in the Gimblett Gravels and Bridge Pa Triangle, it was blended with Viognier (5 per cent) and matured for seven months in tanks and French oak. Full-coloured, it is finely textured, with good depth of plummy, spicy flavours and a finely balanced, smooth finish. Best drinking 2018.

 DRY $22 V+

Trinity Hill Homage Hawke's Bay Syrah ★★★★★

One of the country's most distinguished – and expensive – reds. Harvested by hand, mostly from 19-year-old vines in the Gimblett Gravels, the outstanding 2014 vintage (★★★★★) was matured for 14 months in French oak barriques (mostly new) and 5000-litre oak ovals. Dark and youthful in colour, it is mouthfilling, dense and yet supple, with a floral bouquet and highly concentrated plum, blackcurrant, spice and nut flavours. Impressively rich, complex and savoury, with good tannin backbone, it should flourish with long-term cellaring. The 2015 vintage (★★★★★) is a 'serious', age-worthy red, with a sense of latent power and potential. Deeply coloured, it is floral and mouthfilling, with strong blackcurrant, plum, spice and nut flavours that build across the palate to a firm, lasting finish. Open 2020+.

Vintage	15	14	13	12	11	10	09
WR	7	7	7	NM	NM	7	7
Drink	17-27	17-25	17-25	NM	NM	17-25	17-25

 DRY $130 AV

Turanga Creek Down to Earth Syrah/Viognier   (★★★)

Certified organic, the 2014 vintage (★★★) was estate-grown in South Auckland and made with 'a bit of oak'. It's a medium-bodied, flavoursome, slightly earthy red, with hints of tamarillo and herbs, and some leathery complexity. Ready.

 DRY $25 –V

Vidal Legacy Gimblett Gravels Hawke's Bay Syrah   ★★★★★

The outstanding 2014 vintage (★★★★★) was estate-grown in the Omahu Gravels and Twyford Gravels vineyards, and matured for 18 months in French oak barriques (38 per cent new). Deeply coloured, it is concentrated and silky-textured, with vibrant, densely packed, well-ripened plum and spice flavours, finely integrated oak and supple tannins. A highly refined wine, it's already approachable, but should blossom with long-term cellaring. Best drinking 2020+. (There is no 2015.)

Vintage	15	14	13	12	11	10	09
WR	NM	7	7	NM	7	7	7
Drink	NM	17-28	17-25	NM	17-20	17-20	17-20

 DRY $80 AV

Vidal Reserve Gimblett Gravels Hawke's Bay Syrah   ★★★★

Priced sharply, the 2015 vintage (★★★★☆) was estate-grown and matured for 17 months in French oak barrels (33 per cent new). Dark and youthful in colour, it is floral, fresh and vibrant, with deep blackcurrant, plum and black-pepper flavours, good tannin backbone, and a long, spicy finish. An elegant, tightly structured red, it is very age-worthy; best drinking 2019+.

Vintage	15	14	13	12	11	10	09
WR	7	7	7	6	6	7	7
Drink	17-23	17-23	17-22	17-18	P	P	P

 DRY $25 AV

Villa Maria Cellar Selection Hawke's Bay Syrah   ★★★★★

The refined, bargain-priced 2014 vintage (★★★★★) is an instantly appealing, deliciously rich and smooth-flowing red. Grown in the Gimblett Gravels (two-thirds) and the Bridge Pa Triangle (one-third), it was matured for 17 months in French oak barriques (20 per cent new). Mouthfilling and boldly coloured, it has concentrated plum, spice, liquorice and dark chocolate flavours, excellent fruit/oak balance and a silky-textured, long finish. The 2015 vintage (★★★★☆) was grown almost entirely (94 per cent) in the Gimblett Gravels, and matured for 17 months in French oak barriques (28 per cent new). Boldly coloured, it is full-bodied and supple, with generous, ripe, plummy, spicy flavours, finely integrated oak and an inviting, peppery bouquet.

Vintage	15	14	13	12	11	10	09
WR	7	7	7	6	6	7	7
Drink	18-23	17-24	17-22	17-20	P	P	P

DRY $26 V+

Villa Maria Private Bin Hawke's Bay Shiraz ★★★☆

The 2014 vintage (★★★★) is labelled 'Shiraz', rather than 'Syrah', to attract supermarket shoppers long familiar with Australian Shiraz. Matured in barrels (80 per cent) and tanks (20 per cent), it offers fine value. Boldly coloured, with deep, ripe, well-rounded flavours of spices and liquorice, it has a slightly earthy streak, and good acidity and length.

 DRY $20 AV

Vintage	14	13	12
WR	7	6	5
Drink	17-20	17-19	P

Villa Maria Reserve Gimblett Gravels Hawke's Bay Syrah ★★★★★

The 2014 vintage (★★★★★) is a dark, purple-flushed, densely packed red, matured for 17 months in French oak barriques (35 per cent new). Still very youthful, it offers highly concentrated plum, spice and black-pepper flavours, with lovely fruity sweetness, integrated oak, good tannin support and a long, finely textured finish. Best drinking 2019+.

 DRY $60 AV

Vintage	14	13	12
WR	7	7	6
Drink	19-26	18-25	17-22

Waimarie Huapai Syrah (★★★★)

The sturdy, youthful 2014 vintage (★★★★) was grown at Huapai, in West Auckland, and matured for a year in new American oak casks. Deeply coloured, with a perfumed bouquet, it is mouthfilling and smooth, with ripe blackcurrant, plum and spice flavours, earthy, savoury notes adding complexity, and good tannin backbone. Best drinking 2019+.

 DRY $60 –V

Wairau River Reserve Marlborough Syrah ★★★★

A single-vineyard red, grown on the banks of the Wairau River, the generous, youthful 2015 vintage (★★★★) was matured in French oak casks and bottled unfined and unfiltered. Deeply coloured, it is full-bodied, with fresh, concentrated plum/spice flavours, gentle tannins, good harmony and a lingering finish. Drink now or cellar.

DRY $40 –V

Vintage	15	14
WR	6	7
Drink	17-22	17-23

William Murdoch Syrah ★★★★

Certified organic, the 2014 vintage (★★★★☆) was grown in the Gimblett Gravels, Hawke's Bay, and matured for 15 months in French oak barriques (30 per cent new). Full-coloured, it is a medium to full-bodied style, with fresh, concentrated, distinctly spicy flavours, balanced tannins, good ripeness and density, and the structure to age well. Best drinking 2018+.

 DRY $37 –V

Tannat

Although extremely rare in New Zealand, Tannat is well known in south-west France, especially as a key ingredient in the dark, firm, tannic reds of Madiran. Tannat is also a star variety in Uruguay, yielding firm, fragrant reds with rich blackberry flavours. According to New Zealand Winegrowers' *Vineyard Register Report 2015–2018*, only 2 hectares of Tannat vines will be bearing in 2018, mostly in Auckland, Hawke's Bay and Northland.

De La Terre Grande Reserve Hawke's Bay Tannat (★★★★★)

Notably rich and soft, the 2015 vintage (★★★★★) was estate-grown at Havelock North and matured for 16 months in French oak barriques (50 per cent new). Dark and purple-flushed, it is full-bodied and sweet-fruited, with highly concentrated blackcurrant/plum flavours, a hint of liquorice, and a deliciously smooth, harmonious finish. Drink now or cellar.

DRY $65 AV

De La Terre Hawke's Bay Tannat (★★★★)

The deeply coloured 2014 vintage (★★★★) was estate-grown at Havelock North and matured for over a year in French oak barriques (20 per cent new). Still fresh, it is fruit-packed, with plum and spice flavours, a hint of liquorice, and excellent ripeness and depth.

Vintage	14
WR	6
Drink	17-22

DRY $34 –V

De La Terre Reserve Hawke's Bay Tannat ★★★★☆

Already delicious, the 2015 vintage (★★★★☆) was grown and hand-harvested at Havelock North, and matured for 14 months in French oak barriques (17 per cent new). Full-coloured, it is mouthfilling, fresh and sweet-fruited, with deep, plummy, berryish flavours, a subtle seasoning of oak, gentle tannins and a seductively smooth finish.

Vintage	15	14	13
WR	5	7	7
Drink	17-22	17-28	17-30

DRY $45 –V

Tempranillo

The star grape of Rioja, Tempranillo is grown extensively across northern and central Spain, where it yields strawberry, spice and tobacco-flavoured reds, full of personality. Barrel-aged versions mature well, developing great complexity. The great Spanish variety is starting to spread into the New World, but is still rare in New Zealand, with 20 hectares of bearing vines in 2018, mostly in Hawke's Bay (12 hectares) and Marlborough (3 hectares).

Church Road McDonald Series Hawke's Bay Tempranillo ★★★★★

The powerful 2015 vintage (★★★★☆) is a deeply coloured red, estate-grown in the Redstone Vineyard, in the Bridge Pa Triangle, barrel-aged, and bottled unfined and unfiltered. Still youthful, it is a strapping wine (15.5 per cent alcohol), rich and smooth, with deep blackcurrant, plum and spice flavours, gentle tannins and a well-rounded finish. Drink now or cellar.

DRY $28 V+

Dry River Craighall Vineyard Martinborough Tempranillo ★★★★☆

'In style the wine sits between our Pinot Noir and Syrah', says Dry River. The impressive 2015 vintage (★★★★☆) has promisingly deep, purple-flushed colour. Fragrant, fruit-packed and supple, it has concentrated, youthful, plummy flavours, a hint of tamarillo, a subtle seasoning of oak, fine-grained tannins and excellent depth and harmony. Best drinking 2019+.

DRY $69 –V

Hans Herzog Marlborough Tempranillo ★★★★☆

The top-flight 2013 vintage (★★★★★), estate-grown on the north side of the Wairau Valley, was matured for two years in French oak barriques. Deeply coloured, with a hint of maturity, it is sturdy, savoury and firm, with concentrated blackcurrant, plum and spice flavours, slightly nutty and leathery notes adding complexity, and obvious potential. Best drinking 2018+.

DRY $64 –V

Vintage	13	12	11	10	09
WR	7	7	7	7	7
Drink	17-23	17-22	17-21	17-22	17-21

Kainui Road Bay of Islands Tempranillo ★★★☆

The 2014 vintage (★★★☆) was hand-picked at Kerikeri and matured in French oak casks. Full and bright in colour, it is medium-bodied, with good depth of ripe blackcurrant, plum and spice flavours, toasty oak in evidence, and a smooth finish.

DRY $30 –V

Marsden Bay of Islands Tempranillo ★★★☆

The very easy-drinking 2014 vintage (★★★☆) is a Northland red, matured for a year in French oak barriques. Full and youthful in colour, it is sweet-fruited, with ripe berry, plum and spice flavours, slightly nutty and leathery, gentle tannins, and very good body and depth.

DRY $32 –V

Vintage	14	13
WR	5	6
Drink	17-18	P

Mount Brown Tempranillo   (★★★☆)

Estate-grown at Waipara, the 2016 vintage (★★★☆) is a vibrantly fruity red, full-coloured, with a ripe, slightly earthy bouquet. Enjoyable in its youth, it has very satisfying depth of plummy, spicy, slightly nutty flavours, woven with fresh acidity, and gentle tannins. Best drinking mid-2018+.

DRY $20 AV

Obsidian Estate Waiheke Island Tempranillo   ★★★☆

The 2015 vintage (★★★★) was matured in seasoned French oak barrels (75 per cent) and new American oak barrels (25 per cent). Fragrant, with full, bright, youthful colour, it is a mouthfilling, easy-drinking red with blackcurrant, plum and spice flavours, finely integrated oak, and excellent depth and harmony. The 2016 vintage (★★★☆) is full-coloured, with good body and depth of berry, plum, nut and slight tamarillo flavours, woven with fresh acidity, and a smooth finish.

DRY $39 –V

Rock Ferry Trig Hill Vineyard Tempranillo   ★★★★

Well worth discovering, the 2013 vintage (★★★★☆) was estate-grown at Bendigo, in Central Otago, fermented with indigenous yeasts, and matured for 20 months in French oak puncheons (30 per cent new). Full, bright ruby, it is full-bodied (14.5 per cent alcohol) and vibrantly fruity, with generous, well-ripened plum/spice flavours, youthful, savoury, complex and smooth. Certified organic. The 2014 vintage (★★★★) has deep, moderately youthful colour. Fragrant and full-bodied, it has very satisfying depth of flavour, complex, savoury and slightly herbal, with a fairly firm finish. Ready.

DRY $40 –V

Te Awa Single Estate Hawke's Bay Tempranillo   ★★★★☆

The 2014 vintage (★★★★★) is a classy, youthful Gimblett Gravels red, full-coloured, with strong berry and spice flavours, well-integrated oak adding complexity, and excellent ripeness and depth. A dense, savoury, 'serious' wine, it's well worth cellaring.

DRY $30 AV

Tono Hawke's Bay Tempranillo   (★★★★)

Showing good personality, the 2014 vintage (★★★★) from Salvare Estate was grown at Mangatahi and in the Bridge Pa Triangle. Made in a gently oaked style, it is full-coloured, mouthfilling and supple, with strong, plummy flavours, savoury notes adding complexity, and a finely textured finish. Drink now or cellar.

DRY $25 AV

Trinity Hill Gimblett Gravels Tempranillo ★★★★☆

This is a consistently attractive Hawke's Bay red, full of personality. The youthful 2016 vintage (★★★★☆) was hand-picked and matured for over a year in American and French oak barriques. Full-coloured, it has a fresh bouquet of dark berries, plums and spices. Mouthfilling, it shows very good complexity and harmony, with vibrant, well-ripened plum and spice flavours and a rich, finely textured finish. Best drinking mid-2018+.

Vintage	16	15
WR	7	7
Drink	17-24	17-22

DRY $35 AV

Yealands Estate Single Vineyard Awatere Valley Marlborough Tempranillo ★★★★

Enjoyable young, the 2016 vintage (★★★★) is a rare example of South Island Tempranillo. Estate-grown in the Seaview Valley, it was matured in tanks and seasoned French oak barrels. Full-coloured, it is mouthfilling, with generous, berryish, plummy flavours, very lively, harmonious and well-rounded. Best drinking mid-2018+.

DRY $25 AV

Touriga Nacional

Touriga Nacional is the most prized blending variety in the traditional ports of the Douro Valley of Portugal, and is also used widely in the Dao region for table reds. The low-cropping vines produce small berries that yield sturdy, concentrated, structured wines with high tannin levels. However, Touriga Nacional is extremely rare here and is not listed separately in New Zealand Winegrowers' *Vineyard Register Report 2015–2018*.

Trinity Hill Gimblett Gravels Touriga (★★★★★)

The non-vintage wine (★★★★★) now on sale is a 'port style', blended from Touriga Nacional – the key variety in classic port – Touriga Francesca and Tinta Roriz. From base wines back to 2004, matured in oak barrels for two to nine years, it has dense, inky colour. Highly fragrant, it is robust (19 per cent alcohol), with notably concentrated, spicy, plummy flavours. Overflowing with fruit, it is not a mellow style, but still a lovely mouthful – sweet and delicious.

SW $45 (500ML) AV

Zinfandel

In California, where it is extensively planted, Zinfandel produces muscular, heady reds that can approach a dry port style. It is believed to be identical to the Primitivo variety, which yields highly characterful, warm, spicy reds in southern Italy. There will be only 4 hectares of bearing Zinfandel vines in New Zealand in 2018, clustered in Hawke's Bay, with no expansion projected. Alan Limmer, formerly of Stonecroft winery in Hawke's Bay, believes 'Zin' has potential here, 'if you can stand the stress of growing a grape that falls apart at the first sign of a dubious weather map!'

Stonecroft Gimblett Gravels Hawke's Bay Zinfandel ★★★★

Certified organic, the 2015 vintage (★★★☆) was estate-grown at Roys Hill, in the Gimblett Gravels of Hawke's Bay. Hand-picked from vines planted in 1993 and matured for 18 months in seasoned American oak casks, it is full-coloured, fresh and vibrantly fruity, with mouthfilling body (14.5 per cent alcohol), good depth of youthful, moderately ripe berry/spice flavours, hints of cherries and plums, and gentle tannins. Best drinking mid-2018+.

Vintage	15
WR	6
Drink	17-22

DRY $31 –V

Zweigelt

Austria's most popular red-wine variety is a crossing of Blaufränkisch and St Laurent. It's a naturally high-yielding variety, but cropped lower can produce appealing, velvety reds, usually at their best when young. Zweigelt is extremely rare in New Zealand, with 3 hectares believed to be planted, mostly in Nelson and Marlborough (but the variety is not listed separately in New Zealand Winegrowers' *Vineyard Register Report 2015–2018*).

Hans Herzog Marlborough Zweigelt ★★★★☆

The outstanding 2014 vintage (★★★★★) was estate-grown on the north side of the Wairau Valley and matured for 18 months in French oak barriques. Dark and purple-flushed, with a fragrant bouquet of blackcurrants and spices, it is a powerful, youthful wine. Fleshy, sweet-fruited and smooth, it is packed with cassis, plum and spice flavours, with savoury notes adding complexity, and obvious potential. Best drinking 2018+. Certified organic.

 DRY $53 –V

Vintage	14	13	12	11	10	09
WR	7	7	7	7	7	7
Drink	17-26	17-25	17-24	17-23	17-21	17-21

Seifried Nelson Zweigelt ★★★

The excellent 2014 vintage (★★★★) was matured for a year in new and seasoned French oak barriques. Full-coloured, it is sturdy and firmly structured, with strong, ripe plum/spice flavours, showing a touch of complexity, and definite cellaring potential.

DRY $21 –V

Vintage	14
WR	5
Drink	17-19

Index of Wine Brands

This index should be especially useful when you are visiting wineries as a quick way to find the reviews of each company's range of wines. It also provides links between different wine brands made by the same producer (for example, Amisfield and Lake Hayes).

Visit Michael Cooper's
New Zealand
Wines
website

www.michaelcooper.co.nz

TRY OUR FREE FULL-ACCESS 7-DAY TRIAL

BECOME A MEMBER and have access to over 22,000 of Michael's tasting notes from his annually updated, best-selling *New Zealand Wines*, plus new reviews throughout the year (based on the finest quality and best-value wines tasted). Get detailed, region-by-region vintage reports, vintage charts, and regional maps from the prize-winning *Wine Atlas of New Zealand*. Enjoy the use of the My Wines function, where you can save, organize and make notes about your favourite wines.

GET FREE ACCESS to news about forthcoming wine events; a monthly 'Best Buy' and 'Treat Yourself'; notes on grape varieties and wine regions; cellaring guidelines; a list of Classic Wines of Zealand; Best Buys of the Year; and vintage reports.